Microsoft® Official Academic Course

Windows Server® 2008 Administrator (70-646)

Craig Zacker

WILEY

Credits

EXECUTIVE EDITOR	John Kane
DIRECTOR OF MARKETING AND SALES	Mitchell Beaton
MICROSOFT STRATEGIC RELATIONSHIPS MANAGER	Merrick Van Dongen of Microsoft Learning
DEVELOPMENT AND PRODUCTION	Custom Editorial Productions, Inc.
EDITORIAL PROGRAM ASSISTANT	Jennifer Lartz
PRODUCTION MANAGER	Micheline Frederick
PRODUCTION EDITOR	Kerry Weinstein
CREATIVE DIRECTOR	Harry Nolan
COVER DESIGNER	Jim O'Shea
TECHNOLOGY AND MEDIA	Lauren Sapira/Elena Santa Maria

This book was set in Garamond by Aptara, Inc. and printed and bound by Bind Rite Graphics. The covers were printed by Phoenix Color.

ISBN 978-0-470-22511-0

Printed in the United States of America

10 9 8 7

Foreword from the Publisher

Wiley's publishing vision for the Microsoft Official Academic Course series is to provide students and instructors with the skills and knowledge they need to use Microsoft technology effectively in all aspects of their personal and professional lives. Quality instruction is required to help both educators and students get the most from Microsoft's software tools and to become more productive. Thus our mission is to make our instructional programs trusted educational companions for life.

To accomplish this mission, Wiley and Microsoft have partnered to develop the highest quality educational programs for Information Workers, IT Professionals, and Developers. Materials created by this partnership carry the brand name "Microsoft Official Academic Course," assuring instructors and students alike that the content of these textbooks is fully endorsed by Microsoft, and that they provide the highest quality information and instruction on Microsoft products. The Microsoft Official Academic Course textbooks are "Official" in still one more way—they are the officially sanctioned courseware for Microsoft IT Academy members.

The Microsoft Official Academic Course series focuses on *workforce development*. These programs are aimed at those students seeking to enter the workforce, change jobs, or embark on new careers as information workers, IT professionals, and developers. Microsoft Official Academic Course programs address their needs by emphasizing authentic workplace scenarios with an abundance of projects, exercises, cases, and assessments.

The Microsoft Official Academic Courses are mapped to Microsoft's extensive research and job-task analysis, the same research and analysis used to create the Microsoft Certified Technology Specialist (MCTS) exam. The textbooks focus on real skills for real jobs. As students work through the projects and exercises in the textbooks they enhance their level of knowledge and their ability to apply the latest Microsoft technology to everyday tasks. These students also gain resume-building credentials that can assist them in finding a job, keeping their current job, or in furthering their education.

The concept of life-long learning is today an utmost necessity. Job roles, and even whole job categories, are changing so quickly that none of us can stay competitive and productive without continuously updating our skills and capabilities. The Microsoft Official Academic Course offerings, and their focus on Microsoft certification exam preparation, provide a means for people to acquire and effectively update their skills and knowledge. Wiley supports students in this endeavor through the development and distribution of these courses as Microsoft's official academic publisher.

Today educational publishing requires attention to providing quality print and robust electronic content. By integrating Microsoft Official Academic Course products, *WileyPLUS*, and Microsoft certifications, we are better able to deliver efficient learning solutions for students and teachers alike.

Bonnie Lieberman

General Manager and Senior Vice President

Welcome to the Microsoft Official Academic Course (MOAC) program for Microsoft Windows Server 2008. MOAC represents the collaboration between Microsoft Learning and John Wiley & Sons, Inc. publishing company. Microsoft and Wiley teamed up to produce a series of textbooks that deliver compelling and innovative teaching solutions to instructors and superior learning experiences for students. Infused and informed by in-depth knowledge from the creators of Windows Server 2008, and crafted by a publisher known worldwide for the pedagogical quality of its products, these textbooks maximize skills transfer in minimum time. Students are challenged to reach their potential by using their new technical skills as highly productive members of the workforce.

Because this knowledgebase comes directly from Microsoft, architect of the Windows Server operating system and creator of the Microsoft Certified Technology Specialist and Microsoft Certified Professional exams (www.microsoft.com/learning/mcp/mcts), you are sure to receive the topical coverage that is most relevant to students' personal and professional success. Microsoft's direct participation not only assures you that MOAC textbook content is accurate and current; it also means that students will receive the best instruction possible to enable their success on certification exams and in the workplace.

■ The Microsoft Official Academic Course Program

The *Microsoft Official Academic Course* series is a complete program for instructors and institutions to prepare and deliver great courses on Microsoft software technologies. With MOAC, we recognize that, because of the rapid pace of change in the technology and curriculum developed by Microsoft, there is an ongoing set of needs beyond classroom instruction tools for an instructor to be ready to teach the course. The MOAC program endeavors to provide solutions for all these needs in a systematic manner in order to ensure a successful and rewarding course experience for both instructor and student—technical and curriculum training for instructor readiness with new software releases; the software itself for student use at home for building hands-on skills, assessment, and validation of skill development; and a great set of tools for delivering instruction in the classroom and lab. All are important to the smooth delivery of an interesting course on Microsoft software, and all are provided with the MOAC program. We think about the model below as a gauge for ensuring that we completely support you in your goal of teaching a great course. As you evaluate your instructional materials options, you may wish to use the model for comparison purposes with available products.

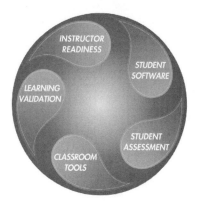

■ Pedagogical Features

The MOAC textbook for Windows Server 2008 Administrator is designed to cover all the learning objectives for that MCTS exam, which is referred to as its "objective domain." The Microsoft Certified Information Technology Professional (MCITP) exam objectives are highlighted throughout the textbook. Many pedagogical features have been developed specifically for *Microsoft Official Academic Course* programs.

Presenting the extensive procedural information and technical concepts woven throughout the textbook raises challenges for the student and instructor alike. The Illustrated Book Tour that follows provides a guide to the rich features contributing to *Microsoft Official Academic Course* program's pedagogical plan. Following is a list of key features in each lesson designed to prepare students for success on the certification exams and in the workplace:

- Each lesson begins with an **Objective Domain Matrix.** More than a standard list of learning objectives, the Domain Matrix correlates each software skill covered in the lesson to the specific MCITP "objective domain."

- Concise and frequent **Step-by-Step** instructions teach students new features and provide an opportunity for hands-on practice. Numbered steps give detailed, step-by-step instructions to help students learn software skills. The steps also show results and screen images to match what students should see on their computer screens.

- **Illustrations:** Screen images provide visual feedback as students work through the exercises. The images reinforce key concepts, provide visual clues about the steps, and allow students to check their progress.

- **Key Terms:** Important technical vocabulary is listed at the beginning of the lesson. When these terms are used later in the lesson, they appear in bold italic type and are defined. The Glossary contains all of the key terms and their definitions.

- Engaging point-of-use **Reader aids,** located throughout the lessons, tell students why this topic is relevant (*The Bottom Line*), provide students with helpful hints (*Take Note*), or show alternate ways to accomplish tasks (*Another Way*). Reader aids also provide additional relevant or background information that adds value to the lesson.

- **Certification Ready?** features throughout the text signal students where a specific certification objective is covered. They provide students with a chance to check their understanding of that particular MCITP objective and, if necessary, review the section of the lesson where it is covered. MOAC offers complete preparation for MCITP certification.

- **Knowledge Assessments** provide three progressively more challenging lesson-ending activities.

■ Lesson Features

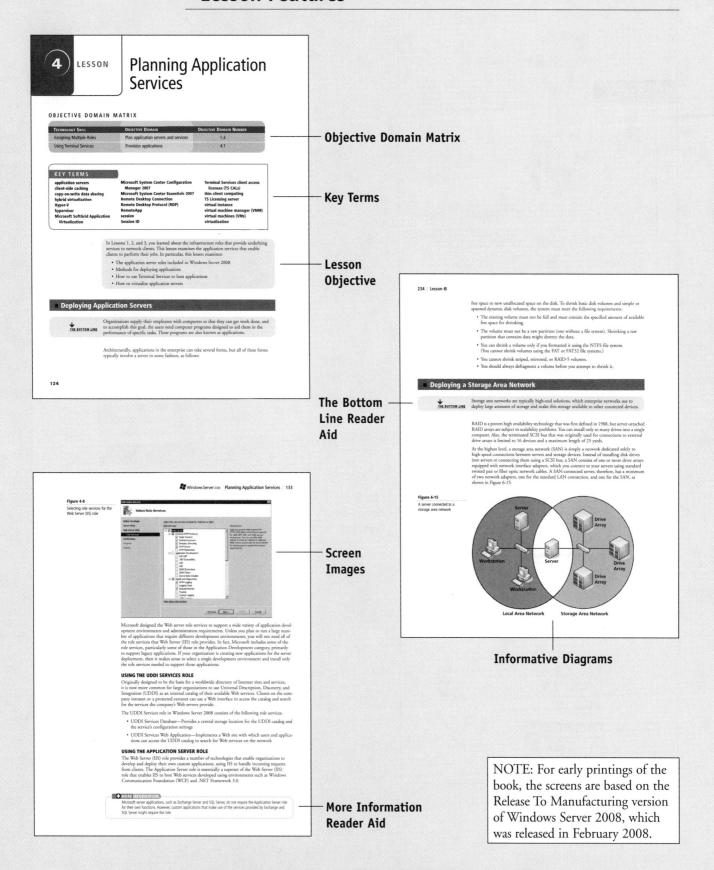

Objective Domain Matrix

Key Terms

Lesson Objective

The Bottom Line Reader Aid

Screen Images

Informative Diagrams

More Information Reader Aid

NOTE: For early printings of the book, the screens are based on the Release To Manufacturing version of Windows Server 2008, which was released in February 2008.

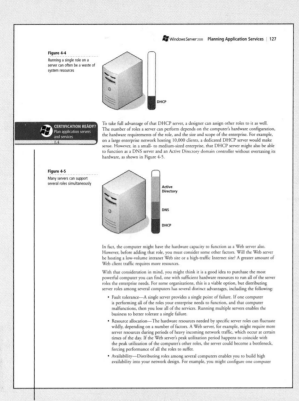

Figure 4-4

Running a single role on a server can often be a waste of system resources

DHCP

CERTIFICATION READY?
Plan application servers and services
1.4

To take full advantage of that DHCP server, a designer can assign other roles to it as well. The number of roles a server can perform depends on the computer's hardware configuration, the hardware requirements of the role, and the size and scope of the enterprise. For example, on a large enterprise network hosting 10,000 clients, a dedicated DHCP server would make sense. However, in a small- to medium-sized enterprise, that DHCP server might also be able to function as a DNS server and an Active Directory domain controller without overtaxing its hardware, as shown in Figure 4-5.

Figure 4-5

Many servers can support several roles simultaneously

Active Directory

DNS

DHCP

In fact, the computer might have the hardware capacity to function as a Web server also. However, before adding that role, you must consider some other factors. Will the Web server be hosting a low-volume intranet Web site or a high-traffic Internet site? A greater amount of Web client traffic requires more resources.

With that consideration in mind, you might think it is a good idea to purchase the most powerful computer you can find, one with sufficient hardware resources to run all of the server roles the enterprise needs. For some organizations, this is a viable option, but distributing server roles among several computers has several distinct advantages, including the following:

- Fault tolerance—A single server provides a single point of failure. If one computer is performing all of the roles your enterprise needs to function, and that computer malfunctions, then you lose all of the services. Running multiple servers enables the business to better tolerate a single failure.

- Resource allocation—The hardware resources needed by specific server roles can fluctuate wildly, depending on a number of factors. A Web server, for example, might require more server resources during periods of heavy incoming network traffic, which occur at certain times of the day. If the Web server's peak utilization period happens to coincide with the peak utilization of the computer's other roles, the server could become a bottleneck, forcing performance of all the roles to suffer.

- Availability—Distributing roles among several computers enables you to build high availability into your network design. For example, you might configure one computer

MCTS Certification Objective Alert

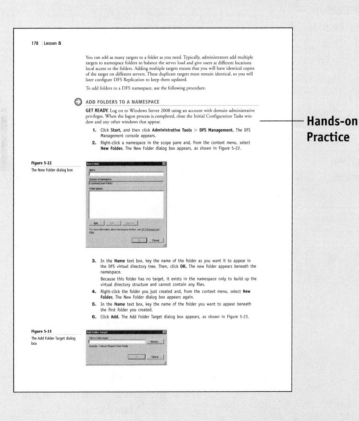

178 | Lesson 5

You can add as many targets to a folder as you need. Typically, administrators add multiple targets to namespace folders to balance the server load and give users at different locations local access to the folders. Adding multiple targets means that you will have identical copies of the target on different servers. These duplicate targets must remain identical, so you will later configure DFS Replication to keep them updated.

To add folders to a DFS namespace, use the following procedure.

ADD FOLDERS TO A NAMESPACE

GET READY. Log on to Windows Server 2008 using an account with domain administrative privileges. When the logon process is completed, close the Initial Configuration Tasks window and any other windows that appear.

1. Click **Start**, and then click **Administrative Tools > DFS Management.** The DFS Management console appears.

2. Right-click a namespace in the scope pane and, from the context menu, select **New Folder.** The New Folder dialog box appears, as shown in Figure 5-22.

Figure 5-22

The New Folder dialog box

Hands-on Practice

3. In the **Name** text box, key the name of the folder as you want it to appear in the DFS virtual directory tree. Then, click **OK.** The new folder appears beneath the namespace.

Because this folder has no target, it exists in the namespace only to build up the virtual directory structure and cannot contain any files.

4. Right-click the folder you just created and, from the context menu, select **New Folder.** The New Folder dialog box appears again.

5. In the **Name** text box, key the name of the folder you want to appear beneath the first folder you created.

6. Click **Add.** The Add Folder Target dialog box appears, as shown in Figure 5-23.

Figure 5-23

The Add Folder Target dialog box

Another Way Reader Aid

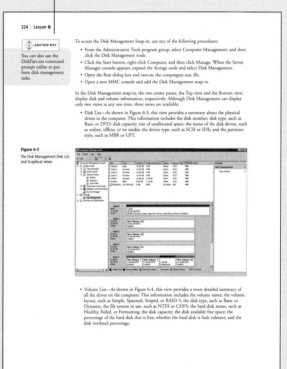

224 | Lesson 6

ANOTHER WAY

You can also use the DiskPart.exe command prompt utility to perform disk management tasks.

To access the Disk Management Snap-in, use any of the following procedures:

- From the Administrative Tools program group, select Computer Management, and then click the Disk Management node.
- Click the Start button, right-click Computer, and then click Manage. When the Server Manager console appears, expand the Storage node and select Disk Management.
- Open the Run dialog box and execute the compmgmt.msc file.
- Open a new MMC console and add the Disk Management snap-in.

In the Disk Management snap-in, the two center panes, the Top view and the Bottom view, display disk and volume information, respectively. Although Disk Management can display only two views at any one time, three views are available:

- Disk List—As shown in Figure 6-3, this view provides a summary about the physical drives in the computer. This information includes the disk number; disk type, such as Basic or DVD; disk capacity; size of unallocated space; the status of the disk device, such as online, offline, or no media; the device type, such as SCSI or IDE; and the partition style, such as MBR or GPT.

Figure 6-3

The Disk Management Disk List and Graphical views

- Volume List—As shown in Figure 6-4, this view provides a more detailed summary of all the drives on the computer. This information includes the volume name; the volume layout, such as Simple, Spanned, Striped, or RAID-5; the disk type, such as Basic or Dynamic; the file system in use, such as NTFS or CDFS; the hard disk status, such as Healthy, Failed, or Formatting; the disk capacity; the disk available free space; the percentage of the hard disk that is free; whether the hard disk is fault tolerant; and the disk overhead percentage.

Warning Reader Aid

Windows Server 2008 Planning Storage Solutions | 229

- Converts basic disk primary partitions and logical drives in the extended partition to simple volumes
- Marks any free space in a basic disk extended partition as unallocated

Creating a Simple Volume

Technically speaking, you create partitions on basic disks and volumes on dynamic disks. This is not just an arbitrary change in nomenclature. Converting a basic disk to a dynamic disk actually creates one big partition, occupying all of the space on the disk. The volumes you create on the dynamic disk are logical divisions within that single partition.

Earlier versions of Windows use the correct terminology in the Disk Management snap-in. The menus enable you to create partitions on basic disks and volumes on dynamic disks. Windows Server 2008 uses the term volume for both disk types, and enables you to create any of the available volume types, whether the disk is basic or dynamic. If the volume type you select is not supported on a basic disk, the wizard converts it to a dynamic disk (with your permission) as part of the volume creation process.

Despite the menus that refer to basic partitions as volumes, the traditional rules for basic disks remain in effect. The New Simple Volume menu option on a basic disk creates up to three primary partitions. When you create a fourth volume, the wizard actually creates an extended partition and a logical drive of the size you specify. If there is any remaining space on the disk, you can create additional logical drives in the extended partition.

WARNING When you use *DiskPart.exe*, a command line utility included with Windows Server 2008, to manage basic disks, you can create four primary partitions or three primary partitions, and one extended partition. The DiskPart.exe utility contains a superset of the commands supported by the Disk Management snap-in. In other words, DiskPart can do everything Disk Management can do, and more. However, while the Disk Management snap-in prevents you from unintentionally performing actions that might result in data loss, DiskPart has no safeties, and so does not prohibit you from performing such actions. For this reason, Microsoft recommends that only advanced users use DiskPart and that they use it with due caution.

To create a new simple volume on a basic or dynamic disk, use the following procedure.

CREATE A NEW SIMPLE VOLUME

GET READY. Log on to Windows Server 2008 using an account with Administrator privileges. When the logon process is completed, close the Initial Configuration Tasks window and any other windows that appear.

1. Open the Disk Management snap-in if necessary.
2. In the Graphical View, right-click an unallocated area in the volume status column for the disk on which you want to create a volume and, from the context menu, select **New Simple Volume.** The New Simple Volume Wizard appears.

X Ref Reader Aid

Windows Server 2008 Planning Storage Solutions | 233

X REF

See the "Create a New Simple Volume" procedure, in the preceding section, for more information about the options on the Assign Drive Letter or Path and Format Partition pages.

6. Specify whether you want to assign a drive letter or path, and then click **Next.** The *Format Partition* page appears.
7. Specify if or how you want to format the volume, and then click **Next.** The *Completing the New Simple Volume Wizard* page appears.
8. Review the settings to confirm your options, and then click **Finish.** If any of the disks you selected to create the volume are basic disks, a Disk Management message box appears, warning you that the volume creation process will convert the basic disks to dynamic disks.
9. Click **Yes.** The wizard creates the volume according to your specifications.

CLOSE the Disk Management snap-in.

The commands that appear in a disk's context menu depend on the number of disks installed in the computer and the presence of unallocated space on them. For example, at least two disks with unallocated space must be available to create a striped, spanned, or mirrored volume, and at least three disks must be available to create a RAID-5 volume.

EXTENDING AND SHRINKING VOLUMES

To extend or shrink a volume, you simply right-click a volume and select Extend Volume or Shrink Volume from the context menu or from the Action menu.

Windows Server 2008 extends existing volumes by expanding them into adjacent unallocated space on the same disk. When you extend a simple volume across multiple disks, the simple volume becomes a spanned volume. You cannot extend striped volumes.

TAKE NOTE

You must be a member of the Backup Operator or the Administrators group to extend or shrink any volume.

To extend a volume on a basic disk, the system must meet the following requirements:

- A volume of a basic disk must be either unformatted or formatted with the NTFS file system.
- If you extend a volume that is actually a logical drive, the console first consumes the contiguous free space remaining in the extended partition. If you attempt to extend the logical drive beyond the confines of its extended partition, the extended partition expands to any unallocated space left on the disk.
- You can extend logical drives, boot volumes, or system volumes only into contiguous space, and only if the hard disk can be upgraded to a dynamic disk. The operating system will permit you to extend other types of basic volumes into noncontiguous space, but will prompt you to convert the basic disk to a dynamic disk.

To extend a volume on a dynamic disk, the system must meet these requirements:

- When extending a simple volume, you can use only the available space on the same disk, if the volume is to remain simple.
- You can extend a simple volume across additional disks if it is not a system volume or a boot volume. However, after you expand a simple volume to another disk, it is no longer a simple volume; it becomes a spanned volume.
- You can extend a simple or spanned volume if it does not have a file system (a raw volume) or if you formatted it using the NTFS file system. (You cannot extend volumes using the FAT or FAT32 file systems.)
- You cannot extend mirrored or RAID-5 volumes, although you can add a mirror to an existing simple volume.

When shrinking volumes, the Disk Management console frees up space at the end of the volume, relocating the existing volume's files, if necessary. The console then converts that

Take Note Reader Aid

---

212 | Lesson 6

There are a variety of storage technologies that are better suited for server use, and the process of designing a storage solution for a server depends on several factors, including the following:

- The amount of storage the server needs
- The number of users that will be accessing the server at the same time
- The sensitivity of the data to be stored on the server
- The importance of the data to the organization

The following sections examine these factors and the technologies you can choose when creating a plan for your network storage solutions.

How Many Servers Do I Need?

CERTIFICATION READY?
Plan storage
5.1

When is one big file server preferable to several smaller ones?

One of the most frequently asked questions when planning a server deployment is whether it is better to use one big server or several smaller ones. In Lesson 4, "Planning Application Services," you learned about the advantages and disadvantages of using one server to perform several roles versus distributing the roles among several smaller servers, so you should now have some idea of which arrangement would be better suited to your organization.

If you are considering one large server, or if your organization's storage requirements are extremely large, you must also consider the inherent storage limitations of Windows Server 2008, which are listed in Table 6-1.

Table 6-1

Windows Server 2008 Storage Limitations

Easy-to-Read Tables

STORAGE CHARACTERISTIC	LIMITATION
Maximum basic volume size	2 terabytes
Maximum dynamic volume size (simple and mirrored volumes)	2 terabytes
Maximum dynamic volume size (spanned and striped volumes)	64 terabytes (2 terabytes per disk, with a maximum of 32 disks)
Maximum dynamic volume size (RAID-5 volumes)	62 terabytes (2 terabytes per disk, with a maximum of 32 disks, and 2 terabytes reserved for parity information)
Maximum NTFS volume size	2^{32} clusters minus 1 cluster (using the default 4 kilobyte cluster size, the maximum volume size is 16 terabytes minus 64 kilobytes; using the maximum 64 kilobyte cluster size, the maximum volume size is 256 terabytes minus 64 kilobytes)
Maximum number of clusters on an NTFS volume	2^{32} (4,294,967,296)
Maximum NTFS file size	2^{44} bytes (16 terabytes) minus 64 kilobytes
Maximum number of files on an NTFS volume	2^{32} minus 1 file (4,294,967,295)
Maximum number of volumes on a server	Approximately 2,000 (1,000 dynamic volumes and the rest basic)

The number of sites your enterprise network encompasses and the technologies you use to provide network communication between those sites can also affect your plans. If, for

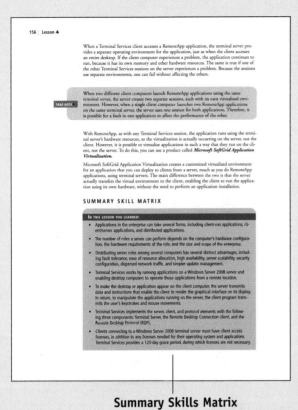

Summary Skills Matrix

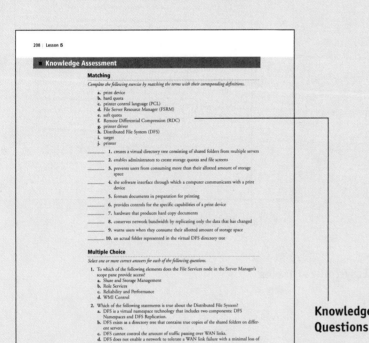

Knowledge Assessment Questions

Review Questions

Case Scenarios

Conventions and Features Used in This Book

This book uses particular fonts, symbols, and heading conventions to highlight important information or to call your attention to special steps. For more information about the features in each lesson, refer to the Illustrated Book Tour section.

CONVENTION	MEANING
NEW FEATURE ✓	This icon indicates a new or greatly improved Windows feature in this version of the software.
↓ **THE BOTTOM LINE**	This feature provides a brief summary of the material to be covered in the section that follows.
CLOSE	Words in all capital letters and in a different font color than the rest of the text indicate instructions for opening, saving, or closing files or programs. They also point out items you should check or actions you should take.
CERTIFICATION READY?	This feature signals the point in the text where a specific certification objective is covered. It provides you with a chance to check your understanding of that particular MCTS objective and, if necessary, review the section of the lesson where it is covered.
TAKE NOTE	Reader aids appear in shaded boxes found in your text. *Take Note* provides helpful hints related to particular tasks or topics.
✦ **ANOTHER WAY**	*Another Way* provides an alternative procedure for accomplishing a particular task.
X REF	These notes provide pointers to information discussed elsewhere in the textbook or describe interesting features of Windows Server 2008 that are not directly addressed in the current topic or exercise.
Alt + Tab	A plus sign (+) between two key names means that you must press both keys at the same time. Keys that you are instructed to press in an exercise will appear in the font shown here.
A *shared printer* can be used by many individuals on a network.	Key terms appear in bold italic.
Key **My Name is**.	Any text you are asked to key appears in color.
Click **OK**.	Any button on the screen you are supposed to click on or select will also appear in color.

The *Microsoft Official Academic Course* programs are accompanied by a rich array of resources that incorporate the extensive textbook visuals to form a pedagogically cohesive package. These resources provide all the materials instructors need to deploy and deliver their courses. Resources available online for download include:

- The **MSDN Academic Alliance** is designed to provide the easiest and most inexpensive developer tools, products, and technologies available to faculty and students in labs, classrooms, and on student PCs. A free 3-year membership is available to qualified MOAC adopters.

  Note: Microsoft Windows Server 2008 can be downloaded from MSDN AA for use by students in this course

- **Windows Server 2008 Evaluation Software.** DVDs containing an evaluation version of Windows Server 2008 is bundled inside the back cover of this text.

- The **Instructor's Guide** contains Solutions to all the textbook exercises as well as chapter summaries and lecture notes. The Instructor's Guide and Syllabi for various term lengths are available from the Book Companion site (http://www.wiley.com/college/microsoft) and from *WileyPLUS*.

- The **Test Bank** contains hundreds of questions in multiple-choice, true-false, short answer, and essay formats and is available to download from the Instructor's Book Companion site (http://www.wiley.com/college/microsoft) and from *WileyPLUS*. A complete answer key is provided.

- **PowerPoint Presentations and Images.** A complete set of PowerPoint presentations is available on the Instructor's Book Companion site (http://www.wiley.com/college/micro-soft) and in *WileyPLUS* to enhance classroom presentations. Tailored to the text's topical coverage and Skills Matrix, these presentations are designed to convey key Windows Server concepts addressed in the text.

  All figures from the text are on the Instructor's Book Companion site (http://www.wiley.com/college/microsoft) and in *WileyPLUS*. You can incorporate them into your PowerPoint presentations, or create your own overhead transparencies and handouts.

  By using these visuals in class discussions, you can help focus students' attention on key elements of Windows Server and help them understand how to use it effectively in the workplace.

- When it comes to improving the classroom experience, there is no better source of ideas and inspiration than your fellow colleagues. The Wiley Faculty Network connects teachers with technology, facilitates the exchange of best practices, and helps to enhance instructional efficiency and effectiveness. Faculty Network activities include technology training and tutorials, virtual seminars, peer-to-peer exchanges of experiences and ideas, personal consulting, and sharing of resources. For details visit www.WhereFacultyConnect.com.

WileyPLUS

Broad developments in education over the past decade have influenced the instructional approach taken in the Microsoft Official Academic Course program. The way that students learn, especially about new technologies, has changed dramatically in the Internet era. Electronic learning materials and Internet-based instruction is now as much a part of classroom instruction as printed textbooks. *WileyPLUS* provides the technology to create an environment where students reach their full potential and experience academic success that will last them a lifetime!

WileyPLUS is a powerful and highly-integrated suite of teaching and learning resources designed to bridge the gap between what happens in the classroom and what happens at home and on the job. *WileyPLUS* provides instructors with the resources to teach their students new technologies and guide them to reach their goals of getting ahead in the job market by having the skills to become certified and advance in the workforce. For students, *WileyPLUS* provides the tools for study and practice that are available to them 24/7, wherever and whenever they want to study. *WileyPLUS* includes a complete online version of the student textbook, PowerPoint presentations, homework and practice assignments and quizzes, image galleries, test bank questions, gradebook, and all the instructor resources in one easy-to-use Web site.

Organized around the everyday activities you and your students perform in the class, *WileyPLUS* helps you:

- **Prepare & Present** outstanding class presentations using relevant PowerPoint slides and other *WileyPLUS* materials—and you can easily upload and add your own.
- **Create Assignments** by choosing from questions organized by lesson, level of difficulty, and source—and add your own questions. Students' homework and quizzes are automatically graded, and the results are recorded in your gradebook.
- **Offer context-sensitive help to students, 24/7.** When you assign homework or quizzes, you decide if and when students get access to hints, solutions, or answers where appropriate—or they can be linked to relevant sections of their complete, online text for additional help whenever—and wherever they need it most.
- **Track Student Progress:** Analyze students' results and assess their level of understanding on an individual and class level using the *WileyPLUS* gradebook, or export data to your own personal gradebook.
- **Administer Your Course:** *WileyPLUS* can easily be integrated with another course management system, gradebook, or other resources you are using in your class, providing you with the flexibility to build your course, your way.

Please view our online demo at **www.wiley.com/college/wileyplus.** Here you will find additional information about the features and benefits of *WileyPLUS*, how to request a "test drive" of *WileyPLUS* for this title, and how to adopt it for class use.

MSDN ACADEMIC ALLIANCE—FREE 3-YEAR MEMBERSHIP AVAILABLE TO QUALIFIED ADOPTERS!

The Microsoft Developer Network Academic Alliance (MSDN AA) is designed to provide the easiest and most inexpensive way for universities to make the latest Microsoft developer tools, products, and technologies available in labs, classrooms, and on student PCs. MSDN AA is an annual membership program for departments teaching Science, Technology, Engineering, and Mathematics (STEM) courses. The membership provides a complete solution to keep academic labs, faculty, and students on the leading edge of technology.

Software available in the MSDN AA program is provided at no charge to adopting departments through the Wiley and Microsoft publishing partnership.

As a bonus to this free offer, faculty will be introduced to Microsoft's Faculty Connection and Academic Resource Center. It takes time and preparation to keep students engaged while giving them a fundamental understanding of theory, and the Microsoft Faculty Connection is designed to help STEM professors with this preparation by providing articles, curriculum, and tools that professors can use to engage and inspire today's technology students.

* Contact your Wiley rep for details.

For more information about the MSDN Academic Alliance program, go to:

http://msdn.microsoft.com/academic/

Note: Microsoft Windows Server 2008 can be downloaded from MSDN AA for use by students in this course.

Important Web Addresses and Phone Numbers

To locate the Wiley Higher Education Rep in your area, go to the following Web address and click on the "*Who's My Rep?*" link at the top of the page.

http://www.wiley.com/college

Or Call the MOAC Toll Free Number: 1 + (888) 764-7001 (U.S. & Canada only).

To learn more about becoming a Microsoft Certified Professional and exam availability, visit www.microsoft.com/learning/mcp.

Book Companion Web Site (www.wiley.com/college/microsoft)

The students' book companion site for the MOAC series includes any resources, exercise files, and Web links that will be used in conjunction with this course.

WileyPLUS

WileyPLUS is a powerful and highly-integrated suite of teaching and learning resources designed to bridge the gap between what happens in the classroom and what happens at home and on the job. For students, *WileyPLUS* provides the tools for study and practice that are available 24/7, wherever and whenever they want to study. *WileyPLUS* includes a complete online version of the student textbook, PowerPoint presentations, homework and practice assignments and quizzes, image galleries, test bank questions, gradebook, and all the instructor resources in one easy-to-use Web site.

WileyPLUS provides immediate feedback on student assignments and a wealth of support materials. This powerful study tool will help your students develop their conceptual understanding of the class material and increase their ability to answer questions.

- A **Study and Practice** area links directly to text content, allowing students to review the text while they study and answer.

- An **Assignment** area keeps all the work you want your students to complete in one location, making it easy for them to stay on task. Students have access to a variety of interactive self-assessment tools, as well as other resources for building their confidence and understanding. In addition, all of the assignments and quizzes contain a link to the relevant section of the multimedia book, providing students with context-sensitive help that allows them to conquer obstacles as they arise.

- A **Personal Gradebook** for each student allows students to view their results from past assignments at any time.

Please view our online demo at www.wiley.com/college/wileyplus. Here you will find additional information about the features and benefits of *WileyPLUS*, how to request a "test drive" of *WileyPLUS* for this title, and how to adopt it for class use.

Wiley Desktop Editions

Wiley MOAC Desktop Editions are innovative, electronic versions of printed textbooks. Students buy the desktop version for 50% off the U.S. price of the printed text, and get the added value of permanence and portability. Wiley Desktop Editions provide students with numerous additional benefits that are not available with other e-text solutions.

Wiley Desktop Editions are NOT subscriptions; students download the Wiley Desktop Edition to their computer desktops. Students own the content they buy to keep for as long as they want. Once a Wiley Desktop Edition is downloaded to the computer desktop, students have instant access to all of the content without being online. Students can also print out the sections they prefer to read in hard copy. Students also have access to fully integrated resources within their Wiley Desktop Edition. From highlighting their e-text to taking and sharing notes, students can easily personalize their Wiley Desktop Edition as they are reading or following along in class.

Windows Server 2008 Evaluation Edition

All MOAC Windows Server 2008 textbooks are packaged with an evaluation edition of Windows Server 2008 on the companion DVDs. Installing the Windows Server Evaluation Edition provides students with the state-of-the-art system software, enabling them to use a full version of Windows Server 2008 for the course exercises. This also promotes the practice of learning by doing, which can be the most effective way to acquire and remember new computing skills.

Evaluating Windows Server 2008 software does not require product activation or entering a product key. The Windows Server 2008 Evaluation Edition provided with this textbook may be installed without activation and evaluated for an initial 60 days. If you need more time to evaluate Windows Server 2008, the 60-day evaluation period may be reset (or re-armed) three times, extending the original 60-day evaluation period by up to 180 days for a total possible evaluation time of 240 days. After this time, you will need to uninstall the software or upgrade to a fully licensed version of Windows Server 2008.

System Requirements

The following are estimated system requirements for Windows Server 2008. If your computer has less than the minimum requirements, you will not be able to install this product correctly. Actual requirements will vary based on your system configuration and the applications and features you install.

PROCESSOR

Processor performance depends not only on the clock frequency of the processor, but also on the number of processor cores and the size of the processor cache. The following are the processor requirements for this product:

> **TAKE NOTE***
>
> An Intel Itanium 2 processor is required for Windows Server 2008 for Itanium-Based Systems.

- Minimum: 1 GHz (for x86 processors) or 1.4 GHz (for x64 processors)
- Recommended: 2 GHz or faster

RAM

The following are the RAM requirements for this product:

- Minimum: 512 MB
- Recommended: 2 GB or more
- Maximum (32-bit systems): 4 GB (for Windows Server 2008 Standard) or 64 GB (for Windows Server 2008 Enterprise or Windows Server 2008 Datacenter)
- Maximum (64-bit systems): 32 GB (for Windows Server 2008 Standard) or 2 TB (for Windows Server 2008 Enterprise, Windows Server 2008 Datacenter, or Windows Server 2008 for Itanium-Based Systems)

Disk space requirements

TAKE NOTE *

Computers with more than 16 GB of RAM will require more disk space for paging, hibernation, and dump files.

The following are the approximate disk space requirements for the system partition. Itanium-based and x64-based operating systems will vary from these estimates. Additional disk space may be required if you install the system over a network. For more information, see http://www.microsoft.com/windowsserver2008.

- Minimum: 10 GB
- Recommended: 40 GB or more
- DVD-ROM drive
- Super VGA (800 x 600) or higher-resolution monitor
- Keyboard and Microsoft mouse (or other compatible pointing device)

Important Considerations for Active Directory Domain Controllers

The upgrade process from Windows Server 2003 to Windows Server 2008 requires free disk space for the new operating system image, for the Setup process, and for any installed server roles.

For the domain controller role, the volume or volumes hosting the following resources also have specific free disk space requirements:

- Application data (%AppData%)
- Program files (%ProgramFiles%)
- Users' data (%SystemDrive%\Documents and Settings)
- Windows directory (%WinDir%)

The free space on the %WinDir% volume must be equal or greater than the current size of the resources listed above and their subordinate folders when they are located on the %WinDir% volume. By default, dcpromo places the Active Directory database and log files under %Windir%—in this case, their size would be included in the free disk space requirements for the %Windir% folder.

However, if the Active Directory database is hosted outside of any of the folders above, then the hosting volume or volumes must only contain additional free space equal to at least 10% of the current database size or 250 MB, whichever is greater. Finally, the free space on the volume that hosts the log files must be at least 50 MB.

A default installation of the Active Directory directory service in Windows Server 2003 has the Active Directory database and log files under %WinDir%\NTDS. With this configuration, the NTDS .DIT database file and all the log files are temporarily copied over to the quarantine location and then copied back to their original location. This is why additional free space is required for those resources. However, the SYSVOL directory, which is also under %WinDir% (%WinDir%\SYSVOL), is moved and not copied. Therefore, it does not require any additional free space.

After the upgrade, the space that was reserved for the copied resources will be returned to the file system.

WARNING Although you can reset the 60-day evaluation period, you cannot extend it beyond 60 days at any time. When you reset the current 60-day evaluation period, you lose whatever time is left on the previous 60-day evaluation period. Therefore, to maximize the total evaluation time, wait until close to the end of the current 60-day evaluation period before you reset the evaluation period.

Installing and Re-Arming Windows Server 2008

Evaluating Windows Server 2008 software does not require product activation. The Windows Server 2008 Evaluation Edition may be installed without activation, and it may be evaluated for 60 days. Additionally, the 60-day evaluation period may be reset (re-armed) three times. This action extends the original 60-day evaluation period by up to 180 days for a total possible evaluation time of 240 days.

How To Install Windows Server 2008 Without Activating It

1. Run the Windows Server 2008 Setup program.

2. When you are prompted to enter a product key for activation, do not enter a key. Click No when Setup asks you to confirm your selection.

3. You may be prompted to select the edition of Windows Server 2008 that you want to evaluate. Select the edition that you want to install.

4. When you are prompted, read the evaluation terms in the Microsoft Software License Terms, and then accept the terms.

5. When the Windows Server 2008 Setup program is finished, your initial 60-day evaluation period starts. To check the time that is left on your current evaluation period, run the Slmgr.vbs script that is in the System32 folder. Use the **-dli** switch to run this script. The **slmgr.vbs -dli** command displays the number of days that are left in the current 60-day evaluation period.

How To Re-Arm the Evaluation Period

This section describes how to extend, or re-arm, the Windows Server 2008 evaluation period. The evaluation period is also known as the "activation grace" period.

When the initial 60-day evaluation period nears its end, you can run the Slmgr.vbs script to reset the evaluation period. To do this, follow these steps:

1. Click **Start**, and then click **Command Prompt**.

2. Type **slmgr.vbs -dli**, and then press **ENTER** to check the current status of your evaluation period.

3. To reset the evaluation period, type **slmgr.vbs –rearm**, and then press **ENTER**.

4. Restart the computer.

This resets the evaluation period to 60 days.

How To Automate the Extension of the Evaluation Period

You may want to set up a process that automatically resets the evaluation period every 60 days. One way to automate this process is by using the Task Scheduler. You can configure the Task Scheduler to run the Slmgr.vbs script and to restart the server at a particular time. To do this, follow these steps:

1. Click **Start**, point to **Administrative Tools**, and then click **Task Scheduler**.

2. Copy the following sample task to the server, and then save it as an .xml file. For example, you can save the file as **Extend.xml**.

```xml
<?xml version="1.0" encoding="UTF-16"?> <Task version="1.2"
xmlns="http://schemas.microsoft.com/windows/2004/02/mit/task">
<RegistrationInfo> <Date>2007-09-17T14:26:04.433</Date>
<Author>Microsoft Corporation</Author> </RegistrationInfo>
<Triggers> <TimeTrigger id="18c4a453-d7aa-4647-916b-
af0c3ea16a6b"> <Repetition> <Interval>P59D</Interval>
<StopAtDurationEnd>false</StopAtDurationEnd> </Repetition>
<StartBoundary>2007-10-05T02:23:24</StartBoundary>
<EndBoundary>2008-09-17T14:23:24.777</EndBoundary>
<Enabled>true</Enabled> </TimeTrigger> </Triggers>
<Principals> <Principal id="Author">
<UserId>domain\alias</UserId>
```

```
<LogonType>Password</LogonType>
<RunLevel>HighestAvailable</RunLevel> </Principal>
</Principals> <Settings> <IdleSettings>
<Duration>PT10M</Duration> <WaitTimeout>PT1H</WaitTimeout>
<StopOnIdleEnd>true</StopOnIdleEnd>
<RestartOnIdle>false</RestartOnIdle> </IdleSettings>
<MultipleInstancesPolicy>IgnoreNew</MultipleInstancesPolicy>
<DisallowStartIfOnBatteries>true</DisallowStartIfOnBatteries>
<StopIfGoingOnBatteries>true</StopIfGoingOnBatteries>
<AllowHardTerminate>true</AllowHardTerminate>
<StartWhenAvailable>false</StartWhenAvailable>
<RunOnlyIfNetworkAvailable>false</RunOnlyIfNetworkAvailable>
<AllowStartOnDemand>true</AllowStartOnDemand>
<Enabled>true</Enabled> <Hidden>false</Hidden>
<RunOnlyIfIdle>false</RunOnlyIfIdle>
<WakeToRun>true</WakeToRun>
<ExecutionTimeLimit>P3D</ExecutionTimeLimit>
<DeleteExpiredTaskAfter>PT0S</DeleteExpiredTaskAfter>
<Priority>7</Priority> <RestartOnFailure>
<Interval>PT1M</Interval> <Count>3</Count>
</RestartOnFailure> </Settings> <Actions Context="Author">
<Exec> <Command>C:\Windows\System32\slmgr.vbs</Command>
<Arguments>-rearm</Arguments> </Exec> <Exec>
<Command>C:\Windows\System32\shutdown.exe</Command>
<Arguments>/r</Arguments> </Exec> </Actions> </Task>
```

3. In the sample task, change the value of the following "UserID" tag to contain your domain and your alias:

   <UserId>domain\alias</UserId>

4. In the Task Scheduler, click **Import Task** on the **Action** menu.

5. Click the sample task .xml file. For example, click **Extend.xml**.

6. Click **Import**.

7. Click the **Triggers** tab.

8. Click the **One Time** trigger, and then click **Edit**.

9. Change the start date of the task to a date just before the end of your current evaluation period.

10. Click **OK**, and then exit the Task Scheduler.

The Task Scheduler will now run the evaluation reset operation on the date that you specified.

Preparing to Take the Microsoft Certified Information Technology Professional (MCITP) Exam

The Microsoft Certified Information Technology Professional (MCITP) certifications enable professionals to target specific technologies and to distinguish themselves by demonstrating in-depth knowledge and expertise in their specialized technologies. Microsoft Certified Information Technology Professionals are consistently capable of inplementing, building, troubleshooting, and debugging a particular Microsoft Technology.

For organizations, the new generation of Microsoft certifications provides better skills verification tools that help with assessing not only in-demand skills on Windows Server, but also the ability to quickly complete on-the-job tasks. Individuals will find it easier to identify and work towards the certification credential that meets their personal and professional goals.

To learn more about becoming a Microsoft Certified Professional and exam availability, visit www.microsoft.com/learning/mcp.

Microsoft Certifications for IT Professionals

The new Microsoft Certified Technology Specialist (MCTS) and Microsoft Certified IT Professional (MCITP) credentials provide IT professionals with a simpler and more targeted framework to showcase their technical skills in addition to the skills that are required for specific developer job roles.

The Microsoft Certified Database Administrator (MCDBA), Microsoft Certified Desktop Support Technician (MCDST), Microsoft Certified System Administrator (MCSA), and Microsoft Certified Systems Engineer (MCSE) credentials continue to provide IT professionals who use Microsoft SQL Server 2000, Windows XP, and Windows Server 2003 with industry recognition and validation of their IT skills and experience.

Microsoft Certified Technology Specialist

The new Microsoft Certified Tehnology Specialist (MCTS) credential highlights your skills using a specific Microsoft technology. You can demonstrate your abilities as an IT professional or developer with in-depth knowledge of the Microsoft technology that you use today or are planning to deploy.

The MCTS certifications enable professionals to target specific technologies and to distinguish themselves by demonstrating in-depth knowledge and expertise in their specialized technologies. Microsoft Certified Technology Specialists are consistently capable of implementing, building, troubleshooting, and debugging a particular Microsoft technology.

You can learn more about the MCTS program at www.microsoft.com/learning/mcp/mcts.

Microsoft Certified IT Professional

The new Microsoft Certified IT Professional (MCITP) credential lets you highlight your specific area of expertise. Now, you can easily distinguish yourself as an expert in database administration, database development, business intelligence, or support.

By becoming certified, you demonstrate to employers that you have achieved a predictable level of skill not only in the use of the Windows Server operating system, but with a comprehensive set of Microsoft technologies. Employers often require certification either as a condition of employment or as a condition of advancement within the company or other organization.

You can learn more about the MCITP program at www.microsoft.com/learning/mcp/mcitp.

The certification examinations are sponsored by Microsoft but administered through Microsoft's exam delivery partner Prometric.

Preparing to Take an Exam

Unless you are a very experienced user, you will need to use a test preparation course to prepare to complete the test correctly and within the time allowed. The *Microsoft Official Academic Course* series is designed to prepare you with a strong knowledge of all exam topics, and with some additional review and practice on your own, you should feel confident in your ability to pass the appropriate exam.

After you decide which exam to take, review the list of objectives for the exam. You can easily identify tasks that are included in the objective list by locating the Objective Domain Matrix at the start of each lesson and the Certification Ready sidebars in the margin of the lessons in this book.

To take the MCITP test, visit www.microsoft.com/learning/mcp/mcitp to locate your nearest testing center. Then call the testing center directly to schedule your test. The amount of advance notice you should provide will vary for different testing centers, and it typically depends on the number of computers available at the testing center, the number of other testers who have already been scheduled for the day on which you want to take the test, and the number of times per week that the testing center offers MCITP testing. In general, you should call to schedule your test at least two weeks prior to the date on which you want to take the test.

When you arrive at the testing center, you might be asked for proof of identity. A driver's license or passport is an acceptable form of identification. If you do not have either of these items of documentation, call your testing center and ask what alternative forms of identification will be accepted. If you are retaking a test, bring your MCITP identification number, which will have been given to you when you previously took the test. If you have not prepaid or if your organization has not already arranged to make payment for you, you will need to pay the test-taking fee when you arrive.

About the Author

Craig Zacker is a writer, editor, and networker whose computing experience began in the days of teletypes and paper tape. After making the move from minicomputers to PCs, he worked as an administrator of Novell NetWare networks and as a PC support technician while operating a freelance desktop publishing business. After earning a Master's Degree in English and American Literature from New York University, Craig worked extensively on integrating Microsoft Windows operating systems into existing internetworks, supported fleets of Windows workstations, and was employed as a technical writer, content provider, and webmaster for the online services group of a large software company. Since devoting himself to writing and editing full-time, Craig has authored or contributed to dozens of books on networking topics, operating systems, and PC hardware, including the Microsoft Official Academic Courses for *Windows Vista Configuration Exam 70-620* and *Windows Server 2008 Applications Infrastructure Configuration Exam 70-643*. He has developed educational texts for college courses, designed online training courses for the Web, and published articles with top industry publications.

Acknowledgments

MOAC Instructor Advisory Board

We would like to thank our Instructor Advisory Board, an elite group of educators who has assisted us every step of the way in building these products. Advisory Board members have acted as our sounding board on key pedagogical and design decisions leading to the development of these compelling and innovative textbooks for future Information Workers. Their dedication to technology education is truly appreciated.

Charles DeSassure, Tarrant County College

Charles DeSassure is Department Chair and Instructor of Computer Science & Information Technology at Tarrant County College Southeast Campus, Arlington, Texas. He has had experience as a MIS Manager, system analyst, field technology analyst, LAN Administrator, microcomputer specialist, and public school teacher in South Carolina. DeSassure has worked in higher education for more than ten years and received the Excellence Award in Teaching from the National Institute for Staff and Organizational Development (NISOD). He currently serves on the Educational Testing Service (ETS) iSkills National Advisory Committee and chaired the Tarrant County College District Student Assessment Committee. He has written proposals and makes presentations at major educational conferences nationwide. DeSassure has served as a textbook reviewer for John Wiley & Sons and Prentice Hall. He teaches courses in information security, networking, distance learning, and computer literacy. DeSassure holds a master's degree in Computer Resources & Information Management from Webster University.

Kim Ehlert, Waukesha County Technical College

Kim Ehlert is the Microsoft Program Coordinator and a Network Specialist instructor at Waukesha County Technical College, teaching the full range of MCSE and networking courses for the past nine years. Prior to joining WCTC, Kim was a professor at the Milwaukee School of Engineering for five years where she oversaw the Novell Academic Education and the Microsoft IT Academy programs. She has a wide variety of industry experience including network design and management for Johnson Controls, local city fire departments, police departments, large church congregations, health departments, and accounting firms. Kim holds many industry certifications including MCDST, MCSE, Security+, Network+, Server+, MCT, and CNE.

Kim has a bachelor's degree in Information Systems and a master's degree in Business Administration from the University of Wisconsin Milwaukee. When she is not busy teaching, she enjoys spending time with her husband Gregg and their two children—Alex, 14, and Courtney, 17.

Penny Gudgeon, Corinthian Colleges, Inc.

Penny Gudgeon is the Program Manager for IT curriculum at Corinthian Colleges, Inc. Previously, she was responsible for computer programming and web curriculum for twenty-seven campuses in Corinthian's Canadian division, CDI College of Business, Technology and Health Care. Penny joined CDI College in 1997 as a computer programming instructor at one of the campuses outside of Toronto. Prior to joining CDI College, Penny taught productivity software at another Canadian college, the Academy of Learning, for four years. Penny has experience in helping students achieve their goals through various learning models from instructor-led to self-directed to online.

Before embarking on a career in education, Penny worked in the fields of advertising, marketing/sales, mechanical and electronic engineering technology, and computer programming. When not working from her home office or indulging her passion for lifelong learning, Penny likes to read mysteries, garden, and relax at home in Hamilton, Ontario, with her Shih-Tzu, Gracie.

Margaret Leary, Northern Virginia Community College

Margaret Leary is Professor of IST at Northern Virginia Community College, teaching Networking and Network Security Courses for the past ten years. She is the co-Principal Investigator on the CyberWATCH initiative, an NSF-funded regional consortium of higher education institutions and businesses working together to increase the number of network security personnel in the workforce. She also serves as a Senior Security Policy Manager and Research Analyst at Nortel Government Solutions and holds a CISSP certification.

Margaret holds a B.S.B.A. and MBA/Technology Management from the University of Phoenix, and is pursuing her Ph.D. in Organization and Management with an IT Specialization at Capella University. Her dissertation is titled "Quantifying the Discoverability of Identity Attributes in Internet-Based Public Records: Impact on Identity Theft and Knowledge-based Authentication." She has several other published articles in various government and industry magazines, notably on identity management and network security.

Wen Liu, ITT Educational Services, Inc.

Wen Liu is Director of Corporate Curriculum Development at ITT Educational Services, Inc. He joined the ITT corporate headquarters in 1998 as a Senior Network Analyst to plan and deploy the corporate WAN infrastructure. A year later he assumed the position of Corporate Curriculum Manager supervising the curriculum development of all IT programs. After he was promoted to the current position three years ago, he continued to manage the curriculum research and development for all the programs offered in the School of Information Technology in addition to supervising the curriculum development in other areas (such as Schools of Drafting and Design and Schools of Electronics Technology). Prior to his employment with ITT Educational Services, Liu was a Telecommunications Analyst at the state government of Indiana working on the state backbone project that provided Internet and telecommunications services to the public users such as K-12 and higher education institutions, government agencies, libraries, and healthcare facilities.

Wen Liu has an M.A. in Student Personnel Administration in Higher Education and an M.S. in Information and Communications Sciences from Ball State University, Indiana. He used to be the director of special projects on the board of directors of the Indiana Telecommunications User Association, and used to serve on Course Technology's IT Advisory Board. He is currently a member of the IEEE and its Computer Society.

Jared Spencer, Westwood College Online

Jared Spencer has been the Lead Faculty for Networking at Westwood College Online since 2006. He began teaching in 2001 and has taught both on-ground and online for a variety of institutions, including Robert Morris University and Point Park University. In addition to his academic background, he has more than fifteen years of industry experience working for companies including the Thomson Corporation and IBM.

Jared has a master's degree in Internet Information Systems and is currently ABD and pursuing his doctorate in Information Systems at Nova Southeastern University. He has authored several papers that have been presented at conferences and appeared in publications such as the Journal of Internet Commerce and the Journal of Information Privacy and Security (JIPC). He holds a number of industry certifications, including AIX (UNIX), A+, Network+, Security+, MCSA on Windows 2000, and MCSA on Windows 2003 Server.

MOAC Windows Server Reviewers

We also thank the many reviewers who pored over the manuscript, providing invaluable feedback in the service of quality instructional materials.

Windows Server® 2008 Administrator Exam 70-646

Mark Babineau, CompuCollege — Moncton Campus
Brian Bordelon, Lantec Computer Training Center
John Crowley, Bucks County Community College
Fidelis Ngang, Houston Community College — Central Campus
Hermine Turner, Focus: HOPE
Bonnie Willy, Ivy Tech

Focus Group and Survey Participants

Finally, we thank the hundreds of instructors who participated in our focus groups and surveys to ensure that the Microsoft Official Academic Courses best met the needs of our customers.

Jean Aguilar, Mt. Hood Community College
Konrad Akens, Zane State College
Michael Albers, University of Memphis
Diana Anderson, Big Sandy Community & Technical College
Phyllis Anderson, Delaware County Community College
Judith Andrews, Feather River College
Damon Antos, American River College
Bridget Archer, Oakton Community College
Linda Arnold, Harrisburg Area Community College–Lebanon Campus
Neha Arya, Fullerton College
Mohammad Bajwa, Katharine Gibbs School–New York
Virginia Baker, University of Alaska Fairbanks
Carla Bannick, Pima Community College
Rita Barkley, Northeast Alabama Community College
Elsa Barr, Central Community College–Hastings
Ronald W. Barry, Ventura County Community College District
Elizabeth Bastedo, Central Carolina Technical College
Karen Baston, Waubonsee Community College
Karen Bean, Blinn College
Scott Beckstrand, Community College of Southern Nevada
Paulette Bell, Santa Rosa Junior College
Liz Bennett, Southeast Technical Institute
Nancy Bermea, Olympic College
Lucy Betz, Milwaukee Area Technical College
Meral Binbasioglu, Hofstra University
Catherine Binder, Strayer University & Katharine Gibbs School–Philadelphia
Terrel Blair, El Centro College
Ruth Blalock, Alamance Community College
Beverly Bohner, Reading Area Community College

Henry Bojack, Farmingdale State University
Matthew Bowie, Luna Community College
Julie Boyles, Portland Community College
Karen Brandt, College of the Albemarle
Stephen Brown, College of San Mateo
Jared Bruckner, Southern Adventist University
Pam Brune, Chattanooga State Technical Community College
Sue Buchholz, Georgia Perimeter College
Roberta Buczyna, Edison College
Angela Butler, Mississippi Gulf Coast Community College
Rebecca Byrd, Augusta Technical College
Kristen Callahan, Mercer County Community College
Judy Cameron, Spokane Community College
Dianne Campbell, Athens Technical College
Gena Casas, Florida Community College at Jacksonville
Jesus Castrejon, Latin Technologies
Gail Chambers, Southwest Tennessee Community College
Jacques Chansavang, Indiana University–Purdue University Fort Wayne
Nancy Chapko, Milwaukee Area Technical College
Rebecca Chavez, Yavapai College
Sanjiv Chopra, Thomas Nelson Community College
Greg Clements, Midland Lutheran College
Dayna Coker, Southwestern Oklahoma State University–Sayre Campus
Tamra Collins, Otero Junior College
Janet Conrey, Gavilan Community College
Carol Cornforth, West Virginia Northern Community College
Gary Cotton, American River College
Edie Cox, Chattahoochee Technical College
Rollie Cox, Madison Area Technical College

David Crawford, Northwestern Michigan College

J.K. Crowley, Victor Valley College

Rosalyn Culver, Washtenaw Community College

Sharon Custer, Huntington University

Sandra Daniels, New River Community College

Anila Das, Cedar Valley College

Brad Davis, Santa Rosa Junior College

Susan Davis, Green River Community College

Mark Dawdy, Lincoln Land Community College

Jennifer Day, Sinclair Community College

Carol Deane, Eastern Idaho Technical College

Julie DeBuhr, Lewis-Clark State College

Janis DeHaven, Central Community College

Drew Dekreon, University of Alaska–Anchorage

Joy DePover, Central Lakes College

Salli DiBartolo, Brevard Community College

Melissa Diegnau, Riverland Community College

Al Dillard, Lansdale School of Business

Marjorie Duffy, Cosumnes River College

Sarah Dunn, Southwest Tennessee Community College

Shahla Durany, Tarrant County College–South Campus

Kay Durden, University of Tennessee at Martin

Dineen Ebert, St. Louis Community College–Meramec

Donna Ehrhart, State University of New York–Brockport

Larry Elias, Montgomery County Community College

Glenda Elser, New Mexico State University at Alamogordo

Angela Evangelinos, Monroe County Community College

Angie Evans, Ivy Tech Community College of Indiana

Linda Farrington, Indian Hills Community College

Dana Fladhammer, Phoenix College

Richard Flores, Citrus College

Connie Fox, Community and Technical College at Institute of Technology West Virginia University

Wanda Freeman, Okefenokee Technical College

Brenda Freeman, Augusta Technical College

Susan Fry, Boise State University

Roger Fulk, Wright State University–Lake Campus

Sue Furnas, Collin County Community College District

Sandy Gabel, Vernon College

Laura Galvan, Fayetteville Technical Community College

Candace Garrod, Red Rocks Community College

Sherrie Geitgey, Northwest State Community College

Chris Gerig, Chattahoochee Technical College

Barb Gillespie, Cuyamaca College

Jessica Gilmore, Highline Community College

Pamela Gilmore, Reedley College

Debbie Glinert, Queensborough Community College

Steven Goldman, Polk Community College

Bettie Goodman, C.S. Mott Community College

Mike Grabill, Katharine Gibbs School–Philadelphia

Francis Green, Penn State University

Walter Griffin, Blinn College

Fillmore Guinn, Odessa College

Helen Haasch, Milwaukee Area Technical College

John Habal, Ventura College

Joy Haerens, Chaffey College

Norman Hahn, Thomas Nelson Community College

Kathy Hall, Alamance Community College

Teri Harbacheck, Boise State University

Linda Harper, Richland Community College

Maureen Harper, Indian Hills Community College

Steve Harris, Katharine Gibbs School–New York

Robyn Hart, Fresno City College

Darien Hartman, Boise State University

Gina Hatcher, Tacoma Community College

Winona T. Hatcher, Aiken Technical College

BJ Hathaway, Northeast Wisconsin Tech College

Cynthia Hauki, West Hills College – Coalinga

Mary L. Haynes, Wayne County Community College

Marcie Hawkins, Zane State College

Steve Hebrock, Ohio State University Agricultural Technical Institute

Sue Heistand, Iowa Central Community College

Heith Hennel, Valencia Community College

Donna Hendricks, South Arkansas Community College

Judy Hendrix, Dyersburg State Community College

Gloria Hensel, Matanuska-Susitna College University of Alaska Anchorage

Gwendolyn Hester, Richland College

Tammarra Holmes, Laramie County Community College

Dee Hobson, Richland College

Keith Hoell, Katharine Gibbs School–New York

Pashia Hogan, Northeast State Technical Community College

Susan Hoggard, Tulsa Community College

Kathleen Holliman, Wallace Community College Selma

Chastity Honchul, Brown Mackie College/ Wright State University

Christie Hovey, Lincoln Land Community College

Peggy Hughes, Allegany College of Maryland

Sandra Hume, Chippewa Valley Technical College

John Hutson, Aims Community College

Celia Ing, Sacramento City College

Joan Ivey, Lanier Technical College

Barbara Jaffari, College of the Redwoods

Penny Jakes, University of Montana College of Technology

Eduardo Jaramillo, Peninsula College

Barbara Jauken, Southeast Community College

Susan Jennings, Stephen F. Austin State University

Leslie Jernberg, Eastern Idaho Technical College

Linda Johns, Georgia Perimeter College

Brent Johnson, Okefenokee Technical College

Mary Johnson, Mt. San Antonio College

Shirley Johnson, Trinidad State Junior College–Valley Campus

Sandra M. Jolley, Tarrant County College

Teresa Jolly, South Georgia Technical College

Dr. Deborah Jones, South Georgia Technical College

Margie Jones, Central Virginia Community College

Randall Jones, Marshall Community and Technical College

Diane Karlsbraaten, Lake Region State College

Teresa Keller, Ivy Tech Community College of Indiana

Charles Kemnitz, Pennsylvania College of Technology

Sandra Kinghorn, Ventura College

Bill Klein, Katharine Gibbs School–Philadelphia

Bea Knaapen, Fresno City College

Kit Kofoed, Western Wyoming Community College

Maria Kolatis, County College of Morris

Barry Kolb, Ocean County College

Karen Kuralt, University of Arkansas at Little Rock

Belva-Carole Lamb, Rogue Community College

Betty Lambert, Des Moines Area Community College

Anita Lande, Cabrillo College

Junnae Landry, Pratt Community College

Karen Lankisch, UC Clermont

David Lanzilla, Central Florida Community College

Nora Laredo, Cerritos Community College

Jennifer Larrabee, Chippewa Valley Technical College

Debra Larson, Idaho State University

Barb Lave, Portland Community College

Audrey Lawrence, Tidewater Community College

Deborah Layton, Eastern Oklahoma State College

Larry LeBlanc, Owen Graduate School– Vanderbilt University

Philip Lee, Nashville State Community College

Michael Lehrfeld, Brevard Community College

Vasant Limaye, Southwest Collegiate Institute for the Deaf – Howard College

Anne C. Lewis, Edgecombe Community College

Stephen Linkin, Houston Community College

Peggy Linston, Athens Technical College

Hugh Lofton, Moultrie Technical College

Donna Lohn, Lakeland Community College

Jackie Lou, Lake Tahoe Community College

Donna Love, Gaston College

Curt Lynch, Ozarks Technical Community College

Sheilah Lynn, Florida Community College– Jacksonville

Pat R. Lyon, Tomball College

Bill Madden, Bergen Community College

Heather Madden, Delaware Technical & Community College

Donna Madsen, Kirkwood Community College

Jane Maringer-Cantu, Gavilan College

Suzanne Marks, Bellevue Community College

Carol Martin, Louisiana State University– Alexandria

Cheryl Martucci, Diablo Valley College

Roberta Marvel, Eastern Wyoming College

Tom Mason, Brookdale Community College

Mindy Mass, Santa Barbara City College

Dixie Massaro, Irvine Valley College

Rebekah May, Ashland Community & Technical College

Emma Mays-Reynolds, Dyersburg State Community College

Timothy Mayes, Metropolitan State College of Denver

Reggie McCarthy, Central Lakes College

Matt McCaskill, Brevard Community College

Kevin McFarlane, Front Range Community College

Donna McGill, Yuba Community College

Terri McKeever, Ozarks Technical Community College

Patricia McMahon, South Suburban College

Sally McMillin, Katharine Gibbs School–Philadelphia

Charles McNerney, Bergen Community College

Lisa Mears, Palm Beach Community College

Imran Mehmood, ITT Technical Institute–King of Prussia Campus

Virginia Melvin, Southwest Tennessee Community College

Jeanne Mercer, Texas State Technical College

Denise Merrell, Jefferson Community & Technical College

Catherine Merrikin, Pearl River Community College

Diane D. Mickey, Northern Virginia Community College

Darrelyn Miller, Grays Harbor College

Sue Mitchell, Calhoun Community College

Jacquie Moldenhauer, Front Range Community College

Linda Motonaga, Los Angeles City College

Sam Mryyan, Allen County Community College

Cindy Murphy, Southeastern Community College

Ryan Murphy, Sinclair Community College

Sharon E. Nastav, Johnson County Community College

Christine Naylor, Kent State University Ashtabula

Haji Nazarian, Seattle Central Community College

Nancy Noe, Linn-Benton Community College

Jennie Noriega, San Joaquin Delta College

Linda Nutter, Peninsula College

Thomas Omerza, Middle Bucks Institute of Technology

Edith Orozco, St. Philip's College

Dona Orr, Boise State University

Joanne Osgood, Chaffey College

Janice Owens, Kishwaukee College

Tatyana Pashnyak, Bainbridge College

John Partacz, College of DuPage

Tim Paul, Montana State University–Great Falls

Joseph Perez, South Texas College

Mike Peterson, Chemeketa Community College

Dr. Karen R. Petitto, West Virginia Wesleyan College

Terry Pierce, Onandaga Community College

Ashlee Pieris, Raritan Valley Community College

Jamie Pinchot, Thiel College

Michelle Poertner, Northwestern Michigan College

Betty Posta, University of Toledo

Deborah Powell, West Central Technical College

Mark Pranger, Rogers State University

Carolyn Rainey, Southeast Missouri State University

Linda Raskovich, Hibbing Community College

Leslie Ratliff, Griffin Technical College

Mar-Sue Ratzke, Rio Hondo Community College

Roxy Reissen, Southeastern Community College

Silvio Reyes, Technical Career Institutes

Patricia Rishavy, Anoka Technical College

Jean Robbins, Southeast Technical Institute

Carol Roberts, Eastern Maine Community College and University of Maine

Teresa Roberts, Wilson Technical Community College

Vicki Robertson, Southwest Tennessee Community College

Betty Rogge, Ohio State Agricultural Technical Institute

Lynne Rusley, Missouri Southern State University

Claude Russo, Brevard Community College

Ginger Sabine, Northwestern Technical College

Steven Sachs, Los Angeles Valley College

Joanne Salas, Olympic College

Lloyd Sandmann, Pima Community College–Desert Vista Campus

Beverly Santillo, Georgia Perimeter College

Theresa Savarese, San Diego City College

Sharolyn Sayers, Milwaukee Area Technical College

Judith Scheeren, Westmoreland County Community College

Adolph Scheiwe, Joliet Junior College

Marilyn Schmid, Asheville-Buncombe Technical Community College

Janet Sebesy, Cuyahoga Community College

Phyllis T. Shafer, Brookdale Community College

Ralph Shafer, Truckee Meadows Community College

Anne Marie Shanley, County College of Morris

Shelia Shelton, Surry Community College

Merilyn Shepherd, Danville Area Community College

Susan Sinele, Aims Community College

Beth Sindt, Hawkeye Community College

Andrew Smith, Marian College

Brenda Smith, Southwest Tennessee Community College

Lynne Smith, State University of New York–Delhi

Rob Smith, Katharine Gibbs School–Philadelphia

Tonya Smith, Arkansas State University–Mountain Home

Del Spencer – Trinity Valley Community College

Jeri Spinner, Idaho State University

Eric Stadnik, Santa Rosa Junior College

Karen Stanton, Los Medanos College

Meg Stoner, Santa Rosa Junior College

Beverly Stowers, Ivy Tech Community College of Indiana

Marcia Stranix, Yuba College

Kim Styles, Tri-County Technical College

Sylvia Summers, Tacoma Community College

Beverly Swann, Delaware Technical & Community College

Ann Taff, Tulsa Community College

Mike Theiss, University of Wisconsin–Marathon Campus

Romy Thiele, Cañada College

Sharron Thompson, Portland Community College

Ingrid Thompson-Sellers, Georgia Perimeter College

Barbara Tietsort, University of Cincinnati–Raymond Walters College

Janine Tiffany, Reading Area Community College

Denise Tillery, University of Nevada Las Vegas

Susan Trebelhorn, Normandale Community College

Noel Trout, Santiago Canyon College

Cheryl Turgeon, Asnuntuck Community College

Steve Turner, Ventura College

Sylvia Unwin, Bellevue Community College

Lilly Vigil, Colorado Mountain College

Sabrina Vincent, College of the Mainland

Mary Vitrano, Palm Beach Community College

Brad Vogt, Northeast Community College

Cozell Wagner, Southeastern Community College

Carolyn Walker, Tri-County Technical College

Sherry Walker, Tulsa Community College

Qi Wang, Tacoma Community College

Betty Wanielista, Valencia Community College

Marge Warber, Lanier Technical College–Forsyth Campus

Marjorie Webster, Bergen Community College

Linda Wenn, Central Community College

Mark Westlund, Olympic College

Carolyn Whited, Roane State Community College

Winona Whited, Richland College

Jerry Wilkerson, Scott Community College

Joel Willenbring, Fullerton College

Barbara Williams, WITC Superior

Charlotte Williams, Jones County Junior College

Bonnie Willy, Ivy Tech Community College of Indiana

Diane Wilson, J. Sargeant Reynolds Community College

James Wolfe, Metropolitan Community College

Marjory Wooten, Lanier Technical College

Mark Yanko, Hocking College

Alexis Yusov, Pace University

Naeem Zaman, San Joaquin Delta College

Kathleen Zimmerman, Des Moines Area Community College

We also thank Lutz Ziob, Jim DiIanni, Merrick Van Dongen, Jim LeValley, Bruce Curling, Joe Wilson, Rob Linsky, Jim Clark, and Scott Serna at Microsoft for their encouragement and support in making the Microsoft Official Academic Course programs the finest instructional materials for mastering the newest Microsoft technologies for both students and instructors.

Brief Contents

Contents

Planning Server Deployments

OBJECTIVE DOMAIN MATRIX

TECHNOLOGY SKILL	OBJECTIVE DOMAIN	OBJECTIVE DOMAIN NUMBER
Installing Microsoft Assessment and Planning Solution Accelerator	Plan server installations and upgrades	1.1
Understanding the deployment process	Plan for automated server deployment	1.2

KEY TERMS

answer file
boot image
image group
imageX.exe
install image
master computer
Microsoft Assessment
   and Planning Solution
   Accelerator (MAP)

Microsoft Deployment Toolkit
   (MDT) 2008
preboot execution
   environment (PXE)
Server Core
single instance storage
technician computer
unattend file
Windows Automated

Installation Kit (AIK)
Windows Deployment Services
   (WDS)
Windows PE (Preinstallation
   Environment) 2.1
Windows RE (Recovery
   Environment)
Windows System Image
   Manager (Windows SIM)

The primary focus of the server administrator's job includes the day-to-day operation of an organization's servers. Before that task begins, however, the administrator might also be responsible for deploying those servers on the network. While it is possible to create Windows Server 2008 servers simply by performing a manual installation on each individual computer, this can be time-consuming and impractical for large-scale deployments. To support deployments of a large number of servers and workstations, Microsoft has created a number of specialized tools. In this lesson, you will study various elements of the Windows Server 2008 deployment process in an enterprise environment, including the following:

- Selecting a Windows Server 2008 edition
- Performing a hardware inventory
- Creating and deploying answer files and image files
- Planning large-scale deployment projects

■ Selecting a Windows Server 2008 Edition

↓
THE BOTTOM LINE
Microsoft now releases all of its operating systems in multiple editions, which provides consumers with varying price points and feature sets.

When planning a server deployment for a large enterprise network, the operating system edition you choose for your servers must be based on multiple factors, including the following:

- The hardware in the computers
- The features and capabilities you require for your servers
- The price of the operating system software

Depending on how you care to count them, there are as many as 13 Windows Server 2008 products available. The four basic editions are as follows:

- Windows Web Server 2008—Designed specifically for computers functioning as Internet or intranet Web servers, this edition includes all of the Internet Information Services 7.0 capabilities, but it cannot function as an Active Directory domain controller, and it lacks some of the other features found in the other editions as well. The licensing terms for this product forbid you to run client/server applications that are not Web-based.
- Windows Server 2008 Standard—The Standard edition includes nearly the full set of Windows Server 2008 features, lacking only some high-end components, such as server clustering and Active Directory Federation Services. Standard edition is also limited to computers with up to 4 GB of RAM (in the x86 version) and up to four processors.
- Windows Server 2008 Enterprise—The Enterprise edition includes the full set of Windows Server 2008 features, and supports computers with up to eight processors and up to 64 GB of RAM (in the x86 edition). Enterprise also supports up to four virtual images with Hyper-V (in the 64-bit version) and an unlimited number of network connections.
- Windows Server 2008 Datacenter—The Datacenter edition is designed for large and powerful servers with up to 64 processors and fault tolerance features such as hot add processor support. As a result, this edition is available only from original equipment manufacturers (OEMs), bundled with a server.

Each of these editions is available in two versions, supporting x86 and x64 processors. The x64 Standard, Enterprise, and Datacenter editions are also available in a version without the Hyper-V virtualization feature, at a slightly reduced price. Finally, there are two additional versions for specialized platforms:

- Windows Server 2008 for Itanium-Based Systems—This edition, designed especially for computers with Itanium processors, is intended for enterprise-class servers with up to 64 processors, typically running large database or line of business applications.
- Windows HPC Server 2008—A 64-bit version of Windows Server 2008 for high performance computing, capable of supporting thousands of processing cores, and designed with special tools to help administrators manage and monitor high-end server hardware platforms.

Introducing Windows Server 2008 Features and Capabilities

The various editions of Windows Server 2008 differ primarily in their feature sets.

The features and capabilities of the five main Windows Server 2008 editions are listed in Table 1-1.

Table 1-1

Features and Capabilities of Windows Server 2008 Editions

FEATURE	WEB	STANDARD	ENTERPRISE	DATACENTER	ITANIUM
Number of processors supported	4	4	8	32 (x86) / 64 (x64)	64
Maximum RAM (x86)	4 GB	4 GB	64 GB	64 GB	N/A
Maximum RAM (x64)	32 GB	32 GB	2 TB	2 TB	N/A
Maximum RAM (IA64)	N/A	N/A	N/A	N/A	2 TB
Hot add/replace memory support	No	No	Yes (add only)	Yes	Yes
Hot add/replace processor support	No	No	No	Yes	Yes
Maximum failover cluster nodes	N/A	N/A	16	16	8
Fault tolerant memory sync	No	No	Yes	Yes	Yes
Cross-file replication	No	No	Yes	Yes	Yes
Network Policy and Access Services	No	Yes	Yes	Yes	No
Maximum Routing and Remote Access Services (RRAS) Connections	N/A	250	Unlimited	Unlimited	2
Maximum Internet Authentication Services (IAS) connections	N/A	50	Unlimited	Unlimited	N/A
Hyper-V support (64-bit only)	No	Yes	Yes	Yes	No
Virtual Image Use Rights	N/A	1	4	Unlimited	Unlimited
Terminal Services Gateway and RemoteApp	No	Yes	Yes	Yes	No
Maximum Terminal Services Gateway Connections	N/A	250	Unlimited	Unlimited	N/A
Network Access Protection	No	Yes	Yes	Yes	No
Windows Deployment Services	No	Yes	Yes	Yes	No
Server Core support	Yes	Yes	Yes	Yes	No
Terminal Services	No	Yes	Yes	Yes	No
Distributed File Services	No	Yes (one DFS root)	Yes	Yes	No
Active Directory Domain Services	No	Yes	Yes	Yes	No
Active Directory Lightweight Directory Services	No	Yes	Yes	Yes	No
Active Directory Federation Services	No	No	Yes	Yes	No
Active Directory Rights Management Services (RMS)	No	Yes	Yes	Yes	No
Active Directory Certificate Services	No	Yes (creates CAs only	Yes	Yes	No

(continued)

Table 1-1 *(continued)*

FEATURE	WEB	STANDARD	ENTERPRISE	DATACENTER	ITANIUM
DHCP Server	No	Yes	Yes	Yes	No
DNS Server	No	Yes	Yes	Yes	No
Windows Internet Naming Service (WINS)	No	Yes	Yes	Yes	No
Fax Server	No	Yes	Yes	Yes	No
UDDI Services	No	Yes	Yes	Yes	No
Print Services	No	Yes	Yes	Yes	No
Application Server	No	Yes	Yes	Yes	Yes
Windows Clustering	No	No	Yes	Yes	Yes
Simple Mail Transfer Protocol	Yes	Yes	Yes	Yes	No
Subsystem for UNIX-Based Applications	No	Yes	Yes	Yes	Yes
Microsoft Message Queuing	No	Yes	Yes	Yes	Yes
BitLocker Drive Encryption	No	Yes	Yes	Yes	Yes
iSNS Server Service	Yes	Yes	Yes	Yes	No
Multipath I/O	No	Yes	Yes	Yes	Yes
BITS Server Extensions	No	Yes	Yes	Yes	Yes
Removable Storage Management	No	Yes	Yes	Yes	Yes

For most administrators planning a server deployment, the main operating system decision will be between Windows Server 2008 Standard or Windows Server 2008 Enterprise. In some cases, hardware is the deciding factor. If, for example, you plan to use computers with more than four x86 processors or more than 4 GB of memory, either now or in the future, then you will need Windows Server 2008 Enterprise. Hardware will also dictate whether you choose the x86 or x64 version, or Windows Server 2008 for Itanium-Based Systems.

Features can be the deciding factor in the selection of an operating system edition once you have a fully developed network deployment plan. For example, you are not likely to know if you will need the server clustering or Active Directory Federation Services capabilities of Windows Server 2008 Enterprise until you have server deployment and directory services plans in hand.

These plans can also affect the hardware you select for your servers, which in turn can affect your operating system selection. For example, if your organization decides to make a major commitment to Terminal Services, this could mean that your network will require more powerful servers and less powerful workstations. Servers with more processors can handle more simultaneous Terminal Services clients. Windows Server 2008 Enterprise supports more processors than Windows Server 2008 Standard, and it supports an unlimited number of Terminal Services Gateway connections. Network design decisions of this type are inevitably interlocked with hardware and software purchasing decisions, so selecting the correct Windows Server 2008 edition will be a crucial aspect of the planning phase.

Using Server Core

Many enterprise networks today use servers that are dedicated to a particular role. When a server is performing a single role, does it really make sense to have so many other processes running on the server that contribute little to that role?

Computer users today have become so accustomed to graphical user interfaces (GUIs) that many are unaware that there was ever any other way to operate a computer. When the first version of Windows NT Server appeared in 1993, many network administrators complained about wasting server resources on graphical displays and other elements that they deemed unnecessary. Up until that time, server displays were usually minimal, character-based, mono-chrome affairs. In fact, many servers had no display hardware at all, relying instead on text-based remote administration tools, such as Telnet.

INTRODUCING SERVER CORE

Windows Server 2008 includes an installation option that addresses those old complaints. When you select the Windows *Server Core* installation option in Windows Server 2008, you get a stripped-down version of the operating system. There is no Start menu, no desktop Explorer shell, no Microsoft Management Console, and virtually no graphical applications. All you see when you start the computer is a single window with a command prompt.

  Server Core is not a separate product or edition. It is an installation option included with the Windows Server 2008 Standard, Enterprise, and Datacenter Editions, in both the x86 and x64 versions. Note that Hyper-V is available only on x64 versions of Server Core.

In addition to omitting most of the graphical interface, a Server Core installation omits some of the server roles and features found in a full installation. Tables 1-2 and 1-3 list the roles and features that are available and not available in a Server Core installation.

Table 1-2

Windows Server 2008 Server Core Roles

ROLES AVAILABLE IN SERVER CORE INSTALLATION	ROLES NOT AVAILABLE IN SERVER CORE INSTALLATION
Active Directory Domain Services	Active Directory Certificate Services
Active Directory Lightweight Directory Services	Active Directory Federation Services
DHCP Server	Active Directory Rights Management Services
DNS Server	Network Policy and Access Services
File Services	Windows Deployment Services
Print Services	Application Server
Web Server (IIS)	Fax Server
Streaming Media Services	Terminal Services
Hyper-V (Virtualization)	UDDI Services

Table 1-3

Windows Server 2008 Server Core Features

FEATURES AVAILABLE IN SERVER CORE INSTALLATION	FEATURES NOT AVAILABLE IN SERVER CORE INSTALLATION
BitLocker Drive Encryption	.NET Framework 3.0
Failover Clustering	BITS Server Extensions
Multipath I/O	Connection Manager Administration Kit
Network Load Balancing	Desktop Experience
QoS (Quality of Service) (qWave)	Internet Printing Client
Removable Storage Manager	Internet Storage Name Server
SNMP Services	LPR Port Monitor
Subsystem for UNIX-based Applications	Message Queuing
Telnet Client	Peer Name Resolution Protocol
Windows Server Backup	Remote Assistance
Windows Internet Name Service (WINS) Server	Remote Server Administration Tools
	RPC Over HTTP Proxy
	Simple TCP/IP Services
	SMTP Server
	Storage Manager for SANs
	Telnet Server
	Trivial File Transfer Protocol Client
	Windows Internal Database
	Windows Process Activation Service
	Windows System Resource Manager
	Wireless LAN Service

ADMINISTERING SERVER CORE

Obviously, with so much of the operating system scaled down, a computer running Server Core can devote more of its resources to its server functions. However, the missing elements provide most of the traditional Windows Server management and administration tools, such as MMC consoles. To work with a Server Core computer, you must rely primarily on either the extensive collection of command prompt tools Microsoft includes with Windows Server 2008 or use MMC consoles on another system to connect to the server.

A few graphical applications can still run on Server Core. Notepad still works, so you can edit scripts and batch files. Registry Editor runs as well, enabling you to modify registry settings, because it has no command line equivalent. Task Manager runs, enabling you to load programs and monitor processes. Some elements of the Control Panel work as well, including the Date and Time application and the Regional and Language Options.

JUSTIFYING SERVER CORE

The next logical question to ask about Server Core is whether it is worth the inconvenience of learning a completely new management paradigm and giving up so much server functionality to save some memory and processor clock cycles. The answer is that there are other benefits to using Server Core besides hardware resource conservation.

As mentioned earlier, many Windows Server computers on enterprise networks are dedicated to a single role, but they still have a great many other applications, services, and processes running on them all the time. You can take it as an axiom that the more complex a system is, the more ways it can go wrong. Despite the fact that all of those extra software elements are performing no useful purpose, it is still necessary to maintain and update them, and that introduces the potential for failure. By removing many of these elements and leaving only the functions needed to perform the server's role, you diminish the failure potential, reduce the number of updates you need to apply, and increase the computer's reliability.

Another drawback to having all of those unnecessary processes running on a server is that they provide increased attack avenues into the computer. The more processes a computer is running, the more exploits there are to attack. Removing the unneeded software elements makes the server more secure.

USING SERVER CORE FOR APPLICATION SERVERS

It is clear from Tables 1-2 and 1-3, earlier in this section, that the Server Core installation option is limited when it comes to application services. In fact, Server Core is not intended as a platform for running server applications, only for running mission-critical server roles. The removal of the Application Server and Terminal Services roles means that you cannot use Server Core to deploy many applications or Terminal Services connections. However, the Server Core option does provide a viable alternative for file and print servers, DHCP and DNS servers, domain controllers at branch offices, and a few other roles.

■ Inventorying Hardware

 THE BOTTOM LINE   Deploying Windows Server 2008 on a large network can often mean evaluating a large number of existing servers, to determine whether they have the appropriate hardware for the operating system.

Performing a hardware inventory can be a daunting task, especially when you have servers with many different hardware configurations, located at distant sites. ***Microsoft Assessment and Planning Solution Accelerator (MAP)*** is a new tool that adds to the capabilities of its predecessor, Windows Vista Hardware Assessment Solution Accelerator, so that you can evaluate the hardware on servers as well as workstations.

Unlike some other products of its type, MAP is capable of performing a hardware inventory on computers with no agent software required on the client side. This means that you can install MAP on one system, and it will connect to any or all of the other computers on your network and add information about their hardware to a database. MAP can then evaluate the hardware information and create reports that perform tasks such as the following:

- Identify computers that are capable of running Windows Server 2008
- Identify computers needing upgrade to Office 2007
- Migrate specific roles and services to Windows Server 2008
- Capture performance metrics for servers and workstations
- Prepare recommendations for server consolidation using Windows Server 2008 Hyper-V or Virtual Server 2005 R2
- Prepare recommendations for application virtualization using Microsoft Application Virtualization

The following sections examine the process of installing and using MAP.

Installing Microsoft Assessment and Planning Solution Accelerator

MAP has several installation and licensing prerequisites that you must meet before you can successfully install the software.

CERTIFICATION READY?
Plan server installations and upgrades
1.1

MAP is essentially a database application based on Microsoft SQL Server 2005 Express, a scaled-down, free version of SQL Server 2005. MAP can run on the 32-bit version of the following operating systems:

- Windows Vista
- Windows XP Professional with Service Pack 2
- Windows Server 2003 R2

TAKE NOTE*

Microsoft Assessment and Planning Solution Accelerator (MAP) is available as a free download from Microsoft's Web site at http://www.microsoft.com/downloads

MAP also requires that you install Microsoft Office 2007 or Microsoft Office 2003 SP2 on the computer, and that you install all available updates for both Windows and Office.

The performance of MAP depends both on the number of computers you plan to inventory and the resources in the computer running MAP. Table 1-4 lists Microsoft's hardware recommendations for the MAP computer, based on the number of computers on your network. Microsoft SQL Server 2005 Express is limited to using no more than 1 GB of RAM and can create databases up to 4 GB in size. To inventory an enterprise network consisting of 20,000 computers or more, you should run MAP on a server with SQL Server 2005 Standard installed.

Table 1-4

Hardware and Software Recommendations for Microsoft Assessment and Planning Solution Accelerator (MAP)

Number of Computers to Inventory	Operating System	Database Manager	Processor	RAM
1 to 4,999	Windows Vista Windows XP Windows Server 2003 R2	SQL Server 2005 Express	1.5 GHz +	1.5 GB + (2 GB + for Vista)
5,000 to 9,999	Windows Vista Windows XP Windows Server 2003 R2	SQL Server 2005 Express	1.5 GHz +	2.5 GB +
10,000 to 19,999	Windows Vista Windows XP Windows Server 2003 R2	SQL Server 2005 Express	1.5 GHz +	4 GB +
20,000 to 49,999	Windows Server 2003 R2	SQL Server 2005 Standard	1.5 GHz +	4 GB +
50,000 plus	Windows Server 2003 R2	SQL Server 2005 Standard	2.0 GHz +	4 GB +

When you run the Microsoft_Assessment_and_Planning_Solution_Setup.exe file, the Microsoft Assessment and Planning Solution Accelerator Setup Wizard appears, as shown in Figure 1-1.

Figure 1-1

The Microsoft Assessment and Planning Solution Accelerator Setup Wizard

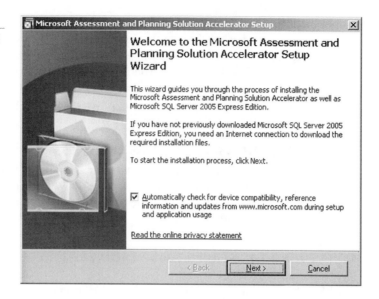

In addition to installing the MAP program itself, the wizard also downloads and installs Microsoft SQL Server 2005 Express, if necessary, as well as other required components, such as Microsoft .NET Framework 2.0. Once the wizard has completed the installation process, you can start working with MAP, as discussed in the next section.

Using Microsoft Assessment and Planning Solution Accelerator

MAP uses a console-based interface to configure its information gathering and report processing tasks.

When you start MAP, the Microsoft Assessment and Planning Solution Accelerator console appears, as shown in Figure 1-2.

Figure 1-2

The Microsoft Assessment and Planning Solution Accelerator console

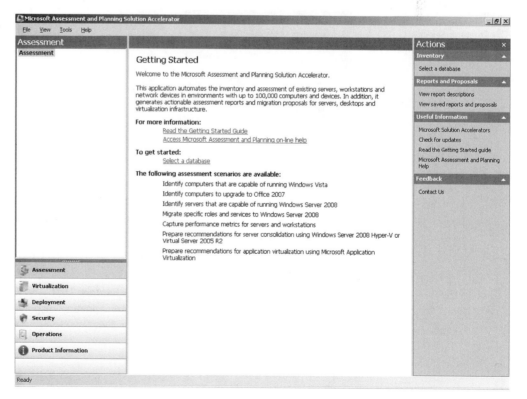

Before you do anything else, you must either create a new database or select an existing one. MAP requires a new database instance for its exclusive use, so unless you have already created a database during a previous MAP session, you should opt to create a new one. Once you have configured MAP with a database, you can select one of the pre-configured assessment reports in the details pane. This launches the Assessment Wizard, which performs the actual inventory of the network hardware, according to the parameters you select, and uses the information to compile a report on the subject you selected.

ASSESSING WINDOWS SERVER 2008 READINESS

MAP is capable of producing a number of different assessment reports, but all of these reports are based on the inventory information the Assessment Wizard collects. To determine which of the computers on your network have the hardware needed to run Windows Server 2008, use the following procedure.

 ASSESS WINDOWS SERVER 2008 READINESS

GET READY. Log on to the computer running MAP using an account with administrative privileges.

1. Click **Start,** and then click **All Programs** > **Microsoft Assessment and Planning Solution Accelerator** > **Microsoft Assessment and Planning Solution Accelerator.** The Microsoft Assessment and Planning Solution Accelerator console appears.

TAKE NOTE * The steps in this procedure assume that the MAP computer is running Windows Server 2003 R2. If the MAP computer is running Windows Vista or XP, some of the steps might be slightly different.

2. In the actions pane, click **Select a Database.** The Create or Select a Database To Use dialog box appears, as shown in Figure 1-3.

Figure 1-3

The Create or Select a Database To Use dialog box

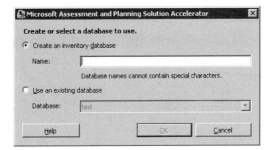

3. Select one of the following options and click **OK.**
   - Create an inventory database—Enables you to create a new database by using the SQL Server 2005 Express or SQL Server 2005 Standard engine installed on the computer
   - Use an existing database—Enables you to select the existing SQL Server database that you want MAP to use

4. In the details pane, click **Identify Servers That Are Capable Of Running Windows Server 2008.** The Assessment Wizard appears, displaying the *Select Reports and Proposals* page, as shown in Figure 1-4.

Figure 1-4

The Select Reports and
Proposals page of the
Assessment Wizard

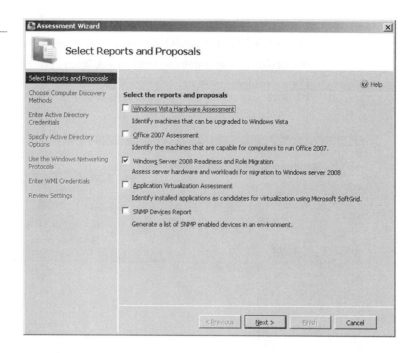

5. Leave the **Windows Server 2008 Readiness Role and Migration** checkbox selected
and click **Next.** The *Choose Computer Discovery Methods* page appears, as shown in
Figure 1-5.

Figure 1-5

The Choose Computer
Discovery Methods page of the
Assessment Wizard

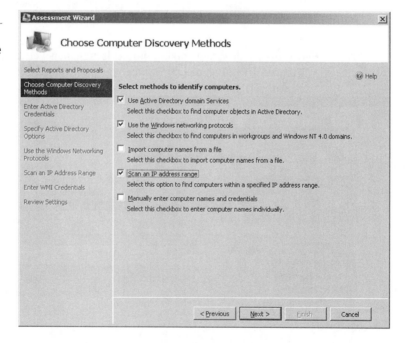

TAKE NOTE* You can select additional reports and proposals on this page, if desired. The hardware
inventory process remains essentially the same, but MAP creates additional reports, based
on the information it collects and compiles.

6. Select one or more of the following options and click **Next.** The wizard displays a configuration page (or pages) for each option you select.

- Use Active Directory domain services—After supplying Active Directory credentials, you can select the domains, containers, and organizational units in which you want the wizard to search for computers, as shown in Figure 1-6.

Figure 1-6

The Specify Active Directory Options page of the Assessment Wizard

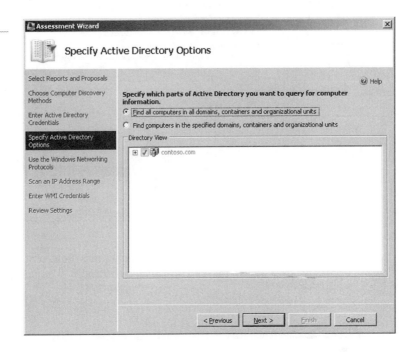

- Use the Windows networking protocols—Enables you to specify the workgroups and Windows NT 4.0 domains in which you want the wizard to search for computers, as shown in Figure 1-7.

Figure 1-7

The Use the Windows Networking Protocols page of the Assessment Wizard

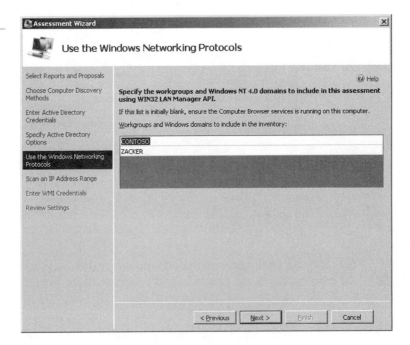

- Import computer names from a file—Enables you to specify the name of a text file containing a list of host names, NetBIOS names, or fully qualified domain names identifying the computers you want the wizard to inventory, as shown in Figure 1-8.

Figure 1-8

The Import Computer Names From a File page of the Assessment Wizard

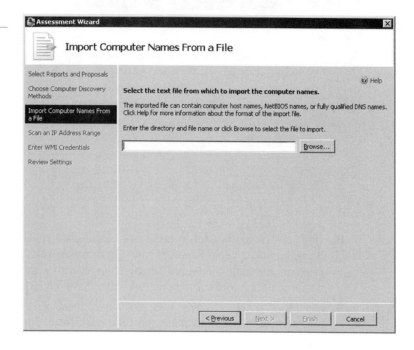

- Scan an IP address range—Enables you to specify one or more ranges of IP addresses that you want the wizard to search for computers, as shown in Figure 1-9.

Figure 1-9

The Scan an IP Address Range page of the Assessment Wizard

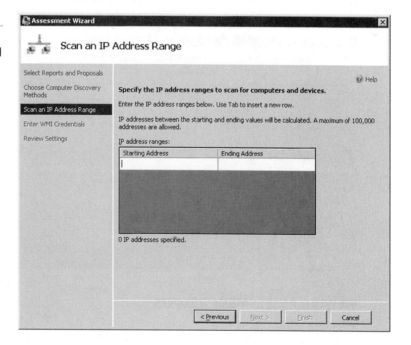

- Manually enter computer names and credentials—Enables you to specify the names of the computers you want the wizard to inventory.

7. On the *Enter WMI Credentials* page, click **New Account**. The Inventory Account dialog box appears, as shown in Figure 1-10.

Figure 1-10

The Inventory Account dialog box

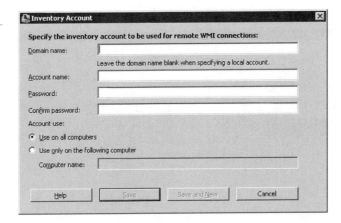

8. Enter the credentials for a domain or local administrative account in the Domain Name, Account Name, Password, and Confirm Password text boxes. Then, specify whether you want the wizard to use the credentials on all of the computers it finds, or on a specific computer, and click **Save**.

9. Add as many sets of credentials, domain or local, that the wizard will need to access the computers it finds, and then click **Next**. The *Review Settings* page appears.

Click **FINISH**.

A Status window appears, as shown in Figure 1-11, displaying the wizard's progress as it performs the inventory and creates the reports you selected.

Figure 1-11

The Assessment Wizard's Status window

Status			
The collection of information and preparation of the requested reports and proposals is running.			
Updates			
Hardware Compatibility List:			Completed
Reference Materials:			Completed
Computer Discovery			
Discovered by Active Directory:			3
Discovered by Windows Network Protocol:			13
IP addresses to scan:			254
Identified by User:			0
WMI - Retry from previous inventory:			0
Windows Management Instrumentation (WMI)			
Successfully inventoried:	12	of	267
Failed to connect:	255	of	267
Reports and Proposals			
Assessment:			Completed
Workbooks Generated: 0 of 0 worksheets completed	0	of	2
Proposals Generated:	0	of	1
			Cancel

VIEWING ASSESSMENT RESULTS

When the wizard completes the assessment process, the console's details pane, shown in Figure 1-12, displays links to resources that enable you to do the following:

- Determine why specific computers were not inventoried successfully
- Access the reports and proposals created by the Assessment Wizard
- Run the Assessment Wizard again to create additional reports and proposals

Figure 1-12

The MAP console, after completion of the Assessment Wizard

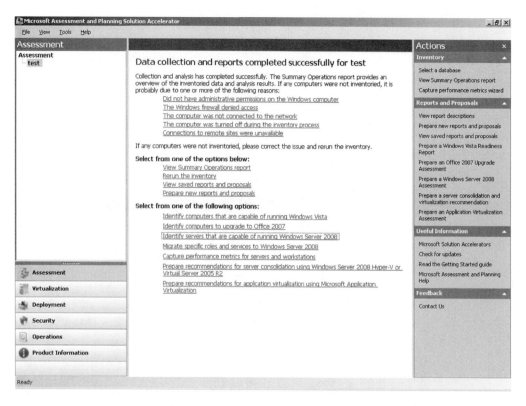

To view the documents that the Assessment Wizard just created, click View Saved Reports and Proposals. An Explorer window appears, displaying the contents of a folder named for the MAP database. The folder includes the following:

- WS2008 Proposal—A Microsoft Word document, as shown in Figure 1-13, which includes general information about deploying Windows Server 2008 on your network computers, with charts, tables, and other data compiled from the inventory added

Figure 1-13

The WS2008 Proposal file

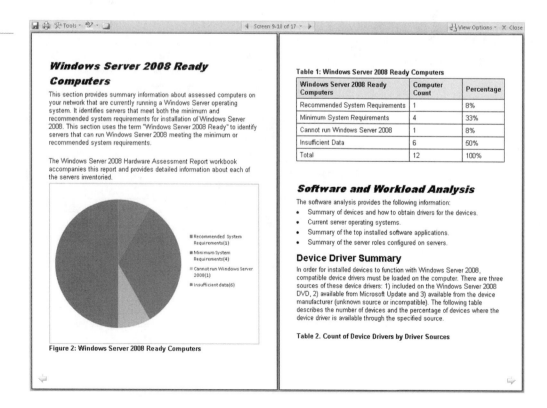

- WS2008 Hardware Assessment—A Microsoft Excel spreadsheet, as shown in Figure 1-14, which contains the detailed inventory of the computers found on the network, including system information, a device summary, device details, and discovered applications

Figure 1-14

The WS2008 Hardware Assessment file

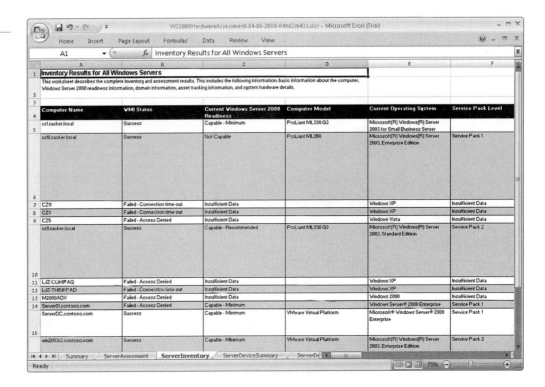

- WS2008 Role Assessment—A Microsoft Excel spreadsheet, as shown in Figure 1-15, which lists the roles currently installed on each server

Figure 1-15

The WS2008 Role Assessment file

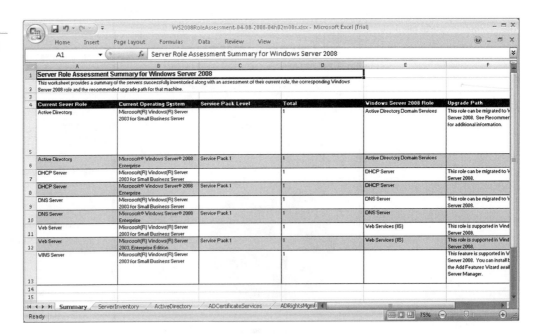

In addition to comparing each computer to the basic system requirements for Windows Server 2008, to determine whether the computer has a sufficiently fast processor and an appropriate amount of RAM, the Assessment Wizard also inventories the various peripheral devices in the system, such as disk drive interfaces and network interface adapters. The WS2008 Hardware Assessment spreadsheet lists all of the devices in each computer and specifies whether Windows Server 2008 includes drivers for them.

■ Automating Server Deployments

THE BOTTOM LINE

Microsoft provides a variety of tools that enable network administrators to deploy the Windows operating systems automatically, using file-based images.

After you have determined which of the servers on your network will run Windows Server 2008, it is time to begin thinking about the actual server deployment process. For small networks, manual server installations, in which you run the Windows Server 2008 DVD on each computer separately, might be the most practical solution. However, if you have many servers to install, you might benefit from automating the installation process, using tools such as the Windows Deployment Services role included with Windows Server 2008 or using the Windows Automated Installation Kit (AIK).

Using Windows Deployment Services

Windows Deployment Services enables administrators to perform attended and unattended operating system installations on remote computers.

Windows Deployment Services (WDS) is a role included with Windows Server 2008. This role enables you to perform unattended installations of Windows Server 2008 and other operating systems on remote computers, using network-based boot and installation media. This means that you can deploy a new computer with no operating system or local boot device on it by installing image files stored on a server running Windows Deployment Services.

WDS is a client/server application in which the server supplies operating system image files to clients on the network. However, unlike most client/server applications, the WDS server is also responsible for providing the remote computer with the boot files it needs to start up and the client side of the application.

For this to be possible, the client computer must have a network adapter that supports a *preboot execution environment (PXE)*. In a PXE, the computer, instead of booting from a local drive, connects to a server on the network and downloads the boot files it needs to run. In the case of a WDS installation, the client downloads a boot image file that loads *Windows PE (Preinstallation Environment) 2.1,* after which it installs the operating system by using another image file.

INSTALLING WINDOWS DEPLOYMENT SERVICES

To use WDS, you must install the Windows Deployment Services role, configure the service, and add the images you want to deploy. WDS is a standard role that you can install from the Initial Configuration Tasks window or the Server Manager console. The Windows Deployment Services role includes the following two role services:

- Deployment Server
- Transport Server

✚ MORE INFORMATION

The image files that WDS uses are highly compressed archives with a .wim extension. Unlike most image file formats, WIM images are file-based, not bit-based, which means that you can modify the image by adding or removing files as needed. For example, you can add an application or an updated device driver to an operating system image without re-creating it from scratch.

The Deployment Server role service provides a full WDS installation and requires installation of the Transport Server role service as well. If you select Transport Server by itself, you install only the core networking elements of WDS, which you can use to create namespaces that enable you to transmit image files using multicast addresses. You must choose the Deployment Server role service to perform full remote operating system installations.

The Add Roles Wizard enforces no other dependencies for the Windows Deployment Services role, but the role has several other prerequisites, as follows:

- Active Directory—The Windows Deployment Services computer must be a member of, or a domain controller for, an Active Directory domain.
- Dynamic Host Configuration Protocol (DHCP)—The network must have an operational DHCP server that is accessible by the WDS clients.
- Domain Name Service (DNS)—A DNS server must be on the network for the WDS server to function.
- NTFS—The WDS server must have an NTFS drive to store the image files.

The process of installing the Windows Deployment Services role does not add configuration pages to the Add Roles Wizard, but you must configure the server before clients can use it, as discussed in the following sections.

CONFIGURING THE WDS SERVER

After you install Windows Deployment Services, it remains inactive until you configure the service and add the images that the server will deploy to clients. To configure the server, use the following procedure.

 CONFIGURE A WDS SERVER

GET READY. Log on to Windows Server 2008 using an account with Administrative privileges. When the logon process is completed, close the Initial Configuration Tasks window and any other windows that appear.

1. Click **Start,** and then click **Administrative Tools** > **Windows Deployment Services.** The Windows Deployment Services console appears, as shown in Figure 1-16.

Figure 1-16

The Windows Deployment Services console

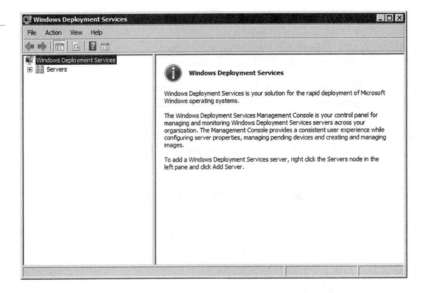

2. In the scope (left) pane, expand the **Servers** node. Right-click your server and, from the context menu, select **Configure Server.** The Windows Deployment Services Configuration Wizard appears.

3. Click **Next** to bypass the Welcome page. The *Remote Installation Folder Location* page appears, as shown in Figure 1-17.

Figure 1-17

The Remote Installation Folder Location page

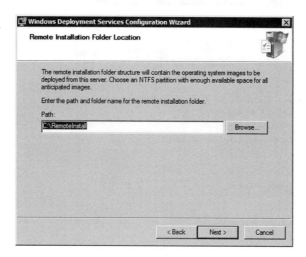

4. In the Path text box, key or browse to the folder where you want to locate the WDS image store. The folder you select must be on an NTFS drive and must have sufficient space to hold all of the images you want to deploy. Microsoft also recommends that you replace the default value with an image store location that is not on the system drive.

5. Click **Next** to continue. The *DHCP Option 60* page appears, as shown in Figure 1-18.

Figure 1-18

The DHCP Option 60 page

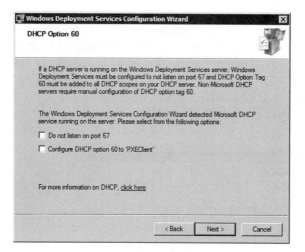

> **TAKE NOTE** *
>
> For a client computer to obtain a boot image from a WDS server, it must be able to locate that server on the network. Because the clients have no stored configuration or boot files when they start, they must use DHCP to discover the name or address of the WDS server.

6. If the DHCP role is running on the same server as the Windows Deployment Services role, select the **Do not listen on port 67** and **Configure DHCP option 60 to 'PXEClient'** checkboxes. Then click **Next.** The *PXE Server Initial Settings* page appears, as shown in Figure 1-19.

Figure 1-19

The PXE Server Initial Settings page

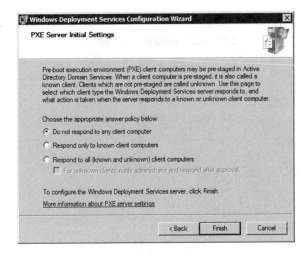

7. Select one of the following options:

Do not respond to any client computer—Prevents the WDS from providing boot access to any clients.

Respond only to known client computers—Configures the WDS server to provide boot access only to clients that you have prestaged in Active Directory by creating computer objects for them. This requires knowing the globally unique identifiers (GUIDs) of the computers, which you can obtain using the Bcdedit.exe program.

Respond to all (known and unknown) client computers—Configures the WDS server to provide access to all clients, whether you have prestaged them or not. Selecting the For unknown clients, notify administrator and respond after approval checkbox requires an administrator to approve each client connection attempt before the server provides it with boot access.

8. Click **Next** to complete the configuration process. The *Configuration Complete* page appears, as shown in Figure 1-20.

Figure 1-20

The Configuration Complete page

9. Select the **Add images to the Windows Deployment Server now** checkbox to launch the Add Image Wizard. Then click **Finish** to complete the Windows Deployment Services Configuration Wizard.

CLOSE the Windows Deployment Services console.

After the Windows Deployment Services Configuration Wizard has completed its tasks, the server has the proper environment to store image files and listen for incoming requests from clients. However, you still must populate the image store with image files, as described in the next section.

ADDING IMAGE FILES

Windows Deployment Services requires two types of image files to perform remote client installations: a boot image and an install image. A ***boot image*** contains the files needed to boot the computer and initiate an operating system installation. The Windows Server 2008 installation DVD includes a boot image file called boot.wim, located in the \Sources folder, which loads Windows PE 2.1 on the client computer. You can use this boot image file for virtually any operating system deployment without modification.

An ***install image*** contains the operating system that WDS will install on the client computer. Windows Server 2008 includes a file named install.wim in the \Sources folder on the installation DVD. This file contains install images for different operating system editions. You can apply these images to a new computer to perform a standard Windows Server 2008 setup, just as if you had used the DVD to perform a manual installation.

To add boot and install images into the image store of your WDS server, use the following procedure.

 ADD IMAGE FILES

GET READY. Log on to Windows Server 2008 using an account with Administrative privileges. When the logon process is completed, close the Initial Configuration Tasks window and any other windows that appear.

1. Click **Start,** and then click **Administrative Tools** > **Windows Deployment Services.** The Windows Deployment Services console appears.

2. Expand the Server node and the node for your server. Then, right-click the **Boot Images** folder and, from the context menu, select **Add Boot Image.** The Windows Deployment Services—Add Image Wizard appears, showing the *Image File* page, as shown in Figure 1-21.

Figure 1-21

The Image File page in the Windows Deployment Services—Add Image Wizard

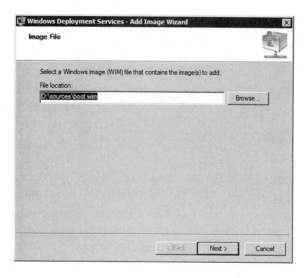

3. Key or browse to the location of the boot image you want to add to the store and then click **Next.** The *Image Metadata* page appears, as shown in Figure 1-22.

Figure 1-22

The Image Metadata page

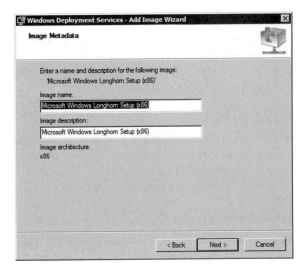

4. Specify different Image Name and Image Description values for the image file you selected, if desired. Then click **Next** to continue. The *Summary* page appears.

5. Click **Next** to continue. The *Task Progress* page appears, as the wizard adds the image to the store.

6. When the operation is complete, click **Finish.** The image appears in the detail pane of the console.

7. Now right-click the **Install Images** folder and, from the context menu, select **Add Install Image.** The Windows Deployment Services—Add Image Wizard appears, showing the *Image Group* page, as shown in Figure 1-23.

Figure 1-23

The Image Group page in the Windows Deployment Services —Add Image Wizard

> **TAKE NOTE** *
>
> An *image group* is a collection of images that use a single set of files and the same security settings. Using an image group, you can apply updates and service packs to all of the files in the group in one process.

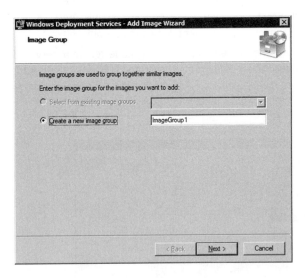

8. With the default Create a New Image Group option selected, supply a name for the group, if desired, and then click **Next.** The *Image File* page appears.

9. Key or browse to the location of the install image you want to add to the store and then click **Next.** The List of Available Images page appears, as shown in Figure 1-24, containing a list of the images in the file you selected. A single image file can contain multiple operating system images, using single instance storage to save space.

Single instance storage is a Windows technology that enables a .wim file to maintain a single copy of a particular operating system file and yet use it in multiple operating system images. This eliminates the need to store multiple copies of the same file.

Figure 1-24

The List of Available Images page

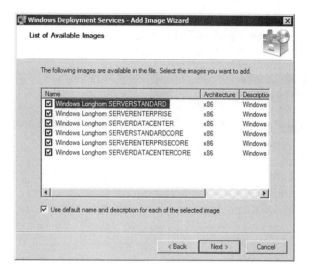

10. Select the images you want to add to the store and then click **Next.** The *Summary* page appears.

11. Click **Next** to continue. The *Task Progress* page appears, as the wizard adds the image to the store.

12. When the operation is complete, click **Finish.** The image group you created and the images you selected appear in the detail pane of the console.

CLOSE the Windows Deployment Services console.

At this point, the WDS server is ready to service clients.

⊕ MORE INFORMATION

If you want to deploy an operating system to a computer that is not PXE-enabled, you can add a boot image to the store, and then convert it to a discover boot image by right-clicking the image and selecting Create a Discover Image from the context menu. A discover image is an image file that you can burn to a CD-ROM, flash drive, or other boot medium. When you use the discover image disk to boot the client computer, the computer loads Windows PE, connects to the WDS server, and proceeds with the operating system installation process.

CONFIGURING A CUSTOM DHCP OPTION

The WDS server configuration procedure discussed earlier in this lesson assumes that an administrator has installed DHCP on the same computer as Windows Deployment Services. In many instances, this is not the case. When you are using another computer as your DHCP server, you should clear the Do Not Listen on Port 67 and Configure DHCP Option 60 to 'PXEClient' checkboxes on the *DHCP Option 60* page of the Windows Deployment Services Configuration Wizard.

When you are using an external DHCP server, you must also configure it manually to include the custom option that provides WDS clients with the name of the WDS server. To configure this option on a Windows Server 2008 DHCP server, use the following procedure.

CONFIGURE A CUSTOM DHCP OPTION

GET READY. Log on to Windows Server 2008 using an account with Administrative privileges. When the logon process is completed, close the Initial Configuration Tasks window and any other windows that appear.

1. Click **Start**, and then click **Administrative Tools** > **DHCP**. The DHCP console appears, as shown in Figure 1-25.

Figure 1-25

The DHCP console

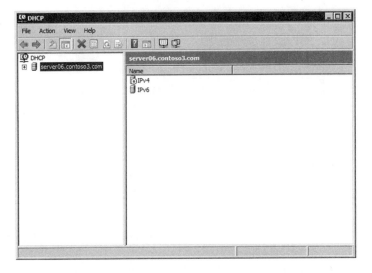

2. In the scope pane, expand the node for your server. Then, right-click the **IPv4** node and, from the context menu, select **Set Predefined Options**. The Predefined Options and Values dialog box appears, as shown in Figure 1-26.

Figure 1-26

The Predefined Options and Values dialog box

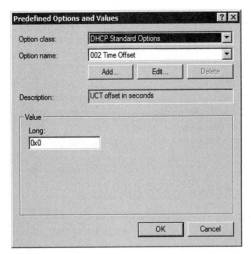

TAKE NOTE ✱

For a DHCP server running Windows Server 2003, you must right-click the server node (instead of the IPv4 node) and select Set Predefined Options from the context menu. You can then continue with the rest of the procedure.

3. Click **Add.** The Option Type dialog box appears, as shown in Figure 1-27.

Figure 1-27

The Option Type dialog box

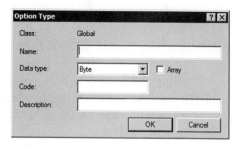

4. In the Name text box, key **PXEClient.**

5. From the Data Type dropdown list, select **String.**

6. In the Code text box, key **060.**

7. Click **OK.**

8. Click **OK** again to close the Predefined Options and Values dialog box.

9. In the scope pane, right-click the **Server Options** node and, from the context menu, select **Configure Options**. The Server Options dialog box appears.

10. In the Available Options list box, scroll down and select the **060 PXEClient** option you just created, as shown in Figure 1-28.

Figure 1-28

The Server Options dialog box

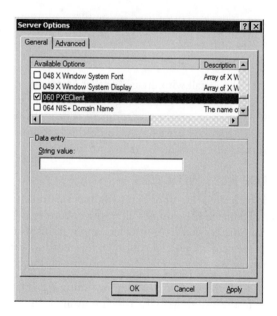

11. In the String Value text box, key the name or IP address of your WDS server. Then, click **OK.**

CLOSE the DHCP console.

This procedure adds the 060 custom option value you defined to all of the DHCPOFFER packets the DHCP server sends out to clients. When a client computer boots from a local device, such as a hard drive or CD-ROM, the 060 option has no effect. However, when a client performs a network boot, after receiving and accepting an offered IP address from the DHCP server, it connects to the WDS server specified in the 060 PXEClient option and uses it to obtain the boot image file it needs to start.

PERFORMING A WDS CLIENT INSTALLATION

After you have installed and configured your WDS server and added images to the store, it is ready to service clients. In a properly configured WDS installation, the client operating system deployment process proceeds as follows:

1. The client computer starts and, finding no local boot device, attempts to perform a network boot.
2. The client computer connects to a DHCP server on the network, from which it obtains a DHCPOFFER message containing an IP address and other TCP/IP configuration parameters, plus the 060 PXEClient option, containing the name of a WDS server.
3. The client connects to the WDS server and is supplied with a boot image file, which it downloads using the Trivial File Transfer Protocol (TFTP).
4. The client loads Windows PE and the Windows Deployment Services client from the boot image file onto a RAM disk (a virtual swap space created out of system memory) and displays a boot menu containing a list of the install images available from the WDS server.
5. The user on the client computer selects an install image from the boot menu, and the operating system installation process begins.
6. From this point, the setup process proceeds just like a manual installation.

Customizing WDS Client Installations

> WDS enables you to deploy customized image files and use unattend scripts to perform unattended installations.

As mentioned earlier, the install.wim image file that Microsoft supplies on the Windows Server 2008 DVD performs a basic operating system installation on the client. However, the real strength of WDS in an enterprise environment is its ability to create and deploy custom image files by using unattended procedures. To do this, you must create your own image files and unattend scripts, as discussed in the following sections.

CREATING IMAGE FILES WITH WDS

An install image is basically a snapshot of a computer's hard drive taken at a particular moment in time. The image file contains all of the operating system files on the computer, plus any updates and drivers you have installed, applications you have added, and configuration changes you have made. Creating your own image files is essentially a matter of setting up a computer the way you want it and then capturing an image of the computer to a file.

You can use several tools to create image files, including the ImageX.exe command line utility Microsoft provides in the Windows AIK, which is available from the Microsoft Downloads Center at http://www.microsoft.com/downloads. To use ImageX.exe, you must boot the target computer to Windows PE and run the tool from the command line. However, the Windows Deployment Center console provides another method for creating image files, using the same WDS infrastructure you used to install images.

WDS enables you to create your own image files by modifying an existing boot image, such as the boot.wim image Microsoft provides with Windows Server 2008, and turning it into a tool that boots the target computer and runs the Windows Deployment Service Capture Utility instead of an operating system's Setup program. The utility then creates an image file and writes it out to the computer's drive, after which you can copy it to the WDS server and deploy it to other computers in the usual manner.

CREATING A CAPTURE BOOT IMAGE

To modify a boot image to perform image file captures, use the following procedure.

 CREATE A CAPTURE BOOT IMAGE

GET READY. Log on to Windows Server 2008 using an account with Administrative privileges. When the logon process is completed, close the Initial Configuration Tasks window and any other windows that appear.

1. Click **Start,** and then click **Administrative Tools > Windows Deployment Services.** The Windows Deployment Services console appears.

2. Expand the **Server** node and the node for your server. Then, select the **Boot Images** folder.

3. If you have not done so already, add the Windows Server 2008 boot.wim image to the Boot Images store, using the procedure described earlier in this lesson.

4. In the detail pane, right-click the boot image and select **Create Capture Boot Image** from the context menu. The Windows Deployment Server—Create Capture Image Wizard appears, as shown in Figure 1-29.

Figure 1-29

The Windows Deployment Server—Create Capture Image Wizard

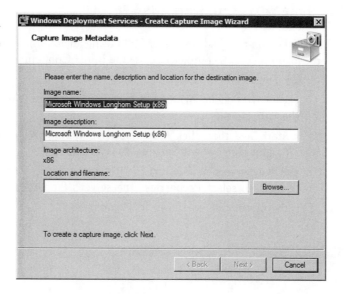

5. On the Capture Image Metadata page, specify a name and description for the new image, and a location and filename for the new image file.

6. Click **Next.** The *Task Progress* page appears as the wizard creates the new image file.

7. Once the image has been created successfully, click **Finish.**

CLOSE the Windows Deployment Services console.

You can now add the new capture image to the Boot Image store in the normal manner. To complete the imaging process, you must prepare the target computer with the Sysprep.exe utility and then reboot the system by using the capture image. A wizard then appears on the computer, guiding you through the process of capturing an image of the computer and uploading it to the WDS server.

USING ANSWER FILES

WDS by itself enables you to perform a standard operating system installation, but the setup process is still interactive, requiring someone at the workstation, like an installation from the DVD. To perform an unattended installation using WDS, you must use answer files, sometimes known as *unattend files.* An *answer file* is a script containing responses to all of the prompts that appear on the WDS client computer during the installation process. To create answer files, Microsoft recommends using the Windows System Image Manager (Windows SIM) tool in the Windows AIK.

To install an operating system on a client using WDS with no interactivity, you must have two answer files, as follows:

- WDS client answer file—This answer file automates the WDS client procedure that begins when the client computer loads the boot image file.
- Operating system answer file—This is an answer file for a standard operating system installation, containing responses to all of the prompts that appear after the client computer loads the install image file.

To use answer files during a WDS operating system deployment, use the following procedure.

 CONFIGURE WDS TO USE AN ANSWER FILE

GET READY. Log on to Windows Server 2008 using an account with Administrative privileges. When the logon process is completed, close the Initial Configuration Tasks window and any other windows that appear.

1. Copy your WDS client answer file to the \RemoteInstall\WDSClientUnattend folder on the WDS server.
2. Click **Start**, and then click **Administrative Tools > Windows Deployment Services.** The Windows Deployment Services console appears.
3. Expand the **Servers** node. Then, right-click the node for your server and, from the context menu, select **Properties.** The server's Properties sheet appears.
4. Click the **Client** tab, as shown in Figure 1-30.

Figure 1-30

The Client tab of a WDS server's Properties sheet

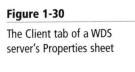

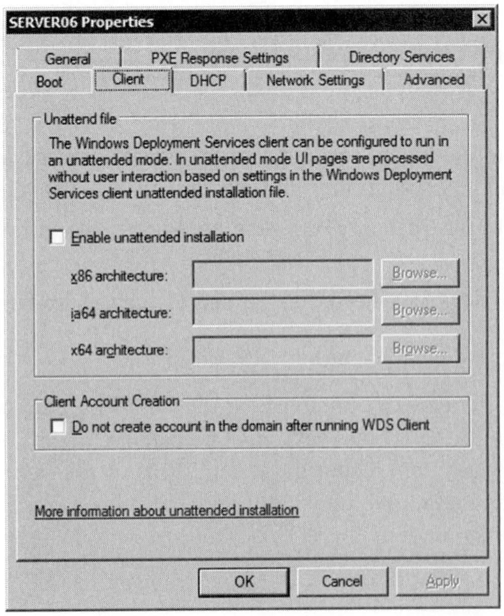

5. Select the **Enable unattended installation** checkbox.
6. Click the **Browse** button corresponding to the processor architecture of the client computer.
7. Browse to your answer file and then click **Open.**
8. Click **OK** to close the server's Properties sheet.
9. Expand the node for your server and the **Install Images** node and locate the image you want to associate with an answer file.
10. Right-click the image file and, from the context menu, select **Properties.** The Image Properties sheet appears, as shown in Figure 1-31.

Figure 1-31

The Image Properties sheet

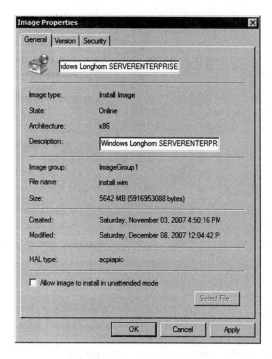

11. Select the **Allow image to install in unattended mode** checkbox.
12. Click **Select File.** The Select Unattend File dialog box appears, as shown in Figure 1-32.

Figure 1-32

The Select Unattend File dialog box

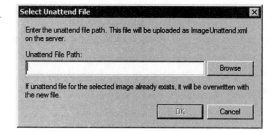

13. Key or browse to the answer file you want to use and then click **OK.**
14. Click **OK** to close the Image Properties sheet.

CLOSE the Windows Deployment Services console.

At this point, if your answer files are properly configured, the entire operating system installation process on the client should require no interaction, except for turning on the computer.

Using the Windows Automated Installation Kit

> Windows AIK provides the tools needed to perform unattended Windows Server 2008 and Windows Vista installations on remote computers.

The *Windows Automated Installation Kit (AIK)* is a set of tools and documents that enable network administrators to plan, create, and deploy operating system image files to new computers on the network. Windows AIK is not included with Windows Server 2008; it is a separate, free download available from the Microsoft Downloads Center at http://www.microsoft.com/downloads.

Windows AIK is a highly flexible collection of tools that you can use to deploy operating systems on almost any scale, from small business networks to large enterprises. The primary tools included in the kit are as follows:

<table>
<tr><td>

TAKE NOTE *

Although this lesson is concerned with deploying Windows Server 2008 servers, you can also use the Windows AIK and Windows Deployment Services to install Windows Vista workstations, using essentially the same procedures.

</td></tr>
</table>

- *ImageX.exe*—A command line program that can capture, transfer, modify, and deploy file-based images from the Windows PE environment.
- Windows Preinstallation Environment (Windows PE)—A stripped-down, command line version of the Windows operating system that provides a boot environment from which you can perform a full operating system installation. Unlike DOS, which earlier versions of Windows used for a boot environment, Windows PE provides full internal support for 32- or 64-bit device drivers, TCP/IP networking, NTFS drives, and various scripting languages.
- *Windows Recovery Environment (Windows RE)*—A command line operating system, similar to Windows PE, in which you can run diagnostic and recovery tools.
- *Windows System Image Manager (Windows SIM)*—A graphical utility that creates and modifies the answer files you can use to perform unattended operating system installations on remote computers.

Sysprep.exe, another tool that you need to build automated deployment solutions, is included with Windows Server 2008 itself.

UNDERSTANDING THE DEPLOYMENT PROCESS

Windows AIK is designed primarily to facilitate new operating system installations. The basic deployment process that the AIK uses assumes that you will be installing Windows on a computer with a new, unformatted hard disk, or one with a disk that you will reformat during the installation.

<table>
<tr><td>

TAKE NOTE *

Windows AIK does not actually include Windows PE and Windows RE, but it does provide the tools you need to build them.

</td></tr>
</table>

<table>
<tr><td>

TAKE NOTE *

</td><td>

The process of upgrading or migrating existing computers to Windows Server 2008 or Windows Vista is more complex than a new installation, and is not covered in the Windows AIK documentation. However, *Microsoft Deployment Toolkit (MDT) 2008* does document these subjects and uses the AIK tools to perform these types of operating system installations.

</td></tr>
</table>

The basic image creation and deployment process, as defined by the Windows AIK, consists of the following steps:

1. Build a lab environment—The lab environment is where you have a *technician computer,* on which you install Windows AIK, and a *master computer,* which serves as the model from which you will create your answer files and images.

2. Create an answer file—On the technician computer, using Windows System Image Manager (Windows SIM), you create and configure a new *answer file.* The answer file contains all of the configuration settings and other information that an installer would normally supply during a manual operating system installation.

3. Build a master installation—Using the Windows Server 2008 installation DVD and the answer file you created, you install the operating system on the master computer, and then use Sysprep.exe to generalize it.

4. Create an image—After creating a Windows PE boot disk, you start the master computer and use the ImageX.exe program to capture an image of the master installation and store it on a network share.

5. Deploy the image—To deploy the image on additional computers, you start them with a Windows PE boot disk, copy the image file you created from the network share to the local drive, and use ImageX.exe to apply the image to that computer. You can also use WDS to deploy the image file.

The following sections describe these steps more fully.

INSTALLING THE WINDOWS AIK

The first step to deploying new computers with the Windows AIK is to download and install Windows AIK on the technician computer in your lab. The technician computer must have .NET Framework 2.0 and MSXML 6.0 installed and must also be running one of the following operating systems:

- Windows Server 2008
- Windows Vista
- Windows Server 2003 Service Pack 2
- Windows XP Professional Service Pack 2 with KB926044

The Windows AIK is available as a free download, in the form of a DVD image file with a .iso extension. Before you can install the Windows AIK, you must download the image file from the Microsoft Downloads Center and burn the image file to a disk. You can then proceed with the installation, using the following procedure.

 INSTALL THE WINDOWS AIK

GET READY. Log on to your technician computer using an account with Administrative privileges. When the logon process is completed, close the Initial Configuration Tasks window and any other windows that appear.

1. Insert the Windows AIK disk you created intro the computer's DVD drive. A Welcome to Windows Automated Installation Kit window appears, as shown in Figure 1-33.

Figure 1-33

The Welcome to the Windows Automated Installation Kit Setup Wizard page

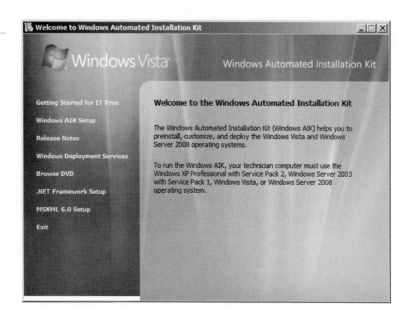

---

2. Click **Windows AIK Setup.** The Windows Automated Installation Kit Setup Wizard appears.

3. Click **Next** to bypass the *Welcome to the Windows Automated Installation Kit Setup Wizard* page. The *License Terms* page appears.

4. Select the **I Agree** option and click **Next.** The *Select Installation Folder* page appears, as shown in Figure 1-34.

Figure 1-34

The Select Installation Folder page of the Windows Automated Installation Kit Setup Wizard

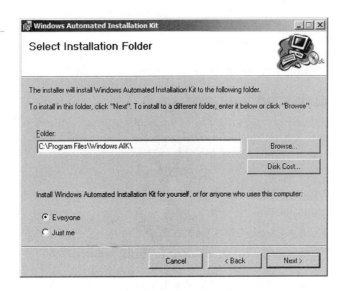

5. Click **Next** to accept the default settings. The *Confirm Installation* page appears.

6. Click **Next** to begin the installation. The wizard installs the Windows AIK, and then the *Installation Complete* page appears.

Click **CLOSE**.

The installation process adds a Microsoft Windows AIK program group to the start menu, which contains shortcuts to the Windows System Image Manager application, a Windows PE Tools command prompt, and the Windows AIK documentation.

CREATING AN ANSWER FILE

Once you have installed Windows AIK, you can use Windows System Image Manager to create the answer file for your master computer installation. The master computer will be the template for the image file you capture later. You are essentially building the computer that you will clone to all of the other new computers you install later.

Answer files can be simple or quite complex, depending on the operating environment you want to deploy to the new computers on your network. In addition to the basic settings you configure when performing a basic Windows Server 2008 installation, you can add many other settings to your answer file. Examples of some of these settings are shown in the following sample procedure.

 CREATE AN ANSWER FILE

GET READY. Log on to your technician computer using an account with Administrative privileges. When the logon process is completed, close the Initial Configuration Tasks window and any other windows that appear.

1. Insert your Windows Server 2008 installation DVD into the computer's drive.

2. Open Windows Explorer, browse to the \Sources folder on the DVD, and copy the Install.wim image file to a folder on the computer's local drive.

TAKE NOTE*

If you plan to customize your master computer before creating an image of it, you might want to create another answer file after you have completed the customization and generalization processes.

3. Click **Start.** Then click **All Programs** > **Microsoft Windows AIK** > **Windows System Image Manager**. The Windows System Image Manager window appears, as shown in Figure 1-35.

Figure 1-35

The Windows System Image Manager window

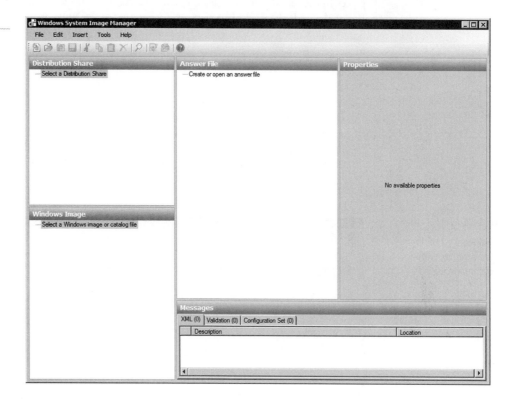

4. Click **File** > **Select Windows Image.** The Select a Windows Image combo box appears.

5. Browse to the folder on your local drive where you copied the Install.wim image file, select the file, and click **Open.** The Select an Image dialog box appears, as shown in Figure 1-36.

Figure 1-36

The Select an Image dialog box

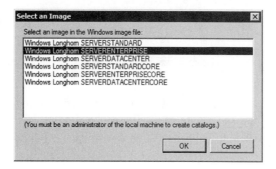

6. Select the Windows Server 2008 edition you plan to install and click **OK.** A Windows System Image Manager message box appears, warning that the program could not find a catalog file for the edition you selected.

TAKE NOTE*

The single Install.wim image file on the Windows Server 2008 installation DVD contains both full and Server Core installation options for the Standard, Enterprise, and Datacenter editions of the operating system, in both the regular and Server Core versions. This is one of the few places in the initial product release where Microsoft has neglected to replace the code name Longhorn with the final product name Windows Server 2008. When deploying Windows Server 2008 using the Windows AIK, you must select the operating system edition and version for which you have purchased licenses.

7. Click **Yes** to create a new catalog file. A catalog file is a binary file with a .clg extension that contains all of the settings for an image file and their values. The Windows Server 2008 edition you selected appears in the Windows Image pane with two subordinate folders, called Components and Packages, as shown in Figure 1-37.

Figure 1-37

The Windows System Image Manager window, with a Windows image added

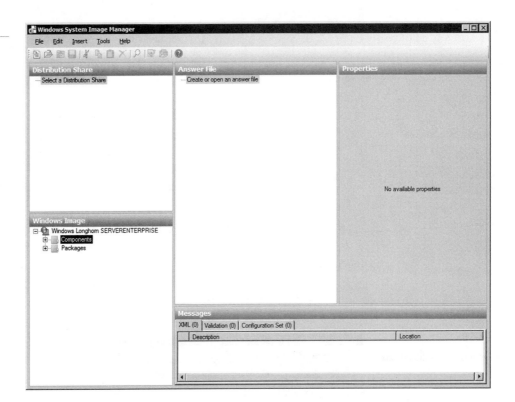

8. Click **File > New Answer File.** A new, untitled heading appears in the Answer File pane, as shown in Figure 1-38. The subheadings in the Components folder represent the phases of the installation process, called configuration passes.

Figure 1-38

The Windows System Image Manager window, with a new answer file added

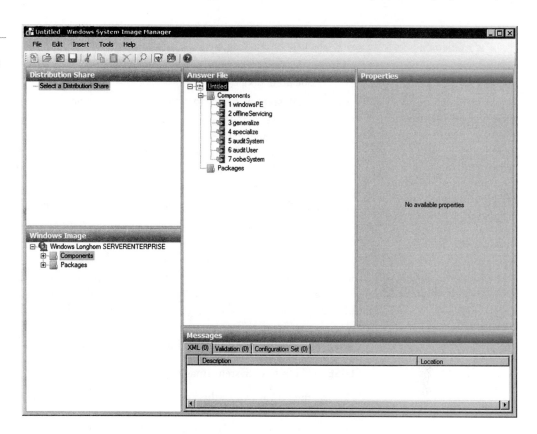

At this point, the answer file exists, but it contains no settings. To populate the answer file, you must select settings in the Windows Image pane and add them to the appropriate configuration pass in the Answer File pane.

9. In the Windows Image pane, expand the **Components** folder and browse to the component you want to add to the answer file. Then, right-click the component and, from the context menu, select one of the active configuration passes. The component appears in the Answer File pane, as shown in Figure 1-39.

Figure 1-39

The Windows System Image Manager window, with a setting added to the answer file

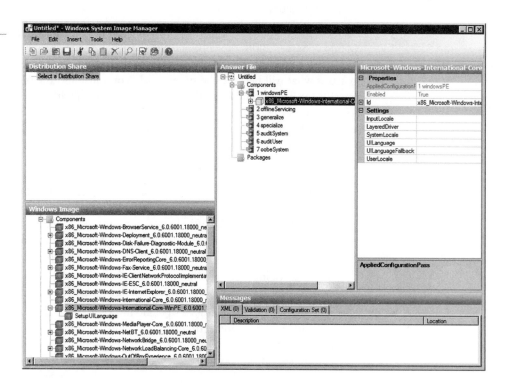

10. In the Answer File pane, select the setting you added. A Properties pane appears, named for that setting.

11. In the Properties pane, select one of the listed settings, and key a value in the associated text box.

12. Repeat steps 9 to 11 to add all of the settings you need to the answer file.

13. Click **Tools > Validate Answer File.** The program checks the values of all the settings you added to the answer file and provides feedback in the Messages pane, either indicating the success of the validation or identifying the settings that are in error. Double-clicking an error message sends you to the appropriate setting, where you can correct the error and then revalidate.

14. Click **File > Save Answer File As.** A Save As combo box appears.

15. Save the answer file to a local drive using the name Autounattend.xml.

TAKE NOTE*

Press the F1 key to open the Unattended Windows Setup Reference help file, which contains explanations and possible values for all of the answer file settings.

TAKE NOTE*

Both Unattend.ml and Autounattend.xml are valid answer file names. However, when you use the name Autounattend.xml, the system applies the settings in the file during the Windows PE configuration pass, before it copies files to the hard disk. Therefore, if your answer file includes disk actions, such as partitioning, you should use Autounattend.xml.

16. Copy the answer file to a floppy disk or flash drive.

CLOSE the Windows System Image Manager window.

Selecting the settings and values you want to add to your answer file is one of the most complicated parts of the deployment process, as is using the correct configuration pass. The following sections examine these two subjects.

UNDERSTANDING CONFIGURATION PASSES

As anyone who has performed a Windows installation knows, there are several phases to the Windows Setup process, and the configuration passes in an answer file enable you to specify during which phase of the installation the setup program should apply each of your selected settings. For many of the answer file settings, you have no choice, as the setting can only apply to one configuration pass. However, there are some settings from which you can select two or more configuration passes, and in some circumstances, you must select the correct pass for the installation to succeed.

For example, if you are deploying computers that require a disk driver not supplied with Windows Server 2008, the configuration pass you use to install that driver should depend on when it is needed. If the disk driver is boot-critical, that is, if the computer needs the driver to access what will become the system disk, you must add the setting to the answer file's windowsPE configuration pass so that the system loads the driver at boot time. If the computer does not need the driver until after the operating system is loaded, then you can add the setting to the offlineServicing configuration pass, which will add the driver to the Windows driver store, so it is available after Windows starts.

The configuration passes you can specify in your answer files are as follows:

* windowsPE—Configures options used during the Windows PE phase of the installation process, including the resolution of the Windows PE screen and the location of the installation log file; and Windows Setup options, including the selection, partitioning, and formatting of the system disk, the name and location of the image file to install, the product key, and administrator password values to apply.

* offlineServicing—Applies unattended installation settings to an offline image, as well as enables you to add updates, hotfixes, language packs, and drivers to the image file.

* specialize—Applies computer-specific information to the Windows installation such as network configuration settings, international settings, and the name of the domain the computer will join. The specialize configuration pass runs after the system runs the generalize pass and reboots.

- generalize—Specifies the settings that will persist after you run the Sysprep.exe program with the /generalize parameter. When you run the sysprep /generalize command, all machine-specific settings are removed from the computer configuration, such as the security ID (SID) and all hardware settings. This enables you to create an image file that does not include settings that will cause network conflicts when you apply it to multiple computers. The generalize configuration pass, and its accompanying specialize configuration pass, run only when you execute the sysprep /generalize command.

- auditSystem—Applies unattended setup settings when the computer is running in the system context of an audit mode startup, before a user has logged on. The auditSystem configuration pass runs only when you configure Windows to start up in audit mode, by running Sysprep.exe with the /audit parameter or by adding the Reseal component to the answer file with the value Audit in the Mode setting. Audit mode is an additional installation phase that occurs with a separate system startup after the operating system installation and before Windows Welcome. OEMs and system builders typically use audit mode to install additional device drivers, applications, and other updates.

- auditUser—Applies unattended setup settings when the computer is running in the user context of an audit mode startup, after a user has logged on. The auditUser configuration pass is typically used to run scripts, applications, or other executables.

- oobeSystem—Applies settings during the first system boot after the Windows installation or the audit mode phase, also known as the Out-of-Box-Experience (OOBE) or Windows Welcome. The oobeSystem configuration pass runs only when you start the computer in OOBE mode, by running Sysprep.exe with the /oobe parameter or by adding the Reseal component to the answer file with the value OOBE in the Mode setting.

SELECTING ANSWER FILE SETTINGS

Unattended operating system installations can be relatively simple or extremely complex. For a basic Windows Server 2008 installation, in which the computer requires no additional drivers or other software, you can create an answer file that contains only the settings needed to apply an image to a local disk drive. Some of the answer file settings that you might need for this part of an unattended Windows Setup process are listed in Table 1-5.

Table 1-5

Unattended Windows PE Phase Answer File Settings

COMPONENT	VALUE	FUNCTION
Microsoft-Windows-International-Core-WinPE	UILanguage = <Language>	Specifies the language to use for the installed Windows operating system.
Microsoft-Windows-International-Core-WinPE\SetupUILanguage	UILanguage = <Language>	Specifies the language to use in the Windows Setup program.
Microsoft-Windows-Setup \UserData	AcceptEula = true|false	When set to true, causes Windows Setup to automatically accept the Windows licensing terms.
Microsoft-Windows-Setup \UserData\ProductKey	Key = <product key>	Specifies the product key that the Setup program will use to select the image to install. The key is then stored on the computer and used later to activate Windows.
Microsoft-Windows-Setup \UserData\ProductKey	WillShowUI = Always|OnError|Never	When set to OnError, causes Windows Setup to display the appropriate Windows Setup interface page if the value specified in the Key setting is invalid.
Microsoft-Windows-Shell-Setup	ProductKey = <product key>	Specifies the product key that the operating system will use when activating Windows. Use this setting only when you want to specify different product keys for installation and activation. Not needed if you are using the Key Management Service (KMS) to activate volume licensed media.
Microsoft-Windows-Setup\DiskConfiguration	WillShowUI = Always|OnError|Never	When set to OnError, causes Windows Setup to display the appropriate Windows Setup interface page if an error occurs during the disk configuration process.
Microsoft-Windows-Setup\DiskConfiguration\Disk	DiskID = <integer>	Identifies (by number) the disk that the Windows Setup program should add or edit.
Microsoft-Windows-Setup\DiskConfiguration\Disk	WillWipeDisk = true|false	When set to true, deletes all partitions from the disk specified by the DiskID setting before performing any other disk configuration tasks.
Microsoft-Windows-Setup\DiskConfiguration\Disk\CreatePartitions\CreatePartition	Extend = true|false	Creates a partition and extends it to fill the entire disk.
Microsoft-Windows-Setup\DiskConfiguration\Disk\CreatePartitions\CreatePartition	Order = <integer>	Specifies the order in which Windows Setup creates partitions.
Microsoft-Windows-Setup\DiskConfiguration\Disk\CreatePartitions\CreatePartition	Size = <integer>	Creates a partition of a specified size (in megabytes).

COMPONENT	VALUE	FUNCTION
Microsoft-Windows-Setup\DiskConfiguration\Disk\CreatePartitions\CreatePartition	Type = Primary|EFI|Extended|Logical|MSR|	Specifies the type of partition Windows Setup should create.
Microsoft-Windows-Setup\DiskConfiguration\Disk\ModifyPartitions\ModifyPartition	Active = true|false	When set to true, causes Windows Setup to mark the partition specified by the PartitionID setting as active.
Microsoft-Windows-Setup\DiskConfiguration\Disk\ModifyPartitions\ModifyPartition	Extend = true|false	When set to true, causes Windows Setup to extend the partition specified by the PartitionID setting to fill the entire disk.
Microsoft-Windows-Setup\DiskConfiguration\Disk\ModifyPartitions\ModifyPartition	Format = NTFS|FAT32	Causes Windows Setup to format the partition specified by the PartitionID setting using the specified file system.
Microsoft-Windows-Setup\DiskConfiguration\Disk\ModifyPartitions\ModifyPartition	Label = <label name>	Causes Windows Setup to apply the specified label name to the partition specified by the PartitionID setting.
Microsoft-Windows-Setup\DiskConfiguration\Disk\ModifyPartitions\ModifyPartition	Letter = <drive letter>	Causes Windows Setup to apply the specified drive letter to the partition specified by the PartitionID setting.
Microsoft-Windows-Setup\DiskConfiguration\Disk\ModifyPartitions\ModifyPartition	Order = <integer>	Specifies the order in which Windows Setup modifies partitions.
Microsoft-Windows-Setup\DiskConfiguration\Disk\ModifyPartitions\ModifyPartition	PartitionID = <integer>	Identifies (by number) the partition on the disk specified by the DiskID setting that the Windows Setup program should modify.
Microsoft-Windows-Setup\ImageInstall\OSImage\InstallTo	DiskID = <integer>	Specifies the disk on which Windows Setup should install Windows.
Microsoft-Windows-Setup\ImageInstall\OSImage\InstallTo	PartitionID = <integer>	Specifies the partition on which Windows Setup should install Windows.
Microsoft-Windows-Setup\ImageInstall\OSImage	InstallToAvailablePartition = true|false	Causes Windows Setup to install Windows on the first available partition with sufficient space, and which does not already have a Windows installation on it.
Microsoft-Windows-Deployment\Reseal	ForceShutdownNow = true|false	Specifies whether the computer should shut down immediately after applying the Mode setting.
Microsoft-Windows-Deployment\Reseal	Mode = Audit|OOBE	Specifies the mode that the computer will start in after the next reboot.

If your answer file contains the Mode = OOBE value in the Reseal setting, or if you run Sysprep.exe with the /oobe parameter, the computer on which you are installing Windows will reboot into the Windows Welcome phase. In an attended installation, this is the phase in which the server prompts the user to supply the computer's operational settings. In a Windows Vista installation, the user must supply a computer name and create a local user account. In Windows Server 2008, the user must change the local Administrator password.

It is possible to automate the Windows Welcome phase with an answer file, just as you can the Windows PE phase. Most of the answer file settings for this phase must run during the oobeSystem configuration pass. Table 1-6 contains some of the most important Windows Server 2008 answer file settings for this phase.

Table 1-6

Unattended Windows Welcome Phase Answer File Settings

Component	Value	Function
Microsoft-Windows-International-Core	InputLocale = <Language>	Specifies the language and keyboard layout to use for the Windows installation.
Microsoft-Windows-International-Core	SystemLocale = <Language>	Specifies the default language the system should use for non-Unicode programs.
Microsoft-Windows-International-Core	UILanguage = <Language>	Specifies the language the system should use for the Windows user interface.
Microsoft-Windows-International-Core	UserLocale = <Language>	Specifies the per-user settings that Windows should use to format dates, times, and currency.
Microsoft-Windows-Shell-Setup\OOBE	HideEULAPage = true|false	Specifies whether to display the Microsoft Software License Terms page.
Microsoft-Windows-Shell-Setup	ComputerName = <Name>	Specifies the name assigned to the computer.
Microsoft-Windows-Shell-Setup\UserAccounts\AdministratorPassword	Value = <Name>	Specifies the password to be assigned to the Administrator account.

For more complex deployments, there are many other settings you can add to an answer file, including those which expand the installation to include an audit phase, so that you can install additional drivers and other software on the computer during the unattended installation.

CREATING A MASTER INSTALLATION

Once you have created your answer file, you can proceed to install Windows Server 2008 on your master computer. This creates the master installation that you will later duplicate by creating an image file.

To install Windows Server 2008 using an answer file, use the following procedure.

 CREATE A MASTER INSTALLATION

GET READY. Turn on your master computer.

1. Insert your Windows Server 2008 installation DVD into the computer's drive.
2. Insert the floppy disk or flash drive containing your answer file.
3. Restart the computer by pressing **CTRL+ALT+DEL.** The unattended installation proceeds.
4. When the installation is completed, check the system to make sure that all of the customizations you specified in the answer file have been completed.
5. Open a Command Prompt window and, at the command prompt, key **c:\windows\system32\sysprep\sysprep.exe /oobe /generalize /shutdown** and press **Enter.** The Sysprep.exe program prepares the computer for the imaging process by removing out-of-box drivers and machine specific settings, and then shuts down the system.

REMOVE the Windows Server 2008 DVD and the answer file disk.

The environment on the master computer is now ready to be imaged.

CAPTURING AN IMAGE FILE

With the master computer installed and generalized, you are now ready to capture the image file that you will use to deploy the operating system on other computers. To do this, you must boot the master computer into the Windows PE operating system and run the ImageX. exe program from the Windows PE command line. To create a Windows PE boot disk and run ImageX.exe, use the following procedure.

 CAPTURE AN IMAGE FILE

GET READY. Log on to your technician computer using an account with Administrative privileges. When the logon process is completed, close the Initial Configuration Tasks window and any other windows that appear.

1. Open Windows Explorer and create a new folder called C:\Images.

2. Share the C:\Images folder using the share name Images and grant the Everyone special identity the Allow Full Control Permission to the share.

3. Open a Command Prompt window and switch to your PETools folder by typing the following command and pressing **Enter:**

   ```
   cd\Program Files\Windows AIK\Tools\PETools
   ```

4. Run the Copype.cmd script by typing the following command and pressing **Enter.** This command creates a WinPE folder on your local drive containing the Windows PE boot files. If you are running a 64-bit version of Windows on your technician computer, use the parameter **amd64** or **ia64,** instead of **x86.**

   ```
   copype.cmd x86 c:\WinPE
   ```

5. Copy the ImageX.exe program to the Windows PE boot files folder by typing the following command and pressing **Enter.**

   ```
   copy "c:\Program
   Files\Windows AIK\Tools\x86\imagex.exe"
   c:\WinPE\iso\
   ```

6. Using Notepad, create a new text file containing the following instructions and save it to the C:\WinPE\iso folder, using the file name Wimscript.ini. ImageX.exe automatically searches for a file with this name when creating an image, and omits the files and folders in the [Exclusion List] section from the image it creates. These files are not needed in the image because Windows Server 2008 creates them automatically when it starts. The filespecs in the [CompressionExclusionList] section represent files that are already compressed, so it is not necessary for ImageX.exe to try to compress them again.

   ```
   [ExclusionList]

   ntfs.log

   hiberfil.sys

   pagefile.sys

   "System Volume Information"

   RECYCLER

   Windows\CSC
   ```

```
[CompressionExclusionList]

*.mp3

*.zip

*.cab

\WINDOWS\inf\*.pnf
```

7. Switch to your PETools folder by typing the following command and pressing **Enter.**

   ```
   cd\program files\Windows AIK\Tools\PETools\
   ```

8. Create a Windows PE boot disk image by typing the following command and pressing **Enter.**

   ```
   oscdimg -n -bc:\winpe\etfsboot.com c:\winpe\ISO
   c:\winpe\winpe.iso
   ```

9. Burn the Winpe.iso image file in the C:\WinPE folder to a CD-ROM using third-party CD-burning software. This creates a Windows PE boot disk that you can use to start your master computer.

10. On your master computer, insert your Windows PE boot disk into the drive and restart the system, making sure that it boots from the CD-ROM, not the hard drive. The computer boots to a Windows PE command prompt.

11. Create an image file of your master computer and save it to your C: drive using the name Winstall.wim by typing the following command and pressing **Enter.**

    ```
    d:\tools\imagex.exe /compress fast /capture c:
    c:\winstall.wim "Windows Server 2008 Install" /verify
    ```

12. Map a drive to the Images share you created on your technician computer by typing the following command and pressing **Enter.**

    ```
    net use z: \\computer_name\images
    ```

13. Copy the image file you created to your technician computer by typing the following command and pressing **Enter.**

    ```
    copy c:\winstall.wim z:
    ```

SHUT DOWN your master computer and **CLOSE** all open windows on your technician computer. The image you created is now ready to be deployed on other computers.

DEPLOYING AN IMAGE FILE

To deploy the image you created on another computer you must first boot the new system using your Windows PE disk and prepare the disk to receive the image, as detailed in the following procedure.

 DEPLOY AN IMAGE FILE

GET READY. Start your technician computer.

1. Turn on the new computer and insert your Windows PE boot disk into the computer's drive. The computer boots to a Windows PE command prompt.

2. Key **diskpart** at the command prompt and press **Enter.** A DISKPART prompt appears.

3. Enter each of the following diskpart commands at the prompt, pressing **Enter** after each one. These commands create a new 40-GB partition on the computer's local disk, make the partition active, and format it.

   ```
   select disk 0

   clean
   ```

```
create partition primary size=40000

select partition 1

active

format

exit
```

4. Map a drive to the share you created on your technician computer by typing the following command and pressing **Enter.**

   ```
   net use z: \\computer_name\images
   ```

5. Copy the image file you created earlier to the computer's local drive by typing the following command and pressing **Enter.**

   ```
   copy z:\winstall.wim c:
   ```

6. Use the ImageX.exe program to apply the image to the computer by typing the following command and pressing **Enter.**

   ```
   d:\imagex.exe /apply c:\winstall.wim 1 c:
   ```

SHUT DOWN your new computer.

Windows Server 2008 is now deployed on the new computer and ready to run.

SUMMARY SKILL MATRIX

IN THIS LESSON YOU LEARNED:

- When planning a server deployment for a large enterprise network, the operating system edition you choose for your servers must be based on multiple factors, including the hardware in the computers, the features and capabilities you require for your servers, and the price of the operating system software.

- Microsoft Assessment and Planning Solution Accelerator (MAP) is a new tool that is capable of performing a hardware inventory on computers with no agent software required on the client side, and adding information about the hardware to a database. MAP can then evaluate the hardware information and create reports that specify which computers are capable of running Windows Server 2008.

- Windows Deployment Services (WDS) is a role included with Windows Server 2008, which enables you to perform unattended installations of Windows Server 2008 and other operating systems on remote computers, using network-based boot and installation media.

- The Windows Automated Installation Kit (AIK) is a set of tools and documents that enable network administrators to plan, create, and deploy operating system image files to new computers on the network.

- An unattend file is a script containing responses to all of the prompts that appear on the WDS client computer during the installation process. To create unattend files, Microsoft recommends using the Windows System Image Manager (Windows SIM) tool in the Windows AIK.

- You can use several tools to create image files, including the ImageX.exe command line utility Microsoft provides in the Windows AIK. To use ImageX.exe, you must boot the target computer to Windows PE and run the tool from the command line.

Knowledge Assessment

Matching

Complete the following exercise by matching the terms with their corresponding definitions.

- **a.** ImageX.exe
- **b.** Microsoft Assessment and Planning Solution Accelerator (MAP)
- **c.** master computer
- **d.** preboot execution environment (PXE)
- **e.** Server Core
- **f.** unattend file
- **g.** Windows Automated Installation Kit (AIK)
- **h.** Windows Deployment Services (WDS)
- **i.** Windows PE (Preinstallation Environment) 2.1
- **j.** Windows System Image Manager (Windows SIM)

_____ **1.** Includes boot files and image deployment tools

_____ **2.** Enables you to install an operating system on a computer with no boot disk

_____ **3.** A Windows Server 2008 role

_____ **4.** Command line program that can capture an entire operating system installation to a single file

_____ **5.** Contains answers to questions asked during an operating system installation

_____ **6.** Provides boot disks with network and 32-bit driver support

_____ **7.** Performs agentless inventories of computer hardware

_____ **8.** Creates and modifies answer files

_____ **9.** Command line–based Windows Server 2008 installation

_____ **10.** The system where you create an image file

Multiple Choice

Select the correct answer for each of the following questions.

1. Which of the following services does a Windows Deployment Services client computer use to locate a WDS server?
   - **a.** DHCP
   - **b.** DNS
   - **c.** Active Directory
   - **d.** WINS

2. Which of the following programs can you use to remove the machine-specific settings from a Windows computer prior to creating an image file?
   - **a.** ImageX.exe
   - **b.** Sysprep.exe
   - **c.** Windows Deployment Services
   - **d.** Windows SIM

3. Which of the following configuration passes runs only when you execute the sysprep/ generalize command?
   - **a.** windowsPE
   - **b.** offlineServicing
   - **c.** specialize
   - **d.** oobeSystem

4. Which of the following tools can you not run on a Windows Server 2008 Server Core installation?
   - **a.** Task Manager
   - **b.** Notepad
   - **c.** DiskPart
   - **d.** Server Manager

5. Which of the following programs do you use to create a Windows PE disk image?
   - **a.** Oscdimg.exe
   - **b.** ImageX.exe
   - **c.** Diskpart.exe
   - **d.** Copype.cmd

6. During which configuration pass should an answer file for a Windows Server 2008 installation create the system disk partition?

    a. windowsPE   **b.** oobeSystem

    c. generalize   **d.** offlineServicing

7. Which of the following is not required to implement a Windows Deployment Services server?

    a. DHCP

    b. DNS

    c. Active Directory Domain Services

    d. Active Directory Certificate Services

8. Which of the following editions of the Windows Server 2008 operating system can support up to 64 processors?

    a. Windows Server 2008 Enterprise

    b. Windows Server 2008 Datacenter (x86)

    c. Windows Server 2008 Datacenter (x64)

    d. Windows Server 2008 Itanium

9. When using Windows AIK, which of the following tasks do you perform on the technician computer?

    a. Create a Windows PE boot disk

    b. Create an answer file

    c. Create an image file

    d. Deploy an image file

10. How many computers can you inventory with Microsoft Assessment and Planning Solution Accelerator (MAP) using SQL Server Express 2005?

    a. Up to 5,000   **b.** Up to 10,000

    c. Up to 20,000   **d.** Up to 50,000

Review Questions

1. List the steps involved in deploying a Windows Server 2008 computer using the Windows AIK, in the correct order.

2. List three advantages to starting a computer using a Windows PE boot disk, rather than a DOS boot disk.

■ Case Scenario

Scenario 1-1: Selecting a Windows Server 2008 Edition

You are a private computer consultant, and Ed, a new client who owns a software company, has approached you about upgrading his network. The network currently consists of eight servers, all running either Windows 2000 Server or Windows Server 2003, and 150 workstations running Windows XP. All of the servers have 32-bit processors running at speeds ranging from 1.8 to 2.66 gigahertz and 2 gigabytes of memory. Two of the servers function as domain controllers for the company's single Active Directory domain, and two are Web servers providing product information, service, and support to users on the Internet. One of the remaining servers is currently running a database manager application that the company uses for order entry, customer service, and technical support. Ed wants to update all of the servers to Windows Server 2008 as economically as possible, but he also wants to enhance the capabilities of the network. First, he wants to create a two-node failover cluster for the database application, and second, he wants to use Hyper-V to virtualize some of the other roles running on his servers. Another consultant has recommended that Ed install Windows Server 2008, Standard Edition on all of his servers. Will this recommendation enable Ed to achieve all of his goals? Why or why not? If not, what Windows Server 2008 versions would you recommend instead for Ed's network, keeping in mind that he has a limited budget?

Planning Infrastructure Services

OBJECTIVE DOMAIN MATRIX

TECHNOLOGY SKILL	OBJECTIVE DOMAIN	OBJECTIVE DOMAIN NUMBER
Planning Infrastructure Services	Plan infrastructure services server roles	1.3

KEY TERMS

80/20 rule
automatic allocation
caching-only server
centralized DHCP
  infrastructure
conditional forwarding
DHCP relay agent
distributed DHCP
  infrastructure
DNS forwarder
domain
dynamic allocation

Dynamic Host Configuration
  Protocol (DHCP)
forwarder
full zone transfer (AXFR)
fully qualified domain name
  (FQDN)
host
host table
incremental zone transfer
  (IXFR)
infrastructure server
iterative query

manual allocation
name resolution
recursive query
referral
resolver
resource record
reverse name resolution
root name servers
scope
zone
zone transfer

An *infrastructure server* is a computer that provides services that support the primary functions of a network. File servers, application servers, and the like provide users with the tools they need to do their jobs, but infrastructure servers work behind the scenes to facilitate user access to those file and application servers.

Generally speaking, infrastructure servers can be said to provide services to network administrators. For example, every computer on a TCP/IP network must have a unique IP address, and several other TCP/IP configuration settings. Dynamic Host Configuration Protocol (DHCP) servers support the TCP/IP infrastructure by automatically assigning IP addresses and other settings to the computers on a network. Without them, administrators would have to manually configure each individual computer.

This lesson is devoted to the deployment of the various Windows infrastructure servers on a large enterprise network, including the following:

- Dynamic Host Configuration Protocol (DHCP)

- Domain Name System (DNS)

CERTIFICATION READY?
Plan infrastructure
services server roles
1.3

Deploying DHCP Servers

As mentioned earlier, the ***Dynamic Host Configuration Protocol (DHCP)*** is a service that automatically configures the Internet Protocol (IP) address and other TCP/IP settings on network computers by assigning addresses from a pool (called a ***scope***) and reclaiming them when they are no longer in use.

Aside from being a time-consuming chore, manually configuring TCP/IP clients can result in typographical errors that cause addressing conflicts that interrupt network communications. DHCP prevents these errors and provides many other advantages, including automatic assignment of new addresses when computers are moved from one subnet to another and automatic reclamation of addresses that are no longer in use.

DHCP consists of three components, as follows:

- A DHCP server application, which responds to client requests for TCP/IP configuration settings
- A DHCP client, which issues requests to a server and applies the TCP/IP configuration settings it receives to the local computer
- A DHCP communications protocol, which defines the formats and sequences of the messages exchanged by DHCP clients and servers

All of the Microsoft Windows operating systems include DHCP client capabilities, and all of the server operating systems (including Windows Server 2008) include the Microsoft DHCP Server. Microsoft's DHCP implementation is based on public domain standards published by the Internet Engineering Task Force (IETF) as RFC 2131, "Dynamic Host Configuration Protocol" and RFC 2132, "DHCP Options and BOOTP Vendor Extensions," and is interoperable with other DHCP implementations.

> ➕ **MORE INFORMATION**
>
> The standards on which TCP/IP communication is based are published in public domain documents called Requests For Comments (RFCs) by the Internet Engineering Task Force. These documents are freely available on the Internet at http://www.ietf.org and many other sites. Unlike many other networking standards, which are highly technical and directed at engineers, a lot of the RFCs are comprehensible to students and beginning networkers, and are well worth examining.

The DHCP standards define three different IP address allocation methods, which are as follows:

- ***Dynamic allocation***—The DHCP server assigns an IP address to a client computer from a scope, or range of IP addresses, for a specified length of time. DHCP servers using dynamic allocation lease addresses only to clients. Each client must periodically renew the lease to continue using the address. If the client allows the lease to expire, the address is returned to the scope for reassignment to another client.
- ***Automatic allocation***—The DHCP server permanently assigns an IP address to a client computer from a scope. Once the DHCP server assigns the address to the client, the only way to change it is to manually reconfigure the computer. Automatic allocation is suitable for networks where you do not often move computers to different subnets. It reduces network traffic by eliminating the periodic lease renewal messages needed for dynamic allocation. In the Windows Server 2008 DHCP server, automatic allocation is essentially dynamic allocation with an indefinite lease.

- *Manual allocation*—The DHCP server permanently assigns a specific IP address to a specific computer on the network. In the Windows Server 2008 DHCP server, manually allocated addresses are called reservations. You use manually allocated addresses for computers that must have the same IP address at all times, such as Internet Web servers that have specific IP addresses associated with their host names in the DNS namespace. Although you can just as easily configure such computers manually, DHCP reservations prevent the accidental duplication of permanently assigned IP addresses.

Understanding DHCP Communications

> To design a DHCP strategy for an enterprise network and deploy it properly requires an understanding of the communications that occur between DHCP clients and servers.

The DHCP communication protocol defines eight different message types, as follows:

- DHCPDISCOVER—Used by clients to request configuration parameters from a DHCP server
- DHCPOFFER—Used by servers to offer IP addresses to requesting clients
- DHCPREQUEST—Used by clients to accept or renew an IP address assignment
- DHCPDECLINE—Used by clients to reject an offered IP address
- DHCPACK—Used by servers to acknowledge a client's acceptance of an offered IP address
- DHCPNAK—Used by servers to reject a client's acceptance of an offered IP address
- DHCPRELEASE—Used by clients to terminate an IP address lease
- DHCPINFORM—Used by clients to obtain additional TCP/IP configuration parameters from a server

On Windows computers, the DHCP client is enabled by default, although it is not mentioned by name in the interface. The Obtain an IP address automatically option in the Internet Protocol Version 4 (TCP/IPv4) Properties sheet (as shown in Figure 2-1), and the Obtain an IPv6 address automatically option in the Internet Protocol Version 6 (TCP/IPv6) Properties sheet control the client for IPv4 and IPv6, respectively.

+ MORE INFORMATION

DHCP is an extension of the Bootstrap Protocol (BOOTP), which was designed to enable diskless workstations to retrieve an IP address and other TCP/IP configuration settings from a network server. The primary limitation of BOOTP is that an administrator must manually enter the configuration parameters for each workstation on the server. DHCP improves on this concept by dynamically assigning IP addresses to clients from a range of addresses specified by an administrator.

Figure 2-1

The Internet Protocol Version 4 (TCP/IPv4) Properties sheet

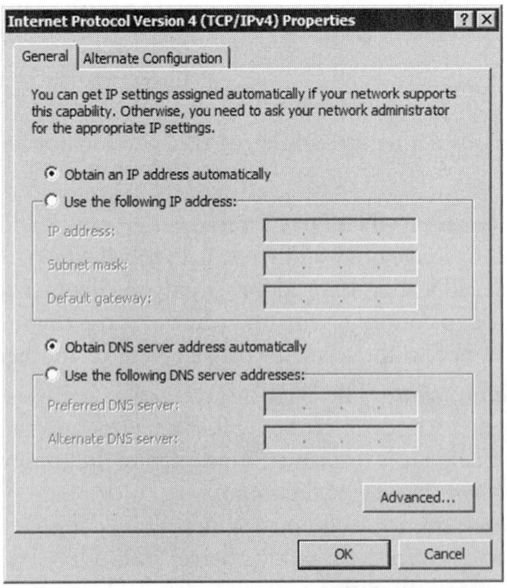

DHCP communications are always initiated by the client, as shown in Figure 2-2, and proceed as follows:

Figure 2-2

The DHCP IP address assignment process

DHCP Client   **DHCP Server**

1. When a computer boots for the first time with the DHCP client active, the client generates a series of DHCPDISCOVER messages to solicit an IP address assignment from a DHCP server and broadcasts them on the local network. At this point, the client has no IP address and is said to be in the *init state*.

2. All DHCP servers receiving the DHCPDISCOVER broadcast messages generate DHCPOFFER messages containing an IP address and whatever other TCP/IP configuration parameters the server is configured to supply, and transmit them to the client. Because the client broadcasts its DHCPDISCOVER messages, it may receive DHCPOFFER responses from multiple servers.

3. After a specified period of time, the client stops broadcasting and signals its acceptance of one of the offered addresses by generating a DHCPREQUEST message, containing the address of the server from which it is accepting the offer along with the offered IP address, and broadcasting it on the local network. This broadcast notifies the selected server that the client is accepting the offered address and also notifies any other servers on the network that the client is rejecting their offers.

4. When the server offering the accepted IP address receives the DHCPREQUEST message, it adds the offered IP address and other settings to its database using a combination of the client's hardware address (its Media Access Control Address, hard-coded on the network interface card) and the offered IP address as a unique identifier for the assignment. This is known as the *lease identification cookie*.

5. The server then transmits a DHCPACK message to the client, acknowledging the completion of the process. If the server cannot complete the assignment for any reason (because it has already assigned the offered IP address to another system, for example), it transmits a DHCPNAK message to the client and the whole process begins again.

6. As a final test, the client transmits the offered IP address in a broadcast using the Address Resolution Protocol (ARP), to ensure that no other system on the network is using the same address. If the client receives no response to the ARP broadcast, the DHCP transaction is completed and the client enters what is known as the *bound* state. If another system does respond to the ARP message, the client discards the IP address and transmits a DHCPDECLINE message to the server, nullifying the transaction. The client then restarts the entire process with a new series of DHCPDISCOVER messages.

TAKE NOTE*

If a Windows DHCP client is unable to contact a DHCP server, it self-assigns an IP address using a feature called Automatic Private IP Addressing (APIPA). Computers on the same subnet can communicate using APIPA addresses, but they are not an effective solution for routed internetworks.

By default, the DHCP Server service in Windows Server 2008 uses dynamic allocation, leasing IP addresses to clients for six-day periods. At periodic intervals during the course of the lease, the client attempts to contact the server to renew the lease, as shown in Figure 2-3, using the following procedure:

Figure 2-3

The DHCP IP address renewal process

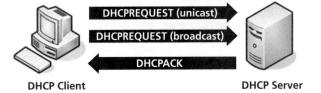

DHCP Client   DHCP Server

1. When the DHCP client reaches the 50 percent point of the lease's duration (called the renewal time value or T1 value), the client enters the *renewing* state and begins generating DHCPREQUEST messages and transmitting them as unicasts to the DHCP server holding the lease. DHCP clients also renew their leases each time they restart.

2. If the server does not respond by the time the client reaches the 87.5 percent point of the lease's duration (called the rebinding time value or T2 value), the client enters the rebinding state and begins transmitting its DHCPREQUEST messages as broadcasts, in an attempt to solicit an IP address assignment from any DHCP server on the network.

3. If the server receives the DHCPREQUEST message from the client, it can responds with either a DHCPACK message, approving the lease renewal request, or a DHCPNAK message, which terminates the lease. If the client receives no responses to its DHCPREQUEST messages by the time the lease expires, or if it receives a DHCPNAK message, the client releases its IP address and returns to the *init* state. All TCP/IP communication then ceases, except for the transmission of DHCPDISCOVER broadcasts.

TAKE NOTE *

The DHCP message formats and communication processes are not Microsoft-specific. They are defined in the RFC 2131 document, and are therefore interoperable with the DHCP server and client implementations in all earlier versions of Microsoft Windows, as well as with those in other implementations based on the same standards.

Designing a DHCP Infrastructure

The Windows Server 2008 DHCP Server service is theoretically capable of supporting many thousands of clients. However, for several reasons, virtually all enterprise networks require more than one DHCP server.

The primary reason for distributing the DHCP Server service is its reliance on broadcast messaging. When a DHCP client starts for the first time, it has no IP address of its own and no way of knowing the addresses of the DHCP servers on the network. Therefore, it can send its DHCPDISCOVER messages only as broadcast transmissions. By definition, broadcast transmissions are limited to the local subnet on which they are transmitted; routers do not propagate them to other networks. As a result, a client's DHCPDISCOVER messages are capable of reaching only DHCP servers on the local subnet.

USING A DISTRIBUTED DHCP INFRASTRUCTURE

Because of this limitation, it might seem at first that you must have a DHCP server on each of your enterprise network's subnets. On some networks, this is a viable DHCP deployment strategy, called a distributed DHCP infrastructure. In a ***distributed DHCP infrastructure,*** shown in Figure 2-4, you install at least one DHCP server on each of your subnets so that all of your clients have access to a local DHCP server.

Figure 2-4

A distributed DHCP
infrastructure

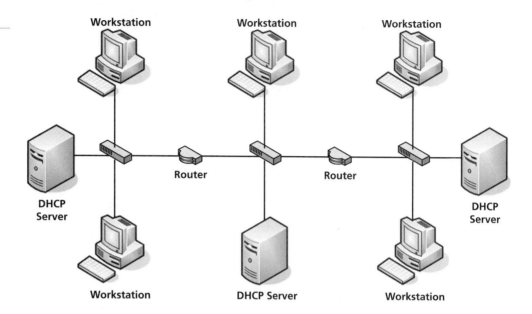

There are distinct advantages to the distributed DHCP infrastructure. Your clients have ready access to their DHCP servers, and you do not have to worry about DHCP traffic adding to the burden of your routers, because all of the client/server traffic is local. The potential disadvantage of this arrangement is the need to install and configure a large number of DHCP servers. This is especially true if you plan to have multiple servers on each subnet, for fault tolerance.

A distributed DHCP infrastructure does not necessarily mean that you must have a separate server dedicated to DHCP on every subnet, however. The DHCP Server role in Windows Server 2008 co-exists well with other roles. Because each DHCP server has to support only the local subnet, the impact of the role on each server's disk subsystem and network traffic burden is significant, but relatively light. If your network design already calls for at least one server on every subnet, adding the DHCP Server role to each subnet can be an acceptable solution.

USING A CENTRALIZED DHCP INFRASTRUCTURE

Despite the limitation of DHCP broadcast traffic, it is possible to design a DHCP infrastructure that does not have a separate DHCP server on every subnet. In a ***centralized DHCP infrastructure,*** the DHCP servers are all placed in a single location, such as a server closet or data center. To enable the broadcast traffic on each subnet to reach the DHCP servers, you must install a DHCP relay agent on each subnet, as shown in Figure 2-5.

Figure 2-5

A centralized DHCP infrastructure

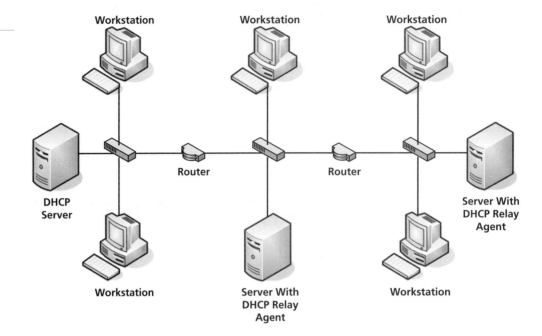

A **DHCP relay agent** is a software component that receives the DHCP broadcast traffic on a subnet and then sends it on to particular DHCP servers on one or more other subnets.

The DHCP servers then process the incoming DHCPREQUEST messages in the normal manner and transmit their replies back to the relay agent, which sends them on to the DHCP client.

> **+ MORE INFORMATION**
>
> The functionality of a DHCP relay agent is essentially unchanged from the original BootP relay agent, as defined in RFC 1542, "Clarifications and Extensions for BOOTP." The RFC 1542 standard defines the term "relay agent," to distinguish the function from the process of IP forwarding. DHCP relay agents do not "forward" DHCP messages in the same way that routers forward IP datagrams. Instead, the relay agent is actually considered to be the final recipient of a DHCP message, after which it generates a completely new message, which it transmits to the destination DHCP server or client.

TAKE NOTE*

To conform with the RFC 1542 standard, a relay agent must be disabled by default, and provide the ability to configure multiple DHCP server addresses on other subnets. Therefore, you must always activate and configure your relay agents, whether they are router-based or Windows-based.

Most IP routers have DHCP relay agent capabilities built into them. If the routers connecting your subnets can be configured to relay DHCP messages, you can use them as relay agents, eliminating the need for a DHCP server on each subnet. If your routers cannot function as DHCP relay agents, you can use the relay agent capability built into the Windows server operating systems. In Windows Server 2008, the DHCP relay agent capability is built into the Network Policy and Access Services role.

The advantages of a centralized DHCP infrastructure include a reduced administrative burden, because there are fewer DHCP servers to install, configure, manage, and monitor. DHCP relay agents incur virtually no additional burden on your servers or routers, so there is no need to scale up your hardware to accommodate them.

There are disadvantages to a centralized DHCP infrastructure, though. The DHCP Server services impose a burden both on the servers running it, and on the subnet to which they are connected. When you consolidate your DHCP Server deployment to a relatively small number of servers, all located on the same subnet, the burden on those servers, and on that subnet, increases accordingly.

On a large enterprise network, a centralized DHCP infrastructure can result in a large convergence of network traffic on the single subnet hosting the DHCP servers. Depending on your organization's work schedule, DHCP traffic can be particularly heavy at the beginning of the day, when a large number of users are turning on their workstations at nearly the same time. This burden can have a negative effect on the performance of other servers on the same subnet, as well as on the routers connecting that subnet to the rest of the network.

For example, if you were to have your high-volume DHCP servers in a data center on the same subnet as your file or application servers, your users might have trouble accessing the tools they need during periods of peak DHCP usage. This traffic congestion can be particularly burdensome if you have DHCP clients on remote subnet accessing DHCP over wide area network (WAN) links. WAN connections are, in most cases, relatively slow and relatively expensive, and burdening them with DHCP traffic can be a big problem, both in terms of performance and expense.

USING A HYBRID DHCP INFRASTRUCTURE

The distributed and centralized DHCP infrastructure represents the extremes at opposite ends of the design spectrum. In practice, as with most things, the ideal solution resides somewhere between those two extremes. A hybrid DHCP infrastructure is one that uses multiple DHCP servers on different subnets, but does not necessarily require a DHCP server on every subnet.

By scattering the DHCP servers on subnets throughout the enterprise, you can avoid the traffic congestion common to a centralized design, and by substituting DHCP relay agents for DHCP servers on some of your subnets, you can reduce the administrative burden of your design.

Take as an example an enterprise network that consists of a home office and a large number of branch offices in remote cities, connected by WAN links. A centralized infrastructure with all of the DHCP servers located in the home office would result in massive amounts of traffic on the WAN links connecting the branch offices to the home office. A distributed infrastructure would eliminate the WAN traffic congestion, but having a separate DHCP server for each subnet at each branch office could be prohibitively expensive, in terms of hardware, and generate a huge administrative burden for the IT staff working remotely from the home office.

A compromise between the two infrastructure designs, with one DHCP server and several relay agents at each branch office, would seem to be an ideal solution in this case. All users would have access to a local DHCP server, the WAN links would be free of DHCP traffic, and the administrators would have to set up and manage only one DHCP server at each remote location.

Thus, by designing an infrastructure that uses DHCP servers on some subnets and relay agents on others, you can exercise control over the amount of internetwork traffic DHCP generates, without incurring too much additional hardware expense and creating an administrative bottleneck.

REGULATING DHCP NETWORK TRAFFIC

As you have learned, the number of DHCP servers on a network, and their locations, can have an affect on the amount of network traffic passing through potential bottlenecks, such as routers and WAN links. Distributing your DHCP servers on different subnets is one way to prevent large amounts of traffic from converging on a single location.

Another way of reducing DHCP traffic levels is to adjust the length of your IP address leases. The default lease interval for a Windows Server 2008 DHCP server is six days, which means that clients enter the renewing state and start transmitting renewal messages every three days. The handful of messages generated by one client might not seem like a lot, but when you multiply that by many thousands of clients, DHCP can generate a significant amount of traffic. By increasing the length of your DHCP leases, you increase the amount of time between lease renewals, and therefore reduce the amount of renewal traffic.

When you consider how long to make your DHCP leases, you might begin to wonder whether it is necessary to use dynamic allocation at all. When you set the lease duration for a scope to Unlimited, you are, in effect, switching that scope to automatic allocation. Whether this is a viable solution for your network depends on factors such as the following:

- The number of IP addresses you have available on each subnet
- The number of computers you have on each subnet
- How often you move computers from one subnet to another

The main reason for leasing IP addresses, rather than assigning them permanently, is so that you can reclaim them for assignment to other computers. If nearly all of the available IP addresses in each of your subnets are allocated, then you are better off keeping your lease intervals relatively short, because you might have need for the unallocated addresses at any time. However, if you have a large number of unused addresses on each subnet, you can safely increase the lease intervals, because you are unlikely to experience a shortage of addresses.

One of the advantages of DHCP is that you can move a computer from one subnet to another, and it will automatically retrieve an appropriate IP address on the new subnet. When the old address lease expires, it will return to the old subnet's scope. DHCP also simplifies the process of merging subnets together and splitting them apart.

The frequency of computer relocations on your network is another factor you should consider when configuring your lease durations. If your network consists largely of mobile computers that move frequently from one subnet to another, as on a university network supporting student laptops, then it is better to keep the lease intervals short. For networks with computers that rarely change locations, long leases are appropriate.

PLANNING FOR FAULT TOLERANCE

This far in this lesson, you have learned how it can be beneficial to distribute multiple DHCP servers around an enterprise network, to provide users with local server access and to control the amount of DHCP message traffic passing through your routers. Another reason to have multiple DHCP servers, as with any type of server, is fault tolerance. If a DHCP server should fail, a fault tolerant network will always have another one available to take its place.

In some cases, you might question how necessary it is to have secondary DHCP servers. After all, if you use the default six-day lease interval for your scopes, and the only DHCP server for a particular network should go offline, you will most likely have several days to repair the server before clients begin losing their leases and dropping off of the network. This might be true, but if you use shorter leases for your scopes, or if you frequently move computers between subnets, access to DHCP services can be critical.

Unlike many other types of servers, you cannot have DHCP servers with identical scopes running at the same time. Although Windows Server 2008 DHCP servers must be authorized on an Active Directory network, they do not store their data in the Active Directory database, nor do they communicate directly with each other. If you were to create identical scopes on two DHCP servers, the potential would exist for each server to assign the same IP address to a different computer, resulting in address conflicts and network communication errors.

There are three techniques you can use to provide fault tolerance for DHCP servers, as discussed in the following sections.

SPLITTING SCOPES

Splitting scopes is the most common method of providing fault tolerance to DHCP servers. To do this, you create identical scopes on two DHCP servers, and then create opposite exclusion ranges that divide the scopes addresses between the two. The most common ratio for scope splitting is 80:20, with 80 percent of the scope's addresses available from one server and 20 percent from the other. For example, if you were using Class C subnets on your network, you would configure the DHCP servers as shown in Table 2-1.

Table 2-1

Scope Splitting on a Class C Network

	DHCP Server A	DHCP Server B
Scope range	192.168.1.1 to 192.168.1.254	192.168.1.1 to 192.168.1.254
Exclusion range	192.168.1.204 to 192.168.1.254	192.168.1.1 to 192.168.1.203
Number of addresses available	203	51
Percentage of addresses available	80%	20%

In this example, Server A and Server B have identical scopes on them, but 20 percent of the scope addresses are excluded from assignment by Server A and the remaining 80 percent is excluded from Server B. This way, both servers are capable of assigning addresses from the same scope, without the possibility of conflict.

When splitting scopes using the ***80/20 rule,*** it is not necessary to deploy multiple DHCP servers on each subnet. The reason for splitting the scope in this way is to have the server with 80 percent of the scope (Server A) located on the subnet it is servicing, while the 20 percent server (Server B) is located on another subnet and accesses the clients through a DHCP relay agent.

When clients on the subnet generate DHCPDISCOVER messages, the messages will reach Server A first, because that server is on the same subnet. The messages will reach Server B as well, but there will be a slight delay as they pass through the relay agent and the router. DHCP clients always accept the first IP address they are offered, so the computers on that subnet will, under normal circumstances, obtain their addresses from Server A. If Server A should fail, however, the DHCPDISCOVER messages will still reach Server B, and the clients will still be able to obtain addresses.

TAKE NOTE * If necessary, you can configure a delay into the Windows Server 2008 DHCP relay agent, using the Boot Threshold setting, to ensure that DHCP clients always obtain their addresses from the local server when it is available.

You can use the 80/20 rule to provide fault tolerance on any DHCP infrastructure. To split scopes on a large enterprise network, you must deploy each scope on two servers, whether the servers are located on the subnets they serve or not. Just make sure that, when both servers are available, clients tend to access the servers containing the 80 percent scope for their subnet first.

As one example of an 80/20 infrastructure design, you might want to have two DHCP servers, with each functioning as the 80 percent server for two scopes and the 20 percent server for two other scopes, as shown in Table 2-2.

Table 2-2

Scope Splitting on an Enterprise Network

Scope	DHCP Server A	DHCP Server B
192.168.2.0	192.168.2.1 to 192.168.2.203 (80%)	192.168.2.204 to 192.168.1.254 (20%)
192.168.3.0	192.168.3.204 to 192.168.3.254 (20%)	192.168.3.1 to 192.168.3.203 (80%)
192.168.4.0	192.168.4.1 to 192.168.4.203 (80%)	192.168.4.204 to 192.168.4.254 (20%)
192.168.5.0	192.168.5.204 to 192.168.5.254 (20%)	192.168.5.1 to 192.168.5.203 (80%)

Even if neither of the servers is located on the subnets they serve, you can still configure the Boot Threshold settings on the DHCP relay agents so that the DHCPDISCOVER messages from each server always reach the 80 percent server for that subnet first.

FAILOVER CLUSTERING

To ensure continued DHCP service with virtually no downtime, you can create a failover cluster in which the DHCP Server service is replicated on two or more computers. A failover cluster uses a shared storage medium, such as an iSCSI or Fibre Channel storage area network (SAN), to hold the application data, which in this case is the DHCP Server's database. The DHCP server on one of the servers in the cluster is always active, while the others remain dormant. In the event that the active server fails, another server in the cluster activates its DHCP server, using the same data.

Generally speaking, failover clustering can be considered to be overkill for the DHCP Server service, except in the case of large enterprises. End-user productivity is not usually interrupted by a DHCP server failure, even if the server is down for several hours. However, for the rare situation in which DHCP service is mission-critical, a failover cluster might be justified.

USING STANDBY SERVERS

A standby server is a computer with the DHCP Server role installed and configured, but not activated. If one of the active DHCP servers should fail, an administrator manually activates the appropriate scopes on the standby server to take its place. Because the standby servers are performing other roles in the meantime, they are an inexpensive way of providing DHCP fault tolerance without splitting scopes. However, because there is no automatic failover mechanism in this method, administrators cannot take action until they are aware that a DHCP server has failed.

ASSIGNING STATIC IP ADDRESSES

While DHCP is an excellent TCP/IP configuration solution for most of the computers on a network, there are a few for which it is not. Domain controllers, Internet Web servers, and DHCP servers themselves need static IP addresses. Because the DHCP dynamic allocation method allows for the possibility that a computer's IP address could change, it is not appropriate for these particular roles. However, it is still possible to assign addresses to these computers with DHCP, by using manual, instead of dynamic, allocation.

In a Windows DHCP server, a manually allocated address is called a *reservation*. You create a reservation by specifying the IP address you want to assign and associating it with the client computer's MAC address, which is hard-coded into its network interface adapter, as shown in Figure 2-6.

> **TAKE NOTE** *
>
> When you have two identical DHCP scopes on different servers, you must configure the servers to use server-side address conflict detection by specifying a value for the Conflict Detection Attempts setting on the Advanced tab in the IPv4 Properties sheet.

Figure 2-6

A DHCP server's New Reservation dialog box

Of course, it is also possible to manually configure the computer's TCP/IP client, but creating a DHCP reservation ensures that all of your IP addresses are managed by your DHCP servers. In a large enterprise, where various administrators might be dealing with DHCP and TCP/IP configuration issues, the IP address that one technician manually assigns to a computer might be included in a DHCP scope by another technician, resulting in potential addressing conflicts. Reservations create a permanent record of the IP address assignment on the DHCP server.

ASSIGNING IPv6 ADDRESSES

When the Internet Protocol (IP) was designed, the 32-bit IP address space seemed enormous, but as the decades passed and the Internet exploded in popularity, that vast address space seemed destined for depletion. Therefore, work commenced on a new IP standard that expands the address space from the original 32 bits of IP version 4 (IPv4) to 128 bits. The new standard is known as IP version 6, or IPv6.

IPv6 addresses are notated as follows:

XX:XX:XX:XX:XX:XX:XX:XX

Each X is a hexadecimal representation of a single byte. Some examples of IPv6 addresses are as follows:

3FFE:2900:D005:3210:FEDC:BA98:7654:3210

3FFE:FFFF:0:0:8:800:200C:417A

Leading zeros can be omitted from individual byte values, and repeated zero-byte values can be replaced with the "::" symbol (but only once in an address). Thus, the second address listed above could also be expressed as follows:

3FFE:FFFF::8:800:200C:417A

The IPv6 unicast addresses assigned to registered computers are split into six variable-length sections instead of the two or three sections (network, subnet, and host) that IPv4 addresses use. These sections are as follows:

- Format prefix—Specifies the type of address, such as provider-based unicast or multicast. (There is also a new type of address called an *anycast* that causes a message to be sent to only one of a specified group of interfaces.)
- Registry ID—Identifies the Internet address registry that assigned the Provider ID.
- Provider ID—Identifies the ISP that assigned this portion of the address space to a particular subscriber.
- Subscriber ID—Identifies a particular subscriber to the service provided by the ISP specified in the Provider ID field.
- Subnet ID—Identifies all or part of a specific physical link on the subscriber's network. Subscribers can create as many subnets as needed.
- Interface ID—Identifies a particular network interface on the subnet specified in the Subnet ID field.

The DHCP Server service in Windows Server 2008 supports both IPv4 and IPv6 address assignments. When you install the DHCP Server role, a Configure DHCPv6 Stateless Mode page appears in the Add Roles Wizard, enabling you to choose from the following two options:

- Enable DHCPv6 stateless mode for this server—IPv6 clients do not obtain addresses from the DHCP server, but they can obtain other TCP/IP configuration settings from the server.
- Disable DHCPv6 stateless mode for this server—IPv6 clients obtain addresses, as well as other TCP/IP configuration settings, from the DHCP server.

The DHCP server assumes that IPv6 clients operating in stateless mode obtain their addresses from an alternative source, typically either autoconfiguration or a manually assigned static address. In the stateless autoconfiguration configuration process, routers advertise prefixes that enable the host to assign themselves an IPv6 address on the appropriate subnet.

Deploying a DHCP Server

DHCP servers operate independently, so you must install the service and configure scopes on every computer that will function as a DHCP server.

The DHCP Server service is packaged as a role in Windows Server 2008, which you can install using the Add Roles Wizard, accessible from the Initial Configuration Tasks windows or the Server Manager console. To install the DHCP Server service on a Windows Server 2008 computer with Server Manager, use the following procedure.

⊙ DEPLOY A DHCP SERVER

GET READY. Log on to Windows Server 2008 using an account with Administrative privileges. When the logon process is completed, close the Initial Configuration Tasks window and any other windows that appear.

1. Click **Start**, and then click **Administrative Tools** > **Server Manager**. The Server Manager console appears.
2. Select the **Roles** node and, in the details pane, click **Add Roles**. The Add Roles Wizard appears.
3. Click **Next** to bypass the *Before You Begin* page. The *Select Server Roles* page appears, as shown in Figure 2-7.

Figure 2-7

The Select Server Roles page of the Add Roles Wizard

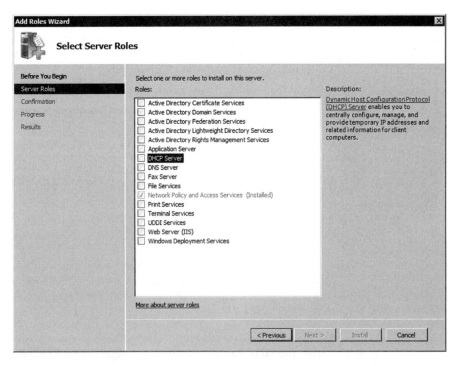

TAKE NOTE *

If your computer does not have a static IP address, a message box appears, recommending that you reconfigure the TCP/IP client with a static address before you install the DHCP Server role.

4. Select the **DHCP Server** checkbox and click **Next**. The *Introduction to DHCP Server* page appears.

5. Click **Next** to bypass the introduction page. The *Select Network Connection Bindings* page appears, as shown in Figure 2-8.

Figure 2-8

The Select Network Connection Bindings page of the Add Roles Wizard

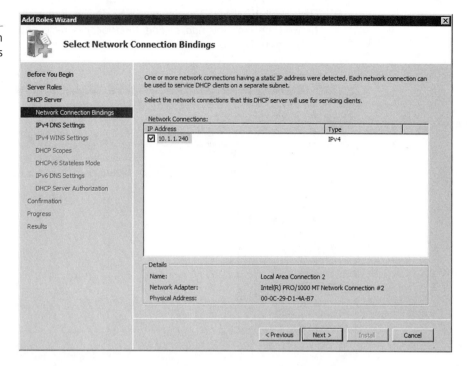

6. Select the checkboxes of the networks containing DHCP clients you want the server to service and click **Next**. The *Specify IPv4 DNS Server Settings* page appears, as shown in Figure 2-9.

Figure 2-9

The Specify IPv4 DNS Server Settings page of the Add Roles Wizard

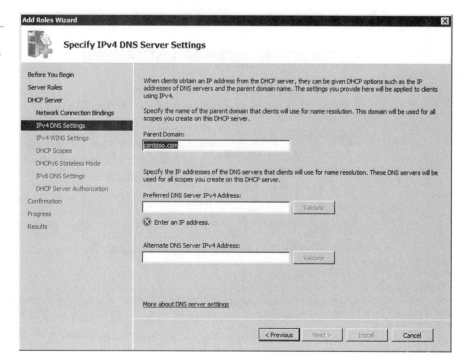

7. Key the IP addresses of your DNS servers in the **Preferred DNS Server IPv4 Address** and **Alternate DNS Server IPv4 Address** text boxes and click **Validate.** Then click **Next**. The *Specify IPv4 WINS Server Settings* page appears.

8. Click **Next** to accept the default WINS Is Not Required For Applications On This Network option. The *Add or Edit DHCP Scopes* page appears, as shown in Figure 2-10.

Figure 2-10

The Add or Edit DHCP Scopes page of the Add Roles Wizard

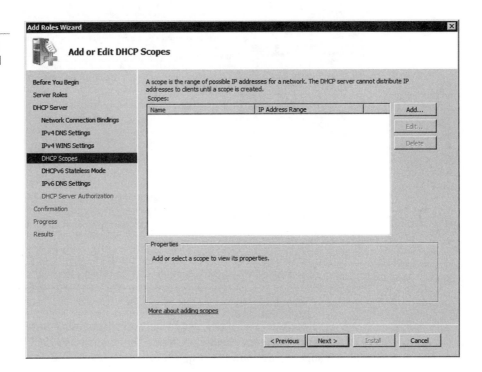

9. Click **Add.** The Add Scope dialog box appears, as shown in Figure 2-11.

Figure 2-11

The Add Scope dialog box

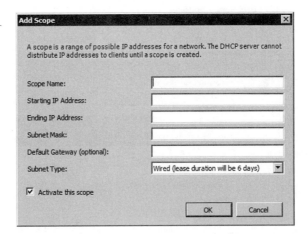

10. In the Add Scope dialog box, create a scope by supplying values for the following settings:
    - Scope Name—Specify a descriptive name identifying the scope.
    - Starting IP Address—Specify the first address in the range of IP addresses you want the scope to assign.
    - Ending IP Address—Specify the last address in the range of IP addresses you want the scope to assign.

- Subnet Mask—Specify the subnet mask value you want the server to assign with the scope addresses.
- Default Gateway—Specify the IP address of the router on the subnet that provides access to the rest of the network.
- Subnet Type—Specify the lease duration for the scope by selecting either Wired (lease duration will be six days) or Wireless (lease duration will be eight hours).

TAKE NOTE *

The Add Roles Wizard provides only a small subset of the settings and options you can assign to a DHCP scope. Once you have installed the role, you can create and modify scopes using the DHCP console. This console enables you to exclude specific addresses from the scope range, specify any value for the lease duration, and configure a large assortment of DHCP options to be supplied to clients with their IP addresses.

---

11. Select the **Activate this scope** checkbox and click **OK**. Then, back on the *Add or Edit DHCP Scopes* page, click **Next**. The *Configure DHCPv6 Stateless Mode* page appears.

12. Specify whether you want your clients to configure their own IPv6 addresses using stateless mode, and click **Next**. If the server is already a member of a domain, the *Authorize DHCP Server* page appears, as shown in Figure 2-12.

TAKE NOTE *

If you opt to enable stateless mode, a Specify IPv6 DNS Server Settings page appears in which you must specify the IP addresses of your DNS servers.

Figure 2-12

The Authorize DHCP Server page of the Add Roles Wizard

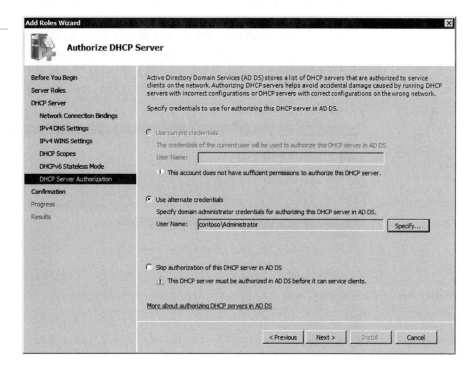

13. Specify the administrative credentials you want to use to authorize the DHCP server in Active Directory, and click **Next**. The *Confirm Installation Selections* page appears.

14. Click **Install**. The wizard installs the DHCP Server role.

CLOSE the Server Manager console when the installation is complete.

Once the role installation is completed, all of the DHCP clients on the subnet identified in the scope you created can obtain their IP addresses and other TCP/IP configuration settings via DHCP. You can also use the DHCP console to create additional scopes for other subnets.

Deploying a DHCP Relay Agent

If you opt to create a centralized or hybrid DHCP infrastructure, you will need a DHCP relay agent on every subnet that does not have a DHCP server on it.

Most routers are capable of functioning as DHCP relay agents, but in situations where they are not you can configure a Windows Server 2008 computer to function as a relay agent using the following procedure.

 DEPLOY A DHCP RELAY AGENT

GET READY. Log on to Windows Server 2008 using an account with Administrative privileges. When the logon process is completed, close the Initial Configuration Tasks window and any other windows that appear.

1. Click **Start**, and then click **Administrative Tools** > **Server Manager**. The Server Manager console appears.

2. Select the **Roles** node and, in the details pane, click **Add Roles**. The Add Roles Wizard appears.

3. Click **Next** to bypass the *Before You Begin* page. The *Select Server Roles* page appears.

4. Select the **Network Policy and Access Services** checkbox and click **Next**. The *Introduction to Network Policy and Access Services* page appears.

5. Click **Next** to bypass the introduction page. The *Select Role Services* page appears, as shown in Figure 2-13.

Figure 2-13

The Select Role Services page of the Add Roles Wizard

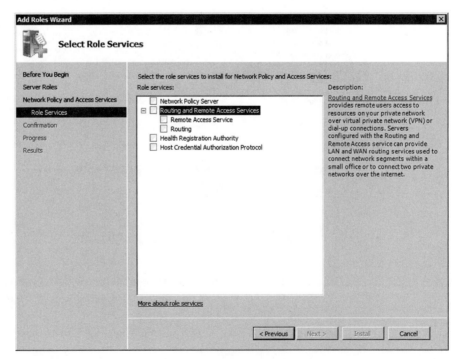

6. Select the **Routing and Remote Access Services** checkbox and click **Next**. The *Confirm Installation Selections* page appears.

7. Click **Install**. The wizard installs the Network Policy and Access Services role.

8. Click **Close** to terminate the wizard.

9. Close the Server Manager console.

10. Click **Start**, and then click **Administrative Tools > Routing and Remote Access**. The Routing and Remote Access console appears.

11. Right-click the server node and, on the context menu, select **Configure and Enable Routing and Remote Access**. The Routing and Remote Access Server Setup Wizard appears.

12. Click **Next** to bypass the Welcome page. The *Configuration* page appears, as shown in Figure 2-14.

Figure 2-14

The Configuration page of the Routing and Remote Access Server Setup Wizard

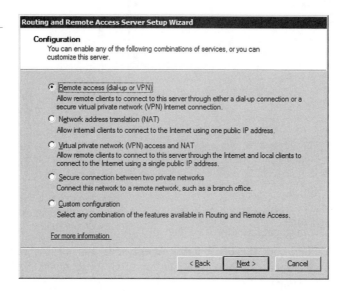

13. Select **Custom Configuration** and click **Next**. The *Custom Configuration* page appears, as shown in Figure 2-15.

Figure 2-15

The Custom Configuration page of the Routing and Remote Access Server Setup Wizard

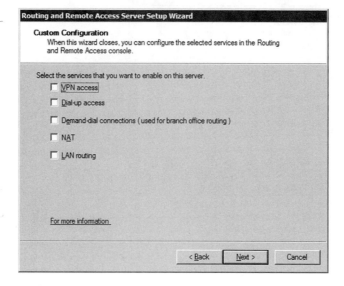

14. Select the **LAN Routing** checkbox and click **Next**. The *Completing the Routing and Remote Access Server Setup Wizard* page appears.

15. Click **Finish**. A Routing and Remote Access message box appears, prompting you to start the service.

16. Click **Start Service**.

17. Expand the IPv4 node. Then, right-click the **General** node and, in the context menu, select **New Routing Protocol**. The New Routing Protocol dialog box appears, as shown in Figure 2-16.

Figure 2-16

The New Routing Protocol dialog box

18. Select **DHCP Relay Agent** and click **OK**. A DHCP Relay Agent node appears, subordinate to the IPv4 node.

19. Right-click the **DHCP Relay Agent** node and, on the context menu, select **New Interface**. The New Interface for DHCP Relay Agent dialog box appears, as shown in Figure 2-17.

Figure 2-17

The New Interface for DHCP Relay Agent dialog box

20. Select the interface to the subnet on which you want to install the relay agent and click **OK**. The DHCP Relay Properties sheet for the interface appears, as shown in Figure 2-18.

Figure 2-18

The DHCP Relay Properties sheet for a selected interface

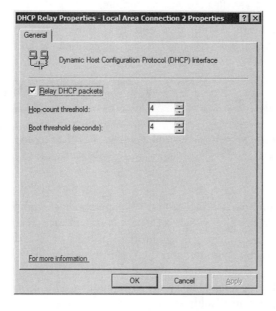

21. Leave the **Relay DHCP Packets** checkbox selected, and configure the following settings, if needed.

- Hop-count threshold—Specifies the maximum number of relay agents that DHCP messages can pass through before being discarded. The default value is 4 and the maximum value is 16. This setting prevents DHCP messages from being relayed endlessly around the network.

- Boot threshold—Specifies the time interval (in seconds) that the relay agent should wait before forwarding each DHCP message it receives. The default value is 4 seconds. This setting enables you to control which DHCP server processes the clients for a particular subnet.

22. Click **OK**.

23. Right-click the **DHCP Relay Agent** node and, on the context menu, select **Properties**. The DHCP Relay Agent Properties sheet appears, as shown in Figure 2-19.

Figure 2-19

The DHCP Relay Agent Properties sheet

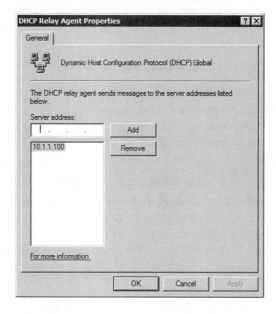

24. Key the IP address of the DHCP server to which you want the agent to relay messages and click **Add.** Repeat this step to add additional servers, if necessary.

25. Click **OK.**

CLOSE the Routing and Remote Access console.

At this point, the server is configured to relay DHCP messages from client computers on the local subnet to the DHCP server addresses you specified.

Deploying DNS Servers

THE BOTTOM LINE
The Domain Name System is a crucial element of both Internet and Active Directory communications.

All TCP/IP communication is based on IP addresses. Each computer on a network has at least one network interface, which is called a *host*, and each host has an IP address that is unique on that network. Every datagram transmitted by a TCP/IP system contains the IP address of the sending computer and the IP address of the intended recipient. However, when users access a shared folder on the network or a Web site on the Internet, they do so by specifying or selecting a host name, not an IP address. This is because names are far easier to remember and use than IP addresses.

For TCP/IP systems to use these friendly host names, they must have some way to discover the IP address associated with a specific name. In the early days of TCP/IP networking, each computer had a list of names and their equivalent IP addresses, called a *host table*. At that time, there were few enough computers on the fledgling Internet for the maintenance and distribution of a single host table to be practical.

Today, there are many millions of computers on the Internet, and the idea of maintaining and distributing a single file containing names for all of them is absurd. Instead of a host table stored on every computer, TCP/IP networks today use Domain Name System (DNS) servers to convert host names into IP addresses. This conversion process is referred to as *name resolution*.

Understanding the DNS Architecture

When the developers of what became the Internet recognized the increasing impracticality of the host table, they set about devising a solution that would not only solve their immediate maintenance and distribution problems, but would also remain a viable solution for decades to come.

The objectives of the name resolution project were as follows:

* To create a means for administrators to assign host names to their computers without duplicating the names of other systems
* To store the host names in a database that would be accessible by any system, anywhere on the network
* To distribute the host name database among servers all over the network
* To avoid creating traffic bottlenecks and a single point of failure
* To create a standardized system for host naming accessing electronic mailboxes
* To allow name changes to be dynamically updated to all participating computers

The resulting solution was the Domain Name System (DNS), as defined and published in 1983 in two documents: RFC 882, "Domain Names: Concepts and Facilities," and RFC

883, "Domain Names: Implementation Specification." These documents were updated in 987, published as RFC 1034 and RFC 1035, respectively, and ratified as an IETF standard. Since that time, the IETF has published numerous other RFCs that update the information in the standard to address current networking issues.

At its core, DNS is still a list of names and their equivalent IP addresses, but the methods for creating, storing, and retrieving those names is very different from those in a host table. DNS consists of three elements, as follows:

- The DNS name space—The DNS standards define a tree-structured namespace in which each branch of the tree identifies a *domain*. Each domain contains a collection of *resource records* that contain host names, IP addresses, and other information. Query operations are attempts to retrieve specific resource records from a particular domain.

- Name servers—A DNS server is an application running on a server computer that maintains information about the domain tree structure and (usually) contains authoritative information about one or more specific domains in that structure. The application is capable of responding to queries for information about the domains for which it is the authority, and also of forwarding queries about other domains to other name servers. This enables any DNS server to access information about any domain in the tree.

- Resolvers—A *resolver* is a client program that generates DNS queries and sends them to a DNS server for fulfillment. A resolver has direct access to at least one DNS server and can also process referrals to direct its queries to other servers when necessary.

TAKE NOTE *

The term "domain," in the context of DNS, has a different meaning than it does when used in the Microsoft Windows directory services. A Windows Server 2008 domain is a grouping of Windows computers and devices that are administered as a unit. In DNS, a domain is a group of hosts and possibly subdomains that represents a part of the DNS namespace.

In its most basic form, the DNS name resolution process consists of a resolver submitting a name resolution request to its designated DNS server. When the server does not possess information about the requested name, it forwards the request to another DNS server on the network. The second server generates a response containing the IP address of the requested name and returns it to the first server, which relays the information in turn to the resolver, as shown in Figure 2-20. In practice, however, the DNS name resolution process can be considerably more complex, as you will learn in the following sections.

Figure 2-20

DNS servers relay requests and replies to other DNS servers

Resolver   DNS Server   Authoritative DNS Server

UNDERSTANDING DNS NAMING

To facilitate the continued growth of the namespace, the developers of the DNS created a two-tiered system, consisting of domain names and host names. The basic principle is that the administrators of individual networks obtain domain names from a centralized authority, and then assign the host names within that domain themselves. This enables administrators to assign host names without worrying about duplication, as long as each host name is unique within its domain.

In the days of host tables, if two administrators each named one of their computers Server01, a conflict would have occurred, resulting in misdirected data packets. Today, the two administrators can both use the host name Server01, as long as the two hosts are in different domains. Each computer is uniquely identified by the combination of its host name and its domain name.

One of the most common examples of this principle is found in the Internet Web sites you see every day. It is common for the administrators of Web sites to assign the host name www to their Web servers. There are therefore millions of Web servers on the Internet with identical host names. However, when you enter a Uniform Resource Locator (URL) such as http://www.contoso.com in your browser, it is the domain name, contoso.com, that distinguishes that particular www server from www.contoso.com and millions of others.

> **➕ MORE INFORMATION**
>
> When you study the structure of a DNS name, notice the similarity between DNS named and IP addresses, which also consist of two parts: a network identifier and a host identifier. This two-part hierarchy is a recurring theme in the architecture of TCP/IP networks, because it enables administrative responsibilities to be distributed throughout the network. In the same way that administrators receive the network identifiers for their IP addresses and are responsible for assigning the host identifiers on that network, administrators also receive DNS domain names, and are responsible for assigning host names within that domain.

The domain name part of a DNS name is hierarchical, and consists of two or more words, separated by periods. The DNS namespace takes the form of a tree that, much like a file system, has its root at the top. Just beneath the root is a series of top-level domains, and beneath each top-level domain is a series of second-level domains, as shown in Figure 2-21. At minimum, the complete DNS name for a computer on the Internet consists of a host name, a second-level domain name, and a top-level domain name, written in that order and separated by periods. The complete DNS name for a particular computer is called its *fully qualified domain name (FQDN)*.

Figure 2-21

The DNS domain hierarchy

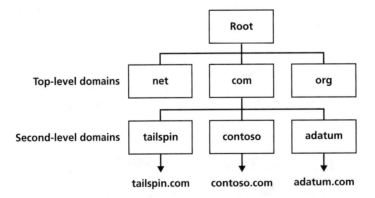

Unlike an IP address, which places the network identifier first and follows it with the host, the notation for an FQDN places the host name first, followed by the domain name, with the top-level domain name last. In the example cited earlier, the FQDN www.contoso.com consists of a host (or computer) called www in the contoso.com domain. In the contoso.com domain name, com is the top-level domain and contoso is the second-level domain. Technically, every FQDN should end with a period, representing the root of the DNS tree, as follows:

```
www.contoso.com.
```

However, the period is rarely included in FQDNs today.

UNDERSTANDING THE DNS DOMAIN HIERARCHY

The hierarchical nature of the DNS namespace is designed to make it possible for any DNS server on the Internet to locate the authoritative source for any domain name, using a minimum number of queries. This efficiency results from the fact that the domains at each level of the hierarchy are responsible for maintaining information about the domains at the next lower level.

The authoritative source for any domain is the DNS server (or servers) responsible for maintaining that domain's resource records. Each level of the DNS domain hierarchy has name servers responsible for the individual domains at that level.

At the top of the DNS hierarchy are the root name servers. The ***root name servers*** are the highest-level DNS servers in the entire namespace, and they maintain information about the top-level domains. All DNS server implementations are preconfigured with the IP addresses of the root name servers, because these servers are the ultimate source for all DNS information. When a computer attempts to resolve a DNS name, it begins at the top of the namespace hierarchy with the root name servers, and works its way down through the levels until it reaches the authoritative server for the domain in which the name is located.

Just beneath the root name servers are the top-level domains. There are seven primary top-level domains in the DNS namespace, as follows:

- com
- net
- org
- edu
- mil
- gov
- int

In addition to the seven main top-level domains, there are also two-letter international domain names representing most of the countries in the world, such as *it* for Italy and *de* for Germany (Deutschland). There are also a number of newer top-level domains promoted by Internet entrepreneurs, such as biz and info.

The top two levels of the DNS hierarchy, the root and the top-level domains, are represented by servers that exist primarily to respond to queries for information about other domains. There are no hosts in the root or top-level domains, except for the name servers themselves. For example, you will never see a DNS name consisting of only a host and a top-level domain, such as www.com. The root name servers do nothing but respond to millions of requests by sending out the addresses of the authoritative servers for the top-level domains, and the top-level domain servers do the same for the second-level domains.

Each top-level domain has its own collection of second-level domains. Individuals and organizations can purchase these domains for their own use. For example, the second-level domain contoso.com belongs to a company that purchased the name from one of the many Internet registrars now in the business of selling domain names to consumers. For the payment of an annual fee, you can purchase the rights to a second-level domain.

To use the domain name, you must supply the registrar with the IP addresses of the DNS servers that you want to be the authoritative sources for information about this domain. The administrators of the top-level domain servers then create resource records pointing to these authoritative sources so that any com server receiving a request to resolve a name in the contoso.com domain can reply with the addresses of the contoso.com servers.

Once you purchase the rights to a second-level domain, you can create as many hosts as you want in that domain, simply by creating new resource records on the authoritative servers. You can also create as many additional domain levels as you want. For example, once you own the contoso.com domain, you can create the subdomains sales.contoso.com and marketing.contoso.com, and then populate each of these subdomains with hosts, such as www.sales.contoso.com and ftp.marketing.contoso.com. The only limitations to the subdomains and hosts you can create in your second-level domain are as follows:

- Each individual domain name can be no more than 63 characters long.
- The total FQDN (including the trailing period) can be no more than 255 characters long.

For the convenience of users and administrators, most domain names do not even approach these limitations.

UNDERSTANDING DNS COMMUNICATIONS

To better explain the relationship of the DNS servers for various domains in the namespace, a diagram of the Internet name resolution process is shown in Figure 2-22. The resolution of a DNS name on the Internet proceeds as follows:

Figure 2-22

The DNS name resolution process

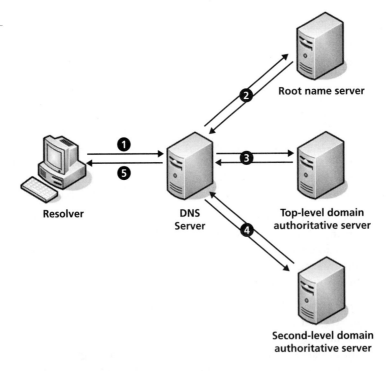

1. An application running on the client computer has a name to resolve and passes it to the DNS resolver running on that system. The resolver generates a DNS name resolution request message and transmits it to the DNS server address specified in its TCP/IP configuration.

2. The client's DNS server, upon receiving the request, checks its own database and cache for the requested name. If the server has no information about the requested name, it forwards the request message to one of the root name servers on the Internet. The root name server, in processing the request, reads only the top-level domain of the requested name, and generates a reply message containing the IP address of an authoritative server for that top-level domain. The root name server then transmits the reply back to the client's DNS server.

3. The client's DNS server now has the IP address of an authoritative server for the requested name's top-level domain, so it transmits the same name resolution request to that top-level domain server. The top-level domain server reads only the second-level domain of the requested name, and generates a reply containing the IP address of an authoritative server for that second-level domain. The top-level server then transmits the reply to the client's DNS server.

4. The client's DNS server now finally has the IP address of an authoritative server for the second-level domain that actually contains the requested host, so it forwards the name resolution request to that second-level domain server. The second-level domain server reads the host in the requested name and transmits a reply containing the resource record for that host back to the client's DNS server.

5. The client's DNS server receives the resource record from the second-level domain server and forwards it to the resolver on the client computer. The resolver then supplies the IP address associated with the requested name to the original application, after which direct communication between the client and the intended destination can begin.

This name resolution process might seem to be incredibly long and tedious, but it actually proceeds very quickly. There are also DNS server mechanisms that help to shorten the name resolution process, including the following:

- Combined DNS Servers—In the DNS name resolution process just described, the process of resolving the top-level and second-level domain names are portrayed as separate steps, but this is often not the case. The most commonly used top-level domains, such as com, net, and org, are actually hosted by the root name servers, which eliminates one entire referral from the name resolution process.

- Name Caching—DNS server implementations typically maintain a cache of information they receive from other DNS servers. When a server possesses information about a requested FQDN in its cache, it responds directly using the cached information, rather than sending a referral to another server. Therefore, if you have a DNS server on your network that has just successfully resolved the name www.contoso.com for a client by contacting the authoritative server for the contoso.com domain, a second user trying to access the same host a few minutes later would receive an immediate reply from the local DNS server's cache, rather than having to wait for the entire referral process to repeat, as shown in Figure 2-23. Caching is a critical part of the DNS, as it reduces the amount of network traffic generated by the name resolution process and reduces the burden on the root name and top-level domain servers.

Figure 2-23

Name caching enables the second name resolution request for the same name to bypass the referral process.

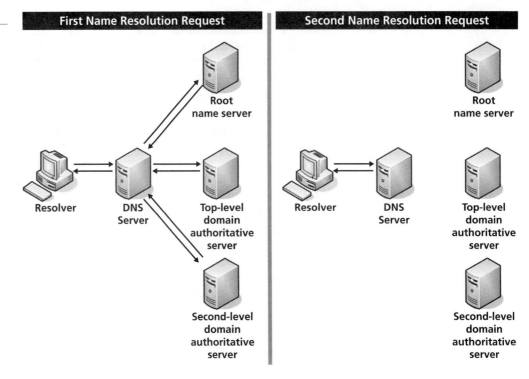

UNDERSTANDING DNS REFERRALS AND QUERIES

The process by which one DNS server sends a name resolution request to another DNS server is called a *referral*. Referrals are essential to the DNS name resolution process. As you noticed in the process described earlier, the DNS client is not involved in the name resolution process at all, except for sending one query and receiving one reply. The client's DNS server might have to send referrals to several servers before it reaches the one that has the information it needs.

DNS servers recognize two types of name resolution requests, as follows:

- Recursive query—In a *recursive query,* the DNS server receiving the name resolution request takes full responsibility for resolving the name. If the server possesses information about the requested name, it replies immediately to the requestor. If the server has no information about the name, it sends referrals to other DNS servers until it obtains the information it needs. TCP/IP client resolvers always send recursive queries to their designated DNS servers.

- Iterative query—In an *iterative query,* the server that receives the name resolution request immediately responds with the best information it possesses at the time. This information could be cached or authoritative, and it could be a resource record containing a fully resolved name or a reference to another DNS server. DNS servers use iterative queries when communicating with each other. In most cases, it would be improper to configure one DNS server to send a recursive query to another DNS server. For example, if DNS servers started sending iterative queries to the root name servers instead of recursive queries, the additional burden on the root name servers would be immense, and probably cause the entire Internet to grind to a halt. The only time a DNS server does send iterative queries to another server is in the case of a special type of server called a forwarder, which is specifically configured to interact with other servers in this way.

UNDERSTANDING REVERSE NAME RESOLUTION

The name resolution process described earlier is designed to convert DNS names into IP addresses. However, there are occasions when it is necessary for a computer to convert an IP address into a DNS name. This is called a *reverse name resolution.* Because domain names break down the domain hierarchy, there is no apparent way to resolve an IP address into a name using iterative queries, except by forwarding the reverse name resolution request to every DNS server on the Internet in search of the requested address, which is obviously impractical.

To overcome this problem, the developers of the DNS created a special domain called in-addr.arpa, specifically designed for reverse name resolution. The in-addr.arpa second-level domain contains four additional levels of subdomains. Each of the four levels consists of subdomains that are named using the numerals 0 to 255. For example, beneath in-addr.arpa, there are 256 third-level domains, which have names ranging from 0.in-addr.arpa to 255. in-addr.arpa. Each of those 256 third-level domains has 256 fourth-level domains beneath it, also numbered from 0 to 255, and each fourth-level domain has 256 fifth-level domains, as shown in Figure 2-24. Each of those fifth-level domains can then have up to 256 hosts in it, also numbered from 0 to 255.

Figure 2-24

The DNS reverse lookup domain

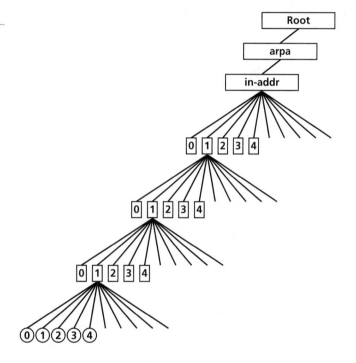

Using this hierarchy of subdomains, it is possible to express the first three bytes of an IP address as a DNS domain name, and to create a resource record named for the fourth byte in the appropriate fifth-level domain. For example, to resolve the IP address 192.168.89.34 into a name, a DNS server would locate a domain called 89.168.192.in-addr.arpa in the usual manner and read the contents of a resource record named 34 in that domain.

Designing a DNS Deployment

> **TAKE NOTE** *
>
> In the in-addr.arpa domain, the IP address is reversed in the domain name because IP addresses have the least pertinent bit (that is, the host identifier) on the right, and in DNS FQDNs the host name is on the left.

All of the DNS information in the preceding sections might seem gratuitous at first, but understanding the structure of the DNS and how the clients and servers communicate is crucial to creating an effective DNS deployment plan.

Every computer on a TCP/IP network needs access to a DNS server, but this does not mean that you absolutely must deploy your own DNS servers on your network. Internet service providers (ISPs) nearly always include the use of their DNS servers in their rates, and in some cases, it might be better to use other DNS servers rather than run your own.

The first factor in designing a DNS deployment is what DNS services your network requires. Consider the information in the following sections as you create your design.

RESOLVING INTERNET NAMES

If you provide your network users with access to the Internet, as most organizations do these days, then every user must have at least one DNS server address specified in its TCP/IP configuration settings. If you use DHCP servers to assign IP addresses to the network computers, you can configure the servers to configure the clients' DNS server addresses as well.

For Internet name resolution purposes, the only functions required of the DNS server are the ability to process incoming queries from resolvers and send its own queries to other DNS servers on the Internet. A DNS server that performs only these functions is known as a *caching-only server*, because it is not the authoritative source for any domain and hosts no resource records of its own.

Installing your own caching-only DNS server is a simple matter, or you can use the DNS servers supplied by your ISP. The important factor to consider in this decision is the amount of traffic generated by the server's query process. In the DNS name resolution process, the client resolver and its DNS server exchange one query message and one reply. If the clients on your local network use the DNS servers on your ISP's network, then your Internet connection has to handle only those two messages, as shown in Figure 2-25.

Figure 2-25

Using an ISP's caching-only DNS server

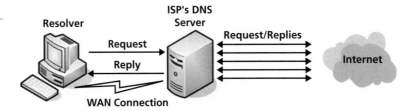

If, however, you install a DNS server on your local network, the recursive queries the server receives from clients cause it to send numerous iterative queries to various other DNS servers on the Internet. These multiple message exchanges must all pass over the Internet connection, as shown in Figure 2-26. When you have hundreds or thousands of clients using the DNS server, the amount of iterative query traffic the server generates can overburden your Internet connection or greatly increase its cost.

Figure 2-26

Using your own caching-only DNS server

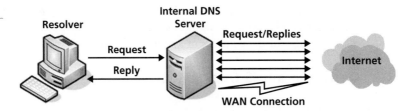

As a general rule, if your network requires no DNS services other than name resolution, you should consider using off-site DNS servers. However, it is also possible to split the name resolution tasks between on-site and off-site servers by using a **DNS forwarder**. When you configure a DNS server to function as a forwarder, it receives name resolution requests from clients and sends them on to another DNS server, specified by the administrator, using recursive, not iterative, queries.

Conditional forwarding is a variation included in Windows Server 2008 that enables you to forward requests for names in certain domains to specific DNS servers. Using conditional forwarding, you can, for example, send all requests for your Internet domain to your local, authoritative DNS server, while all other requests go to your ISP's DNS server on the Internet.

HOSTING INTERNET DOMAINS

If you plan to host a domain on the Internet, you must pay an annual fee to register a second-level domain name with one of the many commercial registrars and supply them with the IP addresses of your DNS servers. These servers will be the authoritative source for information about your domain. They must therefore have registered IP addresses and be accessible from the Internet at all times.

The two main reasons for registering an Internet domain name are to host Web servers and to create email addresses. The authoritative DNS servers for the domain must have resource records that can provide Internet users the IP addresses of your Web servers and email servers. If the authoritative DNS servers are ever offline, Internet users might be unable to access your Web servers, and email messages destined for your domain could bounce back to their senders.

TAKE NOTE*

Because DNS servers cache the information that they obtain from other DNS servers, it might sometimes be possible for Internet users to resolve your domain name, even though your servers are offline. However, DNS servers purge their cached information after a period of time, so if the authoritative servers are down for more than a few hours, no one will be able to resolve your domain name.

As with name resolution, the DNS servers you use to host your domain can be computers on your own network, or servers supplied by a commercial entity. The DNS servers that host your domain do not have to be located in that domain, nor do they have to be supplied by the registrar from whom you obtained your domain name. You can usually pay an additional fee to your domain registrar, and have them host the domain on their servers, or you can use you ISP's servers, also for an additional fee.

Using a commercial domain hosting service usually provides greater reliability than installing your own, in the form of redundant servers and Internet connections, so your DNS records are always available. The same traffic issue discussed in the previous section also applies here; using commercial DNS servers keeps the incoming queries from the Internet off of your local network.

One advantage to hosting your domain on your own DNS servers is the ability to modify your resource records at will, using familiar controls. Before you select a commercial service provider to host your domain, be sure to check their policies regarding DNS resource record modifications. Some companies provide a Web-based interface that enables you to manage your resource records yourself, while others might require you to call them to make DNS changes, and might even charge you an additional fee for each modification.

HOSTING ACTIVE DIRECTORY DOMAINS

If you plan to run Active Directory on your network, you must have at least one DNS server on the network that supports the Service Location (SRV) resource record, such as the DNS Server service in Windows Server 2008. When you install the Active Directory Domain Services role on a Windows Server 2008 computer, the Active Directory Domain Services Installation Wizard checks for an appropriate DNS server, and the wizard offers to install one if none is available.

+ MORE INFORMATION

The SRV resource record was not part of the original DNS standards; it is a relatively recent development. As a result, you might encounter DNS server implementations that do not support this record type. Before you deploy an Active Directory network, be sure your DNS servers support RFC 2052, "A DNS RR for Specifying the Location of Services (DNS SRV)," published by the IETF.

Computers on the network running Windows 2000 and later versions use DNS to locate Active Directory domain controllers. To support Active Directory clients, the DNS server does not have to have a registered IP address or an Internet domain name.

For Active Directory domain hosting, it is nearly always preferable to deploy your own DNS servers on the network. It would be pointless to force your Active Directory clients on the local network to send queries to a DNS server on the Internet so that they can locate a domain controller on the same local network as themselves. This would introduce an unnecessary delay into the already complex Active Directory communications process, and also add to the traffic on your Internet connection for no good reason.

INTEGRATING DHCP AND DNS

To resolve a DNS name into an IP address, the DNS server must have a resource record for that name, which contains the equivalent address. The original DNS specifications call for administrators to manually create the DNS resource records. The use of DHCP complicates this process, however.

When computers lease their IP addresses from DHCP servers, the possibility exists for a particular computer's address to change. For example, a computer that is offline for some time might come back online after its lease has expired, and the DHCP server, having given the computer's address to another client, might assign it a different address. However, a manually created DNS resource record would still contain the old IP address, leading to name resolution errors.

To address this problem, the DNS server included in Windows Server 2008 is compliant with the RFC 2136 document called "Dynamic Updates in the Domain Name System (DNS UPDATE)." The dynamic update standard enables a DNS server to modify resource records at the request of DHCP servers and clients. Therefore, when a DHCP server assigns an address to a client, it can also send the appropriate commands to the DNS server, enabling it to create or update the resource records for that client. The dynamic update standard also enables Active Directory domain controllers to create their own SRV resource records.

This relationship between the DNS and DHCP server services is another reason to run your own DNS servers on your network.

SEPARATING DNS SERVICES

As you have learned in the previous sections, the name resolution and Internet domain hosting functions are often better served by DNS servers that are external to the enterprise network, while organizations that use Active Directory and DHCP typically require internal DNS servers. In many cases, a network requires some or all of these DNS functions, and you must decide which ones you want to implement yourself and which you want to delegate.

It is possible to use a single DNS server to host both Internet and Active Directory domains, as well as to provide clients with name resolution services and DHCP support. However, just because you need all four of these services does not mean that you must compromise by choosing to deploy only internal or external DNS servers.

Because the services are independent from each other, you might also want to consider splitting up these functions by using several DNS servers. For example, you can use your ISP's DNS servers for client name resolution, to conserve your network's Internet bandwidth, even if you are running your own DNS servers for other purposes. You can also use a commercial service provider to host your Internet domain, while keeping your Active Directory domain hosting and dynamic update services internal.

⊕ MORE INFORMATION

The client computers on the network can send their queries only to a single DNS server, so you must use the server's configuration capabilities to delegate the various DNS functions among multiple servers. For example, a **forwarder** is a DNS server that receives queries from other DNS servers that are explicitly configured to send them. With Windows Server 2008 DNS servers, the forwarder requires no special configuration. However, you must configure the other DNS servers to send queries to the forwarder. By using a forwarder, you can configure all of the clients on your network to use the local domain controller as a DNS server, and then have the domain controller forward Internet domain name resolution requests as recursive queries to the ISP's DNS server.

However, when you deploy your own DNS servers for any reason, you should always run at least two instances to provide fault tolerance.

Creating Internet Domains

Designing a DNS namespace for your organization's Internet presence is usually the easiest part of deploying DNS. Most organizations register a single second-level domain and use it to host all their Internet servers.

In most cases, the selection of a second-level domain name depends on what is available. A large portion of the most popular top-level domain, com, is already depleted, and you might find that the name you want to use is already taken. In this case, you have three alternatives:

- Choose a different domain name.
- Register the name in a different top-level domain.
- Attempt to purchase the domain name from its current owner.

If you are certain that you want to use the second-level domain name you have chosen, such as when the name is a recognizable brand of your organization, your best bet is usually to register the name in another top-level domain. Although the org and net domains are available to anyone, these domains are traditionally associated with non-profit and network infrastructure organizations, respectively, and might not fit your business. As an alternative, a number of countries around the world with attractive top-level domain names have taken to registering second-level domains commercially.

Some organizations maintain multiple sites on the Internet, for various reasons. Your organization might be involved in several separate businesses that warrant individual treatment, or your company might have independent divisions with different sites. You might also want to create different sites for retail customers, wholesale customers, and providers. Whatever the reason, there are two basic ways to implement multiple sites on the Internet:

- Register a single second-level domain name and then create multiple subdomains beneath it. For the price of a single domain registration, you can create as many third-level domains as you need, and you can also maintain a single brand across all your sites. For example, a company called Contoso Pharmaceuticals might register the contoso.com domain, and then create separate Web sites for doctors and patients in domains called doctors.contoso.com and patients.contoso.com.

⊕ MORE INFORMATION

For an extensive list of the Internet domain name registrars that the Internet Corporation for Assigned Names and Numbers (ICANN) has accredited, see http://www.icann.org/registrars/accredited-list.html.

- Register multiple second-level domains—If your organization consists of multiple, completely unrelated brands or operations, this is often the best solution. You must pay a separate registration fee for each domain name you need, however, and you must maintain a separate DNS namespace for each domain. A problem might also arise when you try to integrate your Internet domains with your internal network. You can select one of your second-level domains to integrate with your internal namespace, or you can leave your internal and external namespaces completely separate, as discussed later in this lesson.

Creating Internal Domains

In many ways, using DNS on an internal Windows Server 2008 network is similar to using DNS on the Internet. You can create domains and subdomains to support the organizational hierarchy of your network in any way you want.

When you are designing a DNS namespace for a network that uses Active Directory, the DNS domain name hierarchy is directly related to the directory service hierarchy. For example, if your organization consists of a headquarters and a series of branch offices, you might choose to create a single Active Directory tree and assign the name contoso.com to the root domain in the tree. Then, for the branch offices, you create subdomains beneath contoso.com with names like seattle.contoso.com and pittsburgh.contoso.com. These names correspond directly to the domain hierarchy in your DNS namespace.

When selecting names for your internal domains, you should try to observe the following rules:

- Keep domain names short—Internal DNS namespaces tend to run to more levels than those found on the Internet, and using long names for individual domains can result in excessively long FQDNs.

- Avoid an excessive number of domain levels—To keep FQDNs a manageable length and to keep administration costs down, limit your DNS namespace to no more than five levels from the root.

- Create a naming convention and stick to it—When creating subdomains, establish a rule that enables users to deduce what the name of a domain should be. For example, you can create subdomains based on political divisions, such as department names, or geographical divisions, such as names of cities, but do not mix the two at the same domain level.

- Avoid obscure abbreviations—Don't use abbreviations for domain names unless they are immediately recognizable by users. Domains using abbreviations such as NY for New York or HR for Human Resources are acceptable, but avoid creating your own abbreviations just to keep names short.

- Avoid names that are difficult to spell—Even though you might have established a domain naming rule that calls for city names, a domain called *albuquerque.contoso.com* will be all but impossible for most people (outside of New Mexico) to spell correctly the first time.

When you are designing an internal DNS namespace for a network that connects to the Internet, consider the following rules:

- Use registered domain names—Although using a domain name on an internal network that you have not registered is technically not a violation of Internet protocol, this practice can interfere with the client name resolution process on your internal network.

- Do not use top-level domain names or names of commonly known products or companies—Naming your internal domains using names found on the Internet can interfere with the name resolution process on your client computers. For example, if you create an internal domain called microsoft.com, you cannot predict whether a query for a name in that domain will be directed to your DNS server or to the authoritative servers for microsoft.com on the Internet.

- Use only characters that are compliant with the Internet standard—The DNS server included with Microsoft Windows Server 2008 supports the use of Unicode characters in UTF-8 format, but the RFC 1123 standard, "Requirements For Internet Hosts—Applications and Support," limits DNS names to the uppercase characters (A–Z), the lowercase characters (a–z), the numerals (0–9), and the hyphen (-). You can configure the Windows Server 2008 DNS server to disallow the use of UTF-8 characters.

➕ MORE INFORMATION

Although the original DNS standards call for a limited character set, there has been, since 2003, a mechanism for including non-ASCII characters, such as diacriticals, in domain names. Called Internationalizing Domain Names in Applications (IDNA), this mechanism works by converting the non-standard characters into ASCII equivalents so that no changes to the underlying DNS mechanism are needed.

CREATING SUBDOMAINS

Owning a second-level domain that you have registered gives you the right to create any number of subdomains beneath that domain. The primary reason for creating subdomains is to delegate administrative authority for parts of the namespace. For example, if your organization has offices in different cities, you might want to maintain a single DNS namespace, but grant the administrators at each site autonomous control over the DNS records for their computers. The best way to do this is to create a separate subdomain for each site, locate it on a DNS server at that site, and delegate authority for the server to local network support personnel. This procedure also balances the DNS traffic load among servers at different locations, preventing a bottleneck that could affect name resolution performance.

COMBINING INTERNAL AND EXTERNAL DOMAINS

When you are designing a DNS namespace that includes both internal and external (that is, Internet) domains, there are three possible strategies you can use, which are as follows:

- Use the same domain name internally and externally—Using the same domain name for your internal and external namespaces is a practice that Microsoft strongly discourages. When you create an internal domain and an external domain with the same name, you make it possible for a computer in the internal network to have the same DNS name as a computer on the external network. This duplication wreaks havoc with the name resolution process.

- Create separate and unrelated internal and external domains—When you use different domain names for your internal and external networks, you eliminate the potential name resolution conflicts that come with using the same domain name for both networks. However, using this solution requires you to register (and pay for) two domain names and to maintain two separate DNS namespaces. The different domain names can also be a potential source of confusion to users who have to distinguish between internal and external resources.

- Make the internal domain a subdomain of the external domain—The solution that Microsoft recommends for combining internal and external networks is to register a single Internet domain name and use it for external resources, and then create a subdomain beneath that domain name and use it for your internal network. For example, if you have registered the name contoso.com, you would use that domain for your external servers and create a subdomain, such as int.contoso.com, for your internal network. If you have to create additional subdomains, you can create fourth-level domains beneath int for the internal network, and additional third-level domains beneath contoso for the external network, as shown in Figure 2-27. The advantages of this solution are that it makes it impossible to create duplicate FQDNs, and it lets you delegate authority across the internal and external domains, which simplifies the DNS administration process. In addition, you have to register and pay for only one Internet domain name.

TAKE NOTE ✱

It is possible to make this arrangement work by copying all the zone data from your external DNS servers to your internal DNS servers, but the extra administrative difficulties make this a less than ideal solution.

Figure 2-27

Internal and external domain names

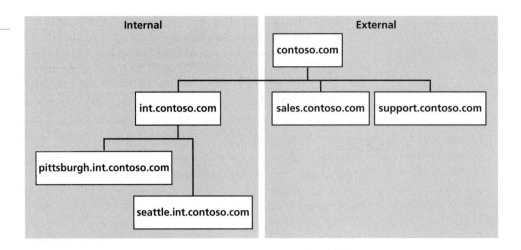

Creating Host Names

Once you have created the domain structure for your DNS namespace, it is time to populate these domains with hosts. You should create hosts the same way you create domains, by devising a naming rule and then sticking to it. In many cases, host-naming rules are based on users, geographical locations, or the function of the computer.

For workstations, a common practice is to create host names (also known as NetBIOS names) from some variation on the user's name, such as a first initial followed by the user's surname. For example, the host name for Mark Lee's computer might be Mlee. Many organizations also use similar naming rules to create user account names and email addresses. Following the same pattern for DNS host names enables users to keep track of only one name. For servers, the most common practice is to create host names describing the server's function or the department that uses it, such as Mail1 or Sales1.

Whatever naming rules you decide to use for your namespace, you should adhere to the following basic practices:

- Create easily remembered names—Users and administrators should be able to figure out the host name assigned to a particular computer by using your naming rules alone.

- Use unique names throughout the organization—Although it is possible to create identical host names as long as they are located in different domains, this practice is strongly discouraged. You might have to move a computer and put it in a new domain that already has a host by that name, causing duplication that interferes with name resolution.

- Do not use case to distinguish names—Although you can use both uppercase and lowercase characters when creating a computer name on a computer running a Windows operating system, DNS itself is not case-sensitive. Therefore, you should not create host names that are identical except for the case of the letters, nor should you create host names that rely on case to be understandable.

- Use only characters supported by all of your DNS servers—As with domain names, avoid using characters that are not compliant with the DNS standard, unless all the DNS servers processing the names support these characters. The NetBIOS namespace supports a larger character set than DNS does. When you are upgrading a Windows network that uses NetBIOS names to one that uses DNS names, you might want to use the Unicode (UTF-8) character support in the Windows Server 2008 DNS server to avoid having to rename all your computers. However, you must not do this on computers that are visible from the Internet; these systems must use only the character set specified in RFC 1123.

Deploying a DNS Server

The process of actually deploying a DNS server on a Windows Server 2008 computer is simply a matter of installing the DNS Server role, using the Initial Configuration Tasks window or the Server Manager console. The actual installation requires no additional input; there are no additional pages in the Add Roles Wizard, no role services to select, and no dependencies.

Once you install the DNS Server role, the computer is ready to perform caching-only name resolution services for any clients that have access to it. The role also installs the DNS Manager console, shown in Figure 2-28, which you use to configure the DNS server's other capabilities. To configure the server to perform other services, consult the following sections.

Figure 2-28

The DNS Manager console

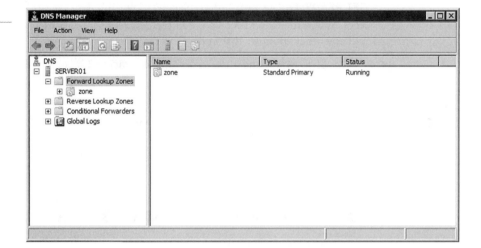

CREATING ZONES

A *zone* is an administrative entity you create on a DNS server to represent a discrete portion of the DNS namespace. Administrators typically divide the DNS namespace into zones to store them on different servers and to delegate their administration to different people. Zones always consist of entire domains or subdomains. You can create a zone that contains multiple domains, as long as those domains are contiguous in the DNS namespace. For example, you can create a zone containing a parent domain and its child, because they are directly connected, but you cannot create a zone containing two child domains without their common parent, because the two children are not directly connected, as shown in Figure 2-29.

Figure 2-29

Valid zones must consist of contiguous domains

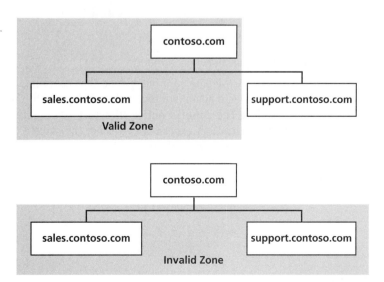

You can divide the DNS namespace into multiple zones and host them on a single DNS server if you want to, although there is usually no persuasive reason to do so. The DNS server in Windows Server 2008 can support as many as 200,000 zones on a single server, although it is hard to imagine what scenario would require this many. In most cases, an administrator creates multiple zones on a server and then delegates most of them to other servers, which then become responsible for hosting them.

Every zone consists of a zone database, which contains the resource records for the domains in that zone. The DNS server in Windows Server 2008 supports three zone types, which specify where the server stores the zone database and what kind of information it contains.

To create a new zone, use the following procedure.

 CREATE A ZONE

GET READY. Log on to Windows Server 2008 using an account with Administrative privileges. When the logon process is completed, close the Initial Configuration Tasks window and any other windows that appear.

1. Click **Start**, and then click **Administrative Tools** > **DNS**. The DNS Manager console appears.

2. Expand the **Server** node and select the **Forward Lookup Zones** folder.

3. Right-click the **Forward Lookup Zones** folder and, from the context menu, select **New Zone**. The New Zone Wizard appears.

4. Click **Next** to bypass the *Welcome* page. The *Zone Type* page appears, as shown in Figure 2-30.

Figure 2-30

The Zone Type page of the New Zone Wizard

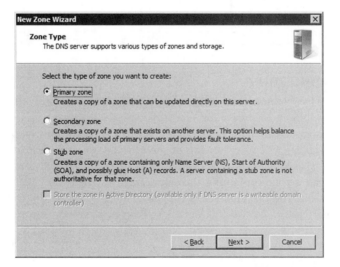

5. Select from the following options:
   • Primary zone—Creates a primary zone that contains the master copy of the zone database, where administrators make all changes to the zone's resource records. If the **Store The Zone In Active Directory (Available Only If DNS Server Is A Domain Controller)** checkbox is cleared, the server creates a primary master zone database file on the local drive. This is a simple text file that is compliant with most non-Windows DNS server implementations.

- Secondary zone—Creates a duplicate of a primary zone on another server. The secondary zone contains a backup copy of the primary master zone database file, stored as an identical text file on the server's local drive. You cannot modify the resource records in a secondary zone manually; you can update them only by replicating the primary master zone database file, using a process called a zone transfer. You should always create at least one secondary zone for each file-based primary zone in your namespace, both to provide fault tolerance and to balance the DNS traffic load.

- Stub zone—Creates a copy of a primary zone that contains the key resource records that identify the authoritative servers for the zone. The stub zone forwards or refers requests. When you create a stub zone, you configure it with the IP address of the server that hosts the zone from which you created the stub. When the server hosting the stub zone receives a query for a name in that zone, it either forwards the request to the host of the zone or replies with a referral to that host, depending on whether the query is recursive or iterative.

- If your DNS server is a domain controller, and you want to store the zone data in the Active Directory database, select the *Store the zone in Active Directory (available only if DNS server is a domain controller)* checkbox.

TAKE NOTE

You can use each of these zone types to create forward lookup zones or reverse lookup zones. As mentioned earlier in this lesson, forward lookup zones contain name-to-address mappings and reverse lookup zones contain address-to-name mappings. If you want a DNS server to perform both name and address resolutions for a particular domain, you must create both forward and reverse lookup zones containing that domain, using the domain name for the forward lookup zone and an in-addr.arpa domain for the reverse lookup zone.

6. Click **Next**. Assuming that you did not opt to store the zone information in the Active Directory database, the *Zone Name* page appears, as shown in Figure 2-31.

Figure 2-31

The Zone Name page of the New Zone Wizard

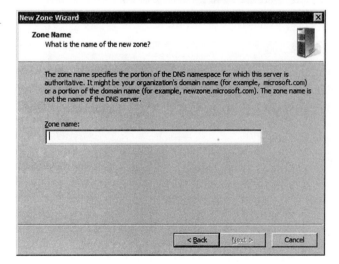

7. Specify the name you want to assign to the zone in the **Zone Name** text box and click **Next**. The *Zone File* page appears, as shown in Figure 2-32.

Figure 2-32

The Zone File page of the New Zone Wizard

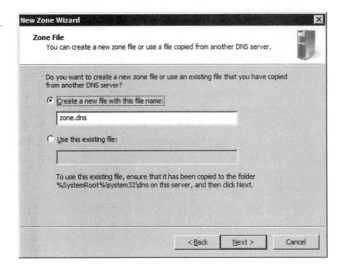

8. Select one of the following options:
   - Create a new file with this file name—Creates a new zone database file using the name you specify.
   - Use this existing file—Uses an existing zone database file of the name you specify, located in the C:\Windows\system32\DNS folder.

   If you selected the Secondary Zone option on the *Zone Type* page, a *Master DNS Servers* page appears, as shown in Figure 2-33, on which you must specify the DNS servers hosting the primary zone(s) you want to replicate.

Figure 2-33

The Master DNS Servers page of the New Zone Wizard

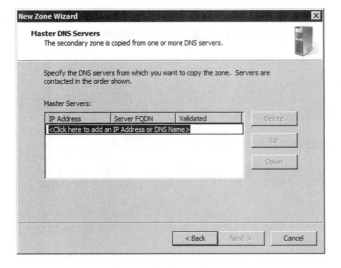

9. Click **Next**. The *Dynamic Update* page appears, as shown in Figure 2-34.

Figure 2-34

The Dynamic Update page of the New Zone Wizard

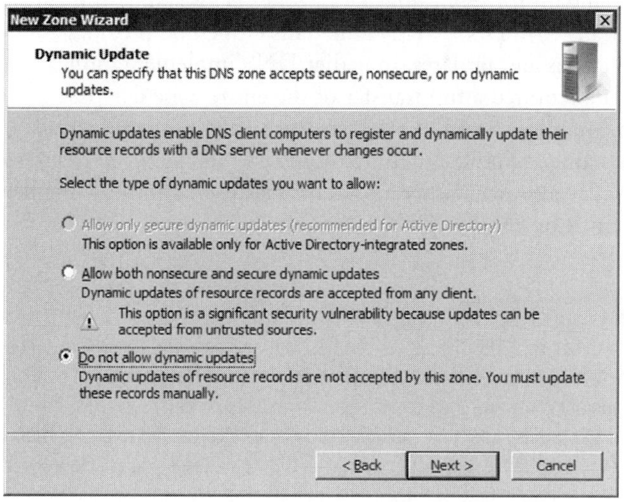

> **New Zone Wizard**
>
> **Dynamic Update**
> You can specify that this DNS zone accepts secure, nonsecure, or no dynamic updates.
>
> Dynamic updates enable DNS client computers to register and dynamically update their resource records with a DNS server whenever changes occur.
>
> Select the type of dynamic updates you want to allow:
>
> ○ Allow only secure dynamic updates (recommended for Active Directory)
> This option is available only for Active Directory-integrated zones.
>
> ○ Allow both nonsecure and secure dynamic updates
> Dynamic updates of resource records are accepted from any client.
> ⚠ This option is a significant security vulnerability because updates can be accepted from untrusted sources.
>
> ● Do not allow dynamic updates
> Dynamic updates of resource records are not accepted by this zone. You must update these records manually.
>
> [< Back] [Next >] [Cancel]

10. Select one of the following options:
  - Allow only secure dynamic updates
  - Allow both nonsecure and secure dynamic updates
  - Do not allow dynamic updates

11. Click **Next**. The *Completing the New Zone Wizard* page appears.

12. Click **Finish**. The wizard creates the zone.

CLOSE the DNS Manager console.

If you have created a primary zone, you can now proceed to create resource records that specify the names of the hosts on the network and their equivalent IP addresses.

REPLICATING ZONE DATA

When you create primary and secondary zones, you must configure zone transfers from the primary to the secondaries, to keep them updated. In a ***zone transfer***, the server hosting the primary zone copies the primary master zone database file to the secondary zone so that their resource records are identical. This enables the secondary zone to perform authoritative name resolutions for the domains in the zone, just as the primary can. You can configure zone transfers to occur when you modify the contents of the primary master zone database file, or at regular intervals.

When you add a new DNS server to the network and configure it as a new secondary master name server for an existing zone, the server performs a ***full zone transfer (AXFR)*** to obtain a full copy of all resource records for the zone. Then, at specified times, the DNS server hosting the primary zone transmits the database file to all the servers hosting secondary copies of that zone. File-based zone transfers use a relatively simple technique, in which the servers transmit the zone database file in its native form, or sometimes with compression.

The Windows Server 2008 DNS Server also supports *incremental zone transfer (IXFR)*, a revised DNS zone transfer process for intermediate changes. IXFR is defined by an additional DNS standard for replicating DNS zones. This standard is called RFC 1995, "Incremental Zone Transfer in DNS." This zone transfer method provides a more efficient way of propagating zone changes and updates. In earlier DNS implementations, any request for an update of zone data required a full transfer of the entire zone database using an AXFR query. With incremental transfers, DNS servers use an IXFR query instead. IFXR enables the secondary master name server to pull only those zone changes it needs to synchronize its copy of the zone with its source, either a primary master or another secondary master copy of the zone maintained by another DNS server.

➕ MORE INFORMATION

A Windows Server 2008 DNS server can host both primary and secondary zones on the same server, so you don't have to install additional servers just to create secondary zones. You can configure each of your DNS servers to host a primary zone, and then create secondary zones on each server for one or more of the primaries on other servers. Each primary can have multiple secondaries located on servers throughout the network. This not only provides fault tolerance, but also prevents all the traffic for a single zone from flooding a single LAN.

Zone transfers are always initiated by the secondary master server for a zone and sent to the DNS server configured as its master server. This master server can be any other DNS name server that hosts the zone, either a primary master or another secondary master server. When the master server receives the request for the zone, it can reply with either a partial or full transfer of the zone.

USING ACTIVE DIRECTORY–INTEGRATED ZONES

When you are running the DNS server service on a computer that is an Active Directory domain controller and you select the Store The Zone In Active Directory (Available Only If DNS Server Is A Domain Controller) checkbox while creating a zone in the New Zone Wizard, the server does not create a zone database file. Instead, the server stores the DNS resource records for the zone in the Active Directory database. Storing the DNS database in Active Directory provides a number of advantages, including ease of administration, conservation of network bandwidth, and increased security.

In Active Directory–integrated zones, the zone database is replicated automatically to other domain controllers, along with all other Active Directory data. Active Directory uses a multiple master replication system so that copies of the database are updated on all domain controllers in the domain. You can modify the DNS resource records on any domain controller hosting a copy of the zone database, and Active Directory will update all of the other domain controllers automatically. You don't have to create secondary zones or manually configure zone transfers, because Active Directory performs all database replication activities.

By default, Windows Server 2008 replicates the database for a primary zone stored in Active Directory to all the other domain controllers running the DNS server in the Active Directory domain where the primary is located. You can also modify the scope of zone database replication to keep copies on all domain controllers throughout the enterprise, or on all domain controllers in the Active Directory domain, whether or not they are running the DNS server. You can also create a custom replication scope that copies the zone database to the domain controllers you specify.

To modify the replication scope for an Active Directory–integrated zone, open the zone's Properties sheet in the DNS Manager console, and on the General tab, click the Change button for Replication: All DNS Servers In the Active Directory Domain to display the Change Zone Replication Scope dialog box, as shown in Figure 2-35.

Figure 2-35

The Change Zone Replication
Scope dialog box

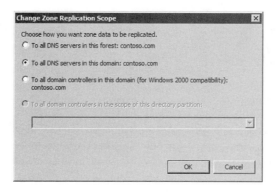

Active Directory conserves network bandwidth by replicating only the DNS data that has
changed since the last replication, and by compressing the data before transmitting it over the
network. The zone replications also use the full security capabilities of Active Directory, which
are considerably more robust than those of file-based zone transfers.

SUMMARY SKILL MATRIX

IN THIS LESSON YOU LEARNED:

• The Dynamic Host Configuration Protocol (DHCP) is a service that automatically configures
the Internet Protocol (IP) address and other TCP/IP settings on network computers by
assigning addresses from a pool (called a scope) and reclaiming them when they are no
longer in use.

• DHCP consists of three components: a DHCP server application, which responds to client
requests for TCP/IP configuration settings; a DHCP client, which issues requests to server
and applies the TCP/IP configuration settings it receives to the local computer; and a DHCP
communications protocol, which defines the formats and sequences of the messages
exchanged by DHCP clients and servers.

• The DHCP standards define three different IP address allocation methods: dynamic allocation,
in which a DHCP server assigns an IP address to a client computer from a scope for a specified
length of time; automatic allocation, in which the DHCP server permanently assigns an IP
address to a client computer from a scope; and manual allocation, in which a DHCP server
permanently assigns a specific IP address to a specific computer on the network.

• In a distributed DHCP infrastructure, you install at least one DHCP server on each of your subnets
so that all of your clients have access to a local DHCP server. In a centralized DHCP infrastructure,
the DHCP servers are all placed in a single location, such as a server closet or data center. To
enable the broadcast traffic on each subnet to reach the DHCP servers, you must install a DHCP
relay agent on each subnet.

• TCP/IP networks today use Domain Name System (DNS) servers to convert host names into
IP addresses. This conversion process is referred to as name resolution.

• The DNS consists of three elements: the DNS namespace, which takes the form of a tree
structure and consists of domains, containing resource records that contain host names, IP
addresses, and other information; name servers, which are applications running on server
computers that maintain information about the domain tree structure; and resolvers, which
are client programs that generate DNS queries and send them to DNS servers for fulfillment.

• The hierarchical nature of the DNS namespace is designed to make it possible for any DNS server
on the Internet to locate the authoritative source for any domain name, using a minimum number
of queries. This efficiency results from the fact that the domains at each level of the hierarchy are
responsible for maintaining information about the domains at the next lower level.

- In a recursive query, the DNS server receiving the name resolution request takes full responsibility for resolving the name. In an iterative query, the server that receives the name resolution request immediately responds with the best information it possesses at the time.

- For Internet name resolution purposes, the only functions required of the DNS server are the ability to process incoming queries from resolvers and to send its own queries to other DNS servers on the Internet. A DNS server that performs only these functions is known as a caching-only server, because it is not the authoritative source for any domain and hosts no resource records of its own.

■ Knowledge Assessment

Matching

Complete the following exercise by matching the terms with their corresponding definitions.

    a. caching-only server
    b. DHCP relay agent
    c. distributed DHCP infrastructure
    d. fully qualified domain name (FQDN)
    e. iterative query
    f. manual allocation
    g. recursive query
    h. resolver
    i. root name servers
    j. zone transfer

_____ **1.** contains a host name and two or more domain names

_____ **2.** a DNS server that is not the authoritative source for a domain

_____ **3.** enables clients on subnets without DHCP servers to obtain IP addresses

_____ **4.** replicates DNS database files

_____ **5.** the ultimate source for information about DNS top-level domains

_____ **6.** known as a reservation on Windows DHCP servers

_____ **7.** generated primarily by DNS clients

_____ **8.** requires a DHCP server on every subnet

_____ **9.** generates DNS queries and transmits them to a designated server

_____ **10.** causes a DNS server to reply with the best information it possesses at the time

Multiple Choice

Select the correct answer for each of the following questions.

1. Which of the following message types is not used during a successful DHCP address assignment?
   a. DHCPDISCOVER
   b. DHCPREQUEST
   c. DHCPACK
   d. DHCPINFORM

2. Which of the following is not one of the techniques you can use to provide fault tolerance for DHCP servers?
   a. splitting scopes
   b. using stand-by servers
   c. DHCP servers using identical scopes
   d. failover clustering

3. Which of the following DHCP infrastructure designs requires the largest number of DHCP server implementations?
   a. hybrid
   b. centralized
   c. dynamic
   d. distributed

4. Which of the following is not one of the elements of the Domain Name System (DNS)?
   a. resolvers
   b. relay agents
   c. name servers
   d. name space

5. What is the maximum length for a fully qualified domain name, including the trailing period?
   a. 50 characters
   b. 63 characters
   c. 255 characters
   d. 255 characters for each individual domain name

6. Which of the following would be the correct FQDN for a resource record in a reverse lookup zone, if the computer's IP address is 10.75.143.88?
   a. 88.143.75.10.in-addr.arpa
   b. 10.75.143.88. in-addr.arpa
   c. in-addr.arpa.88.143.75.10
   d. arpa.in-addr. 10.75.143.88

7. Which of the following are types of zone transfers supported by the DNS server in Windows Server 2008?
   a. network zone transfers
   b. full zone transfers
   c. incremental zone transfers
   d. partial zone transfers

8. In the fully qualified domain name www.sales.contoso.com, which of the following is the second-level domain?
   a. www
   b. sales
   c. contoso
   d. com

9. Which of the following network components are typically capable of functioning as DHCP relay agents?
   a. Windows Vista computers
   b. routers
   c. switches
   d. Windows Server 2008 computers

10. Which of the following types of DHCP address allocation is the equivalent of a reservation in Windows Server 2008?
    a. dynamic allocation
    b. automatic allocation
    c. manual allocation
    d. hybrid allocation

Review Questions

1. List the order in which DHCP messages are exchanged by the client and the server during a successful IP address assignment.

2. For each of the following message exchanges that can occur during a DNS name resolution procedure, specify whether the sending computer generates an iterative query or a recursive query:
   a. resolver to designated DNS server
   b. designated DNS server to top-level domain server
   c. designated DNS server to forwarder
   d. designated DNS server to second-level domain server
   e. forwarder to root name server

■ Case Scenarios

Scenario 2-1: Deploying DNS Servers

Harold is a freelance networking consultant who has designed a network for a small company with a single location. The owner of the company wants to use an Active Directory domain, so Harold installs a Windows Server 2008 domain controller with the Active Directory Domain Services and DNS Server roles. Harold also uses DHCP to configure all of the workstations on the network to use the DNS services provided by the domain controller.

Soon after the installation, however, the owner of the company reports extremely slow Internet performance. After examining the traffic passing over the Internet connection, you determine that it is being flooded with DNS traffic. What can you do to reduce the amount of DNS traffic passing over the internet connection?

Scenario 2-2: Configuring DHCP Servers

After deploying a large number of wireless laptop computers on the network, Taylor, the IT director at Contoso, Ltd., decides to use DHCP to enable the laptop users to move from one subnet to another without having to manually reconfigure their IP addresses. Soon after the DHCP deployment, however, Taylor notices that some of the IP address scopes are being depleted, resulting in some computers being unable to connect to a new subnet. What can Taylor do to resolve this problem without altering the network's subnetting?

Planning an Active Directory Deployment

OBJECTIVE DOMAIN MATRIX

Technology Skill	Objective Domain	Objective Domain Number
Designing an Active Directory Infrastructure	Plan infrastructure services server roles	1.3
Designing a Group Policy Strategy	Plan and implement group policy strategy	2.3

KEY TERMS

Active Directory
attributes
authentication
authorization
container object
Directory Access Protocol
(DAP)
directory schema

domain controller
domain tree
forest
forest root domain
global catalog
leaf object
Lightweight Directory Access
Protocol (LDAP)

multiple-master replication
organizational unit (OU)
Read-Only Domain Controller
(RODC)
root zone method
single-master replication
site
subzone method

In Lesson 2, "Planning Infrastructure Services," you learned how to plan and deploy the Dynamic Host Configuration Protocol (DHCP) and Domain Name System (DNS) services. Now, Lesson 3 is devoted primarily to Active Directory, which is the most pervasive infrastructure service in Windows Server 2008. Active Directory is involved in virtually every transaction conducted by computers on a network that uses it. This lesson examines:

- The basic structure and architecture of an Active Directory installation
- How to design and plan an Active Directory infrastructure
- How to install and configure Active Directory domain controllers
- How to issue and use digital certificates on an Active Directory network

■ Introducing Active Directory

THE BOTTOM LINE

A directory service is a repository of information about the resources—hardware, software, and human—that are connected to a network. Users, computers, and applications throughout the network can access the repository for a variety of purposes, including user authentication, storage of configuration data, and even simple white pages–style information lookups. *Active Directory* is the directory service that Microsoft first introduced in Windows 2000 Server, and which they have upgraded in each successive server operating system release, including Windows Server 2008.

Prior to Windows 2000 Server, the Windows NT operating systems provided a basic directory service that enabled administrators to create organizational divisions called domains. A domain is a logical container of each network component over which you have control and organize in one respective entity. Each domain was hosted by at least one server designated as a *domain controller*. The primary domain controller (PDC) for each domain could replicate its directory information to one or more backup domain controllers (BDC), for fault tolerance and load balancing purposes.

TAKE NOTE *

Although Windows NT uses the term domain, Windows NT domains cannot belong to an Active Directory forest.

Windows NT domains are relatively limited in several ways, including their maximum size, scalability, and replication capabilities. The Active Directory directory service introduced in Windows 2000 Server still uses the domain as its basic administrative division, but it also addresses these shortcomings by expanding the capabilities of the directory in many ways.

Understanding Active Directory Functions

In addition to making services and resources available, the primary functions of Active Directory are to provide authentication and authorization services for hardware and software resources on the network. Simply put, *authentication* is the process of verifying a user's identity and *authorization* is the process of granting the user access only to the resources he or she is permitted to use.

Users that are joined to an Active Directory domain log on to the domain, not an individual computer or application, and are able to access any resources in that domain for which administrators have granted them the proper permissions. Without Active Directory, users must have separate accounts on every computer they access, which results in problems creating and maintaining the accounts, synchronizing passwords, and performing multiple logons.

When a user logs on to an Active Directory domain, the client computer performs an elaborate authentication procedure that involves locating the nearest domain controller and exchanging a series of messages using Kerberos, a complex security protocol. In most cases, users authenticate themselves by supplying a password, but Active Directory networks can also use smart cards and biometrics (such as fingerprint scans) to verify a user's identity.

Once the authentication process is completed (and assuming it is successful), an Active Directory authorization process occurs whenever the user attempts to access a network resource. Network administrators grant users access to resources by assigning them permissions using their Active Directory user objects. There are no transactions between clients and protected resources that do not involve a transaction using a domain controller as a third party. The design of an Active Directory infrastructure, therefore, calls for the distribution of domain controllers around the network so that all clients have ready access to them.

Understanding the Active Directory Architecture

Active Directory is a hierarchical directory service, based on the domain, that is scalable in both directions.

In Active Directory, you can subdivide a domain into organizational units and populate it with objects. You can also create multiple domains and group them into sites, trees, and forests. As a result, Active Directory provides a highly flexible architecture that can accommodate the smallest and the largest organizations, as well as provide a variety of design options.

The following sections examine the components you can use to design and build an Active Directory structure.

UNDERSTANDING OBJECTS AND ATTRIBUTES

An Active Directory domain is a hierarchical structure that takes the form of a tree, much like a file system. The domain consists of objects, each of which represents a logical or physical resource. There are two basic classes of objects: container objects and leaf objects. A ***container object*** is one that can have other objects subordinate to it, while a ***leaf object*** cannot have subordinate objects. The container objects essentially form the branches of the tree, with the leaf objects growing on the branches.

The domain itself is a container object, as are the organizational unit objects within the domain. Leaf objects can represent users, computers, groups, applications, and other resources on the network.

Every object consists of ***attributes,*** which store information about the object. A container object has, as one of its attributes, a list of all the other objects it contains. Leaf objects have attributes that contain specific information about the specific resource the object represents. Some attributes are created automatically, such as the globally unique identifier (GUID) that the domain controller assigns to each object when it creates it, while administrators must supply information for other attributes manually.

For example, a user object can have attributes that specify the user's name, address, telephone number, and other identifying information. This enables Active Directory to function as a directory in the purest sense of the word, much like a telephone book or rolodex. When you open a user object in the Active Directory Users and Computers console, you can see many of its attributes in its Properties sheet, as shown in Figure 3-1.

Figure 3-1

The attributes of a user object, as displayed in its Properties sheet

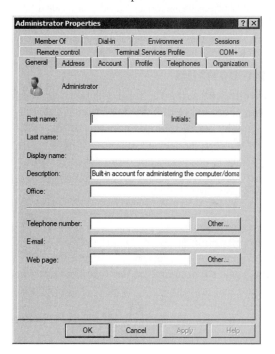

Different object types have different sets of attributes, depending on their functions. The attributes each type of object can possess, both required and optional, the type of data that can be stored in each attribute, and the object's place in the directory tree are all defined in the ***directory schema.*** In Active Directory, unlike Windows NT domains, the directory schema elements are extensible, enabling applications to add their own object types to the directory, or add attributes to existing object types. For example, when you install Microsoft Exchange on an Active Directory network, the application alters the directory schema to add its own attributes to the user object type. When you open a user's Properties sheet after the Exchange installation, as shown in Figure 3-2, you see additional tabs containing the Exchange attributes.

Figure 3-2

Additional user attributes added to the directory schema by Microsoft Exchange

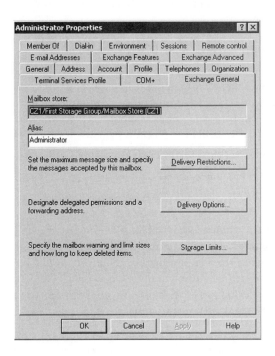

> **➕ MORE INFORMATION**
>
> The hierarchical structure of container and leaf objects used in an Active Directory domain, and the design and composition of the individual objects themselves, are based on a standard called X.500, which was developed by the International Telecommunications Union (ITU) in the late 1980s.

UNDERSTANDING DOMAINS

As mentioned earlier, the domain is the fundamental component of the Active Directory architecture. You can zoom into a domain and create a hierarchy within it, and you can zoom out and create a hierarchy out of multiple domains. In Active Directory, domains function by default as the boundaries for virtually all directory functions, including administration, access control, database management, and replication. You begin the process of designing an Active Directory infrastructure by deciding what domains to create and you begin deploying Active Directory by creating your first domain.

TAKE NOTE* Domains are not security boundaries, in the strict sense of the term. Although it is true that users in one domain cannot access the resources of another domain unless they receive explicit permissions to do so, domains are not completely isolated from one another. An administrator can perform tasks in one domain that affect all of the other domains in the forest. To completely isolate one domain from another, you must create them in different forests. Therefore, it is the forest that functions as the security boundary, not the domain.

ZOOMING IN: ORGANIZATIONAL UNITS

As mentioned earlier, the domain is still the fundamental division in the Active Directory directory service. However, the extreme scalability that Active Directory provides, when compared to Windows NT domains, can often result in domains containing many thousands of objects. When domains grow this large, it can become necessary to divide the security and administrative responsibility for the domain among several divisions or departments. To make this possible, you can create objects within a domain called organizational units.

An *organizational unit (OU)* is a container object that functions in a subordinate capacity to a domain, something like a subdomain, but without the complete separation of security policies. As a container object, OUs can contain other OUs, as well as leaf objects. You can apply separate Group Policy to an OU, and delegate the administration of an OU as needed. However, an OU is still part of the domain, and still inherits policies and permissions from its parent objects.

For example, if you have a company running under a single Active Directory domain, you can create a separate OU for each of the company's divisions, as shown in Figure 3-3, and delegate the responsibility for each one to divisional IT personnel. Each division could then perform its own day-to-day administrative tasks, such as creating and managing user objects, and each division can also configure its own Group Policy settings. The administrators for each division would have control over the objects in their OU, but they would have limited access to the rest of the domain.

Figure 3-3

Organizational units subordinate to a domain

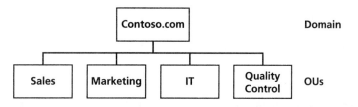

TAKE NOTE

There is another type of container object found in a domain, literally called a container. For example, a newly created domain has several container objects in it, including one called Users, which contains the domain's predefined users and groups, and another called Computers, which contains the computer objects for all of the systems joined to the domain. Unlike organizational units, you cannot assign Group Policy settings to computer objects, nor can you delegate their administration. You also cannot create new container objects using the standard Active Directory administration tools, such as the Active Directory Users and Computers console. You can create container objects using scripts, but there is no compelling reason to do so. Organizational units are the preferred method of subdividing a domain.

ZOOMING IN: GROUPS

Group objects are not containers, as organizational units are, but they perform a similar function, with important differences. Groups are not full-fledged security divisions as OUs are; you cannot apply Group Policy settings to a group object. However, the members of a group—which can be leaf objects, such as users or computers, as well as other groups—do inherit permissions assigned to that group.

One of the most important differences between groups and OUs is that group memberships are independent of the domain's tree structure. A group can have members located anywhere in the domain, and in some cases, it can have members from other domains as well.

For example, you might design a domain with OUs representing the various divisions in your organization. Each division can, therefore, have its own Group Policy settings and permissions that are propagated through the domain tree structure. However, there might also be certain special permissions that you want to assign to the director in charge of each division. You can do this by creating a group object and adding the directors' user objects as members of the group. This prevents you from having to assign permissions to each director individually.

Active Directory supports groups with varying capabilities, as defined by the group type and the group scope. There are two group types in Active Directory, as follows:

- Security groups—Administrators use security groups to assign permissions and user rights to a collection of objects. In the vast majority of cases, the term "group" refers to a security group.
- Distribution groups—Applications use distribution groups for non-security–related functions, such as sending email messages to a collection of users.

The security group is the type you use most often when designing an Active Directory infrastructure. Within the security group type, there are three group scopes, as follows:

- Domain local groups—Most often used to assign permissions to resources in the same domain
- Global groups—Most often used to organize users who share similar network access requirements
- Universal groups—Most often used to assign permissions to related resources in multiple domains

The group nesting capabilities in an Active Directory domain are listed in Table 3-1.

Table 3-1

Group Nesting Capabilities in Active Directory

GROUP SCOPE	GROUP CAN CONTAIN
Global	• User accounts from the same domain • Global groups from the same domain
Domain local	• User accounts from any domain • Global groups from any domain • Universal groups from any domain • Domain local groups from the same domain
Universal	• User accounts from any domain • Universal groups from any domain • Global groups from any domain

AGULP is a traditional mnemonic for remembering the nesting capabilities of Active Directory groups. AGULP stands for:

- Accounts
- Global groups
- Universal groups
- domain Local groups
- Permissions

The order of the elements indicates their nesting capabilities. User accounts can be members of global groups, universal groups, or domain local groups. Global groups can be members of universal or domain local groups. Universal groups can be members of domain local groups, but not global groups. Domain local groups cannot be members of either global or universal groups, but are typically the element to which administrators assign permissions.

ZOOMING OUT: DOMAIN TREES

When designing an Active Directory infrastructure, you might, in some cases, want to create multiple domains. Active Directory scales upward from the domain just as easily as it scales downward.

Active Directory uses the Domain Name System (DNS) naming conventions for its domains. As noted in Lesson 2, "Planning Infrastructure Services," you can create an Active Directory domain using the registered domain name you use on the Internet, or you can create an internal domain name, without registering it.

When you create your first domain on an Active Directory network, you are, in essence, creating the root of a ***domain tree.*** You can populate the tree with additional domains, as long as they are part of the same contiguous namespace, as shown in Figure 3-4. For example, you might create a root domain called contoso.com, and then create additional subdomains for each of the organization's branch offices, with names like baltimore.contoso.com and dallas. contoso.com. These subdomains are said to be part of the same tree as contoso.com, because they use the same top-level and second-level domain names.

Figure 3-4

An internal Active Directory domain tree

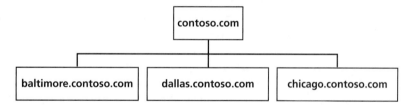

If you are using a registered Internet domain name, you can use it as a parent and create a child, or subdomain, for internal use, such as int.contoso.com, and then create another level of child domains beneath that for the branch offices, as shown in Figure 3-5.

Figure 3-5

An Active Directory domain tree using an Internet domain name

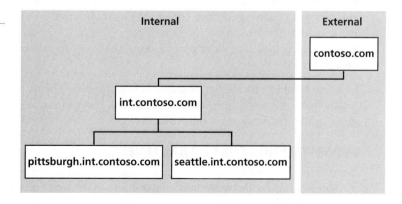

You can add as many domains to the tree as you need, using any number of levels, as long as you conform to the DNS naming limitations, which call for a maximum of 63 characters per domain name and 255 characters for the fully qualified domain name (FQDN).

Each domain in a tree is a separate security entity. They have their own separate Group Policy settings, permissions, and user accounts. However, unlike organizational units, the subdomains in a tree do not inherit permissions and policies from their parent domains. Domains in the same tree do have bidirectional trust relationships between them, though, which Active Directory creates automatically when you create each subdomain. These trust relationships mean that an administrator of a particular domain can grant any user in the tree access to that domain's resources. As a result, there is no need to create duplicate user objects, just because an individual needs access to resources in a different domain.

ZOOMING OUT: FORESTS

An organization might want to use multiple domains that cannot be part of the same tree, because they are not contiguous. For example, a single corporation might run two operations out of the same facilities, each with its own Internet domain name, such as contoso.com and adatum.com. You can create two separate Active Directory domains using these two names, but they cannot be parts of the same tree, because one is not subordinate to the other. You can, however, create two separate domain trees and join them together in a parent structure called a forest.

An Active Directory *forest* consists of one or more separate domain trees, which have the same two-way trust relationships between them as two domains in the same tree. When you create the first domain on an Active Directory network, you are in fact creating a new forest, and that first domain becomes the *forest root domain*. Therefore, if you create the contoso.com domain first, that domain becomes the root of the contoso.com forest. When you create the adatum.com domain in the same forest, it retains its status as a separate domain in a separate tree, but it is still considered to be part of the contoso.com forest.

It is important to understand that separate trees in the same forest still have trust relationships between them, even though they do not share a domain name. If you want to create two domains that are completely separate from one another, you must create each one in a separate forest. Even if this is the case, however, an administrator can still manually create a one-way or two-way trust relationship between domains in different forests, or even a forest trust, which enables all of the domains in one forest to trust all of the domains in the other. In fact, trusts between and among domains in a forest must be explicitly created manually, unlike subdomains in the same domain. If, for example, two companies with separate Active Directory forests should merge, it is possible for the administrators to establish a trust relationship between the two, rather than redesign the entire infrastructure.

INTRODUCING THE GLOBAL CATALOG

Domains function as the hierarchical boundaries for the Active Database, as well. A domain controller maintains only the part of the Active Directory database that defines that domain and its objects. However, Active Directory clients still need a way to locate and access the resources of other domains in the same forest. To make this possible, each forest has a *global catalog*, which is a list of all of the objects in the forest, along with a subset of each object's attributes.

To locate an object in another domain, Active Directory clients perform a search of the global catalog first. This search provides the client with the information it needs to search for the object in the specific domain that contains it.

UNDERSTANDING FUNCTIONAL LEVELS

Every Active Directory forest has a functional level, as does every domain. Functional levels are designed to provide backwards compatibility in Active Directory installations running domain controllers with various versions of the Windows Server operating system. Each successive version of Windows Server includes new Active Directory features, which are incompatible with previous versions. By selecting the functional level representing the oldest Windows version running on your domain controllers, you disable these new features so that the various domain controllers can interoperate properly.

For example, Windows Server 2003 introduced the ability to create a forest trust between two forests. A forest trust enables any domain in one forest to access any domain in another forest, assuming it has the required permissions. Prior to Windows Server 2003, administrators could

create trust relationships only between individual domains in different forests. To enable forest trusts, the forest must be running at the Windows Server 2003 forest functional level. This means that all of the domain controllers in the forest must be running Windows Server 2003 or later.

To raise the forest functional level or domain functional level, you use the Raise Domain Functional Level dialog box in the Active Directory Domains and Trusts console, as shown in Figure 3-6. Once you raise the functional level of a forest or a domain, you cannot lower it again.

Figure 3-6

Raising functional levels

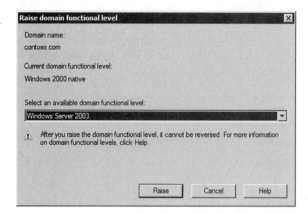

Understanding Active Directory Communications

The Active Directory services are implemented in the network's domain controllers. Each domain controller hosts one (and only one) domain, storing the domain's objects in a database. Active Directory clients—that is, users and computers that are members of a domain—access the domain controller frequently, as they log on to the domain and access domain resources.

Each domain on an Active Directory network should have at least two domain controllers, to ensure that the Active Directory database is available to clients at all times, and to provide clients with ready access to a nearby domain controller. How many domain controllers you install for each of your domains, and where you locate them, is an important part of designing an Active Directory infrastructure. Also important is an understanding of how and why the domain controllers communicate—with each other and with clients.

If a domain has only one domain controller, and it fails, you must restore the Active Directory database from a recent backup. When there are two more domain controllers in a single domain, you can repair or replace a failed domain controller and it will automatically receive a new copy of the database from the other domain controller.

INTRODUCING LDAP

The original X.500 standard calls for the use of a communications protocol called ***Directory Access Protocol (DAP).*** DAP is a highly complex protocol that includes a lot of unnecessary features, requires a great deal of work from the directory service client, and is based on Open Systems Interconnection (OSI) protocol stack. Today, the OSI stack remains a theoretical construct, as the Internet and Windows networks are all based on TCP/IP (Transmission Control Protocol/Internet Protocol) instead.

To avoid the use of DAP and the OSI stack, a team at the University of Michigan worked throughout the 1990s to develop a more practical communications protocol for use with X.500 directory services. This team created a series of standards, published as Requests For Comments (RFCs) by the Internet Engineering Task Force (IETF), which defines the

Lightweight Directory Access Protocol (LDAP). RFC 2251, "Lightweight Directory Access Protocol (v3)," published in December 1997, has become the standard communications protocol for directory service products, including Active Directory.

LDAP defines the format of the queries that Active Directory clients send to domain controllers, as well as providing a naming structure for uniquely identifying objects in the directory.

UNDERSTANDING REPLICATION

When a domain has two or more domain controllers, it is imperative that each one has a database that is identical to those of the others. To stay synchronized, the domain controllers communicate by sending database information to each other, a process called replication. Windows NT domains use a process called *single-master replication*, in which one primary domain controller (the PDC) sends its data to one or more backup domain controllers (BDCs). In this model, shown in Figure 3-7, replication traffic moves in only one direction, so it is possible only to create or modify Active Directory objects on the PDC.

Figure 3-7

Single-master replication

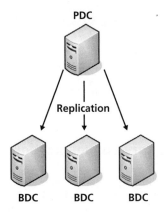

Single-master replication can make it difficult for administrators to manage Active Directory objects, especially if they are located in remote offices and must work over a slow wide area network (WAN) link. To address this problem, Active Directory uses *multiple-master replication,* in which it is possible to make changes to domain objects on any domain controller, which replicates those changes to all of the other domain controllers, as shown in Figure 3-8.

Figure 3-8

Multiple-master replication

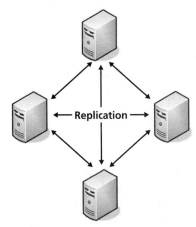

Multiple-master replication is much more complicated than single-master replication, because it is possible for two administrators to be working on the same object at the same time, using different domain controllers. The replication messages exchanged by the domain controllers include timestamps and other transaction identifiers that enable each computer to determine which version of an object is the latest and most relevant.

USING READ-ONLY DOMAIN CONTROLLERS

One of the new Active Directory features in Windows Server 2008 is the ability to create a *Read-Only Domain Controller (RODC)*, which is a domain controller that supports only incoming replication traffic. As a result, it is not possible to create, modify, or delete Active Directory objects using the RODC.

RODCs are intended for use in locations that require a domain controller, but which have less stringent physical security or where there are no administrators present who need read/write access to the Active Directory database. To install an RODC, there must be at least one other domain controller for the domain running Windows Server 2008.

EXPANDING OUTWARD: SITES

To facilitate the replication process, Active Directory includes another administrative division called the site. A *site* is defined as a collection of subnets that have good connectivity between them. Good connectivity is understood to be at least T-1 speed (1.544 megabits per second). Generally speaking, this means that a site consists of all the local area networks (LANs) at a specific location. A different site would be a network at a remote location, connected to the other site using a T-1 or slower WAN technology.

Sites are one of the three Active Directory objects (along with domains and organizational units) that can have their own Group Policy settings assigned to them. However, site divisions are wholly independent of domain, tree, and forest divisions. You can have multiple sites that are part of a single domain, or you can have separate domains, trees, or forests for each site.

The primary reason for creating different sites on an Active Directory network is to control the amount of traffic passing over the relatively slow and expensive WAN links between locations. If your entire network is located in one building or campus, with all of the subnets connected using high-speed, low-cost LAN technologies, there is no need to have more than one site.

If, however, your network spans multiple locations and uses WAN connections running at various speeds, you should create a site topology for your network. A site topology consists of three Active Directory object types, as follows:

- Sites—A site object represents the group of subnets at a single location, with good connectivity.
- Subnets—A subnet object represents an IP network at a particular site.
- Site links—A site link object represents a WAN connection between two sites.

When you create a site topology, you create site objects, specify the subnets located at each site by creating subnet objects, and then specify the access schedules and relative costs (in terms of bandwidth and transmission speed, not monetary costs) of the WAN links between the sites by creating and configuring site link objects.

Once the site topology is in place, Active Directory uses it to provide two regulatory functions, as follows:

- Domain controller location—When an Active Directory client attempts to access a domain controller, it uses its IP address to determine what subnet it belongs to, and which site contains that particular subnet. The client then accesses a domain controller at that same site, or if one is not available, at the remote site with the fastest site link connection. This prevents clients from using slow WAN connections to access a domain controller when a closer one is available.
- Replication traffic control—A component called the Knowledge Consistency Checker (KCC) automatically creates replication links between domain controllers in the same site and schedules their replication activities. When you connect multiple sites using site link objects, you specify the relative cost of each link and the hours during which it can be used for replication. The KCC then creates an intersite replication schedule for each pair of domain controllers, using the routes with coincident schedules and the lowest aggregate costs.

Unlike many other elements of an Active Directory deployment, the creation of a site topology is not automatic. Administrators must manually create and configure the site, subnet, and site link objects.

■ Designing an Active Directory Infrastructure

THE BOTTOM LINE

In Active Directory, Windows Server 2008 provides a highly flexible directory service that can accommodate organizations of virtually any size and complexity. However, it is up to each network's administrators to use the building blocks that Active Directory provides to construct an efficient directory services infrastructure.

The process of designing an Active Directory infrastructure consists of the following basic phases:

- Designing the domain name space—Decide how many domains you need and how to organize them into trees and forests
- Designing the internal domain structure—Decide how many organizational units to create in each domain and how to design the internal tree structure
- Designing a site topology—Divide an Active Directory installation that encompasses multiple locations into sites, and configure the links between them
- Designing a Group Policy strategy—Decide how many group policy objects (GPOs) to create and the objects to which you should link them

The following sections examine each of these phases.

Designing the Domain Name Space

CERTIFICATION READY?
Plan infrastructure
services server roles
1.3

The initial phase of the Active Directory infrastructure design process is to decide how many domains you are going to create, how you plan to integrate them into one or more domain trees and/or forests, and what name you are going to assign them.

The overall objective in your Active Directory design process should be to create as few domains as possible. There are several reasons why this is so. As noted earlier, each domain in an Active Directory installation is a separate administrative entity. The more domains you create, the greater the number of ongoing administration tasks you have to perform. Every domain also requires its own domain controllers, so each additional domain you create increases the overall hardware and maintenance costs of the deployment.

Finally, consider also your applications, which might have problems working in a multi-domain forest. Microsoft Exchange 2000 and 2003, for example, are better suited to a single domain installation. As a general rule, avoid using two domains, two trees, or two forests when one will suffice.

CREATING ADDITIONAL DOMAINS

Before you decide how many domains to create, think about the possible reasons for creating additional domains. Table 3-2 lists the criteria that you should consider to be viable reasons for creating additional domains, as well as those that you should not.

Table 3-2

Reasons to Create (and Not Create) an Additional Active Directory Domain

REASONS TO CREATE ADDITIONAL DOMAINS	REASONS NOT TO CREATE ADDITIONAL DOMAINS
Isolated replication—Using a single domain for multiple sites requires the domain controllers to replicate the entire domain database across the WAN links connecting the sites. If the WAN links are too slow or too expensive to make this practical, then creating a separate domain for each site can reduce the replication traffic.	Size—A single Active Directory domain can easily accommodate millions of objects, so you should not create additional domains because you are concerned that a domain might have too many objects in it (unless they actually do number in the millions).
Unique domain policy—While it is generally possible to assign Group Policy settings to any domain, site, or organizational unit object, there are certain settings that Windows has traditionally restricted to the domain level, such as password and account lockout policies. Windows Server 2008 now makes it possible to create password settings objects (PSOs) and apply them to individual users and groups, but this requires you to modify the Active Directory schema directly. If there are parts of your organization that need different values for these settings, it can often be easier to create separate domains for them.	Administration—You can delegate administrative responsibility for part of a domain by using organizational units, so there is no need to create additional domains for this purpose.
Domain upgrades—If you have an existing Windows NT domain structure, it might be possible to collapse a number of old Windows NT domains into a single Active Directory domain. However, if you do not want to do this right away, you should duplicate the Windows NT domain structure by creating multiple Active Directory domains.	

CHOOSING A DESIGN PARADIGM

The design of a domain name space should be based on the structure of your organization. The most common structural paradigms used in Active Directory designs are the geographic, in which the domain structure is representative of the organization's physical locations, and the political, in which the structure conforms to the divisions or departments within your organization. Generally speaking, you should try to choose one of these options and stick to it throughout your domain design, rather than attempt to combine the two.

The ideal situation for a geographic structure would be one in which the organization has offices in remote locations that are largely autonomous, with each office having its own IT staff, as well as other departments. In this design, you create a domain for each office, and you can then create OUs in each domain to represent the individual departments in each office.

A political structure reverses the two roles. You create domains that represent the autonomous divisions or departments of your organization, and then, if necessary, you can create OUs representing the staff at the various remote offices.

In most cases, organizations fall somewhere between these two perfect extremes. Your organization might have some branch offices that are completely autonomous, while others fall under the administration of the main headquarters. In a case like this, it is up to you to decide which of the following is preferable:

- To create separate domains for the smaller branch offices and suffer the cost of the additional domain controllers and administration
- To install domain controllers for existing domains in the branch offices, and suffer the cost of the additional bandwidth required for intra-domain replication

- To leave the branch offices without domain controllers, forcing the users in those offices to suffer the diminished performance that using a remote domain controller can cause

Another guiding principle to your domain design might be an infrastructure that already exists in your organization. If, for example, you already have a DNS domain hierarchy in place, the best and easiest solution might just be to use that same hierarchy in Active Directory.

DESIGNING A TREE STRUCTURE

As you decide how many domains you are going to create, you should be thinking about how (or if) you are going to arrange them in the form of a tree. Designing a tree structure also includes deciding how you are going to name your domains and which domain will be the forest root.

If you plan to create domains corresponding to remote sites or organizational divisions, the most common practice is to make them all subdomains in the same tree, with a single root domain at the top. Depending on the nature of your organization, the root domain can represent the home office, with the branch offices as subdomains, or you can create a subdomain for each office and leave the root domain empty.

The first domain you create in an Active Directory forest—the forest root domain—is critical, because it has special capabilities. The Schema Administrators group exists only in the forest root domain, and the members of that group have the ability to modify the Active Directory schema, which affects all of the domains in the forest. Therefore, the administrators of the forest root domain, who control the membership of this group, must have sufficient seniority in the organization to warrant that responsibility.

NAMING DOMAINS

Naming domains is an integral part of the tree structure design. The first naming decision you have to make is what to call the tree root domain. Because Active Directory relies on DNS for its naming standard, you should take any existing DNS infrastructure into account when you choose a name for the tree root domain.

For example, if the organization already has a registered second-level domain on the Internet, you can use that domain to implement Active Directory in one of two ways. The first way, called the *root zone method,* is to use your registered domain name for the Active Directory tree root domain. If you choose to do this, you must either use your domain controllers (or other Windows Server 2008 computers) as your DNS servers, in which case you must migrate the resource records from your Internet DNS servers to those machines, or use your Internet DNS servers to host your Active Directory domains. If you choose the latter, you must either turn on dynamic updates on the DNS servers (which is a potential security hazard), or manually create the resource records needed for Active Directory.

The other way to implement Active Directory using an existing DNS infrastructure, which is now recommended by Microsoft, is called the *subzone method,* in which you create a subdomain beneath your registered Internet domain and use that for your Active Directory tree root. For example, if your Internet domain name is contoso.com, you would leave it as it is and create an internal subdomain called something like int.contoso.com, as described in Lesson 2, "Planning Infrastructure Services." This enables you to implement Active Directory without affecting the existing DNS servers.

Using the subzone method, you can leave the Internet DNS servers in place, and use Windows Server 2008 DNS servers to host the zone for the subdomain. The only configuration changes you have to make are the following:

- You must configure the Internet DNS servers to delegate the Active Directory subdomain to the Windows Server 2008 DNS servers.
- You must configure the Windows Server 2008 DNS servers to forward all of the client requests they cannot resolve (that is, requests for names outside of the Active Directory domains) to the Internet DNS servers.

CREATING ADDITIONAL TREES

When you create additional domains to represent your organization's geographical or political boundaries, the general rule is to make those domains part of the same tree. After all, a company's branch offices are subordinate to the main office, so it follows that the branch office subdomains should be subordinate to the root domain that represents the main office.

But what do you do if your organization contains two or more distinct companies, with unrelated names, which are on equal footing? It would seem to follow that you should create separate trees, one for each company. Consider, however, the advantages and disadvantages of such an arrangement.

From a security standpoint, creating separate trees adds nothing. All of the domains in a forest have built-in trust relationships, regardless of the tree structure. The same is true of other reasons often given for creating multiple trees, such as the need to separate resources or use different email addresses. Whether two domains are in the same tree or not has no effect on these things at all.

There are disadvantages to having multiple trees, however. Some applications, such as Microsoft Exchange, can have trouble working in multiple domain trees, and the administration of multiple trees can be considerably more complex than if you combined all of the domains into a single tree.

The lesson to learn here is that although you should try to design an Active Directory infrastructure that conforms to your organization, you should avoid creating additional infrastructure elements that add no value, just to conform to an organizational chart.

CREATING ADDITIONAL FORESTS

Strangely enough, there are more valid reasons for creating multiple forests than there are for creating multiple trees. As mentioned earlier, domains and domain trees are not true security boundaries. If your organization has divisions or departments that you want to be completely isolated, then you must put them in separate forests. The same is true if you want to use different values or configurations for forest-wide attributes. For example, to have different schema configurations or global catalog settings, you must create multiple forests.

Another possible motivation for creating multiple forests is a regulatory one. In some cases, there are legal reasons two divisions in the same organization must be entirely separate. Finally, you must again consider the capabilities of your applications. In some instances, as with certain versions of Microsoft Exchange, it is easier to run the application in a separate forest than in a multidomain or multitree environment.

When you create multiple forests, they are completely separate in every way. While Active Directory creates trust relationships automatically between domains in the same forest, whether they are in the same tree or not, there are no trust relationships at all between separate forests. If you want any interaction between domains in different forests, an administrator must manually create a trust relationship between the domains (or between the two forests).

Designing an Internal Domain Structure

Once you create a design for your Active Directory domains and the trees and forests superior to them, it is time to zoom in on each domain and consider the hierarchy you want to create inside it.

Within a domain, the primary hierarchical building block is the organizational unit. As a general rule, it is easier to build an Active Directory hierarchy using OUs than it is using domains. Unlike domains, it is a simple matter to create new OUs, rename existing ones, and move them around. You can also drag and drop leaf objects, such as users and computers, between OUs, but not between domains. By contrast, as noted earlier, creating a new domain means deploying additional domain controllers; and while it is possible to rename a domain, it is not a simple process.

UNDERSTANDING INHERITANCE

One of the critical differences between a domain tree hierarchy and the OU hierarchy within a domain is inheritance. When you assign Group Policy settings to a domain, the settings apply to all of the leaf objects in that domain, but not to the subdomains that are subordinate to it. However, when you assign Group Policy settings to an OU, those settings apply to all of the leaf objects in the OU, and they are inherited by any subordinate OUs it contains.

The result of this inheritance is that when you have multiple levels of OUs within a domain, individual leaf objects in the lower levels of the hierarchy can conceivably receive settings from each of their parent containers, tracing a path through each level of OUs, up to the parent domain, as shown in Figure 3-9.

Figure 3-9

Group Policy inheritance within a domain

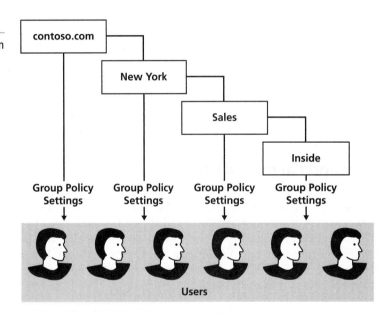

CREATING ORGANIZATIONAL UNITS

Adding organizational units to your Active Directory hierarchy is not as big an issue as adding domains; you do not need additional hardware, and you can easily move or delete an OU at will. However, you should still be conscious of the correct reasons for creating an OU. These reasons include the following:

- Duplicating organizational divisions—The structure of OUs within your domains should be an extension of the model you used to design the Active Directory domain structure. If, for example, you created domains based on a geographical model, you might want to create OUs that correspond to the departments in each domain. Conversely, if you used the political model to create your domains, you might want to create OUs based on the geographical distribution of your objects.

- Assigning Group Policy settings—Another important reason for creating an OU is to assign different Group Policy settings to a particular collection of objects. When you assign Group Policy settings to an OU, every object contained by that OU receives those settings, including other OUs.

- Delegating administration—One of the primary reasons for creating an OU is because you want to grant certain individuals administrative responsibility for a portion of the Active Directory hierarchy, without giving them full access to the entire domain. Once you give someone administrative access to an OU, they can create, modify, and delete any type of object beneath that OU. Every OU should have at least two administrators (in case one becomes locked out).

When designing an internal domain structure, you can create as many organizational unit levels as you need. The name of an OU does not become part of the FQDN for the objects it contains (as the domain name does), so there are no naming limitations that restrict the number of OU layers you can create. Microsoft recommends that you create no more than three layers of OUs, however.

CREATING GROUP OBJECTS

When you want to grant a collection of users permission to access a network resource, such as a file system share or a printer, you cannot assign permissions to an organizational unit; you must use a security group instead. Although they are container objects, groups are not part of the Active Directory hierarchy in the same way that domains and OUs are.

You can create a group object in just about any location and add members from anywhere in the domain, and in most cases, from other domains as well. The members of a group inherit any permissions that you assign to the group, but they do not inherit the Group Policy settings from the group's parent OUs and domain.

The standard strategy when creating groups is to assign the permissions needed to access a network resource to one group and add the users who require the permissions to another group. Then, you make the user group a member of the resource group. This enables you to exercise precise control over the access permissions without having to repeatedly add users to multiple groups.

This strategy, in its original form, called for the use of a domain local group for the resource permissions and a global group for the users. This was due to the group nesting limitations when using Windows NT domain controllers in an Active Directory domain. In Windows Server 2008, the nesting limitations defined in the AGULP rule mentioned earlier in this lesson still apply, but you can conceivably use all global groups or all universal groups, depending on the network's site topology.

The primary difference between global and universal groups is that universal groups add more data to the global catalog, thereby increasing the amount of replication traffic between sites. If your network consists of a single site, then you can use universal groups across the board. For a multisite network, you might want to consider using global groups instead, to reduce the replication traffic.

CREATING USERS AND COMPUTERS

User and computer objects are the leaves at the ends of the tree branches, and the only critical design element that applies to them is the need to formulate appropriate names. The account name you assign to each user and computer object must be unique in the domain. This means that if you delegate the administration of organizational units, you should devise a standardized user naming algorithm and make sure that all of the administrators use it.

One common user naming scheme for smaller organizations is to take the user's first name and append the first letter (or letters) of the surname, as in JohnD or MarkL. For larger organizations, which are more likely to have users with the same first names, the first initial and the surname might be more appropriate, as in JDoe or MLee.

In either case, you should impose a limit on the number of letters in the account name. For example, you might use a naming scheme that calls for the first initial and the first nine letters of the surname so that a user with a long name, such as Sootha Charncherngkha, would have the user name SCharncher. The overall objective is to create a set of naming rules that will enable users and administrators to determine what any user's account name should be, without having to check the actual Active Directory database.

For computers, you might devise a naming scheme that uses a set number of characters to identify the type of computer, and another set of characters for a unique system identifier. For servers, a good naming scheme might specify the server's location, the domain of which it is a member, and its function.

Designing a Group Policy Strategy

> Group Policy is one of the most powerful features of Active Directory. Using Group Policy, you can deploy hundreds of configuration settings to large collections of users at once.

To deploy Group Policy settings, you must create group policy objects (GPOs) and link them to Active Directory domains, organizational units, or sites. Every object in the container to which the GPO is linked receives the settings you configure in it. Linking a GPO to a domain, for example, causes every object in the domain to receive the settings in that GPO.

CERTIFICATION READY?
Plan and implement
group policy strategy
2.3

As noted earlier, Group Policy deployment is one of the main reasons for creating organizational unit objects within a domain. By linking GPOs to OUs, you can deploy different sets of configuration settings to various parts of the domain. When linking GPOs to OUs, the most important element to consider is that the Group Policy settings apply not only to the user and computer objects in the OU, but also to any subordinate OUs and the leaf objects they contain as well. In other words, Group Policy settings flow downward from the linked OU all the way to the bottom of the internal domain hierarchy.

This Group Policy inheritance factor can be a primary influence on the structure of the OUs within your domains. If you have many levels of OUs in a domain, and GPOs assigned to the OUs at each level, then there are two factors you must consider. First, you must think about the possibility of Group Policy settings from different OU levels conflicting in a single leaf object. For example, a user object in an OU five levels deep can have Group Policy settings applied to it by GPOs linked to each of its five parent OUs, as well as GPOs linked to the domain. This need not be a major problem, as long as you understand which Group Policy settings will be active once all of the GPOs are applied.

The other factor to consider is the possibility of delays caused by the application of too many GPOs. Microsoft recommends a maximum of ten OU levels, but the real problem is not with the number of actual OU levels (although too many can lead to administrative confusion), but with the number of GPOs applied to the leaf objects at the bottom of the hierarchy.

GPOs can contain Computer settings, which are applied as the client computer boots, and User settings, which are applied as the user logs on to the domain. The application of Group Policy settings at too many levels can slow down the boot and/or logon processes substantially. Part of the internal domain design process, therefore, consists of deciding where you are going to deploy GPOs and creating a hierarchy that does not apply too many GPOs to individual leaf objects.

■ Deploying Active Directory Domain Services

THE BOTTOM LINE

Once you have created an Active Directory design, it is time to think about the actual deployment process. As with most major network technologies, it is a good idea to install Active Directory on a test network first, before you put it into actual production.

There are a great many variables that can affect the performance of an Active Directory installation, including the hardware you select for your domain controllers, the capabilities of your network, and the types of WAN links connecting your remote sites. In many cases, an Active Directory design that looks good on paper will not function well in your environment, and you might want to modify the design before you proceed with the live deployment.

Active Directory is one of the more difficult technologies to test, because an isolated lab environment usually cannot emulate many of the factors that can affect the performance of a directory service. Most test labs cannot duplicate the network traffic patterns of the production

environment, and few have the WAN links necessary to simulate an actual multisite network. Wherever possible, you should try to test your design under real-life conditions, using your network's actual LAN and WAN technologies, but limiting the domain controllers and Active Directory clients to laboratory computers.

To create a new forest or a new domain, or to add a domain controller to an existing domain, you must install the Active Directory Domain Services role on a Windows Server 2008 computer, and then run the Active Directory Domain Services Installation Wizard.

To use a Windows Server 2008 computer as a domain controller, you must configure it to use static IP addresses, not addresses supplied by a Dynamic Host Configuration Protocol (DHCP) server. In addition, if you are creating a domain in an existing forest, or adding a domain controller to an existing domain, you must configure the computer to use the DNS server that hosts the existing forest or domain, at least during the Active Directory installation.

Installing the Active Directory Domain Services Role

Although it does not actually convert the computer into a domain controller, installing the Active Directory Domain Services role prepares the computer for the conversion process.

To install the role, use the following procedure.

 INSTALL THE ACTIVE DIRECTORY DOMAIN SERVICES ROLE

GET READY. Log on to Windows Server 2008 using an account with Administrative privileges. When the logon process is completed, close the Initial Configuration Tasks window and any other windows that appear.

1. Click **Start,** and then click **Administrative Tools** > **Server Manager.** The Server Manager console appears.
2. Select the **Roles** node and, in the details pane, click **Add Roles.** The Add Roles Wizard appears.
3. Click **Next** to bypass the *Before You Begin* page. The *Select Server Roles* page appears.
4. Select the **Active Directory Domain Services** checkbox and click **Next.** The *Introduction to Active Directory Domain Services* page appears.
5. Click **Next.** The *Confirm Installation Selections* page appears.
6. Click **Install.** The wizard installs the role and displays the *Installation Results* page.
7. Click **Close.**

CLOSE the Server Manager console.

Once you have installed the role, you can proceed to run the Active Directory Domain Services Installation Wizard. The wizard procedure varies, depending on what the function of the new domain controller will be. The following sections describe the procedures for the most common types of domain controller installations.

Creating a New Forest

When beginning a new Active Directory installation, the first step is to create a new forest, which you do by creating the first domain in the forest, the forest root domain.

To create a new forest, use the following procedure.

CREATE A NEW FOREST

GET READY. Log on to Windows Server 2008 using an account with Administrative privileges. When the logon process is completed, close the Initial Configuration Tasks window and any other windows that appear.

1. Click **Start,** and then click **Administrative Tools** > **Server Manager.** The Server Manager console appears.

2. Expand the **Roles** node and select the **Active Directory Domain Services** node, as shown in Figure 3-10.

Figure 3-10

The Active Directory Domain Services node in the Server Manager console

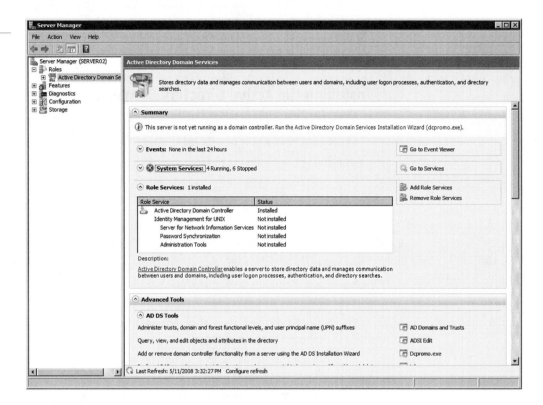

3. Under Advanced Tools, click the **Dcpromo.exe** link. The Active Directory Domain Services Installation Wizard appears, as shown in Figure 3-11.

Figure 3-11

The Active Directory Domain Services Installation Wizard

4. Click **Next** to bypass the Welcome page. The *Operating System Compatibility* page appears.

5. Click **Next.** The *Choose a Deployment Configuration* page appears, as shown in Figure 3-12.

Figure 3-12

The Choose a Deployment Configuration page in the Active Directory Domain Services Installation Wizard

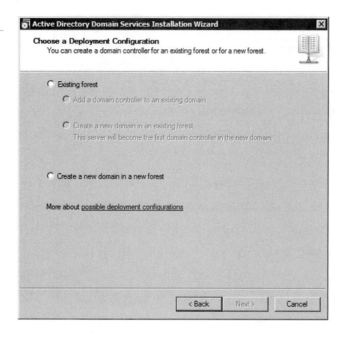

6. Select **Create a New Domain in a New Forest** and click **Next.** The *Name The Forest Root Domain* page appears, as shown in Figure 3-13.

Figure 3-13

The Name The Forest Root Domain page in the Active Directory Domain Services Installation Wizard

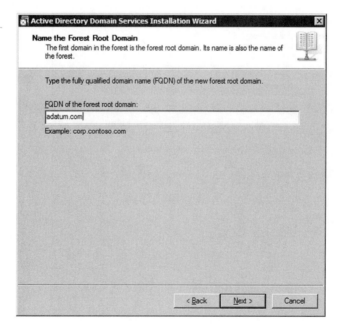

7. In the **FQDN of the Forest Root Domain** text box, key the domain name you selected and click **Next.** The wizard checks to see if the domain name you specified is already in use. The *Domain NetBIOS Name* page appears, as shown in Figure 3-14.

Figure 3-14

The Domain NetBIOS Name page in the Active Directory Domain Services Installation Wizard

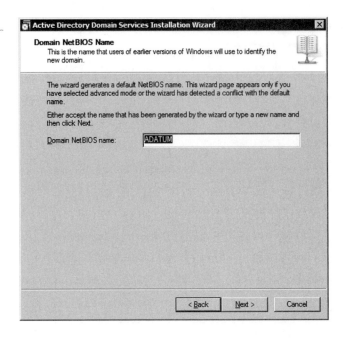

8. Click **Next** to accept the default NetBIOS name. After the wizard verifies the NetBIOS name, the *Set Forest Functional Level* page appears, as shown in Figure 3-15.

Figure 3-15

The Set Forest Functional Level page in the Active Directory Domain Services Installation Wizard

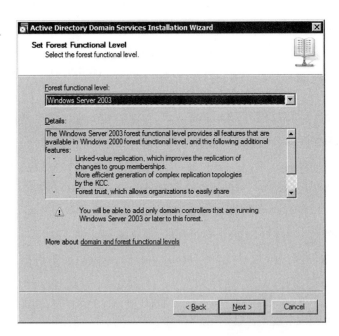

9. In the Forest Functional Level dropdown list, select the oldest operating system that you plan to use on the domain controllers in the forest and click **Next.** The *Set Domain Functional Level* page appears, as shown in Figure 3-16.

Figure 3-16

The Set Domain Functional
Level page in the Active
Directory Domain Services
Installation Wizard

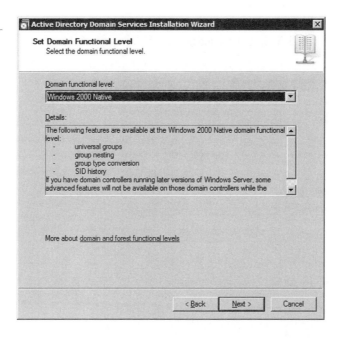

10. In the Domain Functional Level dropdown list, select the functional level you want
to use for the domain and click **Next.** The *Additional Domain Controller Options*
page appears, as shown in Figure 3-17.

Figure 3-17

The Additional Domain
Controller Options page in
the Active Directory Domain
Services Installation Wizard

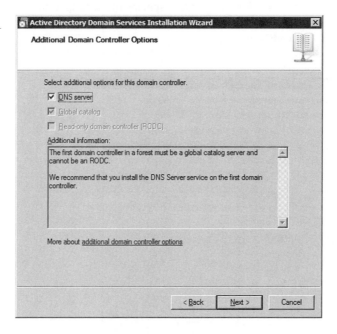

11. If you do not already have a DNS server on the network to host the forest root
domain, leave the **DNS Server** checkbox selected and click **Next.** If the computer
has dynamically assigned or autogenerated IP addresses, a Static IP Assignment
message box appears, recommending the use of static IP addresses. Click **Yes** to
continue. If the FQDN you specified does not have an authoritative parent zone
on an available DNS server, an Active Directory Domain Services Installation Wizard
message box appears, warning you of this. If you are installing the DNS Server
service on the domain controller or creating a new second-level domain, you can

ignore this warning and click **Yes** to continue. The *Location for Database, Log Files, and SYSVOL* page appears, as shown in Figure 3-18.

Figure 3-18

The Location for Database, Log Files, and SYSVOL page in the Active Directory Domain Services Installation Wizard

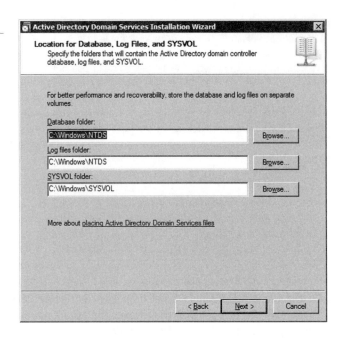

12. In the text boxes provided, specify the locations for the database, log files, and SYSVOL folder. Then click **Next.** The *Directory Services Restore Mode Administrator Password* page appears, as shown in Figure 3-19.

Figure 3-19

The Directory Services Restore Mode Administrator Password page in the Active Directory Domain Services Installation Wizard

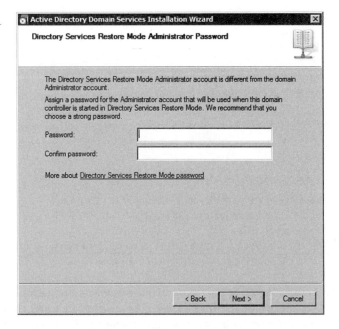

13. In the **Password** and **Confirm Password** text boxes, specify the password you must supply when starting the computer in Directory Services Restore Mode. Then click **Next.** The *Summary* page appears, as shown in Figure 3-20.

Figure 3-20

The Summary page in the Active Directory Domain Services Installation Wizard

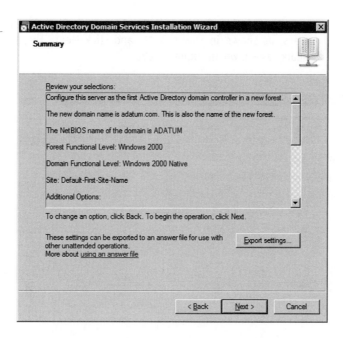

14. Click **Next.** The wizard installs Active Directory, which might take several minutes. Then, the *Completing the Active Directory Domain Services Installation Wizard* page appears.

15. Click **Finish.** An Active Directory Domain Services Installation Wizard message box appears, indicating that you must restart the computer.

RESTART the computer.

With the forest root domain in place, you can now proceed to create additional domain controllers in that domain, or add new domains to the forest.

Creating a New Child Domain in a Forest

Once you have a forest with at least one domain, you can add a child domain beneath any existing domain.

To create a child domain, use the following procedure.

 CREATE A NEW CHILD DOMAIN IN A FOREST

GET READY. Log on to Windows Server 2008 using a domain account with Administrative privileges. When the logon process is completed, close the Initial Configuration Tasks window and any other windows that appear.

1. Click **Start,** and then click **Administrative Tools** > **Server Manager.** The Server Manager console appears.

2. Expand the **Roles** node and select the **Active Directory Domain Services** node.

3. Under Advanced Tools, click the **Dcpromo.exe** link. The Active Directory Domain Services Installation Wizard appears.

4. Click **Next** to bypass the *Welcome* page. The *Operating System Compatibility* page appears.

5. Click **Next.** The *Choose a Deployment Configuration* page appears.

6. Select the **Existing Forest** and **Create a New Domain in an Existing Forest** options, as shown in Figure 3-21, and click **Next.** The *Network Credentials* page appears, as shown in Figure 3-22.

Figure 3-21

The Choose a Deployment Configuration page in the Active Directory Domain Services Installation Wizard

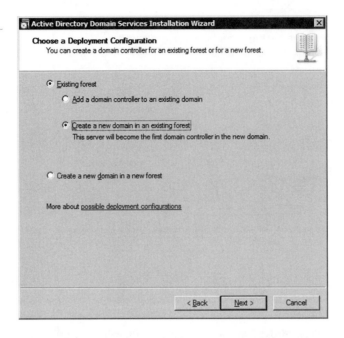

Figure 3-22

The Network Credentials page in the Active Directory Domain Services Installation Wizard

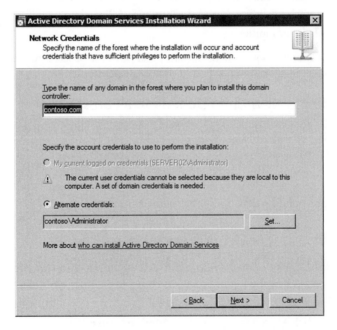

7. In the text box provided, key the name of any domain in the forest to which you want to add the new domain controller. If you want to add the domain controller with an account other than the one you are currently using, select **Alternate Credentials** and click **Set.** A Windows Security dialog box appears in which you can specify the user name and password of the account you want to use. Then click **Next.** The *Name the New Domain* page appears.

8. In the **FQDN of the Parent Domain** text box, key the name of the parent domain beneath which you want to create a new child domain. Then, in the **Single-label DNS Name of the Child Domain** text box, key the name you want to assign to the new child domain, as shown in Figure 3-23, and click **Next.** The wizard checks to see if the domain name you specified is already in use and verifies the NetBIOS equivalent of the name. Then, the *Set Domain Functional Level* page appears.

Figure 3-23

The Name the New Domain page in the Active Directory Domain Services Installation Wizard

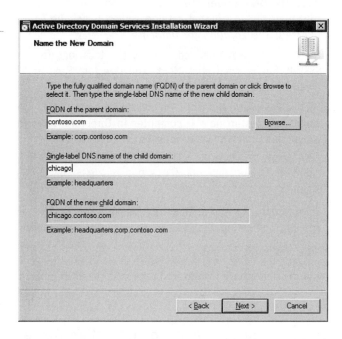

9. In the Domain Functional Level dropdown list, select the functional level you want to use for the domain and click **Next.** The *Select a Site* page appears, as shown in Figure 3-24.

Figure 3-24

The Select a Site page in the Active Directory Domain Services Installation Wizard

10. Select the site in which you want to install the new domain controller. If you want to install the domain controller in a new site, you must first create the site on the existing domain controller, using the Active Directory Sites and Services console. Click **Next** to continue. The *Additional Domain Controller Options* page appears.

11. If you do not already have a DNS server on the network to host the new domain, leave the **DNS Server** checkbox selected and click **Next.** If you want the domain controller to be a global catalog server, leave the **Global Catalog** checkbox selected. The *Location for Database, Log Files, and SYSVOL* page appears.

12. In the text boxes provided, specify the locations for the database, log files, and SYSVOL folder. Then click **Next.** The *Directory Services Restore Mode Administration Password* page appears.

13. In the **Password** and **Confirm Password** text boxes, specify the password you must supply when starting the computer in Directory Services Restore Mode. Then click **Next.** The *Summary* page appears.

14. Click **Next.** The wizard installs Active Directory, which might take several minutes. Then, the *Completing the Active Directory Domain Services Installation Wizard* page appears.

15. Click **Finish.** An Active Directory Domain Services Installation Wizard message box appears, indicating that you must restart the computer.

RESTART the computer.

The new domain you have just created appears beneath the parent domain you specified in step 8.

Adding a Domain Controller to an Existing Domain

Every Active Directory domain should have a minimum of two domain controllers.

To add a domain controller to an existing domain, use the following procedure.

 ADD A DOMAIN CONTROLLER TO AN EXISTING DOMAIN

GET READY. Log on to Windows Server 2008 using a domain account with Administrative privileges. When the logon process is completed, close the Initial Configuration Tasks window and any other windows that appear.

1. Click **Start,** and then click **Administrative Tools** > **Server Manager.** The Server Manager console appears.

2. Expand the **Roles** node and select the **Active Directory Domain Services** node.

3. Under Advanced Tools, click the **Dcpromo.exe** link. The Active Directory Domain Services Installation Wizard appears.

4. Click **Next** to bypass the Welcome page. The *Operating System Compatibility* page appears.

5. Click **Next.** The *Choose a Deployment Configuration* page appears.

6. Select the **Existing Forest** and **Add a Domain Controller to an Existing Domain** options, as shown in Figure 3-25, and click **Next.** The *Network Credentials* page appears.

Figure 3-25

The Choose a Deployment Configuration page in the Active Directory Domain Services Installation Wizard

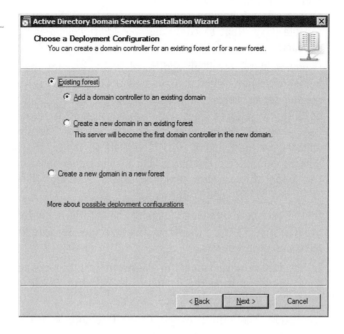

7. In the text box provided, key the name of any domain in the forest to which you want to add the new domain controller. If you want to add the domain controller with an account other than the one you are currently using, select **Alternate Credentials** and click **Set.** A Windows Security dialog box appears in which you can specify the user name and password of the account you want to use. Then click **Next.** The *Select a Domain* page appears, as shown in Figure 3-26.

Figure 3-26

The Select a Domain page in the Active Directory Domain Services Installation Wizard

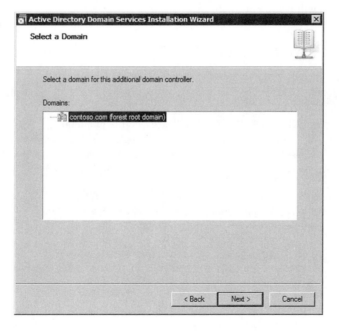

8. Select the domain to which you want to add the new domain controller and click **Next.** The *Select a Site* page appears.

9. Select the site in which you want to install the new domain controller. If you want to install the domain controller in a new site, you must first create the site on the existing domain controller, using the Active Directory Sites and Services console. Click **Next** to continue. The *Additional Domain Controller Options* page appears.

10. If you want to install an additional DNS server for the domain, leave the **DNS Server** checkbox selected. If you want the domain controller to be a global catalog server, leave the **Global Catalog** checkbox selected. Then click **Next.** If the domain you selected does not have an authoritative parent zone on an available DNS server, an Active Directory Domain Services Installation Wizard message box appears, warning you of this. If you are installing the DNS Server service on the domain controller or adding a domain controller for a second-level domain, you can ignore this warning and click **Yes** to continue. The *Location for Database, Log Files, and SYSVOL* page appears.

11. In the text boxes provided, specify the locations for the database, log files, and SYSVOL folder. Then click **Next.** The *Directory Services Restore Mode Administration Password* page appears.

12. In the **Password** and **Confirm Password** text boxes, specify the password you must supply when starting the computer in Directory Services Restore Mode. Then click **Next.** The *Summary* page appears.

13. Click **Next.** The wizard installs Active Directory, which might take several minutes. Then, the *Completing the Active Directory Domain Services Installation Wizard* page appears.

14. Click **Finish.** An Active Directory Domain Services Installation Wizard message box appears, indicating that you must restart the computer.

RESTART the computer.

The domain controller is now configured to service the existing domain. If the new domain controller is located in the same site as the other(s), then Active Directory replication between the two will begin automatically.

SUMMARY SKILL MATRIX

IN THIS LESSON YOU LEARNED:

- A directory service is a repository of information about the resources—hardware, software, and human—that are connected to a network. Active Directory is the directory service that Microsoft first introduced in Windows 2000 Server, and that they have upgraded in each successive server operating system release, including Windows Server 2008.

- Users that are joined to an Active Directory domain log on to the domain, not an individual computer or application, and are able to access any resources in that domain for which administrators have granted them the proper permissions.

- In Active Directory, you can subdivide a domain into organizational units and populate it with objects. You can also create multiple domains and group them into sites, trees, and forests.

- An organizational unit (OU) is a container object that functions in a subordinate capacity to a domain. OUs can contain other OUs, as well as leaf objects. You can apply separate Group Policy to an OU, and delegate the administration of an OU as needed.

- Group objects are containers, just as organizational units are, but groups are not full-fledged security divisions as OUs are; you cannot apply Group Policy settings to a group object.

- When you create your first domain on an Active Directory network, you are, in essence, creating the root of a domain tree. You can populate the tree with additional domains, as long as they are part of the same contiguous name space.

- An Active Directory forest consists of two or more separate domain trees, which have the same two-way trust relationships between them as two domains in the same tree.

- To facilitate the replication process, Active Directory includes another administrative division called the site. A site is defined as a collection of subnets that have good connectivity between them.

- The overall objective in your Active Directory design process should be to create as few domains as possible.

- The design of a domain name space should be based on the structure of your organization. The most common structural paradigms used in Active Directory designs are the geographic, in which the domain structure is representative of the organization's physical locations, and the political, in which the structure conforms to the divisions or departments within your organization.

- One of the critical differences between a domain tree hierarchy and the OU hierarchy within a domain is inheritance. When you assign Group Policy settings to a domain, the settings apply to all of the leaf objects in that domain, but not to the subdomains that are subordinate to it. However, when you assign Group Policy settings to an OU, those settings apply to all of the leaf objects in the OU, and the settings are inherited by any subordinate OUs it contains.

- GPOs can contain Computer settings, which are applied as the client computer boots, and User settings, which are applied as the user logs on to the domain. The application of Group Policy settings at too many levels can slow down the boot and/or logon processes substantially. Part of the internal domain design process, therefore, consists of deciding where you are going to deploy GPOs and creating a hierarchy that does not apply too many GPOs to individual leaf objects.

■ Knowledge Assessment

Matching

Complete the following exercise by matching the terms with their corresponding definitions.

- **a.** directory schema
- **b.** Lightweight Directory Access Protocol (LDAP)
- **c.** multiple-master replication
- **d.** global catalog
- **e.** Read-Only Domain Controller (RODC)
- **f.** single-master replication
- **g.** leaf objects
- **h.** Directory Access Protocol (DAP)
- **i.** organizational unit (OU)
- **j.** container objects

_____ **1.** based on the OSI protocol stack

_____ **2.** organizational units

_____ **3.** specifies the objects and attributes you can create in a domain

_____ **4.** lists all of the objects in a forest

_____ **5.** used for Active Directory communications

_____ **6.** computers and users

_____ **7.** enables administrators to modify objects on any domain controller

_____ **8.** used to create an internal domain infrastructure

_____ **9.** supports only incoming replication traffic

_____ **10.** used by Windows NT PDCs and BDCs

Multiple Choice

Select one or more correct answers for each of the following questions.

1. Which of the following are the primary functions of Active Directory?
   a. to provide authentication and authorization services for hardware resources on the network
   b. to provide only authorization services for hardware resources on the network
   c. to provide only authentication services for software resources on the network
   d. to provide authentication and authorization services for software resources on the network

2. Which of the following can an Active Directory domain controller use to verify a user's identity?
   a. passwords
   b. smart cards
   c. biometrics
   d. all of the above

3. Which of the following cannot contain multiple Active Directory domains?
   a. organizational units
   b. sites
   c. trees
   d. forests

4. What are the two basic classes of Active Directory objects?
   a. resource
   b. leaf
   c. domain
   d. container

5. Which of the following is not true about an object's attributes?
   a. Administrators must manually supply information for certain attributes.
   b. Every container object has, as an attribute, a list of all the other objects it contains.
   c. Leaf objects do not contain attributes.
   d. Active Directory automatically creates the globally unique identifier (GUID).

6. Which of the following is not true of the Lightweight Directory Access Protocol (LDAP)?
   a. LDAP defines the format of the queries that Active Directory clients send to domain controllers.
   b. LDAP provides a naming structure for uniquely identifying objects in the directory.
   c. LDAP is a highly complex protocol that includes many unnecessary features.
   d. LDAP is based on Open Systems Interconnection (OSI) protocol stack.

7. Which of the following is not a reason you should try to create as few domains as possible when designing an Active Directory infrastructure?
   a. Creating additional domains increases the administrative burden of the installation.
   b. Each additional domain you create increases the hardware costs of the Active Directory deployment.
   c. Some applications might have problems working in a forest with multiple domains.
   d. You must purchase a license from Microsoft for each domain you create.

8. Which of the following is not a correct reason for creating an organizational unit?
   a. to create a permanent container that cannot be moved or renamed
   b. to duplicate the divisions in your organization
   c. to delegate administration tasks
   d. to assign different Group Policy settings to a specific group of users or computers

9. Which of the following does an Active Directory client use to locate objects in another domain?
   a. DNS   b. Global catalog
   c. PDC   d. Site link

10. Which of the following Active Directory elements provide a true security boundary?
    a. organizational units   b. domains
    c. domain trees   d. forests

Review Questions

1. List the Active Directory objects you must create to deploy domain controllers at remote locations and explain how each one contributes to the process by which a client locates the nearest domain controller.

2. Explain the roles of site and site link objects in the Active Directory replication process.

■ Case Scenarios

Scenario 3-1: Assigning Permissions

Robert is designing a new Active Directory infrastructure for a company called Litware, Inc., which has its headquarters in New York and two additional offices in London and Tokyo. The London office consists only of sales and marketing staff; they do not have their own IT department. The Tokyo office is larger, with representatives from all of the company departments, including a full IT staff. The Tokyo office is connected to the headquarters using a 64 Kbps demand-dial link, while the London office has a 512 Kbps frame relay connection. The company has registered the litware.com domain name, and Robert has created a subdomain called inside.litware.com for use by Active Directory.

Based on this information, design an Active Directory infrastructure for Litware, Inc. that is as economical as possible, specifying how many domains to create, what to name them, how many domain controllers to install, and where. Explain each of your decisions.

4 LESSON

Planning Application Services

OBJECTIVE DOMAIN MATRIX

TECHNOLOGY SKILL	OBJECTIVE DOMAIN	OBJECTIVE DOMAIN NUMBER
Assigning Multiple Roles	Plan application servers and services	1.4
Using Terminal Services	Provision applications	4.1

KEY TERMS

application servers
client-side caching
copy-on-write data sharing
hybrid virtualization
Hyper-V
hypervisor
Microsoft SoftGrid Application
    Virtualization

Microsoft System Center Configuration
    Manager 2007
Microsoft System Center Essentials 2007
Remote Desktop Connection
Remote Desktop Protocol (RDP)
RemoteApp
session
Session ID

Terminal Services client access
    licenses (TS CALs)
thin client computing
TS Licensing server
virtual instance
virtual machine manager (VMM)
virtual machines (VMs)
virtualization

In Lessons 1, 2, and 3, you learned about the infrastructure roles that provide underlying services to network clients. This lesson examines the application services that enable clients to perform their jobs. In particular, this lesson examines:

- The application server roles included in Windows Server 2008
- Methods for deploying applications
- How to use Terminal Services to host applications
- How to virtualize application servers

■ Deploying Application Servers

THE BOTTOM LINE

Organizations supply their employees with computers so that they can get work done, and to accomplish this goal, the users need computer programs designed to aid them in the performance of specific tasks. These programs are also known as applications.

Architecturally, applications in the enterprise can take several forms, but all of these forms typically involve a server in some fashion, as follows:

- Client-run applications—Some applications run wholly on client computers, such as office productivity applications. However, in an enterprise environment, they typically use services provided by network servers, such as file and print servers, as shown in Figure 4-1.

Figure 4-1

Applications running on a client computer utilize file and print resources provided by application servers

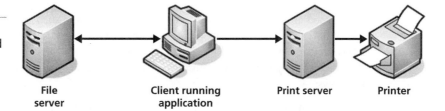

File server   Client running application   Print server   Printer

- Client/Server applications—Sometimes, an application runs on a single server, to which clients all over the network send requests for services. For example, a single server might run a database application that supplies information to all of the clients on the network, as shown in Figure 4-2.

Figure 4-2

A client computer accessing an application running on a single application server

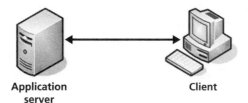

Application server   Client

- Distributed applications—In some cases, a single application might use multiple servers to run its various services, which provide different functions that work together. For example, a server hosting a Web site can function as the intermediary between clients on the front end and a database server on the back end, as shown in Figure 4-3.

Figure 4-3

A client computer accessing an application server, which retrieves information from a database server

Database server   Application server   Client

A typical business network will use two or even all three of these application types, and will therefore need a variety of servers. As with infrastructure servers, it is possible to combine multiple application services on a single computer, enabling administrators to choose between a large number of small servers or a few powerful ones. It is even possible to combine application services with infrastructure services on the same computer.

Therefore, to plan for an efficient enterprise network, IT personnel must consider what applications the users will require, how many users will run each application, and what server resources those applications need to run properly. Typically, administrators refer to the servers that provide these resources, not surprisingly, as ***application servers.*** Conducting an inventory of the users' needs enables the network designers to address basic design questions such as the following:

- How many application servers do I need?
- What hardware should the application servers contain?
- Where should the application servers be located?

Introducing Application Service Roles

The roles included in Windows Server 2008 can be divided into three distinct categories: infrastructure services, directory services, and application services.

You learned about some of the infrastructure service roles, such as the Domain Name System (DNS) and the Dynamic Host Configuration Protocol (DHCP) in Lesson 2, "Planning Infrastructure Services," and the directory services roles in Lesson 3, "Planning an Active Directory Deployment." The Windows Server 2008 roles that define application services are as follows:

- Application Server—Provides an integrated environment for deploying and running server-based business applications designed within (or expressly for) the organization, such as those requiring the services provided by Internet Information Services (IIS), Microsoft .NET Framework 2.0 and 3.0, COM+, ASP.NET, Message Queuing, or Windows Communication Foundation (WCF).
- Fax Server—Enables administrators to manage fax devices and enables clients to send and receive faxes over the network.
- File Services—Installs tools and services that enhance Windows Server 2008's basic ability to provide network clients with access to files stored on server drives, including Distributed File System (DFS), DFS Replication, Storage Manager for Storage Area Networks (SANs), fast file searching, and file services for UNIX clients.
- Hyper-V—Enables Windows Server 2008 to host virtual machines, each of which has its own virtual hardware resources, and a completely separate copy of the operating system.
- Print Services—Provides clients with access to printers attached to the server or to the network, as well as centralized network printer and print server management, and printer deployment using Group Policy.
- Streaming Media Services—Enables the server to transmit digital media content to network clients in real time. (This role is not included with Windows Server 2008, but it is available as a free download from Microsoft's Web site.)
- Terminal Services—Enables clients on the network or on the Internet to remotely access server-based applications or the entire Windows desktop, using server resources.
- UDDI Services—Implements Universal Description, Discovery, and Integration (UDDI), which enables the organization to publish information about its Web services for use by intranet, extranet, and/or Internet clients.
- Web Server (IIS)—Installs Internet Information Services (IIS) 7.0, which enables the organization to publish Web sites and ASP.NET, WCF, or Windows SharePoint–based applications for use by intranet, extranet, and/or Internet clients.

Assigning Multiple Roles

Windows Server 2008 computers can perform multiple roles at the same time.

The concept of assigning multiple roles to a single Windows Server 2008 computer makes it possible to utilize each computer's hardware resources more efficiently. For example, a computer that is functioning only as a DHCP server will probably utilize only a small percentage of its CPU resources, as shown in Figure 4-4. This is because the only thing the DHCP service has to do is assign TCP/IP configuration settings to computers as they start, and then renew those settings, usually several days later. Most of the time, the service is idle.

Figure 4-4

Running a single role on a server can often be a waste of system resources

DHCP

To take full advantage of that DHCP server, a designer can assign other roles to it as well. The number of roles a server can perform depends on the computer's hardware configuration, the hardware requirements of the role, and the size and scope of the enterprise. For example, on a large enterprise network hosting 10,000 clients, a dedicated DHCP server would make sense. However, in a small- to medium-sized enterprise, that DHCP server might also be able to function as a DNS server and an Active Directory domain controller without overtaxing its hardware, as shown in Figure 4-5.

Figure 4-5

Many servers can support several roles simultaneously

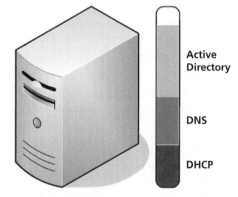

Active Directory

DNS

DHCP

In fact, the computer might have the hardware capacity to function as a Web server also. However, before adding that role, you must consider some other factors. Will the Web server be hosting a low-volume intranet Web site or a high-traffic Internet site? A greater amount of Web client traffic requires more resources.

With that consideration in mind, you might think it is a good idea to purchase the most powerful computer you can find, one with sufficient hardware resources to run all of the server roles the enterprise needs. For some organizations, this is a viable option, but distributing server roles among several computers has several distinct advantages, including the following:

- Fault tolerance—A single server provides a single point of failure. If one computer is performing all of the roles your enterprise needs to function, and that computer malfunctions, then you lose all of the services. Running multiple servers enables the business to better tolerate a single failure.

- Resource allocation—The hardware resources needed by specific server roles can fluctuate wildly, depending on a number of factors. A Web server, for example, might require more server resources during periods of heavy incoming network traffic, which occur at certain times of the day. If the Web server's peak utilization period happens to coincide with the peak utilization of the computer's other roles, the server could become a bottleneck, forcing performance of all the roles to suffer.

- Availability—Distributing roles among several computers enables you to build high availability into your network design. For example, you might configure one computer with the Web server role, and another computer to perform infrastructure roles, such as DHCP and DNS. To add high availability to the design, you would install the Web server role on the infrastructure server and the DHCP and DNS roles on the Web server, disabling the redundant services for the time being. This way, in the event that either server fails, the other one can take over its roles at a few minutes notice.

- Scalability—Having multiple servers on the network enables administrators to reallocate resources as needed. If, for example, a sudden increase in traffic to the company's Internet Web server causes that computer's CPU utilization to consistently spike at 100 percent, you could conceivably redeploy the Web server role on one of the company's other servers, one with a faster processor. Alternatively, you could add a second Web server and configure the two computers to split the traffic load between them.

- Security—Different roles can have different security requirements. For example, you might have a server functioning as an Active Directory domain controller that has sufficient resources to take on another role, but it would be a bad idea to use that computer as an Internet Web server. Computers exposed to the Internet are points of vulnerability, and for that reason, many enterprises put them on perimeter networks, isolated from internal resources, such as infrastructure servers. Generally speaking, the more roles a server has to perform, the more ports it has to leave open for incoming network traffic, and more open ports increase the attack surface of the computer.

- Network traffic—Running a variety of roles on a single server can consolidate a lot of network traffic onto a single subnet. Even if the server itself is capable of handling many different types of requests from clients all over the enterprise, the network might become a serious performance bottleneck. Distributing roles among servers on different subnets can prevent too much traffic from converging on a single location.

- Update management—It is far easier to keep servers updated with the latest operating system patches if each computer is running as few roles as is practical. In addition, fewer problems occur if an update has deleterious side effects.

X REF

In addition to combining application server roles on a single computer, it is also possible to deploy applications and application servers using other Windows Server 2008 technologies, such as Terminal Services and Hyper-V virtualization, as discussed later in this lesson.

Selecting Application Service Roles

Most Windows Server 2008 roles include a variety of options that you can use to customize the installation.

As mentioned earlier in this lesson, the complexity of the design and implementation process for an enterprise network's application servers is largely dependent on the types of applications the users need. The first step of the planning process is to inventory those needs. Then, you can consider the various ways of providing for those needs.

The application services Microsoft includes with Windows Server 2008 provide administrators with several ways to deploy even the simplest applications. The method you choose depends on several factors, including economy, security, and ease of administration. The following sections examine the major application service roles listed earlier in this lesson, list the services that compose each one, and discuss how to use them to implement applications on an enterprise network.

USING THE FILE SERVICES ROLE

Virtually all enterprise networks have some (or maybe all) users who spend much of their time working with standard, off-the-shelf productivity applications, such as word processors, spreadsheets, email clients, and so forth. Even though the simplest way to deploy these applications is to install them on the users' individual workstations, employees can make use of application servers on the network in several ways.

The first consideration is where the users will store their documents. Storing document files on local workstation drives is a simple solution, but one with significant drawbacks. If users want to collaborate on documents, they must create shares on their local drives. This could result in dozens or hundreds of additional shares on the network, making navigation difficult. This practice also creates access control problems; the users would have to either set their own permissions or rely on administrators to do so. Finally, storing documents on workstation drives complicates the process of backing them up on a regular basis.

The more common, and more practical, solution is to have users store their documents on network servers, which means deploying one or more file servers on the network. Windows Server 2008 does not need a special role to provide basic file sharing services. Administrators can share folders on any server drive and make them available to users by assigning the appropriate permissions.

However, installing the File Services role on a Windows Server 2008 computer provides additional capabilities that can aid in the management of document storage, such as the following:

- Distributed File System—Consists of two role services: DFS Namespace, which enables administrators to create a virtual directory tree consisting of folders stored on different servers, and DFS Replication, which maintains duplicate copies of the DFS namespace in remote locations.

- File Server Resource Manager (FSRM)—Enables administrators to create and enforce storage quotas, specify file types that are permitted on network volumes, and generate storage reports.

- Services for Network File System—Implements the Network File System (NFS) on the Windows Server 2008 computer. NFS is the standard file-sharing solution for UNIX-based operating systems, so this service enables UNIX clients to access files stored on a Windows server.

- Windows Search Service—Creates an index that enables clients to rapidly search for files stored on server drives, without having to access each drive in turn.

- Windows Server 2003 File Services—Provides downlevel replication and indexing services that enable the server to participate on legacy networks with Windows Server 2003 storage services.

- Share and Storage Management—A new snap-in for Microsoft Management Console (MMC) that provides a centralized administration tool for file server resources.

X REF

For more information on Windows Server 2008 storage technologies, see Lesson 6, "Planning Storage Solutions."

USING THE TERMINAL SERVICES ROLE

Installing productivity applications on an individual workstation is a simple task, unless you have to repeat the process on hundreds or thousands of computers. In addition, after you have installed the applications, you must consider the prospect of maintaining and upgrading them as needed. Automating the deployment and maintenance of applications on large groups of computers can require extensive planning and preparation, as well as the additional expense of a management software product.

Windows Server 2008 provides an alternative to individual workstation installations in the form of Terminal Services. Terminal Services is a technology that enables users working at another computer on the company network or on the Internet to establish a connection to a server and open an application or desktop session there.

Using Terminal Services to deploy applications offers several advantages to the network administrator, including the following:

X REF

For more information on using Terminal Services, see "Using Terminal Services" later in this lesson.

TAKE NOTE *

Microsoft provides the Remote Desktop feature, based on Terminal Services, with the Windows XP Professional and Windows Vista desktop operating systems.

- Single application installation—Because the applications run on the Terminal Services server, it is necessary to install them only on that one computer. This ensures that all of the users are running the same application versions, and simplifies maintenance and upgrade tasks for the administrators, because they have to work only on a single installation.

- Low bandwidth consumption—Unlike virtual private network (VPN) or direct dial-up connections, a Terminal Services connection uses relatively little network bandwidth because the applications are running on the server computer. The only data exchanged by the Terminal Services client and the server is data needed to relay the keyboard, mouse, and display information.

- Broad-based client support—A user connecting to the Terminal Services server has to run only a simple client program because the resources needed to run the applications are on the server. This means that the client workstations can be low-end computers, non-Windows computers, or even thin client devices, which are minimal computers designed only for server communication.

- Conservation of licenses—Instead of purchasing application licenses for individual workstations, which might or might not be in use at any given time, you can maintain a pool of licenses on the Terminal Services server, which the system allocates to users as they log on. For example, an office with 100 workstations would require 100 licenses for an application installed on each computer, even if there were never more than 50 users running the application at any one time. Using Terminal Services, 50 application licenses would be sufficient, because only the users actually connected to the server need a license.

USING THE HYPER-V ROLE

Virtualization is the process of deploying and maintaining multiple instances of an operating system, called *virtual machines (VMs),* on a single computer. Each virtual machine contains a completely separate copy of the operating system with its own virtual hardware resources, device drivers, and applications. To the network, each virtual machine looks like a separate computer with its own name and IP address. As a result, you are not combining the security risks of multiple roles in a single operating system instance. You update each instance of the operating system separately. Windows Server 2008 supports virtualization in the form of the *Hyper-V* role.

TAKE NOTE *

Using Terminal Services might yield savings on application licenses, but a computer connecting to a terminal server requires a Microsoft Terminal Server client access license (CAL) as well. The only exceptions to this are the two client licenses included with Windows Server 2008 for Remote Desktop administration purposes.

Using virtual machines also makes it easier to manage the distribution of your roles among your physical servers. On a virtualized computer, the hardware resources allocated to each virtual machine are abstracted from the actual physical resources in the computer. This means that you can copy a virtual machine from one computer to another, and it will run without modification, even if the two computers have different physical hardware. Therefore, if you have three roles installed on a single computer in three separate virtual machines, you can simply move one virtual machine to another computer if their combined usage levels begin to overwhelm the hardware.

Virtualization provides other advantages as well, including the following:

- Server consolidation—Running applications or services on separate virtual machines makes it possible to derive the greatest utility from each server in the enterprise. By running several virtual machines on a single computer, you can consolidate the functions of several servers and easily test the resource utilization of various application and service combinations.

- Backups—Backing up individual virtual machines is no more difficult than backing up multiple roles on a single computer. However, virtual machines can greatly simplify the process of restoring a server in the event of a disaster. If a Hyper-V server goes down, you can restore the virtual machines to other Hyper-V servers immediately, as a temporary measure or a permanent solution. You can also maintain dormant copies of your virtual machines on other servers, which you can bring online any time they are needed.

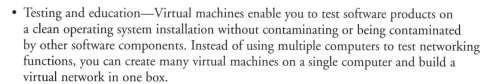

TAKE NOTE

While Microsoft has designed Hyper-V to be a role included with the Windows Server 2008 operating system, Hyper-V is not included in the initial Windows Server 2008 release. Instead, Microsoft provides it as a separate download that adds the Hyper-V role to the operating system.

• Testing and education—Virtual machines enable you to test software products on a clean operating system installation without contaminating or being contaminated by other software components. Instead of using multiple computers to test networking functions, you can create many virtual machines on a single computer and build a virtual network in one box.

• Compatibility—A single host computer can run virtual machines with different operating systems. Therefore, if you want to upgrade your servers to the latest operating system version, you can still maintain downlevel virtual machines to support applications that require a previous version.

Hyper-V is a Windows Server 2008 role like any other, which you can install using the Server Manager console, once you have applied the appropriate update package. However, Hyper-V has hardware and licensing requirements that go beyond those for the Windows Server 2008 operating system. In practice, the technology will largely be limited to enterprise deployments that are willing to make a substantial hardware investment in virtualization technology.

After you have the appropriate hardware and the required licenses, you can add the Hyper-V role using Server Manager. Microsoft recommends that you do not install other roles with Hyper-V. Adding the role installs the virtualization software, as well as the management interface, which is a Microsoft Management Console (MMC) snap-in called Hyper-V Manager.

Using Hyper-V Manager, you can create new virtual machines and define the hardware resources that the system should allocate to them. In the settings for a particular virtual machine, depending on the physical hardware available in the computer and the limitations of the guest operating system, administrators can specify the number of processors and the amount of memory a virtual machine should use, install virtual network adapters, and create virtual disks using a variety of technologies, including SANs.

Each virtual machine on a Hyper-V server can run a different operating system, if necessary. Hyper-V supports both 32-bit and 64-bit Windows versions as guest OSes, as well as Linux distributions.

REF

For more information on using Hyper-V, see "Using Virtualization" later in this lesson.

USING THE WEB SERVER (IIS) ROLE

Originally, Web servers were designed to respond to requests for Hypertext Markup Language (HTML) files generated by client browsers. These HTML files, when interpreted by the browser, display Web page content. Eventually, Web pages grew in complexity, incorporating images into their content, and then audio and video, and finally applications. Today, organizations use Web servers for a huge variety of applications, servicing clients on intranets, extranets, and the Internet.

While standalone applications certainly have their uses, many applications rely on the client/server model, particularly when many users have to access the same resources. For example, it would be possible to create a standalone database application that runs entirely on a single workstation and enables the user to access the company's customer list. However, to add a new customer, it would be necessary to update the database on each user's workstation, as shown in Figure 4-6, which would be highly impractical.

Figure 4-6

Running standalone applications with duplicate databases on every workstation is not a practical solution

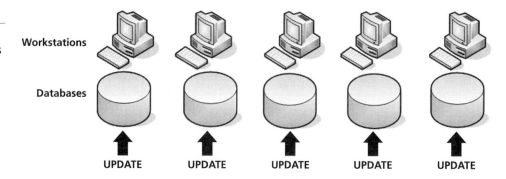

It makes far more sense to store a single copy of the customer list in a database on a central server and have each of the users run a client program that sends requests to the server, as shown in Figure 4-7. This way, administrators have to make modifications to only a single copy of the database, and all of the users can obtain the updated information immediately.

Figure 4-7

Running a single database application enables all of the workstations to retrieve updated information

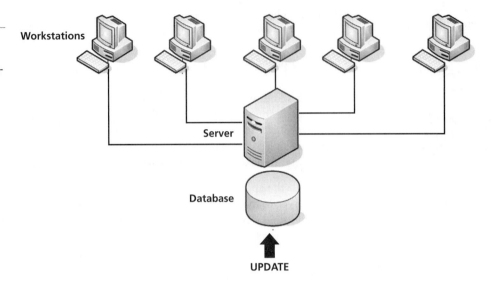

The question remains, however, of where a Web server fits into this client/server model. The simple answer is that Web servers and Web browsers eliminate the need for application developers to reinvent existing technologies. Web browsers are clients that send requests for information to Web servers, which respond by replying with the requested information. To implement the client/server database application described earlier from scratch, developers would have to create a client program that generates database requests and a server program that processes those requests, accesses the desired information in the database, and generates replies.

By using the existing Internet Information Services (IIS) Web server and Internet Explorer Web browser applications already included with the Windows operating systems, database application developers can concentrate on the back end server application, which manages the database itself. They do not have to create a client interface or a server to receive and interpret the client requests.

The client/server model implemented by IIS and Internet Explorer can support many types of applications other than databases. Custom-designed business applications can run on the same computer as the Web server, on a different server, or on the client workstation itself.

Therefore, the client/server model in this type of arrangement consists of three elements:

- An Internet Explorer client browser running on the workstation

- An IIS server running on a Windows Server 2008 computer

- An application that makes use of the services provided by the Web server and the client browser

The Web Server (IIS) role in Windows Server 2008 implements, as its core, Internet Information Services 7.0. IIS 7 provides the basic Web server functionality that enables you to publish a standard Web site on the Internet or on a private network. However, IIS 7 also includes a large number of optional role services that provide support for virtually any type of Web-based application deployment, as well as management, diagnostic, and security functions.

Unlike some of the other Windows Server 2008 roles, installing the Web Server (IIS) role is not an all-or-nothing proposition. The Add Roles Wizard enables you to select a combination of optional role services, as shown in Figure 4-8, while enforcing any dependencies that might exist between them. This enables you to install the capabilities that your applications require, without wasting server resources running a lot of unnecessary code.

Figure 4-8

Selecting role services for the Web Server (IIS) role

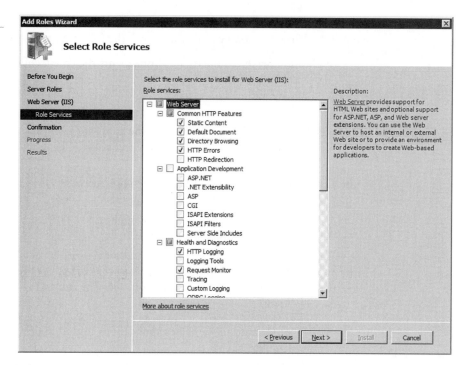

Microsoft designed the Web server role services to support a wide variety of application development environments and administration requirements. Unless you plan to run a large number of applications that require different development environments, you will not need all of the role services that Web Server (IIS) role provides. In fact, Microsoft includes some of the role services, particularly some of those in the Application Development category, primarily to support legacy applications. If your organization is creating new applications for the server deployment, then it makes sense to select a single development environment and install only the role services needed to support those applications.

USING THE UDDI SERVICES ROLE

Originally designed to be the basis for a worldwide directory of Internet sites and services, it is now more common for large organizations to use Universal Description, Discovery, and Integration (UDDI) as an internal catalog of their available Web services. Clients on the company intranet or a protected extranet can use a Web interface to access the catalog and search for the services the company's Web servers provide.

The UDDI Services role in Windows Server 2008 consists of the following role services:

- UDDI Services Database—Provides a central storage location for the UDDI catalog and the service's configuration settings

- UDDI Services Web Application—Implements a Web site with which users and applications can access the UDDI catalog to search for Web services on the network

USING THE APPLICATION SERVER ROLE

The Web Server (IIS) role provides a number of technologies that enable organizations to develop and deploy their own custom applications, using IIS to handle incoming requests from clients. The Application Server role is essentially a superset of the Web Server (IIS) role that enables IIS to host Web services developed using environments such as Windows Communication Foundation (WCF) and .NET Framework 3.0.

➕ MORE INFORMATION

Microsoft server applications, such as Exchange Server and SQL Server, do not require the Application Server role for their own functions. However, custom applications that make use of the services provided by Exchange and SQL Server might require the role.

Installing the Application Server role automatically installs .NET Framework 3.0, and the Add Roles Wizard enables you to select from the following role services:

- **Application Server Foundation**—Implements the core technologies needed to support .NET 3.0 applications, including WCF, Windows Presentation Foundation (WPF), and Windows Workflow Foundation (WWF). This is the only role service installed with the role by default.
- **Web Server (IIS) Support**—Enables the application server to host internal or external Web sites, as well as Web applications and services using technologies such as ASP.NET and WCF.
- **COM+ Network Access**—Enables the application server to host applications built with COM+ or Enterprise Services components.
- **TCP Port Sharing**—Enables multiple applications to share a single TCP port so that they can coexist on a single computer.
- **Windows Process Activation Service Support**—Enables the Application Server to invoke applications remotely over the network so that the applications can start and stop dynamically in response to incoming traffic. The individual traffic types WAS supports are as follows:

  - **HTTP Activation**—Enables applications to start and stop dynamically in response to incoming HTTP traffic
  - **Message Queuing Activation**—Enables applications to start and stop dynamically in response to incoming Message Queuing traffic
  - **TCP Activation**—Enables applications to start and stop dynamically in response to incoming TCP traffic
  - **Named Pipes Activation**—Enables applications to start and stop dynamically in response to incoming named pipes traffic

- **Distributed Transactions**—Implements services that help to ensure the successful completion of transactions involving multiple databases hosted by different computers. The individual services are as follows:

  - **Incoming Remote Transactions**—Provides support for transactions that applications on remote servers propagate
  - **Outgoing Remote Transactions**—Enables the server to propagate the transactions that it generates itself to remote servers
  - **WS-Atomic Transactions**—Provides support for applications that use two-phase commit transactions based on Simple Object Access Protocol (SOAP) exchanges

USING THE PRINT SERVICES ROLE

Sharing printers was one of the original applications that inspired the development of local area networks (LANs), and it is a common requirement on enterprise networks today. You can share a printer connected to a Windows Server 2008 computer without installing the Print Services role, but the role provides centralized tools that enable an administrator to monitor printer activities all over the network. The Print Services role includes the following optional role services:

- **Print Server**—Installs the Print Management snap-in for MMC, which provides centralized printer management for an entire enterprise network
- **LPD Service**—Enables UNIX client computers running the line printer remote (LPR) application to send jobs to Windows Server 2008 printers
- **Internet Printing**—Implements a Web-based printer management interface and enables remote users on the Internet to send print jobs to Windows Server 2008 printers

USING THE FAX SERVER ROLE

Sending and receiving faxes through the network can be an enormous convenience and Windows Server 2008 includes a Fax Server role that includes the Fax Service Manager application, which enables administrators to monitor fax devices, create fax rules and policies, and manage all of the faxes for the organization. The Fax Server role has no optional role services from which to choose. However, it does require the installation of the Print Services role.

USING THE STREAMING MEDIA SERVICES ROLE

The Streaming Media Services role enables an application server to provide digital audio and video content to network clients in real time, using HTTP or the Real Time Streaming Protocol (RTSP). The clients run a media player application that processes the content as they receive it from the server.

Unlike earlier versions of Windows Server, the Streaming Media Services role is not included with the operating system. You must download an update from the Microsoft Web site to add the role to the Server Manager application. When you install the role, you can choose from the following role services:

- Windows Media Server—Enables the application server to stream media to clients on the network

- Web-based Administration—Provides a Web-based interface for managing media server functions

- Logging Agent—Enables the media server to maintain logs of statistics received from clients

■ Deploying Applications

THE BOTTOM LINE
When you install application service roles on a Windows Server 2008 computer, you are creating an appropriate server environment for running applications, but you still have to install the applications themselves.

In a large enterprise network environment, administrators generally do not perform manual application installations on individual computers, even on servers. Depending on the nature of the applications you intend to deploy, the installation process can involve server components, workstation components, or both. The following sections examine some of the tools you can use to automate the application deployment process. With the exception of Group Policy, these tools are separate Microsoft products, not included with Windows Server 2008. In addition, there are third-party products you can use to perform the same tasks.

Deploying Applications Using Group Policy

Windows Server 2008 includes a basic Software Installation feature, incorporated into Group Policy, which you can use to automate application deployments to all or part of a network.

While not as elaborate or capable as solutions designed for large and complex enterprise deployments, such as Microsoft System Center Configuration Manager, the Software Installation policy is an easy-to-use and economical solution that can save you from having to perform individual application installations.

The process of deploying software using Group Policy consists of the following basic steps:

1. Create or obtain an installation package for the application you want to install. An installation package is a Windows Installer file with a .msi extension. Some applications include installation packages. For those that do not, you must create

your own using a third party utility. It is also possible to create transform files, with a .mst extension, which enable you to customize the installation process. The Microsoft Office Resource Kit, for example, includes a Custom Installation Wizard that you can use to create transform files.

2. Copy the application installation files to a network share. All of the computers that will install the application must have at least the Allow Read permissions to both the share and the NTFS drive hosting the installation files.

3. Create a group policy object (GPO) and add the application package to the Software Installation policy. You can create Software Installation policies for computers, users, or both.

4. Link the GPO to the domain, site, or organizational unit where you want to deploy the software.

Once you have completed this process, the target computers install the software package the next time they apply the GPO as a foreground process.

UNDERSTANDING THE LIMITATIONS

Although useful, Group Policy Software Installation is subject to some critical limitations. The foremost of these limitations is its inability to deploy software to computers running the Microsoft Windows Server operating systems. Only Windows Vista, Windows XP Professional, and Windows 2000 Workstation clients can process the Software Installation policy. Therefore, you can use Group Policy to deploy client applications only to workstations running these operating systems.

Group Policy software deployments also lack any type of scheduling and multicasting capabilities, which can potentially cause network traffic congestion problems. Because computers process Software Installation policies only during system startup or user logon, there are likely to be a lot of systems accessing the share containing the application files at the same time, generating a great deal of network traffic to the server hosting the share. Because no multicasts are possible, each client must also establish its own connection to the share. One way of addressing this problem is to replicate the installation share on multiple servers using the Distributed File System (DFS).

Finally, Group Policy Software Installation policies are relatively inflexible in that they apply by default to all of the users or computers in the domain, site, or organizational unit object to which the GPO is linked. However, you can work around this limitation by using permissions to limit the application of a GPO to specific security groups. Denying a group the Apply Group Policy permission, using the interface shown in Figure 4-9, prevents the application of all policy settings in the GPO.

TAKE NOTE

Windows computers process the Software Installation policy only when the computer first starts (in the case of Computer Configuration policies) or when the user logs on (in the case of User Configuration policies). They do not process the policy during background Group Policy refreshes.

X REF

For more information on using DFS replication, see "Configuring DFS Replication" in Lesson 5, "Planning File and Print Services."

Figure 4-9

Regulating policy application using permissions

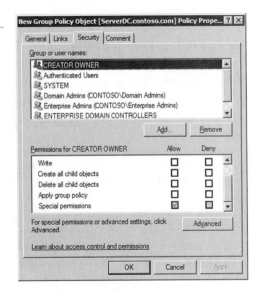

CREATING A SOFTWARE INSTALLATION GPO

Once you have your installation package ready on your installation share, you can proceed to create the group policy object that will contain the Software Installation policies. As a general rule, it is best to create separate GPOs for software deployments, rather than combining the Software Installation policies with other Group Policy settings.

To create Software Installation policies in a GPO, use the following procedure.

 CREATE A SOFTWARE INSTALLATION GPO

GET READY. Log on to Windows Server 2008 using an account with administrative privileges. When the logon process is completed, close the Initial Configuration Tasks window and any other windows that appear. If the computer is not a domain controller, make sure the Group Policy Management feature is installed.

1. Click **Start** > **Administrative Tools** > **Group Policy Managment.** The Group Policy Management console appears, as shown in Figure 4-10.

Figure 4-10

The Group Policy Management console

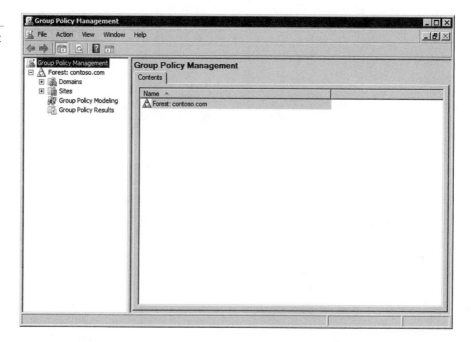

2. Expand the **Domains** container and the node representing your domain.
3. Right-click the **Group Policy Objects** container and, from the context menu, select **New.** A New GPO dialog box appears, as shown in Figure 4-11.

Figure 4-11

The New GPO dialog box

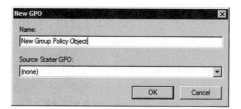

4. In the **Name** text box, key the name you want to assign to the GPO and click **OK.** The New GPO appears in the Group Policy Objects list.

5. Right-click the GPO you just created and, from the context menu, select **Edit.** The Group Policy Management Editor console appears, as shown in Figure 4-12.

Figure 4-12

The Group Policy Management Editor console

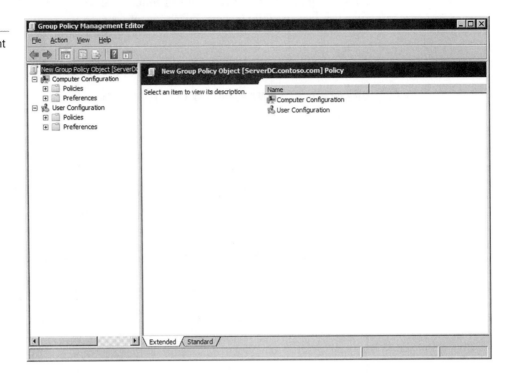

6. Browse to the Computer Configuration > Policies > Software Settings or User Configuration > Policies > Software Settings folder.
7. Right-click the **Software Installation** policy and, from the context menu, select **New > Package.** The **Open** combo box appears.
8. In the **File Name text** box, key the path to the location of your Windows Installer package, select the file, and click **Open.** The Deploy Software dialog box appears, as shown in Figure 4-13.

Figure 4-13

The Deploy Software dialog box

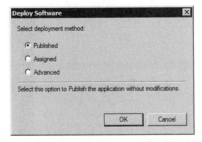

TAKE NOTE*

You must use the Universal Naming Convention (UNC) notation, as in \\server\share\folder, when keying the path to the network share on which you have placed the Windows Installer package and the application files. This is so that the client computers processing the GPO can access the share.

9. Select one of the following options and click **OK.**

  • Published—Provides the computers with access to the application so that users can install it through the Control Panel

- Assigned—Causes the client computer to automatically install the application the next time the computer starts or the user logs on
- Advanced—Opens a Properties sheet for the application, as shown in Figure 4-14, which enables administrators to configure advanced deployment options

Figure 4-14

The Deployment tab in the application's Properties sheet

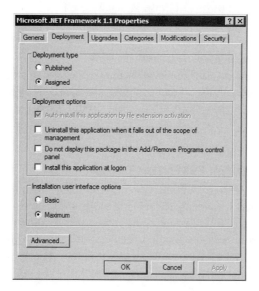

10. In the Group Policy Management console, right-click the domain, site, or organizational unit object where you want to deploy the software and, from the context menu, select **Link an existing GPO.** The Select GPO dialog box appears, as shown in Figure 4-15.

Figure 4-15

The Select GPO dialog box

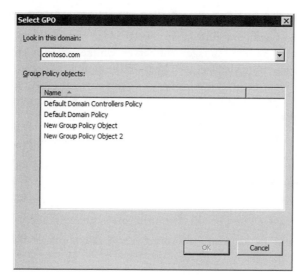

11. Select the GPO you just created and click **OK.**

CLOSE the Group Policy Management Editor and Group Policy Management consoles.

The computers and/or users in the domain, site, or organizational unit object you selected will process the GPO during the next system start or user logon.

Deploying Applications Using System Center Tools

For more extensive application deployment capabilities, you have to turn to network management products outside of Windows Server 2008. Microsoft's System Center products provide a range of network management features that includes application deployment capabilities that exceed those of Group Policy by itself.

Microsoft System Center Essentials 2007, designed for medium-sized organizations, and *Microsoft System Center Configuration Manager 2007,* designed for large enterprises, are both products that you can use to deploy applications, as well as perform a wide variety of other network management tasks. Both of these products rely on Windows Server Update Services 3.0 and use SQL Server databases to store information about the computers on the network.

USING SYSTEM CENTER ESSENTIALS 2007

Because System Center Essentials 2007 is intended for medium-sized organizations, it is limited to 30 servers and 500 clients. To manage a larger network, you must use a product like System Center Configuration Manager 2007. System Center Essentials requires an SQL Server database. If you have SQL Server already installed on the computer, System Center Essentials will use it to create its own database when you install the product. Otherwise, System Center Essentials installs SQL Server 2005 Express, the "light" version of SQL Server that Microsoft provides free of charge.

System Center Essentials provides a wizard-based software deployment tool that enables you to install a wider variety of software components than Group Policy, including applications with or without Windows Installer (.msi) packages, drivers, hotfixes, and operating system updates. The product also provides more granular control over the software deployment process, enabling you to select the individual groups that you want to receive the software.

USING SYSTEM CENTER CONFIGURATION MANAGER 2007

System Center Configuration Manager 2007 is the name now assigned to the product that used to be called System Management Server. Unlike System Center Essentials 2007, System Center Configuration Manager 2007 has no limitations to the number of servers and work-stations it can manage. However, because of this extended capability, it cannot use SQL Server 2005 Express; you must have a full version of SQL Server installed on the computer before you install the Configuration Manager application.

System Center Configuration Manager can perform a wide variety of network management tasks, including the following:

- Deploy operating systems
- Deploy applications
- Deploy updates and patches for operating systems and applications
- Create and maintain an inventory of network computers' hardware and software
- Meter software license usage
- Monitor client compliance to preset configuration parameters

Using Terminal Services

↓
THE BOTTOM LINE Terminal Services is the modern equivalent of mainframe computing, in which servers perform most of the processing and clients are relatively simple devices that provide the user interface.

As noted in the previous sections, deploying applications on a large number of computers can be a highly complicated undertaking. One way to simplify the process is to use Terminal Services to provide your client computers with access to the applications they need. With Terminal Services, client computers can connect to a server and run individual applications or an entire desktop environment. In this arrangement, the server does all of the application computing; the clients function only as terminals. Because the only application running on the client computer is a small communications program, this is also known as **thin client computing.**

CERTIFICATION READY?
Provision applications
4.1

Understanding the Terminal Services Architecture

At the highest level, Terminal Services works by running applications on a Windows Server 2008 server and enabling desktop computers to operate those applications from a remote location.

With Terminal Services, a client program running on the desktop computer establishes a connection to a terminal server, and the server creates a session for that client. The session can provide the client with a full-featured Windows desktop, a desktop containing one application, or (new to Windows Server 2008) a single application in its own window, appearing exactly as if the application was running on the client computer.

A single terminal server can support multiple clients. The number depends on the hardware resources in the server and the clients' application requirements. Thus, the server functions as the equivalent of a mainframe and the clients, as terminals.

To make the desktop or application appear on the client computer, the server transmits data and instructions that enable the client to render the graphical interface on its own display. In return, to manipulate the applications running on the server, the client program transmits the user's keystrokes and mouse movements. As a result, no application data passes between the client and the server; instead, only the client user input and the application output are transmitted in graphical form.

Terminal services is itself a client/server application, and all client/server applications, by definition, require three basic elements: a server program, a client program, and a protocol that enables the two programs to communicate. Windows Server 2008 Terminal Services implements these elements in the following three components:

- Terminal Server—A service that runs on a Windows Server 2008 computer, which enables multiple clients to connect to the server and run individual desktop or application sessions.
- **Remote Desktop Connection** client—In most cases, a program running on a desktop computer that establishes a connection to a terminal server using Remote Desktop Protocol (RDP) and displays a session window containing a desktop or application. Thin clients, which are terminals designed specifically to connect to terminal servers, are also available.
- **Remote Desktop Protocol (RDP)**—A networking protocol that enables communication between the terminal server and the client.

The following sections examine these components in more detail.

INTRODUCING TERMINAL SERVER

To configure a Windows Server 2008 computer to function as a terminal server, you install the Terminal Services role using the Add Roles Wizard in Server Manager, as shown in Figure 4-16. Like any server application, a terminal server listens for incoming client requests. In this case, client connection requests arrive over TCP port 3389, which is the well-known port number for the RDP protocol.

Figure 4-16

Installing Terminal Services using the Add Roles Wizard

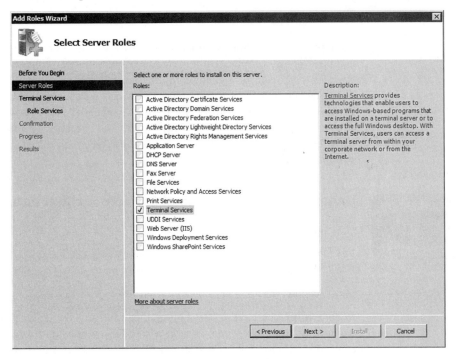

The Terminal Services role provides the computer with multi-session capability. A *session* is a collection of processes that form an individual user environment running on the server. When two or more Terminal Services clients connect to the terminal server, each client has its own session, complete with individual instances of the Win32 subsystem and other processes. This means that every Terminal Services client has an individual desktop, with its user profile settings that remain completely separated from those of other clients. Even when two clients are running the same application, the processes are completely separate.

USING SESSION IDs

To keep the client processes for individual sessions separate, the terminal server assigns each session a unique identifier called a *Session ID.* In Windows Server 2008, Session ID 0 is always dedicated to the system services running on the computer, which isolates them from applications for security reasons. The system then assigns Session IDs, starting with number 1, to each interactive user logging on to the computer from the local console or a remote system.

➕ MORE INFORMATION

This dedication of Session ID 0 to the system services, called *session 0 isolation,* is a new feature in Windows Server 2008 and Windows Vista. In Windows Server 2003, the system services and the local console user share Session ID 0, which allows applications to run in the same session as the system services. This is inherently dangerous because an application could take advantage of the elevated privileges assigned to the services. By isolating the services in their own session, Windows Server 2008 and Windows Vista protect those elevated privileges from unruly or malicious applications.

When the Terminal Services service starts, it always creates two new sessions with unique IDs before any users connect. These two sessions remain dormant until Terminal Services clients connect to the server. As the clients connect, the server creates additional dormant sessions, so it is always ready to accept new clients and connect them as quickly as possible.

Despite the separate sessions and processes, the clients connected to a terminal server still share a single computer's processor(s), memory, disk space, and operating system. Obviously, the server must allocate sufficient resources to each client session to keep them running smoothly. Each session has a high-priority thread for its server-to-client display output and its client-to-server keyboard/mouse input, to which the server allocates resources on a round-robin basis.

ALLOCATING RESOURCES FOR APPLICATIONS

Allocating resources to applications, however, can be a bit trickier. While each session has individual instances of certain processes, such as the Win32 subsystem, applications usually do not. For example, if several clients connect to a terminal server and run a word processing application, loading a complete and separate copy of the entire application for each client would consume an enormous amount of memory to no real benefit.

Most of the application files remain unchanged while users work with a word processor, so there is no reason to load multiple copies of these files into memory when the client sessions could just as easily share access to a single copy of each file. However, this is not a perfect solution either. What happens to the few files that do change? When one client modifies an application file, the modifications should logically affect all of the other clients running that application as well. They do not, though, because Windows Server 2008 uses a memory management technique called *copy-on-write data sharing.*

As the name implies, copy-on-write means that when a client attempts to write to a shared application file, the operating system creates a copy of that file, allocates it for the exclusive use of that client, and writes the changes to the copy. This minimizes the amount of memory utilized by each client and enables the applications to run normally.

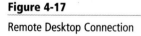

Not all applications are suitable for use on terminal servers. Some applications might not function properly with multiple clients sharing a single set of files. Some require a full copy of the application in each client session, while others might not function at all. An extensive testing period is imperative for all Terminal Services deployments.

INTRODUCING REMOTE DESKTOP CONNECTION (RDC)

Remote Desktop Connection (also known as the Terminal Services Client) is a Win32 application that enables a Windows computer to establish a connection to a terminal server, authenticate a user, and access an application or desktop session running on the server. The latest version of Remote Desktop Connection, version 6.1, as shown in Figure 4-17, is included with all versions of Windows Server 2008, Windows Vista Service Pack 1, and Windows XP Service Pack 3.

Figure 4-17

Remote Desktop Connection

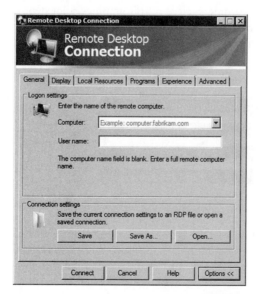

Basically, the RDC program sends the user's keystrokes and mouse movements to the terminal server, and receives information from the server to create the display. However, as noted earlier, many aspects of the Terminal Services model can complicate this relatively simple process.

One factor is the sheer amount of data required to create the display on the client. During an active Terminal Services session, the client display refreshes approximately 20 times per second. When the session is idle, the server reduces the refresh rate to 10 times per second. Depending on the client's configured display resolution, transmitting an entire screen of graphic information 10 or 20 times per second can add up to a tremendous amount of data. To avoid flooding the network with display data, RDC uses a technique called client-side caching.

In *client-side caching,* RDC stores screen elements that remain unchanged from one refresh to the next in a cache on the client system. This way, the terminal server transmits only new display elements to the client during each refresh. As the cache grows in size, the client deletes the oldest elements.

In addition to the standalone client, Terminal Services supports a Web-based client based on an ActiveX control that is now supplied with the Remote Desktop Connection program. In previous versions of Windows, users had to download the ActiveX control from an IIS Web site on the terminal server. This caused problems because many administrators prefer to configure client computers to block ActiveX downloads for security reasons. With RDC version 6.0 and later, clients do not have to download anything; they can access Web-equipped terminal servers using Internet Explorer at any time.

TAKE NOTE*

By default, Windows Server 2008 Terminal Services includes the downloadable ActiveX control for clients that are not running Remote Desktop Connection 6.0 or later. This includes all computers running Windows operating systems prior to Windows XP SP2, and Windows XP SP2 computers that don't have RDC 6.0 installed.

INTRODUCING REMOTE DESKTOP PROTOCOL (RDP)

After you have a server and a client, the only remaining component is the protocol that the two use to communicate. RDP, now in version 6.0, is based on the T.120 protocol standards published by the International Telecommunications Union (ITU). It provides multi-channel communication between Terminal Services clients and servers.

Multi-channel means that the protocol separates the traffic for the Terminal Services functions into logical divisions called channels, as shown in Figure 4-18. The keyboard, mouse, and display traffic occupies one channel, and the various additional features supported by Terminal Services use others. For example, a separate RDP channel carries audio output from the server to the client, enabling the client to play the audio through its local speakers. Traffic for local device mapping and features, such as 32-bit graphics color depth and clipboard mapping, also utilize separate channels. RDP can support up to 64,000 separate channels, although nowhere near that many are currently in use.

Figure 4-18

Multi-channel communications in the RDP

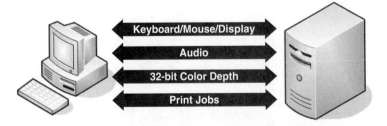

Keyboard/Mouse/Display
Audio
32-bit Color Depth
Print Jobs

The development of new RDP versions coincides with the development of the Terminal Services client and server components. To implement a new feature, all three of the components have to support it. As a result, version control is an important part of administering a

Terminal Services installation. When you install Terminal Services on a Windows Server 2008 computer, you can't take advantage of its new features unless you are running the RDC 6.0 client or later, both of which implement the RDP 6.0 protocol.

Planning a Terminal Services Deployment

Terminal Services represents a fundamental shift in PC networking philosophy. Some people think of it as a step backward, while others consider it to be a return to the good old mainframe days.

You can use Terminal Services in various ways on your network. You can solve specific problems with the technology or completely change the way your network operates. It is relatively simple matter to install Terminal Services on a server and configure it to provide clients with a simple application. However, implementing a fully functional production environment using Terminal Services can be much more complicated because it raises many additional issues, such as the following:

- Security—How secure are the individual client sessions? How secure is the server from the clients?

- Licensing—How does Terminal Services handle client licensing? Are application licenses necessary for individual sessions?

- Local resources—How can clients use locally attached printers, drives, and other devices while working in a Terminal Services session?

- Memory management—How does the terminal server keep multiple copies of the same application separated?

Configuring Terminal Services to be as secure as necessary and to provide clients with all the resources they need can require a lot of configuration and testing.

IDENTIFYING THE ADVANTAGES OF TERMINAL SERVICES

Deploying Terminal Services offers several advantages to the network administrator, including the following:

- Reduced client hardware requirements—Terminal Services client computers have to run only a single application: the RDC program. The hardware requirements for the client computer are therefore minimal. This enables administrators to purchase inexpensive computers for desktop users and avoid constant hardware upgrades to support the latest versions of desktop operating systems and applications.

- Simplified application deployment—Deploying applications on a large fleet of computers can be a long and difficult undertaking, even with distribution tools such as Group Policy and Microsoft Systems Management Services (SMS). Terminal Services enables administrators to deploy applications to as many clients as needed by installing them only on servers.

- Easy configuration and updates—Terminal Services eliminates the need to install, configure, and update applications on individual desktop computers. When an administrator configures or updates a single copy of an application on a terminal server, all of the clients reap the benefits.

- Low network bandwidth consumption—Terminal Services connections use relatively little network bandwidth because most of the data exchanged by the clients and servers consist of keystroke, mouse, and display instructions, instead of large application and data files. For remote users accessing terminal servers over the Internet, much less bandwidth is required than that required for a virtual private network (VPN) or direct dial-up connection.

- Support for thin clients—The availability of thin client devices enables administrators to install terminals in environments that are unsuitable for standard PCs. Dusty environments, such as warehouses, can clog a computer's air intakes. Public environments, such as airports and lobbies, invite computer misuse and theft. Sterile environments, such as clean rooms, can be contaminated by a computer's air circulation. Thin clients are more suitable for these, and many other, problematic locations.

- Conservation of licenses—Instead of purchasing application licenses for all individual workstations, which might not be in use at any given time, you can maintain a pool of licenses on the Terminal Services server, which the system allocates to users as they log on. For example, an office with 100 workstations would require 100 licenses for an application installed on each computer, even if more than 50 users never run the application at any one time. Using Terminal Services, 50 application licenses would be sufficient because only the users actually connected to the server need a license.

- Power savings—A network consisting of standard desktops and servers consumes substantially greater power than a typical Terminal Services installation, which can use client computers with slower processors and less memory. The use of thin clients can increase the savings even more.

- No client backups—In a typical Terminal Services installation, users access all of their applications and data files from servers. As a result, it is usually not necessary to back up the client computers, which yields savings in time and backup media.

- Remote control help and training—Terminal Services enables administrators to tap into a client session (with the client's permission) to observe the user's activity or to interact with the user in real time. Administrators can, therefore, demonstrate procedures to a user for help and training purposes without traveling to the user's location.

USING TERMINAL SERVICES IN VARIOUS SCENARIOS

Network administrators use the capabilities that Terminal Services provides in various ways. Some adopt Terminal Services wholeheartedly, as a complete client solution. Instead of installing and configuring applications on each desktop computer, they have users run an RDC client, connect to a terminal server, and access a remote desktop. When you configure Terminal Services properly, many users do not know that the applications are not running on the local computer.

Whether this is a practical solution for a particular network depends largely on the hardware in the computers involved. If you spent large amounts of money purchasing high-end desktop computers for your users, then it makes little sense to use that powerful hardware just to run the RDC program. However, if you are building a new network, or if your desktops are low-powered or outdated, Terminal Services can be a viable and economical alternative to purchasing new desktops or upgrading the old ones.

TAKE NOTE * Keep in mind that while Terminal Services might save money on desktop hardware, you might have to upgrade your servers (or purchase additional ones) to support the Terminal Services traffic, and you will certainly have to purchase Terminal Services client access licenses (TS CALs) for your users or devices.

X REF

For more information on RemoteApp, see "Virtualizing Applications" later in this lesson.

Even if it is not practical to adopt Terminal Services for your clients' entire desktops, you might use it for individual applications. You can use Terminal Services to deploy some of your applications, automatically deploy a desktop containing only a single application, or use Terminal Services RemoteApp role service to deploy applications directly to client windows without remoting the entire desktop.

Generally, however, you should deploy desktops with individual applications only when your users spend all or most of their time using just one Terminal Services application. You can, for example, have clients open individual Terminal Services sessions for each application they run, and from a user perspective, this might seem like a viable solution. However, from an administrative standpoint, it is highly wasteful of server resources because each session uses a separate copy of the Win32 subsystem. By comparison, a single Terminal Services session running multiple applications uses only one copy of the Win32 subsystem and therefore requires much less server memory.

RemoteApp applications handle memory differently, however. When a single user opens multiple RemoteApp applications, they all run within the same session. This is an advantage over full Remote Desktop sessions because multiple sessions load duplicate code and consume more memory and processor cycles.

In addition to using the RDC client, users can access Terminal Services sessions with a standard Web browser, such as Internet Explorer. The Terminal Services Web Access role service configures a terminal server to use Internet Information Services (IIS) to publish a Web page that provides access to remote desktop sessions or individual RemoteApp applications, as shown in Figure 4-19. When a user double-clicks an icon for a RemoteApp application on the Web page, the application launches in a separate window, just like the RDC client, not in the browser window.

Figure 4-19

A Terminal Services (TS) Web Access Web page

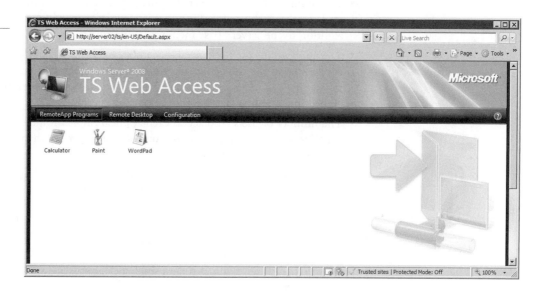

For relatively unsophisticated users, TS Web Access greatly simplifies the process of connecting to Terminal Services desktops and applications. Instead of instructing users how to connect to a particular terminal server and access applications using RDC, simply provide a URL in any of the usual ways, including shortcuts, favorites, hyperlinks, or an icon.

For administrators that don't want or need Terminal Services as an internal solution, it can also enable remote users to access applications and desktops. The new Terminal Services Gateway role service enables users on the Internet to connect to terminal servers, despite the existence of intervening firewalls and Network Address Translation (NAT) routers.

Deploying Terminal Services

Deploying Terminal Services can be a simple solution to a minor requirement or a fundamental shift in the way you deploy applications to your network users.

As mentioned earlier, you can deploy Terminal Services relatively simply at the high level, but configuring the details can become complicated. Many of these details are dependent on the number of clients you must support, the number and types of applications the clients will run, and the users' other needs.

Selecting Server Hardware

The basic philosophy of Terminal Services calls for client applications to run on servers instead of client desktops, which leads naturally to the need for more powerful servers and less powerful clients.

How much more powerful the servers need to be and how much less power is needed for the clients is a difficult question that is better answered through testing and experience than hard and fast rules.

The system requirements that Microsoft specifies for Windows Server 2008 are sufficient to run the Terminal Services role, but not enough to support more than one or perhaps two Terminal Services clients. When you run applications on a server instead of a client, you must shift the resources the applications require from the client to the server as well.

The selection of appropriate hardware for a terminal server should be based on the following factors:

- The number of users connected to the server at any one time—Before you consider the applications, each client session requires a minimum of 64 megabytes of memory in addition to the server's base memory requirements.
- The applications the users need—Memory loads for applications can vary greatly, depending on the size of the application and how the user runs it. Using a word processor to type a letter, for example, probably requires far less memory than spell-checking, embedding graphics, and performing a mail merge.
- The number of users who access each application—A number of clients running different (but equivalent) applications requires more memory than the same number of clients running the same application.
- Using RemoteApp vs. complete remote desktops—Deploying an entire desktop using Terminal Services requires more server resources than deploying an individual application using RemoteApp.

Most major applications can support multiple users on a terminal server without loading a complete copy of the application for each user. This means that such an application will require more hardware resources than a single desktop user installation needs, but less than the total needed for the desktop installations of all your users combined.

As for any computer, selecting hardware for a terminal server is a matter of achieving a balance of performance across all of the major components to avoid any component creating a performance bottleneck.

Installing Terminal Services

After your hardware is in place, the first step in deploying a terminal server is installing the Terminal Services role.

You must install the Terminal Services role before you install the applications that you plan to deploy on the terminal server. If you install the applications first, they might not function properly in the multi-user terminal server environment.

When you install the Terminal Services role using Server Manager, the Add Roles Wizard enables you to select from the following role services.

TAKE NOTE*

If you do have applications installed before you add the Terminal Services role, you should uninstall and reinstall them after the role is in place.

- Terminal Server—Provides the core Terminal Services functionality that enables users running the RDC client to run full desktop sessions. This role service also includes the RemoteApp feature, which enables clients to run individual applications in separate windows.

- TS Licensing—Configures the computer to function as a Terminal Services Licensing Server, which enables it to allocate client access licenses (CALs) to clients. You must have a Licensing Server on your network to use Terminal Services. You can install TS Licensing on the same computer as the other role services or another computer.
- TS Session Broker—Balances the client load among multiple terminal servers and saves session state information so that clients can reconnect to the same session from which they disconnected.
- TS Gateway—Enables RDC clients on the Internet to connect to a terminal server through a firewall or NAT router by tunneling RDP traffic within Secure Hypertext Transfer Protocol (HTTPS) packets.
- TS Web Access—Creates an IIS Web site that enables users to access Terminal Services desktops and RemoteApp applications without running the RDC client.

Selecting from the available Terminal Services role services causes the Add Roles Wizard to prompt you to install dependent roles and features, generate additional wizard pages, install system services, and add snap-ins for the Microsoft Management console.

INSTALLING APPLICATIONS

After you have installed the Terminal Services role, you can install the applications that the terminal server will deploy to your clients. Install the applications in the usual manner, typically by using the application's setup program.

 TAKE NOTE

> Install applications that are designed to work together on the same terminal server. For example, install the entire Microsoft Office suite on one terminal server; do not install Microsoft Word on one server and Microsoft Excel on another.

Terminal Services has two operational modes: Execution and Install. By default, the Add Roles Wizard leaves newly installed terminal servers in Execution mode. Before you begin to install applications, you must switch the server to Install mode, using the following procedure.

⊙ INSTALL AN APPLICATION

GET READY. Log on to Windows Server 2008 using a domain account with Administrator privileges. When the logon process is completed, close the Initial Configuration Tasks window and any other windows that appear.

1. Click **Start**, and then click **All Programs** > **Accessories** > **Command Prompt**. A Command Prompt window appears.
2. In the command prompt window, key **change user /install** and press **Enter.** A *User session is ready to install applications* message appears.
3. Install your application using the setup program supplied by the manufacturer.
4. In the command prompt window, key **change user /execute** and press **Enter.** A *User session is ready to execute applications* message appears.

CLOSE the Command Prompt window.

If your application is packaged as a Microsoft Installer (msi) file, you do not have to change Terminal Services to Install mode before installing it.

UNDERSTANDING TERMINAL SERVICES LICENSING

Windows Server 2008 includes a limited form of Terminal Services that you can use for remote administration, whether you install the Terminal Services role or not. This feature enables up to two users to connect to the server, using the Remote Desktop Connection client, with no licenses or restrictions. To use the Terminal Services role for multiple user connections, you must purchase the appropriate number of **Terminal Services client access licenses (TS CALs)** and install a **TS Licensing server** to deploy them. A client access license (CAL) is a document that grants a single client access to a specific software program, in this case, a Terminal Services server.

Clients connecting to a Windows Server 2008 terminal server must have Terminal Services client access licenses, in addition to any licenses needed for their operating system and applications. Terminal Services provides a 120-day grace period, during which licenses are not necessary, but after that period, clients must have a license to access a Terminal Services server.

When a client without a TS CAL attempts to connect, the terminal server directs it to the TS Licensing server, which issues a permanent license. If a TS Licensing server is not available or if the TS Licensing server does not have available TS CALs, the connection attempt fails.

Like Windows Server 2008 itself, Terminal Services supports two types of licensing:

- Per Device—Permits one client device, such as a computer, terminal, or handheld, to connect to the terminal server, no matter who is using it
- Per User—Permits one user to connect to the terminal server, no matter what device the user is running

When you install the Terminal Server role service, the Add Roles Wizard displays a *Specify Licensing Mode* page, as shown in Figure 4-20. On this page, you specify whether you want to have your clients retrieve Per Device or Per User licenses from your License Server. You can also choose to configure the licensing mode later.

Figure 4-20

The Specify Licensing Mode page in the Add Roles Wizard

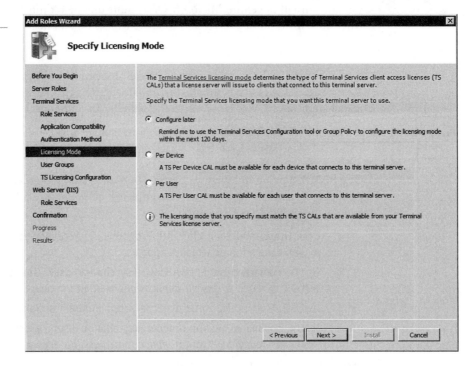

A Terminal Services deployment needs only one TS Licensing server for the entire installation regardless of the number of terminal servers on your network. The process of installing a TS Licensing server and preparing it for use consists of the following basic steps:

1. Install the TS Licensing role service.
2. Activate the TS Licensing server.
3. Install the TS CALs on the TS Licensing server.
4. Configure the licensing settings on the terminal servers.

The resource requirements for the TS Licensing role service are minimal. TS Licensing does not check whether a client possesses a license; the Terminal Services service performs that task. The TS Licensing service requires only about 10 megabytes of memory and the license database requires 1 megabyte of storage space for every 1,200 licenses. The processor requirements are negligible because the service issues a license to each client only once.

> **✚ MORE INFORMATION**
>
> The TS Licensing role service included with Windows Server 2008 can provide licensing services for terminal servers running on Windows Server 2003 and Windows 2000 Server computers. However, a downlevel server cannot provide licensing services for Windows Server 2008 terminal servers. If you are running a Windows Server 2008 terminal server, you must install a Windows Server 2008 TS Licensing server.

For a small Terminal Services deployment, you can run the TS Licensing role service on the same computer as the other Terminal Services role services. A terminal server can always locate a TS Licensing server running on the same computer. For larger deployments with multiple terminal servers, you can install TS Licensing on one of the terminal servers or any other server.

■ Using Virtualization

 THE BOTTOM LINE
Virtualization enables administrators to deploy server roles on separate virtual machines that run on a single computer. This enables each role to operate within its own protected environment.

Earlier in this lesson, you learned how you can distribute roles among your Windows Server 2008 computers, combining roles as needed to take full advantage of the computers' hardware resources. However, running multiple roles on a single computer can lead to problems, such as the following:

- Security—The more roles a server performs, the greater the number of ports you have to leave open. This increases the attack surface of the computer, making it more vulnerable to unauthorized intrusion.

- Updates—Running multiple roles requires you to apply more updates, resulting in a greater potential for software conflicts that can affect the system's performance.

- Peak usage—Different roles have different usage cycles, and the more roles a computer performs, the more complex the convergence of those cycles becomes. A system might have sufficient resources to support multiple roles when they are at rest or one role is running at its peak, but can the system support several roles operating at their peaks simultaneously?

Virtualization is a potential solution to these problems that is becoming increasingly popular in the enterprise networking world. Available for some time in the form of separate applications such as Microsoft Virtual Server and Virtual PC, Windows Server 2008 is the first Windows version to include support for virtualization at the operating system level, using a new feature called Hyper-V.

Virtualization is the process of deploying and maintaining multiple instances of an operating system, called *virtual machines (VMs)*, on a single computer. Each virtual machine contains a completely separate copy of the operating system with its own virtual hardware resources, device drivers, and applications. To the network, each virtual machine looks like a separate computer with its own name and IP address. As a result, you are not combining the security risks of multiple roles in a single operating system instance. You also update each instance of the operating system separately.

Using virtual machines also makes it easier to manage the distribution of your roles among your physical servers. On a virtualized computer, the hardware resources allocated to each virtual machine are abstracted from the actual physical resources in the computer. This means that you can copy a virtual machine from one computer to another, and it will run without modification, even if the two computers have different physical hardware. Therefore, if you have three roles installed on a single computer in three separate virtual machines, you can simply move one virtual machine to another computer if their combined usage levels begin to overwhelm the hardware.

Understanding Virtualization Architectures

> Virtualization products can use several different architectures that enable them to share a computer's hardware resources among several virtual machines.

Virtualization products, including Microsoft Virtual PC and Virtual Server, have been available for several years. With these products, you first install a standard operating system on a computer. This becomes the "host" operating system. Then, you install the virtualization product, which adds a component called a ***virtual machine manager (VMM).*** The VMM essentially runs alongside the host OS, as shown in Figure 4-21, and enables you to create as many virtual machines as you have hardware to support.

Figure 4-21

A hybrid VMM sharing hardware access with a host OS

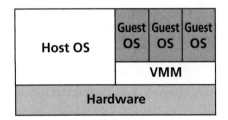

With the VMM, you create a virtual hardware environment for each virtual machine. You can specify how much memory to allocate to each VM, create virtual disk drives using space on the computer's physical drives, and provide access to peripheral devices. You then install a "guest" OS on each virtual machine, just as if you were deploying a new computer.

This type of arrangement is called ***hybrid virtualization.*** The host OS essentially shares access to the computer's processor with the VMM, with each taking the clock cycles it needs and passing control of the processor back to the other. Hybrid virtualization is an improvement over an earlier technology called *Type 2 virtualization,* which virtualized individual guest applications, not entire operating system installations.

While hybrid virtualization provides adequate virtual machine performance, particularly in educational and testing environments, it does not provide the same performance as separate physical computers. Therefore, it is not generally recommended for high-traffic servers in production environments.

The virtualization capability built into Windows Server 2008, called ***Hyper-V,*** uses a different type of architecture. Hyper-V uses *Type 1 virtualization,* in which the VMM is called a ***hypervisor,*** an abstraction layer that interacts directly with the computer's physical hardware. The hypervisor creates individual environments called *partitions,* each of which has its own operating system installed, and accesses the computer's hardware via the hypervisor. Unlike hybrid virtualization, no host OS shares processor time with the VMM. Instead, the hypervisor designates the first partition it creates as the parent partition, and all subsequent partitions as child partitions, as shown in Figure 4-22.

Figure 4-22

A Type 1 VMM, with the hypervisor providing all hardware access

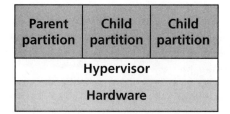

The parent partition accesses the system hardware through the hypervisor, just as the child partitions do. The only difference is that the parent runs the virtualization stack, which creates and manages the child partitions. The parent partition is also responsible for the subsystems that directly affect the performance of the computer's physical hardware, such as Plug and Play, power management, and error handling. These subsystems run in the operating systems on the child partitions as well, but they address only virtual hardware, while the parent, or root, partition handles the real thing.

There are two different forms of Type 1, or hypervisor, virtualization. One form uses a *monolithic hypervisor*, which has the device drivers for the physical hardware installed in the hypervisor layer. The primary disadvantage of this model is that any driver problems affect all of the partitions on the computer. The other form of Type 1 virtualization uses a *microkernelized hypervisor*, in which each individual partition has its own device drivers. This way, a problem driver affects only the partition in which it is running.

Introducing Hyper-V

While Microsoft has designed Hyper-V to be a role included with the Windows Server 2008 operating system, Hyper-V was not included in the initial Windows Server 2008 release. Instead, Microsoft provides it as a separate download that adds the Hyper-V role to the operating system.

TAKE NOTE *

Hyper-V is available as a free download for use with the 64-bit version of Windows Server 2008.

Hyper-V is a Windows Server 2008 role like any other, which you can install using the Server Manager console once you have applied the appropriate update package. However, Hyper-V has hardware and licensing requirements that go beyond those for the Windows Server 2008 operating system. In practice, the technology will largely be limited to enterprise deployments that are willing to make a substantial hardware investment in virtualization technology.

Hyper-V is included in the Windows Server 2008 Standard, Enterprise, and Datacenter products, but only in the 64-bit versions, for computers with x64 processors. There will be no Hyper-V support for computers with 32-bit x86 processors. In addition, the hypervisor requires a processor with hardware support for virtualization, which limits the use of Hyper-V to computers with processors that have a virtualization extension, as well as chipset and BIOS support for virtualization. Intel has named their virtualization extension VT, while AMD calls theirs AMD-V.

In addition to the specialized hardware requirements for Hyper-V, Microsoft has added a licensing requirement. For licensing purposes, Microsoft refers to each virtual machine that you create on a Hyper-V server as a ***virtual instance***. Each Windows Server 2008 version includes a set number of virtual instances; you must purchase licenses to create additional ones. Table 4-1 lists the Windows Server 2008 versions, and the number of virtual instances included with each one.

Table 4-1

Windows Server 2008 Versions and Their Hyper-V Support

OPERATING SYSTEM VERSION	NUMBER OF VIRTUAL INSTANCES INCLUDED
Windows Server 2008 Standard	1
Windows Server 2008 Enterprise	4
Windows Server 2008 Datacenter	Unlimited

After you have the appropriate hardware and the required licenses, you can add the Hyper-V role using Server Manager. Microsoft recommends that you do not install other roles with Hyper-V. Adding the role installs the hypervisor software, as well as the management interface, which takes the form of a Microsoft Management Console (MMC) snap-in called Hyper-V Manager, as shown in Figure 4-23. The Hyper-V Manager MMC snap-in provides administrators with a list of all the virtual machines registered on a Windows Server 2008 system and enables administrators to perform actions on both the Hyper-V server and the virtual machines.

Figure 4-23

The Hyper-V Manager console

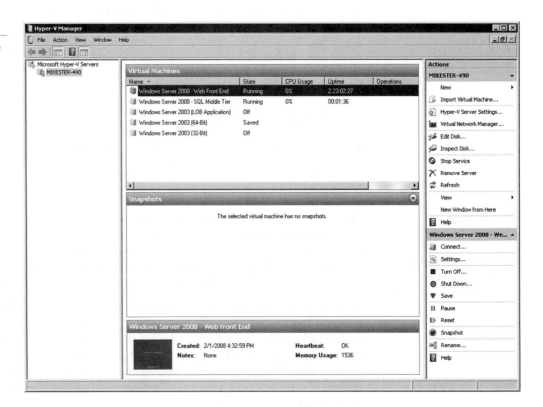

Using Hyper-V Manager, you can create new virtual machines and define the hardware resources that the system should allocate to them, as shown in Figure 4-24. In the settings for a particular virtual machine, depending on the physical hardware available in the computer and the limitations of the guest operating system, administrators can specify the number of processors and the amount of memory a virtual machine should use, install virtual network adapters, and create virtual disks using a variety of technologies, including storage area networks (SANs).

Figure 4-24

The Settings configuration interface for a Hyper-V virtual machine

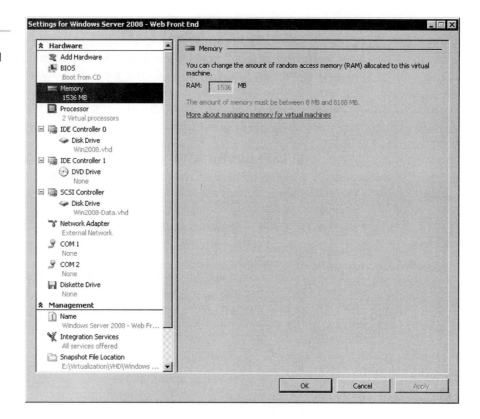

Each virtual machine on a Hyper-V server can run a different operating system, if necessary. Hyper-V supports both 32-bit and 64-bit Windows versions as guest OSes, as well as Linux distributions.

> **TAKE NOTE***
>
> In addition to the Hyper-V Manager console included with the role, you can also manage virtual machines using the Microsoft System Center Virtual Machine Manager product. System Center VMM provides extra features for the administration of Hyper-V virtual machines, including central management and monitoring, and physical-to-virtual machine conversions.

Virtualizing Applications

> Hyper-V and Virtual Server both virtualize entire operating systems, but it is also possible to virtualize individual applications.

When you virtualize an operating system, you create a separate partitioned space with virtual resources that appear just like physical ones to users and applications. You can run as many applications as you need on a single virtual machine, depending on the resources available to it. Virtualizing an application is roughly the same thing, except that you are allocating a set of virtual resources to a single application.

The RemoteApp capability built into Windows Server 2008 Terminal Services is a form of application virtualization. **RemoteApp** is a new Terminal Services feature that enables clients to run terminal server applications within individual windows. The windows are resizable; they have standard system menu and title bar buttons, and they are not constrained by a Terminal Services desktop. In fact, a RemoteApp window is, in most cases, indistinguishable from a window containing a local application.

When a Terminal Services client accesses a RemoteApp application, the terminal server provides a separate operating environment for the application, just as when the client accesses an entire desktop. If the client computer experiences a problem, the application continues to run, because it has its own memory and other hardware resources. The same is true if one of the other Terminal Services sessions on the server experiences a problem. Because the sessions use separate environments, one can fail without affecting the others.

TAKE NOTE*

When two different client computers launch RemoteApp applications using the same terminal server, the server creates two separate sessions, each with its own virtualized environment. However, when a single client computer launches two RemoteApp applications on the same terminal server, the server uses one session for both applications. Therefore, it is possible for a fault in one application to affect the performance of the other.

With RemoteApp, as with any Terminal Services session, the application runs using the terminal server's hardware resources, so the virtualization is actually occurring on the server, not the client. However, it is possible to virtualize applications in such a way that they run on the client, not the server. To do this, you can use a product called ***Microsoft SoftGrid Application Virtualization.***

Microsoft SoftGrid Application Virtualization creates a customized virtualized environment for an application that you can deploy to clients from a server, much as you do RemoteApp applications, using terminal servers. The main difference between the two is that the server actually transfers the virtual environment to the client, enabling the client to run the application using its own hardware, without the need to perform an application installation.

SUMMARY SKILL MATRIX

IN THIS LESSON YOU LEARNED:

- Applications in the enterprise can take several forms, including client-run applications, client/server applications, and distributed applications.

- The number of roles a server can perform depends on the computer's hardware configuration, the hardware requirements of the role, and the size and scope of the enterprise.

- Distributing server roles among several computers has several distinct advantages, including fault tolerance, ease of resource allocation, high availability, server scalability, security configuration, dispersed network traffic, and simpler update management.

- Terminal Services works by running applications on a Windows Server 2008 server and enabling desktop computers to operate those applications from a remote location.

- To make the desktop or application appear on the client computer, the server transmits data and instructions that enable the client to render the graphical interface on its display. In return, to manipulate the applications running on the server, the client program transmits the user's keystrokes and mouse movements.

- Terminal Services implements the server, client, and protocol elements with the following three components: Terminal Server, the Remote Desktop Connection client, and the Remote Desktop Protocol (RDP).

- Clients connecting to a Windows Server 2008 terminal server must have client access licenses, in addition to any licenses needed for their operating system and applications. Terminal Services provides a 120-day grace period, during which licenses are not necessary.

- RemoteApp is a new Terminal Services feature that enables clients to run terminal server applications within individual windows. The windows are resizable; they have standard taskbar buttons, and they are not constrained by a Terminal Services desktop.

- A virtual server is a complete installation of an operating system that runs in a software environment emulating a physical computer. Applications such as Microsoft Virtual Server 2005 and the Windows Server virtualization technology in Windows Server 2008 make it possible for a single computer to host multiple virtual machines, each of which runs in a completely independent environment.

- Hyper-V is a new server role that provides hypervisor-based virtualization on 64-bit Windows Server 2008 computers. This enables the administrator to create multiple virtual machines on a single physical computer, each of which runs a separate operating system.

- You can virtualize individual applications, as well as operating systems, by using Terminal Services RemoteApp or Microsoft SoftGrid Application Virtualization.

■ Knowledge Assessment

Matching

Complete the following exercise by matching the terms with their corresponding definitions.

    a. client that provides users with access to terminal servers
    b. Windows Server 2008's virtualization role
    c. reduces the network bandwidth requirements of Terminal Services
    d. runs alongside the host operating system
    e. enables one copy of an application to service multiple clients
    f. a collection of processes that form an individual user environment running on a terminal server
    g. transmits keystrokes, mouse movements, and display data
    h. client applications running on servers
    i. virtual machine manager in Type I virtualization
    j. launches Terminal Services programs without a remote desktop

_____ **1.** client-side caching

_____ **2.** copy-on-write data sharing

_____ **3.** Hyper-V

_____ **4.** hypervisor

_____ **5.** Remote Desktop Connection

_____ **6.** Remote Desktop Protocol (RDP)

_____ **7.** RemoteApp

_____ **8.** session

_____ **9.** thin client computing

_____ **10.** virtual machine manager (VMM)

Multiple Choice

Select one or more correct answers for each of the following questions.

1. How many days can clients access a Terminal Services server before a client access license is required?
   - **a.** 14 days
   - **b.** 30 days
   - **c.** 90 days
   - **d.** 120 days

2. Session 0 on a Windows Server 2008 terminal server is always devoted to which of the following?
   - **a.** the local console user
   - **b.** the system services running on the computer
   - **c.** the first terminal services client to connect to the server
   - **d.** the first user to log on locally

3. Which of the following features is designed to conserve memory on a terminal server?
   - **a.** thin client computing
   - **b.** copy-on-write data sharing
   - **c.** client-side caching
   - **d.** Execution mode

4. Which of the following does the Remote Desktop Protocol *not* carry between a terminal server and a client?
   - **a.** keystrokes
   - **b.** mouse movements
   - **c.** display information
   - **d.** application data

5. The Remote Desktop Protocol is based on which of the following?
   - **a.** ITU T.120
   - **b.** CredSSP
   - **c.** Win32
   - **d.** HTTPS

6. A client running four RemoteApp applications on the desktop is utilizing how many sessions on the terminal server?
   - **a.** none
   - **b.** one
   - **c.** four
   - **d.** five

7. Windows Server 2008 requires that you install which of the following features for the Application Server role.
   - **a.** .NET Framework 3.0 feature
   - **b.** Network Load Balancing (NLB)
   - **c.** Windows System Resource Manager (WSRM)
   - **d.** Windows Process Activation Service (WPAS)

8. Which of the following is a true statement about limitations Microsoft places on the number of roles a Windows Server 2008 computer can support?
   - **a.** There are no limitations placed on the number of roles a Windows Server 2008 computer can perform.
   - **b.** The number of roles that a Windows Server 2008 computer can run is limited only to the amount of hardware resources available to the server.
   - **c.** A Windows Server 2008 computer can perform only one role.
   - **d.** None of the above.

9. Which of the following types of virtualization provides the best performance for high-traffic servers in production environments?
   - **a.** Type I virtualization
   - **b.** Type II virtualization
   - **c.** Hybrid virtualization
   - **d.** VMM virtualization

10. Which of the following Windows Server 2008 products *cannot* run Hyper-V?
    - **a.** Web Server 64-bit
    - **b.** Standard 32-bit
    - **c.** Enterprise 32-bit
    - **d.** Datacenter 64-bit

Review Questions

1. List five possible advantages to using Terminal Services to deploy applications to clients, rather than running them on individual desktops.

2. Explain the difference between the virtualization used in products such as Microsoft Virtual Server and that used in Windows Server 2008's Hyper-V.

■ Case Scenarios

Scenario 4-1: Deploying Terminal Services

Several months ago, Kathleen installed the Terminal Services role on one of her Windows Server 2008 servers and has been using it to provide clients with access to a custom-designed credit reporting application. This morning, she began receiving calls from users complaining that they could no longer access their Terminal Services desktops. What is the most likely cause of the problem, and what must Kathleen do to resolve it?

Scenario 4-2: Hosting Applications with Terminal Services

Your company is planning to open a second office in another city, and you are part of the team that is designing the new network. The employees in the new office will be performing a wide variety of tasks, and they need a large number of applications installed on their computers. Ralph, your IT director, is having trouble meeting his budget for the new network, due to the high cost of the applications, processor, memory, and disk space resources the workstations will need to run the applications. He is also concerned about supporting and maintaining the workstations because there will be no full-time IT personnel at the new site.

You suggest using Terminal Services to host the applications. Ralph, however, knows nothing about Terminal Services. Explain how using Terminal Services can resolve all of the network design problems Ralph is experiencing.

LESSON | # Planning File and Print Services

OBJECTIVE DOMAIN MATRIX

TECHNOLOGY SKILL	OBJECTIVE DOMAIN	OBJECTIVE DOMAIN NUMBER
Deploying File Servers	Plan file and print server roles	1.5

KEY TERMS

Distributed File System (DFS)
File Server Resource Manager
  (FSRM)
full mesh topology
hard quota
hub/spoke topology

namespace
printer
printer control language (PCL)
printer driver
print device
print server

Remote Differential
  Compression (RDC)
replication group
soft quota
spooler
target

The most common types of application servers found on most enterprise networks are those that provide users with file and print services. This lesson examines the application services that enable servers to share files, printers, and fax devices with users all over the network. This lesson examines:

- How to deploy and configure file servers
- How to implement the Distributed File System
- How to deploy and configure print and fax servers

■ Deploying File Servers

THE BOTTOM LINE

In its most basic form, configuring a Windows Server 2008 computer to function as a file server is the simplest role to implement. All you have to do is share a folder or a drive and, technically, you have a file server.

On an enterprise network, however, things are almost never that simple. File sharing on a large network can be subject to any or all of the following problems:

- Scalability—How much storage space do the users need now, and how much more will they need next year?
- Navigation—On a large network with many shares, how should users find the files they need?
- Protection—How do you control access to network file shares?
- Abuse—How do you prevent users from consuming excessive server storage space?

The File Services role and the other storage-related features included with Windows Server 2008 provide tools that enable system administrators to address problems like these on a scale appropriate to a large enterprise network. However, before you implement the role or use these tools, you should think about your users' needs and how these tools affect user file storage and sharing practices. Implementation of technologies such as Distributed File System and storage quotas requires some idea of how to use the technologies on your enterprise network. Therefore, a period of planning and design is recommended before you start the implementation.

Designing a File-Sharing Strategy

> Decide where users should store their files and who should be permitted to access them.

X REF

One of the most important factors to consider when planning file server roles is what hardware to use in your servers, particularly the storage hardware. For more information on this subject, see Lesson 6, "Planning Storage Solutions."

Why should the administrators of an enterprise network want users to store their files on shared server drives, rather than their local workstation drives? Some of the many answers to this question are as follows:

- To enable users to collaborate on projects by sharing files
- To back up document files more easily
- To protect company information by controlling access to documents
- To reduce the number of shares needed on the network
- To prevent the need to share access to workstations
- To monitor users' storage habits and regulate their disk space consumption
- To insulate users from the sharing and permission assignment processes

If not for these issues, file sharing would simply be a matter of sharing each user's workstation drive and granting everyone full access to it. Because of these issues, however, this practice would lead to chaos, in the form of lost files, corrupted workstations, and endless help calls from confused users.

Server-based file shares can provide users with a simplified data storage solution that they can use to store their files, share files with other users, and easily locate the files shared by their colleagues. Behind the scenes, and unbeknown to the users, administrators can use server-based storage tools to protect everyone's files, regulate access to sensitive data, and prevent users from abusing their storage privileges.

ARRANGING SHARES

One of the most important steps in designing a file-sharing strategy is to decide how many shares to create and where to create them. Simply installing a big hard drive in a server and giving everyone access to it would be as chaotic as sharing everyone's workstation drives. Depending on the size of your organization, you might have one single file server, or many servers scattered around the network.

For many large organizations, departmental or workgroup file servers are a viable solution. Each user has his or her "local" server, the directory layout of which becomes familiar over time. If you have separate file servers for the various departments or workgroups in your organization, it is a good idea to develop a consistent directory structure and duplicate it on all of the servers so that if users have to access a server in another department, they can find their way around.

Generally speaking, a well-designed sharing strategy provides each user with three resources:

- A private storage space, such as a home folder, to which the user has exclusive access
- A public storage space, where each user can store files that they want colleagues to be able to access
- Access to a shared work space for communal and collaborative documents

One way to implement this strategy would be to create one share called Home, with a private folder for each user on it, and a second share called Public, again with a folder for each user. Depending on your network's hardware configuration, you could create both of these shares on a separate server for each department or workgroup, split the shares and folders among multiple servers in each department, or even create one big file server for the entire company, containing all of the shares.

TAKE NOTE*

Even if you split the Home and Public shares among multiple servers, you can still make them appear as a single unified directory tree using the Windows Server 2008 Distributed File System (DFS). See "Using the Distributed File System" later in this lesson for more information.

CONTROLLING ACCESS

On most enterprise networks, the principle of "least privileges" should apply. This principle states that users should have only the privileges they need to perform their required tasks, and no more.

A user's private storage space should be exactly that, private and inaccessible, if not invisible, to other users. This is a place in which each user can store his or her private files, without exposing them to other users. Each user should, therefore, have full privileges to his or her private storage, with the ability to create, delete, read, write, and modify files. Other users should have no privileges to that space at all.

TAKE NOTE*

The easiest way to create private folders with the appropriate permissions for each user is to create a home folder through each Active Directory user object.

Each user should also have full privileges to his or her public folder. This is a space where users can share files informally. For example, when Ralph asks Alice for a copy of her budget spreadsheet, Alice can simply copy the file from her private folder to her public folder. Then, Ralph can copy the file from Alice's public folder to his own private folder, and access it from there. Therefore, public and private folders differ in that other users should be able to list the contents of all public folders and read the files stored there, but not be able to modify or delete files in any folder but their own. Users should also be able to navigate throughout the Public folder tree so that they can read any user's files and copy them to their own folders.

TAKE NOTE*

Although users should have full privileges to their personal folders, you should not leave their storage practices unmonitored or unregulated. Later in this lesson, you will learn how to set quotas limiting users' storage space, prohibit users from storing certain types of files on network servers, and generate reports detailing users' storage habits.

In a shared workspace for collaborative documents, users should have privileges based on their individual needs. Some users need read access only to certain files, while others might have to modify them as well. You might also want to limit the ability to create and delete files to managers or supervisors.

Administrators, of course, must have the privileges required to exercise full control over all users' private and public storage spaces, as well as the ability to modify permissions as needed. Administrators typically use NTFS permissions to assign these privileges on a Windows Server 2008 file server. There is no compelling reason to use the FAT (File Allocation Table) file system in Windows Server 2008. NTFS provides not only the most granular user access control but also other advanced storage features, including file encryption and compression.

To simplify the administration process, you should always assign permissions to security groups and not to individuals. Assigning permissions to groups enables you to add new users or move them to other job assignments without modifying the permissions themselves. On a large Active Directory network, you might also consider the standard practice of assigning the NTFS permissions to a domain local group, placing the user objects to receive the permissions in a global (or universal) group, and making the global group a member of a domain local group.

Except in special cases, it is usually not necessary to explicitly deny NTFS permissions to users or groups. Some administrators prefer to use this capability, however. When various administrators use different permission assignment techniques on the same network, it can become extremely difficult to track down the sources of certain effective permissions. Another way to simplify the administration process on an enterprise network is to establish specific permission assignment policies so that everyone performs tasks the same way and conflicts in permissions have a dedicated administrator for resolution.

In addition to NTFS permissions, it is also necessary for users to have the appropriate share permissions to access a shared folder over a network. The Windows share permission system is completely separate from the NTFS permission system. You can picture the share and NTFS permission systems as two doors that stand between the network users and a shared folder. Unless the users have the keys to both doors (in the form of permissions), they cannot access the shared folder. On many networks, administrators grant everyone the Allow Full Control share permission to all shared folders, essentially leaving one of the two doors unlocked, and relying on the other one, secured by NTFS permissions, for access control.

MAPPING DRIVES

After you have created the folders for each user and assigned permissions to the folders, the next step is to make sure that users can access their folders. One way of doing this is to use the Folder Redirection settings in Group Policy to map each user's Documents folder to his or her home folder on the network share. This process is invisible to the users, enabling them to work with their files without even knowing they are stored on a network drive.

Another way to provide users with easy and consistent access to their files is to map drive letters to each user's directories using the Drive Maps feature in Group Policy so that they can always find their files in the same place, using Windows Explorer. For example, you might consider mapping drive F: to the user's private home folder and drive G: to the user's Public folder. A third drive letter might point to the root of the Public share so that the user can access other people's public folders.

⊕ MORE INFORMATION

To configure Drive Maps, open a group policy object and browse to the User Configuration > Preferences > Windows Settings > Drive Maps node. Then, right-click the node and select New > Mapped Drive from the context menu.

Many computer users do not understand the fundamental concepts of network drive sharing and file management. Often, they just know that they store their files on the F: drive, and are unaware that another user's F: drive might point to a different folder. However, consistent drive letter assignments on every workstation can make it easier to support users experiencing problems storing or retrieving their files.

CREATING FOLDER SHARES

After you have devised a file sharing strategy for your network, you can begin to create the shares that enable users to access your server drives. Your file sharing strategy should include the following information:

- What folders you will share
- What names you will assign to the shares

- What permissions you will grant users to the shares
- What Offline Files settings you will use for the shares

If you are the Creator Owner of a folder, you can share it on a Windows Server 2008 computer by right-clicking the folder in any Windows Explorer window, selecting Share from the context menu, and following the instructions in the File Sharing dialog box, as shown in Figure 5-1.

Figure 5-1

The File Sharing dialog box

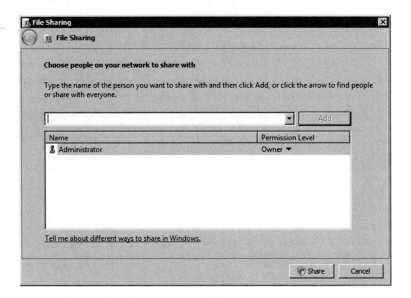

This method of creating shares provides a simplified interface that contains only limited control over elements such as share permissions. If you are not the Creator Owner of the folder, the Share tab of the folder's Properties sheet appears instead, and clicking the Share button launches the wizard. However, to create multiple shares and exercise more granular control over their properties, you can use the Share and Storage Management console, as described in the following procedure.

 TAKE NOTE* For the users on the network to be able to see the shares you create on the file server, you must make sure that the Network Discovery and File Sharing settings are turned on in the Network and Sharing Center control panel.

 CREATE A FOLDER SHARE

GET READY. Log on to Windows Server 2008 using an account with administrative privileges. When the logon process is completed, close the Initial Configuration Tasks window and any other windows that appear.

1. Click **Start** > **Administrative Tools** > **Share and Storage Management.** The Share and Storage Management console appears, as shown in Figure 5-2.

 ANOTHER WAY You can also use the Shared Folders snap-in, accessible from the Computer Management console, to create and manage shares.

Figure 5-2

The Share and Storage
Management console

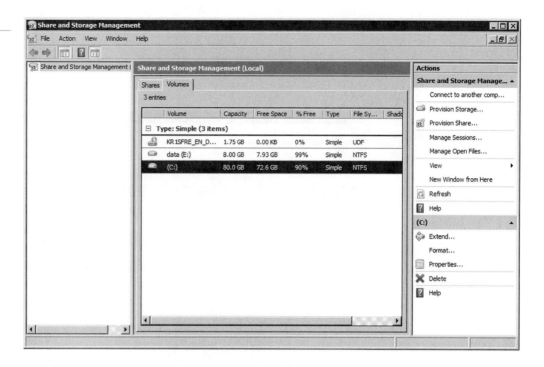

2. In the actions pane, click **Provision Share.** The Provision a Shared Folder Wizard
appears, displaying the *Shared Folder Location* page, as shown in Figure 5-3.

Figure 5-3

The Shared Folder Location
page of the Provision a Shared
Folder Wizard

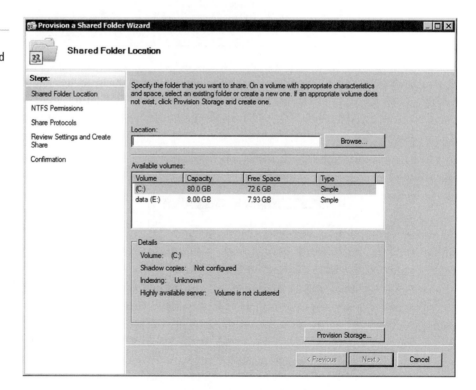

3. In the **Location** text box, key the name of or browse to the folder you want to share, and click **Next.** The *NTFS Permissions* page appears, as shown in Figure 5-4. If necessary, you can create a new volume by clicking **Provision Storage** to launch the Provision Storage Wizard.

Figure 5-4

The NTFS Permissions page of the Provision a Shared Folder Wizard

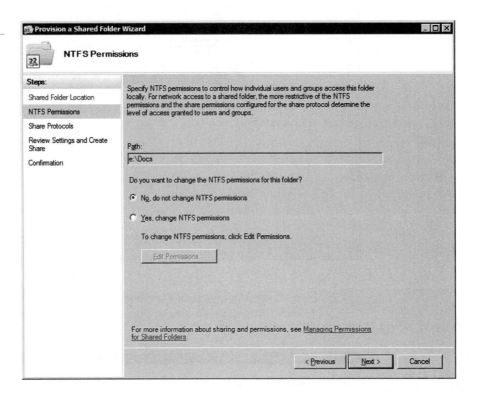

4. To modify the NTFS permissions for the specified folder, select the **Yes, change NTFS permissions** option and click **Edit Permissions.** A Permissions dialog box for the folder appears, as shown in Figure 5-5.

Figure 5-5

An NTFS Permissions dialog box

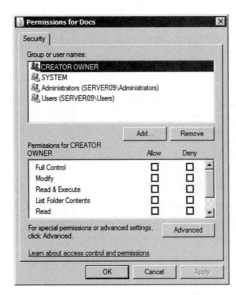

5. Modify the NTFS permissions for the folder as needed and click **OK** to close the Permissions dialog box and return to the *NTFS Permissions* page.

6. On the *NTFS Permissions* page, click **Next** to continue. The *Share Protocols* page appears, as shown in Figure 5-6.

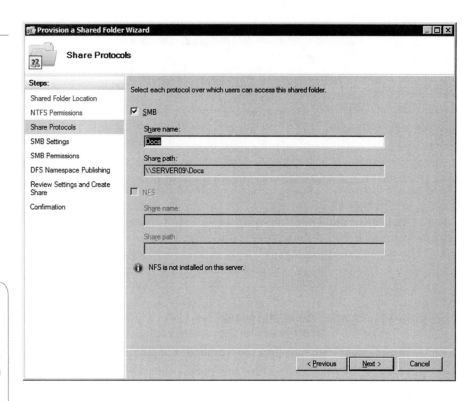

7. With the default **SMB** checkbox selected, key the name you want to assign to the share in the **Share Name** text box and click **Next.** The *SMB Settings* page appears, as shown in Figure 5-7. If you have the File Services role installed, with the Services for Network File System role service, you can also use the *Share Protocols* page to create an NFS share.

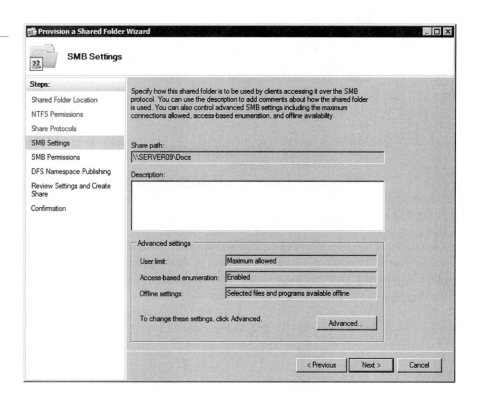

8. Key descriptive text for the share in the Description text box. To modify the default settings for the share, click **Advanced.** The Advanced dialog box appears, as shown in Figure 5-8.

Figure 5-8

The Advanced dialog box

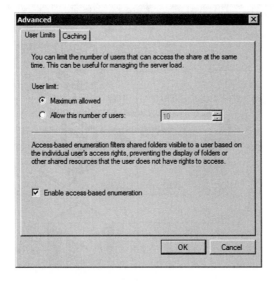

9. Modify the following settings as needed, and click **OK** to return to the *SMB Settings* page:

   • User limit—To limit the number of users that can access the share simultaneously, select **Allow this number of users** and use the spin box to specify a limit.

   • Access-based enumeration—To prevent users from seeing shared resources to which they have no access permissions, select the **Enable access-based enumeration** checkbox.

   • Offline settings—To specify the files and programs that client workstations can save locally using Offline Files, click the **Caching** tab, as shown in Figure 5-9, and select the appropriate option.

➕ **MORE INFORMATION**

Access-based enumeration (ABE), a feature first introduced in Windows Server 2003 R2, applies filters to shared folders based on individual users' permissions to the files and subfolders in the share. Simply, users who cannot access a particular shared resource are unable to see that resource on the network. This feature prevents users from browsing through files and folders they cannot access. You can enable or disable ABE for share at any time by opening the share's Properties sheet in the Sharing and Storage Management console and clicking Advanced, to display the same Advanced dialog box displayed by the Provision a Shared Folder Wizard.

Figure 5-9

The Caching tab of the Advanced dialog box

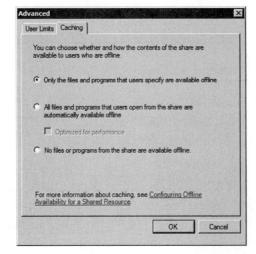

10. On the *SMB Settings* page, click **Next** to continue. The *SMB Permissions* page appears, as shown in Figure 5-10.

Figure 5-10

The SMB Permissions page of the Provision a Shared Folder Wizard

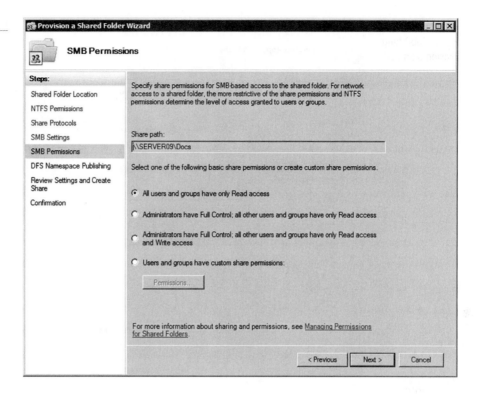

11. Select one of the pre-configured share permission options, or select **Users and groups have custom share permissions** and click **Permissions,** to display the Permissions dialog box for the share, as shown in Figure 5-11.

Figure 5-11

A share Permissions dialog box

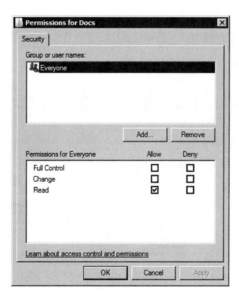

12. Modify the share permissions as needed and click **OK** to close the Permissions dialog box and return to the *SMB Permissions* page.

13. On the *SMB Permissions* page, click **Next** to continue. The *DFS Namespace Publishing* page appears, as shown in Figure 5-12.

Figure 5-12

The DFS Namespace Publishing page of the Provision a Shared Folder Wizard

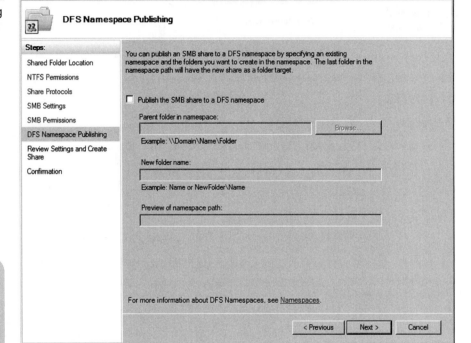

> **TAKE NOTE** *
>
> To add the share to a DFS namespace, you must install the File Services role, with the DFS Namespaces role service. For more information about DFS, see "Using the Distributed File System" later in this lesson.

14. To add the share to a Distributed File System (DFS) namespace, select the **Publish the SMB share to a DFS namespace** checkbox and specify the parent folder and new folder names in the text boxes provided. Then click **Next.** The *Review Settings and Create Share page* appears, as shown in Figure 5-13.

Figure 5-13

The Review Settings and Create Share page of the Provision a Shared Folder Wizard

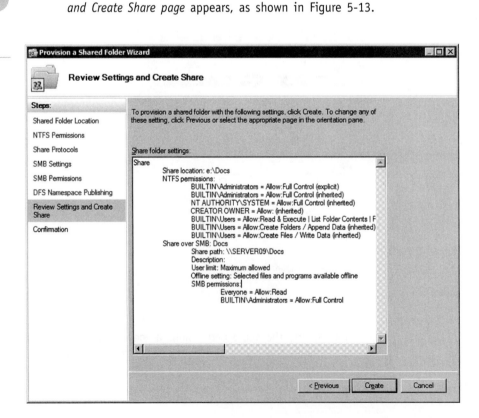

15. Click **Create.** The wizard creates the share and displays a confirmation page.

16. Click **Close** to close the wizard.

CLOSE the Sharing and Storage Management console.

After you create a share with the wizard, the share appears on the Shares tab in the detail (middle) pane of the Share and Storage Management console. You can now use the console to manage the share by opening its Properties sheet, or stop sharing it by clicking Stop Sharing in the actions pane.

Using the Distributed File System

> For users, the Distributed File System simplifies the process of locating files and folders on network servers. For administrators, DFS facilitates traffic control and network backups.

The larger the enterprise, the more file servers the network users are likely to need. However, using a large number of file servers often makes it difficult for users to locate their files. When administrators distribute shared folders among many servers, network users might be forced to browse through multiple domains, servers, and shares to find the files they need. For experienced users who understand something of how a network operates, this can be an exasperating inconvenience. For inexperienced users who are unfamiliar with basic networking principles, it can be overwhelming.

Another common problem for enterprise networks that have multiple sites is providing users with access to their files, while minimizing the traffic passing over expensive wide area network (WAN) connections. Administrators can store files at a central location and let the remote users access them over the WAN, but this solution enables WAN traffic levels to increase without check, and if a WAN connection fails, the remote users are cut off from their files. The other alternative is to maintain local copies of all the files users need at each location. This provides users at every site with local access to their data, minimizes WAN traffic, and enables the network to tolerate a WAN link failure with a minimal loss of productivity. However, to make this solution feasible, it is necessary to synchronize the copies of the files at the different locations so that changes made at one site are propagated to all of the others.

MORE INFORMATION

While the local area networks (LANs) installed within a company site are wholly owned by the company, the WAN links that connect remote sites together nearly always involve a third-party provider, such as a telephone company. The cost of a WAN connection is usually based on the amount of bandwidth needed between the sites, so it is in the company's best interest to minimize the amount of traffic passing over the WAN links as much as possible.

Enterprise administrators also must consider how to implement a backup solution for small branch offices that do not have their own IT staffs. Even if the organization is willing to install a complete backup hardware and software solution at each site, the tasks of changing the media, running the backup jobs, monitoring their progress, and performing any restores that are needed would be left to untrained personnel. The alternative, backing up over the WAN connection to a centrally located backup server, is likely to be slow, costly, and bandwidth-intensive.

The **_Distributed File System (DFS)_** implemented in the Windows Server 2008 File Services role includes two technologies: DFS Namespaces and DFS Replication, which address these problems and enable administrators to do the following:

- Simplify the process of locating files
- Control the amount of traffic passing over WAN links
- Provide users at remote sites with local file server access
- Configure the network to survive a WAN link failure
- Facilitate consistent backups

Each of the two role services that make up the Distributed File System role can work with the other to provide a DFS solution scalable to almost any size network. The DFS Namespaces role service provides basic virtual directory functionality, and the DFS Replication role service enables administrators to deploy that virtual directory on multiple servers, all over the enterprise.

UNDERSTANDING NAMESPACES

At its simplest, DFS is a virtual *namespace* technology that enables administrators to create a single directory tree that contains references to shared folders on various file servers, all over the network. This directory tree is virtual; it does not exist as a true copy of the folders on different servers. Instead, it is a collection of references to the original folders, which users can browse as though it were an actual server share. The actual shared folders are referred to as the *targets* of the virtual folders in the namespace.

For example, Figure 5-14 shows three file servers, each with its own shared folders. Normally, a user looking for a particular file would have to search the folders on each server individually.

Figure 5-14

File server shares integrated into a DFS namespace

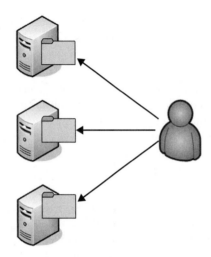

By creating a DFS namespace that contains a virtual representation of the shared folders on all three servers, as shown in Figure 5-15, the user can search through a single directory structure. When the user attempts to open a file in the DFS namespace, the namespace server forwards the access request to the file server where the file is actually stored, which then supplies it to the user.

Figure 5-15

User access requests are forwarded by the DFS server

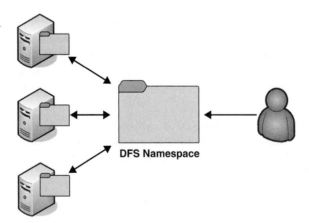

DFS Namespace

Creating a DFS namespace enables users to locate their files more easily, irrespective of where they are actually located. You can create multiple namespaces on a single server and create additional namespace servers for a single namespace.

REPLICATING SHARES

Creating a DFS namespace does not, by itself, affect the actual locations of the files and folders listed in the namespace, nor does it improve file services to remote sites. The DFS

Replication role service performs these tasks. DFS Replication is a multimaster replication engine that can create and maintain copies of shared folders on different servers throughout an enterprise network.

As noted in Lesson 3, "Planning an Active Directory Deployment," multimaster replication is a technique in which duplicate copies of a file are all updated on a regular basis, no matter which copy changes. For example, if a file is duplicated on four different servers, a user can access any one of the four copies and modify the file as needed. The replication engine then takes the changes made to the modified copy and uses them to update the other three copies.

At its simplest, DFS Replication service copies files from one location to another. However, DFS Replication also works in tandem with DFS Namespace to provide unified services, such as the following:

- Data distribution—By replicating shared folders to multiple locations, DFS enables users to access the files they need from a local server, minimizing internetwork traffic and its accompanying delays due to network latency. In addition, by integrating the replicated copies into a DFS namespace, users all over the enterprise can browse the same directory tree. When a user attempts to access a file, the namespace server directs the request to the nearest replica.

- Load balancing—A DFS namespace by itself can simplify the process by which users locate the files they need, but if people all over the network need access to the same file, the requests are still directed to the same file server, which can cause a performance bottleneck in the computer itself or on the subnet where the file server is located. By replicating shared folders to multiple servers, DFS can distribute the access requests, thus preventing any one server from shouldering the entire traffic load.

- Data collection—Instead of installing backup solutions at remote sites or performing backups over a WAN connection, DFS enables administrators to replicate data from remote file servers to a central location, where the backups can take place. Windows Server 2008 DFS uses **Remote Differential Compression (RDC),** a protocol that conserves network bandwidth by detecting changes in files and transmitting only the modified data to the destination. This conserves bandwidth and greatly reduces the time needed for the replication process.

CONFIGURING DFS

Implementing DFS on a Windows Server 2008 computer is more complicated than simply installing the File Services role and the Distributed File System role services. After the role and role services are in place, you have to perform at least some of the following configuration tasks:

- Create a namespace
- Add folders to the namespace
- Create a replication group

The following sections examine these tasks in more detail.

CREATING A NAMESPACE

To create a DFS namespace on a Windows Server 2008 computer, you must have the Distributed File System role and the DFS Namespace role service installed. After you have created a namespace, this computer, the *namespace server,* will maintain the list of shared folders represented in the virtual directory tree and respond to network user requests for access to those shared folders.

In essence, the namespace server functions just like a file server, except that when a user requests access to a file in the DFS directory tree, the namespace server replies not with the file itself, but with a *referral* specifying the file's actual location. The DFS client on the user's computer then sends its access request to the file server listed in the referral, and receives the file in return.

TAKE NOTE*
All versions of the Windows Server 2008 operating system can function as DFS namespace servers. However, the Standard Edition and Web Edition products can host only a single DFS namespace, while the Enterprise Edition and Datacenter Edition versions can host multiple namespaces.

Although the DFS namespace does not include the actual data files of the shared folders that populate it, it does require some storage space of its own to maintain the directory structure that forms the virtual directory tree. The namespace server must have an NTFS volume to create the shared folder that will host the namespace.

The DFS Namespaces role service supports two basic types of namespaces: standalone and domain-based. Domain-based namespaces come in two modes: Windows Server 2008 mode and Windows 2000 Server mode, which are based on the domain functional level of the domain hosting the namespace.

TAKE NOTE *

To raise the domain functional level of a domain, use the Active Directory Domains and Trusts console.

To select the namespace type you should use for your network, consider the following factors:

- If you are deploying DFS on an Active Directory network, you should select the domain-based namespace, unless some of the computers that will be domain controllers are running Windows Server 2003 or an earlier version, and you do not intend to add more than 5,000 folders to the namespace.

- If all of the computers that will be namespace servers are running Windows Server 2008, a domain-based namespace in Windows Server 2008 mode will provide the most fault tolerance and scalability.

- If you are deploying DFS on a network that does not use Active Directory, your only choice is to create a standalone namespace. In this case, you are limited to one namespace server and no DFS replication.

To create a new namespace, use the following procedure.

CREATE A NAMESPACE

GET READY. Log on to Windows Server 2008 using an account with domain administrative privileges. When the logon process is completed, close the Initial Configuration Tasks window and any other windows that appear. Make sure that the File Services role, with the DFS Namespaces role service, is installed on the computer.

1. Click **Start,** and then click **Administrative Tools** > **DFS Management.** The DFS Management console appears, as shown in Figure 5-16.

Figure 5-16

The DFS Management console

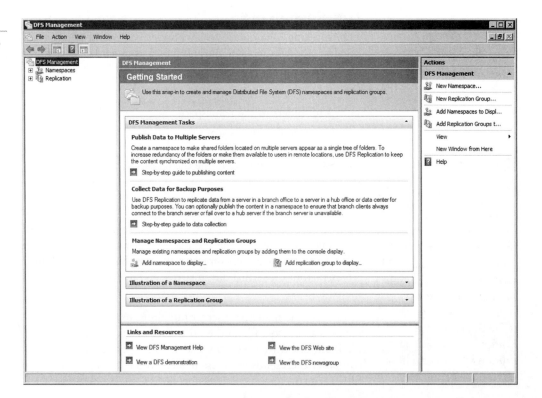

2. In the scope pane, right-click the **Namespaces** node and, from the context menu, select **New Namespace.** The New Namespace Wizard appears and displays the *Namespace Server* page, as shown in Figure 5-17.

Figure 5-17

The Namespace Server page of the New Namespace Wizard

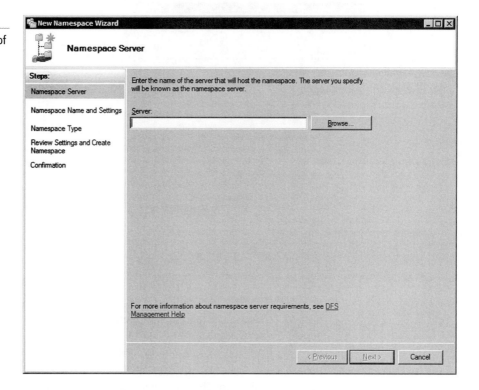

3. In the **Server** text box, key the name of or browse to the server that you want to host the namespace, and then click **Next.** If the DFS Namespace system service is not running on the server you specified, the wizard offers to start the service and set its Startup Type to Automatic. Click **Yes** to continue. The *Namespace Name and Settings* page appears, as shown in Figure 5-18.

Figure 5-18

The Namespace Name and Settings page

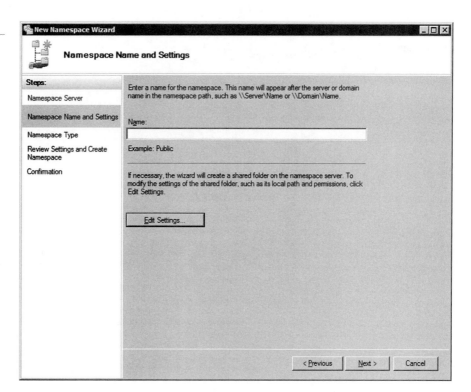

4. In the **Name** text box, key the name that will become the root of the namespace. Then, click **Edit Settings.** The Edit Settings dialog box appears, as shown in Figure 5-19.

Figure 5-19

The Edit Settings dialog box

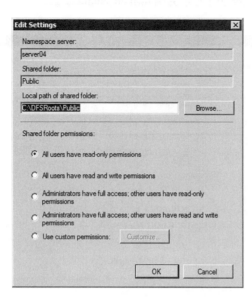

The root of the namespace is an actual share that the wizard will create on the namespace server, containing the referrals that point to the shared folders that populate the namespace. Users on the network will access the DFS namespace by browsing to this share or using its name in the form *server**root* or *domain**root*.

5. Under Shared Folder Permissions, select one of the radio buttons to configure the share permissions for the namespace root. To configure the share permissions manually, select the **Use custom permissions** option and click **Customize.** A Permissions dialog box appears, in which you can configure the share permissions in the usual manner.

6. Click **OK** to close the Permissions dialog box, and click **OK** again to close the Edit Settings dialog box. Then, click **Next.** The *Namespace Type* page appears, as shown in Figure 5-20.

Figure 5-20

The Namespace Type page

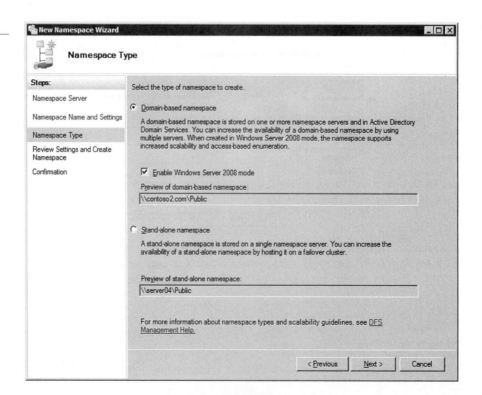

7. Select one of the option buttons to create either a domain-based namespace or a standalone namespace. If you choose the former, use the Enable **Windows Server 2008 Mode** checkbox to specify whether to create the namespace in Windows Server 2008 mode or Windows 2000 mode. Then, click **Next.** *The Review Settings and Create Namespace page appears, as shown in Figure 5-21.*

Figure 5-21

The Review Settings and Create Namespace page

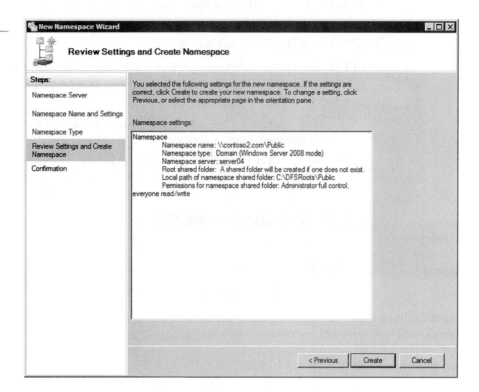

8. Review the settings you have selected and click **Create** to create and configure the namespace. After the process is completed, the *Confirmation* page appears, indicating that the wizard successfully created the namespace, and the namespace appears in the console's scope pane.

CLOSE the DFS Management console.

At any time after you create a domain-based namespace, you can add namespace servers, for load balancing or fault tolerance, by right-clicking the namespace and, from the context menu, selecting Add Namespace Server. Every namespace server must have the DFS Namespaces role service installed and must have an NTFS volume to store the namespace share.

TAKE NOTE*

Adding namespace servers to an existing namespace replicates only the virtual directory structure, not the target folders and files referred to by the virtual folders. To replicate the target folders, you must use DFS Replication, as discussed later in this lesson.

ADDING FOLDERS TO A NAMESPACE

After you have created a namespace, you can begin to build its virtual directory structure by adding folders. You can add two types of folders to a namespace, those with targets and those without. A folder with a target points to one or more shared folders on the same or another server. Users browsing the namespace will see the folder you add, plus all of the subfolders and files that exist in the target folder beneath it. You can also, purely for organizational purposes, create folders in the namespace that do not have targets.

You can add as many targets to a folder as you need. Typically, administrators add multiple targets to namespace folders to balance the server load and give users at different locations local access to the folders. Adding multiple targets means that you will have identical copies of the target on different servers. These duplicate targets must remain identical, so you will later configure DFS Replication to keep them updated.

To add folders to a DFS namespace, use the following procedure.

 ADD FOLDERS TO A NAMESPACE

GET READY. Log on to Windows Server 2008 using an account with domain administrative privileges. When the logon process is completed, close the Initial Configuration Tasks window and any other windows that appear.

1. Click **Start,** and then click **Administrative Tools** > **DFS Management.** The DFS Management console appears.

2. Right-click a namespace in the scope pane and, from the context menu, select **New Folder.** The New Folder dialog box appears, as shown in Figure 5-22.

Figure 5-22

The New Folder dialog box

3. In the **Name** text box, key the name of the folder as you want it to appear in the DFS virtual directory tree. Then, click **OK.** The new folder appears beneath the namespace.

   Because this folder has no target, it exists in the namespace only to build up the virtual directory structure and cannot contain any files.

4. Right-click the folder you just created and, from the context menu, select **New Folder.** The New Folder dialog box appears again.

5. In the **Name** text box, key the name of the folder you want to appear beneath the first folder you created.

6. Click **Add.** The Add Folder Target dialog box appears, as shown in Figure 5-23.

Figure 5-23

The Add Folder Target dialog box

7. Click **Browse.** The Browse for Shared Folders dialog box appears, as shown in Figure 5-24.

Figure 5-24

The Browse for Shared Folders dialog box

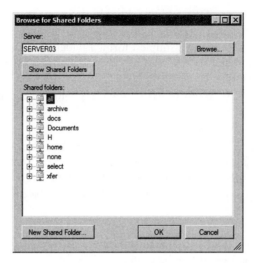

8. Perform one of the following procedures to specify the shared folder that you want to be the target. Then, click **OK** to close the Browse for Shared Folders dialog box.

- Select one of the existing shares in the Shared Folders list on the current server shown in the **Server** text box. Then click **OK.**

- Click **Browse** to select a different server on the network and select one of its shares. Then click **OK.**

- Select a server and click **New Shared Folder** to display the Create Share dialog box, which you can use to create a new shared folder and set its share permissions. Then, click **OK** to close the Create Share dialog box.

> **TAKE NOTE** *
> When referring to folder targets, the term "server" refers to any Windows computer with one or more shared folders on it. Targets for a DFS namespace do not have to be running a Server version of Windows.

9. Click **OK** to close the Add Folder Target dialog box.

10. Repeat steps 6–9 to add additional targets to the folder. When you add multiple targets to a folder, the console prompts you to create a replication group to keep the targets synchronized. Click **No,** because the process of configuring replication is covered later in this lesson.

11. Click **OK** to close the New Folder dialog box. The folder is added to the virtual directory tree in the scope pane.

CLOSE the DFS Management console.

You can continue to populate the namespace by adding more folders to the virtual directory structure or by adding more targets to existing folders. When you select an untargeted folder in the scope pane, you can select New Folder from the context menu to create another subordinate folder (targeted or untargeted). However, to add a subfolder to a targeted folder, you must create the subfolder in the target share, and it will appear in the namespace.

CONFIGURING DFS REPLICATION

When a folder in a DFS namespace has multiple targets, the targets should be identical so that users can access the files from any of the targets invisibly. However, users often modify the files in a folder as they work with them, causing the targets to differ. To resynchronize the target folders, DFS includes a replication engine that automatically propagates changes from one target to all of the others.

To enable replication for a DFS folder with multiple targets, you must create a **replication group,** which is a collection of servers, known as *members,* each of which contains a target for a particular DFS folder. In its simplest form, a folder with two targets requires a replication group with two members: the servers hosting the targets. At regular intervals, the DFS Replication engine on the namespace server triggers replication events between the two members, using the RDC protocol so that their target folders remain synchronized.

TAKE NOTE *

Although terms such as "group" and "member" are typically associated with Active Directory, DFS Replication does not use them to refer to Active Directory objects. In fact, unlike the File Replication Service (FRS) in Windows Server 2003, DFS Replication does not require Active Directory, and can function on standalone, as well as domain-based, namespace servers.

DFS Replication need not be so simple, however, because it is also highly scalable and configurable. A replication group can have up to 256 members, with 256 replicated folders, and each server can be a member of up to 256 replication groups, with as many as 256 connections (128 incoming and 128 outgoing). A member server can support up to one terabyte of replicated files, with up to eight million replicated files per volume.

In addition to scaling the replication process, you can also configure it to occur at specific times and limit the amount of bandwidth it can utilize. This enables you to exercise complete control over the WAN bandwidth utilized by the replication process.

⊕ MORE INFORMATION

For each member server, the number of replication groups multiplied by the number of replicated folders multiplied by the number of simultaneous replication connections should not exceed 1,024. If you are having trouble keeping below this limit, the best solution is to schedule replication to occur at different times for different folders, thus limiting the number of simultaneous connections.

The larger the DFS deployment, the more complicated the replication process becomes. By default, replication groups use a **full mesh topology,** which means that every member in a group replicates with every other member. For relatively small DFS deployments, this is a satisfactory solution, but on larger installations, the full mesh topology can generate a huge amount of network traffic. In such cases, you might want to opt for a **hub/spoke topology,** which enables you to limit the replication traffic to specific pairs of members, as shown in Figure 5-25.

Figure 5-25

The full mesh and hub/spoke replication topologies

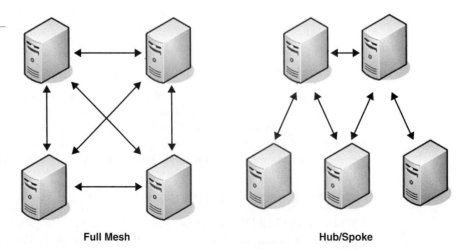

Full Mesh   Hub/Spoke

TAKE NOTE * No matter which topology you use, DFS replication between two members is always bidirectional by default. This means that the Replicate Folder Wizard always establishes two connections, one in each direction, between every pair of computers involved in a replication relationship. This is true in a hub/spoke as well as a full mesh topology. To create unidirectional replication relationships, you can either disable selected connections between the members of a replication group in the DFS Management console or use share permissions to prevent the replication process from updating files on certain member servers.

To create a replication group and initiate the replication process, use the following procedure.

TAKE NOTE * In addition to manually creating replication groups, the system prompts you automatically to create a group when you create a second target for a previously targeted folder.

 CREATE A REPLICATION GROUP

GET READY. Log on to Windows Server 2008 using an account with domain administrative privileges. When the logon process is completed, close the Initial Configuration Tasks window and any other windows that appear.

1. Click **Start,** and then click **Administrative Tools** > **DFS Management.** The DFS Management console appears.
2. Right-click a folder with multiple targets in the scope pane and, from the context menu, select **Replicate Folder.** The Replicate Folder Wizard appears, displaying the *Replication Group and Replicated Folder Name* page, as shown in Figure 5-26.

Figure 5-26

The Replication Group and Replicated Folder Name page of the Replicate Folder Wizard

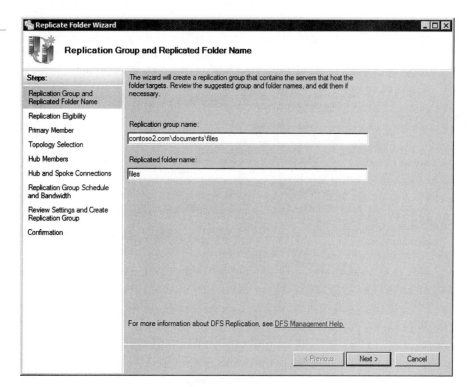

3. Click **Next** to accept the default values for the Replication Group Name and Replicated Folder Name fields. The *Replication Eligibility* page appears, as shown in Figure 5-27.

Figure 5-27

The Replication Eligibility page

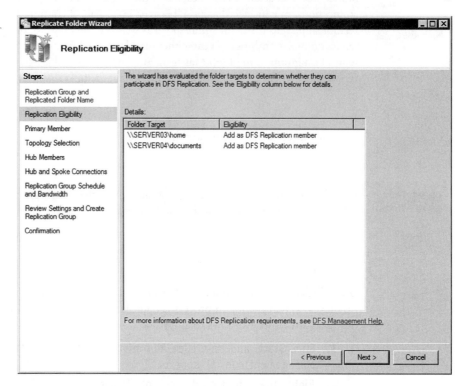

In the **Replication Group Name** text box, the name that the wizard suggests for the replication group consists of the full path from the domain or server to the selected folder. The suggested name for the Replicated Folder Name field is the name of the selected folder. Although it is possible to modify these values, there is usually no compelling reason to do so.

4. Click **Next** to continue. The *Primary Member* page appears, as shown in Figure 5-28. At this time, the wizard examines the targets and specifies whether they are eligible to be added to the replication group.

Figure 5-28

The Primary Member page

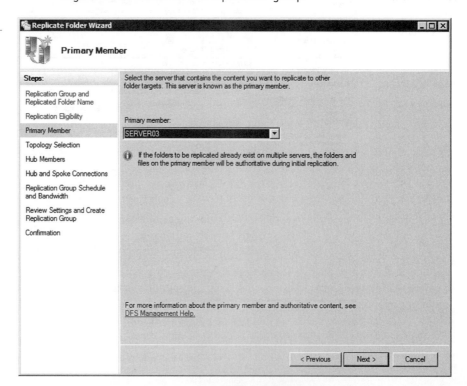

5. In the Primary Member dropdown list, select the target server that you want to be authoritative during the replication process and then click **Next.** The *Topology Selection* page appears, as shown in Figure 5-29.

Figure 5-29

The Topology Selection page

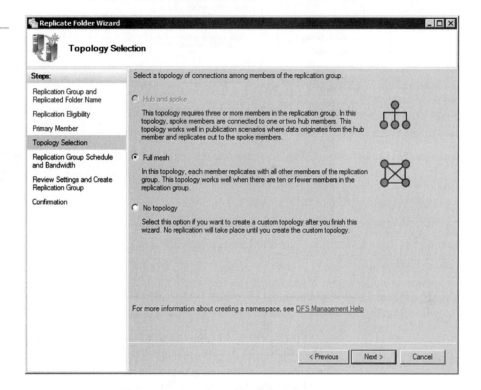

During the replication process, the files from the server that you designate as the primary member will be copied to the other targets in the replication group. If any of the files in one target folder differ from their counterparts in the others, DFS Replication will use the primary member version to overwrite all other versions.

6. Select a replication topology from one of the following options and click **Next.** The *Replication Group Schedule and Bandwidth* page appears, as shown in Figure 5-30.

- Hub and spoke—Each member is designated as a hub or a spoke. Hubs replicate with each other and with spokes, but spokes replicate only with hubs, not with each other. This topology requires the folder to have at least three member servers.

- Full mesh—Every member replicates with every other member. This is the default setting.

- No topology—Indicates that you intend to create a customized topology after the wizard is completed. Replication will not occur until you create a topology.

Figure 5-30

The Replication Group
Schedule and Bandwidth page

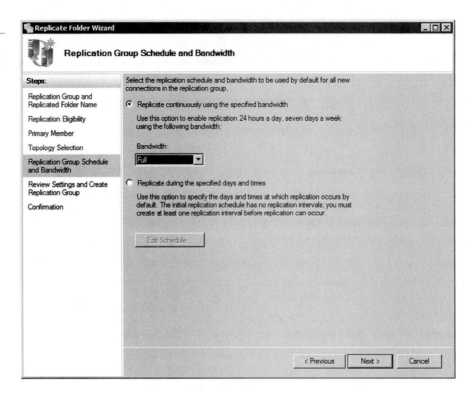

7. Configure one of the following replication scheduling/bandwidth options and then click **Next.** The *Review Settings and Create Replication Group* page appears.

   • Replicate continuously using the specified bandwidth—Select this option and use the Bandwidth dropdown list to specify how much network bandwidth the replication process should be permitted to use.

   • Replicate during the specified days and times—Select this option and click **Edit Schedule** to display the Edit Schedule dialog box shown in Figure 5-31, in which you can specify the days of the week and the hours of the day that replication is permitted to occur.

Figure 5-31

The Edit Schedule dialog box

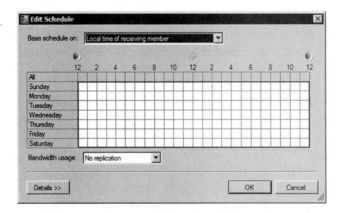

8. Review the settings you selected and click **Create.** When the wizard completes the configuration process, click **Close.** The replication group appears under the Replication node in the scope pane, and the replication process begins as soon as the configuration parameters propagate throughout the domain.

CLOSE the DFS Management console.

After you have created a replication group, it appears under the Replication node in the scope pane of the DFS Management console.

Using File Server Resource Manager

> File Server Resource Manager enables administrators to monitor and regulate the storage consumed by network users.

Although the price of hard disk storage continues to plummet, users still often have a habit of consuming all of the storage space that administrators give them. This is especially true when you consider the large sizes of the audio and video media files that many users store on their drives. In an enterprise environment, it is important to monitor and regulate the amount of storage space consumed by users so that each user receives a fair share and server resources are not overwhelmed by irresponsible user storage practices.

When you install the File Services role with the File Server Resource Manager role service, Windows Server 2008 installs the *File Server Resource Manager (FSRM)* console, first introduced in Windows Server 2003 R2, which provides tools that enable file server administrators to monitor and regulate their server storage, by performing the following tasks:

- Establish quotas that limit the amount of storage space allotted to each user
- Create screens that prevent users from storing specific types of files on server drives
- Create templates that simplify the process of applying quotas and screens
- Automatically send email messages to users and/or administrators when quotas are exceeded or nearly exceeded
- Generate reports providing details of users' storage activities

These tasks are discussed in the following sections.

WORKING WITH QUOTAS

Quotas can warn administrators of excessive storage utilization trends, or apply hard restrictions to user accounts.

In Windows Server 2008, a quota is simply a limit on the disk space a user is permitted to consume in a particular volume or folder. Quotas are based on file ownership. Windows automatically makes a user the owner of all files that he or she creates on a server volume. The quota system tracks all of the files owned by each user and totals their sizes. When the total size of a given user's files reaches the quota specified by the server administrator, the system takes action, also specified by the administrator.

The actions the system takes when a user approaches or reaches a quota are highly configurable. For example, administrators can configure quotas to be hard or soft. A *hard quota* prohibits users from consuming any disk space beyond the allotted amount, while a *soft quota* allows the user storage space beyond the allotted amount and just sends an email notification to the user and/or administrator. Administrators can also specify the thresholds at which the system should send notifications and configure the quota server to generate event log entries and reports in response to quota thresholds.

CREATING A QUOTA TEMPLATE

For enterprise networks, you should create quota templates to manage quota assignments on a large scale. A quota template is a collection of settings that define the following:

- Whether a quota should be hard or soft
- What thresholds FSRM should apply to the quota
- What actions FSRM should take when a user reaches a threshold

The File Server Resource Manager console includes several predefined templates, which you can use to create your own template. To create a quota template, use the following procedure.

⊕ **CREATE A QUOTA TEMPLATE**

GET READY. Log on to Windows Server 2008 using an account with domain administrative privileges. When the logon process is completed, close the Initial Configuration Tasks window and any other windows that appear.

1. Click **Start,** and then click **Administrative Tools** > **File Server Resource Manager.** The File Server Resource Manager console appears, as shown in Figure 5-32.

Figure 5-32

The File Server Resource Manager console

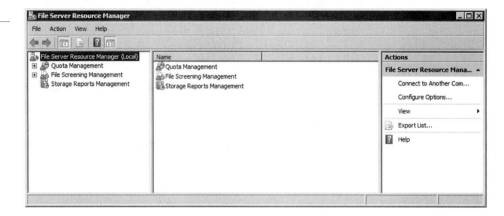

2. Expand the **Quota Management** node, right-click the **Quota Templates** node and, from the context menu, select **Create Quota Template.** The Create Quota Template dialog box appears, as shown in Figure 5-33.

Figure 5-33

The Create Quota Template dialog box

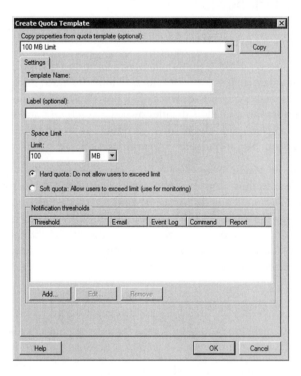

3. If you want to create a new quota template based on the settings in one of the existing templates, click the **Copy properties from quota template** dropdown list to select a template and click **Copy.** The settings from the template appear in the dialog box so that you can modify them as needed.

4. In the **Template Name** text box, key the name you will use to identify the template.

5. Optionally, in the **Label** text box, you can key a term that will be associated with all of the quotas you create using the template.

6. In the **Space Limit** box, specify the amount of storage space you want to allot to each individual user and specify whether you want to create a hard quota or a soft quota.

7. In the **Notification Thresholds** box, click **Add.** The Add Threshold dialog box appears.

8. In the **Generate Notifications When Usage Reaches (%)** text box, specify a threshold in the form of a percentage of the storage quota.

9. Use the controls on the following tabs to specify the actions you want taken when a user reaches the specified threshold:

   - Email Message—Select the appropriate checkbox to specify whether you want the system to send an email message to an administrator, to the user, or both, as shown in Figure 5-34. For administrators, you can specify the email addresses of one or more persons separated by semicolons. For the user, you can modify the text of the default email message.

Figure 5-34

The Email Message tab on the Add Threshold dialog box

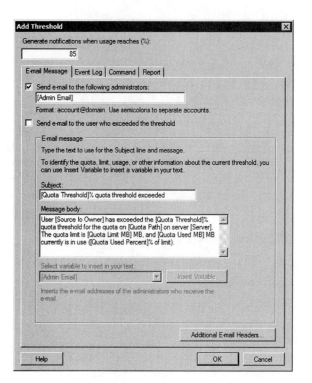

TAKE NOTE *

The Windows Server 2008 computer must be running the Simple Mail Transfer Protocol (SMTP) service to be able to send email messages. To install SMTP, you must use Server Manager to add the SMTP Server feature.

- Event Log—Select the **Send warning to event log** checkbox to create a log entry when a user reaches the threshold, as shown in Figure 5-35. You can modify the wording of the log entry in the text box provided.

Figure 5-35

The Event Log tab on the Add Threshold dialog box

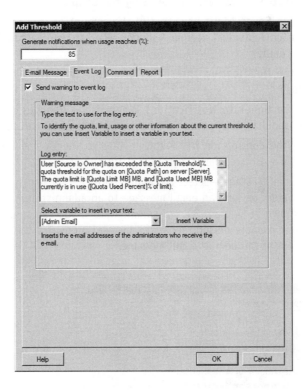

- Command—Select the **Run this command or script** checkbox to specify a program or script file that the system should execute when a user reaches the threshold, as shown in Figure 5-36. You can also specify command arguments, a working directory, and the type of account the system should use to run the program or script.

Figure 5-36

The Command tab on the Add Threshold dialog box

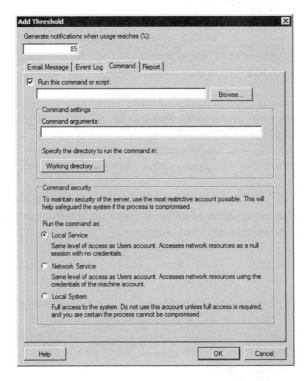

- Report—Select the **Generate reports** checkbox, and then select the checkboxes for the reports you want the system to generate, as shown in Figure 5-37. You can also specify that the system email the selected reports to an administrator or to the user who exceeded the threshold.

Figure 5-37

The Report tab on the Add Threshold dialog box

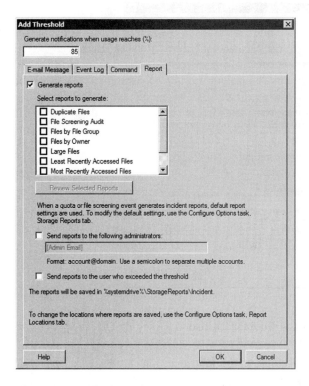

10. Click **OK** to close the dialog box and add the new threshold to the Notification Thresholds list on the Create Quota Template dialog box.

11. Repeat steps 7–10 to create additional thresholds, if desired. When you have created all of the thresholds you need, click **OK** to create the quota template.

CLOSE the File Server Resource Manager console.

Using quota templates simplifies the quota management process, in much the same way as assigning permissions to groups, rather than users. If you use a template to create quotas, and you want to change the properties of all of your quotas at once, you can simply modify the template, and the system applies the changes to all of the associated quotas automatically.

CREATING A QUOTA

After you have created your quota templates, you can create the quotas themselves. To create a quota, use the following procedure.

 CREATE A QUOTA

GET READY. Log on to Windows Server 2008 using an account with domain administrative privileges. When the logon process is completed, close the Initial Configuration Tasks window and any other windows that appear.

1. Click **Start,** and then click **Administrative Tools** > **File Server Resource Manager.** The File Server Resource Manager console appears.

2. Expand the **Quota Management** node, right-click the **Quotas** folder and, from the context menu, select **Create Quota.** The Create Quota dialog box appears, as shown in Figure 5-38.

Figure 5-38

The Create Quota dialog box

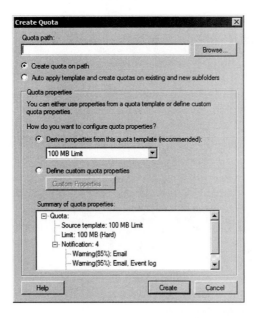

3. In the **Quota Path** text box, key or browse to the name of the volume or folder for which you want to create a quota.

4. Select one of the following application options:

- Create quota on path—Creates a single quota for the specified volume or folder.

- Auto apply template and create quotas on existing and new subfolders—Causes FSRM to automatically create a quota, based on a template, for each subfolder in the designated path, and for every new subfolder created in that path.

5. Select one of the following properties options:

- Derive properties from this quota template—Configures the quota using the settings of the template you select from the dropdown list.

- Define custom quota properties—Enables you to specify custom settings for the quota. Clicking the Custom Properties button opens a Quota Properties dialog box for the selected volume or folder, which contains the same controls as the Create Quota Template dialog box discussed in the previous section.

6. Click **Create.** The new quota appears in the console's details pane.

CLOSE the File Server Resource Manager console.

Even if you do not install the File Server Resource Manager role service, quotas are available on NTFS volumes, but these so-called NTFS quotas are limited to controlling storage on entire volumes on a per-user basis. When you create FSRM quotas for volumes or folders, however, they apply to all users. NTFS quotas are also limited to creating event log entries only, while FSRM quotas can also send email notifications, execute commands, and generate reports, as well as log events.

CREATING A FILE SCREEN

FSRM, in addition to creating storage quotas, enables administrators to create file screens, which prevent users from storing specific types of files on a server drive. Administrators typically use file screening to keep large audio and video files off server drives because they can consume a lot of space and most users do not need them to do their jobs. Obviously, in an organization that utilizes these types of files, screening them would be inappropriate, but you can configure FSRM to screen files of any type.

The process of creating file screens is quite similar to that of creating storage quotas. You choose the types of files you want to screen and then specify the actions you want the server to take when a user attempts to store a forbidden file type. As with quotas, the server can send emails, create log entries, execute commands, and generate reports. Administrators can also create file screen templates that simplify the process of deploying file screens throughout the enterprise.

To create a file screen, use the following procedure.

 CREATE A FILE SCREEN

GET READY. Log on to Windows Server 2008 using an account with domain administrative privileges. When the logon process is completed, close the Initial Configuration Tasks window and any other windows that appear.

1. Click **Start,** and then click **Administrative Tools** > **File Server Resource Manager.** The File Server Resource Manager console appears.

2. Expand the **File Screening Management** node, right-click the **File Screens** folder and, from the context menu, select **Create File Screen.** The Create File Screen dialog box appears, as shown in Figure 5-39.

Figure 5-39

The Create File Screen dialog box

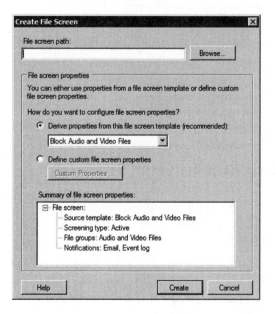

3. In the **File Screen Path** text box, key or browse to the name of the volume or folder that you want to screen.

4. Select one of the following properties options:
   - Derive properties from this file screen template—Configures the file screen using the settings of the template you select from the dropdown list.

- Define custom file screen properties—Enables you to specify custom settings for the file screen. Clicking the Custom Properties button opens a File Screen Properties dialog box for the selected volume or folder, which contains the Settings tab shown in Figure 5-40, plus the same Email Message, Event Log, Command, and Report tabs as the Quota Properties dialog box.

Figure 5-40

The Settings tab of a File Screen Properties dialog box dialog box

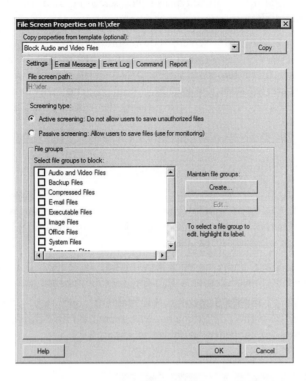

5. Click **Create**. The new file screen appears in the console's details pane.

CLOSE the File Server Resource Manager console.

You can also create file screen exceptions, which override the file screening rules inherited from a parent folder. For example, if you are screening out audio and video files from a particular volume, and you need to store these types of files in one folder, you can create an exception only for that folder.

GENERATING STORAGE REPORTS

Reporting is one of the keys to efficient storage management. File Server Resource Manager is capable of generating a variety of reports that enable administrators to examine the state of their file server volumes and identify transgressors or company storage policies. FSRM can create the following reports:

- Duplicate Files—Creates a list of files that are the same size and have the same last modified date.
- File Screening Audit—Creates a list of the audit events generated by file screening violations for specific users during a specific time period.
- Files By File Group—Creates a list of files sorted by selected file groups in the File Server Resource Manager console.
- Files By Owner—Creates a list of files sorted by selected users that own them.
- Large Files—Creates a list of files conforming to a specified file spec that are a specified size or larger.

- Least Recently Accessed Files—Creates a list of files conforming to a specified file spec that have not been accessed for a specified number of days.

- Most Recently Accessed Files—Creates a list of files conforming to a specified file spec that have been accessed within a specified number of days.

- Quota Usage—Creates a list of quotas that exceed a specified percentage of the storage limit.

Using the FSRM console, you can generate reports on the fly or schedule their creation on a regular basis. To schedule a report, use the following procedure.

 GENERATE A SCHEDULED STORAGE REPORT

GET READY. Log on to Windows Server 2008 using an account with domain administrative privileges. When the logon process is completed, close the Initial Configuration Tasks window and any other windows that appear.

1. Click **Start,** and then click **Administrative Tools** > **File Server Resource Manager.** The File Server Resource Manager console appears.

2. Right-click the **Storage Reports Management** node and, from the context menu, select **Schedule a New Report Task.** The Storage Reports Task Properties dialog box appears, as shown in Figure 5-41.

Figure 5-41

The Settings tab of the Storage Reports Task Properties dialog box

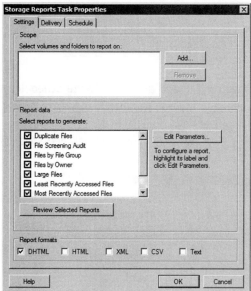

3. On the Settings tab, click **Add** and, in the Browse For Folder dialog box that appears, select the volume or folder on which you want a report. Repeat this step to select multiple volumes or folders, if desired.

4. In the Report Data box, select the reports that you want to generate. When you select a report and click **Edit Parameters,** a Report Parameters dialog box appears, in which you can configure the parameters for that specific report.

5. In the Report Formats box, select the checkboxes for the formats you want FSRM to use when creating the reports.

6. If you want FSRM to send the reports to administrators via email, click the **Delivery** tab, as shown in Figure 5-42, select the **Send reports to the following administrators** checkbox, and key one or more email addresses (separated by semicolons) in the text box.

Figure 5-42

The Delivery tab of the Storage Reports Task Properties dialog box

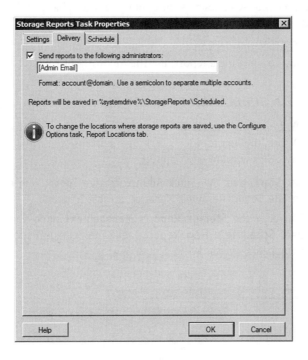

7. Click the **Schedule** tab and then click **Create Schedule.** A Schedule dialog box appears.

8. Click **New,** and use the Schedule Task, Start Time, and Schedule Task Daily controls to specify when you want FSRM to create the reports, as shown in Figure 5-43. You can also click **Advanced** for more detailed scheduling options.

Figure 5-43

The Schedule dialog box

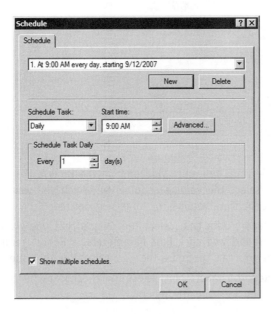

9. Click **OK** to close the Schedule dialog box and click **OK** again to close the Storage Reports Task Properties dialog box.

CLOSE the File Server Resource Manager console.

The report is now added to the schedule. The system will generate it at the specified time.

■ Deploying Print and Fax Servers

THE BOTTOM LINE

Like the file-sharing functions discussed in the previous lessons, print device sharing is one of the most basic applications for which local area networks were designed.

Printing and faxing are relatively simple functions that can become complicated when deployed on an enterprise scale. Installing, sharing, monitoring, and managing a single network print device is relatively simple, but when you are responsible for dozens or even hundreds of print devices on a large enterprise network, these tasks can be overwhelming.

Understanding the Windows Print Architecture

It is important to understand the terms that Microsoft uses when referring to the various components of the network printing architecture.

Printing in Microsoft Windows typically involves the following four components:

- Print device—A **print device** is the actual hardware that produces hard-copy documents on paper or other print media. Windows Server 2008 supports both *local print devices,* which are directly attached to computer ports, and *network interface print devices,* which are connected to the network, either directly or through another computer.

- Printer—In Windows, a **printer** is the software interface through which a computer communicates with a print device. Windows Server 2008 supports numerous physical interfaces, including Universal Serial bus (USB), IEEE 1394 (FireWire), parallel (LPT), serial (COM), Infrared Data Access (IrDA), Bluetooth ports, and network printing services such as lpr, Internet Printing Protocol (IPP), and standard TCP/IP ports.

- Print server—A **print server** is a computer (or standalone device) that receives print jobs from clients and sends them to print devices that are either locally attached or connected to the network.

- Printer driver—A **printer driver** is a device driver that converts the print jobs generated by applications into an appropriate string of commands for a specific print device. Printer drivers are designed for a specific print device and provide applications with access to all of the print device's features.

TAKE NOTE✷

"Printer" and "print device" are the most commonly misused terms of the Windows printing vocabulary. Obviously, many sources use "printer" to refer to the printing hardware. However, in Windows, printer and print device are not equivalents. For example, you can add a printer to a Windows Server 2008 computer without a physical print device being present. The computer can then host the printer, print server, and printer driver. These three components enable the computer to process the print jobs and store them in a print queue until the print device is available.

UNDERSTANDING WINDOWS PRINTING

These four components work together to process the print jobs produced by Windows applications and turn them into hard-copy documents, as shown in Figure 5-44.

Figure 5-44

The Windows print architecture

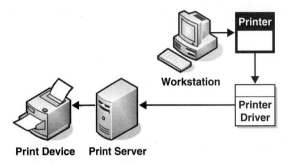

Before you can print documents in Windows, you must install at least one printer. To install a printer in Windows, you must do the following:

- Select the print device's specific manufacturer and model
- Specify the port (or other interface) the computer will use to access the print device
- Supply a printer driver specifically created for that print device

When you print a document in an application, you select the printer that will be the destination for the print job.

The printer is associated with a printer driver that takes the commands generated by the application and converts them into a ***printer control language (PCL),*** a language understood by the printer. PCLs can be standardized, like the PostScript language, or they can be proprietary languages developed by the print device manufacturer.

The printer driver enables you to configure the print job to use the various capabilities of the print device. These capabilities are typically incorporated into the printer's Properties sheet. For example, your word-processing application does not know if your print device supports color or duplex printing. It is the printer driver that provides support for features such as these.

After the printer processes a print job, it stores the job in a print queue, known as a ***spooler.*** Depending on the arrangement of the printing components, the spooled jobs might be in PCL format, ready to go to the print device, or in an interim format, in which case the printer driver must process the spooled jobs into the PCL format before sending them to the device. If other jobs are waiting to be printed, a new job might wait in the spooler for some time. When the server finally sends the job to the print device, the device reads the PCL commands and produces the hard-copy document.

UNDERSTANDING THE FLEXIBILITY OF WINDOWS PRINTING

The flexibility of the Windows print architecture is manifested in the different ways that you can deploy the four printing components. A single computer can perform all of the tasks (except for that of the print device, of course), or you can distribute them about the network. The following sections describe four fundamental configurations that are the basis of most Windows printer deployments. You can scale these configurations up to accommodate a network of virtually any size.

DIRECT PRINTING

The simplest print architecture consists of one print device connected to one computer, also known as a *locally attached print device,* as shown in Figure 5-45. When you connect a print device directly to a Windows Server 2008 computer and print from an application running on that system, the computer supplies the printer, printer driver, and print server functions.

Figure 5-45

A locally attached print device

LOCALLY ATTACHED PRINTER SHARING

In addition to printing from an application running on that computer, you can also share the printer (and the print device) with other users on the same network. In this arrangement, the computer with the locally attached print device functions as a print server. Figure 5-46 shows the other computers on the network, the print clients.

Figure 5-46

Sharing a locally attached printer

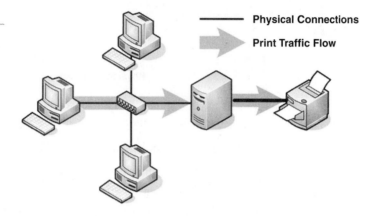

Physical Connections

Print Traffic Flow

In the default Windows Server 2008 printer-sharing configuration, each client uses its own printer and printer driver. As before, the application running on the client computer sends the print job to the printer and the printer driver renders the job, based on the capabilities of the print device.

The main advantage of this printing arrangement is that multiple users, located anywhere on the network, can send jobs to a single print device, which is connected to a computer functioning as a print server. The downside is that processing the print jobs for many users can impose a significant burden on the print server. Although any Windows computer can function as a print server, you should use a workstation for this purpose only when you have no more than a handful of print clients to support or a very light printing volume.

When you use a server computer as a print server, you must be aware of the system resources that the print server role will require. Dedicating a computer solely to print server duties is only necessary when you have several print clients or a high volume of printing to support. In most cases, Windows servers that run the Print Services role perform other functions as well. However, you must be judicious in your role assignments.

NETWORK-ATTACHED PRINTING

The printing solutions discussed thus far involve print devices connected directly to a computer, using a Universal Serial Bus (USB) or other port. Print devices do not necessarily have to be attached to computers, however. You can connect a print device directly to the network instead. Many print device models are equipped with network interface adapters, enabling you to attach a standard network cable. Some print devices have expansion slots into which you can install a network printing adapter, purchased separately. Finally, for print devices with no networking capabilities, standalone network print servers are available, which enable you to attach one or more print devices and connect to the network. Print devices so equipped have their own IP addresses and typically an embedded Web-based configuration interface.

With *network-attached print devices,* the primary deployment decision that the administrator must make is to decide which computer will function as the print server. One simple, but often less than practical, option is to let each print client function as its own print server, as shown in Figure 5-47. Each client processes and spools its own print jobs, connects to the print device using a TCP (Transmission Control Protocol) port, and sends the jobs directly to the device for printing.

Figure 5-47

A network-attached print device with multiple print servers

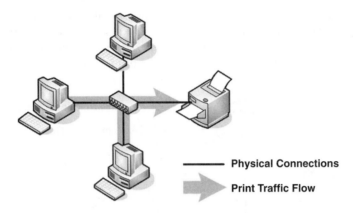

Even individual end users with no administrative assistance will find this arrangement simple to set up. However, the disadvantages are many, including the following:

- Users examining the print queue see only their own jobs.
- Users are oblivious of the other users accessing the print device. They have no way of knowing what other jobs have been sent to the print device, or how long it will be until the print device completes their jobs.
- Administrators have no way of centrally managing the print queue, because each client has its own print queue.
- Administrators cannot implement advanced printing features, such as printer pools or remote administration.
- Error messages appear only on the computer that originated the job the print device is currently processing.
- All print job processing is performed by the client computer, rather than being partially offloaded to an external print server.

For these reasons, this arrangement is only suitable for small workgroup networks that do not have dedicated administrators supporting them.

NETWORK-ATTACHED PRINTER SHARING

The other, far more popular, option for network-attached printing is to designate one computer as a print server and use it to service all of the print clients on the network. To do this, you install a printer on one computer, the print server, and configure it to access the print device directly through a TCP port. Then, you share the printer, just as you would a locally attached print device, and configure the clients to access the print share.

As you can see in Figure 5-48, the physical configuration is exactly the same as in the previous arrangement, but the logical path the print jobs take on the way to the print device is different. Instead of going straight to the print device, the jobs go to the print server, which spools them and sends them to the print device in order.

Figure 5-48

A network-attached print device with a single, shared print server

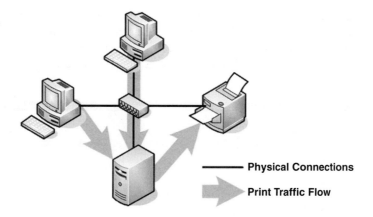

Physical Connections

Print Traffic Flow

With this arrangement, virtually all of the disadvantages of the multiple print server arrangement become advantages, as follows:

- All of the client jobs are stored in a single print queue so that users and administrators can see a complete list of the jobs waiting to be printed.
- Part of the job rendering burden is shifted to the print server, returning control of the client computer to the user more quickly.
- Administrators can manage all of the queued jobs from a remote location.
- Print error messages appear on all client computers.
- Administrators can implement printer pools and other advanced printing features.
- Administrators can manage security, auditing, monitoring, and logging functions from a central location.

Using the Print Services Role

Printer sharing is possible on any Windows Server 2008 computer in its default installation configuration. However, installing the Print Services role on the computer provides additional tools that are particularly useful to administrators involved with network printing on an enterprise scale.

When you install the Print Services role using Server Manager's Add Roles Wizard, you can select from the following role services:

- Print Server—Installs the Print Management console for Microsoft Management Console (MMC), which enables administrators to deploy, monitor, and manage printers throughout the enterprise. This is the only role service that is required when you add the Print Services role.
- LPD Service—Enables UNIX clients running the LPR (line printer remote) program to send their print jobs to Windows printers.
- Internet Printing—Creates a Web site that enables users on the Internet to send print jobs to shared Windows printers.

To install the Internet Printing role service, you must also install the Web Server (IIS) role, with certain specific role services, as well as the Windows Process Activation Service feature. The Add Roles Wizard enforces these dependencies automatically when you select the Internet Printing role service.

As always, Windows Server 2008 adds a new node to the Server Manager console when you install a role. The Print Services node contains a filtered view of print-related event log entries, a status display for the role-related system services and role services, and recommended configuration tasks and best practices, as shown in Figure 5-49.

Figure 5-49

The Print Services node in Server Manager

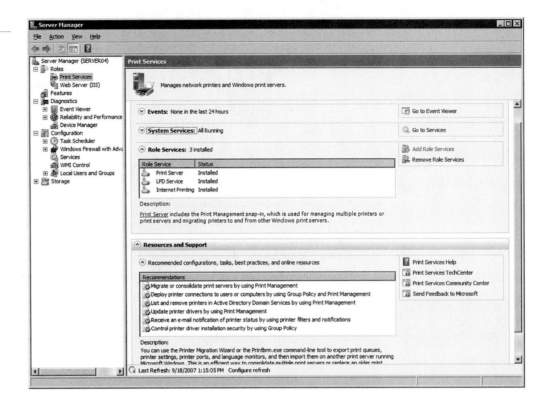

Once you have installed the Print Services role, adding a printer in the traditional way automatically shares it and sets the Printer Sharing option in the Network and Sharing Center to On. Once added, you can manage the printer using the Print Management console.

For older printers, you initiate the installation process by clicking Add Printer Wizard in the Printers control panel. However, most of the print devices on the market today use either a USB connection to a computer or an Ethernet connection to a network.

In the case of a USB-connected printer, you plug the print device into a USB port on the computer and turn on the device to initiate the installation process. For network-attached print devices, an installation program supplied with the product locates the print device on the network, installs the correct drivers, creates a printer on the computer, and configures the printer with the proper IP address and other settings.

USING THE PRINT MANAGEMENT CONSOLE

The Print Management snap-in for MMC consolidates the controls for the printing components throughout the enterprise into a single console. With this tool, you can access the print queues and Properties sheets for all of the network printers in the enterprise, deploy printers to client computers using Group Policy, and create custom views that simplify the process of detecting print devices that need attention due to errors or depleted consumables.

Windows Server 2008 installs the Print Management console when you add the Print Services role to the computer. You can also install the console without the role by adding the Print Services Tools feature, found under Remote Server Administration Tools > Role Administration Tools in Server Manager.

When you launch the Print Management console, the default display, shown in Figure 5-50, includes the following three nodes in the scope (left) pane:

- Custom Filters—Contains composite views of all the printers hosted by the print servers listed in the console, regulated by customizable filters
- Print Servers—Lists all of the print servers you have added to the console, and all of the drivers, forms, ports, and printers for each print server
- Deployed Printers—Lists all of the printers you have deployed with Group Policy using the console

Figure 5-50

The Print Management console

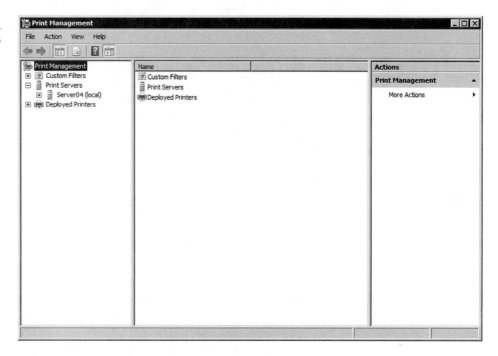

The following sections demonstrate some of the administration tasks you can perform with the Print Management console.

SHARING A PRINTER

To manually share a printer on the network with the Print Management console, use the following procedure.

 SHARE A PRINTER

GET READY. Log on to Windows Server 2008 using a domain account with Administrator privileges. When the logon process is completed, close the Initial Configuration Tasks window and any other windows that appear.

1. Click **Start,** and then click **Administrative Tools** > **Print Management.** The Print Management console appears.
2. Expand the **Print Servers** node and the node representing your print server.

3. In the detail (middle) pane, right-click the printer you want to share and, from the context menu, select **Manage Sharing.** The printer's Properties sheet appears, displaying the Sharing tab, as shown in Figure 5-51.

Figure 5-51

The Sharing tab of a printer's Properties sheet

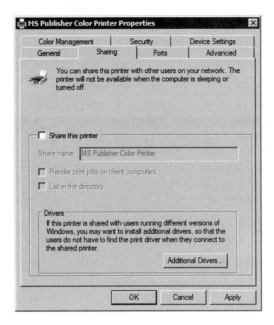

4. Select the **Share this printer** checkbox. The printer name appears in the **Share Name text** box. You can accept the default name or supply one of your own.

5. Select one or both of the following optional checkboxes:

   • **Render print jobs on client computers**—Minimizes the resource utilization on the print server by forcing the print clients to perform the bulk of the print processing.

   • **List in the directory**—Creates a new printer object in the Active Directory database, enabling domain users to locate the printer by searching the directory. This option appears only when the computer is a member of an Active Directory domain.

6. Click **Additional Drivers.** The Additional Drivers dialog box appears, as shown in Figure 5-52. This dialog box enables you to load printer drivers for other versions of the operating system, such as Itanium and x64. When you install the alternate drivers, the print server automatically supplies them to clients running those operating system versions.

Figure 5-52

The Additional Drivers dialog box

7. Select any combination of the available checkboxes and click **OK.** For each checkbox you selected, Windows Server 2008 displays a Printer Drivers dialog box.

8. In each Printer Drivers dialog box, key or browse to the location of the printer drivers for the selected operating system, and then click **OK.**

9. Click **OK** to close the Additional Drivers dialog box.

10. Click **OK** to close the Properties sheet for the printer.

CLOSE the Print Management console.

At this point, the printer is available to clients on the network.

DEPLOYING PRINTERS WITH GROUP POLICY

Configuring a print client to access a shared printer is a simple matter of browsing the network or the Active Directory tree and selecting the printer you want the client to use. However, when you have to configure hundreds or thousands of print clients, the task becomes more complicated. One way to simplify the process of deploying printers to large numbers of clients is to use Active Directory.

Listing printers in the Active Directory database enables users and administrators to search for printers by name, location, or model (as long as you populate the Location and Model fields in the printer object). To create a printer object in the Active Directory database, you can either select the List in the Directory checkbox while sharing the printer, or right-click a printer in the Print Management console and, from the context menu, select List in Directory.

To use Active Directory to deploy printers to clients, you must configure the appropriate policies in a group policy object (GPO). You can link a GPO to any domain, site, or organizational unit (OU) in the Active Directory tree. When you configure a GPO to deploy a printer, all of the users or computers in that domain, site, or OU will receive the printer connection when they log on.

To deploy printers with Group Policy, use the following procedure.

 DEPLOY PRINTERS WITH GROUP POLICY

GET READY. Log on to Windows Server 2008 using a domain account with Administrator privileges. When the logon process is completed, close the Initial Configuration Tasks window and any other windows that appear.

1. Click **Start,** and then click **Administrative Tools** > **Print Management.** The Print Management console appears.

2. Right-click a printer in the console's scope pane and, from the context menu, select **Deploy with Group Policy.** The Deploy with Group Policy dialog box appears, as shown in Figure 5-53.

Figure 5-53

The Deploy with Group Policy dialog box

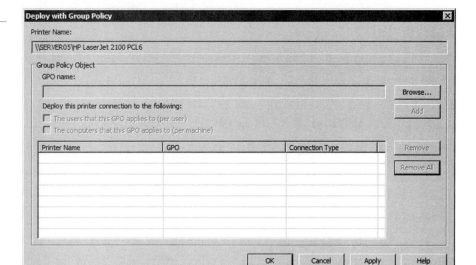

3. Click **Browse.** The Browse for a Group Policy Object dialog box appears, as shown in Figure 5-54.

Figure 5-54

The Browse for a Group Policy Object dialog box

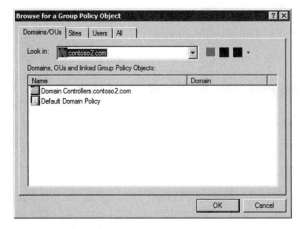

4. Select the group policy object you want to use to deploy the printer and click **OK.** The GPO you selected appears in the GPO Name field.

5. Select the appropriate checkbox to select whether to deploy the printer to the users associated with the GPO, the computers, or both. Then click **Add.** The new printer/GPO associations appear in the table.

Deploying the printer to the users means that all of the users associated with the GPO will receive the printer connection, no matter what computer they use to log on. Deploying the printer to the computers means that all of the computers associated with the GPO will receive the printer connection, no matter who logs on to them.

6. Click **OK.** A Print Management message box appears, informing you that the operation has succeeded.

7. Click **OK,** then click **OK** again to close the Deploy with Group Policy dialog box.

CLOSE the Print Management console.

The next time the Windows Server 2008 or Windows Vista users and/or computers associated with the GPO refresh their policies or restart, they will receive the new settings, and the printer will appear in the Printers control panel.

TAKE NOTE *

Clients running earlier versions of Windows, including Windows XP and Windows Server 2003, do not support automatic policy-based printer deployments. To enable the GPO to deploy printers on these computers, you must configure the systems to run a utility called PushPrinterConnections.exe. The most convenient way to do this is to configure the same GPO you used for the printer deployment to run the program from a user logon script or machine script.

Deploying a Fax Server

Sending faxes, receiving faxes, waiting for faxes, and even walking back and forth to the fax machine can be an enormous drain on productivity in many organizations. Windows Server 2008 includes a Fax Server role that enables users to send faxes from and receive them to their desktops.

By installing the Fax Server role, you enable a Windows Server 2008 computer to send and receive faxes for clients. The clients send their faxes using a standard printer interface, which connects to a fax server on the network as easily as connecting to a local fax modem.

The basic steps involved in setting up a fax server are as follows:

- Add the Fax Server role—Creates the Fax printer and installs the Fax service and the Fax Service Manager console
- Add the Desktop Experience feature—Installs the Windows Fax and Scan application
- Share the fax printer—Makes the printer available to network users
- Configure the fax device—Configures the fax modem or other device that will physically send and receive the fax transmissions
- Configure incoming fax routing—Specifies the actions the server should take when incoming faxes arrive
- Designate fax users—Specifies which users are permitted to send and receive faxes using the server

The following sections examine each of these steps.

USING THE FAX SERVICES ROLE

To use a Windows Server 2008 computer as a fax server, you must add the Fax Server role, using Server Manager console. The Fax Server role consists of only a single role service, which is dependent on the Print Services role.

Installing the Fax Server role adds the Fax Service Manager snap-in to the Server Manager console. Using the Fax Service Manager, administrators can perform the following tasks:

- View and configure fax devices, such as modems
- Specify routing policies for inbound faxes
- Specify rules for outbound faxes
- Manage fax users
- Configure fax logging and archiving

ADDING THE DESKTOP EXPERIENCE FEATURE

The Fax Service Manager can configure various fax server functions, but it cannot actually send outgoing faxes or view incoming ones. To send and view faxes, you must use the Windows Fax and Scan program, shown in Figure 5-55.

Figure 5-55

The Windows Fax and Scan program

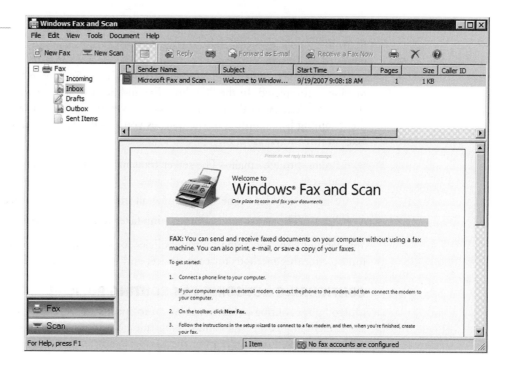

Windows Fax and Scan is included with Windows Server 2008, but it is not installed by default. Instead, Windows Fax and Scan is packaged as part of a single feature called Desktop Experience, along with other non-essential elements, such as desktop themes and Windows Media Player. The assumption is that most servers do not need these applications, and administrators would prefer not to have them installed unnecessarily.

When you add the Desktop Experience feature on a computer running the Fax Server role, the Windows Fax and Scan program is activated and appears in the Start menu. However, if you want to use a Windows Server 2008 computer as a fax client, installing the Desktop Experience feature does not enable any of the elements by default. You must enable them individually as you use them.

SHARING THE FAX PRINTER

Adding the Fax Server role installs a Fax printer, which is what clients use to send outgoing faxes. When a client selects the Fax printer instead of a standard printer, the print job goes to the fax server instead of to a print server or print device. However, while adding the role creates the Fax printer, it does not share it. You must share the fax printer manually, using the same procedure described earlier in this lesson, in "Sharing a Printer."

CONFIGURING A FAX DEVICE

For a Windows Server 2008 computer to function as a fax server, it must have a hardware device capable of sending and receiving faxes over a telephone line, such as a modem. Depending on the fax volume it must support, a fax server's hardware can range from a standard, single fax modem to a rack-mounted device containing many modems.

The Fax printer created by the Fax Server role represents all of the fax devices installed on the computer. If there are multiple devices, the server can distribute outgoing faxes among a group of devices, but there is only one single fax job queue on the system.

When you run the Fax Service Manager console, the fax devices appear in the Devices folder automatically. By default, the server configures all devices to send faxes only. To receive faxes, you must configure the device to do so.

In addition to at least one fax device, a fax server also needs a provider, which manages the devices and controls fax processing. Windows Server 2008 includes the Microsoft Modem Device Provider, which provides basic functionality for devices that conform to the Unimodem driver standard. Third-party providers might include additional features.

CONFIGURING INCOMING FAX ROUTING POLICIES

Fax routing policies provide administrators with various ways to give incoming faxes to their intended recipients. When you configure the fax devices on a Windows Server 2008 fax server to receive faxes, an inbound document first goes to an incoming fax queue, until the transmission is completed. In the Windows Fax and Scan window, this queue corresponds to the Incoming folder. After the fax device has received the entire transmission, the server routes the incoming fax according to the policies you specify. The fax server can route incoming faxes in three ways, as follows:

- Route through email—The server transmits all incoming faxes to a specified email address.
- Store in a folder—The server copies all incoming faxes to a specified hard disk folder.
- Print—The server sends all incoming faxes to a specified printer.

You configure the incoming routing policies for each fax device individually. You can enable multiple routing methods for each device, and set their respective priorities.

CONFIGURING OUTGOING FAX ROUTING POLICIES

Outgoing fax routing policies enable you to specify the sending parameters for fax transmissions, including cover pages and dialing rules. You can configure the properties the server should apply to outgoing faxes in the Fax Service Manager console.

It is also possible to use outgoing fax policies to specify which fax devices the server should use when dialing specific locations. To do this, you must create one or more routing groups and one or more rules. The routing group contains at least one of the server's fax devices, and the rule consists of a country code and/or area code, with the group that the server should use when dialing those codes.

SELECTING FAX USERS

For users to access the fax server, an administrator must create accounts for them in the Fax Service Manager console, using the Create New Account dialog box, as shown in Figure 5-56.

Figure 5-56

The Create New Account dialog box

SUMMARY SKILL MATRIX

IN THIS LESSON YOU LEARNED:

- The Distributed File System (DFS) includes two technologies: DFS Namespaces and DFS Replication, which can simplify the process of locating files, control the amount of traffic passing over WAN links, provide users at remote sites with local file server access, configure the network to survive a WAN link failure, and facilitate consistent backups.

- DFS is a virtual namespace technology that enables you to create a single directory tree that contains references to shared folders located on various file servers, all over the network.

- DFS Replication works in tandem with DFS Namespaces to provide unified services, such as data distribution, load balancing, and data collection.

- The File Server Resource Manager console provides tools that enable file server administrators to monitor and regulate their server storage, by establishing quotas that limit the amount of storage space allotted to each user, creating screens that prevent users from storing specific types of files on server drives, and generating reports providing details of users' storage activities.

- Printing in Microsoft Windows typically involves the following four components: print device, printer, print server, and print driver.

- The simplest form of print architecture consists of one print device connected to one computer, known as a locally attached print device. You can share this printer (and the print device) with other users on the same network.

- With network-attached print devices, the administrator's primary deployment decision is which computer will function as the print server.

- The Print Management snap-in for MMC is an administrative tool that consolidates the controls for the printing components throughout the enterprise into a single console.

- Windows Server 2008 includes a Fax Server role that enables users to send faxes from and receive them to their desktops.

■ Knowledge Assessment

Matching

Complete the following exercise by matching the terms with their corresponding definitions.

    a. print device
    b. hard quota
    c. printer control language (PCL)
    d. File Server Resource Manager (FSRM)
    e. soft quota
    f. Remote Differential Compression (RDC)
    g. printer driver
    h. Distributed File System (DFS)
    i. target
    j. printer

_____ **1.** creates a virtual directory tree consisting of shared folders from multiple servers

_____ **2.** enables administrators to create storage quotas and file screens

_____ **3.** prevents users from consuming more than their allotted amount of storage space

_____ **4.** the software interface through which a computer communicates with a print device

_____ **5.** formats documents in preparation for printing

_____ **6.** provides controls for the specific capabilities of a print device

_____ **7.** hardware that produces hard copy documents

_____ **8.** conserves network bandwidth by replicating only the data that has changed

_____ **9.** warns users when they consume their allotted amount of storage space

_____ **10.** an actual folder represented in the virtual DFS directory tree

Multiple Choice

Select one or more correct answers for each of the following questions.

1. To which of the following elements does the File Services node in the Server Manager's scope pane provide access?
    a. Share and Storage Management
    b. Role Services
    c. Reliability and Performance
    d. WMI Control

2. Which of the following statements is true about the Distributed File System?
    a. DFS is a virtual namespace technology that includes two components: DFS Namespaces and DFS Replication.
    b. DFS exists as a directory tree that contains true copies of the shared folders on different servers.
    c. DFS cannot control the amount of traffic passing over WAN links.
    d. DFS does not enable a network to tolerate a WAN link failure with a minimal loss of productivity.

3. Which of the following is *not* a task that file server administrators can perform by using the File Server Resource Manager (FSRM) console?
   a. monitor file systems for access by intruders
   b. generate reports providing details of users' storage activities
   c. create quota templates and file screens
   d. establish quotas that limit the amount of storage space allotted to each user

4. Which of the following statements is true about printer control languages (PCLs)?
   a. PCLs are controlled by industry-wide standards developed by the Institute of Electrical and Electronics engineers (IEEE).
   b. PCLs ensure that spooled jobs are in PCL format, ready to go directly to the print device.
   c. PCL can be based on industry standards.
   d. PCLs can be proprietary languages developed by print device manufacturers.

5. Which of the following is *not* true with regard to a fax server?
   a. You must install the Print Services role before, or with, the Fax Server role.
   b. Clients send their faxes via the standard fax interface.
   c. If a fax server has multiple fax devices, the system can distribute outgoing faxes among a group of devices, but there is only one fax job queue for the entire system.
   d. The Fax Server role installs the Fax Service Manager console.

6. The Distributed File System enables administrators to do which of the following?
   a. facilitate consistent backups
   b. simplify the process of locating files
   c. provide users at remote sites with local file server access
   d. do all of the above

7. Which is *not* an accurate statement about quota templates?
   a. Quota templates limit the disk space an administrator permits a user to consume on a specified volume or folder.
   b. Quota templates specify what the actions Windows Server 2008 should take when a user reaches a specified storage threshold.
   c. You can use quota templates to configure a soft quota, which prohibits users from consuming disk space beyond the allotted amount.
   d. In enterprise networks, administrators use quota templates to manage quota assignments on a large scale.

8. After installing the role and role services for DFS, which of the following configuration tasks might you need to perform?
   a. task scheduling
   b. adding folders to the namespace
   c. creating a replication group
   d. configuring referral order

9. Which of the following describes the most common use for file screens?
   a. prevent users from storing audio and video files on network server drives
   b. protect database files from unauthorized access
   c. prevent users from consuming too much storage space on network server drives
   d. generate reports about users' storage habits

10. Which of the following steps involved in setting up a fax server should come first?
    a. share the fax printer
    b. add the Fax Server role
    c. configure the fax device
    d. configure incoming fax routing

Review Questions

1. Describe how the Distributed File System is able to conserve WAN bandwidth by replicating shared folders to file servers at remote locations.

■ Case Scenarios

Scenario 5-1: Creating FSRM Quotas

Kathleen has installed the File Server Resource Manager role service on her Windows Server 2008 file servers and created a number of quotas to limit the server disk space each user can consume. In each quota, she has configured FSRM to send email messages to the user and to the administrator if any user exceeds a quota. She has also configured FSRM to create a Quota Usage report each Friday. The next week, on examining the report, she discovers that several users have exceeded their quotas, but she has received no emails to that effect. What is the most likely reason that Kathleen did not receive the FSRM emails and what can she do about it?

Planning Storage Solutions

OBJECTIVE DOMAIN MATRIX

TECHNOLOGY SKILL	OBJECTIVE DOMAIN	OBJECTIVE DOMAIN NUMBER
Planning Server Storage.	Plan storage	5.1

KEY TERMS

arbitrated loop (FC-AL)	external drive array	logical unit numbers (LUNs)
ATA (Advanced Technology Attachment)	Fibre Channel	Network attached storage (NAS)
	Fibre Channel Protocol (FCP)	partition style
basic disks	file-based I/O	serial ATA (SATA)
block I/O access	Internet Storage Name Service (iSNS)	Small Computer System Interface (SCSI)
direct-attached storage		
disk duplexing	iSCSI initiator	storage area network (SAN)
disk mirroring	iSCSI target	switched fabric (FC-SW)
DiskPart.exe	JBOD (Just a Bunch of Disks)	VDS hardware provider
dynamic disk	logical unit number (LUN)	

Storage is one of the most important elements of server performance. No matter what role a server plays on the network, its performance relies on an efficient storage subsystem. This lesson examines some of the storage technologies commonly found on Microsoft Windows Server 2008 computers, including the following:

- Planning a storage strategy
- Using Redundant Array of Independent Disks (RAID)
- Preparing disks in Windows Server 2008
- Using Windows storage management tools
- Building a storage area network

■ Planning Server Storage

THE BOTTOM LINE

A Windows server can conceivably perform its tasks using the same type of storage as a workstation, that is, one or more standard hard disks connected to a standard drive interface such as Serial ATA (SATA). However, the I/O burdens of a server are quite different from those of a workstation, and a standard storage subsystem can easily be overwhelmed by file requests from dozens or hundreds of users. In addition, standard hard disks offer no fault tolerance and are limited in their scalability.

There are a variety of storage technologies that are better suited for server use, and the process of designing a storage solution for a server depends on several factors, including the following:

- The amount of storage the server needs
- The number of users that will be accessing the server at the same time
- The sensitivity of the data to be stored on the server
- The importance of the data to the organization

The following sections examine these factors and the technologies you can choose when creating a plan for your network storage solutions.

CERTIFICATION READY?
Plan storage
5.1

How Many Servers Do I Need?

When is one big file server preferable to several smaller ones?

One of the most frequently asked questions when planning a server deployment is whether it is better to use one big server or several smaller ones. In Lesson 4, "Planning Application Services," you learned about the advantages and disadvantages of using one server to perform several roles versus distributing the roles among several smaller servers, so you should now have some idea of which arrangement would be better suited to your organization.

If you are considering one large server, or if your organization's storage requirements are extremely large, you must also consider the inherent storage limitations of Windows Server 2008, which are listed in Table 6-1.

Table 6-1

Windows Server 2008 Storage Limitations

STORAGE CHARACTERISTIC	LIMITATION
Maximum basic volume size	2 terabytes
Maximum dynamic volume size (simple and mirrored volumes)	2 terabytes
Maximum dynamic volume size (spanned and striped volumes)	64 terabytes (2 terabytes per disk, with a maximum of 32 disks)
Maximum dynamic volume size (RAID-5 volumes)	62 terabytes (2 terabytes per disk, with a maximum of 32 disks, and 2 terabytes reserved for parity information)
Maximum NTFS volume size	2^{32} clusters minus 1 cluster (using the default 4 kilobyte cluster size, the maximum volume size is 16 terabytes minus 64 kilobytes; using the maximum 64 kilobyte cluster size, the maximum volume size is 256 terabytes minus 64 kilobytes)
Maximum number of clusters on an NTFS volume	2^{32} (4,294,967,296)
Maximum NTFS file size	2^{44} bytes (16 terabytes) minus 64 kilobytes
Maximum number of files on an NTFS volume	2^{32} minus 1 file (4,294,967,295)
Maximum number of volumes on a server	Approximately 2,000 (1,000 dynamic volumes and the rest basic)

The number of sites your enterprise network encompasses and the technologies you use to provide network communication between those sites can also affect your plans. If, for example, your organization has branch offices scattered around the world and uses relatively expensive wide area networking (WAN) links to connect them, it would probably be more economical to install a server at each location than to have all of your users access a single server using the WAN links.

Within each site, the number of servers you need can depend on how often your users work with the same resources and how much fault tolerance and high availability you want to build into the system. For example, if each department in your organization typically works with its own applications and documents and rarely needs access to those of other departments, deploying individual servers to each department might be preferable. If everyone in your organization works with the same set of resources, a single server might be a better choice.

Estimating Storage Requirements

The amount of storage space you need in a server depends on a variety of factors, not just the initial requirements of your applications and users.

In the case of an application server, start by allocating the amount of space needed for the application files themselves, plus any other space the application needs, as recommended by the developer. If users will be storing documents on the server, then allocate a specific amount of space for each user the server will support. Then, factor in the potential growth of your organization and your network, both in terms of additional users and additional space required by each user, and of the application itself, in terms of data files and updates.

In addition to the space allocated to applications and individual users, you must also consider the storage requirements for the following server elements:

- Operating system—The size of the operating system installation depends on the roles and features you choose to install. A typical Windows Server 2008 installation with the File Services role takes just over 7 GB, but the system requirements for Windows Server 2008 recommend 40 GB and state that 80 GB is optimal. For a Server Core installation, 10 GB is recommended and 40 GB is optimal.
- Paging file—By default, the paging file on a Windows Server 2008 computer is 1.5 times the amount of memory installed in the computer.
- Memory dump—When Windows Server 2008 experiences a serious malfunction, it offers to dump the contents of the system memory to a file, which technicians can use for diagnostic purposes. The maximum size for a memory dump file is the amount of memory installed in the computer plus one megabyte.
- Log files—Be sure to consider any applications that maintain their own logs, in addition to the operating system logs. You can configure the maximum log size for the Windows event logs and for most application logs, and add those values to calculate the total log space required.
- Shadow copies—The Windows Server 2008 shadow copies feature automatically retains copies of files on a server volume in multiple versions from specific points in time. Shadow copies can utilize up to 10 percent of a volume, by default. However, Microsoft recommends enlarging this value for volumes containing files that are frequently modified.
- Fault tolerance—Fault-tolerance technologies, such as disk mirroring and RAID, can profoundly affect disk consumption. Mirroring disks cuts the effective storage size in half, and RAID 5 can reduce it by as much as one third.

Selecting a Storage Technology

Planning for server storage encompasses both hardware and software elements. You must make decisions about how much storage space you need, as well as how much and what type of fault tolerance, and then select appropriate hardware to implement your decisions.

The following sections examine some of the storage technologies you can choose from when designing a server storage subsystem.

SELECTING A DISK TECHNOLOGY

As of this writing, standard hard drives up to 1 terabyte in size are available, and higher capacities are no doubt on the way. Most computers, including servers, use *direct-attached storage,* that is, the hard drives are located inside the computer case. For servers that require more storage space than a standard computer case can hold, or that have special availability requirements, there are a variety of external storage hardware options available.

Of the many specifications that hard disk manufacturers provide for their products, the best gauge of the drive's performance is the rotational speed of the spindle that holds the platters. Typical desktop workstation hard drives have rotational speeds of 7,200 or 10,000 revolutions per minute (rpm). For a server, 10,000 should be considered the minimum acceptable speed; many higher-end server drives run at 15,000 rpm, which is preferable but costly.

Just as important as the speed and capacity of the hard disks you select is the interface the disks use to connect to the computer. A server on an enterprise network often has to handle large numbers of disk I/O requests simultaneously, far more than a workstation drive with a single user ever would. For that reason, an interface that might be more than sufficient for a workstation, such as the *ATA (Advanced Technology Attachment)* interface that most workstation drives use, would perform poorly under a file server load.

ATA devices are limited to a maximum transmission speed of 133 megabytes/second (MB/sec), which is relatively slow by server standards. The other big problem with ATA devices is that only a single command can be on the cable at any one time. If you have two drives connected to an ATA cable, a command sent to the first drive has to be completed before the system can send a command to the second drive. For a server that must handle requests from many simultaneous users, this is an inherently inefficient arrangement.

The newer *serial ATA (SATA)* standard increases the maximum transmission speed to 300 MB/sec and addresses the ATA unitasking problem with a technology called Native Command Queuing (NCQ). NCQ enables a drive to optimize the order in which it processes commands, to minimize drive seek times. However, SATA supports only a single drive per channel, and can utilize NCQ only when the computer has a motherboard and chipset that supports the Advanced Host Controller Interface (AHCI) standard. Computers that do not comply with this standard run the drives in an "IDE emulation" mode, which disables their NCQ and hot plugging capabilities. While SATA drives are more efficient than ATA, and can be a viable solution for relatively low-volume servers, they are not suitable for large enterprise servers.

Small Computer System Interface (SCSI) is the most commonly used storage interface for enterprise servers. SCSI offers transmission rates up to 640 MB/sec, support for up to 16 devices on a single bus, and the ability to queue commands on each device. This enables multiple drives connected to one SCSI host adapter to process commands simultaneously and independently, which is an ideal environment for a high-volume server.

There are many different SCSI standards, with different bus types, transmission speeds, and cable configurations. To use SCSI on a server, all of the devices and host adapters must support the same standard. You connect SCSI devices to a host adapter using a daisy chain cable arrangement called a SCSI bus. Many host adapters enable you to connect both internal and external devices, so you can expand the bus as needed, even if the computer case does not have room for additional drives. Every device on a SCSI bus has an identifier called a SCSI ID, which the host adapter uses to send commands to the device. Subcomponents of a SCSI device, such as individual drives in an array, are identified using *logical unit numbers (LUNs)*.

SCSI hard drives are usually quite a bit more expensive than those using any of the other disk interfaces, despite the fact that the disk assemblies are virtually identical; only the electronics are different. However, for most administrators of large enterprise networks, the enhanced performance of SCSI drives in a high-traffic environment is worth the added expense.

TAKE NOTE*

Hard drives using the ATA interface are also commonly referred to as Integrated Drive Electronics (IDE) or Enhanced IDE (EIDE) drives.

TAKE NOTE*

With the introduction of the serial ATA interface, the original ATA interface has been retroactively named parallel ATA, in reference to the way in which these devices transmit data over 16 connections simultaneously.

USING EXTERNAL DRIVE ARRAYS

High capacity servers often store hard drives in a separate housing, called an ***external drive array***, which typically incorporates a disk controller, power supply, cooling fans, and cache memory into an independent unit. Drive arrays can connect to a computer using a disk interface, such as SCSI (Small Computer System Interface), IEEE 1394 (FireWire), or USB 2.0, or a network interface, such as iSCSI or Fibre Channel.

Drive arrays enable a server to contain more hard drives than a normal computer case can hold, and often include additional fault-tolerance features, such as hot-swappable drives, redundant power supplies, and hardware-based RAID. Obviously, the more features the array has, and the more drives it can hold, the higher the cost. Large arrays intended for enterprise networks can easily run into the five-figure price range.

Drive arrays typically operate in one of two configurations:

- ***Storage area network (SAN)***—A SAN is a separate network dedicated solely to storage devices, such as drive arrays, magnetic tape autochangers, and optical jukeboxes, as shown in Figure 6-1. SANs use a high speed networking technology, such as SCSI, iSCSI, or Fibre Channel to enable them to transmit large amounts of data very quickly. Therefore, a server connected to a SAN will have two separate network interfaces, one to the SAN and one to the standard local area network (LAN). A SAN provides block-based storage services to the computers connected to it, just as if the storage devices were installed inside the computer. The storage hardware on a SAN might provide additional capabilities, such as RAID, but the file system used to store and protect data on the SAN devices is implemented by the computer.

Figure 6-1

A SAN is a separate network dedicated to file servers and external storage devices

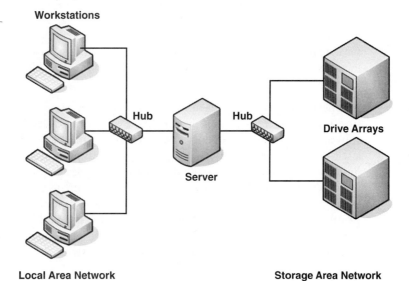

- ***Network attached storage (NAS)***—A NAS drive array differs from a SAN array primarily in its software. NAS devices are essentially dedicated file servers that provide file-based storage services directly to clients on the network. A NAS array connects to a standard LAN, using traditional Fast Ethernet or Gigabit Ethernet hardware, as shown in Figure 6-2, and does not require a computer to implement the file system or function as a file server. In addition to the storage subsystem, the NAS device has its own processor and memory hardware, and runs its own operating system with a Web interface for administrative access. The operating system is typically a stripped-down version of

UNIX designed to provide only data storage, data access, and management functions. Most NAS devices support both the Server Message Block (SMB) protocol used by Windows clients and the Network File System (NFS) protocol used by most UNIX and Linux distributions.

Figure 6-2

A NAS device connects directly to the LAN and functions as a self-contained file server

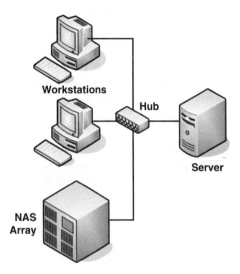

SANs and NAS devices are both technologies designed to provide scalability and fault tolerance to network data storage systems. Generally speaking, a SAN is more complicated and more expensive to implement, but it can provide excellent performance, due to its use of a separate network medium and virtually unlimited storage capacity. Windows Server 2008 includes several new SAN management features and tools, which are discussed later in this lesson.

Adding a NAS device to your network is a simple way to provide your users with additional storage and reduce the processing burden on your servers. Despite its almost plug-and-play convenience, however, NAS does have some significant drawbacks. Because the NAS array is a self-contained device with its own processing hardware and operating system, it has inherent limitations. NAS devices typically do not have upgradeable processors, memory, or network interfaces. If a NAS device is overburdened by too many users or I/O requests, it can reach its performance limit, and there is nothing you can do except purchase another NAS device. By contrast, direct-attached storage and SANs both use standard computers to serve files, which you can upgrade in all the usual ways: by adding or replacing hardware, moving the drives to a more powerful computer, or adding an additional server to a cluster.

Planning for Storage Fault Tolerance

How valuable is your data, and how much are you willing to spend to protect it from disaster?

Depending on the nature of your organization, fault tolerance for your servers might be a convenience or an absolute requirement. For some businesses, a server hard drive failure might mean a few hours of lost productivity. For an order entry department, it could mean lost income. For a hospital records department, it could mean lost lives. Depending on where in this range your organization falls, you might consider using a fault tolerance mechanism to make sure that your users always have access to their applications and data.

The essence of fault tolerance is immediate redundancy. If one copy of a file becomes unavailable due to a disk error or failure, another copy online can take its place almost immediately. A variety of fault tolerance mechanisms provide this redundancy in different ways. Some create redundant blocks, redundant files, redundant volumes, redundant drives, and even redundant servers.

As with many computer technologies, fault tolerance is a tradeoff between performance and expense. The mechanisms that provide the most fault tolerance are usually the most expensive. And it is up to you and your organization to decide the value of continuous access to your data.

The following sections discuss some of the most common fault tolerance mechanisms used by and for servers.

USING DISK MIRRORING

Disk mirroring, in which the computer writes the same data to identical volumes on two different disks, is one of the simplest forms of fault tolerance to implement and manage, but it is also one of the more expensive solutions. By mirroring volumes, you are essentially paying twice as much for your storage space.

Little or no performance penalty is associated with mirroring volumes, as long as you use a hardware configuration that enables the two drives to write their data simultaneously. As discussed earlier in this lesson, SCSI and SATA drives are suitable for disk mirroring, but parallel ATA drives are not, because two ATA drives on the same interface have to write their data sequentially, and not simultaneously, slowing down the volume's performance substantially.

A variation on disk mirroring, called ***disk duplexing***, uses duplicate host adapters as well as duplicate hard drives. Installing the drives on separate host adapters adds an extra measure of fault tolerance, which enables users to continue working if either a drive or a host adapter fails. Duplexing also enables the computer to mirror ATA drives effectively, because each disk is connected to a separate host adapter.

USING RAID

RAID is a group of technologies that use multiple disk drives in various configurations to store redundant data, providing increased performance or fault tolerance, or both. Table 6-2 lists the standard RAID configurations.

Table 6-2

RAID Levels

RAID Level	RAID Functionality	Number of Disks Required	Description
RAID 0	Stripe set without parity	2, minimum	Implemented in Windows Server 2008 as a striped volume, RAID 0 provides no fault tolerance, but it does enhance performance, due to the parallel read and write operations that occur on all of the drives simultaneously. RAID 0 has no error detection mechanism, so the failure of one disk causes the loss of all data on the volume.
RAID 1	Mirror set without parity	2, minimum	Implemented in Windows Server 2008 as a mirrored volume, a RAID 1 array provides increased read performance, as well as fault tolerance. The array can continue to serve files as long as one of the disks remains operational.

(continued)

Table 6-2 (continued)

RAID Level	RAID Functionality	Number of Disks Required	Description
RAID 3	Byte-level stripe set with dedicated parity	3, minimum	Not implemented in Windows Server 2008, a RAID 3 array stripes data at the byte level across the disks, reserving one disk for parity information. A RAID 3 array can survive the loss of any one disk, but because every write to one of the data disks requires a write to the parity disk, the parity disk becomes a performance bottleneck.
RAID 4	Block-level stripe set with dedicated parity	3, minimum	Not implemented in Windows Server 2008, RAID 4 is identical in structure to RAID 3, except that a RAID 4 array uses larger, block-level stripes, which improves performance on the data disks. The parity disk can still be a performance bottleneck, however.
RAID 5	Stripe set with distributed parity	3, minimum	Implemented in Windows Server 2008 as a RAID-5 volume, RAID 5 stripes data and parity blocks across all of the disks, making sure that a block and its parity information are never stored on the same disk. Distributing the parity eliminates the performance bottleneck of the dedicated parity drive in RAID 3 and RAID 4, but the need to calculate the parity information still adds overhead to the system. A RAID 5 array can tolerate the loss of any one of its drives, and rebuild the missing data when the drive is repaired or replaced.
RAID 6	Stripe set with dual distributed parity	4, minimum	Not implemented in Windows Server 2008, RAID 6 uses the same structure as RAID 5, except that it stripes two copies of the parity information with the data. This enables the array to survive the failure of two drives. When a RAID 5 array suffers a drive failure, the array is vulnerable to data loss until the failed drive is replaced and the missing data rebuilt, which in the case of a large volume can take a long time. A RAID 6 array remains protected against data loss, even while one failed drive is rebuilding.

Parity is a mathematical algorithm that some RAID levels use to provide data redundancy in their disk write operations. To calculate the parity information for a RAID array, the system takes the values for the same data bit at a specific location on each of the drives in the array and adds them together to determine if the total is odd or even. The system then uses the resulting total to calculate a value for a parity bit corresponding to those data bits. The system then repeats the process for every bit location on the drives. If one of the drives is lost, due to a hardware failure, the system can restore each lost data bit by calculating its value using the remaining data bits and the parity bit.

For example, in an array with five disks, suppose the first four disks have the values 1, 1, 0, and 1 for their first bit. The total of the four bits is 3, an odd number, so the system sets the first bit of the fifth disk, the parity disk, to 0, indicating an odd result for the total of the bits on the other four disks. Suppose then that one of the disks fails. If the parity disk fails, no actual data is lost, so data I/O can proceed normally. If one of the four data disks is lost, the total of the first bits in the remaining three disks will either be odd or even. If the total is even, then because we know the parity bit is odd, the bit in the missing disk must have been a 1. If the total is odd, the bit in the missing disk must have been a 0. Once the failed disk hardware is replaced, the RAID controller can reconstruct the lost data.

RAID arrays that use parity provide the same fault tolerance as mirrored disks, in that the array can survive the failure of any one drive, but they leave more storage space for data. While mirrored disks only provide half of their total storage capacity for data, the data storage capacity of a RAID array that uses single parity is the size of the disks multiplied by the number of disks in the array, minus one. For example, a RAID 5 array that uses five 200 GB disks has a data storage capacity of 800 GB.

One drawback of the parity system, however, is that the process of recalculating lost bits can degrade the array's performance temporarily. In addition, the process of reconstructing an entire drive can be lengthy.

In addition to the RAID levels listed in the table, there are also hybrid RAID solutions, such as RAID 0+1, which is an array of striped drives mirrored on a duplicate array. Windows Server 2008 only provides support for RAID levels 0, 1, and 5, although the operating system does not refer to RAID 0 and RAID 1 as such, calling them striping and mirroring, respectively. To implement these hybrid RAID solutions, or any standard RAID level other than 0, 1, or 5, you must install a third-party product.

Third-party products can implement RAID functions in software (as Windows Server 2008 does) or in hardware. Most third-party RAID implementations are hardware-based, and can range from a host adapter card that you connect to your own drives to a complete array containing drives and a host adapter. Generally speaking, hardware RAID implementations are more expensive than software implementations, but they provide better performance. This is because a hardware RAID solution offloads the parity calculations and disk manipulation functions from the system processor to the RAID controller itself.

■ Understanding Windows Disk Settings

  When preparing a hard disk for use, Windows Server 2008 servers often require different settings than workstations.

When you install Windows Server 2008 on a computer, the setup program automatically performs all of the preparation tasks for the hard disks in the system. However, when you install additional hard disk drives on a server, or when you want to use settings that differ from the system defaults, you must perform the following tasks manually:

- Select a partitioning style—Windows Server 2008 supports two hard disk partition styles, on both x86- and x64-based computers: the master boot record (MBR) partition style and the GUID (globally unique identifier) partition table (GPT) partition style. You must choose one of these partition styles for a drive; you cannot use both.

- Select a disk type—Windows Server 2008 supports two disk types: basic and dynamic. You cannot use both types on the same disk drive, but you can mix disk types in the same computer.

- Divide the disk into partitions or volumes—Although many professionals use the terms partition and volume interchangeably, it is correct to refer to partitions on basic disks, and volumes on dynamic disks.

- Format the partitions or volumes with a file system—Windows Server 2008 supports the NTFS file system and the FAT file system (including the FAT16, FAT32, and exFAT variants).

The following sections examine the options for each of these tasks.

Selecting a Partition Style

> The term *partition style* refers to the method that Windows operating systems use to organize partitions on the disk.

Windows Server 2008 computers can use either one of the following two hard disk partition styles:

- MBR—The MBR partition style has been around since before Windows and is still the default partition style for x86-based and x64-based computers.
- GPT—GPT has also been around for a while, but no x86 version of Windows prior to Windows Server 2008 and Windows Vista supports it. (Windows XP Professional x64 Edition does support GPT.) Now, you can use the GPT partition style on x86-, as well as x64-based, computers.

Before Windows Server 2008 and Windows Vista, all x86-based Windows computers used only the MBR partition style. Computers based on the x64 platform could use either the MBR or GPT partition style, as long as the GPT disk was not the boot disk.

MBR uses a partition table to point to the locations of the partitions on the disk. The MBR disk partitioning style supports volumes up to 2 terabytes in size, and up to either four primary partitions or three primary partitions and one extended partition on a single drive.

The following systems can use either the MBR or the GPT partition style for their disks:

- Windows Server 2008 computers
- Windows Server 2003 SP1 (or later) x86-based machines
- Windows Vista x86-based computers
- Itanium-based computers
- x64-based computers

Bear in mind, however, that unless the computer's architecture provides support for an Extensible Firmware Interface (EFI)–based boot partition, it is not possible to boot from a GPT disk. If this is the case, the system drive must be an MBR disk, and you can use GPT only on separate non-bootable disks used for data storage.

Itanium-based computers do support EFI; in fact, developers created the EFI specification with the Itanium processor in mind. The Itanium processor's main use is driving applications that require more than 4 GB of memory, such as enterprise databases.

One of the ways that GPT differs from MBR is that partitions, rather than hidden sectors, store data critical to platform operation. In additional, GPT-partitioned disks use redundant primary and backup partition tables for improved integrity. Although GPT specifications permit an unlimited number of partitions, the Windows implementation restricts partitions to 128 per disk. The GPT disk partitioning style supports volumes up to 18 exabytes (1 exabyte = 1 billion gigabytes, or 2^{60} bytes).

➕ MORE INFORMATION

As far as the Windows Server 2008 disk management tools are concerned, there is no difference between creating partitions or volumes in MBR and in GPT. You create partitions and volumes for both by using the same tools to follow the same process.

Table 6-3 compares some of the characteristics of the MBR and GPT partition styles.

Table 6-3

MBR and GPT Partition Style Comparison

Master Boot Record (MBR)	GUID Partition Table (GPT)
Supports up to four primary partitions or three primary partitions and one extended partition, with unlimited logical drives on the extended partition	Supports up to 128 primary partitions
Supports volumes up to 2 terabytes	Supports volumes up to 18 exabytes
Hidden (unpartitioned) sectors store data critical to platform operation	Partitions store data critical to platform operation
Replication and cyclical redundancy checks (CRCs) are not features of MBR's partition table	Replication and CRC protection of the partition table provide increased reliability

Understanding Disk Types

Most personal computers use *basic disks* because they are the easiest to manage.

A basic disk uses primary partitions, extended partitions, and logical drives to organize data. A primary partition appears to the operating system as though it is a physically separate disk and can host an operating system, in which case it is known as the *active partition*.

During the operating system installation, the setup program creates a *system partition* and a *boot partition*. The system partition contains hardware-related files that the computer uses to start. The boot partition contains the operating system files, which are stored in the Windows file folder. In most cases, these two partitions are one and the same, the active primary partition that Windows uses when starting. The active partition tells the computer which system partition and operating system it should use to start Windows.

When you work with basic disks in Windows Server 2008, you can create up to four primary partitions. For the fourth partition, you have the option of creating an extended partition instead, on which you can create as many logical drives as needed. You can format and assign driver letters to logical drives, but they cannot host an operating system. Table 6-4 compares some of the characteristics of primary and extended partitions.

Table 6-4

Primary and Extended Partition Comparison

Primary Partitions	Extended Partitions
A primary partition functions as though it is a physically separate disk and can host an operating system.	Extended partitions cannot host an operating system.
A primary partition can be marked as an active partition. You can have only one active partition per hard disk. The system BIOS looks to the active partition for the boot files it uses to start the operating system.	You cannot mark an extended partition as an active partition.
You can create up to four primary partitions or three primary partitions and one extended partition.	A basic disk can contain only one extended partition, but unlimited logical drives.
You format each primary partition and assign a unique drive letter.	You do not format the extended partition itself, but the logical drives it contains. You assign a unique drive letter to each of the logical drives.

The alternative to using a basic disk is to convert it to a ***dynamic disk.*** The process of converting a basic disk to a dynamic disk creates a single partition that occupies the entire disk. You can then create an unlimited number of volumes out of the space in that partition. Dynamic disks support several different types of volumes, as described in the next section.

Understanding Volume Types

A dynamic disk can contain an unlimited number of volumes that function much like primary partitions on a basic disk, but you cannot mark an existing dynamic disk as active.

When you create a volume on a dynamic disk in Windows Server 2008, you choose from the following five volume types:

- Simple volume—Consists of space from a single disk. After you have created a simple volume, you can extend it to multiple disks to create a spanned or striped volume, as long as it is not a system volume or boot volume. You can also extend a simple volume into any adjacent unallocated space on the same disk or, with some limitations, shrink the volume by deallocating any unused space in the volume.

- Spanned volume—Consists of space from 2 to 32 physical disks, all of which must be dynamic disks. A spanned volume is essentially a method for combining the space from multiple dynamic disks into a single large volume. Windows Server 2008 writes to the spanned volume by filling all of the space on the first disk and then fills each of the additional disks in turn. You can extend a spanned volume at any time by adding disk space. Creating a spanned volume does not increase the disk's read/write performance, nor does it provide fault tolerance. In fact, if a single physical disk in the spanned volume fails, all of the data in the entire volume is lost.

- Striped volume—Consists of space from 2 to 32 physical disks, all of which must be dynamic disks. The difference between a striped volume and a spanned volume is that in a striped volume, the system writes data one stripe at a time to each successive disk in the volume. Striping provides improved performance because each disk drive in the array has time to seek the location of its next stripe while the other drives are writing. Striped volumes do not provide fault tolerance, however, and you cannot extend them after creation. If a single physical disk in the striped volume fails, all of the data in the entire volume is lost.

- Mirrored volume—Consists of an identical amount of space on two physical disks, both of which must be dynamic disks. The system performs all read and write operations on both disks simultaneously, so they contain duplicate copies of all data stored on the volume. If one of the disks fails, the other continues to provide access to the volume until the failed disk is repaired or replaced.

- RAID-5 volume—Consists of space on three or more physical disks, all of which must be dynamic. The system stripes data and parity information across all of the disks so that if one physical disk fails, the missing data can be recreated using the parity information on the other disks. RAID-5 volumes provide improved read performance, because of the disk striping, but write performance suffers, due to the need for parity calculations.

Choosing a Volume Size

Although Windows Server 2008 can support dynamic volumes as large as 64 terabytes, this does not mean that you should create volumes that big, even if you have a server with that much storage. To facilitate the maintenance and administration processes, it is usually preferable to split your server's storage into volumes of manageable size, rather than create a single, gigantic volume.

One common practice is to choose a volume size based on the capacity of your network backup solution. For example, if you perform network backups using tape drives with an 80 GB capacity, creating volumes that can fit onto a single tape can facilitate the backup process. Creating smaller volumes will also speed up the restore process if you have to recover a volume from a tape or other backup medium.

Another factor is the amount of downtime your business can tolerate. If one of your volumes suffers a file system error, and you do not have a fault tolerance mechanism in place to take up the slack, you might have to bring it down so that you can run Chkdsk.exe or some other disk repair utility. The larger the volume, the longer the Chkdsk process will take, and the longer your users will be without their files. For extremely large volumes, running Chkdsk can take hours or even days.

Of course, it is possible to err in the other extreme as well. Splitting a 1-terabyte drive into 100 volumes of 10 GB, for example, would also be an administrative nightmare, in many different ways.

Understanding File Systems

To organize and store data or programs on a hard drive, you must install a file system. A file system is the underlying disk drive structure that enables you to store information on your computer. You install file systems by formatting a partition or volume on the hard disk.

In Windows Server 2008, four file system options are available: NTFS, FAT32, exFAT, and FAT (also known as FAT16). NTFS is the preferred file system for a server; the main benefits are improved support for larger hard drives and better security in the form of encryption and permissions that restrict access by unauthorized users.

Because the FAT file systems lack the security that NTFS provides, any user who gains access to your computer can read any file without restriction. Additionally, FAT file systems have disk size limitations: FAT32 cannot handle a partition greater than 32 GB, or a file greater than 4 GB. FAT cannot handle a hard disk greater than 4 GB, or a file greater than 2 GB. Because of these limitations, the only viable reason for using FAT16 or FAT32 is the need to dual boot the computer with a non-Windows operating system or a previous version of Windows that does not support NTFS, which is not a likely configuration for a server.

■ Working with Disks

 Windows Server 2008 includes tools that enable you to manage disks graphically or from **THE BOTTOM LINE** the command prompt.

Disk Management is a Microsoft Management Console (MMC) snap-in that you use to perform disk-related tasks, such as the following:

- Initializing disks
- Selecting a partition style
- Converting basic disks to dynamic disks
- Creating partitions and volumes
- Extending, shrinking, and deleting volumes
- Formatting partitions and volumes
- Assigning and changing driver letters and paths
- Examining and managing physical disk properties, such as disk quotas, folder sharing, and error checking

ANOTHER WAY

You can also use the DiskPart.exe command prompt utility to perform disk management tasks.

To access the Disk Management Snap-in, use any of the following procedures:

- From the Administrative Tools program group, select Computer Management, and then click the Disk Management node.
- Click the Start button, right-click Computer, and then click Manage. When the Server Manager console appears, expand the Storage node and select Disk Management.
- Open the Run dialog box and execute the compmgmt.msc file.
- Open a new MMC console and add the Disk Management snap-in.

In the Disk Management snap-in, the two center panes, the Top view and the Bottom view, display disk and volume information, respectively. Although Disk Management can display only two views at any one time, three views are available:

- Disk List—As shown in Figure 6-3, this view provides a summary about the physical drives in the computer. This information includes the disk number; disk type, such as Basic or DVD; disk capacity; size of unallocated space; the status of the disk device, such as online, offline, or no media; the device type, such as SCSI or IDE; and the partition style, such as MBR or GPT.

Figure 6-3

The Disk Management Disk List and Graphical views

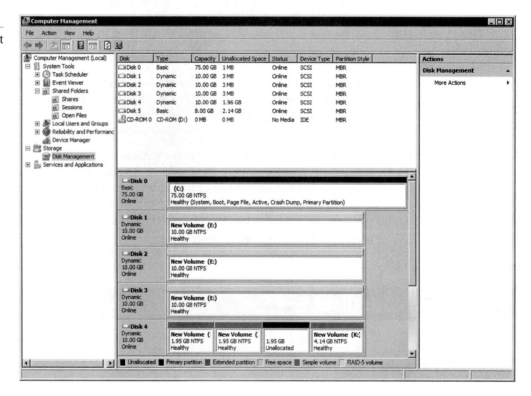

- Volume List—As shown in Figure 6-4, this view provides a more detailed summary of all the drives on the computer. This information includes the volume name; the volume layout, such as Simple, Spanned, Striped, or RAID-5; the disk type, such as Basic or Dynamic; the file system in use, such as NTFS or CDFS; the hard disk status, such as Healthy, Failed, or Formatting; the disk capacity; the disk available free space; the percentage of the hard disk that is free; whether the hard disk is fault tolerant; and the disk overhead percentage.

Figure 6-4

The Disk Management Volume
List and Graphical views

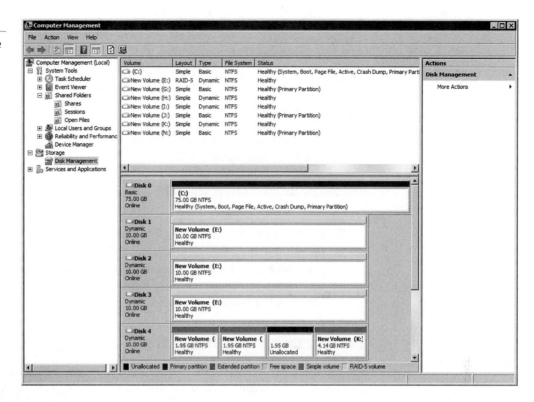

- Graphical view—This view displays a graphical representation of all the physical disks, partitions, volumes, and logical drives available on the computer. The Graphical view is divided into two columns: the disk status (left column) and the volume status (right column). The disk status column displays the number, type, capacity, and status of each disk. The volume status column displays the name, size, file system, and status of each volume.

By default, the Top pane contains the Volume List view, and the Bottom pane contains the Graphical view. You can change the views to suit your purposes by clicking the View menu, selecting either Top or Bottom, and then selecting the desired view. You can hide the Bottom view by clicking the Hidden menu option.

Adding a New Disk

When you add a new hard disk to a Windows Server 2008 computer, you must initialize the disk before you can access its storage.

To add a new secondary disk, shut down your computer and install or attach the new physical disk per the manufacturer's instructions. Then, use the following procedure to initialize the new disk and choose a partition style.

 ADD A NEW DISK

GET READY. Log on to Windows Server 2008 using an account with Administrator privileges. When the logon process is completed, close the Initial Configuration Tasks window and any other windows that appear.

1. Open the Disk Management snap-in. If the disk does not have a disk signature, the console automatically opens the Initialize Disk dialog box, as shown in Figure 6-5.

Figure 6-5

The Initialize Disk dialog box

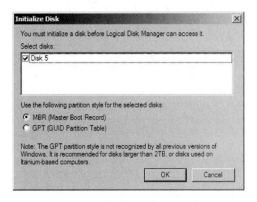

2. In the Select Disk box, verify that the checkbox for the new disk is selected.

3. For the Use The Following Partition Style For The Selected Disks Option, select either **MBR (Master Boot Record) or GPT (GUID Partition Table)** and click **OK.** The snap-in initializes the disk, causing its status to appear as Unallocated, as shown at the bottom of Figure 6-6.

Figure 6-6

The Disk Management snap-in, with a newly initialized disk

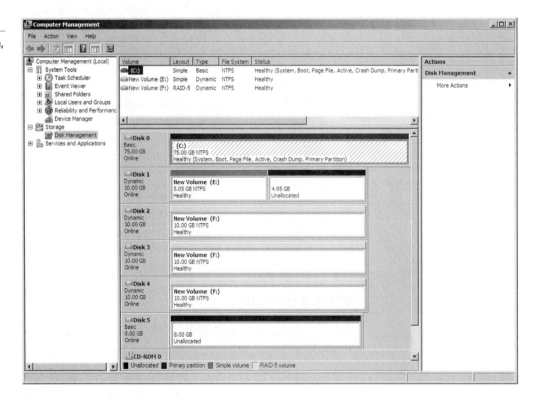

CLOSE the console containing the Disk Management snap-in.

You can convert a disk from one partition style to another at any time by right-clicking the disk you need to convert in the Disk List view and then, from the context menu, selecting Convert to GPT Disk or Convert to MBR Disk. However, be aware that converting the disk partition style is a destructive process. You can perform the conversion only on an unallocated disk, so if the disk you want to convert contains data, you must back up the disk, and then delete all existing partitions or volumes before you begin the conversion.

Converting a Basic Disk to a Dynamic Disk

Newly installed disks always appear as basic disks first.

You can convert a basic disk to a dynamic disk at any time without affecting the data stored on the disk. However, before you convert a basic disk to a dynamic disk, you must be aware of the following conditions:

- Make sure that you have enough space available on the disk for the conversion. The conversion will fail if the hard drive does not have at least 1 MB of free space at the end of the disk. The Disk Management console reserves this free space when creating partitions and volumes, but you cannot presume that other disk management tools also preserve that space.
- You should not convert a basic disk to a dynamic disk if you are dual booting operating systems. If you convert to a dynamic disk, you will not be able to start an installed operating system from any volume on the disk except the current boot volume.
- You cannot convert removable media to dynamic disks. You can configure them only as basic disks with primary partitions.
- You cannot convert drives that use an allocation unit size (sector size) greater than 512 bytes unless you reformat the drive with a smaller sector size before upgrading.
- Once you change a basic disk to a dynamic disk, the only way you can change it back again is to back up the entire disk and delete the dynamic disk volumes. When you delete the last volume, the dynamic disk automatically converts back to a basic disk.

To convert a basic disk to a dynamic disk, use the following procedure.

 CONVERT A BASIC DISK TO A DYNAMIC DISK

GET READY. Log on to Windows Server 2008 using an account with Administrator privileges. When the logon process is completed, close the Initial Configuration Tasks window and any other windows that appear.

1. Open the Disk Management snap-in if necessary.
2. In the Disk List view, right-click the basic disk that you want to convert and then, from the context menu, select **Convert to Dynamic Disk.** The Convert to Dynamic Disk dialog box appears, as shown in Figure 6-7.

Figure 6-7

The Convert to Dynamic Disk dialog box

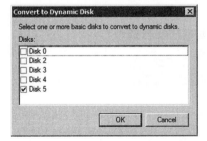

3. Select the checkbox(es) for the disk(s) you want to convert, and then click **OK.** If the disks you selected do not contain formatted partitions, clicking OK immediately converts the disks, and you do not need to follow the remaining steps. If the disks you are converting to dynamic disks have formatted partitions, clicking OK displays the Disks to Convert dialog box, as shown in Figure 6-8, which means that you need to follow the remaining steps to complete the disk conversion.

Figure 6-8

The Disks to Convert dialog box

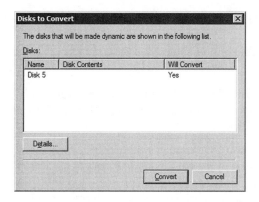

4. The Disks to Convert dialog box lists the disks you chose for conversion for your confirmation. Check the value in the Will Convert column. It should be set to Yes for each of the disks that you are converting. If any of the disks have the value No, then they may not meet Windows conversion criteria.

5. Click **Details.** The Convert Details dialog box appears, as shown in Figure 6-9. This dialog box lists the partitions on the selected drives that Disk Management will convert.

Figure 6-9

The Convert Details dialog box

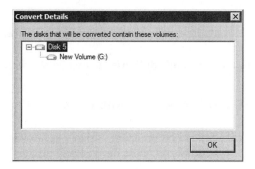

6. Click **OK** when you are ready to continue with the conversion.

7. On the Disks to Convert dialog box, click **Convert** to start the conversion. A Disk Management information box appears, as shown in Figure 6-10, to warn you that after you convert the disks to dynamic disks, you will not be able to boot installed operating systems from any volume other than the current boot volume.

Figure 6-10

A Disk Management information box

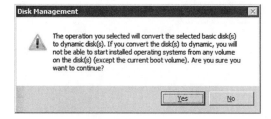

8. If a selected drive contains the boot partition, the system partition, or a partition that is in use, Disk Management prompts you to restart the computer.

CLOSE the console containing the Disk Management snap-in.

When you convert a basic disk into a dynamic disk, Disk Management performs the following tasks:

- Converts basic disk partitions to dynamic disk volumes of equal size

- Converts basic disk primary partitions and logical drives in the extended partition to simple volumes
- Marks any free space in a basic disk extended partition as unallocated

Creating a Simple Volume

Technically speaking, you create partitions on basic disks and volumes on dynamic disks. This is not just an arbitrary change in nomenclature. Converting a basic disk to a dynamic disk actually creates one big partition, occupying all of the space on the disk. The volumes you create on the dynamic disk are logical divisions within that single partition.

Earlier versions of Windows use the correct terminology in the Disk Management snap-in. The menus enable you to create partitions on basic disks and volumes on dynamic disks. Windows Server 2008 uses the term volume for both disk types, and enables you to create any of the available volume types, whether the disk is basic or dynamic. If the volume type you select is not supported on a basic disk, the wizard converts it to a dynamic disk (with your permission) as part of the volume creation process.

Despite the menus that refer to basic partitions as volumes, the traditional rules for basic disks remain in effect. The New Simple Volume menu option on a basic disk creates up to three primary partitions. When you create a fourth volume, the wizard actually creates an extended partition and a logical drive of the size you specify. If there is any remaining space on the disk, you can create additional logical drives in the extended partition.

> ⚠️ **WARNING** When you use *DiskPart.exe,* a command line utility included with Windows Server 2008, to manage basic disks, you can create four primary partitions or three primary partitions and one extended partition. The DiskPart.exe utility contains a superset of the commands supported by the Disk Management snap-in. In other words, DiskPart can do everything Disk Management can do, and more. However, while the Disk Management Snap-in prevents you from unintentionally performing actions that might result in data loss, DiskPart has no safeties, and so does not prohibit you from performing such actions. For this reason, Microsoft recommends that only advanced users use DiskPart and that they use it with due caution.

To create a new simple volume on a basic or dynamic disk, use the following procedure.

 CREATE A NEW SIMPLE VOLUME

GET READY. Log on to Windows Server 2008 using an account with Administrator privileges. When the logon process is completed, close the Initial Configuration Tasks window and any other windows that appear.

1. Open the Disk Management snap-in if necessary.
2. In the Graphical View, right-click an unallocated area in the volume status column for the disk on which you want to create a volume and, from the context menu, select **New Simple Volume.** The New Simple Volume Wizard appears.

3. Click **Next** to bypass the Welcome page. The *Specify Volume Size* page appears, as shown in Figure 6-11.

Figure 6-11

The Specify Volume Size page

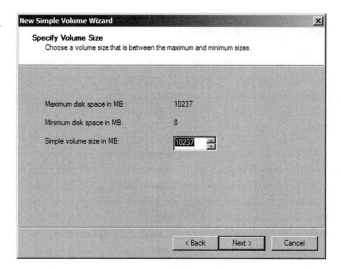

4. Select the size for the new partition or volume, within the maximum and minimum limits stated on the page, using the **Simple Volume Size In MB spin** box, and then click **Next.** The *Assign Drive Letter or Path* page appears, as shown in Figure 6-12.

Figure 6-12

The Assign Drive Letter or Path page

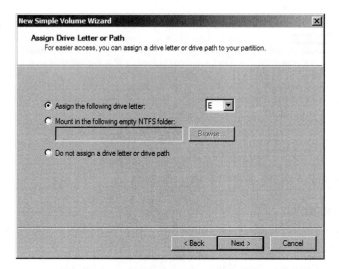

5. Configure one of the following three options.

- Assign the following drive letter—If you select this option, click the associated dropdown list for a list of available drive letters and select the letter you want to assign to the drive.

- Mount in the following empty NTFS folder—If you select this option, either key the path to an existing NTFS folder or click Browse to search for or create a new folder. The entire contents of the new drive will appear in the folder you specify.

- Do not assign a drive letter or drive path—Select this option if you want to create the partition, but are not yet ready to use it. When you do not assign a volume a drive letter or path, the drive is left unmounted and inaccessible. When you want to mount the drive for use, assign a drive letter or path to it.

6. Click **Next.** The *Format Partition* page appears, as shown in Figure 6-13.

Figure 6-13

The Format Partition page

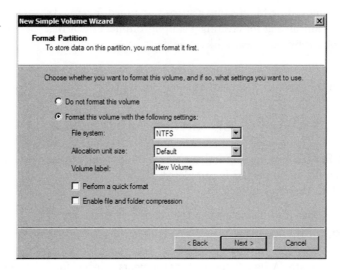

> **➕ MORE INFORMATION**
>
> Mounting drives to NTFS folders is a convenient way to add space to an existing drive or overcome the built-in system limitation of 26 drive letters. When you mount a volume to a folder, it becomes a logical part of the volume containing that folder. To users, the volume is just another folder in the directory tree. They are unaware that the files in that folder (and its subfolders) are actually stored on another volume.

7. Specify whether the wizard should format the volume, and if so, how. If you do not want to format the volume at this time, select the **Do not format this volume** option. If you do want to format the volume, select the **Format this volume with the following settings** option, and then configure the associated options, as follows.

- File system—Select the desired file system: NTFS, FAT, or FAT32.
- Allocation unit size—Specify the file system's cluster size. The cluster size signifies the basic unit of bytes in which the system allocates disk space. The system calculates the default allocation unit size based on the size of the volume. You can override this value by clicking the associated dropdown list and then selecting one of the values. For example, if your client uses consistently small files, you may want to set the allocation unit size to a smaller cluster size.
- Volume label—Specify a name for the partition or volume. The default name is New Volume, but you can change the name to anything you want.
- Perform a quick format—When selected, Windows formats the disk without checking for errors. This is a faster method with which to format the drive, but Microsoft does not recommend it. When you check for errors, the system looks for and marks bad sectors on the disk so that your clients will not use those portions of the disk.
- Enable file and folder compression—Turns on folder compression for the disk. This option is available only for volumes being formatted with the NTFS file system.

8. Click **Next.** The *Completing the New Simple Volume Wizard* page appears.

9. Review the settings to confirm your options, and then click **Finish.** The wizard creates the volume according to your specifications.

CLOSE the console containing the Disk Management snap-in.

After you create a simple volume, you can modify its properties by extending it or shrinking it, as described later in this lesson.

TAKE NOTE

After you initialize and, if necessary, convert your disks using the Disk Administration snap-in, you can also create volumes using the Share and Storage Management console, by selecting Provision Storage in the actions pane.

Creating a Striped, Spanned, Mirrored, or RAID-5 Volume

The procedure for creating a striped, spanned, mirrored, or RAID-5 volume is almost the same as that for creating a simple volume, except that the Specify Volume Size page is replaced by the Select Disks page.

To create a striped, spanned, mirrored, or RAID-5 volume, use the following procedure.

 CREATE A STRIPED, SPANNED, MIRRORED, OR RAID-5 VOLUME

GET READY. Log on to Windows Server 2008 using an account with Administrator privileges. When the logon process is completed, close the Welcome Center window and any other windows that appear.

1. Open the Disk Management snap-in if necessary.
2. In the Graphical View, right-click an unallocated area on a dynamic disk and then, from the context menu, select the command for the type of volume you want to create. A New Volume Wizard appears, named for your selected volume type.
3. Click **Next** to bypass the Welcome page. The *Select Disks* page appears, as shown in Figure 6-14.

Figure 6-14

The Select Disks page

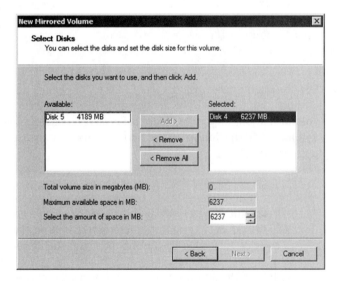

4. On the *Select Disks* page, select the disks you want to use for the new volume from the **Available** list box, and then click **Add.** The disks you chose are moved to the **Selected** list box, joining the original disk you selected when launching the wizard. For a striped, spanned, or mirrored volume, you must have at least two disks in the Selected list; for a RAID-5 volume, you must have at least three.
5. Specify the amount of space you want to use on each disk, using the **Select The Amount Of Space In MB** spin box. Then click **Next.** *The Assign Drive Letter or Path* page appears.
   - If you are creating a spanned volume, you must click each disk in the Selected list and specify the amount of space to use on that disk. The default value for each disk is the size of the unallocated space on that disk.
   - If you are creating a striped, mirrored, or RAID-5 volume, you only specify one value, because these volumes require the same amount of space on each disk. The default value is the size of the unallocated space on the disk with the least amount of space free.

X REF

See the "Create a New Simple Volume" procedure, in the preceding section, for more information about the options on the Assign Drive Letter or Path and Format Partition pages.

6. Specify whether you want to assign a drive letter or path, and then click **Next.** The *Format Partition* page appears.

7. Specify if or how you want to format the volume, and then click **Next.** The *Completing the New Simple Volume Wizard* page appears.

8. Review the settings to confirm your options, and then click **Finish.** If any of the disks you selected to create the volume are basic disks, a Disk Management message box appears, warning you that the volume creation process will convert the basic disks to dynamic disks.

9. Click **Yes.** The wizard creates the volume according to your specifications.

CLOSE the Disk Management snap-in.

The commands that appear in a disk's context menu depend on the number of disks installed in the computer and the presence of unallocated space on them. For example, at least two disks with unallocated space must be available to create a striped, spanned, or mirrored volume, and at least three disks must be available to create a RAID-5 volume.

EXTENDING AND SHRINKING VOLUMES

To extend or shrink a volume, you simply right-click a volume and select Extend Volume or Shrink Volume from the context menu or from the Action menu.

Windows Server 2008 extends existing volumes by expanding them into adjacent unallocated space on the same disk. When you extend a simple volume across multiple disks, the simple volume becomes a spanned volume. You cannot extend striped volumes.

To extend a volume on a basic disk, the system must meet the following requirements:

TAKE NOTE ✱

You must be a member of the Backup Operator or the Administrators group to extend or shrink any volume.

- A volume of a basic disk must be either unformatted or formatted with the NTFS file system.

- If you extend a volume that is actually a logical drive, the console first consumes the contiguous free space remaining in the extended partition. If you attempt to extend the logical drive beyond the confines of its extended partition, the extended partition expands to any unallocated space left on the disk.

- You can extend logical drives, boot volumes, or system volumes only into contiguous space, and only if the hard disk can be upgraded to a dynamic disk. The operating system will permit you to extend other types of basic volumes into noncontiguous space, but will prompt you to convert the basic disk to a dynamic disk.

To extend a volume on a dynamic disk, the system must meet these requirements:

- When extending a simple volume, you can use only the available space on the same disk, if the volume is to remain simple.

- You can extend a simple volume across additional disks if it is not a system volume or a boot volume. However, after you expand a simple volume to another disk, it is no longer a simple volume; it becomes a spanned volume.

- You can extend a simple or spanned volume if it does not have a file system (a raw volume) or if you formatted it using the NTFS file system. (You cannot extend volumes using the FAT or FAT32 file systems.)

- You cannot extend mirrored or RAID-5 volumes, although you can add a mirror to an existing simple volume.

When shrinking volumes, the Disk Management console frees up space at the end of the volume, relocating the existing volume's files, if necessary. The console then converts that free space to new unallocated space on the disk. To shrink basic disk volumes and simple or spanned dynamic disk volumes, the system must meet the following requirements:

- The existing volume must not be full and must contain the specified amount of available free space for shrinking.

- The volume must not be a raw partition (one without a file system). Shrinking a raw partition that contains data might destroy the data.

- You can shrink a volume only if you formatted it using the NTFS file system. (You cannot shrink volumes using the FAT or FAT32 file systems.)

- You cannot shrink striped, mirrored, or RAID-5 volumes.

- You should always defragment a volume before you attempt to shrink it.

■ Deploying a Storage Area Network

THE BOTTOM LINE

Storage area networks are typically high-end solutions, which enterprise networks use to deploy large amounts of storage and make this storage available to other connected devices.

RAID is a proven high availability technology that was first defined in 1988, but server-attached RAID arrays are subject to scalability problems. You can install only so many drives into a single computer. Also, the terminated SCSI bus that was originally used for connections to external drive arrays is limited to 16 devices and a maximum length of 25 yards.

At the highest level, a storage area network (SAN) is simply a network dedicated solely to high-speed connections between servers and storage devices. Instead of installing disk drives into servers or connecting them using a SCSI bus, a SAN consists of one or more drive arrays equipped with network interface adapters, which you connect to your servers using standard twisted pair or fiber optic network cables. A SAN-connected server, therefore, has a minimum of two network adapters, one for the standard LAN connection, and one for the SAN, as shown in Figure 6-15.

Figure 6-15

A server connected to a storage area network

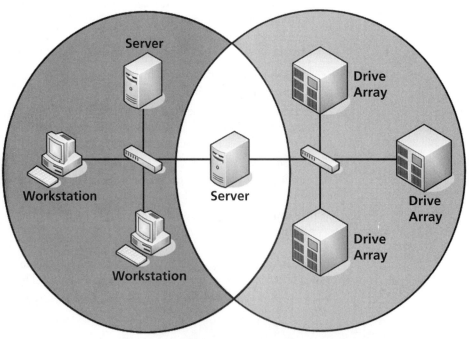

The storage devices on a SAN are nearly always drive arrays, not individual drives, and can include hard disks, optical jukeboxes, tape libraries, or any other type of storage. In most cases, SANs use ***block I/O access,*** which means that a server accesses the storage media on the SAN a block at a time, just as if the storage media were installed in the server computer. This is in contrast to the ***file-based I/O,*** which means that a server accesses the storage media on the SAN a file at a time, typically used by network attached storage.

> **+ MORE INFORMATION**
>
> Block I/O access is preferable for applications that use large data files, such as databases and email stores. With file-based I/O, a database manager application has to retrieve some or all of the database file from the storage device before it can access the information requested by a client. With block I/O access, the database manager can retrieve only the parts of the database file containing the requested information, enhancing the speed at which data is retrieved.

SANs have many advantages. By connecting the storage devices to a network instead of to the servers themselves, you avoid the limitations imposed by the maximum number of devices you can connect directly to a computer. SANs also provide added flexibility in their communication capabilities. Because any device on a SAN can communicate with any other device on the same SAN, high speed data transfers can occur in any of the following ways:

- Server to storage—Servers can access storage devices over the SAN as if they are connected directly to the computer.
- Server to server—Servers can use the SAN to communicate directly with each other at high speeds to avoid flooding the LAN with traffic.
- Storage to storage—Storage devices can communicate amongst themselves without server intervention, such as to perform backups from one medium to another or to mirror drives on different arrays.

Although a SAN is not in itself a high availability technology, you can make it into one by connecting redundant servers to the same network, as shown in Figure 6-16, enabling them to access the same data storage devices. If one server should fail, another can assume its roles by accessing the same data.

Figure 6-16

Multiple servers connected to a SAN

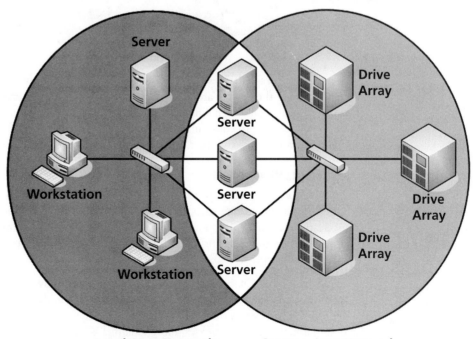

Understanding SAN Technologies

> Because they use standard networking technologies, SANs can greatly extend the distances between servers and storage devices. You can design a SAN that spans different rooms, floors, buildings, or even cities, just as you would with a standard computer network.

External hard drives are now common on servers and workstations alike. The simplest devices consist of a single parallel or serial ATA (Advanced Technology Attachment) drive in a housing that includes a power supply and a Universal Serial Bus (USB) interface. These are suitable for local computer use, but not for the storage of shared data, as on a server.

Hard drive arrays that connect directly to a server are more complex, usually consisting of multiple drives and a SCSI interface. Some arrays include a RAID controller, while others use a simpler arrangement amusingly called ***JBOD (Just a Bunch of Disks)***. This type of array connects to the server using an external SCSI cable, which, when compared to a standard network cable, is thick, heavy, inflexible, and limited in length. Also, the server must have a SCSI host adapter that provides the other connection for the array.

SCSI is still the interface of choice for internal server drives because it enables each drive connected to the SCSI bus to maintain its own command queue, independent of the other drives. The ATA interfaces, by comparison, can handle only one command at a time, which makes them unsuitable for use in servers that might receive dozens or hundreds of I/O requests each minute. However, many of the external hard drive arrays on the market now combine the two interface technologies to form hybrid units. The hard drives might use the high-speed serial ATA (SATA) interface, but the array communicates with servers and other storage devices using SCSI commands.

The drive arrays designed for SANs are more complex than those connecting directly to servers, because in addition to the RAID and SCSI functionality, they include support for networking protocols and intelligent agents that provide advanced functions, such as serverless backups.

TAKE NOTE *

> In a serverless backup, a server is responsible for initiating the backup job, but after the backup begins, the data travels directly from one storage medium on the SAN to another, such as from a hard disk array to a tape library. This type of backup not only eliminates the potential LAN bottleneck by using the SAN for the data transfer, it eliminates the backup server itself as a possible bottleneck.

Servers and storage devices cannot exchange SCSI commands over a SAN connection the way they do when the devices are directly connected using a SCSI cable. The lower level SCSI protocols use parallel signaling and call for a bus topology and relatively short cables with 50 or 68 conductors. To communicate over a SAN, servers and storage devices map their SCSI communications onto another protocol, in most cases either Fibre Channel or iSCSI.

USING FIBRE CHANNEL

Fibre Channel is a high-speed serial networking technology, originally designed for use with supercomputers but now associated primarily with storage area networking. Fibre Channel is a versatile technology, supporting various network media, transmission speeds, topologies, and upper level protocols. Its primary disadvantage is that it requires specialized hardware that can be extremely expensive.

Installing a Fibre Channel SAN means building an entirely new network with its own special medium, switches, and network interface adapters. In addition to the hardware costs, which can easily be ten times that of a traditional Ethernet network, you must consider installation and maintenance expenses. Fibre Channel is a specialized technology, with relatively few

MORE INFORMATION

The British spelling of the word "fibre" in Fibre Channel is deliberate, to distinguish the term from "fiber optic." Fibre Channel can run on twisted pair copper or optical cables. The spelling "fiber" always refers to an optical medium.

experts in the field. To install and maintain a Fibre Channel SAN, an organization must hire experienced staff or train existing personnel on the new technology.

FIBRE CHANNEL MEDIA

A Fibre Channel network can use a variety of network media. Copper alternatives include video or miniature coaxial cable and, more commonly, shielded twisted pair (STP) with DB-9 or HSSDC (High Speed Serial Data Connection) cable connectors. These are distinctly different from the standard unshielded twisted pair (UTP) cables and RJ-45 connectors used for an Ethernet network and require a specialized installation. Fiber optic alternatives include 62.5- or 50-micrometer (or micron) multimode and 7- or 9-micrometer singlemode, all using LC or SC connectors. These are standard fiber optic media options, familiar to any qualified fiber optic contractor. Because Fibre Channel uses serial instead of parallel signaling, it can span much longer distances than a pure SCSI connection, up to 50 kilometers or more, in some cases.

FIBRE CHANNEL SPEEDS

Transmission speeds for Fibre Channel networks range from 133 Mbps (megabits per second) to 1 Gbps (gigabit per second) for copper cables, and up to 10 Gbps for fiber optic. Maximum speeds depend on the type of cable the network uses, the lengths of the cable segments, and, in the case of fiber optic, the type of laser used to transmit the signals.

FIBRE CHANNEL TOPOLOGIES

Fibre Channel networks can use any one of the following three topologies:

- Point-to-point (FC-P2P)—Consists of two devices only, directly connected with a single cable.
- *Arbitrated loop (FC-AL)*—Consists of up to 127 devices, connected in a loop topology, similar to that of a token ring network. The loop can be physical, with each device connected to the next device, or virtual, with each device connected to a hub that implements the loop.
- *Switched fabric (FC-SW)*—Consists of up to 16,777,216 (2^{24}) devices, each of which is connected to a Fibre Channel switch. Unlike Ethernet switches, Fibre Channel switches provide redundant paths between the connected devices, forming a topology called a *mesh* or *fabric*. If a switch or a connection between switches fails, data can find an alternate path through the fabric to its destination.

Until recently, FC-AL was the most popular of the three topologies, because few SANs require more than 127 connections, and the arbitrated loop eliminates the need for expensive switches. However, as of 2007, the prices of Fibre Channel switches have dropped considerably (perhaps due to competition from low-cost iSCSI components) and FC-SW has become the more popular Fibre Channel solution.

FIBRE CHANNEL PROTOCOLS

The Fibre channel standards define five protocol layers, as follows:

- FC0—Defines the physical elements of a Fibre Channel network, including cables, connectors, pinouts, and optical and electrical specifications.
- FC1—Defines the data-link layer transmission protocol, including the 8b/10b encoding method used to generate Fibre Channel network signals.
- FC2—Defines the basic transport mechanism of a Fibre Channel network, including the frame format and three service classes: a connection-oriented class, a connectionless class with acknowledgments, and a connectionless class without acknowledgments.

- FC3—Defines a collection of common services often required by applications using Fibre Channel networks, including data striping, multicasting, and multiport hunt groups.
- FC4—Defines the upper layer protocol mapping rules, which enable Fibre Channel networks to carry SCSI and other types of application layer traffic.

The most critical layer in the operation of a SAN is FC4, which enables the network to carry the SCSI traffic generated by the server and storage devices, replacing the lower layers native to the SCSI protocol. SANs typically use the *Fibre Channel Protocol (FCP)* to transmit SCSI traffic over the network. However, Fibre Channel networks can use a number of other protocols at the FC4 layer for storage area networking, as well as other applications.

USING iSCSI

Fibre Channel networks provide excellent SAN performance, but the expense and special skills required to install and maintain them have made them a rarity in all but the largest enterprise installations. iSCSI is an alternative storage area networking technology that enables servers and storage devices to exchange SCSI traffic using a standard IP network instead of a dedicated Fibre Channel network. This makes iSCSI a far more economical and practical solution, placing SAN technology within reach of small- and medium-sized installations.

Because iSCSI uses a standard IP network for its lower layer functionality, you can use the same cables, network adapters, switches, and routers for a SAN as you would for a LAN or wide area network (WAN), without any modifications. You simply connect your servers and storage devices to an existing Ethernet network or build a new one using low-cost, widely available components.

Because of its relatively low cost and its simplicity, iSCSI has come to dominate the SAN industry. The addition of widespread support for iSCSI in the Windows Server and other operating systems has led to the introduction of many iSCSI storage device products in a wide range of price points. Whereas a SAN at one time required a huge investment in money and time, the technology is now available to modest organizations.

INITIATORS AND TARGETS

iSCSI communication is based on two elements: initiators and targets. An *iSCSI initiator,* so-called because it initiates the SCSI communication process, is a hardware or software device running on a computer that accesses the storage devices on the SAN. On an iSCSI network, the initiator takes the place of the host adapter that traditional SCSI implementations use to connect storage devices to a computer. The initiator receives I/O requests from the operating system and sends them, in the form of SCSI commands, to specific storage devices on the SAN. The only difference between an iSCSI initiator and a SCSI host adapter is that the initiator packages the SCSI traffic in TCP/IP packets, instead of using the native SCSI protocols.

TAKE NOTE*

Windows Server 2008 includes the iSCSI Initiator by default, but for a Windows Server 2003 R2 computer, you must download the latest version of the iSCSI Software Initiator version 2 from the Microsoft Download Center at www.micro-soft.com/downloads.

Hardware-based initiators typically take the form of a host bus adapter (HBA), an expansion card that includes the functionality of a SCSI host adapter and a Gigabit Ethernet network adapter in one device. Hardware-based initiators offload some of the SCSI processing from the computer's main processor.

Initiators can also be software-based, such as the iSCSI Initiator module included in Windows Server 2008. When using a software initiator, you connect the computer to the SAN using a standard Ethernet network adapter.

The other half of the iSCSI equation is the *iSCSI target,* which is integrated into a drive array or computer. The target receives SCSI commands from the initiator and passes them to a storage device, which is represented by a *logical unit number (LUN).* A LUN is essentially an address that SCSI devices use to identify a specific storage resource. A single LUN can represent an entire hard disk, part of a disk, or a slice of a RAID array. Therefore, a single computer or drive array can have many LUNs, represented by multiple targets.

Drive arrays supporting iSCSI have targets implemented in their firmware, automatically making the various volumes in the array available to iSCSI initiators on the SAN. It is also possible for iSCSI targets to be implemented in software, in the form of a service or daemon that makes all or part of a hard disk in a computer available to initiators. You can use various third-party products, both commercial and public domain, to deploy the drives in a computer as iSCSI targets, making them available to initiators on the SAN using block I/O access.

USING iSNS

After the initiators and targets are in place, the only problem remaining in iSCSI communications is how the two locate each other. The *Internet Storage Name Service (iSNS)* makes this possible by registering the presence of initiators and targets on a SAN and responding to queries from iSNS clients. Windows Server 2008 includes an iSNS implementation as a feature, which can provide the identification service for an entire SAN.

iSNS consists of four components, as follows:

- iSNS server—Receives and processes registration requests and queries from clients on the SAN, using the iSNS database as an information store.
- iSNS database—Information store on an iSNS server that contains data supplied by client registrations. The server retrieves the data to respond to client queries.
- iSNS clients—Component in iSCSI initiators and targets that registers information about itself with an iSNS server and sends queries to the server for information about other clients.
- iSNS Protocol (iSNSP)—Protocol used for all registration and query traffic between iSNS servers and clients.

Using Windows Server 2008 with SANs

> Windows Server 2008 provides support for both iSCSI and Fibre Channel SANs and includes the tools and services you need to manage them.

Windows Server 2008 includes several components that enable the computer to interact with devices on a SAN, as follows:

- iSCSI Initiator—Establishes connections with iSCSI targets on the SAN
- Internet Storage Name Server—Registers and locates iSCSI initiators and targets
- Storage Manager for SANs—Enables administrators to manage storage devices on Fibre Channel or iSCSI SANs that are compatible with the Virtual Disk Service (VDS) using a standardized interface
- Storage Explorer—Enables administrators to view and manage the devices on Fibre Channel or iSCSI SANs

These components are discussed in greater detail in the following sections.

INSTALLING iSNS SERVER

iSCSI Initiator is part of the default Windows Server 2008 installation; you don't have to add any roles or features to use it. However, if there are many devices on your SAN, you should use an iSNS server to register your targets and initiators. If you do not have an iSNS server on your SAN already, you can deploy one on your Windows Server 2008 computer by using the following procedure.

⊖ INSTALL iSNS SERVER

GET READY. Log on to Windows Server 2008 using an account with administrative privileges. When the logon process is completed, close the Initial Configuration Tasks window and any other windows that appear.

1. Click **Start**, and then click **Administrative Tools** > **Server Manager.** The Server Manager console appears.

2. Right-click the **Features** node and, from the context menu, select **Add Features.** The Add Features Wizard appears, displaying the *Select Features* page.

3. Select the **Internet Storage Name Server** feature, as shown in Figure 6-17, and click **Next.** The *Confirm Installation Selections* page appears.

Figure 6-17

The Add Features Wizard

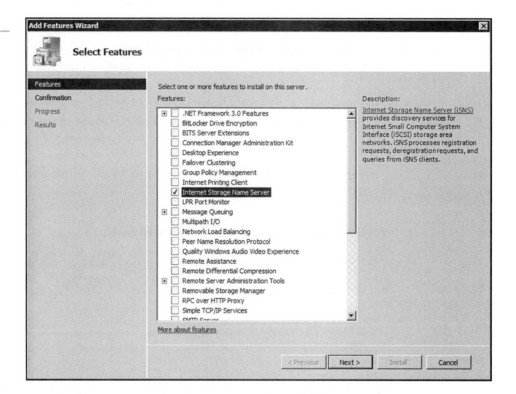

4. Click **Install.** When the installation process is completed, the *Installation Results* page appears.

5. Click **Close.**

CLOSE the Server Manager console.

When the installation process is complete, the iSNS server is ready to accept registrations from iSCSI targets and initiators. After the targets are registered, initiators can send queries to the iSNS server to discover them.

USING iSCSI INITIATOR

Whether or not you plan to use an iSNS server on your SAN, you have to create and/or configure iSCSI targets before your initiators can access the storage devices on the SAN. How you do this depends on the types of storage devices you are using and their iSCSI target capabilities. Drive arrays that support iSCSI have built-in targets and can use a variety of administrative interfaces to configure their functions and register them with the iSNS server. Software-based iSCSI targets that run on Windows and UNIX/Linux computers are also available from third-party vendors.

➕ **MORE INFORMATION**

Windows Server 2008 does not include iSCSI target capabilities, but an embedded version of Windows Storage Server, called Microsoft Windows Unified Data Storage Server, does include iSCSI target capabilities. Windows Unified Data Storage Server is based on Windows Server 2003 and is available only as part of turnkey storage server solutions from original equipment manufacturers (OEMs). As of this writing, Microsoft has not announced plans for a Windows Server 2008 version.

When your targets are configured and registered, you can access them with Windows Server 2008 by configuring iSCSI Initiator, as detailed in the following procedure.

 USE iSCSI INITIATOR

GET READY. Log on to Windows Server 2008 using an account with administrative privileges. When the logon process is completed, close the Initial Configuration Tasks window and any other windows that appear.

1. Click **Start,** and then click **Administrative Tools** > **iSCSI Initiator.** The iSCSI Initiator Properties sheet appears, as shown in Figure 6-18.

Figure 6-18

The iSCSI Initiator Properties sheet

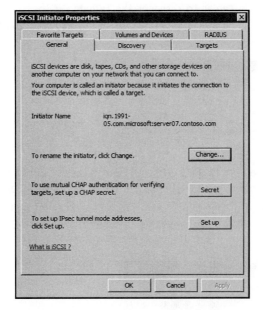

TAKE NOTE * The first time you launch iSCSI Initiator, the system prompts you to start the iSCSI service automatically each time you start the computer and configure Windows Firewall to unblock the port used by the Internet Storage Name Service (iSNS).

2. Click the **Discovery** tab, as shown in Figure 6-19.

Figure 6-19

The Discovery tab of the iSCSI Initiator Properties sheet

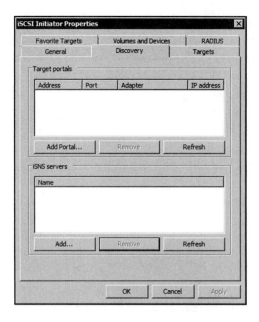

3. To use an iSNS server to discover the targets on the network, click **Add.** The Add iSNS Server dialog box appears, as shown in Figure 6-20.

Figure 6-20

The Add iSNS Server dialog box

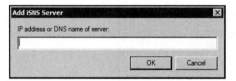

4. In The IP Address Or DNS Name Of Server text box, key the name or address of the iSNS server on your SAN. Then, click **OK.** The server appears in the iSNS Servers box.

5. To connect to a specific target using a target portal, click **Add Portal.** The Add Target Portal dialog box appears, as shown in Figure 6-21.

Figure 6-21

The Add Target Portal dialog box

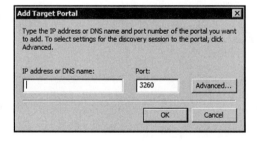

6. In the IP Address Or DNS Name text box, key the name or address of the storage device containing the target to which you want to connect. Leave the Port value set to the default of 3260, unless you changed the port number on your target device. Click **OK.** The new entry appears in the Target Portals box.

7. Click the **Targets** tab, as shown in Figure 6-22. All of the targets accessible through the iSNS servers and/or target portals you added appear in the Targets box.

Figure 6-22

The Targets tab of the iSCSI Initiator Properties sheet

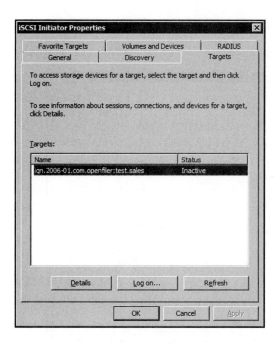

8. Select one of the available targets and click **Log on.** The Log On to Target dialog box appears, as shown in Figure 6-23.

Figure 6-23

The Log On to Target dialog box

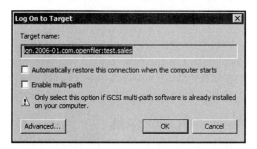

9. Configure the following options, if desired:

- Automatically restore this connection when the computer starts—Creates a persistent connection that enables the computer to access the SCSI target immediately upon starting
- Enable multi-path—Enables the iSCSI initiator to access the target using redundant paths through the SAN so that, if a cable breaks or a component fails, the computer can still access the data stored on the target device
- Advanced—Displays an Advanced Settings dialog box, as shown in Figure 6-24, in which you can configure connection, authentication, and encryption settings

Figure 6-24

The Advanced Settings dialog box

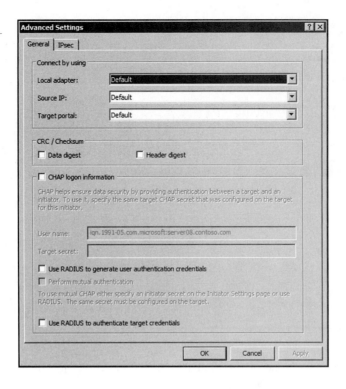

10. Click **OK.** The status of the selected target changes from Inactive to Connected.

CLOSE the iSCSI Initiator Properties sheet by clicking **OK.**

At this point, the target you selected is accessible to the computer, just as if the storage device were installed locally. You can use the Disk Administration snap-in or the Diskpart. exe command line tool to create and manage volumes on the target device, and then access the volumes using any standard tool or application.

USING STORAGE MANAGER FOR SANs

Many of the drive arrays designed for SAN use are very complex devices, not just a bunch of drives in a case. However, they are not full-fledged computers either. SCSI LUNs, RAID, and other features require configuration, but drive arrays do not have their own monitors and keyboards, so they must use other means to provide an administrative interface.

Some drive arrays have RS-232 ports, to which you can connect a terminal, whereas others provide Web-based interfaces that you can access from a browser on any computer connected to the same network. Others use proprietary software interfaces. Windows Server 2008 provides another alternative, however, in the form of Storage Manager for SANs, a Microsoft Management Console (MMC) snap-in that enables you to manage the LUNs and iSCSI targets on a network-attached storage device.

Storage Manager for SANs is limited, however, because it can only manage storage devices that include support for the Microsoft Virtual Disk Service. To be accessible to Storage Manager for SANs, the storage device manufacturer must supply a software component called a *VDS hardware provider*, which you install on the computer you want to use to manage the device. Storage Manager for SANs is therefore not a required tool; it is just one option you can use to manage your storage devices.

Storage Manager for SANs is supplied with Windows Server 2008 as a feature. To manage a storage device, you must install the VDS hardware provider supplied by the device's manufacturer and add the Storage Manager for SANs feature using the Add Features Wizard in Server Manager. Then, when you select Storage Manager for SANs from the Administrative Tools

program group, the console loads the Virtual Disk Service and the VDS hardware provider, and displays the interface shown in Figure 6-25.

Figure 6-25

The Storage Manager for SANs console

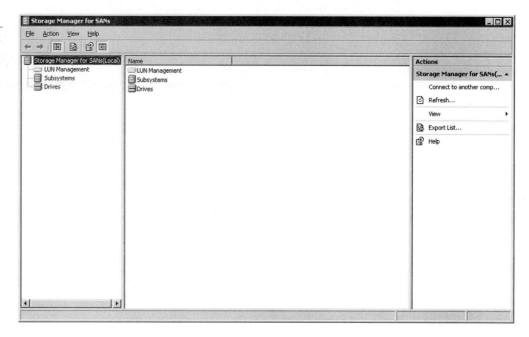

The Storage Manager for SANs console has three nodes, as follows:

- LUN Management—Enables you to manage your iSCSI targets and create LUNs on those targets, as shown in Figure 6-26.

Figure 6-26

Creating LUNs in the Storage Manager for SANs console

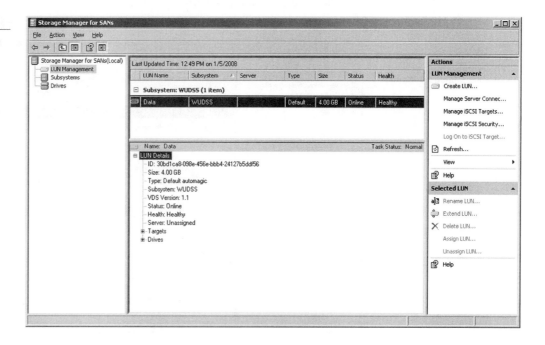

- Subsystems—Displays information about the storage devices on the SAN, including their drives, targets, and portals, as shown in Figure 6-27.

Figure 6-27

Displaying subsystem information in the Storage Manager for SANs console

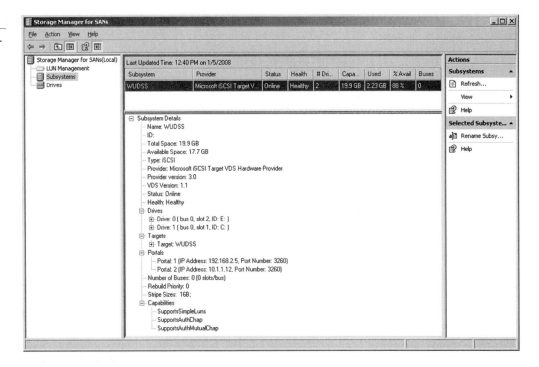

- Drives—Displays information about the drives on the SAN, as shown in Figure 6-28. This option can make the drive light blink, so you can associate the drive listings with the correct physical devices.

Figure 6-28

Displaying drive information in the Storage Manager for SANs console

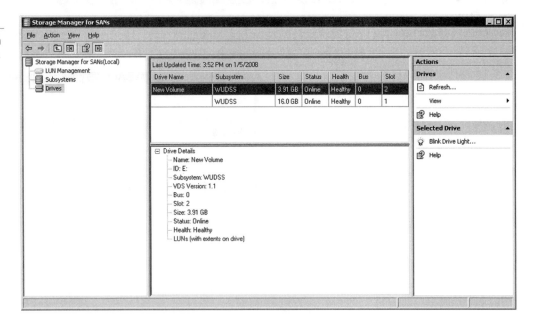

USING STORAGE EXPLORER

Storage Explorer is an MMC console that provides information about SAN resources and enables administrators to perform a variety of management tasks. The console is included in the default Windows Server 2008 installation; it is not part of a role or feature. When you launch Storage Explorer, it crawls the SAN and enumerates the devices it finds there, including servers, storage devices, and such infrastructure components as switches and iSNS servers, as shown in Figure 6-29.

Figure 6-29

The Storage Explorer console

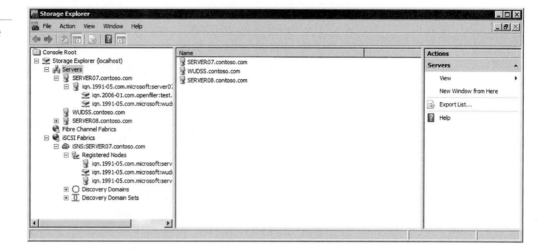

By selecting certain SAN components in the scope (left) pane, you can manipulate their properties by performing such tasks as configuring initiators, as shown in Figure 6-30, and managing iSNS records.

Figure 6-30

Configuring an iSCSI initiator in Storage Explorer

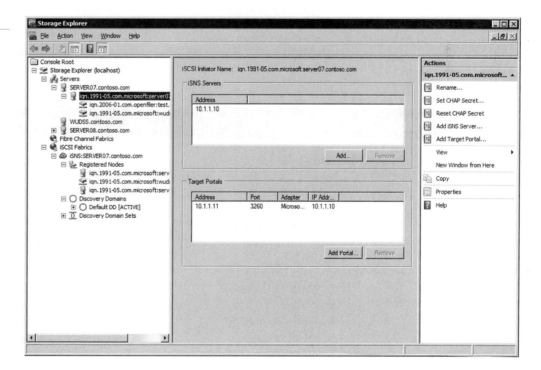

SUMMARY SKILL MATRIX

IN THIS LESSON YOU LEARNED:

- Windows Server 2008 supports two hard disk partition types: MBR and GPT; two disk types: basic and dynamic; five volume types: simple, striped, spanned, mirrored, and RAID-5; and two file systems: NTFS and FAT.

- The Disk Management snap-in is the primary interface you use to initialize, partition, and format disks.

- A storage area network (SAN) is a network dedicated solely to high-speed connections between servers and storage devices.

- Fibre Channel is a high-speed serial networking technology that was originally designed for use with supercomputers but that is now associated primarily with storage area networking.

- iSCSI is an alternative storage area networking technology that enables servers and storage devices to exchange SCSI traffic using a standard IP network instead of a dedicated Fibre Channel network.

- An iSCSI initiator is a hardware or software device running on a computer that accesses the storage devices on the SAN. The other half of the iSCSI equation is the iSCSI target, which receives SCSI commands from the initiator and passes them to a storage device, represented by a logical unit number (LUN).

- The Internet Storage Name Service (iSNS) registers the presence of initiators and targets on a SAN and responds to queries from iSNS clients.

- Storage Manager for SANs can manage only storage devices that include support for the Microsoft Virtual Disk Service. The storage device manufacturer must supply a software component called a VDS hardware provider, which you install on the computer that will manage the device.

- Storage Explorer is an MMC console that provides information about SAN resources and enables administrators to perform a variety of management tasks.

■ Knowledge Assessment

Matching

Complete the following exercise by matching the terms with their corresponding definitions.

    a. switched fabric
    b. VDS hardware provider
    c. disk duplexing
    d. JBOD
    e. logical unit numbers
    f. block I/O access
    g. iSNS
    h. Fibre Channel
    i. iSCSI initiator
    j. direct-attached storage

_____ **1.** enables a database application to access specific records in a database file stored on a SAN drive array

_____ **2.** identifies specific devices in a drive array

_____ **3.** installed by default in Windows Server 2008

_____ **4.** provided with some SAN drive arrays

_____ **5.** supports copper and fiber optic media

_____ **6.** requires redundant drives and redundant host adapters

_____ **7.** a Fibre Channel topology

_____ **8.** a hard drive installed inside a computer

_____ **9.** maintains a database of targets and initiators

_____ **10.** a disk array that does not use RAID

Multiple Choice

Select one or more correct answers for each of the following questions.

1. Which of the following statements are true of striped volumes?
   a. Striped volumes provide enhanced performance over simple volumes.
   b. Striped volumes provide greater fault tolerance than simple volumes.
   c. You can extend striped volumes after creation.
   d. If a single physical disk in the striped volume fails, all of the data in the entire volume is lost.

2. Which of the following are requirements for extending a volume on a dynamic disk?
   a. If you want to extend a simple volume, you can use only the available space on the same disk, if the volume is to remain simple.
   b. The volume must have a file system (a raw volume) before you can extend a simple or spanned volume.
   c. You can extend a simple or spanned volume if you formatted it using the FAT or FAT32 file systems.
   d. You can extend a simple volume across additional disks if it is not a system volume or a boot volume.

3. Which of the following is the application layer protocol used for all communications between Internet Storage Name Service clients and servers?
   a. iSCSI   b. iSNSP
   c. IP   d. FCP

4. Which of the following is *not* true in reference to converting a basic disk to a dynamic disk?
   a. You cannot convert a basic disk to a dynamic disk if you need to dual boot the computer.
   b. You cannot convert drives with volumes that use an allocation unit size greater than 512 bytes.
   c. A boot partition or system partition on a basic disk cannot be extended into a striped or spanned volume, even if you convert the disk to a dynamic disk.
   d. The conversion will fail if the hard drive does not have at least 1 MB of free space at the end of the disk.

5. Which of the following is *not* true about differences between network attached storage (NAS) devices and storage area network (SAN) devices?

   a. NAS devices provide a file system implementation; SAN devices do not.

   b. NAS devices must have their own processor and memory hardware; SAN devices do not require these components.

   c. NAS devices must run their own operating system and typically provide a Web interface for administrative access; SAN devices do not have to have either one.

   d. NAS devices require a specialized protocol, such as Fibre Channel or iSCSI; SAN devices use standard networking protocols.

6. To manage a storage device using Storage Manager for SANs, you must have which of the following?

   a. a Fibre Channel switch   b. an iSCSI target

   c. a VDS hardware provider   d. an iSNS server

7. Which of the following Windows Server 2008 components is intended for use with iSCSI and Fibre Channel SANs?

   a. Internet Storage Name Server   b. Storage Manager for SANs

   c. Storage Explorer   d. iSCSI initiator

8. Which of the following components is not included in the Windows Server 2008 product?

   a. iSCSI initiator   b. iSCSI target

   c. iSNS Server   d. Storage Manager for SANs

9. Which of the following Fibre Channel layers contains the SCSI commands destined for storage devices on the SAN?

   a. FC1   b. FC2

   c. FC3   d. FC4

10. An iSCSI target receives commands from an initiator and passes them to a storage device. Which of the following is used to represent the storage device?

    a. logical unit number   b. iSNS database entry

    c. VDS hardware provider   d. RS-232 port

Review Questions

1. Considering the five dynamic volume types supported by Windows Server 2008, explain why each volume type either does or does not provide fault tolerance.

2. Explain why the block I/O access provided by a storage area network is preferable to the file-based I/O provided by network attached storage when you are running a database or email application.

■ Case Scenario

Scenario 6-1: Using Storage Manager for SANs

Mackenzie is responsible for deploying a test storage area network, using a Windows Server 2008 computer and an iSCSI drive array with a standard Ethernet networking infrastructure. After connecting the server and the drive array to the SAN and configuring an iSCSI target using the Web-based interface provided by the array, Mackenzie uses iSCSI initiator on the server to establish a connection to a target. Mackenzie can now use the Disk Administration snap-in to partition and format the volume on the drive array. Next, Mackenzie attempts to use the Storage Manager for SANs console to create additional LUNs on the drive array, but the console fails to load the Virtual Disk Service. What must Mackenzie do to use Storage Manager for SANs to manage the LUNs on the drive array?

Planning for High Availability

OBJECTIVE DOMAIN MATRIX

Technology Skill	Objective Domain	Objective Domain Number
Planning for Application Resilience	Plan application servers and services	1.4
Using Offline Files	Provision data	4.2
Planning for Data Availability	Plan high availability	5.2

KEY TERMS

application resilience
convergence
DNS Round Robin
failover cluster
heartbeats

network load balancing (NLB)
Offline Files
server farm
Shadow Copies

terminal server farm
TS Session Broker
Windows Installer 4.0
witness disk

In computer networking, high availability refers to technologies that enable users to continue accessing a resource despite the occurrence of a disastrous hardware or software failure. This lesson examines a number of availability mechanisms, including the following:

- Shadow copies and offline files
- Disk redundancy solutions, such as RAID
- Application availability solutions
- Server clustering

■ Planning for Data Availability

THE BOTTOM LINE As the computer component with the most moving parts and the closest physical tolerances, hard disk drives are more prone to failure than virtually any other element of a data network.

CERTIFICATION READY?
Plan high availability
5.2

When a hard disk drive fails, the data stored on it obviously becomes unavailable. Depending on the type of data stored on the disk and the availability technologies implemented on the computer and the network, the effect of a disk failure on user productivity can be transitory, temporary, or permanent.

Backing Up Data

The simplest and most common type of data availability mechanism is the disk backup, that is, a copy of a disk's data stored on another medium. The traditional medium for network backups is magnetic tape, although other options are now becoming more prevalent, including online backups.

While backups are designed to protect data against the outright loss caused by a drive failure, they cannot be considered a high availability mechanism, because in the event of a failure, administrators must restore the data from the backup medium before it is again accessible to users. Depending on the nature of the failure and what files are lost, data might be unavailable for hours or even days before the drive is replaced and the restoration completed.

Despite these drawbacks, however, regular backups are an essential part of any network maintenance program, even when you have other availability mechanisms in place. Disk redundancy cannot provide protection again user error, for example, or computer theft and natural disasters.

For more information on backing up and restoring network data, see Lesson 12, "Backing Up."

Using Shadow Copies

Backups are primarily designed to protect against major losses, such as drive failures, computer thefts, and natural disasters. However, the loss of individual data files is a fairly common occurrence on most networks, typically due to accidental deletion or user mishandling. For backup administrators, the need to locate, mount, and search backup media just to restore a single file can be a regular annoyance, but Windows Server 2008 includes a feature called Shadow Copies that can make recent versions of data files highly available to end-users.

Shadow Copies is a mechanism that automatically retains copies of files on a server volume in multiple versions from specific points in time. When users accidentally overwrite or delete files, they can access the shadow copies to restore earlier versions. This feature is specifically designed to prevent administrators from having to load backup media to restore individual files for users. Shadow Copies is a file-based fault tolerance mechanism that does not provide protection against disk failures, but it does protect against the minor disasters that inconvenience users and administrators on a regular basis.

To use Shadow Copies effectively, you must have your users store their files on server, as opposed to local, volumes. You can automate this practice using File Redirection, which automatically redirects local folders to server volumes.

You can implement Shadow Copies only for an entire volume; you cannot select specific shares, folders, or files. To configure a Windows Server 2008 volume to create Shadow Copies, use the following procedure.

➔ CONFIGURE SHADOW COPIES

GET READY. Log on to Windows Server 2008 using an account with domain administrative privileges. When the logon process is completed, close the Initial Configuration Tasks window and any other windows that appear.

1. Click **Start,** and then click **All Programs** > **Accessories** > **Windows Explorer**. The Windows Explorer window appears.

2. In the **Folders** list, expand the **Computer** container, right-click a volume and, from the context menu, select **Configure Shadow Copies**. The Shadow Copies dialog box appears, as shown in Figure 7-1.

Figure 7-1

The Shadow Copies dialog box

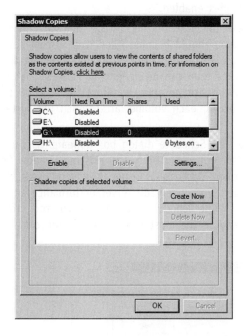

3. In the **Select a volume** box, choose the volume for which you want to enable Shadow Copies. By default, when you enable Shadow Copies for a volume, the system uses the following settings:

- The system stores the shadow copies on the selected volume.
- The system reserves 10 percent of the source volume for the shadow copies.
- The system creates shadow copies at 7:00 AM and 12:00 PM every weekday.

4. To modify the default parameters, click **Settings**. The Settings dialog box appears, as shown in Figure 7-2.

Figure 7-2

The Settings dialog box

5. In the **Storage area** box, specify the volume where you want to store the shadow copies. For a server operating with a high I/O load, such as a file server, Microsoft recommends that, for best performance, you create the Shadow Copies storage area on another volume, preferably a volume on another physical disk that does not have Shadow Copies enabled.

6. Specify the Maximum Size for the storage area, or choose the **No Limit** option. If the storage area should become filled, the system begins deleting the oldest shadow copies, so if a lot of large files are stored on the volume, increasing the size of the storage area can be beneficial. However, no matter how much space you allocate to the storage area, Windows Server 2008 supports a maximum of 64 shadow copies for each volume, after which the system begins deleting the oldest copies.

7. Click **Schedule**. The Schedule dialog box appears, as shown in Figure 7-3. Using the controls provided, you can modify the existing Shadow Copies tasks, delete them, or create new ones, based on the needs of your users. Scheduling shadow copies to occur too frequently can degrade server performance and cause copies to be aged out too quickly, while scheduling them to occur too infrequently can cause users to lose work because the most recent copy is too old.

Figure 7-3

The Schedule dialog box

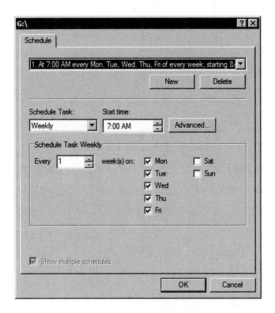

8. Click **OK** twice to close the Schedule and Settings dialog boxes.

9. Click **Enable**. The system enables the Shadow Copies feature for the selected volume and creates the first copy in the designated storage area.

CLOSE any open windows.

After you complete this procedure, the system creates shadow copies of each file on the storage volume you selected at the scheduled times. Shadow copies are block-based; the system copies only the blocks in each file that have changed since the last copy. This means that in most cases, the shadow copies take up far less storage space than the originals.

Once the server begins creating shadow copies, users can open previous versions of files on the selected volumes, either to restore those that they have accidentally deleted or overwritten, or to compare multiple versions of files as they work. To access the shadow copies stored on a server, a computer must be running the Previous Versions Client. This client is included with Windows Vista, Windows XP Service Pack 2, Windows Server 2008, and Windows Server 2003. For pre-SP2 Windows XP and Windows 2000 computers, you can download the client from the Microsoft Download Center at www.microsoft.com/downloads.

To open a shadow copy of a file, a user must select it in any Explorer window and open its Properties sheet. On the Previous Versions tab, all of the available copies of the file appear, along with their dates, as shown in Figure 7-4.

Figure 7-4

The Previous Versions tab of a file's Properties sheet

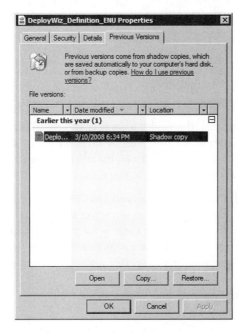

After selecting one of the file versions, the user clicks one of the following buttons to access it:

- Open—Launches the application associated with the file type and loads the file from its current location. You cannot modify the file unless you save it to another location.
- Copy—Copies the file to the system's Clipboard so that you can paste it to any location.
- Restore—Overwrites the current version of the file with the selected previous version. Once done, the current version of the file is lost and cannot be restored.

Using Offline Files

Offline Files is a mechanism that individual users can employ to maintain access to their server files, even if the server becomes unavailable.

Offline Files works by copying server-based folders that users select for offline use to a workstation's local drive. The users then work with the copies, which remain accessible whether the workstation can access the server or not. No matter what the cause, be it a drive malfunction, a server failure, or a network outage, the users can continue to access the offline files without interruption.

When the workstation is able to reconnect to the server drive, a synchronization procedure replicates the files between server and workstation in whichever direction is necessary. If the user on the workstation has modified the file, the system overwrites the server copy with the workstation copy. If another user has modified the copy of the file on the server, the workstation updates its local copy. If there is a version conflict, such as when users have modified both copies of a file, the system prompts the user to specify which copy to retain.

Although an effective availability mechanism, primary control of Offline Files rests with the user, not the administrator, making it a less than reliable solution for an enterprise network. Administrators can configure server shares to prevent users from saving offline copies, but they cannot configure a server to force a workstation to save offline copies.

CERTIFICATION READY?
Provision data
4.2

To use Offline Files, the user of the client computer must first activate the feature, using one of the following procedures:

- Windows XP and Windows Server 2003—Open the Folder Options control panel, click the Offline Files tab, and select the Enable Offline Files checkbox.
- Windows Vista and Windows Server 2008—Open the Offline Files control panel and, on the General tab, click Enable Offline Files.

This control panel interface also provides settings that enable the user to specify how much local disk space is allotted for offline files, when synchronization events should occur, and whether the system should encrypt the locally stored offline files.

Once Offline Files is enabled, the workstation user can right-click any file or folder on a server share and select Always Available Offline or Make Available Offline from the context menu. The workstation will then perform an initial synchronization that copies the contents of the folder to the local disk.

From this point on, Offline Files works automatically for that selected folder. If the user is working on a protected file when access to the server share is interrupted, the system indicates that the server is no longer available, but there is no interruption to the file access, because the user is actually working with the offline copy. When the server share is once again available, the system notifies the user and offers to perform a synchronization.

Using Disk Redundancy

> Shadow copies and offline files are both effective mechanisms for maintaining data availability. However, for mission critical data that must be continuously available, using a mechanism controlled by administrators, not end users, there is no better solution than to have redundant disks containing the same data online at once.

In Lesson 6, "Planning Storage Solutions," you learned about how storage technologies such as disk mirroring and RAID (Redundant Array of Independent Disks) enable servers to maintain multiple copies of data files online at all times so that in the event of a disk failure, users can still access their files.

Disk redundancy is the most common type of high availability technology currently in use. Even organizations with small servers and modest budgets can benefit from redundant disks, by installing two or more physical disk drives in a server and using the disk mirroring and RAID-5 capabilities built into Windows Server 2008. For larger servers, external disk arrays and dedicated RAID hardware products can provide more scalability, better performance, and a greater degree of availability.

Generally speaking, when you plan for high availability, you must balance three factors: fault tolerance, performance, and expense. The more fault tolerance you require for your data, the more you must spend to achieve it, and the more likely you are to suffer degraded performance as a result of it.

Disk mirroring is the simplest form of disk redundancy, and typically does not have a negative effect on performance, as long as you use a disk technology, such as SCSI (Small Computer System Interface) or serial ATA (SATA), that enables the computer to write to both disks at the same time. However, mirroring reduces the amount of storage space you realize from the array by half, which is less efficient than parity-based RAID technologies, in this respect, and more expensive in the long run. However, the price per gigabyte of hard disk storage continues to fall, which makes disk mirroring a viable high availability solution.

Parity-based RAID is the most commonly used high availability solution for data storage, primarily because it is far more scalable than disk mirroring and it enables you to realize more storage space from your hard disks. In fact, the more physical disks you add to the array, the greater the percentage of space that can be devoted to actual storage.

TAKE NOTE *

Disk duplexing is strictly a hardware modification that adds a further degree of fault tolerance to a mirrored disk environment. By mirroring disks connected to different host adapters, the system can continue to function, even if one of the host adapters fails. This is admittedly a far less likely occurrence than a hard drive failure, but fault tolerance is all about planning for unlikely occurrences.

For example, a RAID-5 array that consists of three 250 GB disks (a total of 750 GB) yields 500 GB of available space, that is, 66 percent of the total storage. This is because, for each bit on the three disks, one must be devoted to the parity data that provides the fault tolerance. However, if you add a fourth 250 GB disk to the array, for a total of 1000 GB, you get 750 GB of storage, or 75 percent, because there is still only one out of each four bits devoted to parity information. In the same way, a five-disk array will realize 80 percent of its total as usable storage.

Windows Server 2008 supports RAID-5 as its only parity-based data availability mechanism. While RAID-5 is more scalable than disk mirroring (because you can always add another drive to the array) and more economical (because you realize more usable storage), you must accept a performance hit.

Because RAID-5 distributes the parity information among the drives in the array, disk write performance is not heavily affected, as it is with RAID levels 3 and 4, which use dedicated parity disks. However, you must consider the processing burden required to calculate the parity information. The RAID-5 implementation included with Windows Server 2008 uses the system's processor and memory resources to perform all of the parity calculations, and depending on the amount of I/O traffic the server must handle, this additional processor burden can be significant.

If you intend to use only the data availability mechanisms built into Windows Server 2008, you should consider carefully whether you want to use disk mirroring, and pay a larger price per gigabyte of usable storage, or use RAID-5, and possibly pay more for a server with sufficient memory and processor speed to handle the parity calculations.

The alternative to the Windows Server 2008 RAID-5 mechanism is to purchase a hardware-based RAID solution, either in the form of a host adapter card that you install in the server, or an external disk array, which you connect to the server. The downside to this solution, obviously, is the additional cost. RAID adapter cards range in cost from under $50 to well over $1000, while drive arrays (without the hard drives) start at just over $100 and rise quickly to stratospheric levels. The inexpensive products are suitable for workstations and the smallest servers, however.

The advantages to hardware-based RAID are improved performance and flexibility. These solutions include dedicated hardware that performs the parity calculations, so there is no additional burden placed on the computer's own resources. Third-party products often provide additional RAID capabilities as well, such as RAID-6, which maintains two copies of the parity data, enabling the array to survive the failure of two drives without service interruption or data loss. Some third-party RAID implementations also include hybrid RAID technologies, such as mirrored stripe sets or other proprietary combinations of striping, mirroring, and/or parity.

When selecting a data high availability solution, consider questions like the following:

- How much data do you have to protect?
- How critical is the data is to the operation of your enterprise?
- How long an outage can your organization comfortably endure?
- How much you can afford to spend?

Remember that none of these high availability mechanisms are intended to be replacements for regular system backups. For document files that are less than critical, or files that see only occasional use, it might be more economical to keep some spare hard drives on hand and rely on your backups. If a failure occurs, you can replace the malfunctioning drive and restore it from your most recent backup, usually in a matter of hours. However, if access to server data is critical to your organization, the expense of a RAID solution might be seen as minimal, when compared to the lost revenue or even more serious consequences of a disk failure.

■ Planning for Application Availability

THE BOTTOM LINE
High availability is not limited to data; applications, too, must be available for users to complete their work.

Application availability can mean different things, depending on the nature of the applications your users run. Lesson 4, "Planning Application Services," classifies applications into three categories: client-run, client/server, and distributed, and it describes the server interaction needed by each one. Keeping each of these application types available to users at all times requires different strategies and mechanisms, some of which are simply a matter of setting configuration parameters, while others call for additional hardware and an elaborate deployment. As with data availability, the solutions you select must depend on how important the applications are to your organization and how much you can afford to spend.

When a standalone application is installed on a client workstation, it will obviously continue to run, even if the computer is disconnected from the network for any reason. However, an application might still require access to the network at least occasionally, to download service packs and updates needed to keep it current. Network connectivity aside, a standalone application can also be rendered unavailable by a local disk failure or an accidentally deleted executable or other application file.

Client/server applications are more likely to be rendered unavailable than client-run applications, because they require both the client and server components to function properly, and the two must also be able to communicate. As a result, damage to either component or any sort of network outage can prevent the application from functioning. Distributed applications are even more sensitive, because they have more components that can go wrong.

For example, a Web-based application that accesses a database requires three separate application components (the Web browser, the Web server, and the database server) to function properly on three different computers. There are also two network connections (browser to Web server and Web server to database server) that must be operational as well. If any one of these components or connections fails, the application becomes unavailable.

The following sections examine some of the ways that you can ensure the continued availability of your applications.

Increasing Application Availability

An application running on workstations, whether it is a standalone application or the client half of a client/server application, is left to the responsibility of the end users. If a user deletes the wrong file or damages the computer in some other way, he or she might disable the application.

One way of protecting workstation applications and ensuring their continued availability is to run them using Terminal Services. Lesson 4 describes how, with Terminal Services, users can access applications that are actually running on a server, rather than their own workstations. Because the server administrators have ultimate control over the application files, they can protect them against accidental deletion and other types of damage.

In addition, deploying applications using Terminal Services makes it far easier to replace a workstation that has experienced a catastrophic failure of some type. For example, if a user's workstation experiences a complete hard disk failure, the applications on the computer are obviously rendered unavailable. The user's productivity stops.

X REF

Terminal Services can also enhance application availability by running on a server cluster. For more information on server clustering, see "Planning for Server Availability" later in this lesson.

Replacing or repairing the computer and installing all of the applications the user needs can be a lengthy process, during which the user sits idle. If the applications are deployed on terminal servers, you can supply the user with a temporary workstation containing just the operating system. The user can then run his or her applications from the terminal servers and get back to work almost immediately.

Virtualization, such as that provided by the Hyper-V feature in Windows Server 2008, is another way of increasing application availability. Administrators can move virtual machines from one computer to another relatively easily, in the event of a hardware failure, or when the applications running on the virtual machines require more or different hardware resources.

Planning for Application Resilience

Application resilience refers to the ability of an application to maintain its own availability by detecting outdated, corrupted, or missing files and automatically correcting the problem.

CERTIFICATION READY?
Plan application servers and services
1.4

There are a number of methods you can use to make applications resilient, most of which are integrated into application deployment tools. The following sections examine some of these methods.

ENHANCING APPLICATION AVAILABILITY USING GROUP POLICY

As discussed in Lesson 4, administrators can use Group Policy to deploy application packages to computers and/or users on the network. When you assign a software package to a computer, the client installs the package automatically when the system boots. When you assign a package to a user, the client installs the application when the user logs on to the domain, or when the user invokes the software by double-clicking an associated document file.

Both of these methods enforce a degree of application resilience, because even if the user manages to uninstall the application, the system will reinstall it during the next startup or domain logon. This is not a foolproof system, however. Group Policy will not recognize the absence of a single application file, as some other mechanisms do.

ENHANCING APPLICATION AVAILABILITY USING WINDOWS INSTALLER

X REF

Another way to improve application resilience is by using Windows Server Update Services (WSUS) to automatically apply updates. For more information on using WSUS, see Lesson 10, "Managing Servers."

Windows Installer 4.0 is the component in Windows Server 2008 that enables the system to install software packaged as files with a .msi extension. One of the advantages of deploying software in this manner is the built-in resiliency that Windows Installer provides to the applications.

When you deploy a .msi package, either manually or using an automated solution, such as Group Policy or System Center Configuration Manager 2007, Windows Installer creates special shortcuts and file associations that function as entry points for the applications contained in the package. When a user invokes an application using one of these entry points, Windows Installer intercepts the call and verifies the application to make sure that its files are intact and all required updates are applied before executing it.

Implementing this resilience is up to the developers of the application. In organizations that create their own software in-house, the server administrators should make sure that the application developers are aware of the capabilities built into Windows Installer so that they can take advantage of them.

Planning for Server Availability

THE BOTTOM LINE

Server clustering can provide two forms of high availability on an enterprise network. In addition to providing fault tolerance in the event of a server failure, it can provide network load balancing for busy applications.

As mentioned earlier in this lesson, high availability is typically a matter of using redundant components to ensure the continued functionality of a particular network resource. A database stored on a RAID array remains available to users, even if one of the hard disk drives fails. An application installed on a terminal server is readily available to users from any workstation.

Servers themselves can suffer failures that render them unavailable. Hard disks are not the only computer components that can fail, and one way of keeping servers available is to equip them with redundant components other than hard drives. The ultimate in fault tolerance, however, is to have entire servers that are redundant so that if anything goes wrong with one computer, another one can take its place almost immediately. In Windows Server 2008, this is known as a *failover cluster*.

Another type of clustering, useful when a Web server or other application becomes overwhelmed by a large volume of users, is *network load balancing (NLB)*, in which you deploy multiple identical servers, also known as a *server farm*, and distribute the user traffic evenly among them.

Using Hardware Redundancy

Servers contain the same basic components as workstations: processors, memory, hard disks, and so forth. In many cases, what differentiates a server from a workstation, apart from the size, speed, and expense of the individual components, is the inclusion of secondary hardware that provides enhanced or redundant functions.

Servers often have faster processors than workstations, or multiple processors. They also tend to have more, and larger, hard drives installed. One of the byproducts of this extra hardware is additional heat. There is nothing that can kill a computer faster than uncontrolled heat generation, and many server computers are equipped with cooling systems that include multiple redundant fans that can run at various speeds.

When the computer's motherboard senses a temperature rise inside the case, it can switch the fans to a higher speed and, in some cases, warn an administrator of the problem. Because there are multiple cooling fans in most servers, this variable speed capability can also compensate for the failure of one or more fans.

Another critical component to server operation that is known to be fallible is the computer's power supply. The power supply connects to an AC power source and provides all of the components in the computer with the various voltages they need to operate. Power supplies can fail due to factors such as power surges or excessive heat, which cause the computer to stop. To prevent this, some servers have redundant power supplies so that the system can continue running, even if one fails.

There are other types of specialized hardware often found in servers as well. Some of these, such as hot swappable drive arrays, are designed to enable administrators to effect repairs while the server is still running.

Using Failover Clustering

> A failover cluster is a collection of two or more servers that perform the same role or run the same application and appear on the network as a single entity.

Windows Server 2008 includes a Failover Cluster Management console that enables you to create and configure failover clusters after you have set up an appropriate environment. Before you can create a failover cluster in Windows Server 2008, you must install the Failover Clustering feature using the Add Features Wizard in Server Manager. Because Failover Clustering is a feature, and not a role, it is relatively simple to add clustering to roles such as file, print, and DHCP servers.

UNDERSTANDING FAILOVER CLUSTER REQUIREMENTS

Failover clusters are intended for critical applications that must keep running. If an organization is prepared to incur the time and expense required to deploy a failover cluster, Microsoft assumes that the organization is prepared to take every possible step to ensure the availability of the application. As a result, the recommended hardware environment for a failover cluster calls for an elaborate setup, including the following:

- Duplicate servers—The computers that will function as cluster nodes should be as identical as possible in terms of memory, processor type, and other hardware components.
- Shared storage—All of the cluster servers should have exclusive access to shared storage, such as that provided by a Fibre Channel or iSCSI storage area network. This shared storage will be the location of the application data so that all of the cluster servers have access to it. The shared storage can also contain the *witness disk*, which holds the cluster configuration database. This too should be available to all of the servers in the cluster.
- Redundant network connections—Connect the cluster servers to the network in a way that avoids a single point of failure. You can connect each server to two separate networks or build a single network using redundant switches, routers, and network adapters.

Shared storage is a critical aspect of server clustering. In a pure failover cluster, all of the servers must have access to the application data on a shared storage medium, but you cannot have two instances of the application accessing the same data at the same time. For example, if you are running a database application on a failover cluster, only one of the cluster servers is active at any one time. If two servers accessed the same database file at the same time, they could modify the same record simultaneously, causing data corruption.

In addition to the hardware recommendations, the cluster servers should use the same software environment, which consists of the following elements:

- Operating system—All of the servers in a cluster must be running the same edition of the same operating system.
- Application—All of the cluster servers must run the same version of the redundant application.
- Updates—All of the cluster servers must have the same operating system and application updates installed.
- Active Directory—All of the cluster servers must be in the same Active Directory domain, and they must be either member servers or domain controllers. Microsoft recommends that all cluster servers be member servers, not domain controllers. Do not mix member servers and domain controllers in the same failover cluster.

Before you create a failover cluster using the Failover Cluster Management console, you should connect all of the hardware to the networks involved and test the connectivity of each

---

TAKE NOTE

To create a failover cluster, the computers must be running Windows Server 2008 Enterprise or Datacenter. The Standard and Web editions do not support failover clustering.

device. Make sure that every cluster server can communicate with the other servers and with the shared storage device.

VALIDATING A FAILOVER CLUSTER CONFIGURATION

The Failover Cluster Management console is included as a feature with Windows Server 2008. You must install it using the Add Features Wizard in Server Manager. Afterward, you can start to create a cluster by validating your hardware configuration. The Validate a Configuration Wizard performs an extensive battery of tests on the computers you select, enumerating their hardware and software resources and checking their configuration settings. If any elements required for a cluster are incorrect or missing, the wizard lists them in a report.

To validate a cluster configuration, use the following procedure.

 VALIDATE A FAILOVER CLUSTER CONFIGURATION

GET READY. Log on to Windows Server 2008 using an account with administrative privileges. When the logon process is completed, close the Initial Configuration Tasks window and any other windows that appear.

1. Click **Start**, and then click **Administrative Tools** > **Failover Cluster Management.** The Failover Cluster Management console appears, as shown in Figure 7-5.

Figure 7-5

The Failover Cluster Management console

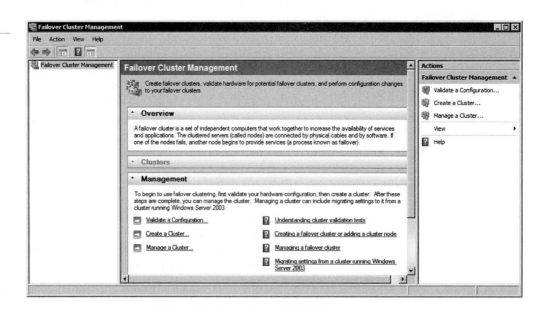

2. In the detail (middle) pane, in the **Management** box, click **Validate a Configuration.** The Validate a Configuration Wizard appears, as shown in Figure 7-6.

Figure 7-6

The Validate a Configuration Wizard

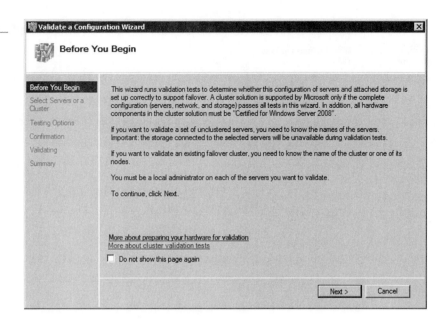

3. Click **Next** to bypass the *Before You Begin* page. The *Select Servers or a Cluster* page appears, as shown in Figure 7-7.

Figure 7-7

The Select Servers or a Cluster page of the Validate a Configuration Wizard

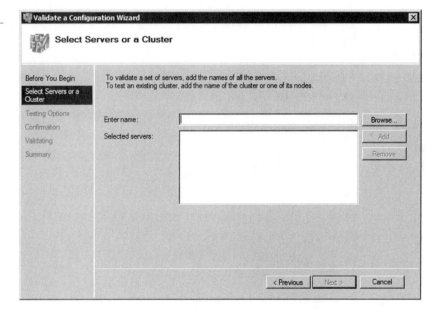

4. Key or browse to the name of the first server you want to add to the cluster and click **Add**. The server appears in the Selected Servers list.

5. Repeat the process to add the rest of the cluster servers to the Selected Servers list. Then, click **Next**. The *Testing Options* page appears, as shown in Figure 7-8.

Figure 7-8

The Testing Options page of
the Validate a Configuration
Wizard

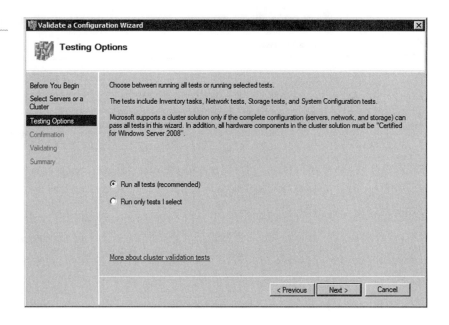

6. Leave the **Run All Tests** option selected and click **Next**. The *Confirmation* page appears, as shown in Figure 7-9.

Figure 7-9

The Confirmation page of
the Validate a Configuration
Wizard

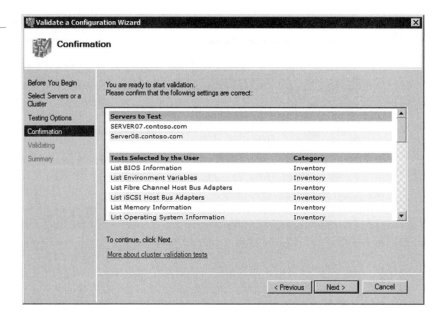

7. Click **Next**. The *Validating* page appears as the wizard performs the testing process. When the testing process is completed, the *Summary* page appears, as shown in Figure 7-10.

Figure 7-10

The Summary page of the Validate a Configuration Wizard

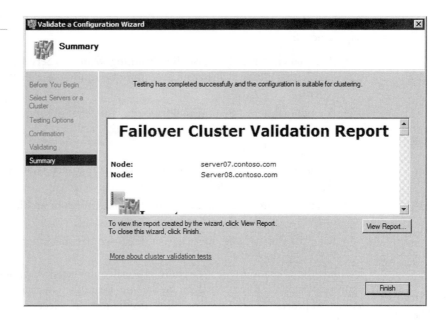

8. Click **View Report**. An Internet Explorer window appears, as shown in Figure 7-11, containing a detailed report of the validation tests.

Figure 7-11

A Failover Cluster Validation Report

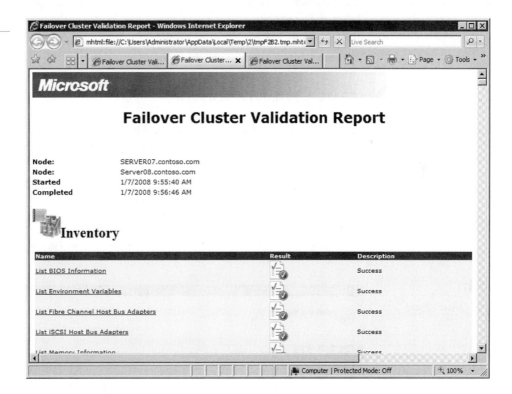

9. Click **Finish**.

CLOSE the Failover Cluster Management console.

To ensure that your validation is successful, your systems should conform to the following requirements:

- Potential cluster nodes must all be running Windows Server 2008 Enterprise edition or Datacenter edition. Cluster nodes cannot be running earlier Windows server operating systems.
- Potential cluster nodes must all have the same level of service pack installed.
- Potential cluster nodes must have computer accounts in the same domain and the same organizational unit.
- Potential cluster nodes must all be either member servers or domain controllers, but a cluster cannot have a mixture of both.
- Potential cluster nodes must all use the same processor architecture, such as x86 or x64 or IA64.
- Potential cluster nodes must have at least two network interface adapters.

Examine the validation report carefully, especially any listed warnings or test failures, and take appropriate actions to correct them before you create the cluster. You can repeat the entire validation process as needed or perform specific tests by selecting Run Only Tests I Select on the *Testing Options* page.

CREATING A FAILOVER CLUSTER

After you validate your cluster configuration and correct any problems, you can create the cluster. A failover cluster is a logical entity that exists on the network, with its own name and IP address, just like a physical computer.

To create a failover cluster, use the following procedure.

CREATE A FAILOVER CLUSTER

GET READY. Log on to Windows Server 2008 using an account with administrative privileges. When the logon process is completed, close the Initial Configuration Tasks window and any other windows that appear.

1. Click **Start**, and then click **Administrative Tools** > **Failover Cluster Management**. The Failover Cluster Management console appears.

2. In the detail (middle) pane, in the **Management** box, click **Create a Cluster**. The *Create Cluster Wizard* page appears, as shown in Figure 7-12.

TAKE NOTE

You can also use the Validate a Configuration Wizard to check a cluster that already exists to ensure that all of the requisite components are still operational.

Figure 7-12

The Create Cluster Wizard

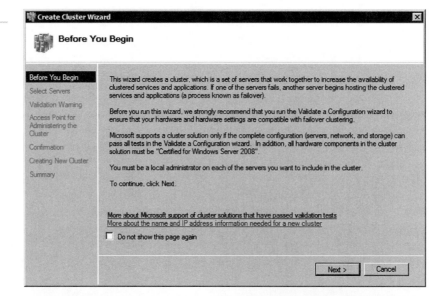

3. Click **Next** to bypass the *Before You Begin* page. The *Select Servers* page appears, as shown in Figure 7-13.

Figure 7-13

The Select Servers page of the Create Cluster Wizard

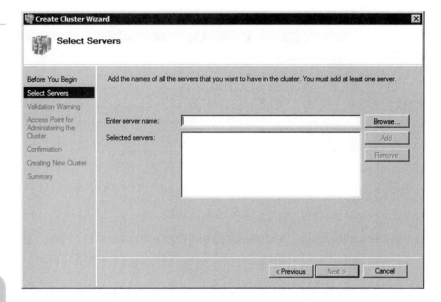

4. Key or browse to the name of the first server you want to add to the cluster and click **Add**. The server appears in the Selected Servers list.

5. Repeat the process to add the rest of the cluster servers to the Selected Servers list. Then, click **Next**. The *Access Point for Administering the Cluster* page appears, as shown in Figure 7-14.

Figure 7-14

The Access Point for Administering the Cluster page of the Create Cluster Wizard

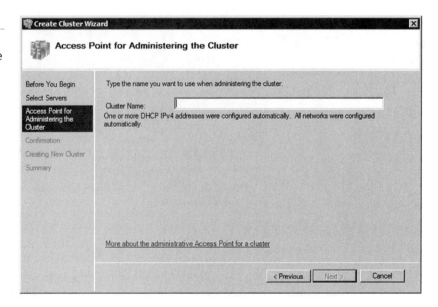

6. In the **Cluster Name** text box, key a name for the cluster and click **Next**. The Wizard obtains an IP address for the cluster on each network using DHCP and the *Confirmation* page appears, as shown in Figure 7-15.

Figure 7-15

The Confirmation page of the Create Cluster Wizard

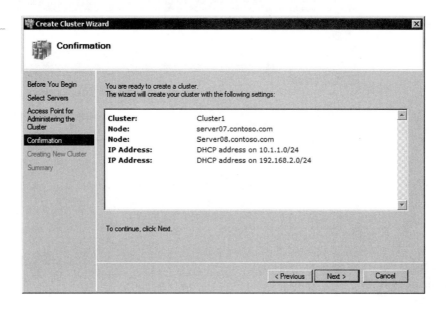

7. Click **Next**. The *Creating New Cluster* page appears.

8. When the cluster creation process is completed, the *Summary* page appears. Click **Finish**. The cluster appears in the console's scope (left) pane, as shown in Figure 7-16.

Figure 7-16

A newly created cluster in the Failover Cluster Management console

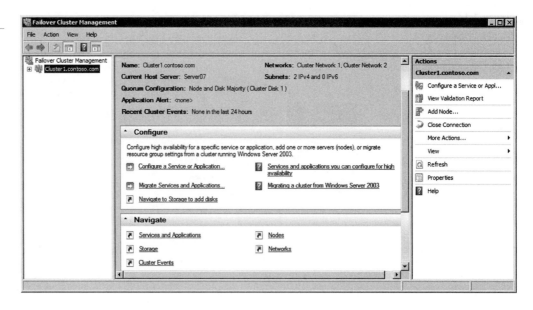

CLOSE the Failover Cluster Management console.

After you create the cluster, you can use the Failover Cluster Management console to specify the applications the cluster will manage. If a server fails, the applications you select are immediately executed on another server to keep them available to clients at all times.

Using Network Load Balancing

> Network load balancing (NLB) differs from failover clustering because its primary function is not fault tolerance, but rather the more efficient support of heavy user traffic.

If you have an Internet Web site that experiences a sudden increase in traffic, the Web server could be overwhelmed, causing performance to degrade. To address the problem, you can add another Web server that hosts the same site, but how do you ensure that the incoming traffic is split equally between the two servers? Network load balancing (NLB) is one possible answer.

In a failover cluster, only one of the servers is running the protected application at any given time. In network load balancing, all of the servers in the cluster are operational and able to service clients. The NLB cluster itself, like a failover cluster, is a logical entity with its own name and IP address. Clients connect to the cluster, rather than the individual computers, and the cluster distributes the incoming requests evenly among its component servers.

Because all of the servers in an NLB cluster can actively service clients at the same time, this type of cluster is not appropriate for database and email applications, which require exclusive access to a data store. NLB is more appropriate for applications that have their own data stores, such as Web servers. You can easily replicate a Web site to multiple servers on a regular basis, enabling each computer to maintain a separate copy of the data it provides to clients.

CREATING AN NLB CLUSTER

To create and manage NLB clusters on a Windows Server 2008 computer, you must first install the Network Load Balancing feature using Server Manager. This feature also includes the Network Load Balancing Manager console. Once you create the NLB cluster itself, you can add servers to and remove them from the cluster as needed.

The process of implementing an NLB cluster consists of the following tasks:

- Creating the cluster
- Adding servers to the cluster
- Specifying a name and IP address for the cluster
- Creating port rules that specify which types of traffic the cluster should balance among the cluster servers

To create an NLB cluster, use the following procedure.

 CREATE AN NLB CLUSTER

GET READY. Log on to Windows Server 2008 using an account with administrative privileges. When the logon process is completed, close the Initial Configuration Tasks window and any other windows that appear.

1. Click **Start,** and then click **Administrative Tools** > **Network Load Balancing Manager.** The Network Load Balancing Manager console appears, as shown in Figure 7-17.

Figure 7-17

The Network Load Balancing
Manager console

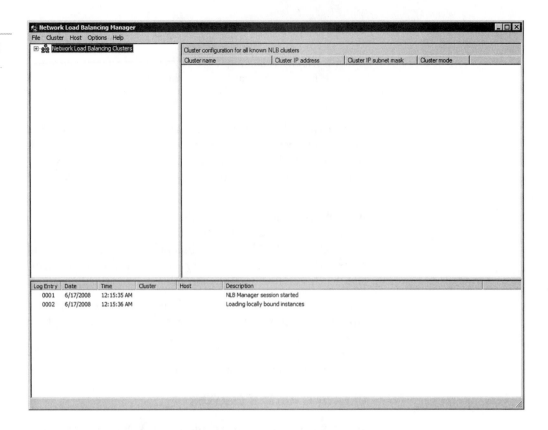

2. In the scope (left) pane, right-click **Network Load Balancing Clusters** and, from
the context menu, select **New Cluster.** The *New Cluster: Connect* page appears, as
shown in Figure 7-18.

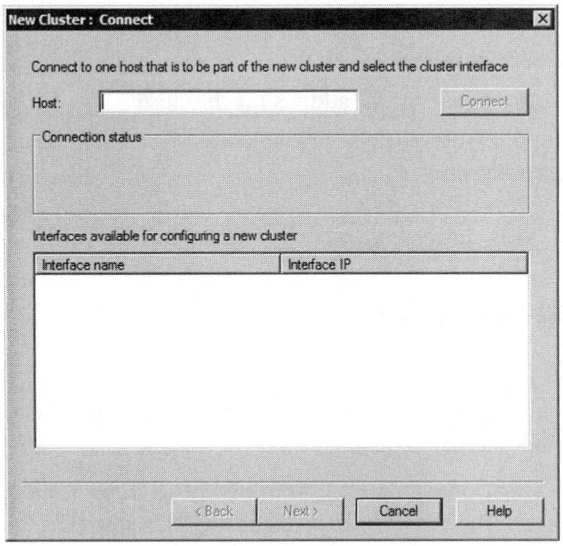

Figure 7-18

The New Cluster: Connect page

3. In the **Host** text box, key the name of the first server you want to add to the
cluster and click **Connect.** The network interfaces in the computer appear.

4. Select the interface over which the server will receive traffic destined for the clustered application and click **Next.** The *New Cluster: Host Parameters* page appears, as
shown in Figure 7-19.

Figure 7-19

The New Cluster: Host Parameters page

The servers that you intend to add to an NLB cluster must have static IP addresses. If the interface you select obtains its IP address from a DHCP server, the wizard disables the DHCP client and instructs you to configure the network connection manually.

5. Configure the following parameters, if necessary:

- Priority—Specifies a unique identifier for each host in the cluster. The host with the lowest identifier handles all of the cluster traffic that is not forwarded by port rules.
- Dedicated IP Addresses—Specifies the IP address and Subnet Mask that the host will use for non-cluster traffic, that is, the original IP address of the server's network interface.
- Initial Host State—Specifies whether the NLB service should start and add the host to the cluster each time Windows starts.

6. Click **Next.** The *New Cluster: Cluster IP Addresses* page appears, as shown in Figure 7-20.

Figure 7-20

The New Cluster: Cluster IP Addresses page

7. Click **Add.** The Add IP Address dialog box appears, as shown in Figure 7-21.

Figure 7-21

The Add IP Address dialog box

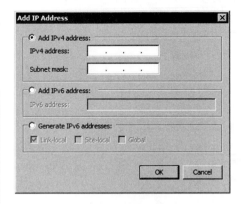

To specify an IPv6 address for the cluster, select the Add IPv6 Address option and key the address in the IPv6 Address field. To have the computer auto-con-figure an IPv6 address, select the Generate IPv6 Addresses option and specify the types of address you want to use by selecting from the three checkboxes.

8. In the **IPv4 Address** and **Subnet Mask** text boxes, specify the IP address you want to use for the NLB cluster and its subnet mask value. This address must be differ-ent from the server's own host address and unique on the network. Then click **OK.** The address you specified appears in the *New Cluster: Cluster IP Addresses* page.

9. Click **Next.** The *New Cluster: Cluster Parameters* page appears, as shown in Figure 7-22.

Figure 7-22

The New Cluster: Cluster Parameters page

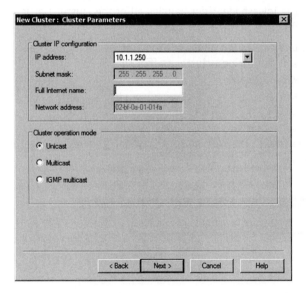

10. In the **Full Internet Name** text box, key the name you want to assign to the cluster, such as cluster.contoso.com. In the **Cluster Operation Mode** box, specify whether you want the cluster's network address to be a unicast or multicast address.

11. Click **Next.** The *New Cluster: Port Rules* page appears, as shown in Figure 7-23.

Figure 7-23

The New Cluster: Port Rules page

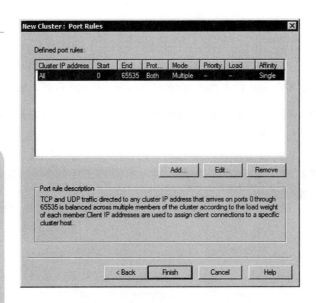

By default, a new cluster has a port rule that balances all incoming traffic amongst the servers in the cluster. If you want to limit the traffic that the cluster will balance, you must modify or remove this default port rule.

12. Click **Add.** The Add/Edit Port Rule dialog box appears, as shown in Figure 7-24.

Figure 7-24

The Add/Edit Port Rule dialog box

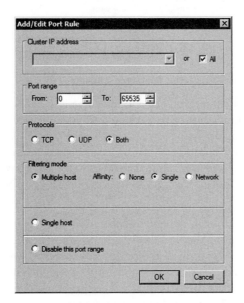

13. Configure the following parameters:

- Cluster IP Address—If the cluster has multiple IP addresses, use this dropdown list to select the one to which the rule should apply.

- Port Range—Specifies the port numbers of the traffic you want to balance among the cluster servers. For example, to balance only standard incoming Web traffic, you would use the values 80 and 80.

- Protocols—Specifies whether you want to balance TCP (Transmission Control Protocol) traffic, UDP (User Datagram Protocol) traffic, or both.

- Multiple Host—When selected, causes the cluster to distribute incoming traffic amongst all of the servers in the cluster.

- Affinity—When the Multiple Host option is selected, specifies that the cluster should forward incoming messages from the same IP address to a single host (the default). The None option specifies that the cluster can forward incoming messages from the same IP address to any host, and the Network option specifies that the cluster should forward incoming messages from the same network address to the same host.

- Single Host—Specifies that the cluster should forward all of the incoming traffic for the port rule to a single host.
- Disable This Port Range—Blocks all traffic conforming to this port rule.

14. Click **OK.** The port rule appears in the Defined Port Rules list.

15. Click **Finish.** The cluster and the server appear in the scope pane, as shown in Figure 7-25.

Figure 7-25

The Network Load Balancing Manager console, with an active cluster

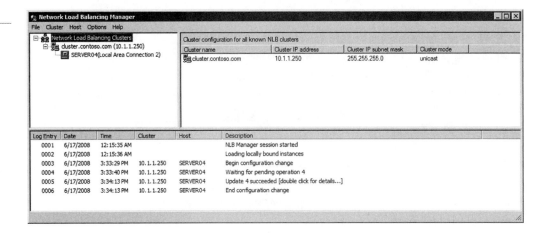

CLOSE the Network Load Balancing Manager console.

After creating the NLB cluster, you can add servers to it at will, using the Network Load Balancing Manager console from any computer. As you add each server, the Network Load Balancing service automatically incorporates it into the cluster, as displayed in the log (bottom) pane. You must install the Network Load Balancing feature on each server before you add it to the cluster, but you can manage the cluster from any server running the Remote Server Administration Tools > Feature Administration Tools > Network Load Balancing Tools feature.

Once the cluster is operational, the only modification on the part of the clients is that they connect to the cluster, using the name or IP address you specified in the New Cluster wizard, not to the individual servers in it. In the case of a Web server, switching from a single server to an NLB cluster would mean changing the DNS (Domain Name System) record for the Web server's name to reflect the IP address of the cluster, not the address of the original Web server. Users would still direct their browsers to the same www.contoso.com URL, for example, but the DNS would resolve that name to the cluster IP address instead of an individual server's IP address.

The servers in an NLB cluster continually exchange status messages with each other, known as *heartbeats*. The heartbeats enable the cluster to check the availability of each server. When a server fails to generate five consecutive heartbeats, the cluster initiates a process called *convergence*, which stops it from sending clients to the missing server. When the offending server is operational again, the cluster detects the resumed heartbeats and again performs a convergence, this time to add the server back into the cluster. These convergence processes are entirely automatic, so administrators can take a server offline at any time, for maintenance or repair, without disrupting the functionality of the cluster.

This type of server clustering is intended primarily to provide a scalable solution that can use multiple servers to handle large amounts of client traffic. However, NLB clustering provides fault tolerance as well. If a server in the cluster should fail, you can simply remove it from the cluster, and the other servers will take up the slack.

The main thing to remember when managing this type of cluster is that when you make any changes to a clustered application on one server, you must change the other servers in the same way. For example, if you add a new page to your Web site, you must update all of the servers in the cluster with the new content.

LOAD BALANCING TERMINAL SERVERS

Windows Server 2008 supports the use of network load balancing for terminal servers in a slightly different manner. In Lesson 4, you learned how to deploy Windows desktops to clients using Terminal Services. For any organization with more than a few Terminal Services clients, multiple terminal servers are required. Network load balancing can ensure that the client sessions are distributed evenly among the servers.

One problem inherent in the load balancing of terminal servers is that a client can disconnect from a session (without terminating it) and be assigned to a different terminal server when he or she attempts to reconnect later. To address this problem, the Terminal Services role includes the *TS Session Broker* role service, which maintains a database of client sessions and enables a disconnected client to reconnect to the same terminal server.

The process of deploying Terminal Services with network load balancing consists of two parts:

- Creating a terminal server farm
- Creating a network load balancing cluster

The following sections describe these procedures.

CREATING A TERMINAL SERVER FARM

To create a load balanced *terminal server farm,* you must install the Terminal Services role with the Terminal Server role service on at least two Windows Server 2008 computers. You must also install the TS Session Broker role service on one computer. The computer running TS Session Broker can be, but does not have to be, one of the terminal servers. The Terminal Services computers are subject to the following requirements:

- The Terminal Services computers must be running Windows Server 2008.
- The terminal servers and the computer running TS Session Broker must be members of the same Active Directory domain.
- The terminal servers must be configured identically, with the same installed applications.
- Clients connecting to the terminal server farm must run Remote Desktop Connection (RDC) version 5.2 or later.

When you install the TS Session Broker role service, the Add Roles Wizard installs the Terminal Services Session Broker system service and creates a local group called Session Directory Computers. For a computer to participate in a terminal server farm, you must add it to the Session Directory Computers group and then complete the following procedure on each of your terminal servers.

 CREATE A TERMINAL SERVER FARM

GET READY. Log on to Windows Server 2008 using an account with administrative privileges. When the logon process is completed, close the Initial Configuration Tasks window and any other windows that appear.

1. Click **Start,** and then click **Administrative Tools** > **Terminal Services** > **Terminal Services Configuration.** The Terminal Services Configuration console appears, as shown in Figure 7-26.

Figure 7-26

The Terminal Services
Configuration console

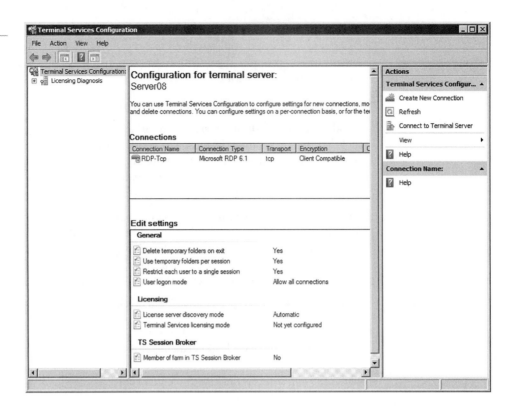

2. In the detail (middle) pane, under TS Session Broker, double-click **Member of farm in TS Session Broker**. The Properties sheet appears, displaying the TS Session Broker tab, as shown in Figure 7-27.

Figure 7-27

The TS Session Broker tab in
the Properties sheet

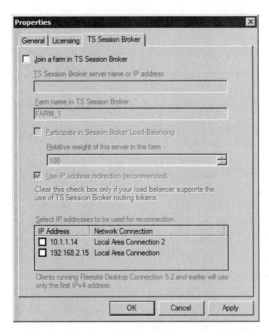

3. Select the **Join a farm in TS Session Broker** checkbox.

4. In the TS Session Broker Server Name or IP Address text box, specify the name or address of the computer on which you installed the TS Session Broker role service.

5. In the Farm **Name In TS Session Broker** text box, key the name of the server farm you want to use. If a farm by the name you specify does not exist on the TS Session Broker server, the console creates it. If the farm does exist, the console adds the terminal server to it.

6. Select the **Participate in Session Broker Load-Balancing** checkbox.

7. In the **Relative Weight Of The Server In The Farm** spin box, specify the priority of this terminal server in relation to the others in the farm.

8. If you use DNS round robin or Network Load Balancing redirection, leave the default **Use IP Address Redirection** checkbox selected. Clear this checkbox if you use a network load balancing solution that supports routing token redirection.

9. If the terminal server is connected to more than one network, select the checkbox for the IP address you want TS Session Broker to use when redirecting sessions to the server.

10. When the configuration is complete, as shown in Figure 7-28, click **OK.**

Figure 7-28

A completed TS Session Broker tab in the Properties sheet

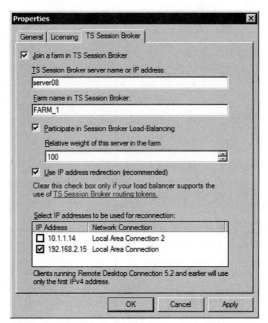

CLOSE the Terminal Services Configuration console.

You must repeat this procedure on each of your terminal servers to join them to the server farm. To automate the configuration process, you can apply these settings to an organization unit (OU) using Group Policy. The TS Session Broker settings are located in the Computer Configuration/Policies\Administrative Templates\Windows Components\Terminal Services\ Terminal Server\TS Broker Session node of a Group Policy Object, as shown in Figure 7-29.

Figure 7-29

Group Policy settings for TS
Session Broker

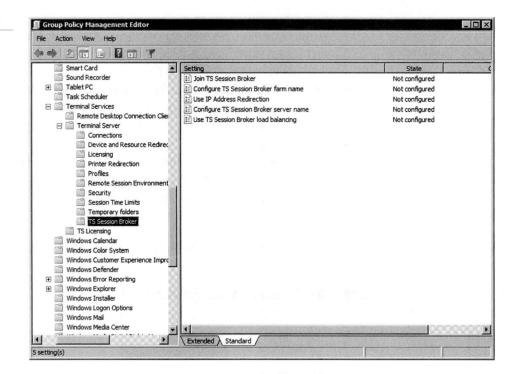

BALANCING THE TRAFFIC LOAD

When you configure your terminal servers to use the load balancing capability built in to TS
Session Broker, the client connection process proceeds as follows:

1. A client attempts to connect to one of the terminal servers in the server farm.

2. The terminal server sends a query to the TS Session Broker server, identifying the
   client attempting to connect.

3. The TS Session Broker searches its database to see if the specified client is
   already in an existing session.

4. The TS Session Broker server sends a reply to the terminal server, instructing it
   to redirect the connection to one of the servers in the farm. If a session already
   exists for the client, the TS Session Broker server redirects it to the terminal
   server running that session. If a session does not exist for the client, the TS Session Broker server redirects it to the terminal server with the fewest sessions.

5. The terminal server forwards the client connection to the computer specified by
   the TS Session Broker server.

USING DNS ROUND ROBIN

While TS Session Broker is an effective method for keeping the sessions balanced among the
terminal servers, it does nothing to control which terminal server receives the initial connection requests from clients on the network. To balance the initial connection traffic amongst
the terminal servers, you can use an NLB cluster, as described earlier in this lesson, or you can
use another, simpler load balancing technique called DNS Round Robin.

When a client connects to a server, the user typically specifies the server by name. The
client's computer then uses the Domain Name System (DNS) to resolve the name into an
IP address, and then uses the address to establish a connection to the server. Under normal
circumstances, the DNS server has one resource record for each host name. The resource
record equates the name with a particular IP address, enabling the server to receive requests
for the name and respond with the address. Therefore, when the DNS server receives a
request for a given name, it always responds with the same IP address, causing all clients to
connect initially to the same server.

For more information on the DNS name resolution process, see Lesson 2, "Planning Infrastructure Services."

In the case of a terminal server, this is undesirable, even if there is a TS Session Broker server in place. In the *DNS Round Robin* technique, you create multiple resource records using the same name, with a different server IP address in each record. When clients attempt to resolve the name, the DNS server supplies them with each of the IP addresses in turn. As a result, the clients are evenly distributed among the servers.

For example, to distribute traffic among five Web servers using DNS Round Robin, you would create five Host (A) resource records in the contoso.com zone, all with the name www. Each resource record would have the IP address of one of the five servers. By doing this, you are essentially creating a cluster called www.contoso.com, although there is no software entity representing that cluster, as there is in Network load balancing. Once you activate the DNS Round Robin feature on the DNS server, incoming name resolution requests for the www. contoso.com name use each of the five IP address associated with that name in turn.

To configure a Windows Server 2008 DNS server to use DNS Round Robin, use the following procedure.

 CONFIGURE DNS ROUND ROBIN

GET READY. Log on to a Windows Server 2008 using an account with administrative privileges. When the logon process is completed, close the Initial Configuration Tasks window and any other windows that appear.

1. Click **Start,** and then click **Administrative Tools** > **DNS**. The DNS Manager console appears, as shown in Figure 7-30.

Figure 7-30

The DNS Manager console

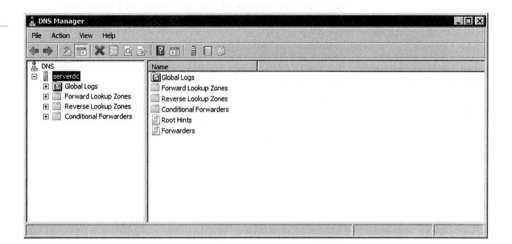

2. Expand the **server** node and the **Forward Lookup Zones** folder.
3. Right-click the zone in which you want to create the resource records and, from the context menu, select **New Host** (A or AAAA). The New Host dialog box appears, as shown in Figure 7-31.

Figure 7-31

The New Host dialog box

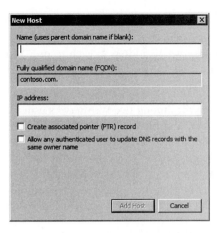

4. In the **Name** text box, key the name you want your clients to use when connecting to the server cluster.

5. In the **IP Address** text box, key the address of the first server in the cluster. Then click **Add Host**. A DNS message box appears, informing you that the new resource record has been created.

6. Repeat steps 4–5 to create additional resource records, each using the same Name value and a different IP Address value. Then click **Done**.

7. Right-click the **server** node and, from the content menu, select **Properties**. The server's Properties sheet appears.

8. Click the **Advanced** tab, as shown in Figure 7-32.

Figure 7-32

The Advanced tab of a DNS server's Properties sheet

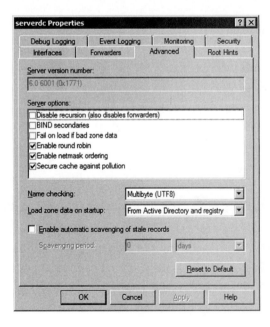

9. To control the DNS Round Robin functionality of the server, select or clear the following checkboxes:

- Enable Round Robin—Causes the server to access multiple resource records for each name resolution request and use each record in turn when resolving the name.

- Enable Netmask Ordering—Causes the server to examine the IP address of incoming name resolution requests and attempt to supply the requestor with an IP address on the same subnet.

10. Click **OK.**

CLOSE the DNS Manager console.

DNS Round Robin is a simple mechanism, one which enables administrators to create a basic network load balancing cluster without installing additional services or performing elaborate configurations. However, when compared with the Network Load Balancing service, round robin has several disadvantages.

The main disadvantage of DNS Round Robin is that the DNS server has no connection with the servers in the cluster. This means that if one of the servers fails, the DNS server will continue trying to send clients to it, until an administrator deletes that server's resource record. The DNS server also has no conception of how the clients make use of the servers in the cluster.

For example, some clients might connect to a Web server cluster and view one Web page, while others might download huge video files. The DNS server balances the incoming client connection requests among the servers in the cluster evenly, regardless of the burden on each server.

Another disadvantage is that DNS servers cache resource records for reuse by subsequent clients. When a client on the Internet connects to a round robin cluster, its DNS server only caches one of the resource records, not all of them. Therefore, any other clients using the DNS server will all connect to the same server, throwing off the distribution of cluster addresses.

Generally speaking, the Network Load Balancing service is far superior to DNS Round Robin in its capabilities, and that is much more difficult to implement.

SUMMARY SKILL MATRIX

IN THIS LESSON YOU LEARNED:

- In computer networking, high availability refers to technologies that enable users to continue accessing a resource despite the occurrence of a disastrous hardware or software failure.

- Shadow copies is a mechanism that automatically retains copies of files on a server volume in multiple versions from specific points in time. When users accidentally overwrite or delete files, they can access the shadow copies to restore earlier versions.

- Offline Files works by copying server-based folders that users select for offline use to a workstation's local drive. The users then work with the copies, which remain accessible whether the workstation can access the server or not.

- When you plan for high availability, you must balance three factors: fault tolerance, performance, and expense. The more fault tolerance you require for your data, the more you must spend to achieve it, and the more likely you are to suffer degraded performance as a result of it.

- Disk mirroring is the simplest form of disk redundancy, and typically does not have a negative effect on performance, as long as you use a disk technology, such as SCSI (Small Computer System Interface) or serial ATA (SATA), that enables the computer to write to both disks at the same time.

- Parity-based RAID is the most commonly used high availability solution for data storage, primarily because it is far more scalable than disk mirroring and enables you realize more storage space from your hard disks.

- One way of protecting workstation applications and ensuring their continued availability is to run them using Terminal Services.

- Windows Installer 4.0 is the component in Windows Server 2008 that enables the system to install software packaged as files with a .msi extension. One of the advantages of deploying software in this manner is the built-in resiliency that Windows Installer provides to the applications.

- A failover cluster is a collection of two or more servers that perform the same role or run the same application and appear on the network as a single entity.

- The NLB cluster itself, like a failover cluster, is a logical entity with its own name and IP address. Clients connect to the cluster, rather than the individual computers, and the cluster distributes the incoming requests evenly among its component servers.

- The Terminal Services role includes the TS Session Broker role service, which maintains a database of client sessions and enables a disconnected client to reconnect to the same terminal server.

- In the DNS Round Robin technique, you create multiple resource records using the same name, with a different server IP address in each record. When clients attempt to resolve the name, the DNS server supplies them with each of the IP addresses in turn. As a result, the clients are evenly distributed among the servers.

■ Knowledge Assessment

Fill in the Blank

Complete the following exercise by filling in the blanks with the appropriate terms from this lesson.

1. The network load balancing method that assigns multiple IP addresses to a single host name is called _____.

2. The application high availability method that uses redundant servers with only one active at any time is called a _____.

3. The Windows Server 2008 feature that enables end users to store copies of server-based documents on a local drive is called _____.

4. The servers in a network load balancing cluster continually exchange status messages called _____.

5. Windows Server 2008 servers can maintain multiple versions of a volume's files using a feature called _____.

6. The process by which servers are automatically added to and removed from a network load balancing cluster is called _____.

7. A failover cluster stores its configuration database on a _____.

8. The role service that enables disconnected Terminal Services clients to reconnect to the same server is called _____.

9. The application high availability mechanism that uses redundant servers, with all running simultaneously, is called _____.

10. The Windows Server 2008 feature that enables a computer to verify an application before launching it is called _____.

Multiple Choice

Select one or more correct answers for each of the following questions.

1. In addition to the application data, which of the following is stored on a failover cluster's shared storage?

   a. the Failover Cluster management console
   b. the witness disk
   c. the TS Session Broker database
   d. the Shadow Copies database

2. Which of the following Windows Server 2008 features enables users to access files that they have accidentally overwritten?

   a. Offline Files   b. parity-based RAID
   c. Windows Installer 4.0   d. Shadow Copies

3. Which of the following server clustering solutions can make use of a storage area network?

   a. a failover cluster
   b. a terminal server farm
   c. a network load balancing cluster
   d. DNS Round Robin

4. Which of the following RAID levels yields the largest percentage of usable disk space?

   a. RAID-0   b. RAID-1
   c. RAID-5   d. RAID-6

5. To use Shadow Copies, you must enable the feature at which of the following levels?

   a. the file level   b. the folder level
   c. the volume level   d. the server level

6. How many heartbeat messages must a server in an NLB cluster miss before it is removed from the cluster?

   a. 1   b. 5
   c. 50   d. 500

7. Which of the following is not a requirement to use the TS Session Broker role service?

   a. All of the Terminal Services computers must be running Windows Server 2008.
   b. All of the Terminal Services computers must be configured identically.
   c. The TS Session Broker role service must be installed on one of the terminal servers.
   d. The Terminal Services computers must all be member of the same Active Directory domain.

8. Which of the following statements is true about DNS Round Robin load balancing?

   a. DNS Round Robin requires you to create multiple resource records containing the same host name.
   b. When one of the servers in the cluster fails, the Windows Server 2008 DNS server performs a convergence and disables the resource record for that server.
   c. To use DNS Round Robin, you must first create a cluster resource record specifying the cluster name.
   d. When the Windows Server 2008 DNS server receives a name resolution request for a cluster, it replies with all of the resource records for that cluster name.

9. Which of the following statements best defines the function of the port rules in an NLB cluster?

   a. Port rules specify what types of application traffic are allowed through the cluster's firewall.
   b. Port rules specify the name of the servers that are to be members of the cluster.
   c. Port rules enable the cluster to detect server failures and initiate a convergence.
   d. Port rules specify what application traffic is to be distributed among the cluster servers.

10. Which of the following operating systems does not include the Previous Versions client needed to access Shadow Copies files?

    a. Windows XP
    b. Windows Server 2003
    c. Windows Vista
    d. Windows Server 2008

Review Questions

1. Explain the primary difference between a failover cluster and a network load balancing cluster.

2. List three of the disadvantages of DNS Round Robin, as compared to Network Load Balancing.

■ Case Scenario

Scenario 7-1: Deploying a Terminal Services Server Farm

Wingtip Toys has recently decided to deploy all office productivity applications to its internal users with terminal servers. Robert, a member of the IT staff, has been given the responsibility for installing and configuring a server farm on the company network that consists of 12 new terminal servers running Windows Server 2008. Robert installs the Terminal Services role, with the Terminal Server role service, on all 12 computers. He also installs the TS Session Broker role service on one of the computers. After adding each of the 12 terminal servers to a TS Session Broker farm and installing the office applications on the server, Robert begins a test deployment, adding groups of users to gradually increase the terminal server traffic load. Later, when examining the traffic statistics, Robert notices that one of the servers is experiencing much higher traffic levels than the others and it is not the server running TS Session Broker. What could be the problem and how should Robert resolve it?

Planning Server and Network Security

OBJECTIVE DOMAIN MATRIX

Technology Skill	Objective Domain	Objective Domain Number
Using BitLocker	Plan server installations and upgrades	1.1
Securing Network Access	Monitor and maintain security and policies	3.3

KEY TERMS

access control entries (ACEs)
access control list (ACL)
biometrics
BitLocker Drive Encryption
centralized authentication
decentralized authentication
dictionary attacks
firewall
effective permissions
Kerberos

Key Distribution Center (KDC)
port numbers
program exception
public key encryption
secret key encryption
Security Accounts Manager (SAM)
security identifiers (SIDs)
security principal
single sign-on (SSO)

smart card
social engineering
special permissions
standard permissions
ticket granting tickets (TGTs)
Trusted Platform Module (TPM)
trusts
tunneling

Security is an omnipresent concern for server administrators. Every application, every file, and every feature must be protected from unauthorized access. This lesson examines a number of Windows Server 2008 security issues, including the following:

- physical server security
- firewalls
- BitLocker Drive Encryption
- authentication
- authorization

■ Securing Servers

THE BOTTOM LINE Security is a concern on many levels, but for the server administrator, the first concern is the security of the individual server itself.

Before you begin to consider the security of your network as a whole, you should think about protecting the individual servers on the network. Mail servers, database servers, Web servers, and other application servers are prime targets for attack, both from inside and outside the organization. For many businesses, compromised servers can mean lost production, lost income, or even loss of life. While administrators have to be concerned about the security of their workstations and the network as a whole, server security is critical.

The following sections examine some of the security issues of particular concern to server administrators.

Physically Securing Servers

In a rush to work with the many security mechanisms provided by Windows Server 2008, some individuals forget about the most basic security principle: the physical security of the server itself.

No matter how carefully you secure software resources, such as files, applications, and directory services, physical security must come first. Bulletproof applications and complex passwords are no help if someone can simply pick up your server and walk off with it. Before you consider any other security mechanisms, or even operating system and application deployments, you should take steps to ensure that your servers are stored in a location that is physically secure.

CONTROLLING ACCESS

In most cases, the term *access control* refers to mechanisms that regulate access to computers, software, or other resources. However, server administrators must understand that the term also applies to the physical access that users are granted to computers and other equipment. Protecting servers against theft is an important consideration; servers and other network equipment should always be kept under lock and key. However, physical access control can also protect against other occurrences, including fire, natural disasters, and even simple accidents.

The facilities dedicated to server storage typically vary depending on the size of the organization that owns them. Small businesses are less likely to have elaborate computer centers, and they often leave their servers in common areas that are freely accessible by anyone. The danger of this type of arrangement is not just from theft; accidental damage is far more common when servers are used as work surfaces, footstools, and plant stands.

Servers containing important data, routers, and other crucial networking components should always be stored in locked server closets or a secured computer center, to protect against theft and damage. However, it is all too often that the so-called computer center in a small office consists simply of the rooms occupied by the IT department, perhaps with an extra air conditioning unit and a combination lock on the door. In these facilities, the servers might be scattered amidst workers' desks and the security door left open during business hours, for the sake of convenience. Server closets can be an equally inappropriate, when computers have to share unheated storage space with cleaning products and other supplies.

Locking the door of the computer center at night and leaving the air conditioning on can provide a relatively secure environment that defeats the casual thief, but IT workers are no less likely to spill their cups of coffee than anyone else, and having the servers out in the open during working hours is an inherently dangerous practice. In the same way, a service closet that is regularly accessed by maintenance workers and other personnel provides little or no protection.

USING PHYSICAL BARRIERS

A properly designed computer center or server closet is one in which physical barriers prevent access by anyone but authorized personnel, and only when they have a specific reason to enter. Even authorized IT workers should not have to be in the same room as sensitive networking equipment because their desks are nearby or because supplies are stored in there. In fact, servers should need very little physical access at all, because administrators can perform most maintenance and configuration tasks remotely.

For more information on remote server administration, see Lesson 10, "Managing Servers."

An installation with proper physical security should consist of multiple physical barriers of increasing strength, with the most sensitive resources stored in the most protected area. The combination lock on the computer center door is still a good idea, protecting the entire IT department from casual intruders. The door should be closed and locked at all times, however, perhaps with a buzzer to admit screened outsiders.

Inside the computer center, the actual location of the servers and other critical components should be protected by still another locked door, with monitored access. At its simplest, this monitoring could take the form of a paper log in which users sign in and out of the locked room. If more security is required, you can add magnetic key cards, video cameras, or even security guards. No one should be entering the secured area without a specific purpose, and without their presence being logged for later reference.

The actual nature of the physical barriers used to secure servers and networking equipment is also an important consideration. Typical office construction standards—hollow doors, flimsy drywall, and drop ceilings—might defeat the casual intruder, but a determined intruder can easily penetrate them. A state-of-the-art electronic lock is of little value when you can easily put your fist through the wall, or crawl over the doorway through a drop ceiling into the secured area.

The innermost part of your security area should provide protection on all six sides of the room, meaning that doors should be solid and walls should be reinforced and run vertically from slab to slab, through drop ceilings and raised floors. In some cases, even these precautions might be insufficient protection against intruders with heavy tools; an alarm system or security cameras can provide additional protection.

USING BIOMETRICS

For installations requiring extreme security, the standard mechanisms used to control access to the secured area, such as metal keys, magnetic keycards, combinations, and passwords, might be insufficient. Keys and keycards can be lent, lost, or stolen, and passwords and combinations written down, shared, or otherwise compromised. One increasingly popular alternative is *biometrics,* the automatic identification of individuals based on physiological characteristics.

Biometric technologies can be used for two different purposes: verification and identification. Biometric verification is a matter of confirming the identity supplied by an individual. For example, a biometric verification lock might require an individual to enter a user identification number on a keypad, and then supply a fingerprint to verify that the person corresponding to that number is actually there.

Biometric identification is the process of establishing an individual's identity based on biometric information, essentially asking the system to indicate who the person is. An example of this would be a lock that requires only a fingerprint scan. The system then identifies the individual belonging to that fingerprint and decides whether to grant access. While both of these functions have their own complexities, most biometric security systems are designed to verify individuals, because the process is inherently simpler.

The complexities involved in biometric identification depend largely on the size of the system's user base. When there are a relatively small number of individuals to be identified, the biometric scan can immediately isolate specific minutiae in the individual's physiology and compare them with a database of known records. When the system must authenticate any one of thousands of individuals, the system typically categorizes the scanned biometric data first, reducing the size of the database sampling that the system has to search. Biometric verification, on the other hand, does not require the system to compare a sampling to all of the records in an entire database. Instead, it needs only to compare the sampling to the one specific record belonging to whomever the individual claims to be.

Biometric authentication devices can use a number of different characteristics to identify individuals. Some of the biometric technologies in use today include the following:

- Fingerprint matching—The fingerprint scan is the oldest of the biometric technologies and still the most popular. Because each individual's fingerprints are unique, fingerprint scans can be used for identification or verification. The image enhancement technologies developed over the years have helped to eliminate many of the problems resulting from inadequate scanning or variances in finger pressure and position during the scan.

- Hand geometry—Hand geometry is a verification technique based on a scan of an individual's hand shape, taking into account various characteristics such as length, thickness, and curvature of fingers. An individual's hand geometry is not unique, however, as fingerprints are, so this technique cannot be used for identification, only for verification. However, hand geometry scans are much faster, cleaner, and less invasive than fingerprint scans, making them a much more convenient mechanism.

- Iris or retinal scans—Scans of unique eyeball characteristics, such as iris and retina patterns, are usable for both verification and identification, but the scans themselves can be difficult to obtain, often requiring special lighting.

- Speech recognition—Voice pattern matching is one of the more complex biometric functions, and it is also easier to spoof (with recordings) than the other technologies listed here. The process of matching voice patterns involves the creation of a voice model for the individual to be authenticated. The voice model is a baseline pattern that accounts for the variations in utterances spoken by the same person at different times.

- Face recognition and facial thermograms—Facial recognition systems and thermograms are not yet as accurate as fingerprints and other unique human attributes, but they have the potential of becoming a fast and uninvasive biometric verification system.

Some of the biometric systems on the market use a combination of physiological factors, for various reasons. For example, a system that can perform both hand geometry and fingerprint scans can use the former for rapid identity verifications and the latter for the identification of individuals. Other systems combine two or more biometric technologies to create a combined accuracy rate and performance time that exceeds those of the technologies working individually.

SOCIAL ENGINEERING

All security mechanisms are essentially a compromise between the need to protect valuable resources and the need to provide access to them with a minimum of inconvenience. It would not be difficult to seal your servers inside a bank vault, run all of your network cables through heavy steel conduits, and assign complex 20-character passwords to all your user accounts. The result would almost certainly be greater security than you have now. However, the expense of the installation and the revolt of users faced with the inconvenience of remembering passwords and unlocking the vault makes extreme measures like these impractical.

Although it is administrators and managers who are responsible for implementing and enforcing security policies, true security actually rests in the hands of the people who use the protected systems every day. The object of all your security procedures is to make people understand the importance of protecting sensitive resources and to urge them to work with you in providing that protection. No matter how stringent your password policies, for example, there's nothing you can do to stop users from writing down their passwords in inappropriate places or sharing them with the wrong people except to educate them in the dangers of these practices.

Social engineering is a term used to describe the process of circumventing security barriers by persuading authorized users to provide passwords or other sensitive information. In many cases, users are duped into giving an intruder access to a protected system through a phone call in which the intruder claims to be an employee in another department, a customer, or a

hardware vendor. A user might give out a seemingly innocent piece of information, which the intruder then uses to elicit more information from someone else.

For example, in the first phone call, an innocent user might supply the information that Deepak Kumar, manager of the IT department, is out on vacation for the week, and that Wendy Kahn is the acting manager. In the next call, to Wendy Kahn, the intruder might identify himself as the IT manager of one of the company's other offices, saying that Deepak had promised to fax him the details of the office's firewall configuration. Would it be possible for you to fax it to me at this number? Or the intruder might identify himself as the salesman for a router manufacturer, and by getting a network administrator to chat about their current router needs, get the information needed to penetrate the company's defenses.

Attitude and confidence is everything when it comes to social engineering. These seemingly obvious and transparent techniques can be amazingly effective at eliciting confidential information when the intruder is adept at sounding confused, hurried, confident, or imperious. Many of the most successful computer criminals obtained confidential information using their social engineering skills as much as their technical expertise.

You can't protect your network against social engineers with locked doors or passwords or firewalls. The only true protection is to educate your users about the techniques used by social engineers and the need to verify people's identities before disclosing any information to them. However, a telephone system that is capable of recording calls for later examination can sometimes act as a deterrent.

CONTROLLING THE ENVIRONMENT

The environment in which your servers must operate is an important consideration in the design and construction of the network and in the technologies that you select. In places where high concentrations of sensitive equipment are located, such as computer centers and server closets, the typical office environment is usually augmented with additional air conditioning, air filtration, humidity control, and/or power conditioning. This type of environmental planning is as important to the continued operation of your network as is securing your resources against theft, destruction, and data loss.

In addition to protecting sensitive equipment from theft and maintaining proper operating conditions, fire is a major threat to continued operation of your servers. The damage caused by fire, and by standard firefighting techniques, can result not only in data and equipment loss, but also in damage to the facilities themselves that can take a long time to repair before you can even begin to install replacement equipment.

For large installations, a fire suppression system should be mandatory in the computer center or server room. In the event of a fire, these systems flood the room with an inert gas, displacing the oxygen that the fire needs to burn. This puts the fire out quickly and prevents firefighters from destroying electronic equipment with water or foam. Unfortunately, these systems also displace the oxygen that people need to breathe, so evacuation alarms and emergency air supplies are also a necessary part of the system.

WIRELESS NETWORKING

The increasing use of wireless networking technologies has led to a new class of physical security hazards that administrators should be careful not to underestimate. Because the signals that most wireless networking technologies use today can penetrate walls and other barriers, it is entirely possible for clandestine users outside the building to access servers by using their own equipment. When selecting and installing wireless networking components, and particularly access points that provide access to the cabled network, you should test carefully to ascertain the operational range of the devices and select locations for the antennae that are near the center of the building and as far away from the outside walls as is practical.

Another way of protecting a wireless network from unauthorized connections is to shield the operational area. This can also protect the wireless network from denial of service (DOS) attacks. Depending on the transmission power of the wireless networking equipment and the materials used to construct the building, the walls themselves might function as an effective shield. New buildings can be constructed with integrated shielding, enabling wireless networks to operate inside without fear of a security breech. The problem with using shielding to protect a wireless network is that the signals of other devices, such as cell phones, could be blocked as well.

Building a Firewall

Once you have considered physical protection for your servers, you can start to concern yourself with the other main avenue of intrusion: the network.

You may have locked the door to the computer center in which the servers are located, but the computers are still connected to the network. A network is another type of door, or rather a series of doors, which can allow data out or allow it in. To provide services to your users, some of those doors must be open at least some of the time, but server administrators must make sure that only the right doors are left open.

A *firewall* is a software program that protects a computer by allowing certain types of network traffic in and out of the system while blocking others. A firewall is essentially a series of filters that examine the contents of packets and the traffic patterns to and from the network to determine which packets they should allow to pass through the filter.

Some of the hazards that firewalls can protect against are as follows:

- Network scanner applications that probe systems for unguarded ports, which are essentially unlocked doors that attackers can use to gain access to the system

- Trojan horse applications that open a connection to a computer on the Internet, enabling an attacker on the outside to run programs or store data on the system

- Attackers that obtain passwords by illicit means, such as social engineering, and then use remote access technologies to log on to a computer from another location and compromise its data and programming

For more information about authentication and authorization, see "Securing Network Access" later in this lesson.

The object of a firewall is to permit all of the traffic in and out that legitimate users need to perform their assigned tasks, and block everything else. Note that when you are working with firewalls, you are not concerned with subjects like authentication and authorization. Those are mechanisms that control who is able to get through the server's open doors. The firewall is all about which doors are left open, and which are shut tight.

UNDERSTANDING WINDOWS FIREWALL SETTINGS

Windows Server 2008 includes a firewall program called Windows Firewall, which is activated by default on all Windows Server 2008 systems. By default, Windows Firewall blocks most network traffic from entering the computer. Firewalls work by examining the contents of each packet entering and leaving the computer and comparing the information they find to a series of rules, which specify which packets are allowed to pass through the firewall and which are blocked.

The TCP/IP (Transmission Control Protocol/Internet Protocol) protocols that Windows systems use to communicate function by packaging application data using a series of layered protocols that define where the data comes from and where it is going. The three most important criteria that firewalls can use in their rules are as follows:

- IP addresses—IP addresses identify specific hosts on the network. You can use IP addresses to configure a firewall to allow traffic from only specific computers or networks in and out.

- Protocol numbers—Protocol numbers specify whether the packet contains TCP or UDP (User Datagram Protocol) traffic. You can filter protocol numbers to block packets containing certain types of traffic. Windows computers typically use UDP for brief message exchanges, such as DNS (Domain Name System) and DHCP (Dynamic Host Configuration Protocol) transactions. TCP packets usually carry larger amounts of data, such as the files exchanged by Web, file, and print servers.

- Port numbers—*Port numbers* identify specific applications running on the computer. The most common firewall rules use port numbers to specify the types of application traffic the computer is allowed to send and receive. For example, a Web server usually receives its incoming packets to port number 80. Unless the firewall has a rule opening port 80 to incoming traffic, the Web server cannot function in its default configuration.

Firewall rules can function in two ways, as follows:

- Admit all traffic, except that which conforms to the applied rules
- Block all traffic, except that which conforms to the applied rules

Generally speaking, blocking all traffic by default is the more secure arrangement. From the server administrator's standpoint, you start with a completely blocked system, and then start testing your applications. When an application fails to function properly because network access is blocked, you create a rule that opens up the ports the application needs to communicate.

This is the method that Windows Firewall uses by default for incoming network traffic. The default rules preconfigured into the firewall are designed to admit the traffic used by standard Windows networking functions, such as file and printer sharing. For outgoing network traffic, Windows Firewall uses the other method, allowing all traffic to pass the firewall except that which conforms to a rule.

WORKING WITH WINDOWS FIREWALL

Windows Firewall is a single program with one set of rules, but there are two distinct interfaces you can use to manage and monitor it. The Windows Firewall control panel provides a simplified interface that enables administrators to avoid the details of rules and port numbers. If you just want to turn the firewall on or off (typically for testing or troubleshooting purposes), or work with the firewall settings for a specific Windows role or feature, you can do so simply by using the control panel. For full access to firewall rules and more sophisticated functions, you must use the Windows Firewall with Advanced Security console, as discussed later in this lesson.

In many cases, administrators never have to work directly with Windows Firewall. Many of the roles and features included in Windows Server 2008 automatically open the appropriate firewall ports when you install them. In other situations, the system warns you of firewall issues.

For example, the first time you open Windows Explorer and try to access the network, a warning appears, as shown in Figure 8-1, informing you that Network Discovery and File Sharing are turned off, preventing you from browsing the network.

Figure 8-1

Windows Explorer with Network Discovery and File Sharing turned off

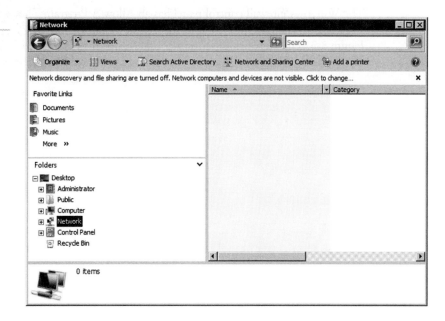

In addition to support for certain discovery protocols, Network Discovery includes a set of firewall rules that regulate the ports Windows uses for network browsing, specifically ports 137, 138, 1900, 2869, 3702, 5355, 5357, and 5358. By default, Windows Server 2008 disables the inbound rules associated with these ports, so the ports are closed, blocking all traffic through them. When you click the warning banner and choose Turn On Network Discovery And File Sharing from the context menu, you are in effect activating these firewall rules, thereby opening the ports associated with them.

In addition to the menu command accessible through the warning banner, you can also control the Network Discovery and File Sharing rules in other ways. The Network and Sharing Center control panel, in its Sharing and Discovery section, provides options that you can use to turn Network Discovery on and off, as shown in Figure 8-2, as well as File Sharing and other basic networking functions.

Figure 8-2

The Network and Sharing Center control panel

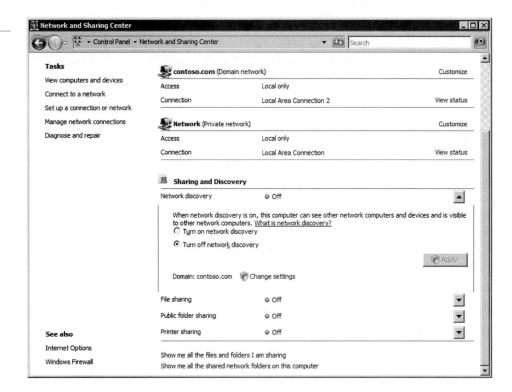

The Windows Firewall control panel has an Allow A Program Through Windows Firewall link, which opens the Exceptions tab in the Windows Firewall Settings dialog box, as shown in Figure 8-3. The Network Discovery checkbox on this tab enables you to control the same set of rules as the Network Discovery control in the Network and Sharing Center.

Figure 8-3

The Exceptions tab of the Windows Firewall Settings dialog box

Finally, you can access the individual Network Discovery rules directly, using the Windows Firewall with Advanced Security console. When you select the Inbound Rules node and scroll down in the list, you can see eighteen different Network Discovery rules, as shown in Figure 8-4. These rules provide not only individual control over each of the ports used by Network Discovery operations, but they also enable you to set different values for the three network profiles supported by Windows Server 2008: domain, public, and private.

Figure 8-4

The Windows Firewall with Advanced Security console

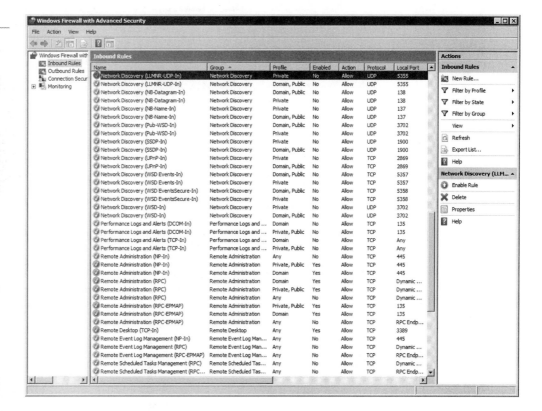

As you can see by examining the rules in the console, Network Discovery is a complex Windows function that would be difficult to control if you had to determine by trial and error which ports it uses. This is why Windows Firewall includes a large collection of rules that regulate the ports that the applications and services included with the operating system need to operate.

USING THE WINDOWS FIREWALL CONTROL PANEL

The Windows Firewall control panel provides the easiest and safest access to the firewall controls. These controls are usually sufficient for most server administrators, unless the system has special requirements or you are working with custom server applications.

When you open the Windows Firewall window from the control panel, as shown in Figure 8-5, you see the following information:

- Whether the Windows Firewall service is currently turned on or off
- Whether inbound and outbound connections are blocked
- Whether users are notified when a program is blocked
- Whether the computer is connected to a domain, private, or public network

Figure 8-5

The Windows Firewall control panel window

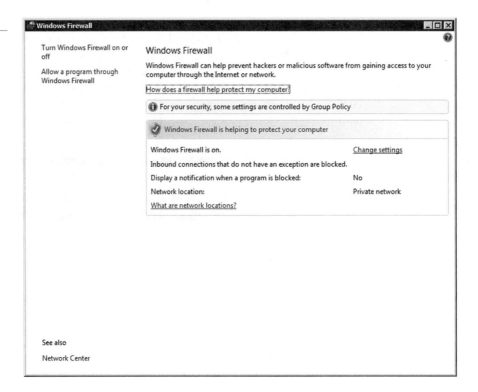

On the left side of the window are two links, one that enables you to turn Windows Firewall on and off, and one that enables you to configure Windows Firewall to allow a specific program through its barrier. This second link, like the Change Settings link, opens the Windows Firewall Settings dialog box, as shown in Figure 8-6.

Figure 8-6

The Windows Firewall Settings
dialog box

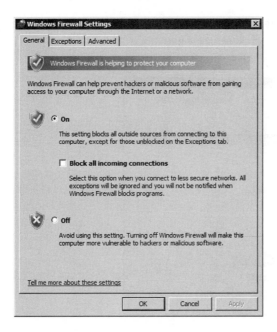

BLOCKING INCOMING CONNECTIONS

The General tab of the Windows Firewall Settings dialog box duplicates some of the control in the Windows Firewall window. In addition to turning the firewall completely on and off, there is a Block All Incoming Connections checkbox that enables you to increase the security of your system by blocking all unsolicited attempts to connect to your computer. Note, however, that this does not prevent you from performing common networking tasks, such as accessing Web site and sending or receiving emails. These activities are not unsolicited connection attempts; they begin with the client contacting the server first. When the firewall detects the outgoing traffic from your Web browser to a Web server on the Internet, for example, it knows that it should admit the incoming response from the server.

CONFIGURING EXCEPTIONS AND PORTS

There are times when administrators might be required to modify the firewall settings in other ways too, typically because a specific application requires access to a port not anticipated by the firewall's preconfigured rules. To do this, you use the Exceptions tab of the Windows Firewall Settings dialog box, as discussed earlier.

Opening up a port in a server's firewall is an inherently dangerous activity. The more open doors you put in a wall, the greater the likelihood that intruders will get in. There are two basic methods for opening a hole in your firewall: opening a port and creating a ***program exception.*** The latter is more desirable, because when you open a port, it stays open permanently. When you create a program exception, the specified port is open only while the program is running. When you terminate the program, the firewall closes the port.

To create an exception using the Windows Firewall Settings dialog box, use the following procedure.

 CREATE A FIREWALL EXCEPTION

GET READY. Log on to Windows Server 2008 using an account with administrative privileges. When the logon process is completed, close the Initial Configuration Tasks window and any other windows that appear.

1. Click **Start,** and then click **Control Panel.** The Control Panel window appears.
2. Double-click the **Windows Firewall** icon. The Windows Firewall window appears.
3. Click **Allow a program through Windows Firewall.** The Windows Firewall Settings dialog box appears, displaying the Exceptions tab.

4. To create a program exception, click **Add Program.** The Add a Program dialog box appears, as shown in Figure 8-7.

Figure 8-7

The Add a Program dialog box

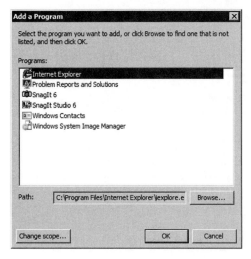

5. Select the program for which you want to create an exception from the Programs list or click **Browse** to locate the program.

6. Click **Change Scope** to limit the exception to a specific network or specific addresses, as shown in Figure 8-8.

Figure 8-8

The Change Scope dialog box

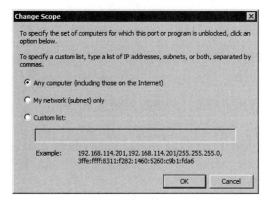

7. Click **OK** to close the Add a Program dialog box. The program you selected appears in the Program or Port list, with its checkbox selected.

8. To open a port, click **Add Port** to open the Add a Port dialog box, as shown in Figure 8-9.

Figure 8-9

The Add a Port dialog box

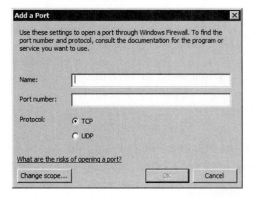

TAKE NOTE *

If you want to control both TCP and UDP traffic, you must add two separate ports.

9. Specify a name for the port, the port number, and whether you want to allow TCP or UDP traffic using that port through the firewall.

10. Click **Change Scope** to limit the exception to a specific network or specific addresses.

11. Click **OK** to close the Add a Port dialog box. The port you specified appears in the Program or Port list, with its checkbox selected.

12. Click **OK** to close the Windows Firewall Settings dialog box.

CLOSE the Windows Firewall window.

Once you have created an exception, you can enable or disable it at will by selecting or clearing its checkbox.

USING THE WINDOWS FIREWALL WITH ADVANCED SECURITY CONSOLE

The Windows Firewall Settings dialog box is designed to enable administrators to create exceptions in the current firewall settings as needed. For full access to the Windows Firewall configuration settings, you must use the Windows Firewall With Advanced Security snap-in for the Microsoft Management Console.

To open the console, shown in Figure 8-10, click Start, and then click Administrative Tools > Windows Firewall With Advanced Security.

Figure 8-10

The Windows Firewall with Advanced Security console

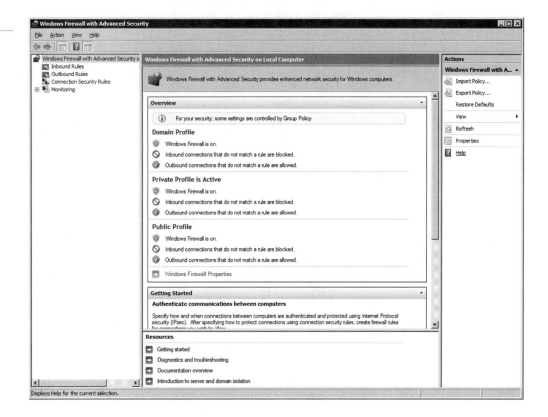

CONFIGURING PROFILE SETTINGS

At the top of the Windows Firewall with Advanced Security console's detail (middle) pane, in the Overview section, are status displays for the computer's three possible network locations. Windows Firewall maintains separate profiles for each of the three possible network locations: domain, private, and public. If you connect the computer to a different network (which is admittedly not likely with a server), Windows Firewall can load a different profile and a different set of rules.

As you can tell from the screen shot, the default Windows Firewall configuration calls for the same basic settings for all three profiles: the firewall is turned on, incoming traffic is blocked unless it matches a rule, and outgoing traffic is allowed unless it matches a rule. You can change this default behavior by clicking the Windows Firewall Properties link, which displays the Windows Firewall with Advanced Security on Local Computer dialog box, as shown in Figure 8-11.

Figure 8-11

The Windows Firewall with Advanced Security on Local Computer dialog box

In this dialog box, each of the three location profiles has a tab with identical controls that enables you to modify the default profile settings. You can, for example, configure the firewall to shut down completely when it is connected to a domain network, and turn the firewall on with its most protective settings when you connect the computer to a public network. You can also configure the firewall's notification options, its logging behavior, and how it reacts when rules conflict.

TAKE NOTE *

In addition to configuring these profile settings directly through the Windows Firewall with Advanced Security console, it is also possible to use Group Policy to configure them for a local computer or an entire enterprise. When you open the Computer Configuration\Policies\Windows Settings\Security Settings\Windows Firewall with Advanced Security folder in a group policy object, you see the exact same interface as in the Windows Firewall with Advanced Security console.

CREATING RULES

The exceptions and ports that you can create in the Windows Firewall Settings dialog box are a relatively friendly method for working with firewall rules. In the Windows Firewall with Advanced Security console, you can work with the rules in their raw form. Selecting either Inbound Rules or Outbound Rules in the scope (left) pane displays a list of all the rules operating in that direction, as shown in Figure 8-12. The rules are organized into groups, which correspond to the exceptions in the Windows Firewall control panel. The rules that are currently operational have a checkmark in a green circle, while the rules not in force are grayed out.

Figure 8-12

The Inbound Rules list in the Windows Firewall with Advanced Security console

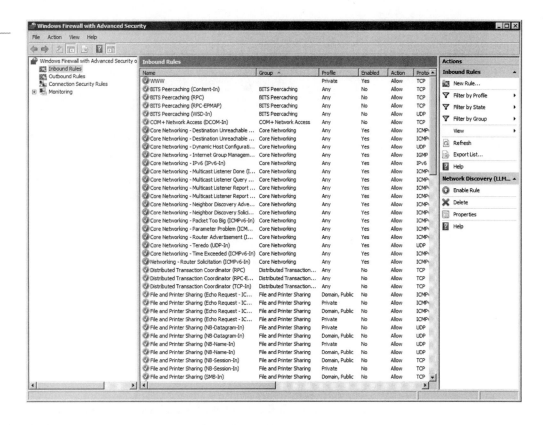

TAKE NOTE*

It is important to remember that in the Windows Firewall with Advanced Security console, you are always working with a complete list of rules for all of the profiles, while in the Windows Firewall Settings dialog box, you are working with only the rules that apply to the currently active profile.

Creating new rules with this interface provides a great deal more flexibility than the Windows Firewall Settings dialog box. When you right-click the Inbound Rules (or Outbound Rules) node and select New Rule from the context menu, the New Inbound (or Outbound) Rule Wizard, shown in Figure 8-13, takes you through the process of configuring the following sets of parameters:

- Rule Type—Specifies whether you want to create a program rule, a port rule, a variant on one of the predefined rules, or a custom rule. This selection determines which of the following pages the wizard displays.
- Program—Specifies whether the rule applies to all programs, to one specific program, or to a specific service.
- Protocol and Ports—Specifies the protocol and the local and remote ports to which the rule applies. This enables you to specify the exact types of traffic that the rule should block or allow.
- Scope—Specifies the IP addresses of the local and remote systems to which the rule applies. This enables you to block or allow traffic between specific computers.
- Action—Specifies the action the firewall should take when a packet matches the rule. You configure the rule to allow traffic if it is blocked by default, or block traffic if it is allowed by default. You can also configure the rule to allow traffic only when the connection between the communicating computers is secured using IPsec.
- Profile—Specifies the profile(s) to which the rule should apply: domain, private, and/or public.
- Name—Specifies a name and (optionally) a description for the rule.

Figure 8-13

The New Inbound Rule wizard

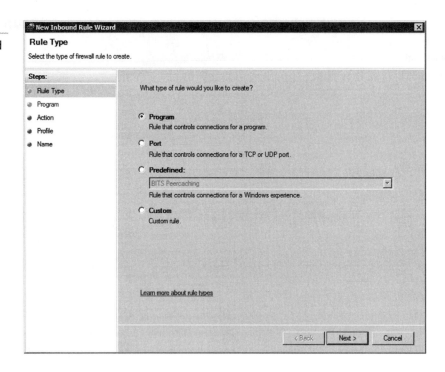

The rules you can create using the wizards range from simple program rules, just like those you can create in the Windows Firewall Settings dialog box, to highly complex and specific rules that block or allow only specific types of traffic between specific computers. The more complicated the rules become, however, the more you have to know about TCP/IP communications in general and the specific behavior of your applications. Modifying the default firewall settings to accommodate some special applications is relatively simple, but creating an entirely new firewall configuration is a formidable task.

USING FILTERS

Although what a firewall does is sometimes referred to as packet filtering, in the Windows Firewall With Advanced Security console, the term *filter* is used to refer to a feature that enables you to display rules according to the profile they apply to, their current state, or the rule group to which they belong.

For example, to display only the rules that apply to the public profile, click Action > Filter By Profile > Filter By Public Profile. The display then changes to show only the rules that apply to the public profile. In the same way, you can apply a filter that causes the console to display only the rules that are currently turned on, or the rules that belong to a particular group. Click Action > Clear All Filters to return to the default display showing all of the rules.

CREATING CONNECTION SECURITY RULES

Windows Server 2008 also includes a feature that incorporates IPsec data protection into the Windows Firewall. The IP Security (IPsec) standards are a collection of documents that define a method for securing data while it is in transit over a TCP/IP network. IPsec includes a connection establishment routine, during which computers authenticate each other before transmitting data, and a technique called *tunneling,* in which data packets are encapsulated within other packets, for their protection.

⊕ MORE INFORMATION

Data protection technologies such as the Encrypting File System (EFS) and BitLocker are designed to protect data while it is stored on a drive. However, they do nothing to protect data while is being transmitted over the network, because they both decrypt the data before sending it. IPsec is the only technology included in Windows Server 2008 that can protect data while it is in transit.

In addition to inbound and outbound rules, the Windows Firewall with Advanced Security console enables you to create connection security rules, using the New Connection Security Rule Wizard. Connection security rules define the type of protection you want to apply to the communications that conform to Windows Firewall rules.

When you right-click the Connection Security Rules node and select New Rule from the context menu, the New Connection Security Rule Wizard, shown in Figure 8-14, takes you through the process of configuring the following sets of parameters:

- Rule Type—Specifies the basic function of the rule, such as to isolate computers based on authentication criteria, to exempt certain computers (such as infrastructure servers) from authentication, to authenticate two specific computers or groups of computers, or to tunnel communications between two computers. You can also create custom rules combining these functions.

- Endpoints—Specifies the IP addresses of the computer that will establish a secured connection before transmitting any data.

- Requirements—Specifies whether authentication between two computers should be requested or required in each direction.

- Authentication Method—Specifies the type of authentication the computers should use when establishing a connection.

- Profile—Specifies the profile(s) to which the rule should apply: domain, private, and/or public.

- Name—Specifies a name and (optionally) a description for the rule.

Figure 8-14

The New Connection Security Rule Wizard

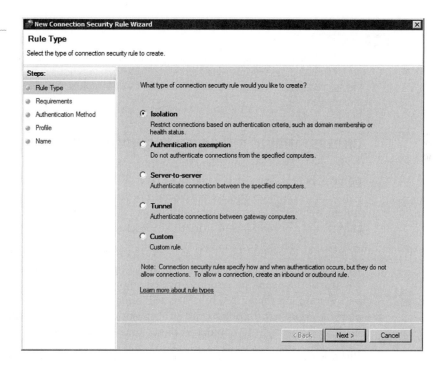

Using BitLocker

Firewalls enable you to specify which doors to your servers are left open and which are locked, but there are some doors that you must leave open, and these require security also. Data encryption mechanisms, such as the Encrypting File System (EFS) and BitLocker Drive Encryption, enable you to protect your data so that even if intruders get through the door, they cannot steal the valuables inside.

The Encrypting File System, which has been available since Windows 2000, enables users to protect specific files and folders so that no one else can access them. ***BitLocker Drive Encryption,*** on the other hand, is a new feature first released in Windows Vista, which makes it possible to encrypt an entire volume.

The full volume encryption provided by BitLocker has distinct advantages, including the following:

- Increased data protection—BitLocker encrypts all of the files on a volume, including operating system and application files, as well as paging files and temporary files, which can also contain sensitive information.

- Integrity checking—BitLocker can perform an integrity check before it permits the system to start, ensuring that the system BIOS, master boot record, boot sector, Boot Manager, and Windows Loader have not been compromised. This means that if someone steals a server, or removes its hard drive and tries to install it in another computer, they will be unable to access any of the volume data.

CERTIFICATION READY?
Plan server installations and upgrades
1.1

Unlike EFS, BitLocker is not designed to protect files for specific users, making it so other users cannot access them. Instead, BitLocker protects entire volumes from being compromised by unauthorized persons. For example, if someone alters the server's boot components, such as by stealing the hard drive and installing it into another computer, BitLocker will lock the protected volumes, preventing all access. However, when the system boots successfully under normal conditions, the BitLocker volumes are accessible to anyone. You must still protect your files and folders using the standard Windows Server 2008 tools, such as NTFS permissions and EFS.

⊕ MORE INFORMATION

According to Microsoft, there is no "back door" in the BitLocker encryption mechanism that would allow third parties (including government and law enforcement agencies) to access a protected volume. However, Microsoft has not made the source code available that would enable independent security analysts to confirm or refute this assertion.

UNDERSTANDING BITLOCKER REQUIREMENTS

To use BitLocker, you must have a computer with the appropriate hardware, and prepare it properly before you install Windows Server 2008. Two of the three available BitLocker modes require the computer to have a ***Trusted Platform Module (TPM),*** version 1.2 or later, and a system BIOS that is compatible with its use. The TPM is a dedicated cryptographic processor chip that the system uses to store the BitLocker encryption keys.

In addition to having the TPM, and before you install Windows Server 2008 or BitLocker, you must create a system partition on the computer, separate from the partition where you will install the operating system. The system partition, which must be an active, primary partition no less than 1.5 GB in size, will remain unencrypted and contain the files needed to boot the computer. In other words, this partition will hold all of the software the computer must access before it has unlocked the volume encrypted with BitLocker.

BitLocker has three operational modes, which define the steps involved in the system boot process. These modes are as follows:

- Transparent operation mode—The system stores the BitLocker volume encryption key on the TPM chip and accesses it automatically when the chip has determined that the boot environment is unmodified. This unlocks the protected volume and the computer continues to boot. No administrative interaction is required during the system boot sequence.

- User authentication mode—The system stores the BitLocker volume encryption key on the TPM chip, but an administrator must supply a PIN or insert a USB flash drive before the system can unlock the BitLocker volume and complete the system boot sequence.

- USB key mode—The BitLocker configuration process stores a startup key on a USB flash drive, which the administrator must insert each time the system boots. This mode does not require the server to have a TPM chip, but it must have a system BIOS that supports access to the USB flash drive before the operating system loads.

INSTALLING BITLOCKER

The basic steps of the BitLocker installation process are as follows.

 INSTALL BITLOCKER

GET READY. Log on to Windows Server 2008 using an account with administrative privileges. When the logon process is completed, close the Initial Configuration Tasks window and any other windows that appear.

1. Install the BitLocker Drive Encryption feature, using the Server Manager console.

2. Open the **Local Group Policy Editor** console, browse to the **Local Computer Policy** > **Computer Configuration** > **Administrative Templates** > **Windows Components** > **BitLocker Drive Encryption** node and open the **Control Panel Setup: Enable advanced startup options** policy.

3. Select the **Enabled** option, as shown in Figure 8-15, and configure the following settings to select an operational mode:

   - Allow BitLocker Without A Compatible TPM
   - Configure TPM Startup Key Option
   - Configure TPM Startup PIN Option

Figure 8-15

The Control Panel Setup: Enable advanced startup options policy

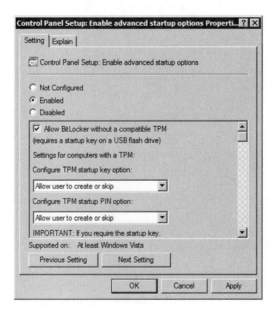

4. Open the BitLocker Drive Encryption control panel, as shown in Figure 8-16, and click **Turn On BitLocker** for the volume you want to encrypt.

Figure 8-16

The BitLocker Drive Encryption
control panel

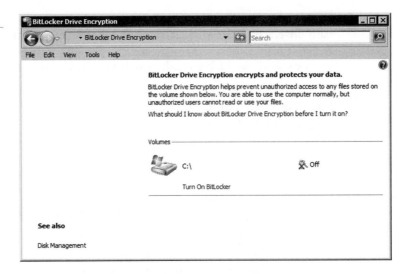

5. On the *Set BitLocker startup preferences* page, as shown in Figure 8-17, select an option that specifies the operational mode. The system then generates a startup key and stores it either on the computer's TPM chip or on a USB flash drive you supply.

Figure 8-17

The Set BitLocker startup preferences page

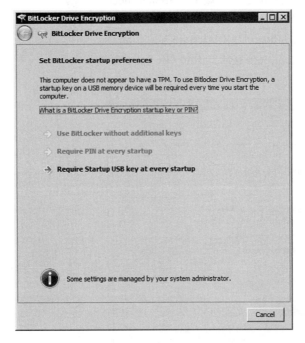

6. On the *Save the recovery password* page, specify where you want to store the password needed to override a locked BitLocker volume.

7. On the *Encrypt the volume* page, click **Continue** and restart the computer.

LOG ON to the computer. BitLocker then performs the encryption.

Once the encryption process is completed, you can open the BitLocker Drive Encryption control panel to ensure that the volume is encrypted, or to turn off BitLocker, such as when performing a BIOS upgrade or other system maintenance.

■ Securing Network Access

 THE BOTTOM LINE

The server security tasks discussed in the previous sections occur mostly during the initial server design and deployment processes. Once the server is operational, it becomes part of the network, and many of the security issues that affect the server are actually network-based.

Although it is possible to operate a Windows Server 2008 server as an independent entity from a security standpoint, with its own user accounts, authentication schemes, and access control mechanisms, this is rare in an enterprise environment. In most Windows enterprise networks, servers and workstations are members of Active Directory domains, which shifts the security emphasis to the network, rather than the individual servers.

When you use Active Directory on an enterprise network, it becomes responsible for two of the most critical security concepts in computing: authentication and authorization. Whether you are withdrawing money from a bank, entering a restricted building, or boarding an airplane, obtaining access to a protected resource requires both authentication and authorization. The two processes are closely related and often confused.

CERTIFICATION READY?
Monitor and maintain security and policies
3.3

To understand the difference between authentication and authorization, consider an example in the physical world that is familiar to most people: boarding an airplane. Before you can board a plane, you must present some means of identification and your ticket. Your identification, typically a driver's license or a passport, enables the airport staff to determine who you are. Validating your identity is the authentication part of the boarding process. The airport staff also checks your ticket to make sure that the flight you are boarding is the correct one. Verifying that you are allowed to board that particular plane is the authorization process.

On computer networks, users generally authenticate themselves by supplying an account name and a password. The account name identifies the user, and the password offers the system some assurance that the user really is who he or she claims to be. After a successful authentication, the computer is satisfied as to the user's identity, but it doesn't yet know whether the user should be allowed to access the resource he or she is requesting. To authorize the user, the computer system typically checks an ***access control list (ACL).*** An ACL is a list of users and/or groups who are permitted to access a resource, as well as the degree of access each user or group is permitted.

The following sections examine the Windows Server 2008 authentication and authorization processes in greater detail.

Understanding Authentication

To authenticate a user on a network with reasonable certainty that the individual is who he or she claims to be, the user needs to provide two pieces of information: identification and proof of identity.

On most networks, users identify themselves with an account name or an email address. The proof of identity can vary, however, depending on the amount of security the network requires.

Proof of identity typically takes one of three forms:

- Something you know—Most commonly, proof of identity takes the form of a password. A password is a type of shared secret. The user knows the password, and the server authenticating the user either has the password stored, or has some information that it can use to validate the password.
- Something you have—Many modern computer networks require greater security to authenticate users by reading information from a smart card. A ***smart card*** is a credit card–sized device that contains memory and embedded circuitry that enables it to store

data, such as a public encryption key. Running the card through an electronic card reader provides an electronic equivalent of a password.

- Something you are—For even greater security, some networks require you to provide proof of identify by confirming a physical attribute using biometrics. A biometric system proves a user's identity by scanning a unique part of the body such as fingerprints, the retina of the eye, or facial features.

Passwords can be guessed, and smart cards can be stolen. One form of authentication alone might not meet your organization's security requirements. Multifactor authentication combines two or more authentication methods, and significantly reduces the likelihood that an attacker will be able to impersonate a user during the authentication process. The most common example of multifactor authentication is combining a smart card with a password. Typically, the user supplies a password to retrieve a key stored on the smart card.

An organization can require smart cards for all users or, to save money, assign them only to specific users. Network administrators are often required to use smart cards because their privileges on the network would provide an attacker with a more significant opportunity than those of a common user.

Requiring smart cards for authentication can cause problems with existing applications. However, if an application includes the Certified for Windows Server 2008 logo, the application has been tested to ensure that it meets Microsoft security standards for Windows Server 2008. One of the security requirements for the Certified for Windows Server 2008 logo is that the application "support smart card login and secure credential management."

To require a user to authenticate using a smart card, use the Active Directory Users and Computers console to open the user object's Properties sheet and select the Account tab, as shown in Figure 8-18. In the Account Options list, select the Smart Card Is Required For Interactive Logon checkbox.

Figure 8-18

The smart card control in a user's Properties sheet

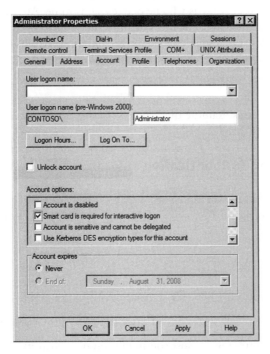

STORING USER CREDENTIALS

The server that authenticates the user must be able to determine that the individual's credentials are valid. To do this, the server must store information that it can use to verify the credentials. How and where the server stores this information are important decisions to make when designing an authentication model.

The way that an authentication server stores credentials can determine how difficult it is for an attacker to misuse the information and whether administrators can migrate those user credentials to a new authentication system in the future. Naturally, it is important that this information remains confidential. Instead of simply storing a list of user passwords on a server and directly comparing the password provided by the user to the one in the list, it is common practice for servers to store an encrypted or hashed version of the user password. If an attacker does gain access to the user credentials stored on the server, the attacker still needs to decrypt the contents before employing them to impersonate a user.

UNDERSTANDING ENCRYPTION

To protect data stored on and transmitted over a network, computers use various types of encryption to encode messages and create digital signatures that verify their authenticity. For one computer to encrypt a message and another computer to decrypt it, both must possess a key.

Encryption is essentially a system in which one character is substituted for another. If you create a key specifying that the letter A should be replaced by Q, the letter B by O, the letter C by T, and so forth, any message you encode using that key can be decoded by anyone else possessing the key. This is called *secret key encryption,* because you must protect the key from compromise. For computer transactions, this simple type of encryption is often useless, because there is usually no practical and secure way to distribute the secret key to all of the parties involved. After all, if the object is to send an encrypted message to a recipient over the network, it would hardly be appropriate to first send the secret encryption key in an unsecured message. However, there are some Windows Server 2008 applications that use secret key encryption effectively, such as the Kerberos authentication protocol, which is described later in this lesson.

For encryption on a data network to be both possible and practical, computers typically use a form of public key encryption. In *public key encryption,* every user has two keys, a public key and a private key. As the names imply, the public key is freely available to anyone, while the private key is carefully secured and never transmitted over the network. The basic premise of a public key encryption system is that data encrypted with the public key can be decrypted only with the private key, and conversely, data encrypted with the private key can be decrypted only using the public key. Data encrypted with a public key cannot be decrypted with that public key, nor can data encrypted with a private key be decrypted using that private key. It is the protection of the private key that guarantees the security of messages encrypted using this system.

If someone wants to send you a message, making sure that no one but you can read it, that person must obtain your public key and use it to encrypt the message. The person can then transmit the message to you over the network, secure in the knowledge that only you possess the private key needed to decrypt it. Even if an intruder were to intercept the message during transmission, it would still be in its encrypted form, and therefore inaccessible. Once you receive the message and decrypt it using your private key, you can reply to it by using the other party's own public key to encrypt your response, which only that person can decrypt, using their private key.

CENTRALIZED AND DECENTRALIZED AUTHENTICATION MODELS

Determining where to store user credentials requires choosing between centralized and decentralized authentication models. In a *decentralized authentication* model, as mentioned earlier, each server maintains its own list of users and their credentials. For users to access resources on multiple servers, they must have a separate account on each server. While a decentralized authentication model provides granular control over which users can authenticate to network resources, it becomes increasingly difficult to manage as networks grow to include more than a handful of servers.

A *centralized authentication* model can provide simpler management for larger networks, which lowers help desk costs related to account management. In a centralized model, all of the servers on the network rely on a single authority to authenticate users. Users attempting to access a particular network resource supply their credentials in the normal manner, and the server hosting the resource relays those credentials to a separate authentication server, which either grants or denies the user access. Centralized authentication is required to create an environment in which users can access all network resources with a single set of credentials, a desirable situation known as *single sign-on (SSO)*. The main potential drawback of the centralized model is that the servers must transmit authentication information over the network, which presents an additional security hazard. Most centralized authentication systems use elaborate forms of encryption to protect this data as it travels over the network.

Microsoft Windows Server 2008, like the other Windows operating systems, is capable of using either a centralized or a decentralized authentication model. All Windows computers have a component called the *Security Accounts Manager (SAM),* which enables them to maintain a list of local users and groups that function as a decentralized authentication system. When you log on to a Windows computer for the first time, you use the local Administrator account, which the computer authenticates using its own SAM.

On Windows networks, centralized authentication is provided by Active Directory domain controllers that store all of the account information for the domain, and are responsible for authenticating all user requests for access to domain resources. Larger networks might use multiple domains, with *trusts* that enable network resources in one domain to authorize users in another domain.

PROTECTING USER CREDENTIALS

Since the earliest computer systems, some of the most widely used security attacks have relied upon the attacker's ability to gain access to the operating system's password file. When multi-user computer systems were first created, security was not a major priority, and operating systems often stored their password files in plain (that is, unencrypted) text. Anyone who could gain access to the password file would easily be able to read every user's password.

Later, operating system developers began to use various forms of encryption and hashing to obscure user credentials. This was a huge step forward, because the casual attacker couldn't read the files without first decrypting them. However, security experts (on both sides of the law) have always put a huge amount of effort into finding ways to uncover user credentials based on a captured password file. Over time, these security experts have found ways to decrypt, in a reasonable amount of time, just about every encryption scheme operating system developers have created for protecting password files. This trend is bound to continue in the future, but you can reduce the risk of someone penetrating your password files by requiring users to employ strong passwords, by requiring regular password changes, and by using the cracking tools yourself to identify easily cracked passwords that should be changed.

NETWORK PLANNING AND AUTHENTICATION

Many organizations have to provide seamless network access for multiple types of users, such as office workers, employees who are traveling, business partners, and customers. At the same time, organizations must protect network resources from potential intruders. A network designed with an eye toward authentication can help you to achieve this complex balance between providing reliable access for users and strong network security for your organization.

When establishing an authentication strategy for your organization, you must become familiar with your current environment. This includes the structure of your organization; the users, computers, and services that require authentication; and the applications and services running on the computers. This will help you to understand the requirements and constraints of your organization.

When evaluating your environment, consider the following:

- The number of domain controllers in your organization—Ensure that there are enough domain controllers to support client logon requests and authentication requests while meeting your redundancy requirements. A sufficient number of domain controllers will ensure that a large volume of authentication requests do not result in authentication failures, even if a domain controller is offline because of a hardware or network failure.

- The type of network connectivity between your organization's sites—Ensure that clients in remote sites are connected well enough to authenticate to domain controllers located in main sites. If connectivity is an issue, consider installing domain controllers in sites that might have logon problems because of slow or unreliable links.
- The number of certification authorities (CAs) that are available in your organization and their locations—Ensure that you have enough CAs to support the anticipated number of certificate requests.

TAKE NOTE*

Many administrators express concern about whether they have enough bandwidth, but it's latency (the time it takes for a packet to travel from a source to a destination) that's more likely to cause authentication problems across wide area network links. Authentication requires very little bandwidth. However, packets must go back and forth across the link several times. If latency causes a significant delay for each round trip, authentication will seem slow.

ENHANCING AUTHENTICATION SECURITY WITH STRONG PASSWORDS

Encryption limits your organization's vulnerability to having user credentials intercepted and misused. Specifically, password encryption is designed to make it extremely difficult for unauthorized users to decrypt captured passwords. Ideally, when accounts use strong passwords, it should take an attacker months, years, or decades to extract a password after capturing the encrypted or hashed data. During that time, the user should have changed the password—thus rendering the cracked password useless.

Weak passwords, on the other hand, can be cracked in a matter of hours or days, even when encrypted. Encryption also cannot protect against passwords that are easily guessable, because weak passwords are vulnerable to **dictionary attacks.** Dictionary attacks encrypt a list of common passwords, and compare the results with the captured cyphertext. If the password appears in the password dictionary, the attacker can identify the password quickly. You can defend against this vulnerability by implementing a strong password policy.

A strong password is one that a user can easily remember but which is also too complex for a stranger to guess. For example, *&_I5y#<.h* might appear to be a good password, but few users would be able to remember it without writing it down, creating a significant security vulnerability. Fortunately, there are techniques for creating strong passwords that the human brain can remember more easily. For example, you could take a password that is easy to remember (and easy to guess), such as *99Butterflies,* and add an easy-to-remember suffix to it to make it more secure: *99Butterflies@complexpassword.com*. You now have a password that is 33 characters long; uses uppercase, lowercase, and symbols; is easy to remember; and that, because of the length, is harder than the *&_I5y#<.h* password to crack.

In the previous example, an email-type suffix was added to the end of the password to make it complex. You can also add phone numbers, addresses, and file path locations (like c:\winnt\system32) to make a password complex.

USING PASSWORD POLICIES

When implementing and enforcing a password policy, consider the users' inability to remember passwords that are too complex, change too often, and are too long. When passwords are too complex or too long, the eventuality that users will use other methods to remember their passwords, such as writing them down, is more likely.

To help network administrators implement strong passwords, Windows Server 2008 provides a series of password settings that you can implement using Group Policy, either locally or through Active Directory. An effective combination of password policies compels users to select appropriate passwords and change them at regular intervals.

To implement password policies on an Active Directory network, you create or modify a group policy object (GPO) using the Group Policy Management Editor console, as shown in

Figure 8-19, and link it to a domain, site, or organizational unit object. All of the container and leaf objects subordinate to the selected object receive the configured policy settings.

Figure 8-19

Password policies in the Group Policy Management Editor

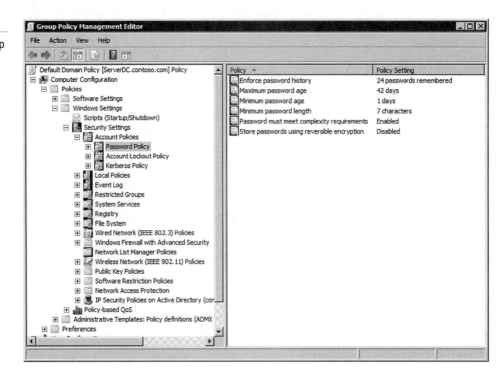

Table 8-1 describes the password policy settings that you can use to implement strong passwords.

Table 8-1

Security Policy Settings for Strong Passwords

SECURITY POLICY SETTING	DEFAULT VALUE	DESCRIPTION
Enforce Password History	24 passwords	Stores the passwords that users have previously supplied and prevents them from reusing those same passwords. Lowering this value is recommended if you also plan to reduce the Maximum Password Age value.
Maximum Password Age	42 days	Determines how long passwords can be used before users are required to change them. Ideally, this value would be lower than the time it takes a commercial password cracking program to compromise the passwords in your organization. Lowering this value decreases the likelihood that a password will be cracked while it is still valid, but doing so may increase the number of support calls relating to forgotten passwords.
Minimum Password Age	1 day	Determines how long a user must keep a password before changing it. This can prevent a user from immediately changing a password to a previous one.
Minimum Password Length	7 characters	Determines the minimum length of a password. Longer passwords are inherently more secure, but can also be more difficult to remember.
Password Must Meet Complexity Requirements	Enabled	Forces users to specify passwords that: • Do not contain all or part of the user's account name • Are at least six characters in length • Contain characters from three of the following four categories: uppercase characters (A through Z), lowercase characters (a through z), base 10 digits (0 through 9), and non-alphabetic characters (such as !, $, #, %)

Table 8-1 (*continued*)

SECURITY POLICY SETTING	DEFAULT VALUE	DESCRIPTION
Store Passwords Using Reversible Encryption	Disabled	Causes the system to store passwords in a form that can be easily decrypted by applications that require access to them, such as the Challenge Handshake Authentication Protocol (CHAP). This option severely compromises the security of the password system and should be disabled except in situations where it is absolutely required.

Although you can enforce strong passwords in Windows Server 2008 Active Directory using password policies, employee education is the only way to keep users from writing down passwords in public locations or using discoverable personal information in passwords.

USING ACCOUNT LOCKOUT POLICIES

Account lockout policies exist to limit your network's vulnerability to password-guessing attacks. When you implement account lockout policies, a user account is automatically locked out after a specified number of incorrect authentication attempts. Windows Server 2008 does not enable account lockouts by default, and for a good reason: enabling account lockouts exposes you to a denial-of-service vulnerability. A malicious attacker with access to user names can guess incorrect passwords and lock everyone's accounts, which denies legitimate users from accessing network resources.

Therefore, you should enable account lockout policies only in environments where the threat from guessed passwords is greater than the threat of a denial-of-service attack. Like password policies, you define account lockout policies using Group Policy, as shown in Figure 8-20. When configuring these policies, you should select values that are sufficiently lax to allow for user input error, but are also stringent enough to prevent attacks on user accounts.

Figure 8-20

Account lockout policies in the Group Policy Management Editor

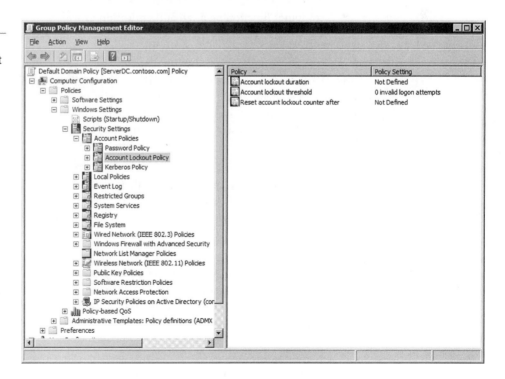

Table 8-2 describes the various account lockout settings that you can use to secure your network.

Table 8-2

Password and Account Lockout Settings

Security Policy Setting	Default Value	Description
Account Lockout Duration	Not defined	Determines how many minutes a locked-out account will remain disabled before being automatically re-enabled. A value of 0 requires an administrator to unlock the account manually.
Account Lockout Threshold	0 invalid logon attempts	Determines how many logon attempts users can make before the account is locked out. This setting does not apply to attempts to log on at the console of a locked workstation or to attempts to unlock a screensaver, because locked workstations cannot be forced to run password-cracking programs.
Reset Account Lockout Counter After	Not defined	Determines the number of minutes that must elapse after a failed logon attempt before the counter is reset to 0 bad logon attempts.

UNDERSTANDING KERBEROS AUTHENTICATION

Enterprise networks that use Active Directory authenticate their users with the *Kerberos* authentication protocol. The Kerberos protocol gets it name from the three-headed dog in Greek mythology that guards the entrance to Hades. The three components of Kerberos, corresponding to the heads of the dog, are as follows:

- The client requesting services or authentication
- The server hosting the services requested by the client
- A computer functioning as an authentication provider, which is trusted by both the client and the server

In the case of a Windows Server 2008 network, the authentication provider is a Windows Server 2008 domain controller running the Kerberos *Key Distribution Center (KDC)* service. The KDC maintains a database of account information for all security principals in the domain. A security principal is any user, computer, or service account that logs on to the domain. The KDC also stores a cryptographic key known only to the security principal and the KDC. This key, derived from a user's logon password, is used in exchanges between the security principal and the KDC and is known as a *long-term key*.

Kerberos authentication is based on specially formatted data packets known as tickets. With Kerberos, computers transmit these tickets over the network instead of passwords. Transmitting tickets instead of passwords makes the authentication process more resistant to attackers who can intercept the network traffic. To generate tickets, the KDC use the following two services:

- Authentication Service (AS)—Issues *ticket granting tickets* (TGTs) to users that supply valid authentication credentials. A TGT remains valid for a limited length of time (typically 10 hours) and prevents the user from having to re-authenticate each time it requests access to a network resource. Whenever the client requires access to a new network resource, it must present its TGT to the KDC.
- Ticket-Granting Service (TGS)—Issues service tickets that provide users with access to specific network resources. Clients requesting access to a network resource must present a valid TGT to the TGS before receiving a service ticket.

In a Kerberos environment, the authentication process consists of three separate message exchanges, which are discussed in the following sections.

THE AUTHENTICATION SERVICE EXCHANGE

The Authentication Service exchange, shown in Figure 8-21, occurs during a user's initial logon to the network, and proceeds as follows:

Figure 8-21

The Kerberos Authentication Service Exchange

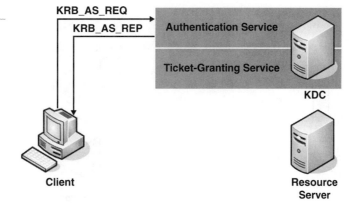

1. When a user logs on by keying an account name and password, the Local Security Authority (LSA) on the client computer creates a *user key* by encrypting the password. The LSA then saves a copy of the user key in its credentials cache, and passes the authentication data to the Kerberos Security Support Provider (SSP), also running on the client computer. The Kerberos SSP is responsible for all communications between the client computer and the KDC running on the domain controller.

2. The Kerberos SSP generates a Kerberos Authentication Service Request (KRB_AS_REQ) and sends it to the Authentication Service on the KDC. The request contains the user's name, the name of the domain, and pre-authentication data (such as a timestamp), which the Kerberos SSP encrypts with the user key it received from the LSA.

3. The KDC looks up the user's name in its account database and accesses the copy of the user key already stored there (when the user specified his or her password). The KDC then decrypts the pre-authentication data using its own copy of the user key. If the pre-authentication data is valid, then the request message must have been encrypted using the same user key, and the user's identity is confirmed. Notice that at no time during this exchange is the actual password transmitted over the network, in encrypted or unencrypted form.

4. Having confirmed the user's identity, the Authentication Service on the KDC generates a Kerberos Authentication Service Reply (KRB_AS_REP) and transmits it back to the client. The reply message contains a TGT and a session key that the client will use for all subsequent transmissions to the Ticket Granting Service (TGS) on the domain controller. The session key is encrypted with the user key and the TGT is encrypted with the KDC's own long-term key. The TGT included in the reply message contains another session key, which the TGS will use to communicate with the client. It also contains authorization data, including security identifiers for the user's account and the groups of which the user is a member.

5. When the client receives the KRB_AS_REP message from the KDC, it decrypts the message using the copy of its user key stored in the credentials cache. The client can now destroy the cached user key, because it will encrypt all subsequent communications to the KDC with the session key it has just received. This session key remains valid until the TGT expires or the user logs off.

At this time, the transaction with the Authentication Service on the KDC is completed, and the user has been authenticated to the domain.

THE TICKET-GRANTING SERVICE EXCHANGE

From this point on, whenever the user wants to access a new network resource, another exchange of messages is required, this time between the client and the Ticket-Granting Service on the KDC. This exchange, shown in Figure 8-22, proceeds as follows:

Figure 8-22

The Kerberos Ticket-Granting Service Exchange

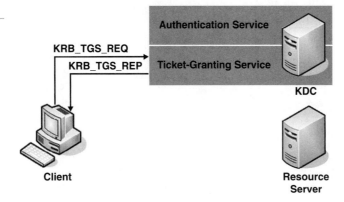

1. When a user on the client computer wants to access a network resource, the client first checks its credentials cache to see if it possesses a service ticket for that resource. If there is no service ticket for that particular resource, the client then searches the cache for a TGT.

2. Finding the TGT it received from the Authentication Service on the KDC, the client generates a Kerberos Ticket-Granting Service Request (KRB_TGS_REQ) message and sends it to the KDC. The request message contains the name and domain of the computer hosting the requested resource, a copy of the TGT, and an authenticator. The *authenticator* contains a timestamp, a checksum, and authorization data, and is encrypted using the TGS session key supplied to the client during the Authentication Service exchange.

3. On receipt of the request message, the Ticket-Granting Service on the KDC decrypts the TGT using its own long-term key, extracts the session key in the TGT, and uses it to decrypt the authenticator. If the KDC can successfully decrypt the authenticator and finds that the information contained inside is valid, it can trust the source of the request message. The inclusion of the authenticator enables the KDC to confirm that the request message was actually generated by the client, and is not a stolen message being transmitted by an imposter. The use of the TGT prevents the KDC from having to look up the user's long-term key in the directory database each time the user requests access to a new resource. Instead, the KDC can use its own long-term key (stored in memory) to decrypt the TGT and validate the user's identity.

4. After successfully decrypting the authenticator and verifying the client's identity, the TGS generates a Kerberos Ticket-Granting Service Reply (KRB_TGS_REP) message and transmits it to the client. The reply message contains a new session key, which the client will use to communicate with the server hosting the requested resource, and a service ticket. The service ticket contains another copy of the same session key and authorization data for the user, copied from the TGT. The client's session key is encrypted using the TGS session key from the Authentication Service exchange, and the service ticket is encrypted using the resource server's own session key.

5. When the client receives the reply message, it decrypts the session key and stores it in its credentials cache. The client also stores the service ticket, still in its encrypted form, in the same cache. The credentials cache on a Kerberos client is

always stored in volatile memory only so that unencrypted keys could never be left on a hard disk in the event of a power failure or other malfunction.

Once the Ticket-Granting Service exchange is completed, no further communication with the KDC is needed until the client needs to access another network resource.

THE CLIENT/SERVER EXCHANGE

Now that the client possesses a service ticket for the requested resource, it can communicate directly with the server hosting that resource, using the following procedure, shown in Figure 8-23:

Figure 8-23

The Kerberos Client/Server
Exchange

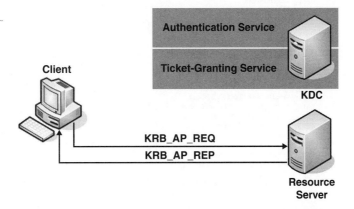

1. To access a network resource, the client searches its credentials cache for a service ticket for that particular resource.

2. When the client finds an appropriate service ticket, it generates a Kerberos Application Request (KRB_AP_REQ) message and transmits it to the server hosting the resource. The request message contains the service ticket, a new authenticator, and application flags specifying the use of the session key and whether the client wants to use mutual authentication. The service ticket is still in the same encrypted form as when the client received it from the KDC, and the authenticator is encrypted using the resource-specific session key the client received in the KRB_TGS_REP message (a copy of which is also included in the service ticket).

3. The resource server, on receipt of the request message, decrypts the service ticket using its own session key, extracts the client's session key from inside the ticket, and uses it to decrypt the authenticator and verify the client's identity, just as the KDC did earlier.

4. Once the resource server successfully verifies the authenticator, it checks to see if the mutual authentication flag was set in the request message. If so, the resource server uses the session key from the service ticket to encrypt the timestamp from the client's authenticator, and transmits it back to the client in a Kerberos Application Reply (KRB_AP_REP) message. If the flag is not set, then no reply message is necessary.

The client is now authenticated, and the resource server can create an access token, which provides the user on the client computer the ability to connect to the desired resource. The next exchange between the client and the server will consist of messages specific to the application that requires access to the network resource.

CONTROLLING KERBEROS AUTHENTICATION USING GROUP POLICIES

Although most of the transactions in a Kerberos authentication are invisible to both users and administrators, there are some Group Policy settings you can use to configure the properties of the Kerberos tickets issued by your domain controllers. Reasonable Kerberos ticket lifetimes must be short enough to prevent attackers from cracking the cryptography that protects the ticket's stored credentials and long enough to ensure that requests for new tickets do not overload the KDC and network.

Table 8-3 lists the Kerberos Group Policy settings, shown in Figure 8-24.

Figure 8-24

Kerberos policies in the Group Policy Management Editor

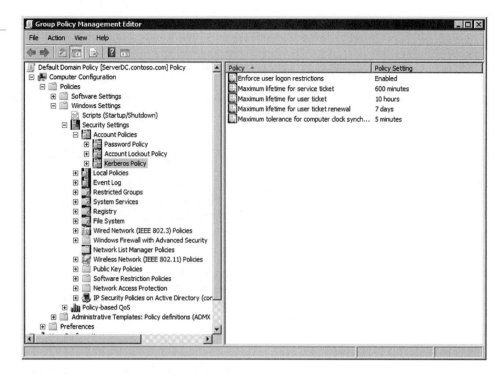

Table 8-3

Security Policy Settings for Kerberos Ticket Policy

SECURITY POLICY SETTING	DEFAULT VALUE	DESCRIPTION
Enforce User Logon Restrictions	Enabled	Determines whether the KDC validates every request for a session ticket by examining the user rights policy on the target computer. This option also serves as a means of ensuring that the requesting account is still valid and was not disabled since the Kerberos ticket was issued. This option could potentially slow down network logons.
Maximum Lifetime For Service Ticket	600 minutes	Determines the amount of time a service ticket is available before it expires. This setting should be set the same as the user ticket setting, unless your users run jobs that are longer then their user tickets would allow.
Maximum Lifetime For User Ticket	10 hours	Determines the amount of time a user ticket is available before it expires. This setting should be set according to the average amount of time a user logs on to a computer at your organization.
Maximum Lifetime For User Ticket Renewal	7 days	Determines the number of days for which a user's TGT can be renewed. The default is seven days. Shortening this interval will increase security but put more load on the KDC.
Maximum Tolerance For Computer Clock Synchronization	5 minutes	Determines the maximum time difference (in minutes) between the time on the user's computer's clock and the time on the domain controller. Raising this value from the default increases vulnerability to replay attacks, in which encrypted credentials captured from the network are resubmitted by a malicious attacker. Lowering this value increases the number of authentication failures caused by unsynchronized or poorly synchronized clocks.

Understanding Authorization

> Authorization is the process of determining whether an authenticated user is allowed to perform a requested action.

Each time a user opens a file, Windows Server 2008 verifies that the user is authorized to open that file. Each time a user prints, Windows Server 2008 verifies that the user has the permissions needed to send jobs to that printer. In fact, Windows Server 2008 verifies a user's authorization to access just about every object imaginable: NTFS files and folders, shared folders, printers, services, Active Directory directory service objects, Terminal Services connections, and registry keys and values.

Understanding how authorization works for each of these different types of resources can be complicated, because each type requires permissions that are specific to its function. For example, you need to control whether users can read files or write to files, but for services, your concern is whether a given user can start or stop the service. Fortunately, Windows Server 2008 simplifies authorization management by using a standard permission model for all types of resources.

Permissions are privileges granted to specific system entities, such as users, groups, or computers, enabling them to perform a task or access a resource. For example, you can grant a specific user permission to read a file, while denying that same user the permissions needed to modify or delete the file.

Windows Server 2008 has several sets of permissions, which operate independently of each other. As a server administrator, you should be familiar with the operation of the following four permission systems:

- Share permissions—Control access to folders over a network. To access a file over a network, a user must have appropriate share permissions (and appropriate NTFS permissions, if the shared folder is on an NTFS volume).
- NTFS permissions—Control access to the files and folders stored on disk volumes formatted with the NTFS file system. To access a file, whether on the local system or over a network, a user must have the appropriate NTFS permissions.
- Registry permissions—Control access to specific parts of the Windows registry. An application that modifies registry settings or a user attempting to manually modify the registry must have the appropriate registry permissions.
- Active Directory permissions—Control access to specific parts of an Active Directory hierarchy. Although file servers typically do not function as Active Directory domain controllers, server administrators might use these permissions when servicing computers that are members of a domain.

All of these permission systems operate independently of each other, and sometimes combine to provide increased protection to a specific resource. For example, an administrator might grant Alice the NTFS permissions needed to access a spreadsheet stored on a file server volume. If Alice sits down at the file server console and logs on as herself, she will be able to access that spreadsheet. However, if Alice is working at her own computer, she will not be able to access the spreadsheet until the administrator creates a share containing the file and grants Alice the proper share permissions as well.

TAKE NOTE

While all of these permissions systems are operating all the time, server administrators do not necessarily have to work with them all on a regular basis. In fact, many administrators might not ever have to manually alter a registry or Active Directory permission. However, many server administrators do have to work with NTFS and share permissions on a daily basis.

UNDERSTANDING THE WINDOWS PERMISSION ARCHITECTURE

Files, folders, shares, registry keys, and Active Directory objects are all protected by permissions. To store the permissions, each of these resources has an access control list (ACL). An ACL is a collection of individual permissions, in the form of *access control entries (ACEs).* Each ACE consists of a *security principal* (that is, the name of the user, group, or computer granted the permissions) and the specific permissions assigned to that security principal. When you manage permissions in any of the Windows Server 2008 permission systems, you are actually creating and modifying the ACEs in an ACL.

It is important to understand that, in all of the Windows operating systems, permissions are stored as part of the protected resource, not the security principal granted access. For example, when you grant a user the NTFS permissions needed to access a file, the ACE you create is stored in the file's ACL; it is not part of the user account. You can move the file to a different location, and its permissions go with it.

To manage permissions in Windows Server 2008, you use a tab in the resource's Properties sheet, like the one shown in Figure 8-25, with the security principals listed at the top and the permissions associated with them at the bottom. Share permissions are typically found on a Share Permissions tab, and NTFS permissions are located on a Security tab. All of the Windows permission systems use the same interface, although the permissions themselves differ.

Figure 8-25

The Security tab of a Properties sheet

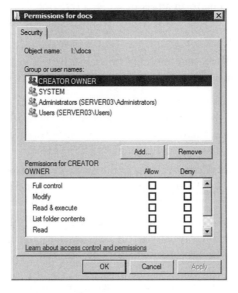

UNDERSTANDING STANDARD AND SPECIAL PERMISSIONS

The permissions protecting a particular system resource are not like the keys to a lock, which provide either full access or no access at all. Permissions are designed to be granular, enabling you to grant specific degrees of access to security principals. For example, you can use NTFS permissions to control not only who has access to a spreadsheet but also the degree of access. You might grant Ralph permission to read and modify the spreadsheet, while Alice can only read it, and Ed cannot see it at all.

To provide this granularity, each of the Windows permission systems has an assortment of permissions that you can assign to a security principal in any combination. Depending on the permission system you are working with, you might have dozens of different permissions available for a single system resource.

Although this might sound extremely complex, in practice it usually is not. Windows provides preconfigured permission combinations suitable for most common access control chores. When you open the Properties sheet for a system resource and look at its Security tab, the NTFS permissions you see are called *standard permissions.* Standard permissions are actually combinations of *special permissions,* which provide the most granular control over the resource.

For example, the NTFS permission system has 14 special permissions that you can assign to a folder or file. However, there are also six standard permissions, which are various combinations of the 14 special permissions. In most cases, administrators work only with standard permissions. Many administrators rarely, if ever, work directly with special permissions.

If you do find it necessary to work with special permissions directly, Windows makes it possible. When you click the Advanced button on the Security tab of any Properties sheet, an Advanced Security Settings dialog box appears, as shown in Figure 8-26, which enables you to access the ACEs for the selected system resource directly.

Figure 8-26

The Advanced Security Settings dialog box

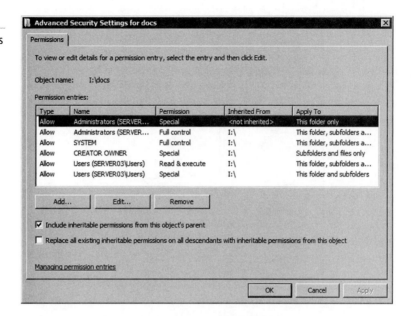

ALLOWING AND DENYING PERMISSIONS

When you assign permissions to a system resource, you are, in effect, creating a new ACE in the resource's ACL. There are two basic types of ACE: *Allow* and *Deny*. This makes it possible to approach permission management tasks from two directions:

- Additive—Start with no permissions and then grant Allow permissions to individual security principals to provide them with the access they need.

- Subtractive—Start by granting all possible Allow permissions to individual security principals, providing them with full control over the system resource, and then grant them Deny permissions for the access you don't want them to have.

Most administrators prefer the additive approach, because Windows, by default, attempts to limit access to important system resources. In a properly designed permission hierarchy, the use of Deny permissions is often not needed at all. Many administrators frown on their use, because combining Allow and Deny permissions in the same hierarchy can often make it difficult to determine the effective permissions for a specific system resource.

INHERITING PERMISSIONS

The most important principle in permission management is that permissions tend to run downward through a hierarchy. This is called permission inheritance. Permission inheritance means that parent resources pass their permissions down to their subordinates. For example, when you grant Alice Allow permissions to access the root of the D: drive, all of the folders and subfolders on the D: drive inherit those permissions, and Alice can access them. The principle of inheritance simplifies the permission assignment process enormously. Without it, you would have to grant security principals individual Allow permissions for every file, folder, share, object, and key they need to access. With inheritance, you can grant access to an entire file system by creating one set of Allow permissions.

In most cases, whether consciously or not, system administrators take inheritance into account when they design their file systems and Active Directory trees. The location of a system resource in a hierarchy is often based on how the administrators plan to assign permissions. For example, the section of a directory tree shown in Figure 8-27 is intended to be a place where network users can temporarily store files that they want other users to access.

Figure 8-27

A sample xfer directory structure

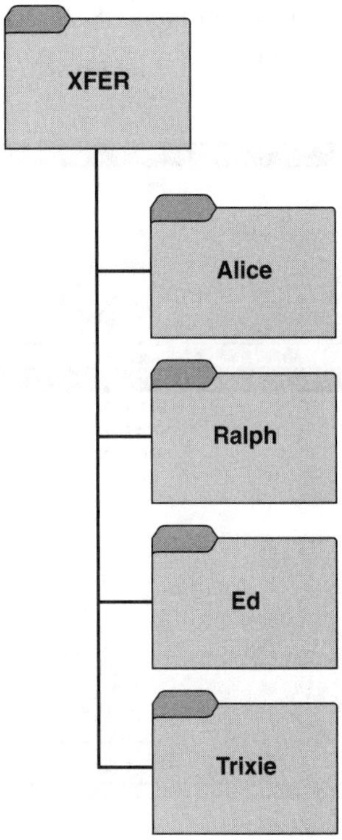

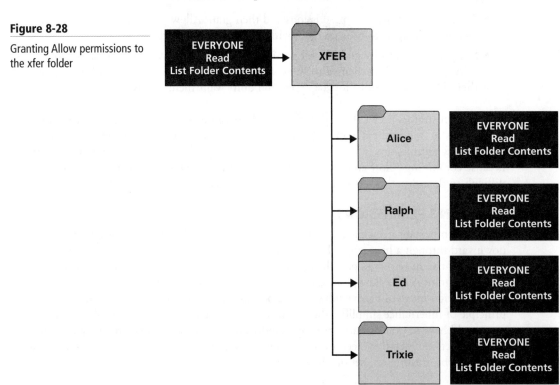

Because the administrator has assigned all users the Allow Read and Allow List Folder Contents standard permission to the xfer folder, as shown in Figure 8-28, everyone is able to read the files in the xfer directory. Because the assigned permissions run downward, all of the subfolders beneath xfer inherit those permissions, so all of the users can read the files in all of the subfolders as well.

Figure 8-28

Granting Allow permissions to the xfer folder

The next step for the administrator is to assign each user the Allow Full Control permission to his or her own subfolder, as shown in Figure 8-29. This enables each user to create, modify, and delete files in his or her own folder, without compromising the security of the other users' folders. Because the user folders are at the bottom of the hierarchy, there are no subfolders to inherit the Full Control permissions.

Figure 8-29

Granting Full Control to individual user folders

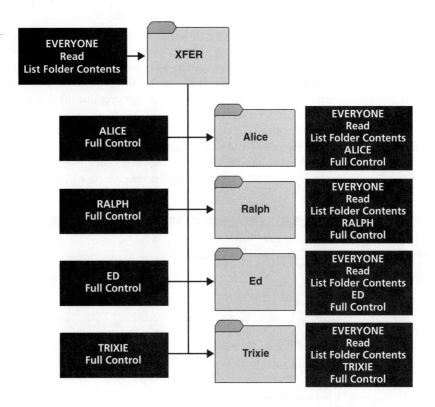

In some situations, an administrator might want to prevent subordinate resources from inheriting permissions from their parents. There are two ways to do this:

- Turn off inheritance—When you assign special permissions, you can configure an ACE not to pass its permissions down to its subordinate resources. This effectively blocks the inheritance process.
- Deny permissions—When you assign a Deny permission to a system resource, it overrides any Allow permissions that the resource might have inherited from its parent objects.

UNDERSTANDING EFFECTIVE PERMISSIONS

A security principal can receive permissions in many ways, and it is important for an administrator to understand how these permissions interact. The combination of Allow permissions and Deny permissions that a security principal receives for a given system resource, whether explicitly assigned, inherited, or received through a group membership, is called the *effective permissions* for that resource. Because a security principal can receive permissions from so many sources, it is not unusual for those permissions to conflict, so rules define how the permissions combine to form the effective permissions. These rules are as follows:

- Allow permissions are cumulative—When a security principal receives Allow permissions from more than one source, the permissions are combined to form the effective permissions. For example, if Alice receives the Allow Read and Allow List Folder Contents permissions for a particular folder by inheriting them from its parent folder, and receives the Allow Write and Allow Modify permissions to the same folder from a group membership, Alice's effective permissions for the folder are the combination of all four permissions. If you then explicitly grant Alice's user account the Allow Full Control permission, this fifth permission is combined with the other four.

- Deny permissions override Allow permissions—When a security principal receives Allow permissions, whether explicitly, by inheritance, or from a group, you can override those permissions by granting the principal Deny permissions of the same type. For example, if Alice receives the Allow Read and Allow List Folder Contents permissions for a particular folder by inheritance, and receives the Allow Write and Allow Modify permissions to the same folder from a group membership, explicitly granting the Deny permissions to that folder prevents her from accessing it in any way.

- Explicit permissions take precedence over inherited permissions—When a security principal receives permissions by inheriting them from a parent or from group memberships, you can override those permissions by explicitly assigning contradicting permissions to the security principal itself. For example, if Alice inherits the Deny Full Access permission for a folder, explicitly assigning her user account the Allow Full Access permission to that folder overrides the denial.

Of course, instead of examining and evaluating all of the possible permission sources, you can just open the Advanced Security Settings dialog box and click the Effective Permissions tab, as shown in Figure 8-30, to display your current effective permissions for the selected file or folder.

Figure 8-30

The Effective Permissions tab of the Advanced Security Settings dialog box

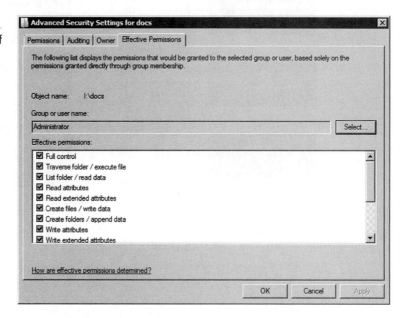

ASSIGNING STANDARD NTFS PERMISSIONS

The majority of Windows installations today use the NTFS file system, as opposed to FAT32. One of the main advantages of NTFS is that it supports permissions, which FAT32 does not. As described earlier, every file and folder on an NTFS drive has an ACL that consists of ACEs, each of which contains a security principal and the permissions assigned to that principal.

In the NTFS permission system, the security principals involved are users and groups, which Windows refers to using *security identifiers (SIDs)*. When a user attempts to access an NTFS file or folder, the system reads the user's security access token, which contains the SIDs for the user's account and all of the groups to which the user belongs. The system then compares these SIDs to those stored in the file or folder's ACEs, to determine what access the user should have. This is how the authorization process works in the NTFS file system.

Most file server administrators work with standard NTFS permissions almost exclusively because there is no need to work directly with special permissions for most common access control tasks. To assign standard NTFS permissions to a shared folder, use the following procedure.

 ASSIGN STANDARD NTFS PERMISSIONS

GET READY. Log on to Windows Server 2008 using an account with domain administrative privileges. When the logon process is completed, close the Initial Configuration Tasks window and any other windows that appear.

1. Click **Start** > **Administrative Tools** > **Share and Storage Management**. The Share and Storage Management console appears.

2. In the detail (middle) pane, click the **Shares** tab. All of the folder shares on the computer appear in the detail pane.

3. Select the share you want to modify and, in the actions pane, select **Properties**. The Properties sheet for the share appears.

4. Click the **Permissions** tab, and then click **NTFS Permissions**. An NTFS Permissions dialog box for the share appears, as shown in Figure 8-31. The top half of the display lists all of the security principals currently possessing permissions to the selected folder. The bottom half lists the permissions held by the selected security principal.

Figure 8-31

An NTFS Permissions dialog box

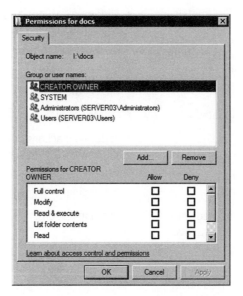

NTFS permissions are not limited to shared folders. Every file and folder on an NTFS volume has permissions. While this procedure describes the process of assigning permissions to a shared folder, you can open the Properties sheet for any folder in a Windows Explorer window, click the Security tab, and work with its NTFS permissions in the same way.

TAKE NOTE*

5. Click **Add**. The Select Users, Computers, or Groups dialog box appears.

6. In the **Enter The Object Names To Select** text box, key the name of the user or group you want to add and click **OK**. The user or group appears on the Permissions dialog box in the Group Or User Names list.

7. Select the user or group you just added and, in the **Permissions** box, select or clear the checkboxes to **Allow** or **Deny** the user any of the standard permissions.

8. Click **OK** twice to close the Permissions dialog box and the Properties sheet.

CLOSE the Share and Storage Management console.

Table 8-4 lists the standard permissions that you can assign to NTFS files or folders, and the capabilities that they grant to their possessors.

 TAKE NOTE *

Assigning permissions to a single folder takes only a moment, but for a folder with a large number of files and subfolders subordinate to it, the process can take a long time, because the system must modify the ACL of each folder and file.

Table 8-4

NTFS Standard Permissions

STANDARD PERMISSION	WHEN APPLIED TO A FOLDER, ENABLES A SECURITY PRINCIPAL TO:VALUE	WHEN APPLIED TO A FILE, ENABLES A SECURITY PRINCIPAL TO:
Full Control	• Modify the folder permissions. • Take ownership of the folder. • Delete subfolders and files contained in the folder. • Perform all actions associated with all of the other NTFS folder permissions.	• Modify the file permissions. • Take ownership of the file. • Perform all actions associated with all of the other NTFS file permissions.
Modify	• Delete the folder. • Perform all actions associated with the Write and the Read & Execute permissions.	• Modify the file. • Delete the file. • Perform all actions associated with the Write and the Read & Execute permissions.
Read and Execute	• Navigate through restricted folders to reach other files and folders. • Perform all actions associated with the Read and List Folder Contents permissions.	• Perform all actions associated with the Read permission. • Run applications.
List Folder Contents	• View the names of the files and subfolders contained in the folder.	• Not applicable.
Read	• See the files and subfolders contained in the folder. • View the ownership, permissions, and attributes of the folder.	• Read the contents of the file. • View the ownership, permissions, and attributes of the file.
Write	• Create new files and subfolders inside the folder. • Modify the folder attributes. • View the ownership and permissions of the folder.	• Overwrite the file. • Modify the file attributes. • View the ownership and permissions of the file.

ASSIGNING SPECIAL NTFS PERMISSIONS

To view and manage the special NTFS permissions for a file, folder, or share, use the following procedure.

 ASSIGN SPECIAL NTFS PERMISSIONS

GET READY. Log on to Windows Server 2008 using an account with domain administrative privileges. When the logon process is completed, close the Initial Configuration Tasks window and any other windows that appear.

1. Open the Properties sheet for a file, folder, or share on an NTFS drive using one of the following procedures:

   - Open Windows Explorer, right-click a file or folder and, from the context menu, select **Properties**. Then, click the **Security** tab.

   - Open the Share and Storage Management console, select a share, and click **Properties**. Click the **Permissions** tab and then click the **NTFS Permissions** button.

2. Click **Advanced**. The Advanced Security Settings dialog box for the selected file or folder appears. This dialog box is as close as the Windows graphical interface can come to displaying the contents of an ACL. Each of the lines in the Permission Entries list is essentially an ACE, and includes the following information:

   - Type—Specifies if the entry allows or denies the permission.

   - Name—Specifies the name of the security principal receiving the permission.

   - Permission—Specifies the name of the standard permission assigned to the security principal. If the entry is used to assign special permissions, the word *Special* appears in this field.

   - Inherited From—Specifies if the permission is inherited and if so, where it is inherited from.

   - Apply To—Specifies if the permission is inherited by subordinate objects and if so, by which ones.

3. Click **Edit**. An editable Advanced Security Settings dialog box appears, as shown in Figure 8-32. This dialog box also contains the following two checkboxes:

   - Include inheritable permissions from this object's parent—Specifies whether the file or folder should inherit permissions from parent objects. This checkbox is selected by default. Deselecting it causes a Windows Security message box to appear, enabling you to choose whether to remove all of the inherited ACEs from the list or copy the inherited permissions from the parents to the file or folder. If you choose the latter, the effective permissions stay the same, but the file or folder is no longer dependent on the parents for permission inheritance. If you change the permissions on the parent objects, the file or folder remains unaffected.

   - Replace all existing inheritable permissions on all descendents with inheritable permissions from this object—Causes subordinate objects to inherit permissions from this file or folder, to the exclusion of all permissions explicitly assigned to the subordinate objects.

Figure 8-32

The editable Advanced Security Settings for docs Folder page

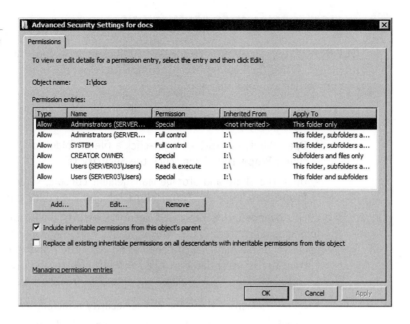

4. Click **Add**. The Select Users, Computers, or Groups dialog box appears.

5. In the **Enter the object names to select** text box, key the name of the user or group you want to add and click **OK**. The Permission Entry dialog box for the user or group appears, as shown in Figure 8-33.

Figure 8-33

The Permission Entry for docs dialog box

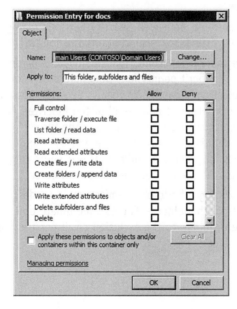

6. In the **Apply To** dropdown list, select which subordinate resources should receive the permissions you assign using this dialog box.

7. In the **Permissions** list, select or clear the checkboxes to **Allow** or **Deny** the user any of the special permissions.

8. Click **OK** four times to close all of the dialog boxes.

CLOSE Windows Explorer or the Share and Storage Management console.

Table 8-5 lists the NTFS special permissions that you can assign to files and folders, and the capabilities that they grant to their possessors.

Table 8-5

NTFS Special Permissions

SPECIAL PERMISSION	FUNCTIONS
Traverse Folder/ Execute File	• The Traverse Folder permission allows or denies security principals the ability to move through folders that they do not have permission to access so that they can reach files or folders that they do have permission to access. This permission applies to folders only. • The Execute File permission allows or denies security principals the ability to run program files. This permission applies to files only.
List Folder/ Read Data	• The List Folder permission allows or denies security principals the ability to view the file and subfolder names within a folder. This permission applies to folders only. • The Read Data permission allows or denies security principals the ability to view the contents of a file. This permission applies to files only.
Read Attributes	Allows or denies security principals the ability to view the NTFS attributes of a file or folder.
Read Extended Attributes	Allows or denies security principals the ability to view the extended attributes of a file or folder.
Create Files/Write Data	• The Create Files permission allows or denies security principals the ability to create files within the folder. This permission applies to folders only. • The Write Data permission allows or denies security principals the ability to modify the file and overwrite existing content. This permission applies to files only.
Create Folders/ Append Data	• The Create Folders permission allows or denies security principals the ability to create subfolders within a folder. This permission applies to folders only. • The Append Data permission allows or denies security principals the ability to add data to the end of the file but not to modify, delete, or overwrite existing data in the file. This permission applies to files only.
Write Attributes	Allows or denies security principals the ability to modify the NTFS attributes of a file or folder.
Write Extended Attributes	Allows or denies security principals the ability to modify the extended attributes of a file or folder.
Delete Subfolders and Files	Allows or denies security principals the ability to delete subfolders and files, even if the Delete permission has not been granted on the subfolder or file.
Delete	Allows or denies security principals the ability to delete the file or folder.
Read Permissions	Allows or denies security principals the ability to read the permissions for the file or folder.
Change Permissions	Allows or denies security principals the ability to modify the permissions for the file or folder.
Take Ownership	Allows or denies security principals the ability to take ownership of the file or folder.
Synchronize	Allows or denies different threads of multithreaded, multiprocessor programs to wait on the handle for the file or folder and synchronize with another thread that might signal it.

As mentioned earlier in this lesson, standard permissions are combinations of special permissions designed to provide frequently needed access controls. Table 8-6 lists all of the standard permissions, and the special permissions that compose them.

Table 8-6

NTFS Standard Permissions and Their Special Permission Equivalents

STANDARD PERMISSIONS	SPECIAL PERMISSIONS
Read	• List Folder/Read Data • Read Attributes • Read Extended Attributes • Read Permissions • Synchronize
Read and Execute	• List Folder/Read Data • Read Attributes • Read Extended Attributes • Read Permissions • Synchronize • Traverse Folder/Execute File
Modify	• Create Files/Write Data • Create Folders/Append Data • Delete • List Folder/Read Data • Read Attributes • Read Extended Attributes • Read Permissions • Synchronize • Write Attributes • Write Extended Attributes
Write	• Create Files/Write Data • Create Folders/Append Data • Read Permissions • Synchronize • Write Attributes • Write Extended Attributes
List Folder Contents	• List Folder/Read Data • Read Attributes • Read Extended Attributes • Read Permissions • Synchronize • Traverse Folder/Execute File

(continued)

Table 8-6 (*continued*)

Standard Permissions	Special Permissions
Full Control	• Change Permissions
	• Create Files/Write Data
	• Create Folders/Append Data
	• Delete
	• Delete Subfolders and Files
	• List Folder/Read Data
	• Read Attributes
	• Read Extended Attributes
	• Read Permissions
	• Synchronize
	• Take Ownership
	• Write Attributes
	• Write Extended Attributes

UNDERSTANDING RESOURCE OWNERSHIP

As you study the NTFS permission system, it might occur to you that it seems possible to lock out a file or folder, that is, to assign a combination of permissions that permits access to no one at all, leaving the file or folder inaccessible. In fact, this is true.

A user with administrative privileges can revoke his or her own permissions, as well as everyone else's, preventing them from accessing a resource. However, the NTFS permissions system includes a "back door" that prevents these orphaned files and folders from remaining permanently inaccessible.

Every file and folder on an NTFS drive has an owner, and the owner always has the ability to modify the permissions for the file or folder, even if the owner has no permissions him- or herself. By default, the owner of a file or folder is the user account that created it. However, any account possessing the Take Ownership special permission (or the Full Control standard permission) can take ownership of the file or folder.

The Administrator user can take ownership of any file or folder, even those from which the previous owner has revoked all of Administrator's permissions. After the Administrator user has taken ownership of a file or folder, the Administrator user cannot assign ownership back to the previous owner. This prevents the Administrator account from accessing other users' files undetected.

The other purpose for file and folder ownership is to calculate disk quotas. When you set quotas specifying the maximum amount of disk space particular users can consume, Windows calculates a user's current disk consumption by adding the sizes of all the files and folders that the user owns.

X REF

For more information on setting file system quotas, see Lesson 5, "Planning File and Print Services."

SUMMARY SKILL MATRIX

IN THIS LESSON YOU LEARNED:

- Before you consider any other security mechanisms, or even operating system and application deployments, you should take steps to ensure that your servers are stored in a location that is physically secure.

- Biometric identification is the process of establishing an individual's identity based on biometric information, essentially asking the system to indicate who the person is.

- A firewall is a software program that protects a computer by allowing certain types of network traffic in and out of the system while blocking others. A firewall is essentially a series of filters that examine the contents of packets and the traffic patterns to and from the network to determine which packets they should allow to pass through the filter.

- The default rules preconfigured into the firewall are designed to admit the traffic used by standard Windows networking functions, such as file and printer sharing. For outgoing network traffic, Windows Firewall allows all traffic to pass the firewall except that which conforms to a rule.

- The Windows Firewall Settings dialog box is designed to enable administrators to create exceptions in the current firewall settings as needed. For full access to the Windows Firewall configuration settings, you must use the Windows Firewall with Advanced Security snap-in for the Microsoft Management console.

- BitLocker Drive Encryption is a new feature, first released in Windows Vista, that makes it possible to encrypt an entire volume.

- When you use Active Directory on an enterprise network, it becomes responsible for two of the most critical security concepts in computing: authentication and authorization.

- On most networks, users identify themselves with an account name or an email address. The proof of identity can vary, however, typically taking one of three forms: something you know, something you have, or something you are.

- To protect data stored on and transmitted over a network, computers use various types of encryption to encode messages and create digital signatures that verify their authenticity. For one computer to encrypt a message and another computer to decrypt it, both must possess a key.

- Windows Server 2008 provides a series of password settings that you can implement using Group Policy, either locally or through Active Directory. An effective combination of password policies compels users to select appropriate passwords and change them at regular intervals.

- Enterprise networks that use Active Directory authenticate their users with the Kerberos authentication protocol.

- Authorization is the process of determining whether an authenticated user is allowed to perform a requested action.

- Files, folders, shares, registry keys, and Active Directory objects are all protected by permissions. To store the permissions, each of these resources has an access control list (ACL). An ACL is a collection of individual permissions, in the form of access control entries (ACEs). Each ACE consists of a security principal (that is, the name of the user, group, or computer granted the permissions) and the specific permissions assigned to that security principal. When you manage permissions in any of the Windows Server 2008 permission systems, you are actually creating and modifying the ACEs in an ACL.

■ Knowledge Assessment

Fill in the Blank

Complete the following exercise by matching the terms with their corresponding definitions.

1. Windows Firewall enables you to create rules that call for the use of IPsec to encapsulate data packets within other packets. This process is called _____.

2. The process of granting users access to file server shares by reading their permissions is called _____.

3. The combination of permissions assigned to a file, plus the permissions inherited from parent folders and group memberships, is called the file's _____ permissions.

4. In the NTFS permission system, _____ permissions are actually combinations of _____ permissions.

5. Kerberos is a _____ authentication method.

6. To use the Windows Firewall control panel to enable traffic for a specific application, you must create a _____.

7. The users, computers, and services to which you assign permissions are also known as _____.

8. The hardware requirements for BitLocker call for either a USB flash drive or a _____.

9. The Advanced Security Settings dialog box displays a list of _____.

10. The software module on an Active Directory domain controller that is primarily responsible for implementing the Kerberos authentication protocol is called the _____.

Multiple Choice

Select one or more correct answers for each of the following questions.

1. Which of the following is the best description of a security principal?
   a. the person granting permissions to network users
   b. the network resource receiving permissions
   c. a collection of individual special permissions
   d. an object that assigns permissions

2. Which of the following is an example of a complex password by Microsoft's definition?
   a. tyia
   b. imsitrjs5itr
   c. passwordpassword
   d. l%@3tty7&

3. Which of the following statements about effective permissions is not true?
   a. Inherited permissions take precedence over explicit permissions.
   b. Deny permissions always override Allow permissions.
   c. When a security principal receives Allow permissions from multiple groups, the permissions are combined to form the effective permissions.
   d. Effective permissions include both permissions inherited from parents and permissions derived from group memberships.

4. Which of the following biometric authentication mechanisms is suitable for verification, but not identification?
   a. fingerprint matching
   b. retinal scans
   c. hand geometry
   d. iris scans

5. Which of the following is the filter criterion most commonly used in firewall rules?
   a. IP addresses
   b. subnet masks
   c. protocol numbers
   d. port numbers

6. Which of the following devices is BitLocker unable to use to store its volume encryption key?
   a. a floppy disk
   b. the system BIOS
   c. a USB flash drive
   d. a trusted platform module

7. Which of the following Group Policy settings prevents users from changing their passwords, and then changing them immediately back again?
   a. Enforce Password History
   b. Maximum Password Age
   c. Password Must Meet Complexity Requirements
   d. Store Passwords Using Reversible Encryption

8. Which of the following statements is not true in reference to resource ownership?
   a. One of the purposes for file and folder ownership is to calculate disk quotas.
   b. Every file and folder on an NTFS driver has an owner.
   c. It is possible for any user possessing the Take Ownership special permission to assume the ownership of a file or folder.
   d. It is possible to lock out a file or folder by assigning a combination of permissions that permits access to no one at all, including the owner of the file or folder.

9. Which of the following statements about public key encryption are true?
   a. Data encrypted with the public key can be decrypted only with the public key.
   b. Data encrypted with the public key can be decrypted only with the private key.
   c. Data encrypted with the private key can only be decrypted using the private key.
   d. Data encrypted with the private key can be decrypted only using the public key.

10. Which of the following statements about permissions are true?
    a. ACLs are composed of ACEs.
    b. Standard permissions are composed of special permissions.
    c. All permissions are stored as part of the protected resource.
    d. All of the above.

Review Questions

1. Is showing your identification to prove that you are old enough to purchase a pack of cigarettes an example of authentication or authorization? Explain your answer.

2. Is showing your identification to a cashier to verify that the credit card you are using belongs to you an example of authentication or authorization? Explain your answer.

■ Case Scenarios

Scenario 8-1: Assigning Permissions

While you are working the help desk for a corporate network, a user named Leo calls to request access to the files for Trinity, a new classified project. The Trinity files are stored in a shared folder on a file server, which is locked in a secured underground data storage facility in New Mexico. After verifying that he has the appropriate security clearance for the project, you create a new group on the file server called TRINITY_USERS and add Leo's user account to that group. Then, you add the TRINITY_USER group to the access control list for the Trinity folder on the file server, and assign the group the following NTFS permissions:
- Allow Modify
- Allow Read & Execute
- Allow List Folder Contents
- Allow Read
- Allow Write

Some time later, Leo calls you to tell you that he is able to access the Trinity folder and read the files stored there, but he has been unable to save changes back to the server. What is the most likely cause of the problem?

Scenario 8-2: Accessing Orphaned Files

Libby, a new hire in the IT department, approaches you, her supervisor, ashen-faced. A few minutes earlier, the president of the company called the help desk and asked Libby to give his new assistant the permissions needed to access his personal budget spreadsheet. As she was attempting to assign the permissions, she accidentally deleted the BUDGET_USERS group from the spreadsheet's access control list. Libby is terrified because that group was the only entry in the file's ACL. Now, no one can access the spreadsheet file, not even the president or the Administrator account. Is there any way to gain access to the file, and if so, how?

Securing Infrastructure Services

OBJECTIVE DOMAIN MATRIX

TECHNOLOGY SKILL	OBJECTIVE DOMAIN	OBJECTIVE DOMAIN NUMBER
Securing Remote Access	Monitor and maintain security and policies	3.3
Using Certificates	Plan infrastructure services server roles	1.3

KEY TERMS

autoenrollment
certificate revocation list (CRL)
certificate templates
certification authority (CA)
Challenge Handshake
  Authentication Protocol
  (CHAP)
Cryptographic Service Provider
  (CSP)
delta CRLs
digital certificate
enrollment
enterprise CA
exit module
Extensible Authentication
  Protocol (EAP)

Extensible Authentication
  Protocol-Transport Level
  Security (EAP-TLS)
intermediate CAs
issuing CAs
Layer 2 Tunneling Protocol
  (L2TP)
Microsoft Challenge
  Handshake Authentication
  Protocol Version 2 (MS-
  CHAPv2)
Password Authentication
  Protocol (PAP)
Point-to-Point Protocol (PPP)
Point-to-Point Tunneling

Protocol (PPTP)
policy module
Protected EAP (PEAP)
public key infrastructure (PKI)
Remote Authentication Dial In
  User Service (RADIUS)
Secure Socket Tunneling
  Protocol (SSTP)
standalone CA
root CA
subordinate CAs
trust chaining
virtual private network (VPN)
Web enrollment

Lesson 8, "Planning Server and Network Security," discussed some of the basic security principles of concern to Windows Server 2008 administrators and described how to configure some of its security mechanisms. This lesson examines some of the infrastructure security mechanisms in Windows Server 2008, including the following:

- Remote access security
- Digital certificates

■ Securing Remote Access

↓ **THE BOTTOM LINE**

The Kerberos authentication mechanism discussed in Lesson 8 is for clients on the local network, clients that have access to Active Directory domain controllers. Users that connect to the network from offsite, such as travelers and telecommuters, cannot use Kerberos. Windows Server 2008 provides remote access capabilities, as part of its Network Policy and Access Services role, which enable users to connect to the network using dial-up or virtual private network (VPN) connections.

CERTIFICATION READY?
Monitor and maintain security and policies
3.3

When you install Remote Access, you are essentially converting the Windows Server 2008 computer into a router. Clients at remote locations connect to the server using modem or Internet connections and, after authenticating them, the server provides the clients with access to its local resources and to the internal network. With a Remote Access connection, users can access their server-based files and network applications from home or from the road.

Understanding Remote Access Connectivity

Windows Server 2008 Remote Access supports two types of remote client connections: dial-up, which typically uses standard asynchronous modems and telephone lines, and VPN, which uses the Internet as the medium connecting the client to the remote access server.

The first step in planning a Remote Access solution for an enterprise network is to decide which of these connection types you plan to use. To use dial-up connections, you must equip your Windows Server 2008 computer with at least one modem and telephone line. For a single-user connection, as for an administrator dialing in from home, a standard off-the-shelf modem is suitable. For multiple connections, there are modular rack-mount modems available that enable you to connect dozens of users at once, if necessary.

➕ **MORE INFORMATION**

The data-link and network layers that this description refers to are two of the seven layers defined by the Open System Interconnection (OSI) reference model. The OSI model is a theoretical construction that defines the various functions required for data network communications. The seven layers, in order from top to bottom, are application, presentation, session, transport, network, data-link, and physical. Together, the seven protocols that implement the functions defined by the seven layers are called a protocol stack.

In the real world, however, hardware and telephone costs and the near-ubiquity of high-speed Internet connections have caused dial-up remote connections to be almost entirely replaced by VPN connections.

UNDERSTANDING VIRTUAL PRIVATE NETWORKING

A dial-up connection is a dedicated link between two modems that remains in place during the entire session, as shown in Figure 9-1. The client and the server establish a *Point-to-Point Protocol (PPP)* connection, during which the server authenticates the client and the computers negotiate a set of communication parameters they have in common. PPP takes the place of the Ethernet protocol at the data-link layer, by encapsulating the datagrams created by the Internet Protocol (IP) at the network layer, to prepare them for their transmission. PPP is much simpler than Ethernet because the two computers are using a dedicated connection, and there is no need to address each packet to a particular destination, as they must do on a local area network (LAN).

Figure 9-1

A dial-up remote access connection

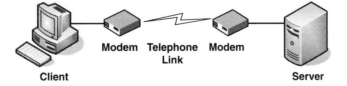

In a ***virtual private network (VPN)*** connection, the remote client and the remote access server are both connected to the Internet, using local service providers, as shown in Figure 9-2. This eliminates the expense of long distance telephone charges common to dial-up connections, as well as the additional hardware expense, since both computers most likely have Internet connections already. The client establishes a connection to the server using the Internet as a network medium and, after authentication, the server grants the client access to the network.

Figure 9-2

A VPN remote access connection

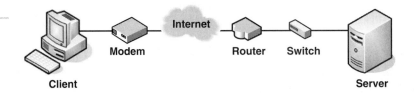

While it is theoretically possible for someone to tap into the telephone line used by a dial-up connection, intercept the analog signals exchanged by the two modems, convert them into digital data packets, and access the data, it is not likely to occur and remote connections are almost never compromised in this manner. Therefore, the data transmitted during a dial-up connection is considered to be relatively secure.

A VPN is another matter, however, because the client and the server transmit their data over the Internet, which makes the data packets accessible to anyone with the equipment needed to capture them. For this reason, VPN clients and servers use a specialized protocol when establishing a connection, which encapsulates their data packets inside another packet, a process called tunneling. The VPN protocol establishes a virtual connection, or tunnel, between the client and the server, which encrypts data encapsulated inside.

In the tunneling process, the two computers establish a PPP connection, just as they would in a dial-up connection, but instead of transmitting the PPP packets over the Internet as they are, they encapsulate the packets again using one of the three VPN protocols supported by Windows Server 2008. As shown in Figure 9-3, the original PPP data packet generated by the computer consists of a network layer IP datagram, encapsulated within a data-link layer PPP frame. The system then encapsulates the entire frame in another IP datagram, which the VPN protocol encrypts and encapsulates one more time, for transmission over the network.

Figure 9-3

VPN protocol encapsulation

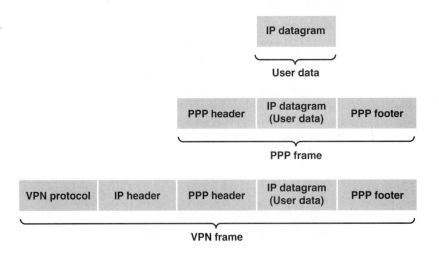

Having a data-link layer frame inside a network layer datagram is a violation of the OSI model's most basic principles, but this is what makes tunneling an effective carrier mechanism for private data transmitted over a public network. Intruders can intercept the transmitted packets, but they cannot decrypt the inner PPP frame, which prevents them from obtaining any of the information inside.

The VPN protocols that Windows Server 2008 supports are as follows:

- *Point-to-Point Tunneling Protocol (PPTP)*—The oldest of the VPN protocols, PPTP takes advantage of the authentication, compression, and encryption mechanisms of PPP, tunneling the PPP frame within a Generic Routing Encapsulation (GRE) header and encrypting it with Microsoft Point-to-Point Encryption (MPPE), using encryption keys generated during the authentication process. PPTP therefore can provide data protection, but not other services, such as packet origin identification or data integrity checking. For authentication, PPTP supports only the Microsoft Challenge Handshake Authentication Protocol version 1 (MS-CHAP v1), Microsoft Challenge Handshake Authentication Protocol version 2 (MS-CHAP v2), Extensible Authentication Protocol (EAP), or Protected Extensible Authentication Protocol (PEAP). Although it can use them (with EAP), one of the advantages of PPTP is that it does not require the use of certificates. In most cases, organizations use PPTP as a fallback protocol for clients running non-Windows operating systems.

- *Layer 2 Tunneling Protocol (L2TP)*—L2TP relies on the IP security extensions (IPsec) for encryption, and as a result performs a double encapsulation. The system adds an L2DP header to the PPP frame and packages it with the User Datagram Protocol (UDP). Then it encapsulates the UDP datagram with the IPsec Encapsulating Security Payload (ESP) protocol, encrypting the contents using the Data Encryption Standard (DES) or Triple DES (3DES) algorithm, with encryption keys generated during IPsec's Internet Key Exchange (IKE) negotiation process. L2TP/IPsec can use certificates or preshared keys for authentication, although administrators typically use the latter only for testing. The end result is that the L2TP/IPsec combination provides a more complete set of services than PPTP, including packet origin identification, data integrity checking, and replay protection. For VPN connections involving Windows XP clients, L2TP/IPsec is the preferred protocol.

- *Secure Socket Tunneling Protocol (SSTP)*—New to Windows Server 2008 and supported only by clients running Windows Vista with Service Pack 1, SSTP encapsulates PPP traffic using the Secure Sockets Layer (SSL) protocol supported by virtually all Web servers. The advantage of this is that administrators do not have to open an additional external port in the server, as SSTP uses the same TCP port 443 as SSL. SSTP uses certificates for authentication, with the EAP-TLS authentication protocol, and in addition to data encryption, provides integrity checking and enhanced key negotiation services.

CHOOSING A REMOTE ACCESS SOLUTION

There are many factors to consider when choosing between dial-up and VPN connections for remote access. Obviously, administrators must compare the upfront and ongoing costs for each solution. VPN access often has a significant cost advantage because implementing a dial-up access solution on a large scale requires the purchase of modem equipment and the leasing of circuits from a telecommunications provider, while VPN access uses the Internet connection that is probably already in place. Although it might be necessary to upgrade the Internet connection to provide sufficient bandwidth for the VPN clients, the cost will almost certainly be lower than building a dial-up infrastructure.

Administrators must also compare the security levels of the two access methods. Many people assume that dial-up access provides greater security than a VPN connection. After all, the idea of allowing clients on the public Internet to access your internal network sounds extremely risky. However, if you analyze the security risks point-by-point, dial-up and VPN access are similar.

- Attackers can methodically identify both dial-up and VPN ports on remote access servers. If attackers want to find an organization's dial-up ports, they use a *war dialer*, which is a program that instructs a modem to dial a given range of telephone numbers in sequence, searching for the handshake tones that indicate the presence of other modems. If attackers want to find VPN ports, they use a *port scanner*, which is a program that sends transmissions to a range of IP addresses and port numbers, searching for the responses that identify the ports that are listening for incoming VPN client connections.

- Once an attacker has identified an organization's dial-up or VPN ports, the next step is to try to authenticate to the remote access server. Dial-up and VPN remote access servers use the same assortment of authentication protocols. However, because of the modem connection delays involved, attackers can send requests to a VPN server faster than they can to a dial-up server. Therefore, dial-up servers have a bit of a security advantage here because their long connection times make them less vulnerable to brute-force attacks.

- Because dial-up servers need not be accessible from the Internet, they are not vulnerable to attack from that avenue. However, dial-up servers are often located behind the network's firewall, so they present a greater risk to the network if intruders do manage to access them.

- Regardless of whether an organization uses dial-up or VPN connections for remote access, it is difficult for an attacker to eavesdrop on a client's traffic. Gaining access either to an ISP or a public telephone provider is not a simple matter. It is much easier for an attacker to eavesdrop on traffic at either end of the remote access connection by installing a protocol analyzer on the remote access client or server.

When you consider these factors, the end result is that VPN servers and dial-up servers present similar security risks, but VPN servers are significantly less expensive to implement and maintain. In the real world, administrators are better off using a VPN and spending the money they save on other security initiatives—such as smart card authentication or an intrusion detection system to detect brute-force attacks against the VPN server.

AUTHENTICATING REMOTE USERS

Remote Access in Windows Server 2008 uses an authentication system that is entirely separate from the Kerberos authentication system that clients on the local network use. However, authentication is even more important for remote access clients than for local ones, because of the increased likelihood of intrusion.

All remote access connections, whether dial-up or VPN, use PPP to package their data, and the PPP connection establishment process includes a sequence in which the client and the server negotiate the use of a specific authentication protocol. In this sequence, each computer sends a list of the authentication protocols it supports to the other, and the two then agree to use the strongest protocol they have in common.

The authentication protocols supported by Windows Server 2008, in order from strongest to weakest, are as follows:

- *Extensible Authentication Protocol (EAP)*—EAP is a shell protocol that provides a framework for the use of various types of authentication mechanisms. The primary advantage of EAP is that it enables a computer to use mechanisms other than passwords for authentication, including public key certificates and smart cards, as well as providing an extensible environment for third-party authentication mechanisms. Windows Server 2008 supports two EAP methods:

  ○ *Protected EAP (PEAP)*—The primary function of PEAP is to use Transport Level Security (TLS) to create an encrypted channel between a wireless client and an authentication server. The use of PEAP is not supported for remote access clients.

  ○ Smart Card or other certificate—Also known as *Extensible Authentication Protocol-Transport Level Security (EAP-TLS),* this method enables the server to support authentication with smart cards or other types of digital certificates. To use EAP-TLS, you must obtain and install a certificate on the remote access server and configure both the server and the client to use smart card authentication. This is the strongest authentication method supported by Windows Server 2008 Remote Access.

• Microsoft Encrypted Authentication Version 2 (MS-CHAPv2)—because it uses a new encryption key for each connection and for each direction in which data is transmitted, *Microsoft Challenge Handshake Authentication Protocol Version 2 (MS-CHAPv2)* is the strongest password-based authentication method supported by Windows Server 2008 Remote Access, and is selected by default. MS-CHAPv2 supports mutual authentication of clients and servers, as well as encryption of both authentication and connection data.

• Encrypted Authentication (CHAP)—The non-Microsoft version of the *Challenge Handshake Authentication Protocol (CHAP)* uses MD5 hashing to encrypt user passwords, but it does not support the encryption of connection data, and the passwords it uses must be stored in a reversibly encrypted format. As a result, CHAP provides relatively weak protection when compared to MS-CHAPv2. Windows Server 2008 does not select CHAP by default, and supports it only to provide compatibility with non-Microsoft clients.

• Unencrypted Password (PAP)—The *Password Authentication Protocol (PAP)* is the least secure of the authentication protocols supported by Windows Server 2008 because it uses simple passwords for authentication, and transmits them in clear text. The advantage of PAP is that it requires no special technology, and virtually every operating system and remote access software product supports it. The disadvantage is that anyone capturing the packets transmitted during the authentication process can read the user's account name password and use it to gain access to the network. In Windows Server 2008 Remote Access, PAP is disabled by default, and its use is strongly discouraged for all connections that can use a more capable authentication protocol.

• Unauthenticated access—Windows Server 2008 also supports unauthenticated access, in which the systems use no authentication protocol at all, and the client does not have to supply a user name or password. Obviously, no authentication is the weakest form of authentication available, and should be used only when there is some other security mechanism in place or when the administrator wants to allow anyone to connect to the server.

Installing Remote Access

To configure a Windows Server 2008 computer to function as a Remote Access server, you must install the Network Policy and Access Services (NPAS) role and configure the Routing and Remote Access Services (RRAS).

Unlike earlier versions of Windows, Windows Server incorporates Routing and Remote Access Services into the larger Network Policy and Access Services role and subdivides RRAS into two separate role services: Remote Access and Routing. As a result, you can configure a Windows Server 2008 computer to function as a Remote Access server, independent of the routing function.

To install the Network Policy and Access Services role, use the following procedure.

 INSTALL THE NETWORK POLICY AND ACCESS SERVICES ROLE

GET READY. Log on to Windows Server 2008 using an account with administrative privileges. When the logon process is completed, close the Initial Configuration Tasks window and any other windows that appear.

1. Click **Start,** and then click **Administrative Tools** > **Server Manager.** The Server Manager console appears.

2. Select the **Roles** node and, in the details pane, click **Add Roles.** The Add Roles Wizard appears.

3. Click **Next** to bypass the *Before You Begin* page. The *Select Server Roles* page appears, as shown in Figure 9-4.

Figure 9-4

The Select Server Roles page of the Add Roles Wizard

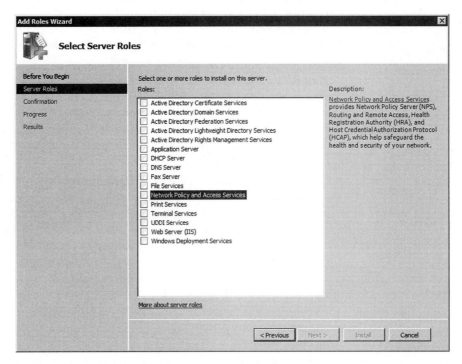

4. Select the **Network Policy and Access Services** checkbox and click **Next.** The *Introduction to Network Policy and Access Services* page appears.

5. Click **Next** to bypass the *Introduction to Network Policy and Access Services* page. The *Select Role Services* page appears, as shown in Figure 9-5.

Figure 9-5

The Select Role Services page of the Add Roles Wizard

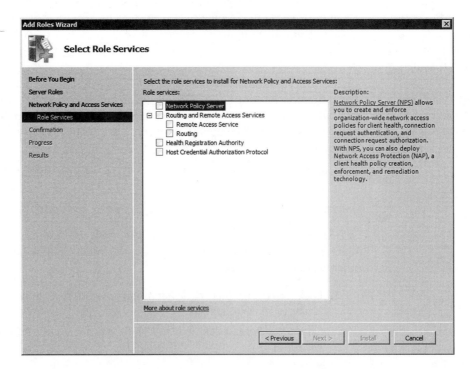

6. Select the **Remote Access Service** checkbox and click **Next.** The *Confirm Installation Selections* page appears.

7. Click **Install.** When the installation is complete, click **Close.**

CLOSE the Server Manager console.

At this point, the Network Policy and Access Services role is installed, but RRAS is not yet running. You must configure RRAS and start the service before the computer can begin to service clients.

CONFIGURING ROUTING AND REMOTE ACCESS

To use Windows Server 2008 as a Remote Access server, you must configure Routing and Remote Access Services, using the following procedure.

 CONFIGURE ROUTING AND REMOTE ACCESS

GET READY. Log on to Windows Server 2008 using an account with administrative privileges. When the logon process is completed, close the Initial Configuration Tasks window and any other windows that appear.

1. Click **Start**, and then click **Administrative Tools** > **Routing and Remote Access.** The Routing and Remote Access console appears, as shown in Figure 9-6.

Figure 9-6

The Routing and Remote Access console

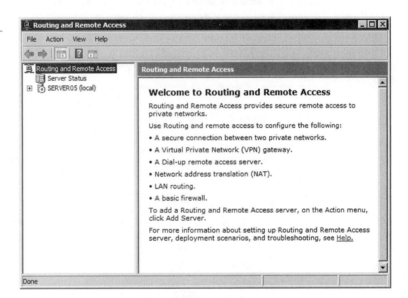

2. Right-click the node representing your server and, on the context menu, click **Configure and Enable Routing and Remote Access.** The Routing and Remote Access Server Setup Wizard appears.

3. Click **Next** to bypass the Welcome page. The *Configuration* page appears, as shown in Figure 9-7.

Figure 9-7

The Configuration page of the Routing and Remote Access Server Setup Wizard

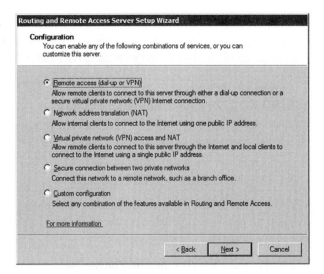

4. Leave the **Remote access (dial-up or VPN)** option selected and click **Next.** The *Remote Access* page appears, as shown in Figure 9-8.

Figure 9-8

The Remote Access page of the Routing and Remote Access Server Setup Wizard

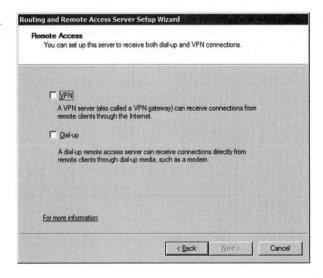

5. Select one or both of the checkboxes to configure the server for VPN and/or dial-up access, and then click **Next.** If you selected the **VPN** option, the *VPN Connection* page appears. If you selected only the **Dial-up** option, the *Network Selection* page appears.

6. On the *VPN Connection* page, shown in Figure 9-9, select the network interface that provides the Internet connection, over which the VPN clients will connect to the server. Leave the **Enable Security On The Selected Interface By Setting Up Static Packet Filters** checkbox selected, unless you want other types of traffic to be able to access the server from the Internet.

Figure 9-9

The VPN Connection page of the Routing and Remote Access Server Setup Wizard

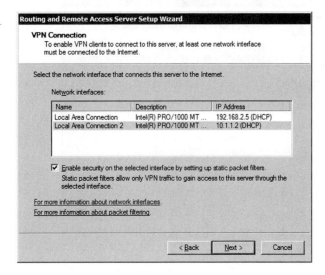

7. On the *Network Selection* page, select the interface that you want the dial-up clients to use to access the network.

8. Click **Next.** The *IP Address Assignment* page appears, as shown in Figure 9-10.

Figure 9-10

The IP Address Assignment page of the Routing and Remote Access Server Setup Wizard

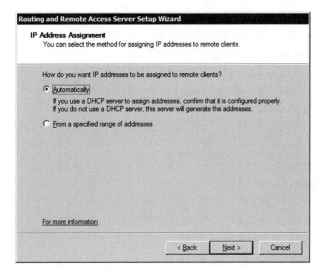

9. Select the **Automatically** option to use the DHCP server on your network to assign IP addresses to remote access clients. Selecting From A Specified Range Of Addresses adds an *Address Range Assignment* page to the wizard, as shown in Figure 9-11, in which you can specify the IP addresses the server should assign to the clients.

Figure 9-11

The Address Range Assignment page of the Routing and Remote Access Server Setup Wizard

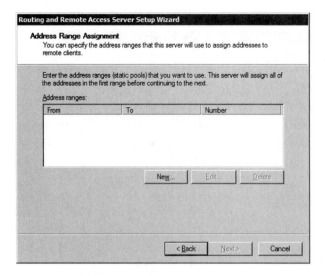

10. Click **Next.** The *Managing Multiple Remote Access Servers* page appears, as shown in Figure 9-12.

Figure 9-12

The Managing Multiple Remote Access Servers page of the Routing and Remote Access Server Setup Wizard

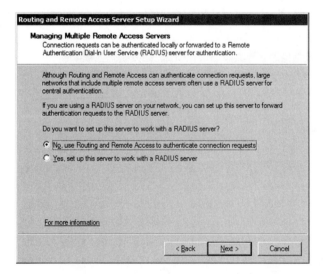

11. Leave the **No, use Routing and Remote Access to authenticate connection requests** option selected to configure the server to authenticate clients. If you have a RADIUS server in your network, select the **Yes, set up this server to work with a RADIUS server** option.

12. Click **Next.** The *Completing the Routing and Remote Access Server Setup Wizard* page appears.

13. Click **Finish.** The wizard configures Routing and Remote Access and starts the service.

CLOSE the Routing and Remote Access console.

Once you have completed this configuration process, the RRAS service starts, and the computer is ready to service clients.

CONFIGURING REMOTE ACCESS AUTHENTICATION

Routing and Remote Access has a great many settings you can alter, once the service is operational. To specify which authentication protocols you want your Remote Access server to support, use the following procedure.

 CONFIGURE REMOTE ACCESS AUTHENTICATION

GET READY. Log on to Windows Server 2008 using an account with administrative privileges. When the logon process is completed, close the Initial Configuration Tasks window and any other windows that appear.

1. Click **Start,** and then click **Administrative Tools > Routing and Remote Access.** The Routing and Remote Access console appears.

2. Right-click the node representing your server and, on the context menu, click **Properties.** The server's Properties sheet appears.

3. Click the **Security** tab, as shown in Figure 9-13.

Figure 9-13

The Security tab of a Remote Access server's Properties sheet

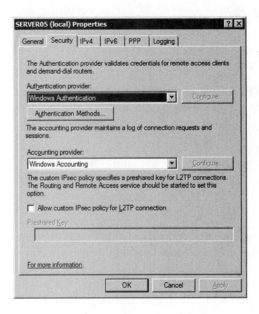

4. Leave the **Windows Authentication** option selected in the **Authentication Provider** dropdown list and click **Authentication Methods.** The Authentication Methods dialog box appears, as shown in Figure 9-14.

Figure 9-14

The Authentication Methods dialog box

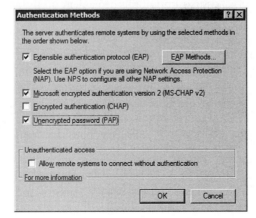

5. Select the checkboxes for the authentication methods you want to enable on the Remote Access server and click **OK.**

6. Click **OK** to close the server's Properties sheet.

CLOSE the Routing and Remote Access console.

When negotiating a PPP connection with a client, the Remote Access server will attempt to use each of the authentication methods listed in the Authentication Methods dialog box in turn until it finds one that is also supported by the client. If the server and the client do not have any authentication methods in common (and the server is configured to deny unauthenticated access), the server denies the client a connection.

Using Certificates

THE BOTTOM LINE

In Lesson 8, "Planning Server and Network Security," you learned how public key encryption uses two keys, one public and one private, to provide digital signing and data encryption services. Windows Server 2008 relies heavily on this ***public key infrastructure (PKI)*** for many of its security mechanisms.

CERTIFICATION READY?
Plan infrastructure
services server roles
1.3

There is one important question about the PKI that we have not yet addressed, and that is the distribution of the public keys. For the system to be truly secure, there must be some way to confirm that the public keys being distributed actually belong to the individual they purport to identify.

If you receive an email from Alice that has been encrypted using your public key, the fact that you can decrypt it using your private key confirms that no one has intercepted the message and read its contents. But how do you know that it actually came from Alice, when your public key is freely available to anyone? For that matter, what is there to stop someone from issuing a public key in your name, causing people to send messages intended for you to someone else?

One of the most common answers to these questions is digital certificates. A ***digital certificate*** is a digitally signed document, issued by a third party called a ***certification authority (CA),*** that binds a user, computer, or service holding a private key with its corresponding public key. When both parties involved in a transaction trust the CA to properly authenticate users before handing out certificates, and believe that the CA protects the privacy of its certificates and keys, then they can both trust in the identity of the certificate holder.

Understanding Certificates

The trustworthiness of the CA is a critical element of a certificate's usefulness, and the selection of the CA that will issue certificates is dependent on the application that requires them.

For example, suppose Litware, Inc. wants to run Remote Access servers to enable its employees to telecommute from home, using EAP-TLS authentication. To use EAP-TLS, both the clients and the Remote Access servers must have certificates, and in this case, the organization could create its own CA and issue its own certificates by installing the Active Directory Certificate Services role on a Windows Server 2008 computer. This is an acceptable solution in this case because the internal CA is trusted by both the clients and the servers.

However, consider another scenario in which Litware wants to distribute an ActiveX control to Internet users through its Web site. The users on the Internet would understandably want to confirm that the software is indeed coming Litware, so they expect the software to be digitally signed using a certificate. Litware could conceivably use its own CA to issue the certificate for the software, but the users would be foolish to accept them. What good is an affirmation of identity that comes from the party whose identity you are trying to affirm? Anyone could install their own CA using the name Litware, and digitally sign any piece of software they want.

The key to using certificates is for both parties to trust the CA, so in this case, the certificates must come from a third party that both the client and the server trust. In most cases, this means that Litware must contact one of the commercial certification authorities, such as VeriSign, Inc., to obtain a certificate for its software. They pay a fee to the CA, and use the certificate to digitally sign the software. The clients accessing the Litware Web site are then informed, before they download the software, that it is digitally signed by VeriSign. Recognizing and trusting the VeriSign name, the user then proceed with the download.

UNDERSTANDING CERTIFICATE FUNCTIONS

Digital certificates can perform a variety of functions, including the following:

- Digital signatures—Certificates can confirm that the individual sending a message, file, or other data is actually the person he or she claims to be. Digital signatures do not protect the data itself from compromise, they only verify the identity of the sender.

- Encrypting File System (EFS) user and recovery certificates—EFS enables users to store data on disk in encrypted form, to prevent other users from accessing it. To prevent a loss of data resulting from users leaving the organization or losing their encryption keys, EFS allows designated recovery agents to create public keys that can decode the encrypted information. As with IPsec, EFS does not have to use the PKI for its encryption keys, but the use of a PKI simplifies the implementation of EFS.

- Internet authentication—You can use the PKI to authenticate clients and servers as they establish connections over the Internet. This enables servers to identify the clients connecting to them and enables clients to confirm that they are connecting to the correct servers.

- IP Security (IPsec)—The IP Security extensions enable you to encrypt and digitally sign communications, to prevent intruders from compromising them as they are transmitted over a network. The Windows Server 2008 IPsec implementation does not have to use a PKI to obtain its encryption keys, but you can use the PKI for this purpose.

- Secure email—Internet email protocols transmit mail messages in plain text, making it relatively easy to intercept them and read their contents. With a PKI, you can secure email communications by encrypting the actual message text using the recipient's public key, and you can digitally sign the messages using your private key.

- Smart card logon—Windows Server 2008 can use a smart card as an authentication device that verifies the identity of a user during logon. The smart card contains the user's certificate and private key, enabling the user to log on to any workstation in the enterprise securely.

- Software code signing—Microsoft's Authenticode is one technology that uses certificates to confirm that the software user's download and install actually come from the publisher and have not been modified.

- Wireless network authentication—The increasing popularity of wireless local area networking (WLAN) technologies, such as those based on the 802.11 standards, raises an important security issue. When you install a WLAN, you must make sure only authorized users can connect to the network and that no one can eavesdrop on the wireless communications. You can use the Windows Server 2008 PKI to protect a wireless network by identifying and authenticating users before they are granted access to the network.

UNDERSTANDING CERTIFICATE COMPONENTS

Digital certificates carry information about their functions and capabilities in a variety of fields, including the following:

- Version—Identifies the version of the X.509 standard used to format the certificate
- Serial number—Specifies a value assigned by the CA that uniquely identifies the certificate
- Signature algorithm—Specifies the algorithm that the CA used to calculate the certificate's digital signature
- Issuer—Specifies the name of the entity that issued the certificate
- Valid from—Specifies the beginning of the period during which the certificate is valid
- Valid to—Specifies the end of the period during which the certificate is valid
- Subject—Specifies the name of the entity for which the certificate is issued
- Public key—Specifies the type and length of the public key associated with the certificate
- Enhanced key usage—Specifies the functions for which the certificate can be used
- Key usage—Specifies additional functions for which the certificate can be used
- Thumbprint algorithm—Specifies the algorithm used to generate a digest of the certificate data
- Thumbprint—Contains a digest of the certificate data, used for digital signing
- Friendly name—Specifies a common name for the entity listed in the Subject field
- Certificate policies—Describes the policy that the CA followed to originally authenticate the subject
- CRL distribution points—Specifies the location of the *certificate revocation list (CRL),* a document maintained and published by a CA that lists certificates that have been revoked

> **TAKE NOTE** *
>
> Not every certificate has all of the fields listed here. The information within a given certificate is based on its origin and its intended purpose.

To view the information in a certificate's fields in Windows Server 2008, you must open it in the Certificates snap-in for Microsoft Management Console (MMC). There is no shortcut to the Certificates snap-in in the Start menu. You must open a blank MMC console and add the Certificates snap-in to it. When you do this, you have to specify the focus of the snap-in as the current user's account, a computer account, or a service account. When you select the current user account option, the snap-in creates an interface like the one shown in Figure 9-15.

Figure 9-15

The Certificates snap-in

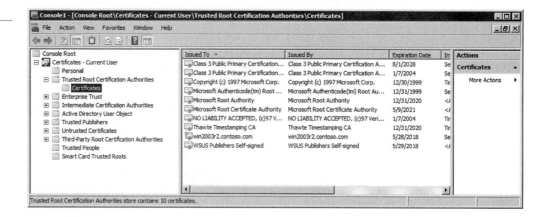

When you double-click one of the certificates listed in the console, a Certificate dialog box appears, containing the following tabs:

• General—Displays a list of the functions the certificate is capable of performing, plus the issuer, the recipient, and the dates of validity, as shown in Figure 9-16

Figure 9-16

The General tab in a Certificates dialog box

• Details—Displays the values for all of the certificate's fields, as shown in Figure 9-17

Figure 9-17

The Details tab in a Certificates dialog box

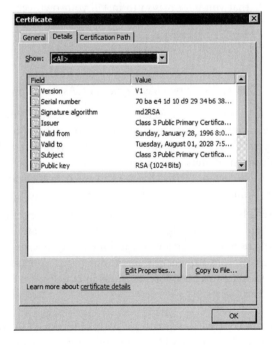

- Certification Path—Contains a tree display of the certificate's issuing CA, and all of its trusted certification authorities leading back to the root, as shown in Figure 9-18

Figure 9-18

The Certification Path tab in a Certificates dialog box

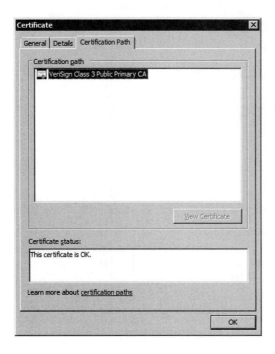

Planning a CA Deployment

After you decide that you have reason to install your own certification authorities, there are a number of decisions you must make to ensure that the CAs you install can perform the tasks you require from them.

Windows Server 2008 supports two basic types of CAs, as follows:

- *Enterprise CA*—Enterprise CAs are integrated into the Windows Server 2008 Active Directory environment. They use certificate templates, publish their certificates and CRLs to Active Directory, and use the information in Active Directory to approve or deny certificate enrollment requests automatically. Because the clients of an enterprise CA must have access to Active Directory to receive certificates, enterprise CAs are not suitable for issuing certificates to clients outside the enterprise.

- *Standalone CA*—Standalone CAs do not use certificate templates or Active Directory; they store their information locally. In addition, by default, standalone CAs do not automatically respond to certificate enrollment requests, as is the case with enterprise CAs. Requests wait in a queue for an administrator to manually approve or deny them. Standalone CAs are intended for situations in which users outside the enterprise submit requests for certificates.

In addition, you can configure each enterprise or standalone CA to function as either a root CA or a subordinate CA. The first CA you install in your organization must always be a root CA. A *root CA* is the parent that issues certificates to the *subordinate CAs* beneath it. If a client trusts the root CA, it must also trust all the subordinate CAs that have been issued certificates by the root CA. The certification path included in every certificate traces the hierarchy from the issuing CA up through any additional CAs to the root.

Every CA must have a certificate of its own, which authorizes it to issue certificates. Root CAs are the only CAs that do not have a certificate issued by a higher authority. A root CA issues its own self-signed certificate, which functions as the top of the certificate chain for all the certificates issued by all the CAs subordinate to the root. When you install a subordinate CA, you must specify the name of a parent CA, which will issue a certificate to the subordinate. The parent does not have to be the root CA.

Because the root CA is the ultimate seat of trust in the public key infrastructure, its security is crucial. If the root CA is compromised, then all of the certificates it issues and all of the certificates issued by the subordinate CAs are compromised as well. For this reason, many administrators install a root CA solely for the purpose of issuing certificates to subordinate CAs, and then shut it down and physically secure it for its own protection, leaving the task of issuing end-user certificates to the subordinates.

> **TAKE NOTE***
>
> The increasing use of server virtualization in the enterprise has made this root protection strategy less costly, and more appealing. You can create a Windows Server 2008 virtual machine, configure it as your root CA, and shut the root CA virtual machine down. Then you can use the computer to run other virtual machines, and activate the root CA only when you need it.

Depending on the size and layout of the organization, you might decide to create many CAs, in multiple levels and in different locations. If your organization has multiple sites, you might decide to create a CA in each office, to give users local access to new certificates, just as you can do with domain controllers. You might also create separate CAs to perform different functions.

As a result of these options, there are four different types of CAs that you can create on a Windows Server 2008 computer:

- Enterprise root
- Enterprise subordinate
- Standalone root
- Standalone subordinate

DETERMINING THE CERTIFICATE LIFE CYCLE

Certificate holders cannot continue to use the same certificates indefinitely. The longer a certificate remains in use, the more time attackers have to work on penetrating the corresponding private key. Certificates have a predefined life cycle and expire at the end of this life cycle. Administrators exercise control over certificates; they can extend the lifetime of a certificate by renewing it, or end the usefulness of a certificate before the expiration date by revoking it.

Administrators should consider a number of factors when choosing the length of a certificate's lifetime, such as the type of certificate, the security requirements of the organization, the standard practices in the industry, and government regulations. In general, using longer encryption keys makes it possible to have longer certificate lifetimes and key lifetimes. Using longer certificate lifetimes reduces administrative overhead, which in turn reduces costs.

When planning certificate and key lifetimes, administrators must consider how vulnerable the keys are to compromise and what the potential consequences of their compromise are. The following factors can influence the lifetimes that an administrator chooses for certificates and keys:

- The length of private keys for certificates—Because longer keys are more difficult to break, they justify longer safe key lifetimes.
- The security of the CAs and their private keys—In general, the more secure the CA and its private key, the longer the safe certificate lifetime. CAs that are kept offline and stored in locked vaults or data centers are the most secure.

- The strength of the technology used for cryptographic operations—In general, stronger cryptographic technology supports longer key lifetimes. You can extend key lifetimes if you enhance private key storage by using smart cards and other hardware-based cryptographic service providers. Some cryptographic technologies provide stronger security, in addition to support for stronger cryptographic algorithms.

- The vulnerability of the CA certification chain—In general, the more vulnerable your CA hierarchy is to attack, the longer the CA private keys should be and the shorter the key lifetimes.

- The users of your certificates—Organizations typically trust their own employees more than they trust employees of other organizations. If you issue certificates to external users, you might want to shorten the lifetimes of those certificates to reduce the time window during which an individual can abuse a compromised private key.

- The number of certificates that have been signed by a dedicated CA—The wider the distribution of the public key that a CA uses to sign its issued certificates, the more vulnerable it becomes to attempts to break its private key.

A CA defines an expiration date for each certificate it issues. An enterprise CA issues certificates with lifetimes that are based on the certificate template for the requested certificate type.

PLANNING CA VALIDITY PERIODS

Because a CA must have a certificate of its own to operate—either self-issued, in the case of a root CA, or issued by a parent—the expiration of the CA's certificate causes the CA itself to expire. This also means that the expiration date of a CA's certificate is more important to the continued function of the PKI than those of other certificates. In addition, a CA cannot issue certificates with expiration dates that are valid beyond the expiration date of its own certificate. Therefore, when a CA's certificate reaches the end of its validity period, all of the certificates it has ever issued also expire. Because of this, if you deliberately do not renew a CA's certificate, you can be assured that all the certificates the now-expired CA issued are no longer usable. In other words, there can be no orphaned certificates that are still valid, when the CA that issued them is no longer valid.

Because a CA that is approaching the end of its own validity period must issue certificates valid for increasingly shorter periods of time, administrators should have a policy in place to renew the CA well before it expires. For example, in the case of Windows Server 2008, a root CA's self-generated certificate defaults to a validity period of five years. Administrators should renew it every four years, however, to prevent the CA from publishing new certificates with lifetimes shorter than a year.

Administrators can reduce the time required to administer a PKI by increasing the validity period of the root CA. As with any certificate, it is best to choose a validity period shorter than the time required for an attacker to break the root CA key's cryptography. Given the current state of computer technology, one can estimate that a 4096-bit private key would take decades to crack. While a determined attacker can eventually crack any private key, the end result is useless if the certificate expires before the attack is successful.

UNDERSTANDING CERTIFICATE REVOCATION

A certificate has a specified lifetime, but CAs can reduce this lifetime by a process known as *certificate revocation*. Every CA publishes a certificate revocation list (CRL) that lists the serial numbers of certificates that it considers to be no longer valid. The specified lifetime of CRLs is typically much shorter than that of a certificate. The CA might also include in the CRL a code specifying the reason the certificate has been revoked. A revocation might occur because a private key has been compromised, because a certificate has been superseded, or because an employee has left the company. The CRL also includes the date the certificate was revoked.

During signature verification and other activities that require certificate access, applications typically check the revocation list on the certificate's CA to determine whether the certificate and its key pair are still trustworthy. Applications can also determine whether the reason for the revocation or the date it occurred affects the use of the certificate in question. For example, if an application is using the certificate to verify a signature, and the date on the signature precedes the date of the revocation of the certificate by the CA, the application can consider the signature to still be valid.

To reduce the number of requests sent to a CA, clients typically cache CRLs, and use them until they expire. If a CA publishes a new CRL, applications that have a valid CRL do not usually use the new CRL until the one they have expires.

Installing Certification Authorities

> When you install the Active Directory Certificate Services Role on a Windows Server 2008 computer, you can create any one of the four types of CA listed earlier.

When you select the CA type, the Add Roles Wizard changes to include various additional configuration pages depending on the type you select. On most enterprise networks that use certificates for their internal applications, the first CA they install will be an enterprise root CA. The following sections describe the process of installing a CA and managing the templates you use to create certificates.

INSTALLING AN ENTERPRISE ROOT CA

To install the first CA on an enterprise network, the enterprise root CA, use the following procedure.

 INSTALL AN ENTERPRISE ROOT CA

GET READY. Log on to Windows Server 2008 using an account with administrative privileges. When the logon process is completed, close the Initial Configuration Tasks window and any other windows that appear.

1. Click **Start**, and then click **Administrative Tools** > **Server Manager.** The Server Manager console appears.

2. Select the **Roles** node and, in the details pane, click **Add Roles.** The Add Roles Wizard appears.

3. Click **Next** to bypass the *Before You Begin* page. The *Select Server Roles* page appears.

4. Select the **Active Directory Certificate Services** checkbox and click **Next.** The *Introduction to Active Directory Certificate Services* page appears.

> **TAKE NOTE***
>
> Although the role is called Active Directory Certificate services, Active Directory is not required to install and run a CA. As noted earlier, standalone CAs need not use Active Directory in any way, and can provide certificates to Internet and other clients outside the enterprise network.

5. Click **Next** to bypass the introduction page. The *Select Role Services* page appears, as shown in Figure 9-19.

Figure 9-19

The Select Role Services page
of the Add Roles Wizard

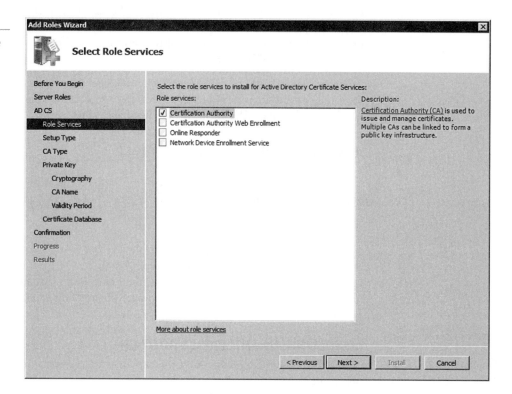

6. Leave the Certification Authority role service selected and click **Next.** The *Specify Setup Type* page appears, as shown in Figure 9-20.

Figure 9-20

The Specify Setup Type page of
the Add Roles Wizard

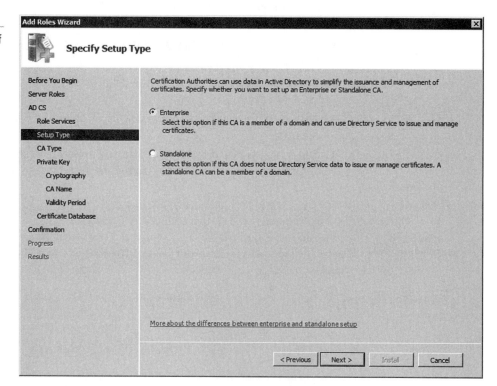

7. Select the **Enterprise** option and click **Next.** The *Specify CA Type* page appears, as shown in Figure 9-21.

Figure 9-21

The Specify CA Type page of the Add Roles Wizard

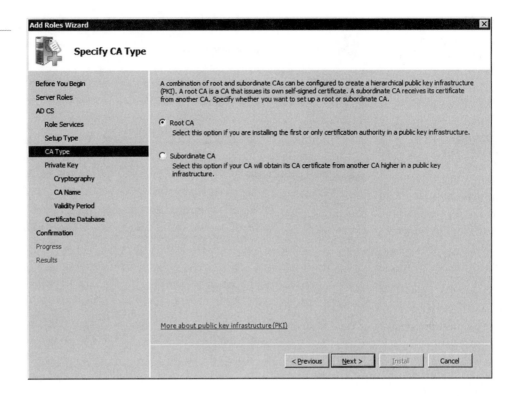

8. Select the **Root CA** option and click **Next.** The *Set Up Private Key* page appears, as shown in Figure 9-22.

Figure 9-22

The Set Up Private Key page of the Add Roles Wizard

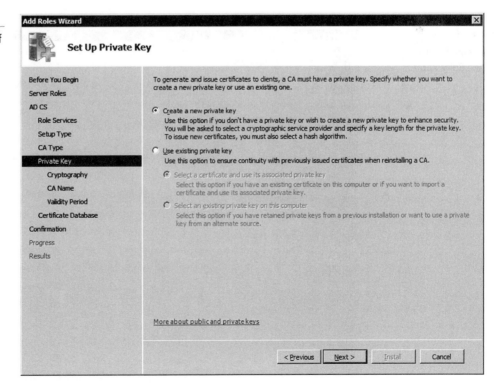

9. Select the **Create a new private key** option and click **Next.** The *Configure Cryptography for CA* page appears, as shown in Figure 9-23.

Figure 9-23

The Configure Cryptography for CA page of the Add Roles Wizard

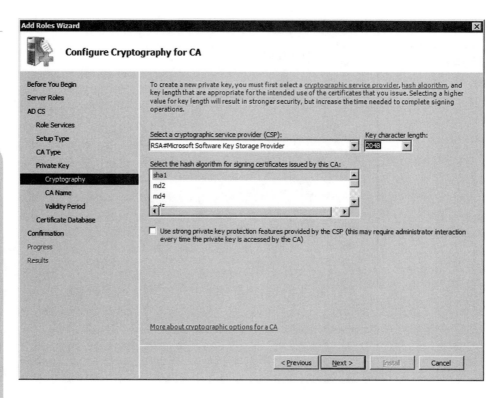

TAKE NOTE*

The Create a New Private Key option instructs the wizard to create a new private key for the CA. The Use Existing Private Key option instructs the wizard to use the private key associated with an existing certificate or stored on the server, which you must import in the *Select Existing Certificate* page. This option adds to the wizard. Select this option when you are reinstalling a CA.

10. Select a cryptographic service provider and a hashing algorithm from the lists provided. Then, specify the **Key character length** you want the CA to use, and click **Next.** The *Configure CA Name* page appears, as shown in Figure 9-24.

Figure 9-24

The Configure CA Name page of the Add Roles Wizard

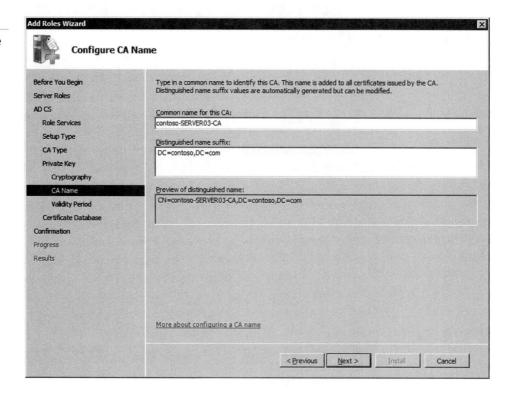

11. The wizard uses the server's name to form the common name of the CA. Specify a different name, if desired, and click **Next**. The *Set Validity Period* page appears, as shown in Figure 9-25.

Figure 9-25

The Set Validity Period page of the Add Roles Wizard

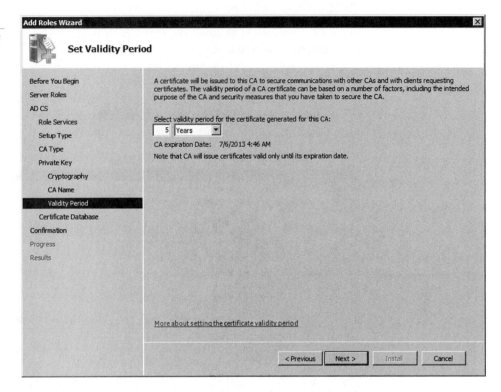

12. Specify a validity period for the certificate that will be self-generated by the CA and click **Next.** The *Configure Certificate Database* page appears, as shown in Figure 9-26.

Figure 9-26

The Configure Certificate Database page of the Add Roles Wizard

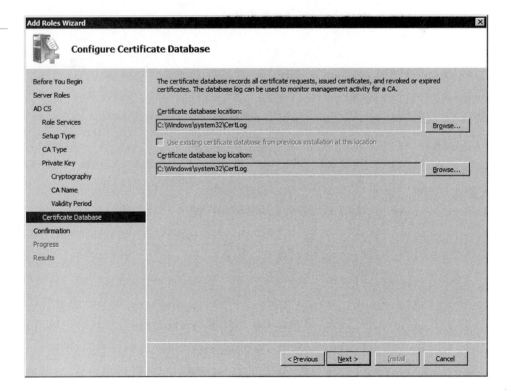

13. Click **Next** to accept the default database location settings. The *Confirm Installation Selections* page appears.

14. Click **Install.** When the installation is complete, click **Close.**

CLOSE the Server Manager console.

Once you have created an enterprise root CA on your network, you can proceed to create as many enterprise subordinate CAs as you need.

INSTALLING AN ENTERPRISE SUBORDINATE CA

The only difference in the installation procedure for an enterprise subordinate CA is the inclusion of a *Request Certificate from a Parent CA* page in the Add Roles Wizard, as shown in Figure 9-27, in place of the *Set Validity Period* page.

Figure 9-27

The Request Certificate from a Parent CA page of the Add Roles Wizard

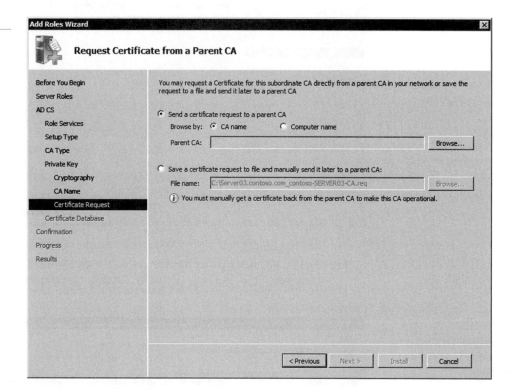

When you create a root CA, the computer generates its own certificate, so the Set Validity Period enables you to specify the life span of that certificate, and consequently the CA's life span. When you create a subordinate CA, you specify the name of a parent CA instead, from which the computer will obtain the certificate it needs to operate as a subordinate. The parent CA can be a root CA or another subordinate CA.

CREATING A CA HIERARCHY

While even a single CA constitutes a PKI, it is common for organizations to use multiple CAs, arranged in a hierarchy, much like Active Directory forests. In a hierarchical CA structure, there is a single root CA at the top, and one or more subordinate CAs beneath it, as shown in Figure 9-28. The root CA provides certificates to the subordinate CAs, which in turn can generate certificates for additional subordinate CAs or for end users. In an Active Directory hierarchy, domains in the same tree automatically trust each other. In a CA hierarchy, *trust chaining* enables clients that trust the root CA to also trust certificates issued by any other CAs subordinate to the root.

Figure 9-28

A simple CA hierarchy

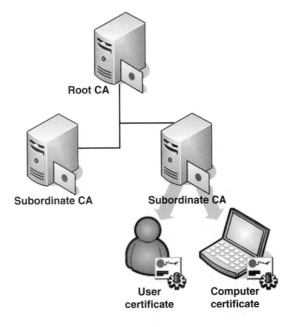

While a CA hierarchy can have just two levels, larger organizations might have three or more levels. When this is the case, there are two distinct types of subordinate CAs, as follows:

- *Intermediate CAs*—Intermediate CAs do not issue certificates to end users or computers; they issue certificates only to other subordinate CAs below them in the certification hierarchy. Intermediate CAs are not required, but using them enables you to take your root CA offline, which greatly increases its security.
- *Issuing CAs*—Issuing CAs provide certificates to end users and computers. Root and intermediate CAs are capable of issuing certificates to end users, but in a three-level arrangement, they typically do not.

TAKE NOTE * Unlike the strictly defined root, subordinate, enterprise, and standalone CAs discussed earlier, intermediate and issuing servers are not roles that you select when you install Active Directory Certificate Services on a Windows Server 2008 computer. These are instead more informal roles that are dictated only by the use you make of a CA you have already installed.

Figure 9-29 displays the relationships between root, intermediate, and issuing CAs in a three-level hierarchy, and the users and computers who use certificates.

Figure 9-29

A three-level CA hierarchy

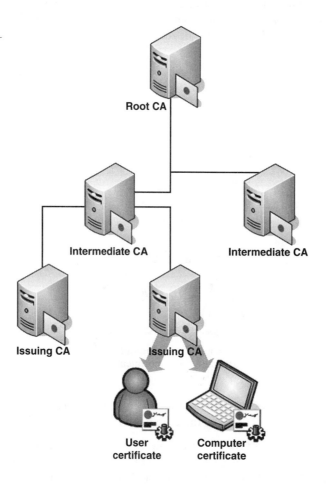

TAKE NOTE* All of the information about installing CAs found in the previous sections is applicable to standalone, as well as enterprise, CAs. However, the following information, on certificate templates, applies only to enterprise CAs.

Managing Certificate Templates

Enterprise CAs might have to issue thousands of certificates to users and computers. If administrators had to provide the configuration settings for each certificate manually, they could easily spend all of their time issuing certificates—and would probably make a large number of mistakes in the process. Fortunately, administrators can use certificate templates to simplify the process of creating certificates and to ensure that they are created consistently across an organization.

Certificate templates are sets of rules and settings that define the format and content of a certificate based on the certificate's intended use. Certificate templates also provide the client with instructions on how to create and submit a valid certificate request. In addition, certificate templates define which security principals are allowed to read, enroll for, or autoenroll for certificates based on that template.

Windows Server 2008 includes a large collection of predefined certificate templates, supporting a variety of functions and applications. You can also customize each template for a specific use or create your own templates to suit the needs of your organization. Only enterprise CAs can issue certificates based on certificate templates; standalone CAs cannot. When an administrator defines a certificate template, the definition must be available to all CAs in the forest. To make the definition available, administrators publish the template in Active Directory and let the Active Directory replication engine propagate the template throughout the enterprise.

WORKING WITH CERTIFICATE TEMPLATES

To modify and publish certificate templates, you use the Certificate Templates snap-in for Microsoft Management Console (MMC), as shown in Figure 9-30, which is only available on a CA server, or a server with the Certification Authority Tools feature installed. Using this snap-in, you can modify templates to suit your needs and deploy them on the network.

Figure 9-30

The Certificate Templates snap-in for MMC

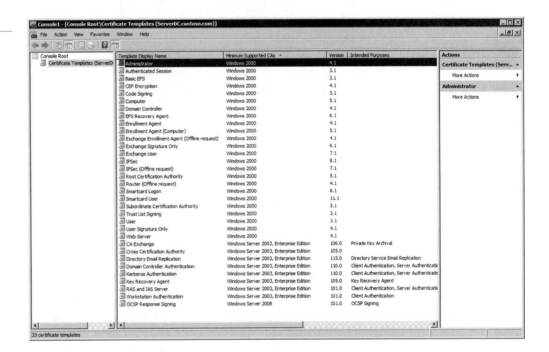

As with the Certificates snap-in mentioned earlier, Windows Server 2008 does not have a shortcut to a Certificate Templates console in the Start menu. You must add the Certificate Templates snap-in to an MMC console yourself to manage templates.

MANAGING CERTIFICATE TEMPLATE PERMISSIONS

Every certificate template has an access control list (ACL) that you can use to allow or deny security principals permission to Read, Write, Enroll, and Autoenroll the certificate template. You set permissions on certificate templates by using the Certificate Templates snap-in to open a template's Properties sheet and click the Security tab, as shown in Figure 9-31. The process of assigning permissions is the same as on any of Windows Server 2008's other permission systems; only the permissions themselves are different.

Figure 9-31

The Security tab of a certificate template's Properties sheet

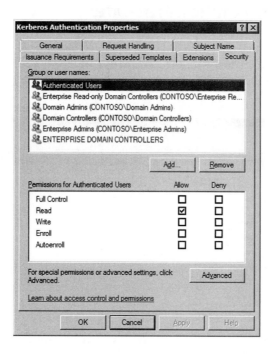

You can allow or deny security principals any combination of the following certificate template permissions:

- Full Control—Enables a security principal to modify all attributes of a certificate template, including its permissions.

- Read—Enables a security principal to find the certificate template in Active Directory when enrolling for a certificate.

- Write—Enables a security principal to modify all the attributes of a certificate template, except for its permissions.

- Enroll—Enables a security principal to enroll for a certificate based on the certificate template. To enroll for a certificate, the security principal must also have the Allow Read permission for the certificate template.

- Autoenroll—Enables a security principal to receive a certificate based on the template through the autoenrollment process. Autoenrollment also requires that the user have both the Allow Read and Allow Enroll permissions.

For autoenrollment to function correctly, you must ensure that all three of the required permissions (Allow Read, Allow Enroll, and Allow Autoenroll) are granted to the same user or group. If you assign Allow Read and Allow Enroll to one group and Allow Autoenroll to another group, users will not be allowed to autoenroll for certificates, even if they have membership in both groups.

This is because permissions for a certificate template are not additive, as they are in the NTFS file system. In this example, because a user is a member of two groups, the CA will treat the group with Allow Read and Allow Enroll permissions separately from the group with Allow

Autoenroll permissions. For best results, create a global or universal group for each certificate template. Then, grant the global or universal group all three permissions, and then add the necessary user groups to this group.

UNDERSTANDING CERTIFICATE TEMPLATE VERSIONS

Windows Server 2008's Active Directory Certificate Services role supports three types of certificate templates: version 1, version 2, and version 3. Version 1 templates provide backward compatibility for CAs running Windows Server 2003, Standard Edition and Windows 2000 family operating systems. Version 1 templates have a major limitation, however: the information they contain is hard-coded in the certificate. You cannot modify version 1 certificate template properties, such as certificate lifetime and key size. With version 2 certificate templates, you can modify these properties.

When you install the first enterprise CA in a forest, most of the templates supplied with Certificate Services are version 1 templates. These version 1 templates provide an immediate certificate solution you can use as soon as the CA is installed because they support many general needs for subject certification. For example, using the default version 1 templates, a CA can create certificates that allow EFS encryption recovery, client authentication, smart card logon, and server authentication. Windows 2000 Server and Windows Server 2003, Standard Edition CAs support only version 1 templates.

Some of the default templates supplied with Active Directory Certificate Services are version 2, however, and you can only use them to issue certificates with a CA running Windows Server 2003, Enterprise Edition; Windows Server 2003, Datacenter Edition; or Windows Server 2008. Version 3 can be issued only by CAs running Windows Server 2008, and can be issued only to clients running Windows Vista and Windows Server 2008.

The certificate templates included with Windows Server 2008's Active Directory Certificate Services role are listed in Table 9-1.

Table 9-1

Windows Server 2008 Certificate Templates

TEMPLATE NAME	TEMPLATE VERSION	SUBJECT TYPE	KEY USAGE	TEMPLATE FUNCTION
Administrator	1	User	Signature and Encryption	Allows user authentication, EFS encryption, secure email, and certificate trust list signing.
Authenticated Session	1	User	Signature	Authenticates a user to a Web server. Uses the private key to sign the authentication request.
Basic EFS	1	User	Encryption	Encrypts and decrypts data by using EFS. Uses the private key to decrypt the file encryption key (FEK) that encrypts and decrypts the EFS-protected data.
CA Exchange	2	Computer	Encryption	Used to store keys that are configured for private key archival.
CEP Encryption	1	Computer	Encryption	Enables the certificate holder to act as a registration authority (RA) for Simple Certificate Enrollment Protocol (SCEP) requests.
Code Signing	1	User	Signature	Used to digitally sign software.

(continued)

Table 9-1 *(continued)*

TEMPLATE NAME	TEMPLATE VERSION	SUBJECT TYPE	KEY USAGE	TEMPLATE FUNCTION
Computer	1	Computer	Signature and Encryption	Provides both client and server authentication abilities to a computer account. The default permissions for this template allow enrollment only by computers running Windows 2000 and Windows Server 2008 family operating systems that are not domain controllers.
Cross-Certification Authority	2	Cross-certified CA	Signature	Used for cross-certification and qualified subordination.
Directory E-mail Replication	2	DirEmailRep	Signature and Encryption	Used to replicate email within Active Directory.
Domain Controller	2	DirEmailRep	Signature and Encryption	Provides both client and server authentication abilities to a computer account. Default permissions allow enrollment by only domain controllers.
Domain Controller Authentication	2	Computer	Signature and Encryption	Used to authenticate Active Directory computers and users.
EFS Recovery Agent	1	User	Encryption	Enables the subject to decrypt files previously encrypted with EFS.
Enrollment Agent	1	User	Signature	Used to request certificates on behalf of another subject.
Exchange Enrollment Agent (Offline request)	1	User	Signature	Used to request certificates on behalf of another subject and supply the subject name in the request.
Exchange Signature Only	1	User	Signature	Used by Exchange Key Management Service to issue certificates to Microsoft Exchange Server users for digitally signing email.
Exchange User	1	User	Encryption	Used by Exchange Key Management Service to issue certificates to Exchange users for encrypting email.
IPsec	1	Computer	Signature and Encryption	Provides certificate-based authentication for computers by using IP Security (IPsec) for network communications.
IPsec (Offline request)	1	Computer	Signature and Encryption	Used by IPsec to digitally sign, encrypt, and decrypt network communication when the subject name is supplied in the request.
Kerberos Authentication	2	Computer	Signature and Encryption	Used to authenticate Active Directory computers and users.
Key Recovery Agent	2	Key Recovery Agent	Encryption	Recovers private keys that are archived on the certification authority.
OCSP Response Signing	3	Computer	Signature	Used by an Online Responder to sign responses to certificate status requests.

(continued)

Table 9-1 *(continued)*

TEMPLATE NAME	TEMPLATE VERSION	SUBJECT TYPE	KEY USAGE	TEMPLATE FUNCTION
RAS and IAS Server	2	Computer	Signature and Encryption	Enables Remote Access Services (RAS) and Internet Authentication Services (IAS) servers to authenticate their identities to other computers.
Root Certification Authority	2	CA	Signature	Used to prove the identity of the certification authorities
Router (Offline request)	1	Computer	Signature and Encryption	Used by a router when requested through SCEP from a certification authority that holds a Certificate Enrollment Protocol (CEP) Encryption certificate.
Smartcard Logon	1	User	Signature and Encryption	Authenticates a user with the network by using a smart card.
Smartcard User	1	User	Signature and Encryption	Identical to the Smartcard Logon template, except that it can also be used to sign and encrypt email.
Subordinate Certification Authority	2	CA	Signature	Used to prove the identity of the certification authorities.
Trust List Signing	1	User	Signature	Enables the holder to digitally sign a trust list.
User	1	User	Signature and Encryption	Used for email, EFS, and client authentication.
User Signature Only	1	User	Signature	Enables users to digitally sign data.
Web Server	1	Computer	Signature and Encryption	Authenticates the Web server to connecting clients. The connecting clients use the public key to encrypt the data that is sent to the Web server when using Secure Sockets Layer (SSL) encryption.
Workstation Authentication	2	Computer	Signature and Encryption	Enables client computers to authenticate their identities to servers.

TAKE NOTE*

In the Certificate Templates snap-in, you can tell the version of a template by looking at the value in the Minimum Supported CAs column. Templates with Windows 2000 in this column are version 1; templates with Windows Server 2003, Enterprise Edition are version 2; and templates with Windows Server 2008 are version 3.

You cannot modify or remove the default version 1 templates installed with Active Directory Certificate Services, but you can duplicate them. When you create a duplicate of a version 1 template, the result is a version 2 template, which you can modify as needed.

The version 1 certificate templates provided by Windows Server 2008 Active Directory Certificate Services are completely compatible with previous versions of Certificate Services. Therefore, a Windows Server 2008 CA installation can work alongside an existing Windows CA infrastructure.

WORKING WITH CERTIFICATE TEMPLATES

Certificates are simply mechanisms for carrying information about users or computers, and as such, they have the potential for use by a wide variety of applications. It is up to the operating system and the applications to use that information to perform functions such as encrypting messages and authenticating connections.

Windows Server 2008's Active Directory Certificate Services includes many different templates designed to create certificates that applications can use for various purposes. To specify how the certificates created with a certificate template can be used, you configure its application policies. Application policies, sometimes known as extended key usage or enhanced key usage, give you the ability to specify which certificates can be used for which purposes. This enables you to issue certificates without being concerned that they will be misused.

For example, when you open the Smartcard User template in the Certificate Templates snap-in, click the Extensions tab, and select Enhanced Key Usage, you can see that a system can use a certificate based on this template to send secure email, to perform client authentication, and to log on by using a smart card, as shown in Figure 9-32. By default, the certificate cannot authenticate a server to a client, recover files, encrypt files, or perform many other tasks that rely on a certificate. Further, the CA can issue the certificate only to a user, not to a computer.

Figure 9-32

The default capabilities of the Smartcard User template

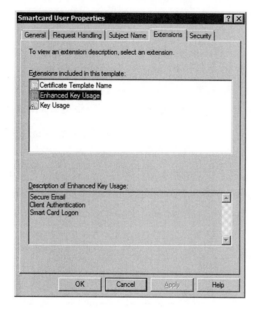

You will notice also that there is no way to modify the policies on the Extensions tab, and if you click on the other tabs, you cannot modify their settings either. This is because Smartcard User is a version 1 certificate template. However, if you create a duplicate of the Smartcard User template, by right-clicking it and selecting Duplicate Template from the context menu, you can choose whether to create a copy that is a version 2 or version 3 template, using the interface shown in Figure 9-33.

Figure 9-33

The Duplicate Template dialog box

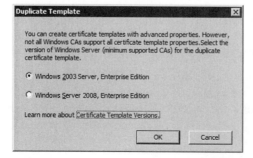

When you look at the duplicate template you have created, you can see that the same capabilities appear as application policies by default, but in this case you can modify the template by adding any of the additional application policies shown in the Edit Application Policies Extension dialog box, shown in Figure 9-34. You can also modify any of the template's other settings, and even create new application policies of your own.

Figure 9-34

Adding application policies to a duplicate template

You have no choice but to create a copy of a version 1 template if you want to modify its properties. However, even if you are working with one of the version 2 templates included with Active Directory Certificate Services, it is a good idea to make a copy before attempting any modifications so that you retain a backup of the original configuration.

Using certificate templates with multiple functions is an excellent way to reduce the number of certificates that administrators have to create and manage to fill an organization's needs. Many certificate templates, however, are single-function only. Single-function certificate templates are typically designed for sensitive operations that have unique requirements. For example, you might want to issue certificates for a sensitive operation, such as key recovery, with a short certificate lifetime of two months. In this case, a single-function template is preferable, because you would not want to combine this function with other functions that are less sensitive, and which can have a much longer lifetime.

You can modify a version 2 or version 3 certificate template at any time. After you make changes, all of the new certificates the CA issues using that template will have the new settings. This is an excellent way to make sweeping changes to certificates deployed to users and computers in your organization. For example, if you discover that a certificate could be compromised in less than one year, you can modify the validity period of the certificate to six months. However, modifying a template does not affect the certificates that the CA has already issued. To ensure that all clients using certificates issued before you modified the template receive the new settings, you must make sure that the CA issues a new certificate to each client. You can do this in two ways:

- Use the Certificates snap-in on each client computer to renew the certificate or request a new certificate.
- Use the Certification Authority snap-in to revoke the old certificates, forcing the client to request a new enrollment.

Enrolling and Revoking Certificates

> Certificate *enrollment* is the process by which a client requests a certificate and a CA generates one.

Although enrollment options might be restricted by network connectivity issues or by the use of a standalone CA, the certificate enrollment process always follows the same high-level procedure, which is as follows:

1. Generating keys—When a client generates a request for a new certificate, the operating system passes the request information to a ***Cryptographic Service Provider (CSP)*** that is installed on the computer. The CSP generates the private key and the public key—referred to as a key pair—for the certificate request. If the CSP is software-based, it generates the key pair on the client computer. If the CSP is hardware-based, such as a smart card CSP, the CSP instructs the hardware device to generate the key pair. The client might also be assigned a key pair by some authority in the organization.

2. Collecting required information—The client collects the information the CA requires to issue a certificate. For an internal CA, this can be authentication information or data stored in the Active Directory database. For an external CA, such as a commercial provider, the information could include the applicant's email address, birth certificate, fingerprints, or other notarized documents—whatever materials the CA needs to confirm the identity of the applicant. CAs with stringent identification requirements produce certificates with high assurance; that is, their certificates generate a high level of confidence. CAs themselves are said to be of high, medium, or low assurance.

3. Requesting the certificate—The client sends a certificate request, consisting of the public key and the additional required information, to the CA. The certificate request might be encrypted using the CA's own public key. Clients can submit certificate enrollment requests to a CA in several ways: automatically, by an application; explicitly, using email, a Web site, or a client program; or by a postal or courier service, when the certificate request or other documents must be notarized.

4. Verifying the information—The CA uses a policy module to process the applicant's certificate request. A ***policy module*** is a set of rules the CA uses to determine whether it should approve the request, deny it, or mark it as pending for later review by an administrator. The policy module also adds an attribute to the certificate containing the source of the CA's own certificate. This enables the client to verify the newly issued certificate by checking the credentials of the CA that issued it. As with the identification requirements, the rules in a CA's policy module influence the amount of confidence generated by the certificates it issues.

5. Creating the certificate—The CA creates a document containing the applicant's public key and other appropriate information and digitally signs it using its own private key. The signed document is the certificate. The digital signature of the CA authenticates the binding of the subject's name to the subject's public key. It enables anyone receiving the certificate to verify its source by obtaining the CA's public key.

6. Sending or posting the certificate—The CA uses an ***exit module*** to determine how it should make the new certificate available to the applicant. Depending on the CA type, the exit module might cause the CA to publish the new certificate in the Active Directory directory service, send it to the applicant in an email message, or store it in a specified folder for later retrieval.

UNDERSTANDING CERTIFICATE ENROLLMENT METHODS

Active Directory Certificate Services supports several certificate enrollment methods. A client's choice of enrollment method for obtaining certificates is typically dictated by the type of CA the client is requesting the certificate from and whether the client and CA can communicate across a network.

When requesting certificates from an enterprise CA, a client can use the following methods:

- *Autoenrollment*—Applications automatically issue a certificate enrollment request and send it to the CA. The CA then evaluates the request and issues or denies a certificate. When everything works properly, the entire process is invisible to the end user.

- *Web enrollment*—When you install Active Directory Certificate Services with the Certification Authority Web Enrollment role service, the setup wizard creates a Web site that clients can use to request certificates from the CA. Although standalone CAs are more likely to use Web enrollment, enterprise CAs support it as well.

- Certificates snap-in—The Certificates snap-in for MMC enables users to manually request certificates, as well as view the certificates they already possess.

Clients requesting certificates from standalone CAs are more limited in their options. Standalone CAs cannot use certificate templates, do not interact with Active Directory, and therefore do not support autoenrollment. Clients also cannot use the Certificates snap-in with a standalone CA, because the snap-in can communicate only with a CA using Active Directory. As a result, clients must use the Web enrollment interface to request a certificate from a standalone CA, and the CA holds the requests in a queue until an administrator evaluates each one individually and either issues or denies the certificate.

Additionally, a client computer that is not connected to the network cannot automatically enroll for a certificate because autoenrollment requires the client to communicate directly to the enterprise CA. In these circumstances, the client must submit all certificates requests to the CA manually.

USING AUTOMATIC ENROLLMENT

Autoenrollment enables organizations to automatically deploy certificates to both users and computers. The autoenrollment feature enables administrators to centrally manage all aspects of the certificate life cycle, including certificate enrollment, certificate renewal, and the modification and superseding of certificates. Autoenrollment also enables faster deployment of PKI applications, such as smart card logon, EFS, SSL, and Signed Multipurpose Internet Mail Extensions (S/MIME), within an Active Directory environment by eliminating the need for interaction with the end user.

Even when clients are manually requesting certificates, using Web enrollment or the Certificates snap-in, autoenrollment enables the CA to automatically issue the certificate without an administrator having to manually grant the request. To control whether a CA should autoenroll clients or queue their requests for manual approval, administrators can allow or deny the Autoenroll permission on the certificate template for the users and groups that will request certificates based on that template.

Some types of certificate enrollment require user interaction to proceed, even when autoenrollment is enabled. For example, smart card certificates require the user to insert the smart card before the CA can generate the certificate. In these cases, you can still use autoenrollment by configuring the version 2 certificate template to prompt the user during enrollment. On the certificate template's Properties sheet, click the Request Handling tab and then select either Prompt The User During Enrollment or Prompt The User During Enrollment And Require User Input When The Private Key Is Used, as shown in Figure 9-35. When a client is autoenrolled, a message window appears, informing the user that interaction is required.

Figure 9-35

The Request Handling tab on a certificate template's Properties sheet

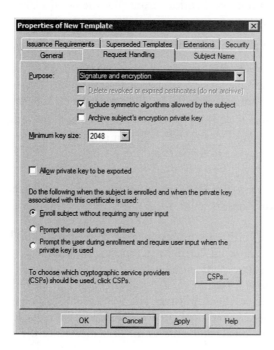

USING MANUAL ENROLLMENT

If you have client computers running operating systems earlier than Windows 2000, you must manually enroll these clients for certificates, even with an enterprise CA, because these client operating systems do not support Group Policy, and therefore cannot take advantage of autoenrollment. As discussed in the previous section, you can manually enroll for certificates by using the Web enrollment interface or the Certificates snap-in.

USING WEB-BASED ENROLLMENT

As mentioned earlier, to manually enroll clients using the Web interface, you must install the Certification Authority Web Enrollment role service on a CA, which causes the Add Role Services Wizard to add the Web Services (IIS) role as well. This configures the computer to function as a Web server, with the Active Server Pages support needed to support Web-based enrollment.

Once the installation is complete, clients can connect to the CA from any Web browser using the URL *http://*servername/*certsrv*. The Web interface, shown in Figure 9-36, enables users to create enrollment requests and retrieve certificates that the CA has issued.

Figure 9-36

The Certification Authority Web Enrollment interface

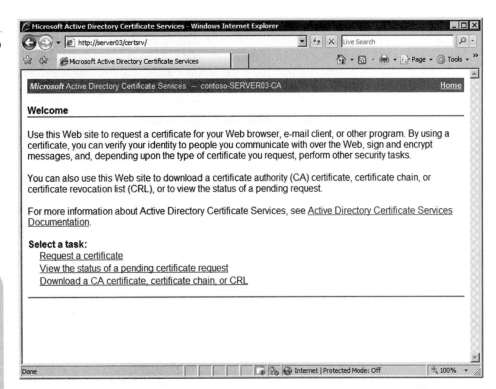

By default, SSL is not enabled on the Web-based interface. For increased security, enable SSL on the certsrv virtual directory using a certificate that is trusted by all clients, such as a certificate issued by a commercial CA.

With an enterprise CA, Web-based enrollment can require no interaction from the administrator, as long as the proper policy settings and permissions are in place. For a standalone CA, however, an administrator must manually approve all Web enrollment requests, using the Certification Authority console.

USING THE CERTIFICATES SNAP-IN

Clients can also enroll for certificates by using the Certificate Enrollment Wizard in the Certificates snap-in to request certificates from an enterprise CA, as shown in Figure 9-37.

Figure 9-37

The Certificate Enrollment Wizard

The Certificates snap-in displays the client's active certificates and other PKI client properties, such as trusted root CAs and existing certificate trust lists. Users with administrative privileges on the computer running the snap-in can manage certificates that are issued to users, computers, and services. Users without administrative privileges can manage only their own user certificates.

ISSUING CERTIFICATES MANUALLY

When users send enrollment requests to an enterprise CA using the Certification Authority Web Enrollment interface, the response is usually immediate, because enterprise CAs use autoenrollment. With a standalone CA, however, the CA queues the requests until an administrator evaluates them and manually issues a certificate or denies the request, using the Certification Authority console.

To manually process an enrollment request, use the following procedure.

 ## ISSUE CERTIFICATES MANUALLY

GET READY. Log on to Windows Server 2008 using an account with administrative privileges. When the logon process is completed, close the Initial Configuration Tasks window and any other windows that appear.

1. Click **Start,** and then click **Administrative Tools** > **Certification Authority.** The Certification Authority console appears.
2. In the scope (left) pane, expand the node representing your server and click the **Pending Requests** folder, as shown in Figure 9-38.

Figure 9-38

The Pending Requests folder of the Certification Authority console

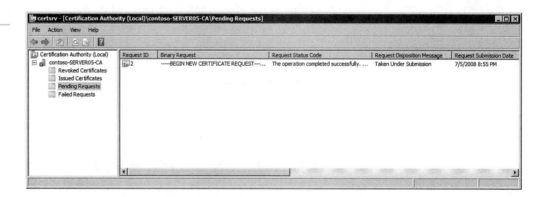

3. In the detail (right) pane, right-click a certificate request and, in the context menu, click **All Tasks** > **Issue.** The request moves to the Issued Certificates folder.

CLOSE the Certification Authority console.

Once the administrator has issued the certificate, the user can check the status of the request in the Certification Authority Web Enrollment site, as shown in Figure 9-39.

Figure 9-39

The Certificate Issued page in the Certification Authority Web Enrollment site

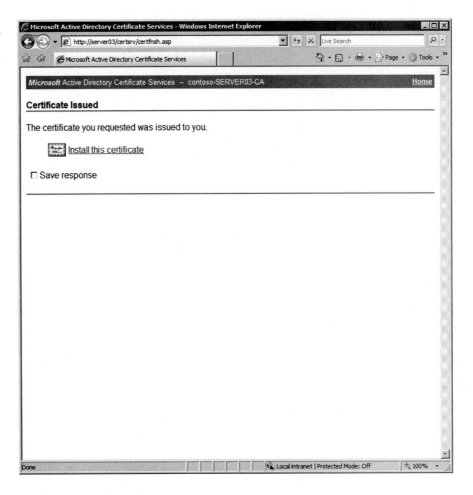

REVOKING CERTIFICATES

Administrators might occasionally need to revoke a certificate because a user has left the organization, because they have decommissioned a computer, or because a private key has been compromised. There are two ways to revoke certificates:

- By using the Certification Authority snap-in
- By using the Certutil.exe command-line program

To revoke a certificate using the Certification Authority snap-in, you select the Issued Certificates node; right-click the certificate you want to revoke; and, from the context menu, select All Tasks > Revoke Certificate to display the Certificate Revocation dialog box, as shown in Figure 9-40.

Figure 9-40

The Certificate Revocation dialog box

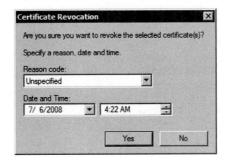

You must choose a reason for revoking the certificate, which will be included in the CRL. You can choose from the following reason codes, which are self-explanatory:

- Unspecified
- Key Compromise
- CA Compromise
- Change Of Affiliation
- Superseded
- Cease Of Operation
- Certificate Hold

TAKE NOTE *

The CRLs that a CA publishes contain the reason codes administrators select when they revoke certificates. Before you select a reason code, think about whether you really want everyone who can access the CRL to know why you revoked it. If you did have a key compromise or a CA compromise, do you want that to be public information? If not, just select Unspecified. In most cases, the reason you select for revoking a certificate has no bearing on the applications that use the certificate.

Applications discover that a certificate has been revoked by retrieving the certificate revocation list (CRL) from the CA. There are two kinds of CRLs: full CRLs, which contain a complete list of all of a CA's revoked certificates, and delta CRLs. *Delta CRLs* are shorter lists of certificates that have been revoked since the last full CRL was published. After an application retrieves a full CRL, it can then download the shorter delta CRL to discover newly revoked certificates.

PUBLISHING CRLS

When you have to download a file from a server, you can often access the file in several different ways. If you are logged onto the computer locally, you can use Windows Explorer to navigate to the folder containing the file. If you are on a different computer on the same network, you might map a drive to the server and download the file from a shared folder. If the server is behind a firewall and running IIS, you can open a Web browser to retrieve the file.

Having multiple ways to retrieve a file from a server is important, especially when the server will be accessed by a variety of different clients. Active Directory Certificate Services enables clients to retrieve CRLs using a variety of different protocols, including the following:

- Shared folders
- Hypertext Transfer Protocol (HTTP)
- File Transfer Protocol (FTP)
- Lightweight Directory Access Protocol (LDAP)

By default, CRLs are published in three different locations.

- The *Servername*\CertEnroll share—Created automatically when you install Active Directory Certificate Services, clients on the network can access this share, as long as they have the required permissions.
- CN=CAName,CN=CAComputerName,CN=CDP,CN=Public Key Services, CN=Services,CN=Configuration,DC=ForestRootNameDN—Clients who need to retrieve the CRL by using LDAP can access it from this address.
- http://*servername*/certenroll—Web clients can retrieve the CRLs from this URL.
- file:// *servername*/certenroll—Web clients can also retrieve the CRLs using the file prefix.

Though these default locations are sufficient for most organizations, you can add locations if necessary. In particular, you must add a location if you are using an offline root CA, since the

CA will not be accessible by clients under normal circumstances. Additionally, if clients use your certificates outside your private network and your CA is behind a firewall, you should publish the CRL to a publicly accessible location.

To simplify administration, you can use variable names when entering CRL locations. After you click the Add button, the Add Location dialog box appears and provides a list of variables that you can use, as shown in Figure 9-41. Descriptions for each variable are provided in the Description Of Selected Variable box.

Figure 9-41

The Add Location dialog box

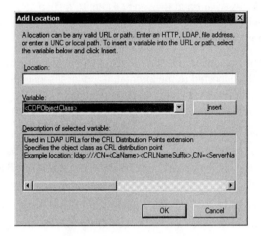

After you revoke a certificate, the CA must publish a new CRL before clients can discover that the certificate has been revoked. By default, Windows Server 2008 CAs publish delta CRLs daily, and full CRLs weekly. You can change these settings using the Certification Authority snap-in by right-clicking the Revoked Certificates node, opening its Properties sheet, and then clicking the CRL Publishing Parameters tab, as shown in Figure 9-42. This tab also shows you when the next scheduled updates will occur.

Figure 9-42

The Properties sheet for a CA's Revoked Certificates node

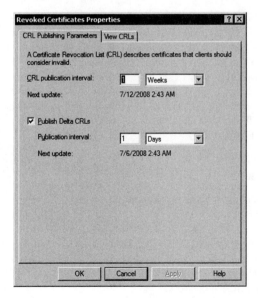

SUMMARY SKILL MATRIX

- Windows Server 2008 provides remote access capabilities, as part of its Network Policy and Access Services role, which enable users to connect to the network using dial-up or virtual private network (VPN) connections. A dial-up connection is a dedicated link between the two modems that remains in place during the entire session.

- The Remote Access client and the server establish a Point-to-Point Protocol (PPP) connection, during which the server authenticates the client and the computers negotiate a set of communication parameters they have in common.

- In a virtual private network (VPN) connection, the remote client and the remote access server are both connected to the Internet, using local service providers. The client establishes a connection to the server using the Internet as a network medium and, after authentication, the server grants the client access to the network.

- In the tunneling process, the two computers establish a PPP connection, just as they would in a dial-up connection, but instead of transmitting the PPP packets over the Internet as they are, they encapsulate the packets again using one of the three VPN protocols supported by Windows Server 2008.

- Remote Access in Windows Server 2008 uses an authentication system that is entirely separate from the Kerberos authentication system that clients on the local network use.

- A digital certificate is a digitally signed document, issued by a third party called a certification authority (CA), that binds a user, computer, or service holding a private key with its corresponding public key.

- When both parties involved in a transaction trust the CA to properly authenticate users before handing out certificates, and believe that the CA protects the privacy of its certificates and keys, then they can both trust in the identity of the certificate holder.

- Windows Server 2008 supports two basic types of CAs: enterprise CAs and standalone CAs.

- You can configure each enterprise or standalone CA to function as either a root CA or a subordinate CA. The first CA you install in your organization must always be a root CA. A root CA is the parent that issues certificates to the subordinate CAs beneath it. If a client trusts the root CA, it must also trust all the subordinate CAs that have been issued certificates by the root CA.

- While a CA hierarchy can have just two levels, larger organizations might have three or more levels. When this is the case, there are two distinct types of subordinate CAs: intermediate CAs and issuing CAs.

- Certificate templates are sets of rules and settings that define the format and content of a certificate based on the certificate's intended use.

- Certificate enrollment is the process by which a client requests a certificate and a CA generates one.

- Active Directory Certificate Services supports several certificate enrollment methods. A client's choice of enrollment method for obtaining certificates is typically dictated by the type of CA the client is requesting the certificate from and whether the client and CA can communicate across a network.

- Applications discover that a certificate has been revoked by retrieving the certificate revocation list (CRL) from the CA. There are two kinds of CRLs: full CRLs, which contain a complete list of all of a CA's revoked certificates, and delta CRLs. Delta CRLs are shorter lists of certificates that have been revoked since the last full CRL was published.

■ Knowledge Assessment

Fill in the Blank

Complete the following exercise by filling in the blanks with the appropriate terms from this lesson.

1. The _____ authentication protocol stores user passwords in clear text.

2. The certificate revocation lists that a CA publishes daily are called _____.

3. A Remote Access connection that uses the Internet for a network medium is called a _____ connection.

4. _____ encapsulates PPP traffic using the Secure Sockets Layer (SSL) protocol.

5. _____ is a shell protocol that provides a framework for the use of various types of authentication mechanisms.

6. A set of rules that a CA uses to determine whether it should approve a certificate request, deny it, or mark it as pending for later review by an administrator, is called a _____.

7. A(n) _____ CA can use Active Directory, but does not require it.

8. The first CA you create in your PKI must be a _____ CA.

9. The default authentication protocol used by Remote Access on a Windows Server 2008 computer is _____.

10. To issue your own certificates, you must install a _____.

Multiple Choice

Select one or more correct answers for each of the following questions.

1. In which of the following scenarios would public key encryption keep a message sent from User A to User B private?
   a. User A encrypts a message with User B's public key.
   b. User A encrypts a message with User A's public key.
   c. User B encrypts a message with User B's private key.
   d. User B encrypts a message with User A's public key.

2. Which of the following is a feature unique to enterprise CAs?
   a. Web enrollment
   b. certificate autoenrollment
   c. certificates can be revoked
   d. certificates can be renewed prior to their expiration date

3. Which of the following tasks can you not perform on a version 1 certificate template?
   a. add a certificate based on the template to a CRL
   b. change the expiration date of the template
   c. duplicate the version 1 template to a version 2 template
   d. change the permissions assigned to the template

4. You are reviewing enrollment methods and have determined that you will implement three methods for certificate enrollment: Web-based enrollment, the Certificate Enrollment Wizard in the Certificates console, and autoenrollment. Which of the following criteria must you meet if you want a client to use the Certificates console to enroll certificates? (Choose all that apply.)
   a. The issuing CA must be an enterprise CA.
   b. The computer running the Certificates console must be a member of an Active Directory domain.
   c. The issuing CA must be a standalone CA.
   d. The client computer must be running Windows 2000 or later.

5. Your organization's security policy has a requirement that passwords not be stored with reversible encryption. Which of the following authentication protocols can you not use for Remote Access connections?

   a. EAP
   b. MS-CHAP v2
   c. CHAP
   d. PAP

6. Which of the following CA types requires administrators to manually issue certificates?

   a. enterprise
   b. root
   c. subordinate
   d. standalone

7. Which of the following VPN protocols uses IPsec for encryption?

   a. Point-to-Point Tunneling Protocol
   b. Extensible Authentication Protocol-Transport Level Security
   c. Layer 2 Tunneling Protocol
   d. Secure Socket Tunneling Protocol

8. Which of the following certificate enrollment methods can a client use to request a certificate from either an enterprise or a standalone CA?

   a. autoenrollment
   b. Web enrollment
   c. Certificate Enrollment wizard
   d. all of the above

9. Which of the following protocols negotiates the authentication method used by a client and a server while establishing a Remote Access connection?

   a. Point-to-Point Tunneling Protocol
   b. Extensible Authentication Protocol
   c. Virtual Private Networking Protocol
   d. Point-to-Point Protocol

10. In a three-level PKI hierarchy, which of the following CA types always receives its own certificate from the root CA?

   a. issuing CA
   b. intermediate CA
   c. subordinate CA
   d. standalone CA

Review Questions

1. Explain the differences in the process of installing an enterprise subordinate CA, as compared to an enterprise root CA.

2. Place the following steps of the certificate enrollment process in the proper order:

   send or post the certificate
   create the certificate
   request the certificate
   verify the information
   generate keys
   collect required information

■ Case Scenario

Scenario 9-1: Installing a Certification Authority

Adatum, Inc. is a large corporation with an Active Directory network that consists of a head-quarters and branch offices in cities throughout the country. The company's IT department is in the process of deploying a new Web-based application that they have developed in-house, and the IT director is concerned about providing users in the branch offices with secured access to the application.

The director has instructed you to install a certification authority (CA) on one of your Windows Server 2008 servers. The CA must enable Active Directory clients in the branch offices to manually submit enrollment requests for certificates using a Web-based interface. The CA should be able to generate the certificates using a custom template based on settings supplied by the application developers. The director also wants all certificate enrollment requests to be manually approved by an administrator before the CA issues the certificates.

Create a list of the tasks you must perform to install and configure the CA the director has requested, along with a reason for performing each task.

Managing Servers

OBJECTIVE DOMAIN MATRIX

TECHNOLOGY SKILL	OBJECTIVE DOMAIN	OBJECTIVE DOMAIN NUMBER
Using Remote Desktop	Plan server management strategies	2.1
Delegating Administration Tasks	Plan for delegated administration	2.2
Updating Servers	Implement patch management strategy	3.1

KEY TERMS

actions pane
Background Intelligent Transfer
  Service (BITS) peer-caching
console
Delegation of Control Wizard
detail pane
extension snap-ins
Initial Configuration Tasks

Microsoft Management Console
  (MMC)
Network Level Authentication
  (NLA)
Remote Desktop
Remote Desktop Connection
  (RDC)

scope pane
snap-ins
standalone snap-ins
Windows Server Update
  Services (WSUS)

As demonstrated throughout this book, Windows Server 2008 includes a large number of roles and features. Many of the previous lessons describe how to set up those roles and features by installing and configuring them. However, once your servers are up and running, there are still management tasks to be performed, and this lesson describes some of the tools and techniques you can use to perform them. This lesson covers the following topics:

- Managing remote servers
- Delegating administration tasks
- Updating servers

■ Using Remote Administration

THE BOTTOM LINE

Server administrators frequently have to work with a lot of different computers, and often those computers are located in other rooms, other buildings, or even other cities. Rather than open a server closet, enter a secured data center, or travel to another site, Windows Server 2008 makes it possible to perform most server management tasks remotely.

When you install a role or a feature on a Windows Server 2008 computer, Server Manager automatically installs the tools you need to manage it. In many cases, the tools are *Microsoft Management Console (MMC)* snap-ins that you can use to manage the local server or any other server on the network running the same role or feature. The following sections examine some of the ways you can access these administration tools, many of which enable you to manage a server without having to travel to the site and work at its console.

Using Server Manager

Server Manager is an MMC console that provides a selection of the most commonly used Windows Server 2008 management tools.

When you start a Windows Server 2008 computer for the first time after installing the operating system, the *Initial Configuration Tasks* window displays. This window presents a consolidated view of the post-installation tasks that, in previous Windows Server versions, you had to perform using various interfaces presented during and after the OS setup process.

After you complete the configuration tasks in sections 1 and 2 of the Initial Configuration Tasks window, you can use the links in the Customize This Server section to install roles and features on the computer. The Add Roles and Add Features links launch the Add Roles Wizard and the Add Features Wizard, respectively.

You can also install and manage roles and features using the Server Manager console. Server Manager is an MMC console that contains a collection of snap-ins most commonly used by Windows Server 2008 administrators, as shown in Figure 10-1. The Server Manager console integrates the ten snap-ins into a single, categorized interface, by default, in the following manner:

- Diagnostics
  - Event Viewer
  - Reliability and Performance
  - Device Manager
- Configuration
  - Task Scheduler
  - Windows Firewall with Advanced Security
  - Services
  - WMI Control
  - Local Users and Groups
- Storage
  - Windows Server Backup
  - Disk Management

You can access each of these snap-ins by selecting it in the Server Manager scope (left) pane, just as if you opened it from the Administrative Tools program group or manually added it to an MMC console.

When you install roles and features with Server Manager, the wizards also install the administration tools associated with those roles and features. Many of these tools are MMC snap-ins as well, and Server Manager enables you to access some of them through its interface. When you expand the Roles node, you see the roles installed on the computer, and by expanding

Figure 10-1

The Server Manager console

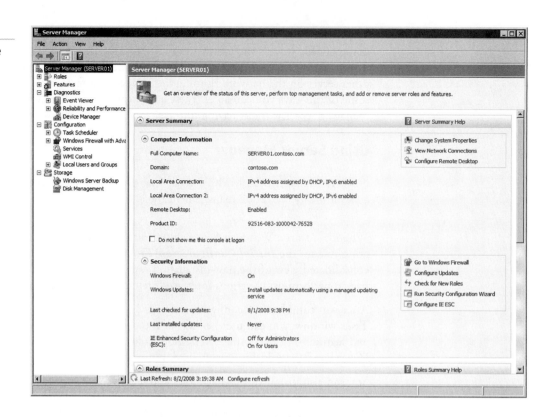

each role, you can access the snap-ins. For example, installing the File Services role (with all of its role services) adds the Share and Storage Management and the File and Server Resource Manager snap-ins, as shown in Figure 10-2.

Figure 10-2

Role-specific snap-ins in the Server Manager console

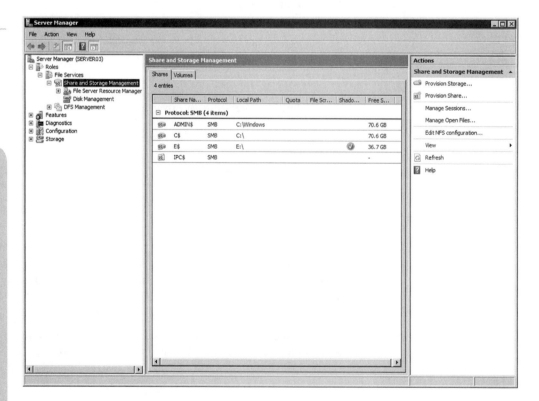

TAKE NOTE *

Be aware that Server Manager does not necessarily display all of the snap-ins associated with a particular role. For example, when you install the File Services role, the Share and Storage Management and the File and Server Resource Manager snap-ins appear in Server Manager, but the Services for Network File System (NFS) snap-in does not appear; you must launch it from the Administrative Tools program group instead.

In addition to the role-specific snap-ins, Server Manager includes a summary page for each installed role that contains the following elements:

- Events—Displays a subset of the computer's System log containing all events related to the role during the past 24 hours, as shown in Figure 10-3. You can configure the filter to display only events with certain levels or event IDs, or specify a different time period. You can also click the Go To Event Viewer link to display the entire Event Viewer snap-in, which is also integrated into the Server Manager console.

Figure 10-3

The Events display for the File Services role

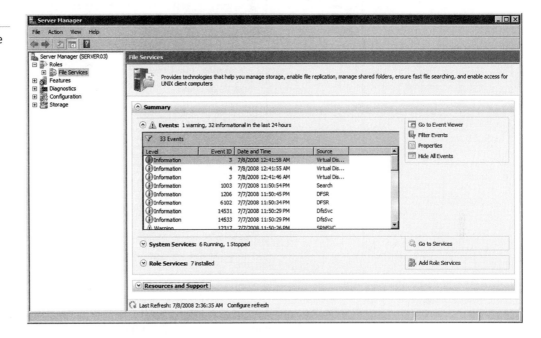

- System Services—Displays all of the system services associated with the role, with the Status and Startup Type of each service, as shown in Figure 10-4. You can start, stop, and restart services as needed.

Figure 10-4

The System Services display for the File Services role

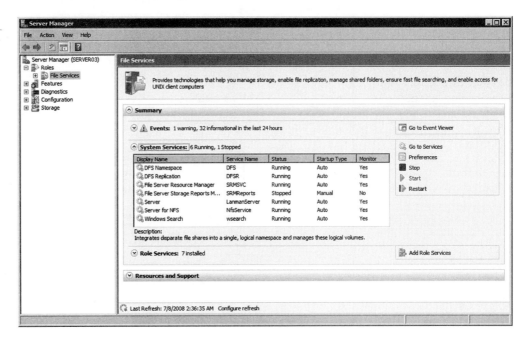

- Role Services—Displays a list of the role services for the role, specifying which role services are currently installed, as shown in Figure 10-5. You can install or remove role services by clicking the provided links to launch the appropriate wizard.

Figure 10-5

The Role Services display for the File Services role

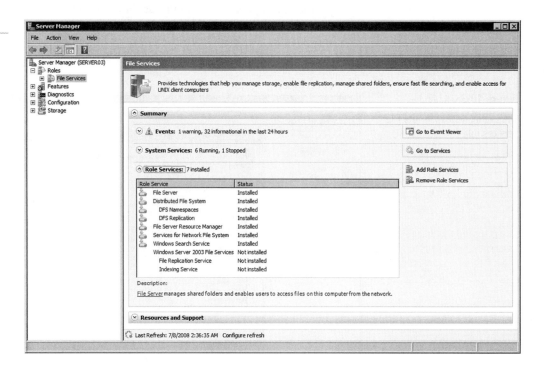

- Resources and Support—Displays a list of role-related tasks and suggestions, as shown in Figure 10-6, which are linked to help files.

Figure 10-6

The Resources and Support display for the File Services role

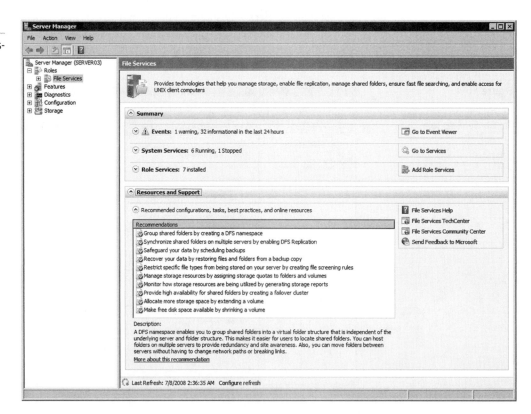

Unlike many MMC consoles, you cannot point Server Manager to another computer to manage it remotely. You can, however, use Remote Desktop to connect to another computer and run Server Manager within the Remote Desktop session. You can also create your own MMC console containing the various snap-ins found in Server Manager, and point it to any other server on the network.

Installing Role Administration Tools

It is not necessary to install a role just to access the tools needed to manage it. Server Manager enables you to install the administration tools for any role on any Windows Server 2008 computer. You can then use the MMC-based tools to connect to any server on the network that is running that role and administer its properties.

To install the administration tools for a role, use the following procedure.

 INSTALL ROLE ADMINISTRATION TOOLS

GET READY. Log on to Windows Server 2008 using an account with administrative privileges. When the logon process is completed, close the Initial Configuration Tasks window and any other windows that appear.

1. Click **Start**, and then click **Administrative Tools** > **Server Manager**. The Server Manager console appears.

2. Select the **Features** node and, in the details pane, click **Add Features.** The Add Features Wizard appears, displaying the *Select Features* page, as shown in Figure 10-7.

Figure 10-7

The Select Features page of the Add Features Wizard

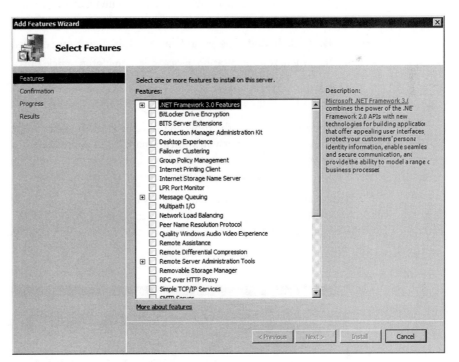

3. Expand the **Remote Server Administration Tools** > **Role Administration Tools** container, as shown in Figure 10-8.

Figure 10-8

The Role Administration Tools container in the Add Features Wizard

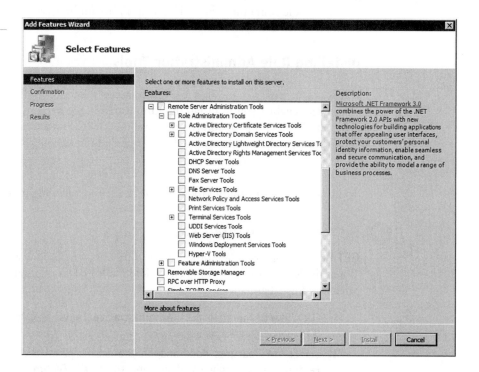

4. Select the checkbox for the role whose tools you want to install. In some cases, you can expand a role and select individual tools within it.

5. Click **Next**. The *Confirm Installation Selections* page appears.

6. Click **Install**. The wizard installs the tools you selected.

7. When the installation process is completed, click **Close**.

CLOSE the Server Manager console. In some cases, the wizard will prompt you to restart the server, to finish the installation process.

When you run one of the tools you have installed in this manner, you might have to direct the console to the server you want to manage. In some cases, this is unnecessary. For example, when you install the Active Directory Domain Services tools, the consoles automatically connect to the domain of which the computer is a member.

However, if you install the File Services tools and run the File Server Resource Manager console, the console appears and attempts to connect to the FSRM service on the local machine. This attempt fails, as shown in Figure 10-9, because you installed only the console, not the entire role.

Figure 10-9

A failed File Server Resource Manager console connection

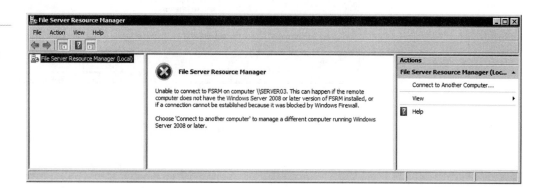

When you click Connect to Another Computer in the actions pane, a Connect to Another Computer dialog box appears, as shown in Figure 10-10, in which you can specify or browse to the computer you want to manage.

Figure 10-10

The Connect to Another Computer dialog box

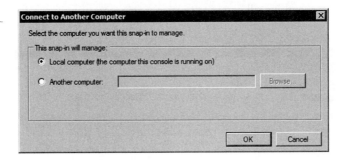

Using MMC Consoles

> Microsoft Management Console is a shell application that Windows Server 2008 uses to provide access to most of its system and network management tools.

MMC provides a standardized, common interface for application modules called ***snap-ins***, which you can use to configure operating system settings, applications, and services. MMC snap-ins are individualized to specific tasks, and you can combine, order, and group them within the MMC shell to your individual preferences. An instance of MMC with one or more snap-ins installed is referred to as a ***console***.

Most of the primary administrative tools in Windows Server 2008 are MMC consoles with collections of snap-ins installed that are suited to a specific purpose. With only a few exceptions, all of the shortcuts that can appear in the Administrative Tools program group on a computer running Windows Server 2008 are links to pre-configured MMC consoles.

For example, when you promote a Windows Server 2008 computer to a domain controller, the Active Directory Domain Services Installation Wizard creates shortcuts to the following three primary management tools for Active Directory:

- Active Directory Domains and Trusts
- Active Directory Sites and Services
- Active Directory Users and Computers
- ADSI Edit

Each of these shortcuts opens an MMC console containing a single snap-in, as shown in Figure 10-11. The Active Directory Users and Computers snap-in, for example, is specifically designed to administer the user, group, and computer objects in an Active Directory domain. It is the snap-ins within the MMC shell, not MMC itself, that provide the administrative tools.

Figure 10-11

The Active Directory Users and Computers console

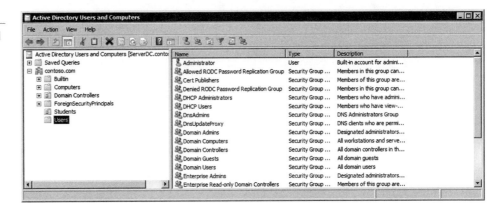

The four Active Directory consoles listed earlier all contain only a single snap-in, but as you have seen in Server Manager, an MMC console is not limited to using one snap-in at a time. In addition to Server Manager, consoles such as Computer Management, found in the Administrative Tools program group on every Windows Server 2008 computer, contain many different snap-ins, all combined into a single, convenient interface, as shown in Figure 10-12.

Figure 10-12

The Computer Management console

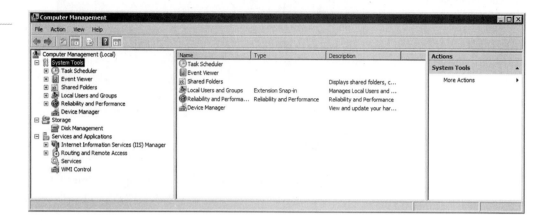

USING THE MMC INTERFACE

The MMC interface uses a three-paned design. The left pane, called the ***scope pane***, contains a hierarchical list of the snap-ins installed in the console and any subheadings that the snap-ins provide. You can expand and contract the elements in the scope pane to display more or less information, just as you can expand and contract folders in Windows Explorer. Selecting an item in the scope pane displays its contents in the console's middle pane, called the ***detail pane***. What you see in the details pane is wholly dependant on the function of the snap-in you are using. The ***actions pane***, on the right side, contains links to the tasks most commonly associated with the content appearing in the detail pane.

Above the three panes, MMC has a standard Windows menu and toolbar. The commands in the menus and the tools in the toolbar vary depending on the snap-in that is currently selected in the scope pane. For example, when you open the Computer Management console and click each of the snap-ins in the scope pane in turn, you see the contents of the toolbar change with each one, as do some of the menu contents.

The primary menu for context-specific functions in an MMC console is the Action menu. When you select a snap-in element in either the scope or the detail pane, the Action menu changes to include commands specific to that element. Most Action menus contain an All Tasks submenu that lets you select any of the possible tasks to perform on the selected element (see Figure 10-13). It is also common to find a New submenu under Action, which enables you to create subelements beneath the selected element. In most cases, the Action menu commands for a selected element are also available from a context menu, accessible by right-clicking the element.

Figure 10-13

The Action menu in an MMC console

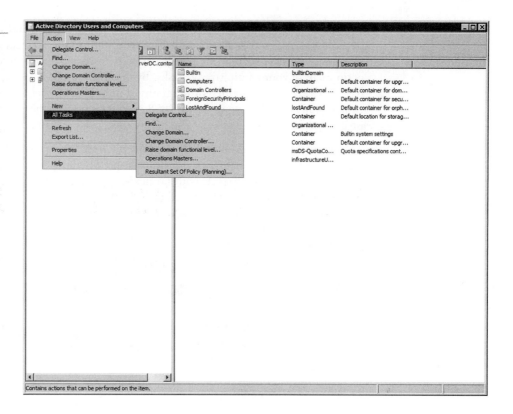

Although it is the Action menu that changes most frequently, other MMC menus can contain context-specific elements as well, most particularly the View menu, which often contains commands that control how the snap-in displays information. For example, there are several MMC snap-ins that display a subset of their available information by default. When an Advanced Features command appears in the View menu, selecting it switches the console to the full display (see Figure 10-14).

Figure 10-14

The Active Directory Users and Computers console with Advanced Features displayed

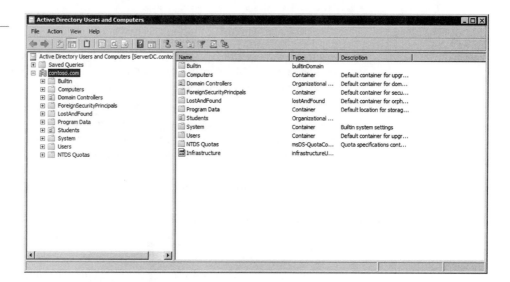

CREATING CUSTOMIZED MMC CONSOLES

Windows Server 2008 includes a large collection of MMC snap-ins, not all of which are immediately accessible using the default shortcuts in the Start menu. There are some extremely powerful tools included with the operating system that you must seek out yourself. It is also possible for third-party software developers to create their own MMC snap-ins and include them with their products.

This leads to one of the most powerful MMC features, which is the ability to create customized consoles containing whatever snap-ins you want to use. You can combine one or more snap-ins or parts of snap-ins in a single console, to create a single interface in which you can perform all of your administrative tasks. By creating a custom MMC console, you do not have to switch between different programs or individual consoles. Customized consoles can contain any of the Windows Server 2008 snap-ins, whether they are already included in a preconfigured console or not, as well as any third party snap-ins you might have.

The executable file for Microsoft Management Console is Mmc.exe. When you run this file from the Run dialog box or a command prompt, an empty console appears, as shown in Figure 10-15. This is a console with no snap-ins, so the menus and toolbar buttons at this point have their default MMC functions. The only element in the console window is the console root object in the scope pane, which is a placeholder representing the top of the console hierarchy. Before you can perform any administrative tasks using the console, you must add one or more snap-ins to it.

Figure 10-15

A blank MMC console

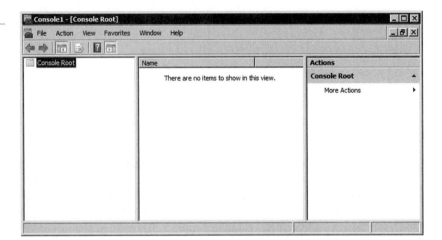

ADDING SNAP-INS

There are two types of MMC snap-ins, as follows:

- *Standalone snap-ins*—A standalone snap-in is a single tool that you can install directly into an empty MMC console. Standalone snap-ins appear in the first level directly beneath the console root in the console's scope pane.

- *Extension snap-ins*—An extension snap-in provides additional functionality to specific standalone snap-ins. You cannot add an extension snap-in to a console without adding an appropriate standalone snap-in first. Extension snap-ins appear beneath the associated standalone snap-in in the console's scope pane.

Some snap-ins offer both standalone and extension functionality. For example, the Event Viewer snap-in appears as an extension in the Computer Management console, beneath the Computer Management object in the scope pane. However, you can also add the Event Viewer snap-in to a custom console as a standalone snap-in so that it appears directly beneath the console root.

To add snap-ins to a custom console, use the following procedure.

 ADD SNAP-IN

GET READY. Log on to Windows Server 2008 using an account with administrative privileges. When the logon process is completed, close the Initial Configuration Tasks window and any other windows that appear.

1. Click **Start**, and then click **Run**. The Run dialog box appears.

2. In the **Open** text box, key **mmc** and click **OK**. An empty MMC console appears.

3. Click **File** > **Add/Remove Snap-in**. The Add or Remove Snap-ins dialog box appears, as shown in Figure 10-16.

Figure 10-16

The Add or Remove Snap-ins dialog box

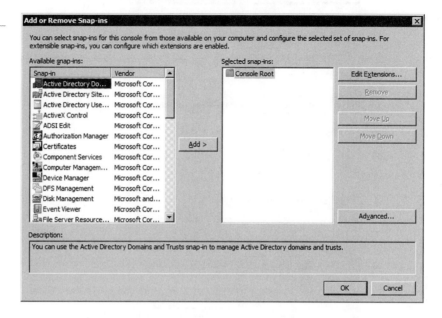

4. In the **Available snap-ins** list, select a snap-in such as Computer Management and click **Add**. A dialog box for the snap-in appears, as shown in Figure 10-17.

Figure 10-17

The Computer Management dialog box

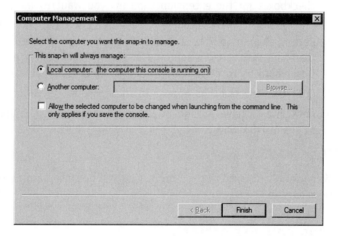

TAKE NOTE *

The snap-ins that appear in the Available snap-ins list depend on the roles and features installed on the computer.

5. Specify the computer you want to manage with the snap-in and click **Finish**. The snap-in appears in the Selected snap-ins list.

TAKE NOTE *

In some cases, such as the Certificates snap-in, the dialog box presents different options, such as whether you want to manage a user or computer account.

6. Select one of the entries in the **Selected snap-ins** list and click **Edit Extensions**. The Extensions dialog box for the selected snap-in appears, as shown in Figure 10-18.

Figure 10-18

The Extensions for Computer Management dialog box

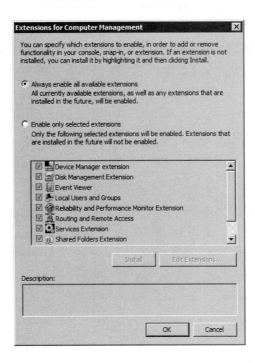

7. To select from the extension snap-ins associated with the selected standalone snap-in, select the **Enable only selected extensions** option and then select the checkboxes for the extension snap-ins you want to include in the console. Then, click **OK**.

8. Repeat steps 4 to 7 to add additional snap-ins to the Selected snap-ins list. When there are two or more snap-ins in the list, you can use the Move Up and Move Down buttons to control the order in which they will appear in the console.

9. Click **OK**. The snap-ins appear in the console.

10. Click **File** > **Save As** and, in the **Save As** combo box, specify a name for the console and click **Save**.

CLOSE the MMC console.

MMC consoles are saved to the Administrative Tools program group in the Start menu, with a .msc extension.

SETTING CONSOLE OPTIONS

Once you have added the snap-ins you want to appear in your custom MMC console, you can set options that determine what changes other users can make to the console's configuration. Selecting File > Options displays the Options dialog box, in which you can specify the name that should appear in the console's title bar and select the console mode.

By default, all new consoles you create are configured to use Author mode, which provides full access to all console functions. The available modes you can choose from are as follows:

- Author Mode—Provides full console access, including adding or removing snap-ins, creating windows, creating taskpad views and tasks, viewing portions of the console tree, changing the options on the console, and saving the console. This is the default mode for new MMC consoles.

- User Mode-Full Access—Allows users to navigate between snap-ins, open windows, and access all portions of the console tree.

- User Mode-Limited Access, Multiple Windows—Prevents users from opening new windows or accessing a portion of the console tree, but allows them to view multiple windows in the console.
- User Mode-Limited Access, Single Window—Prevents users from opening new windows or accessing a portion of the console tree, and allows them to view only one window in the console.

Console modes enable you to create consoles for other users that have limited capabilities, and that the users cannot alter. Console mode settings are why you cannot add snap-ins to the preconfigured consoles supplied with Windows Server 2008.

USING MULTIPLE WINDOWS

If you look at the upper right corner of a custom MMC console, you will see that there are two sets of window manipulation buttons. This is because the snap-ins installed in that console are actually in a separate window that is maximized by default. When you click the Restore Down button (the middle one of the three), the snap-ins revert to a floating window, as shown in Figure 10-19.

Figure 10-19

An MMC console with a floating window

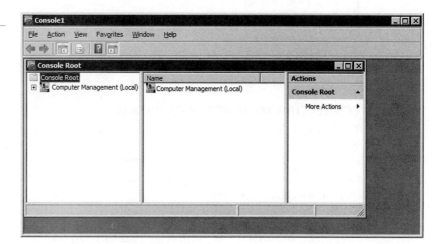

You can create additional windows in the console by selecting Window > New Window. This enables you to create two different views of a single snap-in, or work with two different snap-ins in one console at the same time, as shown in Figure 10-20. You can also select an element in the scope pane and select New Window From Here from the Action menu, to create a new window with the selected element at its root.

Figure 10-20

An MMC console with two open windows

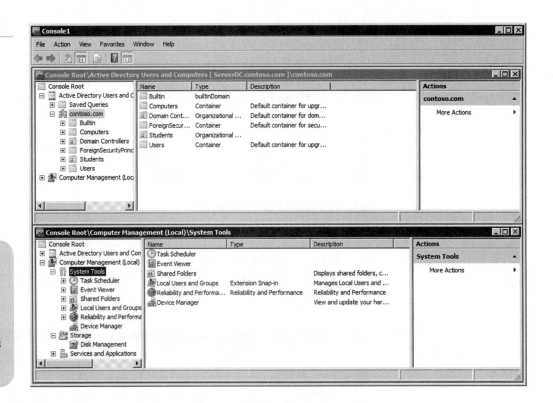

Not all MMC consoles enable you to open multiple windows. It is possible to configure a console to operate in a user mode that prevents the creation of new windows.

CONNECTING TO REMOTE COMPUTERS

The MMC consoles that appear in the Start menu of a computer running Windows Server 2003 are all configured to manage resources on the local system. However, many of the snap-ins supplied with Windows Server 2008 enable you to manage other Windows computers on the network as well. There are two ways to access a remote computer using an MMC snap-in: which are as follows:

- Redirect an existing snap-in to another system
- Create a custom console with snap-ins directed to other systems

To connect to and manage another system using an MMC snap-in, you must launch the console with an account that has administrative credentials on the remote computer. The exact permissions required depend on the functions performed by the snap-in. If your credentials do not provide the proper permissions on the target computer, you will be able to load the snap-in, but you will not be able to read information from or modify settings on the target computer.

REDIRECTING A SNAP-IN

A snap-in that is directed at a specific system has a Connect To Another Computer command in its Action menu. Selecting this command opens a dialog box in which you can specify or browse to another computer on the network. Once you select the name of the computer you want to manage and click OK, the snap-in element in the scope pane changes to reflect the name of the computer you selected.

Not every snap-in has the ability to connect to a remote computer, because some do not need it. For example, the Active Directory Domain Services consoles, as mentioned earlier, automatically locate a domain controller for the current domain and access Active Directory from there. There is no need to specify a computer name. However, you will find Change Domain and Change Domain Controller commands in the Action menu in these consoles, which enable you to manage a different domain or select a specific domain controller in the present domain.

CREATING A REMOTE CONSOLE

Connecting to a remote computer by redirecting an existing console is convenient for impromptu management tasks, but it is limited by the fact that you can access only one computer at a time. You also have to open the console and redirect it every time you want to access the remote system. A more permanent solution is to create a custom console with snap-ins that are already directed at other computers.

When you add a snap-in to a custom console, you select the computer you want to manage with that snap-in. You can also add multiple copies of the same snap-in to a custom console, with each one pointed at a different computer. This adds a whole new dimension to MMC's functionality. Not only can you create custom consoles containing a variety of tools, you can also create consoles containing tools for a variety of computers. For example, you can create a single console containing multiple instances of the Computer Management snap-in, with each one pointing to a different computer. This enables you to manage computers all over the network from a single console.

Using Remote Desktop

In Lesson 4, "Planning Application Services," you learned about how you can use the Terminal Services role to deploy applications to workstations on your network without having to perform an installation for every user. You can also use the Terminal Service capabilities in Windows Server 2008 to manage servers and workstations from remote locations.

In Terminal Services, a computer running a client program opens a session on a server computer and receives access to a fully functional Windows desktop. All of the controls and applications the client uses are actually running on the server. The only data transmitted over the network is that needed to create the interface on the client, that is, keystrokes, mouse movements, and display graphics.

Ever since the Windows Server 2003 release, however, the components that make up the Terminal Services application are fully integrated into the operating system. This means that the Terminal Services capabilities are there, even if you do not have the Terminal Services role installed on the computer. The main reason for this is so administrators can use Terminal Services to manage remote computers without having to travel to a distant location. In Windows, this capability is known as ***Remote Desktop***.

Unlike Terminal Services, which supports multiple simultaneous connections and requires clients to have Terminal Services Client Access Licenses (TS CALs), Windows Server 2008 includes licenses for two Remote Desktop connections. This means that there is no extra cost associated with Windows Server 2008's remote administration capabilities.

To use Remote Desktop to administer a server on the network, you must complete the following tasks:

- Enable Remote Desktop on the server
- Configure ***Remote Desktop Connection (RDC)*** on the client
- Establish a connection between the client and the server

ENABLING REMOTE DESKTOP

For security reasons, Remote Desktop is disabled on Windows Server 2008 computers by default. Before you can connect to a server, you must enable Remote Desktop, using the following procedure.

ENABLE REMOTE DESKTOP

GET READY. Log on to Windows Server 2008 using an account with administrative privileges. When the logon process is completed, close the Initial Configuration Tasks window and any other windows that appear.

1. Click **Start**, and then click **Control Panel.** The Control Panel window appears.

2. Double-click the **System** icon. The System control panel appears, as shown in Figure 10-21.

Figure 10-21

The System control panel

TAKE NOTE*

You can also access the System control panel from the Initial Configuration Tasks window, by clicking Enable Remote Desktop.

3. Click **Remote Settings.** The System Properties sheet appears, displaying the Remote tab, as shown in Figure 10-22.

Figure 10-22

The Remote tab on the System Properties sheet

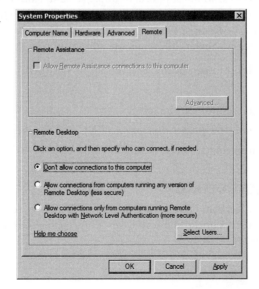

4. In the **Remote Desktop** box, select one of the following options:

- Allow connections from computers running any version of Remote Desktop (less secure)
- Allow connections only from computers running Remote Desktop with Network Level Authentication (more secure)

5. Click **OK.** A message box appears, informing you that you have chosen to enable the Remote Desktop exception for Windows Firewall on all of the computer's network interfaces.

CLOSE the System control panel.

➕ MORE INFORMATION

Network Level Authentication (NLA) is a new security feature introduced in Windows Vista and Windows Server 2008 that confirms the user's identity with the Credential Security Service Provider (CredSSP) protocol before the client and server establish the Remote Desktop connection. This eliminates a potentially hazardous, if momentary, window of opportunity during which the computers are connected before the authentication process begins. To use Network Level Authentication, the Remote Desktop server must be running Windows Server 2008, and the client computer must be running Remote Desktop Connection version 6.0 or above on Windows Vista, Windows Server 2008, or another operating system that supports CredSSP.

By default, the Administrators group on a Windows Server 2008 computer has the permissions needed to establish a Remote Desktop connection. If you want to grant other users the same permissions, you must add them to the Remote Desktop Users group on the server, either by clicking the Select Users button on the Remote tab of the System Properties sheet, or by using the Local Users and Groups MMC snap-in.

Configuring Remote Desktop Connection

Although the RDC client seems simple at first, clicking the Options button expands the Remote Desktop Connection dialog box into a tabbed dialog box containing a variety of configuration settings.

By configuring the options in the RDC client, administrators can use them to improve the client's performance and optimize network bandwidth consumption. The following sections examine these options and their functions.

CONFIGURING GENERAL OPTIONS

On the General tab, shown in Figure 10-23, in addition to specifying the name or address of a terminal server, you can specify a default *User name* value that will appear in the Windows Security dialog box when the user attempts to connect. This can be useful if you intend to create RDP files or shortcuts for users confused by the domain\user name format.

Figure 10-23

The General tab on the expanded Remote Desktop Connection dialog box

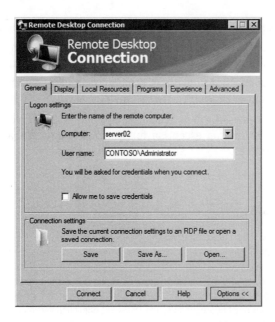

CONFIGURING DISPLAY OPTIONS

On the Display tab, shown in Figure 10-24, you can specify the size of the terminal server desktop, as it appears on the client computer. By default, the Remote Desktop Size slider is set to Full Screen, which causes the client to occupy the client computer's entire display, using the computer's configured display resolution.

Figure 10-24

The Display tab on the expanded Remote Desktop Connection dialog box

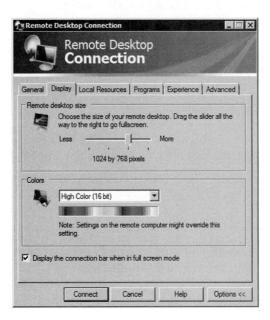

In addition to the desktop size, you can adjust the color depth of the RDC display, using the Colors dropdown list. The settings available in this dropdown list depend on the capabilities of the video display adapter installed in the client computer.

One of the new features implemented in RDP 6.x is support for 32-bit color, which enables clients to run graphic intensive applications, such as image editors, with a full color palette. However, the tradeoff for this ability is the increased network bandwidth required to transmit the display information from the terminal server to the client.

For example, when you configure RDC to use 32-bit color, the client and the terminal server open a special RDP channel just for that color information. This enables the client to assign a lower priority to the extra color information so that it does not interfere with the basic functionality of the client. However, 32-bit color increases the overall bandwidth consumed by the connection substantially. As a general rule, you should set the Colors parameter to the High Color (16-bit) setting, unless the client will be running terminal server applications that can benefit from the additional color information.

CONFIGURING LOCAL RESOURCES OPTIONS

On the Local Resources tab, shown in Figure 10-25, you configure how the RDC client should reconcile the resources on the terminal server with those on the client computer.

Figure 10-25

The Local Resources tab on the expanded Remote Desktop Connection dialog box

CONFIGURING KEYBOARD REDIRECTION

One of the long-standing problems for Terminal Services users is how the client computer should interpret system keyboard combinations during a terminal session. For example, when you press ALT+TAB to switch between the programs running on the computer, do you want to switch the terminal server programs or those on the client computer?

In the Keyboard box, you can control this behavior by selecting one of the following options:

- On the local computer—Causes the client computer to process all system keystrokes.
- On the remote computer—Causes the terminal server computer to process all system keystrokes.
- In full screen mode only—Causes the terminal server computer to process all system keystrokes, but only when the Remote Desktop Size parameter is set to Full Screen. This is the default setting.

If you select the *On the local computer* option, you can use alternative key combinations in the RDC session window, as shown in Table 10-1.

Table 10-1

Terminal Services Key Combinations

TERMINAL SERVICES KEY COMBINATION	WINDOWS KEY COMBINATION EQUIVALENT	FUNCTION
ALT+PAGE UP	ALT+TAB	Switches to the next program to the right in the task list
ALT+PAGE DOWN	ALT+SHIFT+TAB	Switches to the next program to the left in the task list
ALT+HOME	CTRL+ESC	Displays the Start menu
CTRL+ALT+BREAK	N/A	Toggles the client session between a full screen and a window
CTRL+ALT+END	CTRL+ALT+DEL	Displays the Windows Security screen
ALT+INSERT	N/A	Cycles through running programs in the order you launched them
ALT+DELETE	ALT+SPACE	Displays the system menu for the current active window
CTRL+ALT+Plus Sign	PRINT SCREEN	Copies the graphical contents of the desktop to the clipboard
CTRL+ALT+Minus Sign	ALT+PRINT SCREEN	Copies the graphical contents of the active window to the clipboard

CONFIGURING LOCAL RESOURCE REDIRECTION

Terminal Services users often have peripherals connected to their local computers, and over the years, Microsoft has gradually developed the device redirection capabilities of the RDC client. With RDC 6.x, you can use almost any device connected to the client computer in a terminal session.

In the Local Devices and Resources box, you can select which of the following resources on the client computer you want to use in the terminal session:

- Printers—Enables terminal server applications to send print jobs to printers on the client computer
- Clipboard—Enables terminal server applications to copy data to, and paste data from, the clipboard on the client computer

Click the More button to display the dialog box shown in Figure 10-26, which contains the following additional options:

Figure 10-26

The Remote Desktop Connection Local Devices and Resources dialog box

- Smart cards—Enables RDC to use a smart card reader on the client computer for authentication within a terminal session
- Serial ports—Enables terminal server applications to access devices connected to serial ports on the client computer
- Drives—Enables terminal server applications to access selected drives on the client computer
- Supported Plug and Play devices—Enables terminal server applications to access selected Plug and Play devices on the client computer

CONFIGURING EXPERIENCE OPTIONS

On the Experience tab, shown in Figure 10-27, you can specify which standard Windows desktop performance features you want the client to use within a terminal session. These features are as follows:

- Desktop background—Displays the selected desktop wallpaper in the RDC session. When deselected, the desktop appears with only a black background.
- Font smoothing—Also called anti-aliasing, enables the client to display screen fonts without jagged lines.
- Desktop composition—Enables the RDC client to duplicate the graphics rendering capabilities of Windows Vista, most notably the Aero "glass" effect.
- Show contents of window while dragging—Causes the client to move windows fluidly across the desktop when you drag them.
- Menu and window animation—Enables the client to display menu and window effects, such as fades.
- Themes—Enables the client to display the theme elements configured on the terminal server, including backgrounds and icons.
- Bitmap caching—Enables the client to store display information in a cache in local memory so that the server does not have to repeatedly transmit the same data.

Figure 10-27

The Experience tab on the expanded Remote Desktop Connection dialog box

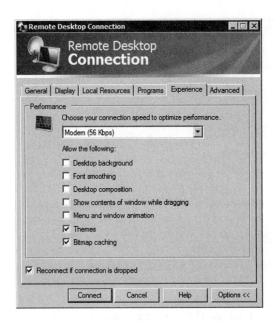

With one exception, these features are strictly cosmetic, and enabling them can degrade the client's performance and increase its network bandwidth consumption. The only exception is bitmap caching, which improves the client's performance and reduces the amount of bandwidth it utilizes. Therefore, you should always enable bitmap caching.

Connecting to a Remote Desktop Server Using RDC

Establishing a connection to a Remote Desktop server is basically a matter of specifying the server name in the RDC client and supplying the appropriate logon credentials.

You can use the same credentials to open a Remote Desktop session as to log on at the remote computer's keyboard. The only special requirement is that the user has either administrative privileges or membership in the Remote Desktop Users group on the terminal server.

To connect to a terminal server, use the following procedure.

 CONNECT TO A REMOTE DESKTOP SERVER USING RDC

GET READY. Log on to Windows Server 2008. When the logon process is completed, close the Initial Configuration Tasks window and any other windows that appear.

1. Click **Start**, and then click **All Programs** > **Accessories** > **Remote Desktop Connection**. The Remote Desktop Connection dialog box appears, as shown in Figure 10-28.

Figure 10-28

The Remote Desktop
Connection dialog box

2. In the **Computer** text box, specify the terminal server to which you want to connect, using a fully-qualified domain name (FQDN), a NetBIOS name, or an IP address.

3. Click **Connect.** A Windows Security dialog box appears, as shown in Figure 10-29.

Figure 10-29

The Windows Security dialog
box

4. In the **User Name** text box, key the name of the account you will use to log on to the terminal server, using the format *servername\username or domainname\ username.*

5. In the **Password** text box, key the password associated with the user account you specified.

6. To configure the RDC client to retain your logon credentials, click the **Remember my credentials** checkbox.

7. Click **OK.** The terminal server desktop appears, occupying the entire display, except for a connection bar at the top, which you can use to control the terminal session.

CLOSE the Remote Desktop Connection window to disconnect from the Terminal Services session.

TAKE NOTE*

When using Remote Desktop, it is important to distinguish between disconnecting from a session and logging off from one. When you disconnect, the session still exists on the remote computer, and any applications you have left open will continue to run. When you log off, the session ends, terminating all running applications.

The RDC client displays the terminal server desktop in full screen mode by default. After the desktop appears, you can use the standard controls at the top right of the connection bar to reduce it to a window or minimize it.

■ Delegating Administration Tasks

THE BOTTOM LINE

As networks grow larger in size, so do the numbers of administrative tasks there are to perform on a regular basis, and so do the IT staffs that are needed to perform them. Delegating administrative tasks to specific individuals is a natural part of enterprise server management, as is assigning those individuals the permissions they need—and only the permissions they need—to perform those tasks.

On smaller networks, with small IT staffs, it is not uncommon for task delegation to be informal, and for everyone in the IT department to have full access to the entire network. However, on larger networks, with larger IT staffs, this becomes increasingly impractical. For example, you might want the newly hired junior IT staffers to be able to create new user accounts, but you do not want them to be able to redesign your Active Directory tree or change the CEO's password.

CERTIFICATION READY?
Plan for delegated administration
2.2

Delegation, therefore, is the practice by which administrators grant other users a subset of the privileges that they themselves possess. As such, delegation is as much a matter of restricting permissions as it is of granting them. You want to provide individuals with the privileges they need, while protecting sensitive information and delicate infrastructure.

The following sections examine some of the Windows Server 2008 tools you can use to control administrative access to Active Directory and other applications.

Delegating File System Permissions

Despite the fact that they are exercised constantly, assigning file system permissions is usually not an everyday task on a properly designed enterprise network. However, there are times when you might want to provide other administrators with the ability to set permissions on files, folders, and shares.

The general rule of thumb for network file system permission assignments is to never assign permissions to individual user accounts. While it is certainly possible to grant each user individual permissions for every file they need, this would require an enormous amount of work, both in the initial setup and in ongoing maintenance.

Instead, the preferred solution for file system permission assignments is to grant permissions to groups, and then add individual user accounts (or other groups) to them as members. The members of each group then inherit the permissions assigned to that group. Once you have created the groups and assigned file system permissions to them, the ongoing maintenance consists mainly of adding users to and removing them from groups.

However, there are occasions in which you might want to delegate the ability to assign file system permissions, such as when someone is installing a new disk drive in a computer or creating a new directory structure on an existing disk. To assign permissions on an NTFS drive, an administrator must have either the Allow Full Control standard permission or the Allow Change Permissions special permission.

TAKE NOTE *

As explained in Lesson 8, "Planning Server and Network Security," the NTFS permission system is based on a series of standard permissions, each of which is a combination of special permissions. In most cases, administrators work with the standard permissions, but in certain circumstances, they might want to exercise more granular control by assigning special permissions directly.

X REF

For more information on working with special permissions, see "Assigning Special NTFS Permissions" in Lesson 8.

Granting administrators the Allow Full Control permission for a disk volume or folder enables them to modify the file system in any way, including assigning permissions to other users or groups. However, there might be situations in which you do not want to give administrators the Allow Full Control permission, such as to prevent them from deleting or taking ownership of files and folders.

To do this, you must work with special permissions. For example, if you grant administrators all of the Allow standard permissions except for Full Control, and then grant them the Allow Change Permissions special permission, they will be able to assign permissions to other users, but will not be able to take ownership of files and folders.

Assigning Group Managers

As mentioned earlier, most organizations assign NTFS permissions to security groups, not to individual users, so managing group memberships is a common administrative task.

Planning a group strategy is an important part of designing an enterprise network, but once the strategy is in place, administrators must maintain it by adding users to the correct groups and removing them as needed. Depending on the size of the organization, the size of the IT staff, and the nature of the business, it might be prudent to allow department managers or staffers to manage group memberships, rather than forcing them to call the IT staff.

To grant individuals the ability to add members to and remove them from a specific Active Directory security group, you can designate them as group managers, using the following procedure.

 ASSIGN GROUP MANAGERS

GET READY. Log on to Windows Server 2008. When the logon process is completed, close the Initial Configuration Tasks window and any other windows that appear. If you have not done so already, install the Remote Server Administration Tools > Role Administration Tools > Active Directory Domain Services Tools feature.

1. Click **Start**, and then click **Administrative Tools** > **Active Directory Users and Computers**. The Active Directory Users and Computers console appears.
2. Browse to the group object you want to manage, right-click the group, and from the context menu, select **Properties**. The group's Properties sheet appears.

3. Display the Managed By tab, shown in Figure 10-30.

Figure 10-30

The Managed By tab in a
group object's Properties sheet

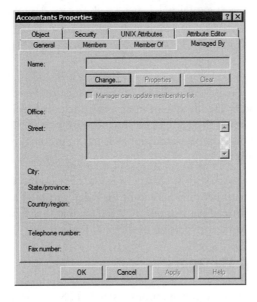

4. Click **Change.** The Select User, Contact, or Group dialog box appears, as shown in
Figure 10-31.

Figure 10-31

The Select User, Contact, or
Group dialog box

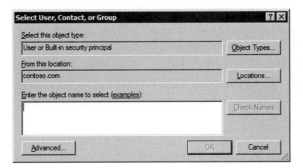

5. Key the name of a user or group in the **Enter The Object Name To Select** text box
and click **OK.**
6. Select the **Manager can update membership list** checkbox and click **OK.**

CLOSE the Active Directory Users and Computers console.

The designated group manager can now add users to and remove them from the group's
member list.

Delegating Active Directory Administrative Privileges

One of the most common ways of delegating administrative responsibility on an Active
Directory network is to give individuals responsibility for branches of the directory tree,
or for individual objects.

Active Directory has its own permissions system, which functions much like that of the
NTFS file system. By granting users and groups permissions to specific Active Directory
objects, you can allow them to perform specific administrative tasks on those objects. As with

NTFS, Active Directory has a set of standard permissions, which are pre-defined collections of special permissions. You can choose to work with either type of permission, or you can simplify the process by using the Delegation of Control Wizard to create permission assignments.

The basic premise behind Active Directory delegation is to provide individual departments or sites or divisions in your organization with administrative control over the Active Directory objects representing those departments, sites, or divisions. For example, if your organization has branch offices in three cities, each of which is represented by an organizational unit object in your Active Directory domain, you can delegate certain privileges to the IT staff in each office so that they can create user objects for new hires, manage group memberships, and so forth.

As with file system permissions, granting branch office administrators permissions to their OU object enables them to manage all of the objects subordinate to that OU. An administrator with the Allow Full Control permission to an OU can not only create users and groups, but also create additional OUs and other objects, creating as complex a hierarchy as they need. This is why it is possible to limit the permissions assigned to the administrator of a branch office.

The privileges you delegate to other individuals must obviously depend on their training and expertise. If your branch offices have full IT staffs, you might want to give them full control over their portions of the Active Directory hierarchy. However, for branch offices without IT personnel, you might be able to train someone to create user objects for new hires and add them to the appropriate groups, and then assign the erstwhile administrator only the permissions needed to complete those tasks.

Active Directory is essentially a database, and Active Directory objects are records in the database that consist of a number of properties. The permission system enables you to specify what objects administrators can create or delete, and whether they can read and write properties for those objects.

When working with standard permissions, the Read and Write permissions enable a security principal (that is, the user or group to which you have assigned the permissions) to view and modify the properties of the specified object and all of its subordinate objects. The ability to create and delete objects is treated as a whole. A security principal with the Create All Child Objects permission, for example, can create any type of object that the schema will allow beneath the specified object. In other words, this permission provides the ability to create any type of leaf object in an OU, or subordinate OU objects, but you cannot create a domain beneath an OU, because the schema will not allow anyone to do that.

➕ MORE INFORMATION

The Active Directory schema is the code that specifies what types of objects can exist in the Active Directory hierarchy, what properties each object possesses, and the relationships between objects in the directory tree. Applications can modify the schema to add custom properties to existing object types or create their own new objects types.

The special permissions provide a more granular approach to the creation and deletion of objects. There are individual special permissions for each of 37 object types in a default Active Directory installation, and installing applications can add more object types to the schema. Using special permissions, you can grant a security principal the ability to create specific types of objects, and prevent them from creating other types. You can therefore enable branch office managers to create new user objects, while preventing them from creating other object types.

As with all of the other permission systems in Windows Server 2008, you can either allow or deny permissions to security principals, and the following effective permission rules still apply:

- Allow permissions are cumulative
- Deny permissions override Allow permissions
- Explicit permissions take precedence over inherited permissions

X REF

For more information on the effective permission rules, see "Understanding Effective Permissions" in Lesson 8.

The standard and special permissions for organizational unit objects are listed in Table 10-2. The permissions for other object types can differ.

Table 10-2

Active Directory Organizational Unit Standard and Special Permissions

STANDARD PERMISSION	EQUIVALENT SPECIAL PERMISSIONS	CAPABILITIES
Full Control	• All special permissions	Enables the security principal to perform all Active Directory object administration tasks, including the creation and deletion of subordinate objects and management of their properties
Read	• List Contents • Read All Properties • Read Permissions	Enables the security principal to view all of the objects beneath the selected object, their properties, and their permissions
Write	• Write All Properties • All Validated Writes	Enables the security principal to write to all of the selected object's properties, as well as those of any subordinate objects
Create All Child Objects	• All 37 of the Create Object special permissions	Enables the security principal to create any type of object supported by Active Directory subordinate to the selected object
Delete All Child Objects	• All 37 of the Delete Object special permissions	Enables the security principal to delete any existing objects subordinate to the selected object
Generate Resultant Set of Policy (Planning)	• Generate Resultant Set of Policy (Planning)	Enables the security principal to run the Group Policy Modeling Wizard in the Group Policy Management Console, which creates a scenario and simulates the application of group policy objects to the users and computers in that scenario
Generate Resultant Set of Policy (Logging)	• Generate Resultant Set of Policy (Logging)	Enables the security principal to run the Group Policy Results Wizard in the Group Policy Management Console, which creates a report listing the policies currently applied to a particular user or computer

ASSIGNING ACTIVE DIRECTORY PERMISSIONS

Administrators can modify Active Directory permissions manually, by opening an object's Properties sheet in the Active Directory users and Computers console and selecting the Security tab, as shown in Figure 10-32. Please note, however, that the Security tab does not appear in the Properties sheet unless you activate the Advanced Features view in the console first. To do this, open the Active Directory Users and Computers console and select View > Advanced Features.

Figure 10-32

The Security tab in a user object's Properties sheet

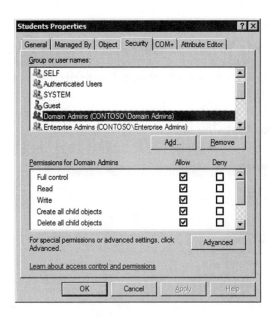

USING THE DELEGATION OF CONTROL WIZARD

The manual Active Directory permission assignment procedure is suitable for creating a few permission assignments, but it can be prone to error. Instead of working directly with individual permissions, you can use the ***Delegation of Control Wizard*** in the Active Directory Users and Computers console to assign permissions based on common administrative tasks.

To assign Active Directory permissions using the Delegation of Control Wizard, use the following procedure.

 USE THE DELEGATION OF CONTROL WIZARD

GET READY. Log on to Windows Server 2008. When the logon process is completed, close the Initial Configuration Tasks window and any other windows that appear. If you have not done so already, install the Remote Server Administration Tools > Role Administration Tools > Active Directory Domain Services Tools feature.

1. Click **Start**, and then click **Administrative Tools** > **Active Directory Users and Computers**. The Active Directory Users and Computers console appears.

2. Browse to the object you want to manage, right-click the object, and from the context menu, select **Delegate Control**. The Delegation of Control Wizard appears.

3. Click **Next** to bypass the Welcome page. The *Users or Groups* page appears, as shown in Figure 10-33.

Figure 10-33

The Users or Groups page in the Delegation of Control Wizard

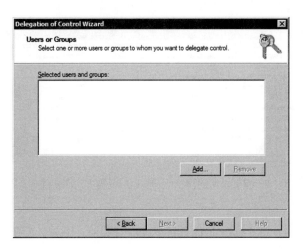

4. Click **Add**. The Select User, Contact, or Group dialog box appears.

5. In the **Enter The Object Name To Select** box, key the name of the security principal (user or group) to which you want to delegate control of the selected object. Then, click **OK**. The security principal you selected appears in the Selected Users And Groups box.

6. Repeat steps 4 and 5 to add additional security principals to the list, if desired. Then, click **Next**. The *Tasks to Delegate* page appears, as shown in Figure 10-34.

Figure 10-34

The Tasks to Delegate page in the Delegation of Control Wizard

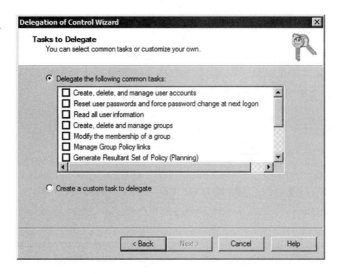

7. Select one or more of the checkboxes in the **Delegate The Following Common Tasks** list and click **Next**. The *Completing the Delegation of Control Wizard* page appears.

8. Click **Finish**. The wizard closes.

CLOSE the Active Directory Users and Computers console.

The Delegation of Control Wizard creates its permission assignments using special permissions. However, you cannot use the wizard to modify or revoke existing permissions. If you want to modify the permissions created by the wizard, you must work with the special permissions directly, by opening the Security tab of the object's Properties sheet and clicking the Advanced button, to display the Advanced Security Settings dialog box for the object, as shown in Figure 10-35.

Figure 10-35

The Advanced Security Settings dialog box for an Active Directory object

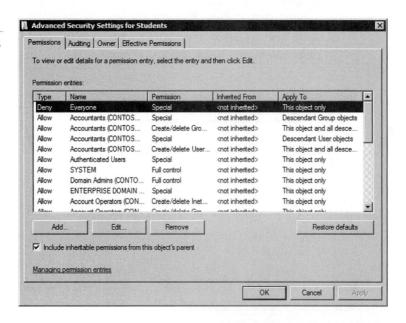

■ Updating Servers

THE BOTTOM LINE

One of the most important ongoing tasks faced by server administrators is keeping the network's servers updated with the latest operating system hotfixes and service packs. Windows Server 2008 includes an Automatic Updates feature that can download and install updates with no user intervention, but this is not always an ideal solution for enterprise network servers.

When enabled, the default behavior of Automatic Updates is to connect to the Microsoft Update Web site at regular intervals and then download and install any new operating system updates. However, this behavior is often not desirable, especially for servers.

First, having each computer download the same updates independently compounds the amount of Internet bandwidth the systems utilize. In the case of service packs, which can run to hundreds of megabytes, the bandwidth needed to update hundreds of computers can be enormous.

Second, Automatic Updates does not give administrators an opportunity to evaluate the updates before deploying them on production servers and workstations. Many administrators prefer to wait some time before installing new updates, to see if any problems arise, while others test the updates themselves on laboratory computers.

CERTIFICATION READY?
Implement patch
management strategy
3.1

Windows Server Update Services (WSUS) is a solution to both these problems. WSUS is a program that downloads updates from the Microsoft Update Web site and stores them for administrative evaluation. An administrator can then select the updates to deploy and computers on the network download them using a reconfigured Automatic Updates client.

Understanding WSUS Architectures

There are several architectural configurations you can use when deploying WSUS on an enterprise network, depending on its size and the number of remote locations.

There are four basic WSUS architecture configurations, as follows:

- Single WSUS server
- Multiple independent WSUS servers
- Multiple synchronized WSUS servers
- Multiple disconnected WSUS servers

USING A SINGLE WSUS SERVER

In the simplest configuration, a single WSUS server downloads updates from the Microsoft Update Web site and all of the other computers on the network download the updates from that WSUS server, as shown in Figure 10-36. A single WSUS server can support as many as 25,000 clients, so this configuration is suitable for most enterprise networks.

Figure 10-36

The WSUS single server
architecture

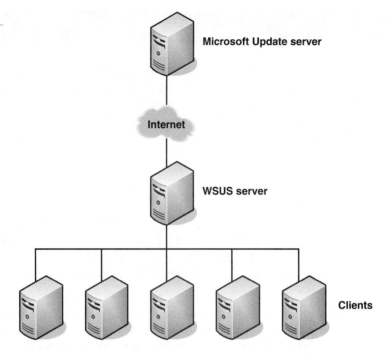

USING MULTIPLE INDEPENDENT WSUS SERVERS

For enterprise networks with remote locations, it might be preferable to run a separate WSUS
server at each site. In the multiple independent architecture, each of the WSUS servers has
its own connection to the Microsoft Update site, as shown in Figure 10-37, and maintains its
own updates. Administrators at each site manage their own WSUS server configuration and
designate the updates they want to release to the production network.

Figure 10-37

The WSUS multiple independent
server architecture

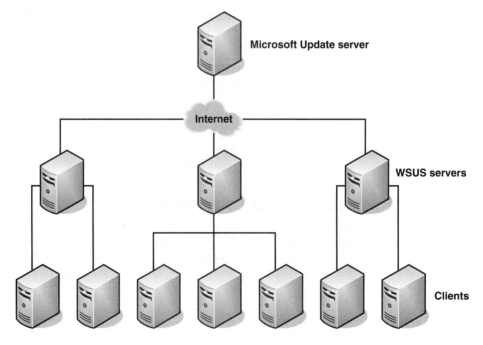

USING MULTIPLE SYNCHRONIZED WSUS SERVERS

It is also possible to use multiple WSUS servers in a synchronized manner. In this configuration, one central WSUS server downloads updates from the Microsoft Update Web site, and the other WSUS servers obtain their updates from that first server, as shown in Figure 10-38. This minimizes the amount of Internet bandwidth expended and enables the administrators of the central server to manage the updates for the entire enterprise.

Figure 10-38

The WSUS multiple synchronized server architecture

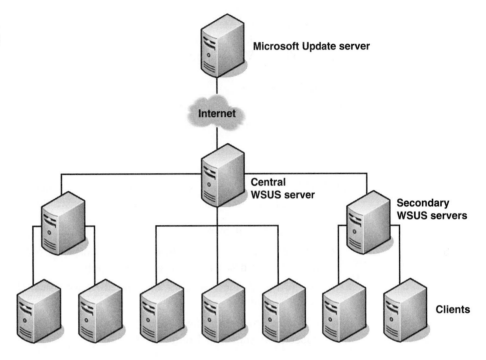

Both of these multiple server architectures are becoming increasingly unnecessary, as the Windows Server 2008 and Windows Vista operating systems become more prevalent in the enterprise. Both of these operating systems support a feature that you can enable with Group Policy called *Background Intelligent Transfer Service (BITS) peer-caching*, which enables computers to share their updates with each other on a peer-to-peer basis, rather than download them all from a WSUS server. As a result, even in the case of remote sites with slow, expensive wide area network (WAN) connections, the update process generates relatively little inter-site communication.

USING MULTIPLE DISCONNECTED WSUS SERVERS

The multiple disconnected WSUS server architecture is the same as the multiple synchronized architecture, except that instead of the central WSUS server transmitting updates directly to the secondary servers, administrators save the updates to an offline medium, such as DVD-ROMs, and ship them to the remote sites.

Deploying WSUS

WSUS 3.0 Service Pack 1 is the first WSUS release that can run on Windows Server 2008.

WSUS 3.0 SP1 is not supplied with the Windows Server 2008 operating system. However, it is a free download from the Microsoft Downloads Web site. You must also download Microsoft Report Viewer 2005 or later and install it before using WSUS.

Automatic Updates clients connect to a WSUS server by accessing a Web site, just as they do when connecting to the Microsoft Update site directly. Therefore, before you install WSUS, you must add the Web Server (IIS) role to the computer. In addition to the default role services, you must also select the following:

- Windows Authentication
- ASP.NET
- IIS 6.0 Management Compatibility
- IIS 6.0 Metabase Compatibility

WSUS requires a database, and if desired, you can use SQL Server 2005 SP1 or later for this purpose. This is optional, however. If there is no database manager installed on the server, WSUS installs the Windows Internal Database feature automatically.

INSTALLING WSUS

Once you have downloaded the WSUS 3.0 SP1 executable and installed all of the prerequisite components, you can proceed with the WSUS installation, using the following procedure.

 INSTALL WSUS

GET READY. Log on to Windows Server 2008. When the logon process is completed, close the Initial Configuration Tasks window and any other windows that appear.

1. Click **Start**, and then click **Run**. The Run dialog box appears.
2. Click **Browse** and, in the **Browse** combo box, locate and select the WSUS executable file you downloaded. Then, click **Open**.
3. In the Run dialog box, click **OK**. The Windows Server Update Services 3.0 SP1 Setup Wizard appears.
4. Click **Next** to bypass the Welcome page. The *Installation Mode Selection* page appears, as shown in Figure 10-39.

Figure 10-39

The Installation Mode Selection page in the Windows Server Update Services 3.0 SP1 Setup Wizard

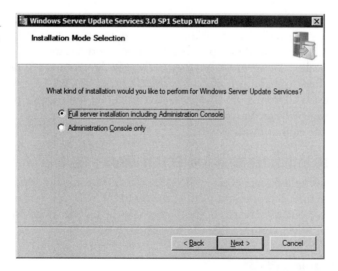

5. Leave the **Full server installation including Administration Console** option selected and click **Next**. The *License Agreement* page appears.
6. Select the **I accept the terms of the License agreement** option and click **Next**. The *Select Update Source* page appears, as shown in Figure 10-40.

Figure 10-40

The Select Update Source page in the Windows Server Update Services 3.0 SP1 Setup Wizard

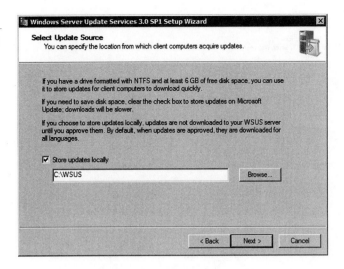

7. Leave the **Store Updates Locally** checkbox selected and specify the name of the folder where you want to store the updates the server downloads from the Microsoft Update Web site. Then, click **Next**. The *Database Options* page appears, as shown in Figure 10-41.

Figure 10-41

The Database Options page in the Windows Server Update Services 3.0 SP1 Setup Wizard

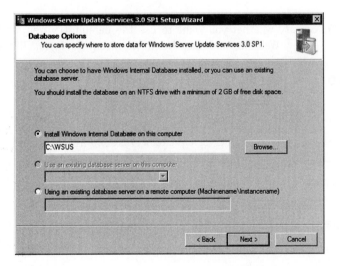

8. Leave the **Install Windows Internal Database On This Computer** option selected and specify the name path to the folder where you want to store the database. Then, click **Next**. The *Web Site Selection* page appears, as shown in Figure 10-42.

Figure 10-42

The Web Site Selection page in the Windows Server Update Services 3.0 SP1 Setup Wizard

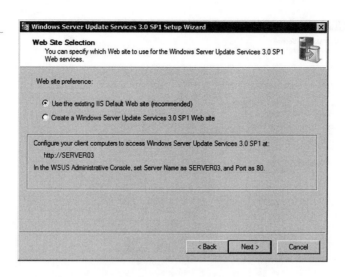

 TAKE NOTE *

If you have SQL Server 2005 SP1 or later installed on your network, you can select the Use an existing database server on a remote computer option and specify the database instance you want to use instead of the Windows Internal Database.

9. Specify whether you want to use the default IIS Web site to host WSUS or create a new Web site and click **Next**. The *Ready To Install Windows Server Update Services 3.0 SP1* page appears.

10. Click **Next**. The Wizard installs WSUS and the *Completing the Windows Server Update Services 3.0 SP1 Setup Wizard* page appears.

11. Click **Finish**.

PAUSE as the Windows Server Update Services 3.0 SP1 Setup Wizard closes and the Windows Server Update Services Configuration Wizard appears.

When the wizard completes the WSUS installation, it automatically launches the configuration wizard, as described in the next section.

CONFIGURING WSUS

To configure WSUS, use the following procedure.

CONFIGURE WSUS

GET READY. Log on to Windows Server 2008. When the logon process is completed, close the Initial Configuration Tasks window and any other windows that appear. Complete the WSUS installation procedure described in the previous section. When the installation is finished, the Windows Server Update Services Configuration Wizard appears, displaying the *Before You Begin* page.

1. Click **Next** twice to bypass the *Before You Begin* page and the *Join the Microsoft Update Improvement Program* page. The *Choose Upstream Server* page appears, as shown in Figure 10-43.

Figure 10-43

The Choose Upstream Server page in the Windows Server Update Services Configuration Wizard

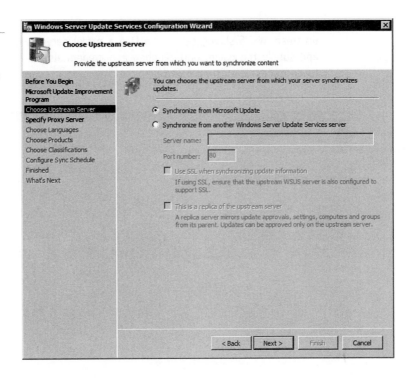

2. Select from the following options:

- Synchronize from Microsoft Update—Configures the server to obtain updates directly from the Microsoft Update Web site on the Internet.

- Synchronize from another Windows Server Update Services server—Configures the server to obtain updates from the WSUS server on the internal network whose Server Name and Port Number you specify in the text boxes provided.

- Use SSL when synchronizing update information—Configures the server to use Secure Sockets Layer (SSL) encryption when communicating with the upstream WSUS server.

- This is a replica of the upstream server—Configures the server to replicate all configuration settings and update approvals from the upstream WSUS server.

3. Click **Next**. The *Specify Proxy Server* page appears, as shown in Figure 10-44.

Figure 10-44

The Specify Proxy Server page in the Windows Server Update Services Configuration Wizard

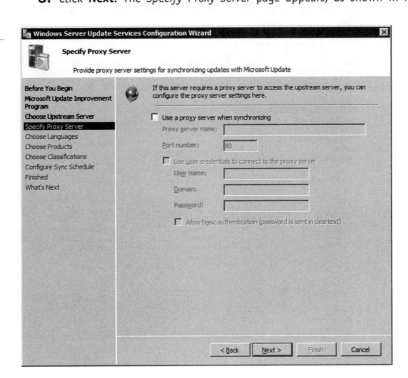

4. If your computer must use a proxy server to connect to the Internet or to the upstream WSUS server, select the **Use a proxy server when synchronizing** option and supply the name, port number, and credentials for the proxy server. Click **Next** to continue. The *Connect To Upstream Server* page appears, as shown in Figure 10-45.

Figure 10-45

The Connect To Upstream Server page in the Windows Server Update Services Configuration Wizard

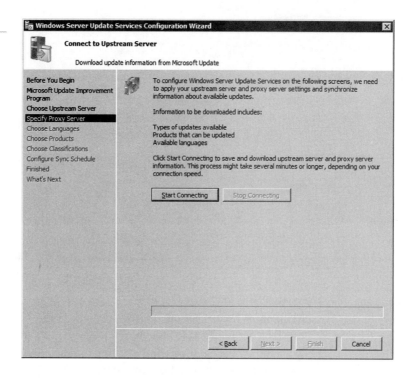

5. Click **Start Connecting**. The wizard connects to the Microsoft Update or upstream WSUS server and downloads information about the updates that are available. When the download is complete, click **Next**. The *Choose Languages* page appears, as shown in Figure 10-46.

Figure 10-46

The Choose Languages page in the Windows Server Update Services Configuration Wizard

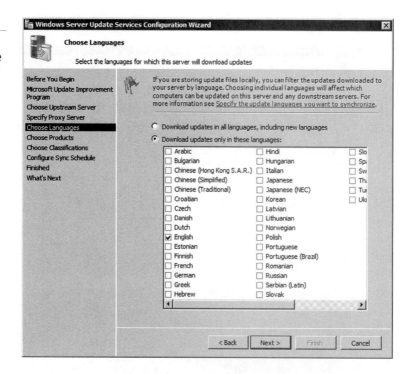

6. Select the checkboxes for any additional languages the computers on your network use and click **Next**. The *Choose Products* page appears, as shown in Figure 10-47.

Figure 10-47

The Choose Products page in the Windows Server Update Services Configuration Wizard

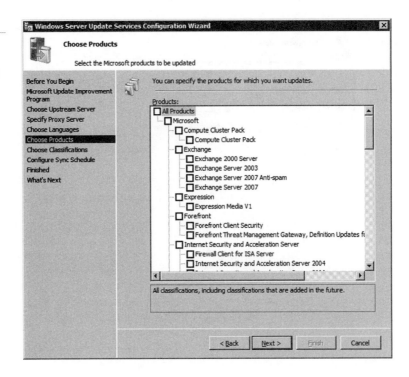

7. Select the checkboxes for the products you want WSUS to update and click **Next**. The *Choose Classifications* page appears, as shown in Figure 10-48.

Figure 10-48

The Choose Classifications page in the Windows Server Update Services Configuration Wizard

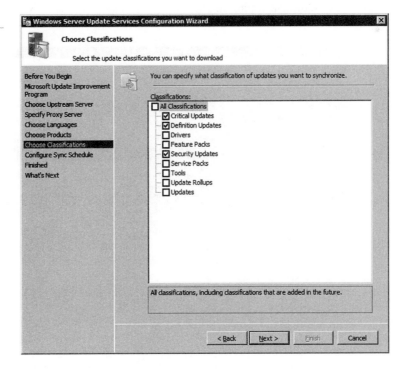

8. Select the types of updates you want WSUS to download and click **Next**. The *Set Sync Schedule* page appears, as shown in Figure 10-49.

Figure 10-49

The Set Sync Schedule page in the Windows Server Update Services Configuration Wizard

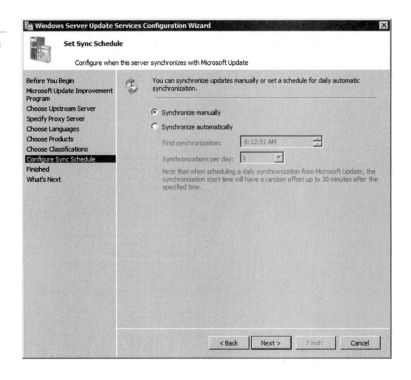

9. To create a synchronization schedule, select the **Synchronize automatically** option and specify a time for the first synchronization and the number of times per day you want WSUS to synchronize. Then, click **Next**. The *Finished* page appears, as shown in Figure 10-50.

Figure 10-50

The Finished page in the Windows Server Update Services Configuration Wizard

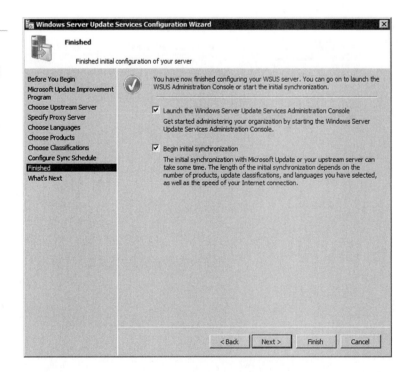

10. Click **Next**. The *What's Next* page appears.

11. Click **Finish**. The Update Services console appears, as shown in Figure 10-51, and WSUS begins its first synchronization.

CLOSE the Update Services console.

Figure 10-51

The Update Services console

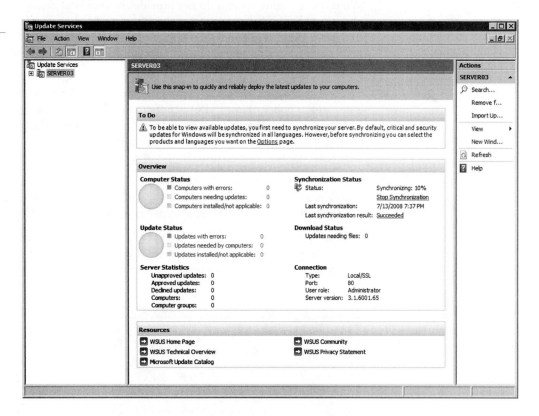

Once the server completes its initial synchronization, an administrator must examine the downloaded updates, as shown in Figure 10-52, and approve the ones to be distributed to clients on the network.

Figure 10-52

The All Updates display in the Update Services console

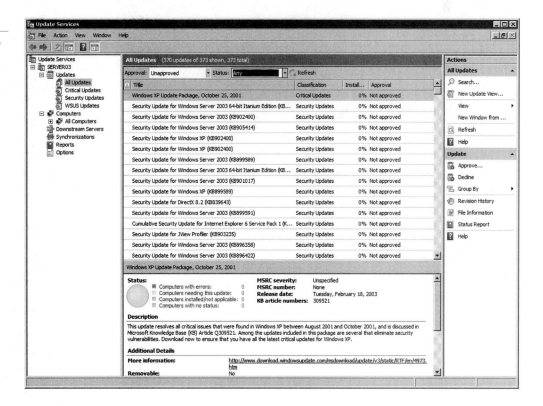

CONFIGURING WSUS CLIENTS

Before the client computers on the network can download updates from the WSUS server, you configure their Automatic Updates clients. The Automatic Updates controls in the Windows operating systems do not provide any means of configuring the client to use an internal WSUS server instead of the Microsoft Update Web site, and even if they did, individual client configuration would not be a practical solution for a large enterprise network. To configure the Automatic Updates clients on your network you must use Group Policy.

To configure Automatic Updates using Group Policy, the recommended practice is to create a new group policy object (GPO); configure the required policy settings; and link the GPO to an appropriate domain, site, or organizational unit object. If you are using multiple WSUS servers, you can distribute the client load among them by creating a separate GPO for each server and linking them to different objects.

The Group Policy settings that control the behavior of the Automatic Updates client are found in the Computer Configuration > Policies > Administrative Templates > Windows Components > Windows Update folder in the Group Policy Management Editor console.

To configure clients to download updates from the WSUS server, enable the Specify intranet Microsoft update service location policy, as shown in Figure 10-53, and specify the URL of your WSUS server in the two text boxes provided.

Figure 10-53

The Specify intranet Microsoft update service location policy

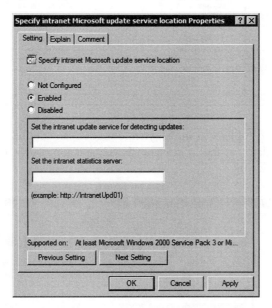

To configure the behavior of your Automatic Updates clients, enable the Configure Automatic Updates policy, as shown in Figure 10-54, and specify the download options, update frequency, and time of day values for your clients.

Figure 10-54

The Configure Automatic
Updates policy

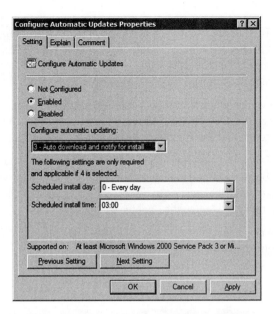

SUMMARY SKILL MATRIX

IN THIS LESSON YOU LEARNED:

- Server Manager is an MMC console that contains a collection of snap-ins most commonly used by Windows Server 2008 administrators. The Server Manager console integrates the ten snap-ins into a single, categorized interface, by default.

- MMC provides a standardized, common interface for application modules called snap-ins, which you can use to configure operating system settings, applications, and services. MMC snap-ins are individualized to specific tasks, and you can combine, order, and group them within the MMC shell to your individual preferences. An instance of MMC with one or more snap-ins installed is referred to as a console.

- There are two types of MMC snap-ins. A standalone snap-in is a single tool that you can install directly into an empty MMC console. Standalone snap-ins appear in the first level directly beneath the console root in the console's scope pane. An extension snap-in provides additional functionality to specific standalone snap-ins. You cannot add an extension snap-in to a console without adding an appropriate standalone snap-in first.

- The MMC consoles that appear in the Start menu of a computer running Windows Server 2003 are all configured to manage resources on the local system. However, many of the snap-ins supplied with Windows Server 2008 enable you to manage other Windows computers on the network as well.

- Ever since the Windows Server 2003 release, the components that make up the Terminal Services application are fully integrated into the operating system. This means that the Terminal Services capabilities are there, even if you do not have the Terminal Services role installed on the computer. The main reason for this is so administrators can use Terminal Services to manage remote computers without having to travel to a distant location. In Windows, this capability is known as Remote Desktop.

- The general rule of thumb for network file system permission assignments is to never assign permissions to individual user accounts. While it is certainly possible to grant each user individual permissions for every file they need, this would require an enormous amount of work, both in the initial setup and in ongoing maintenance.

- Active Directory has its own permissions system, which functions much like that of the NTFS file system. By granting users and groups permissions to specific Active Directory objects, you can allow them to perform specific administrative tasks on those objects.

- As with NTFS, Active Directory has a set of standard permissions, which are pre-defined collections of special permissions. You can choose to work either type of permission, or you can simplify the process by using the Delegation of Control Wizard to create permission assignments.

- Instead of working directly with individual permissions, you can use the Delegation of Control Wizard in the Active Directory Users and Computers console to assign permissions based on common administrative tasks.

- Windows Server Update Services (WSUS) is a program that downloads updates from the Microsoft Update Web site and stores them for administrative evaluation. An administrator can then select the updates to deploy and computers on the network download them using a reconfigured Automatic Updates client.

- Before the client computers on the network can download updates from the WSUS server, you configure their Automatic Updates clients.

■ Knowledge Assessment

Fill in the Blank

Complete the following exercise by filling in the blanks with the appropriate terms from this lesson.

1. The leftmost pane in a Microsoft Management Console window is called the _____ pane.

2. The Terminal Services license included with Windows Server 2008 enables administrators to connect to distant servers using _____.

3. When you run the Mmc.exe program with no additional parameters, a blank _____ appears.

4. To enable the computers on a network to download operating system updates from a server on the local network, you must install _____.

5. The two types of snap-ins that you can add to an MMC console are _____ and _____.

6. To manage permissions for an Active Directory object, you can open the object's Properties sheet or use the _____.

7. The Windows Vista feature that enables computers on the same network to share updates is called _____.

8. The Terminal Services client included with Windows Server 2008 is called _____.

9. _____ is a shell application that Windows Server 2008 uses to provide access to most of its system and network management tools.

10. The first window that appears when you start a Windows Server 2008 computer is called _____.

Multiple Choice

Select one or more correct answers for each of the following questions.

1. Which of the following tools can you use to enable the server side of the Remote Desktop application on a Windows Server 2008 computer?
   a. Terminal Services Manager
   b. The Add Features Wizard in Server Manager
   c. Terminal Services Configuration
   d. System control panel

2. How many users can connect to a Windows Server 2008 computer at the same time using Remote Desktop, without purchasing additional licenses?
   a. none
   b. one
   c. two
   d. ten

3. Which of the following statements about MMC snap-ins is true?
   a. You cannot add a standalone snap-in to a custom MMC console, unless you add an extension snap-in first.
   b. You cannot add an extension snap-in to a custom MMC console, unless you add a standalone snap-in first.
   c. You cannot add an extension snap-in to a custom MMC console once you have added a standalone snap-in.
   d. You cannot add a standalone snap-in to a custom MMC console at all. They run independently.

4. Which of the following Microsoft Management Console panes lists the snap-ins installed in the console?
   a. the scope pane
   b. the detail pane
   c. the actions pane
   d. the snap-in pane

5. Which of the following Windows Server Update Services architectures requires more than one computer to be connected to the Microsoft Update server on the Internet?
   a. single WSUS server
   b. multiple independent WSUS servers
   c. multiple synchronized WSUS servers
   d. multiple disconnected WSUS servers

6. Which of the following is the default mode when you create a new MMC console?
   a. Author mode
   b. User Mode-Full Access
   c. User Mode-Limited Access, Multiple Windows
   d. User Mode-Limited Access, Single Window

7. Which of the following tasks must you complete on your Automatic Updates client computers before they can download updates from a WSUS server?
   a. open the Automatic Updates control panel and reconfigure the client
   b. open the Local Security Policy console and enable the *Specify intranet Microsoft update service location* policy
   c. open Server Manager and install the WSUS Client feature
   d. none of the above

8. Which of the following does not have to be installed to run Windows Server Update Services 3.0 SP1?
   a. the Web Server (IIS) role
   b. SQL Server 2005 SP1 or later
   c. Windows Process Activation Service
   d. Microsoft Report Viewer 2005 or later

9. Which of the following Windows Server Update Services architectures are being used less often because of the increasing use of Background Intelligent Transfer Service (BITS) peer-caching?
   a. single WSUS server
   b. multiple independent WSUS servers
   c. multiple synchronized WSUS servers
   d. multiple disconnected WSUS servers

10. Which of the following is not one of the tasks you must complete to use Remote Desktop to administer a server on the network?
    a. configure Remote Desktop Connection on the client
    b. establish a connection between the client and the server
    c. configure Group Policy settings
    d. enable Remote Desktop on the server

Review Questions

1. Explain how Network Level Authentication can increase the security of a Remote Desktop connection.

2. Why is it not possible to add snap-ins to the Computer Management console, or to the other preconfigured MMC consoles included with Windows Server 2008?

■ Case Scenario

Scenario 10-1: Using Remote Desktop

Robert is a new hire in the IT department of Wingtip Toys. He wants to be able to access all of the Windows Server 2008 servers on the company network from his workstation using Remote Desktop. Robert logs on to his workstation using his personal account, which currently has only domain user privileges.

To give his user account the proper access, he logs onto the company's Active Directory domain with the Administrator account and uses the Active Directory Users and Computers console to create a group called Remote Desktop Users. Then, he adds his domain user account to the group. However, when he logs on to the domain with his user account, the Remote Desktop Connection client is unable to connect to any of the remote servers. What must Robert do to correct the problem?

Monitoring Servers

OBJECTIVE DOMAIN MATRIX

TECHNOLOGY SKILL	OBJECTIVE DOMAIN	OBJECTIVE DOMAIN NUMBER
Using the Reliability and Performance Console	Monitor servers for performance evaluation and optimization	3.2
Using Auditing	Monitor and maintain security and policies	3.3

KEY TERMS

auditing
baseline
bottleneck
channel
data collector set

events
Event Viewer
memory leak
Performance Monitor

Reliability and Performance
    snap-in
Reliability Monitor
Resource Overview

Windows Server 2008 is capable of providing administrators with enormous amounts of information about the status of the computer hardware, the operating system, and the applications running on it. In fact, for the busy administrator wanting to monitor server performance, the real trick is to winnow out the pertinent information from the extraordinary amount of everyday goings-on. This lesson covers the server monitoring tools and their operation:

- Event Viewer console
- Reliability and Performance console
- System Resource Manager

Using the Event Viewer Console

THE BOTTOM LINE The Event Viewer console has been enhanced in Windows Server 2008 to provide easier access to a more comprehensive array of event logs.

It is common practice for software products to save information about their ongoing activities to chronological lists called logs. By examining the logs, administrators can track the activity of the software, document errors, and extract analytical information. Logs are traditionally text files, which administrators open in an editor application, but the Windows operating systems have long used a graphical application for this purpose.

The operating system component that generates the Windows logs is called Windows Eventing. The primary function of the Windows Eventing engine, as always, is to record information about system activities as they occur and package that information in individual units called *events*. The application you use to view the events is called Event Viewer. In Windows Server 2008, Event Viewer takes the form of a Microsoft Management Console (MMC) snap-in.

The *Event Viewer* snap-in appears in Windows Server 2008 as a separate console, accessible from the Administrative Tools program group, and as part of other consoles, including Server Manager, under the Diagnostics node, and Computer Management, under System Tools. As with all snap-ins, you can also add Event Viewer to a custom MMC console. However you choose to access it, the Event Viewer snap-in looks the same and operates in the same way.

Introducing the Windows Server 2008 Event Viewer

Through many of its previous versions, Windows has maintained the same three basic logs: a System log, a Security log, and an Application log. Servers performing certain roles have additional logs, such as those tracking DNS and File Replication activities. The format of these logs has remained consistent, although the Event Viewer application has undergone some changes. It was in the Windows Server 2003 and Windows XP releases that Event Viewer first took the form of an MMC snap-in, rather than an independent application.

Windows Server 2008 and Windows Vista represent the most comprehensive overhaul of the Windows Eventing engine in many years. Windows Eventing 6.0 includes the following enhancements:

- Events now stored in XML format
- The addition of a Setup log documenting the installation and configuration history of applications
- New logs for key applications and services, including DFS Replication and the Key Management Service
- Individual logs for Windows components
- Enhanced querying capabilities that simplify the process of locating specific events
- The ability to attach scheduled tasks to events
- The ability to create subscriptions that enable administrators to collect and store specific types of events from other computers on the network
- Event log sizes now limited only by available disk space

When you first launch the Event Viewer console, you see the Overview and Summary display shown in Figure 11-1.

Figure 11-1

The Overview and Summary screen in the Event Viewer console

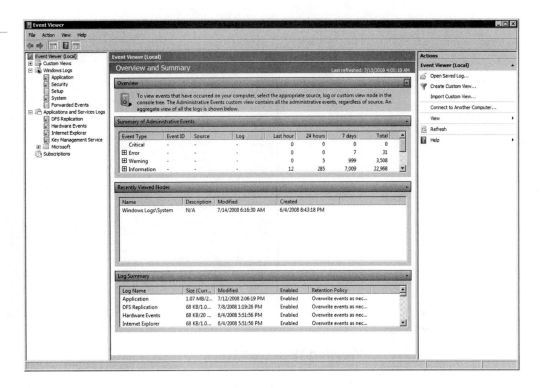

The Summary of Administrative Events displays the total number of events recorded in the last hour, day, and week, sorted by event type. When you expand an event type, the list is broken down by event ID, as shown in Figure 11-2.

Figure 11-2

The Event ID breakdown in the Event Viewer console

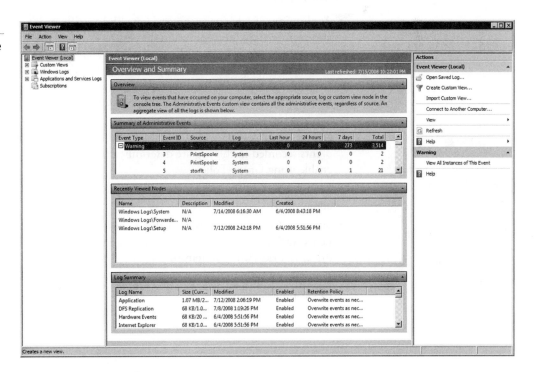

When you double-click one of the event IDs, the console creates a filtered custom view that displays only the events having that ID, as shown in Figure 11-3.

Figure 11-3

A custom view in the Event Viewer console

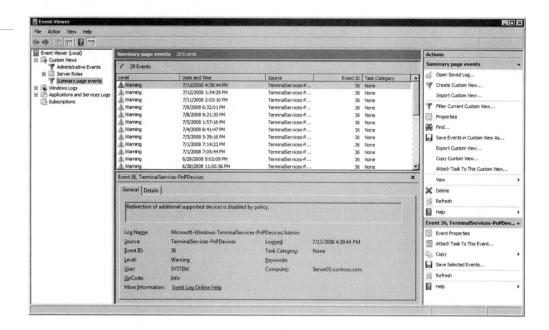

Viewing Windows Logs

In Windows Server 2008, Event Viewer contains more than the three original logs.

When you expand the Windows Logs folder in the Event Viewer console, you see the following logs:

- Application—Contains events generated by specific programs running on the computer, as determined by the application developer. Many of the applications included with Windows Server 2008 record events to this log, as do many other Microsoft applications. Third-party applications can utilize the log, but they are under no obligation to do so. In Windows Server 2008, the Applications and Services Logs folder usually contains more detailed information about application conditions than the Applications log.

- Security—Contains information about security-related events, such as failed logons, attempts to access protected resources, and success or failure of audited events. The events recorded in this log are determined by audit policies, which administrators can enable using Group Policy.

- Setup—Contains information about the installation and setup of roles, services, and applications.

- System—Contains information about events generated by the operating system components, such as services and device drivers. For example, a failure of a service to start or a driver to load during system startup is recorded in the System log.

- Forwarded Events—Contains events received from other computers on the network via subscriptions.

Selecting one of the logs causes a list of the events it contains to appear in the details pane, in reverse chronological order, as shown in Figure 11-4.

Figure 11-4

Contents of a log in the Event Viewer console

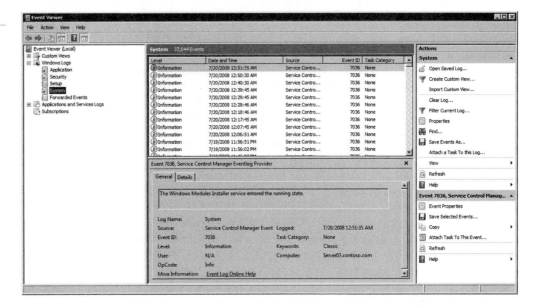

The Windows event logs contain different types of events, which are identified by icons. The four event types are as follows:

- Information—An event that describes a change in the state of a component or process as part of a normal operation.

- Error—An event that warns of a problem that is not likely to affect the performance of the component or process where the problem occurred, but that could affect the performance of other components or processes on the system.

- Warning—An event that warns of a service degradation or an occurrence that can potentially cause a service degradation in the near future, unless you take steps to prevent it.

- Critical—An event warning that an incident resulting in a catastrophic loss of functionality or data in a component or process has occurred.

When you select one of the events in the list of events, its properties appear in the preview pane at the bottom of the list. You can also double-click an event to display a separate Event Properties dialog box, such as that shown in Figure 11-5.

Figure 11-5

An Event Properties dialog box

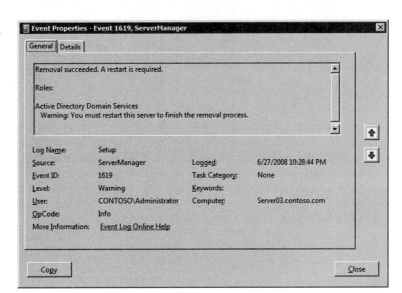

VIEWING APPLICATIONS AND SERVICES LOGS

The Event Viewer console contains a great deal of information, and one of the traditional problems for system administrators and desktop technicians is finding the events they need amidst an embarrassment of riches. Windows Eventing 6.0 includes a number of innovations that can help in this regard, including separate logs for the applications and services running on the computer.

When you expand the Applications and Services Logs folder in the console, you find additional logs for the various applications and services installed on the computer. Many of the roles and features that you can add to a Windows Server 2008 computer include their own logs that appear in this folder. For example, domain controllers include a Directory Service log.

The four types of logs that can appear in this folder are as follows:

- Admin—Contains events targeted at end users or administrators that indicate a problem and offer a possible solution.
- Operational—Contains events that signify a change in the application or service, such as the addition or removal of a printer.
- Analytic—Contains a high volume of events tracking application operation activities.
- Debug—Contains events used by software developers for troubleshooting purposes.

By default, only the Admin and Operational logs are visible in the Event Viewer console, because these are the logs that can be useful to the average administrator. The Analytic and Debug logs are disabled and hidden, because they typically contain large amounts of information that is of interest only to developers and technicians. To display and enable these log types, use the following procedure.

DISPLAY ANALYTIC AND DEBUG LOGS

GET READY. Log on to Windows Server 2008. When the logon process is completed, close the Initial Configuration Tasks window and any other windows that appear.

1. Click **Start.** Then, click **Administrative Tools** > **Event Viewer.** The Event Viewer console appears.

2. Expand the **Applications and Services Logs** folder, as shown in Figure 11-6.

Figure 11-6

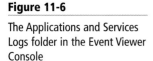

The Applications and Services Logs folder in the Event Viewer Console

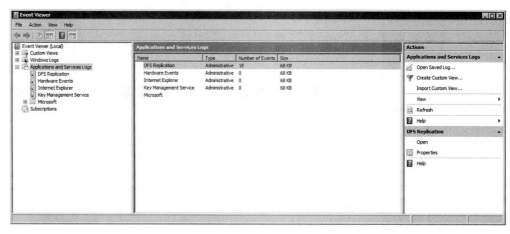

3. Click **View** > **Show Analytic and Debug Logs.** The additional logs appear in new subfolders in the Applications and Services Logs folder, as shown in Figure 11-7, as well as in the \Microsoft\Windows subfolders.

Figure 11-7

The Analytic and Debug log folders in the Event Viewer Console

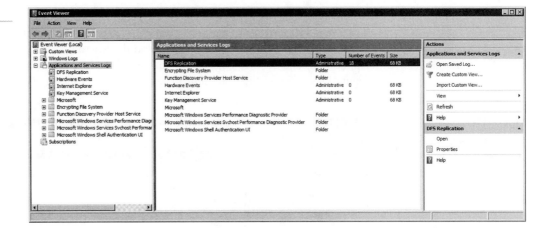

4. Select one of the new subfolders. Then, right-click one of the logs and, from the context menu, select **Properties.** The Properties sheet for the log appears, as shown in Figure 11-8.

Figure 11-8

The Properties sheet for an Analytic log

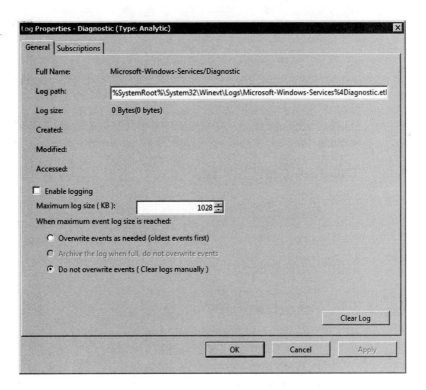

5. Select the **Enable Logging** checkbox and click **OK.**

CLOSE the Event Viewer console.

Analytic logs in particular can generate large amounts of information, so be careful to configure appropriate values for the maximum log size and the overwriting behavior.

VIEWING ADDITIONAL LOGS

Another one of the new logging features in Windows Server 2008 is component-specific logs that enable you to examine the events for a particular operating system component or application. Any component that is capable of recording events in the System log or Application log can also record events in a separate log dedicated solely to that component.

The Event Viewer console comes preconfigured with a large collection of additional logs for Windows Server 2008. When you expand the Microsoft and Windows folders in the Applications and Services Logs folder, you see a long list of Windows components, as shown in Figure 11-9. Each of these components has a pathway, called a *channel,* to its own separate log.

Figure 11-9

Windows component logs in the Event Viewer console

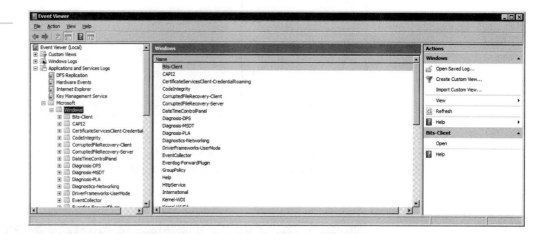

In most cases, the events in the component logs are non-administrative, meaning that they are not indicative of problems or errors. The components continue to save the administrative events to the System log or Application log. The events in the component logs are operational, analytic, or debug events, which means that they are more descriptive entries that document the ongoing activities of the component. The component logs are intended more for use in trouble-shooting long-term problems and for software developers seeking debugging information.

CREATING CUSTOM VIEWS

Another means of locating and isolating information about specific events is to create custom views. A custom view is essentially a filtered version of a particular log, configured to display only certain events. The Event Viewer console now has a Custom Views folder, in which you can create filtered views and save them for later use.

To create a custom view, use the following procedure.

 CREATE A CUSTOM VIEW

GET READY. Log on to Windows Server 2008. When the logon process is completed, close the Initial Configuration Tasks window and any other windows that appear.

1. Click **Start.** Then, click **Administrative Tools** > **Event Viewer.** The Event Viewer console appears.

2. Right-click the **Custom Views** folder and, from the context menu, select **Create Custom View.** The Create Custom View dialog box appears, as shown in Figure 11-10.

Figure 11-10

The Create Custom View dialog box

 ANOTHER WAY

You can also create custom views of specific logs by right-clicking a log and selecting Create Custom View from the context menu.

3. From the **Logged** dropdown list, select the time interval from which you want to display events.

4. In the Event Level area, select the checkboxes for the types of events you want to display.

5. From the **By Log** dropdown list, select the log(s) from which you want to display events. Alternatively, select the **By Source** option and then select the checkboxes for the components about which you want to display events.

6. Optionally, you can then specify event ID numbers, task categories, keywords, and user credentials to narrow your search.

7. Click **OK.** The Save Filter to Custom View dialog box appears, as shown in Figure 11-11.

Figure 11-11

The Save Filter to Custom View dialog box

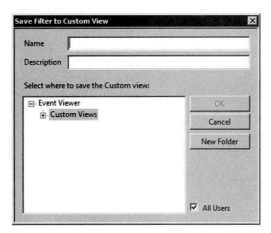

8. Enter a name for the view in the **Name** text box; enter a description, if desired; and select the folder in which you want to create your custom view. You can also create new folders to organize your custom views, if desired. Then, click **OK.** The console adds your view to the folder you selected and displays the view in the detail pane.

CLOSE the Event Viewer console.

Once you have created and saved a custom view, you can access it at any future time from the Custom Views folder.

■ Using the Reliability and Performance Console

THE BOTTOM LINE

A computer's performance level is constantly changing as it performs different combinations of tasks. Monitoring the performance of the various components over a period of time is the only way to get a true picture of the system's capabilities.

While the Event Viewer snap-in enables you to review system events that have already occurred, the *Reliability and Performance snap-in* enables you to view system information on a continuous, real-time basis. Like Event Viewer, Reliability and Performance is an MMC snap-in that you can launch as a separate console from the Administrative Tools program group; view from within another console, such as Server Manager or Computer Management; or add to a custom MMC console.

CERTIFICATION READY?
Monitor servers for performance evaluation and optimization
3.2

Using Resource Overview

The Resource Overview screen is a new feature that provides a quick view of the computer's hardware performance, in real time.

When you launch the Reliability and Performance Monitor console, you see the *Resource Overview* screen, as shown in Figure 11-12. This screen contains four real-time line graphs that display information about four of the server's main hardware components. Each of the four components also has a separate, expandable section below the graphs, displaying more detailed information in text form, such as the resources being utilized by individual applications and processes. The statistics displayed by the graphs and the text sections are listed in Table 11-1.

Figure 11-12

The Resource Overview page of the Reliability and Performance Monitor console

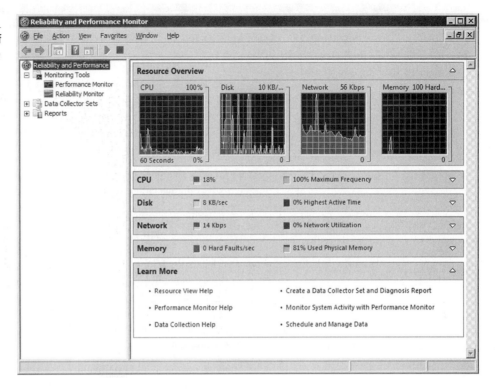

Table 11-1

Resource Overview Line Graph Statistics

COMPONENT	LINE GRAPH STATISTICS	TEXT STATISTICS
CPU	Overall CPU utilization (%)	• Image—The application using CPU resources • PID—The Process ID of the application • Threads—The number of active threads generated by the application • CPU—The number of CPU cycles currently being used by the application • Average CPU—The percentage of the total CPU capacity being used by the application
Disk	Total current disk I/O rate (in KB/sec)	• Image—The application using disk resources • PID—The Process ID of the application • File—The file currently being read or written by the application • Read—The speed of the current read operation (in bytes/min) • Write—The speed of the current write operation (in bytes/min) • I/O Priority—The priority of the I/O task currently being performed by the application • Response Time—The interval between the issuance of a command to the disk and its response (in milliseconds)

(continued)

Table 11-1 *(continued)*

COMPONENT	LINE GRAPH STATISTICS	TEXT STATISTICS
Network	Current total network traffic (in Kb/sec)	• Image—The application using network resources • PID—The Process ID of the application • Address—The network address or computer name of the system with which the computer is communicating • Send—The speed of the current network send operation (in bytes/min) • Receive—The speed of the current network receive operation (in bytes/min) • Total—The combined bandwidth of the current network send and receive processes (in bytes/min)
Memory	Current hard faults per second Percentage of physical memory currently in use (%)	• Image—The application using memory resources • PID—The Process ID of the application • Hard Faults Per Min—The number of hard faults currently being generated by the application • Commit—The amount of memory (in KB) committed by the application • Working Set—The amount of physical memory (in KB) currently being used by the application • Shareable—The amount of memory (in KB) being used by the application that it can share with other applications • Private—The amount of memory (in KB) being used by the application that it cannot share with other applications

Examining the resources utilized by specific applications and processes over time can help you to determine ways to improve the performance of a computer. For example, if all of the system's physical memory is frequently being utilized, then the system is probably being slowed by large amounts of disk paging. Increasing the amount of physical memory or reducing the application load will probably improve the overall performance level of the computer.

Using Performance Monitor

Performance Monitor is another tool within the Reliability and Performance Monitor console that displays system performance statistics in real time. The difference between Performance Monitor and Resource Overview is that Performance Monitor can display hundreds of different statistics (called performance counters) and that you can create a customized graph containing any statistics you choose.

When you select the Performance Monitor node in the console, the detail pane of the snap-in contains a line graph, updated in real time, showing the current level for the % Processor Time performance counter, as shown in Figure 11-13.

Figure 11-13

The default Performance Monitor display

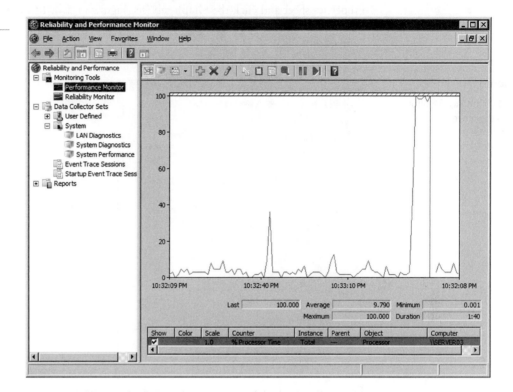

A performance counter is a measure of one specific hardware or software component's current activity. The % Processor Time counter that appears in the Performance Monitor graph by default measures the percentage of the system processor's clock cycles that are being utilized by non-idle tasks. This is one of the basic measures of computer activity. A % Processor Time counter that is consistently pegged at 100% indicates that the processor is unable to keep up with the tasks it has to perform.

There are counters available that measure processor performance in other ways, as well as counters for many other system components. You can add as many counters to the graph as you want, although adding too many can make the display difficult to read. By viewing the statistics generated by these counters, and learning their significance, you can evaluate the performance of the computer in many different ways.

MODIFYING THE GRAPH VIEW

The legend beneath the Performance Monitor graph specifies the line color for each counter added to the display, the scale of values for each counter, and other identifying information. When you select a counter in the legend, its current values appear in numerical form at the bottom of the graph.

TAKE NOTE*

When you have multiple counters in the Performance Monitor graph, clicking the Highlight button in the toolbar (or pressing Ctrl+H) changes the selected counter to a broad line that is easier to distinguish from the others.

If your computer is otherwise idle, you will probably notice that the line in the default graph is hovering near the bottom of the scale, making it difficult to see its exact value. You can address this problem by modifying the scale of the graph's Y (that is, vertical) axis. Click the Properties button in the toolbar (or press Ctrl+Q) to display the Performance Monitor Properties sheet and click the Graph tab (see Figure 11-14). In the Vertical Scale box, you can reduce the maximum value for the Y axis, thereby using more of the graph to display the counter data.

Figure 11-14

The Performance Monitor Properties sheet

Depending on the nature of counters displayed in the graph, you might want to raise or lower the Maximum and Minimum values in the Vertical Scale box to create an ideal range of values. Different counters use different units of measurement for the data they present; they are not all percentages. Part of the skill in using Performance Monitor effectively is selecting counters with units of measurement and value ranges that work well together on the same graph.

On the General tab of the Performance Monitor Properties sheet, you can also modify the sample rate of the graph. By default, the graph updates the counter values every one second, but you can increase this value to display data for a longer period of time on a single page of the graph. This can make it easier to detect long-term trends in counter values.

USING OTHER VIEWS

In addition to the line graph, Performance Monitor has two other views of the same data, a histogram bar graph and a report view. You can change the display to one of these views by clicking the Change Graph Type toolbar button. The histogram view is a bar graph with a separate vertical bar for each counter, as shown in Figure 11-15. In this view, it is easier to monitor large numbers of counters, because the lines do not overlap.

TAKE NOTE *

The Performance Monitor Properties sheet contains a number of other controls that you can use to modify the appearance of the graph. For example, on the Graph tab, you can add axis titles and gridlines, and in the Appearance tab, you can control the graph's background and select a different font.

Figure 11-15

The Performance Monitor histogram view

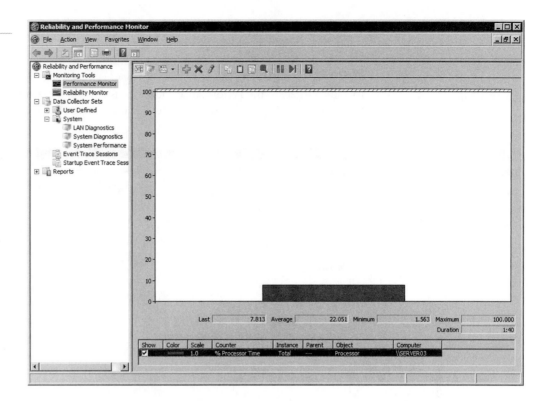

The report view (see Figure 11-16) displays the numerical value for each of the performance counters.

Figure 11-16

The Performance Monitor report view

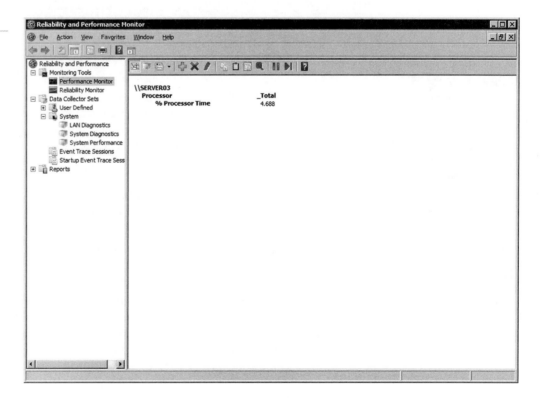

As with the line graph, the histogram and report views both update their counter values at the interval specified in the General tab of the Performance Monitor Properties sheet. The main drawback of these two views, however, is that they do not display a history of the counter values, only the current value. Each new sampling overwrites the previous one in the display, unlike the line graph, which displays the previous values as well.

ADDING COUNTERS

To add counters to the Performance Monitor display, click the Add button in the toolbar or press Ctrl+I to display the Add Counters dialog box, as shown in Figure 11-17.

Figure 11-17

The Add Counters dialog box

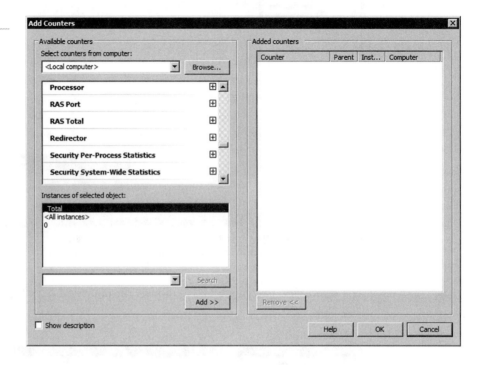

In the Add Counters dialog box, you have to specify the following four pieces of information to add a counter to the display:

- Computer—The name of the computer you want to monitor with the selected counter. Unlike most MMC snap-ins, you cannot redirect the entire focus of Performance Monitor to another computer on the network. Instead, you specify a computer name for each counter you add to the display. This enables you to create a display showing counters for various computers on the network, such as a single graph of processor activity for all of your computers.

- Performance object—A category representing a specific hardware or software component in the computer. Click the plus sign on a performance object to display a selection of performance counters related to that component.

- Performance counter—A statistic representing a specific aspect of the selected performance object's activities.

- Instance—An element representing a specific occurrence of the selected performance counter. For example, on a computer with two network interface adapters, each counter in the Network Interface performance object would have two instances, one for each adapter, enabling you to track the performance of each adapter individually. Some counters also have instances such as Total or Average, enabling you to track the performance of all instances combined or the median value of all instances.

Once you have selected a computer name, a performance object, a performance counter in that object, and an instance of that counter, click Add to add the counter to the Added

TAKE NOTE*

Select the Show Description checkbox to display a detailed explanation of the selected performance counter.

Counters list. The dialog box remains open so that you can add more counters. Click OK when you are finished to update the graph with your selected counters.

The performance objects, performance counters, and instances that appear in the Add Counters dialog box depend on the computer's hardware configuration, the software installed on the computer, and the computer's role on the network.

CREATING AN EFFECTIVE DISPLAY

In most cases, when users first discover Performance Monitor, they see the hundreds of available performance counters and proceed to create a line graph containing dozens of different counters. In most cases, the result is a graph that is crowded and incoherent. The number of counters that you can display effectively depends on the size of your monitor and the resolution of your video display.

Consider the following tips when selecting counters:

- Limit the number of counters—Too many counters make the graph more difficult to understand. To display a large number of statistics, you can display multiple windows in the console and select different counters in each window, or use the histogram or report view to display a large number of counters in a more compact form.

- Modify the counter display properties—Depending on the size and capabilities of your monitor, the default colors and line widths that Performance Monitor uses in its graph might make it difficult to distinguish counters from each other. In the Data tab in the Performance Monitor Properties sheet, you can modify the color, style, and width of each counter's line in the graph, to make it easier to distinguish.

- Choose counters with comparable values—Performance Monitor imposes no limitations on the combinations of counters you can select for a single graph, but some statistics are not practical to display together, because of their disparate values. When a graph contains a counter with a typical value that is under 20 and another counter with a value in the hundreds, it is difficult to arrange the display so that both counters are readable. Choose counters with values that are reasonably comparable so that you can display them legibly. Here again, if you must display counters with different value ranges, you might prefer to use the report view instead of the graph view.

SAVING A SYSTEM MONITOR CONSOLE

Once you are satisfied with the display you have created, you can save it as a console file by clicking File > Save As and specifying a file name with a .msc extension. Launching this console file will open the Reliability and Performance Monitor console and display the Performance Monitor snap-in with all of the counters and display properties you configured before saving it.

Using Reliability Monitor

Reliability Monitor is a new addition to Windows Server 2008 that automatically tracks events that can have a negative effect on system stability and uses them to calculate a stability index.

The default display when you click the Reliability Monitor node contains a System Stability Chart for the most recent days and a System Stability Report, as shown in Figure 11-18. The interface includes a scroll bar and calendar in the form of a dropdown list, either of which you can use to display the reliability information for any 28-day period in the last year.

Figure 11-18

The Reliability Monitor display

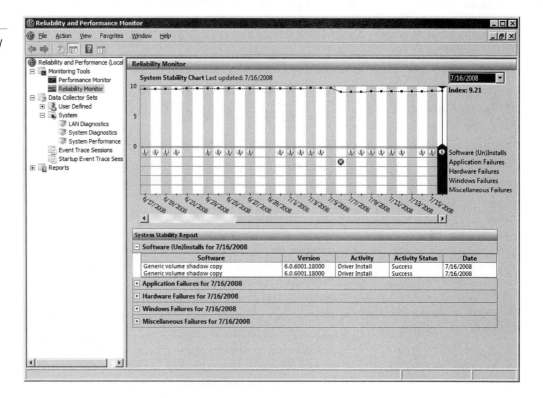

Reliability Monitor gathers information using a hidden scheduled task called Reliability Access Component Agent (RACAgent). The agent collects data from the event logs every hour and updates the Reliability Monitor display every 24 hours. The stability index is a number from 0 to 10 (with 0 representing the least and 10 the most stability) that the system calculates using information about the following types of events:

- Software (Un)Installs—Includes software installations, uninstallations, updates, and configurations for the operating system, applications, and device drivers.
- Application Failures—Includes application hangs, crashes, and terminations of non-responding applications.
- Hardware Failures—Includes disk and memory failures.
- Windows Failures—Includes boot failures, operating system crashes, and sleep failures.
- Miscellaneous Failures—Includes unrequested system shutdowns.
- System Clock Changes—Includes all significant clock time changes. This entry only appears when a significant clock time change has occurred recently.

Pertinent events appear in the System Stability Chart as data points. Clicking one of the points displays information about it in the System Stability Report.

The Reliability Monitor snap-in doesn't actually do anything except present event log information in a new way. It is not possible to configure the snap-in or alter the criteria it uses to evaluate a computer' reliability. If you ever notice that the stability index has decreased, you should check the events that caused the reduction and evaluate for yourself how serious the situation is and what actions you should take, if any.

Locating Bottlenecks

> Once you learn how to operate the Reliability and Performance Monitor console, the next step is to learn how to use it to monitor and troubleshoot a computer.

Server administrators often encounter performance problems that are not attributable to an obvious cause, such as a hardware or service failure. Users might complain that a server's performance is slow at certain times of the day, or that performance has been declining gradually over the course of weeks or months. When this occurs, one of the most common causes is a performance bottleneck somewhere in the server.

A *bottleneck* occurs when a component is not providing an acceptable level of performance compared with the other components in the system. For example, users might complain that their file server performance is slow, and you might spend a great deal of time and money upgrading your network, expecting to see a dramatic improvement. However, if your server is an older computer using an outdated processor, the improvement is likely to be minimal, because it is the server's processor, not the network, that is the bottleneck. All the other components are running well, but the processor cannot keep up with the data flow provided by the new, faster network.

Bottlenecks can appear for a variety of reasons, including the following:

- Increased server load—A server might function adequately in a particular role at first, but as you add more users or more tasks, the inadequacy of one or more components might become more pronounced. For example, a Web server might be sufficient for a company's Web site at first, but then the company introduces a new product and traffic to the site triples. Suddenly, you find that the Web server's disk performance is insufficient to handle the additional traffic.

- Hardware failure—Hardware failures do not always manifest themselves as catastrophic stoppages. A component might malfunction intermittently for a long period of time, causing degraded server performance that is maddeningly inconsistent. For example, a faulty network cable connecting a server to a hub can cause occasional traffic interruptions that show up as degraded performance in the server.

- Changed server roles—Different applications have different resource requirements. You might have a computer that functions adequately as a Web server, but when you change the computer's role to that of a database server, you find that the processor is not fast enough to handle the load that the new application places on it.

Locating the bottleneck that is hindering performance can be a complicated task, but the Reliability and Performance Monitor console provides most of the tools you need. To find a bottleneck, you usually examine the four main subsystems of a computer, which are covered in the following sections.

MONITORING PROCESSOR PERFORMANCE

An inadequate or malfunctioning processor array can cause a server to queue incoming client requests, preventing the server from fulfilling them promptly. For general monitoring of the processor subsystem, use the following performance counters:

- Processor: % Processor time—Specifies the percentage of time that the processor is busy. This value should be as low as possible, with anything remaining below 85 percent most of the time being acceptable. If this value is consistently too high, you should attempt to determine which process is using too much processor time, upgrade the processor, or add another processor, if possible.

- System: Processor Queue Length—Specifies the number of program threads waiting to be executed by the processor. This value should be as low as possible, with values less than 10 being acceptable. If the value is too high, upgrade the processor or add another processor.

- Server Work Queues: Queue Length—Specifies the number of requests waiting to use a particular processor. This value should be as low as possible, with values less than 4 being acceptable. If the value is too high, upgrade the processor or add another processor.

- Processor: Interrupts/sec—Specifies the number of hardware interrupts the processor is servicing each second. The value of this counter can vary greatly and is significant only in relation to an established baseline. A hardware device that is generating too many interrupts can monopolize the processor, preventing it from performing other tasks. If the value increases precipitously, examine the various other hardware components in the system to determine which one is generating too many interrupts.

MONITORING MEMORY PERFORMANCE

An inadequate amount of memory in a server can prevent the computer from caching frequently used data aggressively enough, causing processes to rely on disk reads more than memory reads and slowing down the entire system. Memory is the single most important subsystem to monitor because memory problems can affect all of the other subsystems. For example, when a memory condition causes excessive disk paging, the system might appear to have a problem in the storage subsystem, although memory is actually the culprit.

One of the most common conditions that can cause memory-related problems is a memory leak. A *memory leak* is the result of a program allocating memory for use but not freeing up that memory when it is finished using it. Over time, the computer's free memory can be totally consumed, degrading performance and ultimately halting the system. Memory leaks can be fast, causing an almost immediate degradation in overall server performance, but they can also be slow and difficult to detect, gradually degrading system performance over a period of days or weeks. In most cases, memory leaks are caused by third-party applications, but operating system leaks are not unprecedented.

To monitor basic memory performance, use the following counters:

- Memory: Page Faults/Sec—Specifies the number of times per second that the code or data needed for processing is not found in memory. This value should be as low as possible, with values below 5 being acceptable. This counter includes both soft faults (in which the required page is found elsewhere in memory) and hard faults (in which the requested page must be accessed from a disk). Soft faults are generally not a major problem, but hard faults can cause significant delays because disk accesses are much slower than memory accesses. If this value is too high, you should determine whether the system is experiencing an inordinate number of hard faults by examining the Memory: Pages/Sec counter. If the number of hard page faults is excessive, you should either determine what process is causing the excessive paging or install more random access memory (RAM) in the system.

- Memory: Pages/Sec—Specifies the number of times per second that required information was not in RAM and had to be accessed from disk or had to be written to disk to make room in RAM. This value should be as low as possible, with values from 0 to 20 being acceptable. If the value is too high, you should either determine what process is causing the excessive paging or install more RAM in the system.

- Memory: Available MBytes—Specifies the amount of available physical memory in megabytes. This value should be as high as possible and should not fall below 5 percent of the system's total physical memory, as this might be an indication of a memory leak. If the value is too low, consider installing additional RAM in the system.

- Memory: Committed Bytes—Specifies the amount of virtual memory that has space reserved on the disk paging files. This value should be as low as possible and should always be less than the amount of physical RAM in the computer. If the value is too high, this could be an indication of a memory leak or the need for additional RAM in the system.

- Memory: Pool Non-paged Bytes—Specifies the size of an area in memory used by the operating system for objects that cannot be written to disk. This value should be a stable number that does not grow without a corresponding growth in server activity. If the value increases over time, this could be an indication of a memory leak.

MONITORING DISK PERFORMANCE

A storage subsystem that is overburdened with read and write commands can slow down the rate at which the system processes client requests. The server's hard disk drives carry a greater physical burden than the other three subsystems because in satisfying the I/O requests of many clients, the drive heads must continually move to different locations on the drive platters. The drive head mechanism can move only so fast, however, and once the drive reaches its maximum read/write speed, additional requests can begin to pile up in the queue, waiting to be processed. For this reason, the storage subsystem is a prime location for a bottleneck.

To monitor the storage subsystem in Performance Monitor, you can use the following counters:

- PhysicalDisk: Disk Bytes/sec—Specifies the average number of bytes transferred to or from the disk each second. This value should be equivalent to the levels established in the original baseline readings or higher. A decrease in this value could indicate a malfunctioning disk that could eventually fail. If this is the case, consider upgrading the storage subsystem.

- PhysicalDisk: Avg. Disk Bytes/Transfer—Specifies the average number of bytes transferred during read and write operations. This value should be equivalent to the levels established in the original baseline readings or higher. A decrease in this value indicates a malfunctioning disk that could eventually fail. If this is the case, consider upgrading the storage subsystem.

- PhysicalDisk: Current Disk Queue Length—Specifies the number of pending disk read or write requests. This value should be as low as possible, with values less than 2 being acceptable per disk spindle. High values for this counter can indicate that the drive is malfunctioning or that it is incapable of keeping up with the activities demanded of it. If this is the case, consider upgrading the storage subsystem.

- PhysicalDisk: % Disk Time—Specifies the percentage of time that the disk drive is busy reading or writing. This value should be as low as possible, with values less than 80 percent being acceptable. High values for this counter can indicate that the drive is malfunctioning, that it is incapable of keeping up with the activities demanded of it, or that a memory problem is causing excess disk paging. Check for memory leaks or related problems and, if none are found, consider upgrading the storage subsystem.

- LogicalDisk: % Free Space—Specifies the percentage of free space on the disk. This value should be as high as possible, with values greater than 20 percent being acceptable. If the value is too low, consider adding more disk space.

Most storage subsystem problems, when not caused by malfunctioning hardware, are resolvable by upgrading the storage system. These upgrades can include any of the following measures:

- Install faster hard disk drives.
- Install additional hard disk drives and split your data among them, reducing the I/O burden on each drive.
- Replace standalone drives with a RAID (Redundant Array of Independent Disks) array.
- Add more disk drives to an existing RAID array.

MONITORING NETWORK PERFORMANCE

Monitoring network performance is more complicated than monitoring the other three subsystems because many factors outside the computer can affect network performance. You can use the following counters to try to determine if a network problem exists, but if you suspect one, you should begin looking for causes external to the computer:

- Network Interface: Bytes Total/sec—Specifies the number of bytes sent and received per second by the selected network interface adapter. This value should be equivalent to the levels established in the original baseline readings or higher. A decrease in this value could indicate malfunctioning network hardware or other network problems.
- Network Interface: Output Queue Length—Specifies the number of packets waiting to be transmitted by the network interface adapter. This value should be as low as possible, and preferably zero, although values of two or less are acceptable. If the value is too high, the network interface adapter could be malfunctioning or another network problem might exist.
- Server: Bytes Total/Sec—Specifies the total number of bytes sent and received by the server over all of its network interfaces. This value should be no more than 50 percent of the total bandwidth capacity of the network interfaces in the server. If the value is too high, consider migrating some applications to other servers or upgrading to a faster network.

The bandwidth of the network connections limits the amount of traffic reaching the server through its network interfaces. If these counter values indicate that the network itself is the bottleneck, there are two ways to upgrade the network, and neither one is a simple fix:

- Increase the speed of the network—This means replacing the network interface adapters in all the computers, switches, routers, and other devices on the network, and possibly replacing the cabling as well.
- Install additional network adapters in the server and redistribute the network—If traffic frequently saturates the network interfaces already in the server, the only way to increase the network throughput without increasing the network's speed is to install more network interfaces. However, connecting more interfaces to the same network will not permit any more traffic to reach the server. Instead, you must create additional subnets on the network and redistribute the computers among them so that there is less traffic on each subnet.

ESTABLISHING A BASELINE

As mentioned earlier, performance bottlenecks can develop over a long period of time, and it can often be difficult to detect them by observing a server's performance levels at one particular point in time. This is why it is a good idea to use tools like the Reliability and Performance Monitor console to establish baseline levels for a server. A *baseline* is simply a set of readings, captured under normal operating conditions, which you can save and compare to readings taken at a later time. By comparing the baseline readings to the server's current readings at regular intervals, you can discern trends that might eventually affect the computer's performance.

To capture counter statistics in the Reliability and Performance Monitor console for later review, you must create a data collector set. A *data collector set* is a means of gathering, compiling, and storing information from various sources, including performance counters, event traces, and the Windows registry. At its simplest, data collector sets can function as the equivalent of performance logs in earlier Windows versions. You select the counters you want to monitor, and the console records their information for later evaluation.

In more complex configurations, data collector sets can gather information from different sources and combine them into a single report. For example, when you expand the System node under Data Collector Sets in the Reliability and Performance Monitor console, you can select from three predefined tools that gather diagnostic information by monitoring hardware and software performance, reading configuration values from the registry, and tracing specific event types in the Windows logs.

For more flexibility, the User Defined node enables you to create your own customized data collector sets, for which you can select specific combinations of counters, event traces, and configuration settings you want to monitor. You can also create performance counter alerts that notify an administrator when the values of selected performance counters reach specified

threshold values. Once you have configured a data collector set, you can save it as a template, enabling you to load it again at a later time; or you can save it for use on another computer. Reliability and Performance Monitor also includes some templates for basic system diagnostics and performance monitoring.

To create a simple data collector set that monitors performance counters, use the following procedure.

 CREATE A DATA COLLECTOR SET

GET READY. Log on to Windows Server 2008. When the logon process is completed, close the Initial Configuration Tasks window and any other windows that appear.

1. Click **Start.** Then, click **Administrative Tools** > **Reliability and Performance Monitor.** The Reliability and Performance Monitor console appears.
2. Expand the **Data Collector Sets** folder. Then, right-click the **User Defined** folder and, on the context menu, click **New** > **Data Collector Set.** The Create New Data Collector Set wizard appears, displaying the *How would you like to create this new data collector set?* page, as shown in Figure 11-19.

Figure 11-19

The How would you like to create this new data collector set? page in the Create new Data Collector Set wizard

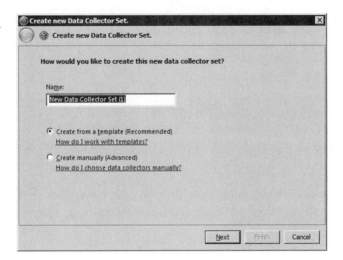

3. In the **Name** text box, key a name for the data collector set. Then, select the **Create manually (Advanced)** option and click **Next.** the *What type of data do you want to include?* page appears, as shown in Figure 11-20.

Figure 11-20

The What type of data do you want to include? page in the Create new Data Collector Set wizard

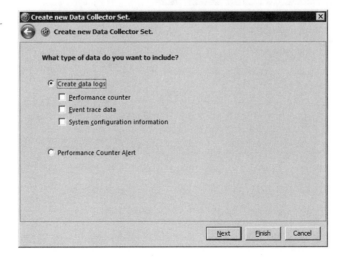

4. Select the **Performance counter** checkbox and click **Next.** The *Which performance counters would you like to log?* page appears, as shown in Figure 11-21.

Figure 11-21

The Which performance counters would you like to log? page in the Create new Data Collector Set wizard

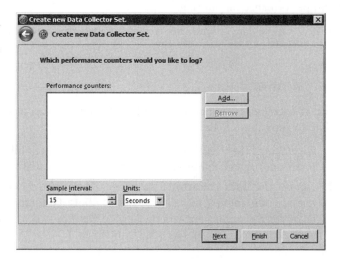

5. Click **Add.** The Add Counters dialog box appears. Select the counters you want to log in the usual manner and click **OK.** The counters appear in the Performance counters box.

> **TAKE NOTE** *
> You can also use the Create New Data Collector Set wizard to create performance counter alerts, which monitor the values of specific counters and perform a task, such as sending an email to an administrator, when the counters reach a specific value.

6. Select the interval at which you want the system to collect samples and click **Next.** The *Where would you like the data to be saved?* page appears, as shown in Figure 11-22.

Figure 11-22

The Where would you like the data to be saved? page in the Create new Data Collector Set wizard

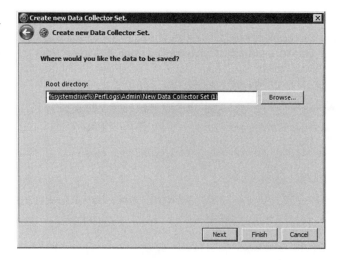

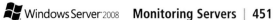

7. Key the name of or browse to the folder where you want to store the data collector set and click **Next.** The *Create the data collector set?* page appears, as shown in Figure 11-23.

Figure 11-23

The Create the data collector set? page in the Create new Data Collector Set wizard

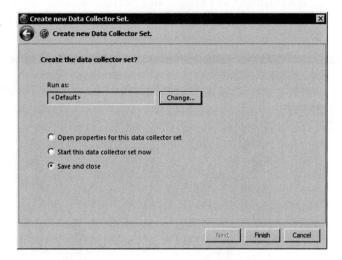

8. If the account you are currently using does not have the privileges needed to gather the log information, click **Change** to display a Reliability and Performance Monitor dialog box in which you can supply alternative credentials.

9. Select one of the following options:

- Open properties for this data collector set—Saves the data collector set to the specified location and opens its Properties sheet, as shown in Figure 11-24, for further modifications

- Start this data collector set now—Saves the data collector set to the specified location and starts collecting data immediately

- Save and close—Saves the data collector set to the specified location and closes the wizard

Figure 11-24

The Properties sheet for a data collector set

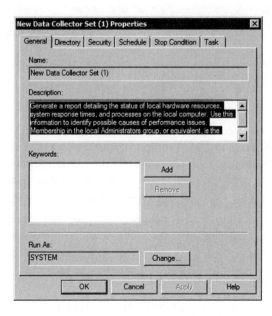

10. Click **Finish.** The new data collector set appears in the User Defined folder.

11. Select the new data collector set and click **Start** in the toolbar. The console begins collecting data until you click **Stop.**

CLOSE the Reliability and Performance Monitor console.

Once you have captured data using the collector set, you can display the data by double-clicking the Performance Monitor file in the folder you specified during its creation. This opens a Reliability and Performance Monitor window containing a graph of the collected data, as shown in Figure 11-25, instead of real-time activity.

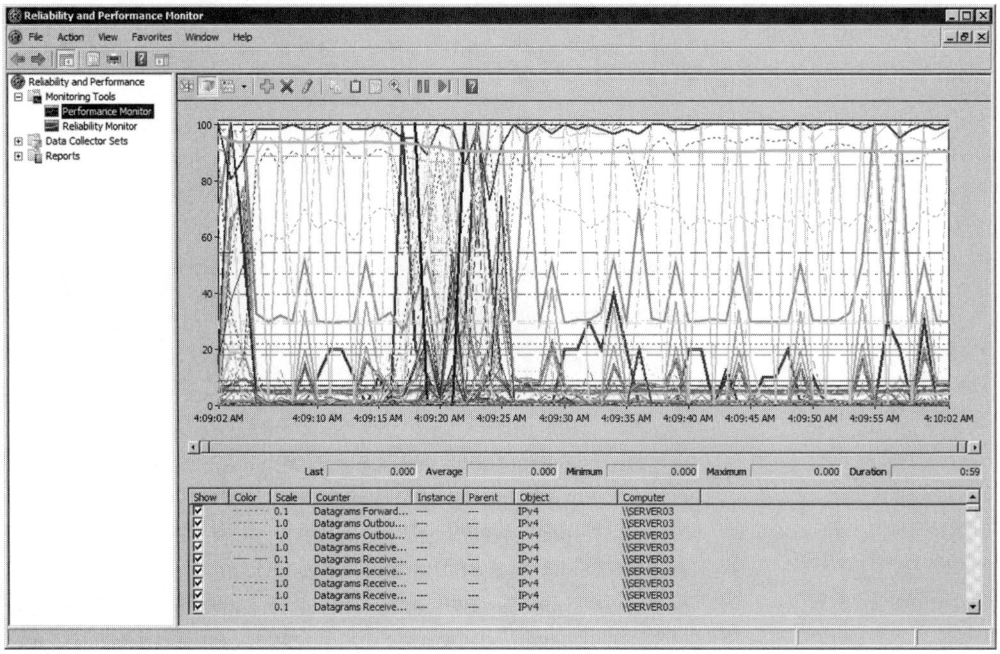

Figure 11-25

Performance Monitor information collected using a data collector set

By repeating this process at a later time and comparing the information in the two data collector sets, you can often detect performance trends that indicate the presence of bottlenecks.

■ Using Auditing

THE BOTTOM LINE

Auditing is the process by which administrators can track specific security-related events on a Windows Server 2008 computer.

Windows Server 2008 can audit a variety of activities for both success and failure. For example, you can audit account logons so that you have a record of every time a user logs on. For security purposes, though, administrators might be interested in auditing logon failures only so that they can tell when someone makes repeated attempts to access a user account and fails. You can configure the system to audit all logons, all successes, or all failures.

Auditing is an elective process that administrators can configure to their own needs. This is primarily because enabling all of the available audit options can generate an enormous amount of data and also negatively affect system performance. Selective auditing enables administrators to avoid monitoring events unnecessarily, and helps them to locate pertinent information more easily.

CERTIFICATION READY?
Monitor and maintain security and policies
3.3

To audit security events, you must enable specific Group Policy settings for a computer. Once you activate these settings, the system tracks the specified activities and records them as events in the Security log, which you can access using the Event Viewer snap-in.

To enable auditing, use the following procedure.

→ **ENABLE AUDITING**

GET READY. Log on to Windows Server 2008 using a domain account with administrative privileges. When the logon process is completed, close the Initial Configuration Tasks window and any other windows that appear. If you are not working on a domain controller, use the Server Manager console to install the Group Policy Management feature, if you have not done so already.

1. Click **Start.** Then, click **Administrative Tools** > **Group Policy Management.** The Group Policy Management console appears.

2. Select or create a group policy object, right-click the object and, from the context menu, select **Edit.** The Group Policy Management Editor console appears.

3. Browse to the **Computer Configuration** > **Policies** > **Windows Settings** > **Security Settings** > **Local Policies** > **Audit Policy** container, as shown in Figure 11-26.

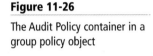

Figure 11-26

The Audit Policy container in a group policy object

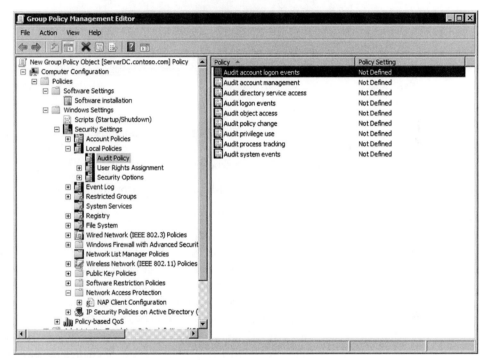

4. Double-click one of the audit policies to open its Properties sheet, as shown in Figure 11-27.

Figure 11-27

The Properties sheet for an audit policy

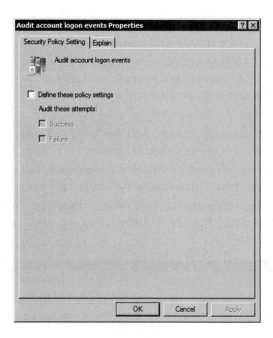

5. Select the **Define these policy settings** checkbox and, under Audit These Attempts, specify whether you want to audit successes, failures, or both, by selecting the appropriate checkboxes. Then click **OK.**

CLOSE the Group Policy Management Editor and Group Policy Management consoles.

Group policy objects contain the following audit policies:

- Audit account logon events—Records successful and/or unsuccessful domain logon attempts in the domain controller's Security log. Logon attempts are recorded only on the domain controller where the attempt occurs. To audit logon attempts for an entire domain, you must examine the Security logs on all of the domain controllers, or use the Subscriptions capability in the Event Viewer console to gather the audit events from all of the domain controllers to a single computer.

- Audit account management—Records successful and/or unsuccessful attempts to create, modify, rename, delete, enable, disable, or change the password of any domain or local user account.

- Audit directory service access—Records successful and/or unsuccessful attempts to access Active Directory objects with their own system access control lists in the domain controller's Security log. In addition to setting this policy, you must configure auditing for the individual Active Directory objects you want to monitor, using the Auditing tab in the object's Advanced Security Settings dialog box, as shown in Figure 11-28.

- Audit logon events—Records successful and/or unsuccessful local logon attempts in the local computer's Security log.

- Audit object access—Records successful and/or unsuccessful attempts to access non–Active Directory objects, such as files, folders, registry keys, and printers, that have their own system access control lists. In addition to setting this policy, you must configure auditing for the individual objects you want to monitor, using the Auditing tab in the object's Advanced Security Settings dialog box.

- Audit policy change—Records successful and/or unsuccessful attempts to change user rights assignments, audit policies, or trust policies.

- Audit privilege use—Records successful and/or unsuccessful attempts to exercise user rights.

- Audit process tracking—Records successful and/or unsuccessful system events, such as process activations, handle duplications, indirect object accesses, and exits from processes.

This policy typically generates an extremely large number of events; you should enable it only for brief periods, when needed for troubleshooting purposes.

- Audit system events—Records successful and/or unsuccessful attempts to restart or shut down the computer, or any other events that affect system security or the Security log.

Figure 11-28

The Auditing tab of an object's Advanced Security Settings for Students dialog box

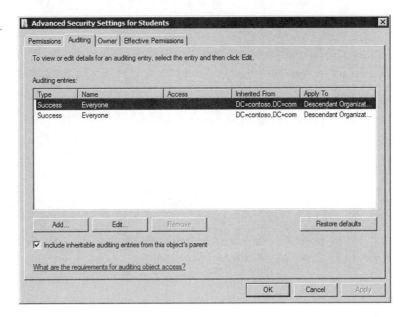

Windows Server 2008 enhances the auditing capabilities of previous Windows versions in several ways. When auditing Active Directory changes, the system can now log both the old and the new values so that you have a record of the previous values, before the changes were made.

Windows Server 2008 also adds subcategories to the global categories listed earlier. For example, the Audit directory service access global category is now divided into four subcategories, as follows:

- Directory service access
- Directory service changes
- Directory service replication
- Detailed directory service replication

Enabling the global category causes the system to enable all four subcategories, but you can use the Auditpol.exe command prompt tool to disable any of the four.

SUMMARY SKILL MATRIX

IN THIS LESSON YOU LEARNED:

- The primary function of the Windows Eventing engine, as always, is to record information about system activities as they occur and package that information in individual units called events. The application you use to view the events is called Event Viewer.

- When you expand the Windows Logs folder in the Event Viewer console, you see the following logs: Application, Security, Setup, System, and Forwarded Events.

- The Windows event logs contain different types of events, as follows: Information, Error, Warning, and Critical.

- Four types of logs can appear in the Applications and Services Logs folder, as follows: Admin, Operational, Analytic, and Debug.

- When you launch the Reliability and Performance Monitor console, you see the Resource Overview screen, which contains four real-time line graphs that display information about four of the server's main hardware components.

- While the Event Viewer snap-in enables you to review system events that have already occurred, the Reliability and Performance snap-in enables you to view system information on a continuous, real-time basis.

- Performance Monitor is a tool within the Reliability and Performance Monitor console that displays system performance statistics in real time. The difference between Performance Monitor and Resource Overview is that Performance Monitor can display hundreds of different statistics (called performance counters) and that you can create a customized graph containing any statistics you choose.

- Reliability Monitor is a new addition to Windows Server 2008 that automatically tracks events that can have a negative effect on system stability and uses them to calculate a stability index.

- A bottleneck occurs when a component is not providing an acceptable level of performance compared with the other components in the system.

- Auditing is the process by which administrators can track specific security-related events on a Windows Server 2008 computer.

■ Knowledge Assessment

Fill in the Blank

Complete the following exercise by filling in the blanks with the appropriate terms from this lesson.

1. You enable _____ using Group Policy and view the results using the Event Viewer console.

2. A condition in which a system allocates memory for a task but does not reclaim all of it when the task ends is called a _____.

3. Counters and instances are elements you use with a tool in the Reliability and Performance snap-in called _____.

4. To capture performance counter readings for later evaluation, you must create a _____.

5. The main display that first appears when you open the Reliability and Performance snap-in is called _____.

6. A set of performance counter readings, captured under normal operating conditions, which you can save and compare to readings taken at a later time, is called a _____.

7. The tool in Windows Server 2008 that automatically calculates a stability index is called _____.

8. Windows Server 2008 packages information about system activities into individual units called _____.

9. A hardware or software component that is operating below par, slowing down the performance of the system, is called a _____.

10. To view the Windows Server 2008 system logs, you must use the _____.

Multiple Choice

Select one or more correct answers for each of the following questions.

1. Which of the following is not one of the event types found in the Windows Server 2008 event logs?
   a. Information
   b. Admin
   c. Warning
   d. Critical

2. Which of the following logs from the Applications and Services Logs folder in the Event Viewer console are disabled and hidden by default?
   a. Analytic
   b. Admin
   c. Debug
   d. Operational

3. Which of the following event logs contains events generated by the Windows Server 2008 auditing policies?
   a. Setup
   b. System
   c. Security
   d. Application

4. Which of the following Performance Monitor views displays a history of counter values?
   a. the graph view only
   b. the graph and histogram views
   c. the histogram and report views
   d. the histogram view only

5. The default graph view in Performance Monitor displays the current state of which system component?
   a. memory
   b. processor
   c. disk
   d. network

6. Which of the following audit policies requires you to modify the system access control lists of the elements you want to audit?
   a. audit account logon events
   b. audit directory service access
   c. audit object access
   d. audit account management

7. Which of the following is not one of the tools included in the Reliability and Performance snap-in?
   a. Resource Overview
   b. Reliability Monitor
   c. data collector sets
   d. subscriptions

8. What is the term that Event Viewer uses to describe the pathways to the separate logs it creates for Windows components?
   a. events
   b. channels
   c. subscriptions
   d. instances

9. Which of the following audit policies is likely to generate the largest number of events when enabled?
   a. audit object access
   b. audit privilege use
   c. audit process tracking
   d. audit system events

10. Which of the following tools should you use to establish a baseline performance level for a Windows Server 2008 computer?
    a. data collector sets
    b. Performance Monitor
    c. Resource Overview
    d. Reliability Monitor

Review Questions

1. Explain why Performance Monitor counters sometimes have multiple instances.

2. What are the four main subsystems of a computer where a performance bottleneck is likely to occur?

■ Case Scenario

Scenario 11–1: Eliminating a Bottleneck

You are a server administrator who has been given the task of determining why a particular Windows Server 2008 server on a local area network is performing poorly. You must also implement a remedy for the problem. The computer is functioning as a file and print server for a small department of eight graphic designers. After monitoring the computer's performance using the Performance Monitor tool, you have determined that the network itself is the bottleneck preventing peak performance. The graphic designers routinely work with very large files, saturating the network with traffic. Give two possible solutions that will remedy the problem and increase the performance level of the computer in question.

Backing Up

OBJECTIVE DOMAIN MATRIX

TECHNOLOGY SKILL	OBJECTIVE DOMAIN	OBJECTIVE DOMAIN NUMBER
Backing Up and Restoring Group Policy Objects	Plan and implement group policy strategy	2.3
Planning a Backup Strategy	Plan for backup and recovery	5.3

KEY TERMS

archive bit
authoritative restore
autoloader
backup
backup targets
backup window

differential backup
Directory Services Restore
   Mode (DSRM)
full backup
Grandfather-Father-Son
   method

helical scanning
incremental backup
linear scanning
non-authoritative restore
shoeshining
tape library

Hard drives fail. They have many more moving parts than most other computer components, and when those parts wear out, the drive fails and the data stored on it is lost. For this reason, backing up the data stored on your computers is an essential part of server administration. This lesson examines some basic backup concepts, as well as backup tools, including:

- Backup hardware options
- Backup software features
- Windows Server Backup

■ Planning a Backup Strategy

THE BOTTOM LINE

A ***backup*** is simply a copy of the data on a computer's hard disks, stored on another medium in case a hard drive fails. If a drive failure occurs, an administrator can repair or replace the drive, and then restore the data from the backup.

CERTIFICATION READY?
Plan for backup and recovery
5.3

Whatever disk technologies your servers happen to be using, they are not a replacement for regular backups. RAID (Redundant Array of Independent Disks) can provide protection against disk failures, but what if a server is stolen, or destroyed in a fire or other disaster? Every server that contains valuable data should be backed up on a regular basis, with a copy of the backup stored offsite.

A backup solution consists of the following two elements:

- One or more backup drives
- A backup software product

Networks can both complicate and simplify the process of performing regular backups. To back up a single Windows Server 2008 computer, you can install a backup drive and use the Windows Server Backup feature to perform either manual or scheduled backups. However, if you are responsible for a network with dozens of servers, this approach quickly becomes impractical. The advantage of the network lies in the fact that you can conceivably use one server to back up the drives on many other servers.

A backup strategy specifies what data you will back up, how often you will back it up, and what medium you will use to store the backups. The decisions you make regarding the backup hardware, software, and administrative policies should depend on how much data you have to back up, how much time you have to back it up, and how much protection you want to provide.

The following sections examine the components of a backup solution and how to use them.

Selecting Backup Hardware

> Although any storage device can theoretically function as a backup drive, some form of removable media is preferable, because it enables you to store a copy of your backups offsite.

The three main criteria to consider when evaluating the suitability of a storage device for backups are as follows:

- Capacity—One of the primary objectives in designing an effective backup strategy is to automate as much of the process as possible. While it is possible to back up a server to individual DVD-ROMs holding 4 or 8 gigabytes (GB) each, a server with several hundred gigabytes of storage will need dozens of disks, and someone will have to be there to swap those disks in an out of the drive for several hours. Therefore, you should select a backup device that is capable of storing as much of your data as possible without having to change media. The ideal situation is one in which an entire backup job needs only one media change. This enables you to schedule backup jobs to run completely unattended. This does not mean, however, that if you are planning a backup strategy for your entire network, you have to purchase a drive that can hold all of the data stored on all of the network's computers. You can be selective about what data you want to back up, so it is important to determine just how much of your data needs protecting, and how often, before you decide on the capacity of your backup device.

- Speed—Backup drives are available in many different speeds, ranging from the slowest magnetic tape drives to the fastest hard drives. Not surprisingly, the faster devices of a particular type are generally more expensive. Many administrators prefer to run backup jobs during periods when the network is not otherwise in use. This ensures that all of the data on the server is available for backup and that productivity will not be affected. The amount of time that you have to perform your backups is sometimes called the *backup window.* The backup device that you choose should depend in part on the amount of data you have to protect and the amount of time that you have to back it up. If, for example, you have 500 GB of data to back up and your company closes down from 5:00 P.M. until 9:00 A.M. the next morning, you have a 16-hour backup window—plenty of time to copy your data, using a medium-speed backup device. However, if your company operates three shifts and only leaves you one hour, from 7:00 A.M. to 8:00 A.M., to back up the same amount of data, you will have to use a much faster device, or in some cases, several devices.

- Cost—Cost is always a factor in selecting any hardware product. You can purchase a writable DVD-ROM or external hard drive for well under $100, which is suitable for backing up a single computer where speed is not a major factor. However, when you move up to drives that have the speed and capacity to make them suitable for large server and network backups, the prices increase dramatically. High-end magnetic tape drives can command prices that run well into five figures. When you evaluate backup devices, you must be aware of the product's extended costs as well. Backup devices that use a removable medium, such as magnetic tapes or blank DVDs, have additional costs to consider. One of the most common methods of evaluating backup devices is to determine the cost per gigabyte of the storage it provides. Divide the price of the medium by the number of gigabytes it can store, and use this figure to compare the relative media cost of various devices. Of course, in some cases you might need to sacrifice economy for speed or capacity.

Some of the storage devices that you can use as backup drives are examined in the following sections.

USING OPTICAL DISKS

As mentioned earlier, it is possible to use a CD-ROM or DVD-ROM drive for backups. Most servers come equipped with a writable DVD-ROM drive, or can easily be retrofitted with one. The drives and media are both relatively inexpensive, and write speeds are reasonably fast.

The primary drawback of optical disks is their capacity. CD-ROMs are limited to approximately 800 megabytes (MB) of storage, which is inadequate for all but the smallest servers. The standard DVD writers supplied with most computers can write 4.7 GB to a single disk, but higher-end DVD standards support up to 17 GB per disk.

Even at this maximum capacity, however, virtually all servers would require multiple DVDs for a full backup. This makes it nearly impossible to automate a backup job, and also complicates the process of cataloging and storing the disks.

USING HARD DISK DRIVES

The ever-increasing capacities of hard disk drives, along with their ever-decreasing prices per gigabyte, have led to their use as the primary backup medium for home users and small networks in recent years. Even more significant than speed and capacity, however, is the ubiquity of the Universal Serial Bus (USB) 2.0 and IEEE 1394 (FireWire) interfaces in today's computers.

Internal hard disk drives can be good for backups. They are fast, they hold a lot of data, and they are inexpensive. However, internal drives are not easily removable, and for backups to be truly secure, it should be possible to store a copy at another location, such as a bank vault. The high-speed USB or FireWire interfaces now included with every computer address this issue, though.

External hard drives, which are basically standard hard disk drives in a simple housing with a USB or FireWire interface and a power supply, are wildly popular products on the home and small business computing markets. Although usable for any storage purpose, they are particularly suitable for backups, because you can easily detach them from the computer and take them offsite.

Individual, external hard drives can serve as an inexpensive and effective backup medium for a single server or even a small network, but are generally not practical for high-capacity servers and enterprise networks. In these cases, a drive array with removable hard disks would be more suitable, such as a network attached storage (NAS) device or a storage area network (SAN) array.

Another possible alternative is the use of external drives that have an External SATA (eSATA) interface, which is a SATA variant with an external connector. Few computers have eSATA interfaces on the motherboard at this time, however, so to use eSATA drives, you have to install an eSATA card in the computer. One advantage to using external eSATA drives is that if you have several of them, you can configure them as a RAID array, something you can't do with external USB or FireWire drives.

For long-term data archiving, hard disk drives are a somewhat less suitable choice. Compared with magnetic tapes or optical disks, hard disks are quite fragile, and it is probably not economically feasible to leave entire hard drives in storage for long periods of time.

USING MAGNETIC TAPE

Magnetic tape is the traditional choice for server and network backups. Tape drives are well suited for backups; they are fast, they can hold a lot of data, they can archive that data for long periods of time, and their media cost per gigabyte is low. Unlike hard disks, floppies, or optical disks, tape drives are not random access devices. A hard drive can access any file on its platters by moving the heads to the appropriate spot. A tape drive must spool through the reel of tape until it locates the desired file. This linear access paradigm makes magnetic tape unsuitable for standard data storage tasks, but it is perfectly fine for backups, which use the medium for writing much more frequently than reading.

You cannot mount a tape drive in a computer's file system, assign it a drive letter, and copy files to it, as you can with a hard disk. You must use a special software program to address the drive and send the data you select to it for storage. This also means that magnetic tape drives are useless for anything other than backups, whereas other types of removable storage media, such as optical disks, can be used for other things.

The computer industry has been using magnetic tape for data storage since the 1950s, and there have been a great many formats and technologies during those years. Open reel tapes and *linear scanning*, in which the drive draws the tape over stationary recording heads, have given way to cartridge drives that use various forms of *helical scanning*, in which the heads are mounted on a rotating drum that records data in diagonal stripes across the tape.

There are many different types of magnetic tape drives that differ greatly in speed, capacity, and price. In recent years, the slower, more inexpensive formats designed for home computer and single workstation backups have largely been forced out of the market by optical disks and external hard drives. Most of the tape drives that are left are intended for backing up large servers and networks, and their high prices reflect those capabilities.

The general rule of magnetic tape drives is that you trade speed and capacity for cost. The higher-end technologies that are still on the market, such as Digital Linear Tape (DLT), Linear Tape-Open (LTO) Ultrium, Advanced Intelligent Tape (AIT), and Digital Data Storage/Digital Audio Tape (DDS/DAT), have all undergone several generations of development, often doubling their speeds and capacities with each step. A state-of-the-art magnetic tape drive today has a single-tape capacity of 800 to 1000 GB and a maximum transfer speed of 60 to 120 MB/sec (megabytes per second). These standards are constantly improving, however, and most of these technologies have announced speed and capacity increases that are planned for the near future.

TAKE NOTE*

The Windows Server Backup utility included in Windows Server 2008 does not support magnetic tape drives. To use a magnetic tape drive with Windows Server 2008, you must purchase a third-party backup software product.

➕ MORE INFORMATION

Magnetic tape drive specifications often list their capacities using two figures, such as 400 GB/800 GB, representing uncompressed and compressed storage. Most tape drives have hardware-based compression built into the unit, which prevents the computer from having to perform the processor-intensive task of compressing the data before writing it to tape. While administrators must treat all hardware specifications as approximate values, compressed tape capacities are particularly variable, because the capacity depends on the nature of the data being compressed. Data can be compressed only once. Files that are already in a compressed form, such as ZIP archives and JPG images, cannot be compressed further by a tape drive. In addition, different file formats compress at different rates. Executables and other program files typically compress at about a 2:1 ratio, while uncompressed images and media files might compress at much higher rates, such as 7:1. The 2:1 ratio that drive manufacturers use is therefore a reasonable average, but you must consider the nature of the data you will be backing up whenever you are evaluating magnetic tape drive capacities.

USING TAPE LIBRARIES

For many network installations, no single magnetic tape drive provides the speed and capacity needed to back up all of the data in the time that is available. The use of multiple drive arrays in large enterprise settings is therefore common. As with hard drive arrays, magnetic tape drive arrays often provide fault tolerance features such as hot-swapping and redundant power supplies. In fact, some drive arrays can handle a combination of hard disk and magnetic tape drives so that administrators can alter their configuration as needed.

Obviously, a magnetic tape drive array moves you up into an even higher price bracket, but that is still not the ultimate in tape backup technology. To minimize the tape changes you have to make to complete your backups and perform restores, you can purchase an ***autoloader***, sometimes called a ***tape library***. An autoloader is a single device that contains one or more magnetic tape drives, as well as a robotic mechanism that inserts tapes into and removes them from the drives.

Smaller autoloaders can handle up to ten tapes with a single drive, while the largest are refrigerator-sized units that can hold 100 tapes and support as many as 12 drives. These high-end units often have bar code readers that can automatically identify the tapes in the slots and present administrators with a menu, allowing them to select any tape for a backup or a restore. Not surprisingly, the prices of these units are stratospheric, easily reaching six figures for an autoloader fully populated with multiple drives.

Autoloaders enable administrators to perform comprehensive backups of entire enterprise networks with full automation. With multiple tape drives operating at the same time, the aggregate data transfer speed can be enormous, enabling backups to occur during smaller backup windows. Autoloaders can also simplify the process of performing restores, because the required tapes are immediately available. In the case of a restore from incremental or differential tapes, the autoloader can take charge of the entire process, inserting each tape as needed.

SELECTING A DRIVE INTERFACE

The interface that a backup device uses to connect to a computer is of particular concern to server administrators. No matter how fast the backup device itself, throughput will be slow if the interface cannot deliver data to the drive at a sufficient rate. Magnetic tape drives, in particular, require a consistent stream of data to write to the tape with maximum effectiveness. If there are constant interruptions in the data stream, as can be the case with a relatively slow interface, the tape drive must repeatedly stop and start the tape (called ***shoeshining***), which reduces its speed and its overall storage capacity.

Backup devices can use any of the standard computer interfaces, such as Parallel Advanced Technology Attachment (PATA), Serial ATA (SATA), USB, IEEE 1394, and Small Computer System Interface (SCSI). In most cases, optical drives and internal hard disk drives use PATA or SATA, and external hard drives use USB or IEEE 1394. Magnetic tape drives are available that use any of these interfaces, but the vast majority of them use SCSI.

SCSI devices operate more independently than those devices that use other interfaces, meaning that the backup process, which might entail reading from one device while writing to another on the same interface, is more efficient. When two PATA devices share a channel, only one operates at a time. Each drive must receive, execute, and complete a command before the other drive can receive its next command. On the other hand, SCSI devices can maintain a queue of commands that they have received from the host adapter and execute them sequentially and independently.

SCSI backup devices are always more expensive than those using alternative interfaces, because the drive requires additional electronics and because you must have a SCSI host adapter installed in the computer. SCSI tape drives are available as internal or external units, the latter of which have their own power supplies, which also adds to the cost. However, for large, mission-critical servers or enterprise networks, a reliable, efficient backup solution is worth the additional expense for SCSI.

Selecting Backup Software

> The Windows Server Backup program is a reasonably adequate full backup solution for a single server, but it lacks many of the features found in more comprehensive third-party backup software products.

Depending on the type of backup device you select for your servers, a backup software product can be a convenience or an absolute necessity. For example, when you use an external hard disk drive for backups, you can simply copy your files to the disk using Windows Explorer. Backup software can simplify and organize the process, but one could conceivably get by without it. If you plan to back up to magnetic tape, however, backup software is essential, because Windows does not include the driver needed for the system to utilize the tape drive.

The following sections examine the main features of a backup software product that is suitable for large server and enterprise network use.

SELECTING TARGETS

One of the most basic functions of a backup software product is to let you select what you want to back up, often called the *backup targets*. Most backup software programs enable you to select any combination of the following:

- Entire servers
- Entire disks
- Entire volumes
- Specific folders
- Specific files

Depending on your disaster recovery planning, it is in most cases not necessary to back up all of a computer's data on a regular basis. If a hard drive is destroyed or its data is completely erased, you will most likely have to reinstall the operating system before you can restore files from a backup, so it might not be worthwhile to include all of the operating system files each time you run a backup job. The same holds true for applications. You can reinstall an application from the original distribution media, so you might want to back up only your data files and configuration settings for that application.

In addition, most operating systems and applications create temporary files as they run, which you do not need to back up. The memory paging file on a Windows server, for example, can be several gigabytes in size. Because this operating system automatically creates this file, you can save space on your backup media by omitting it and files like it from your backup jobs. Judicious selection of backup targets can mean the difference between fitting an entire backup job onto one tape or staying late after work to insert a second tape into the drive.

USING A TREE DISPLAY

Most backup programs provide a tree display, with checkboxes that you can use to select the targets for a backup job, although the Windows Server Backup utility in Windows Server 2008 does not. However, the Windows Server 2003 Backup program uses a tree-based target selection interface, as shown in Figure 12-1.

Figure 12-1

The Backup tab in the Windows
Server 2003 Backup program

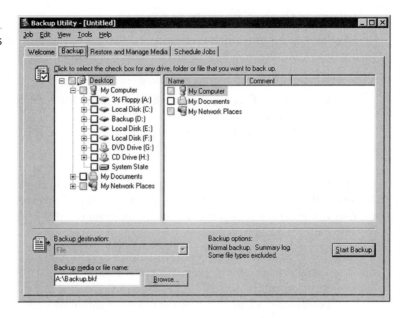

USING FILTERS

Individually selecting the files, folders, and volumes that you want to back up can be quite
tedious on a large network installation, so many backup programs provide other ways to
specify targets. One common method is to use filters that enable the software to evaluate
each file and folder on a drive and decide whether to back it up. Backup software products
that support filtering typically enable you to use the filters inclusively or exclusively; that is, a
filter can identify the files you want to back up or the files that you want to exclude from the
backup.

A good backup program provides a variety of filters that enable you to select targets based on
any of the following criteria:

- File and folder name—Specifying individual file and folder names using filters is not
  easier than using a tree display, but the ability to use wildcard characters in file and
  folder names makes this a powerful feature. You can use the standard question mark (?)
  and asterisk (*) to represent single characters and multiple characters respectively. For
  example, creating an exclude filter using the file mask *.tmp would exclude all files with
  a tmp extension (which is commonly used for temporary files) from the backup job.

- File size—Filtering based on file size enables you to exclude zero-length files from your
  backups, or extremely large files, such as the Windows memory paging file.

- File dates/times—All file systems maintain at least one date and time for each file stored,
  typically specifying when the file was most recently modified. Some file systems, such
  as the Windows NTFS file system, include multiple dates and times for each file, such
  as when the file was created, when it was last accessed, and when it was last modified.
  Filtering based on these dates enables you to back up only the files that have changed
  since a given date and time, or only the files that are older than a certain date.

- File attributes—Attributes are one-bit flags attached to files that identify specific
  characteristics about them. Most file systems support the four standard DOS attributes,
  which are H for hidden, R for read-only, S for system, and A for archive, but some file
  systems include other attributes as well. Most backup programs rely primarily on archive
  attribute filtering for performing backups, which enables them to back up only the files
  that have changed since the last backup. This type of filter is the basis for incremental
  and differential backup jobs.

UNDERSTANDING BACKUP JOB TYPES

Most backup software products include a collection of standard backup job types that are actually preset filter combinations. The most common of these job types are the following:

- Full—Backs up all files to the storage medium and resets their archive bits
- Differential—Backs up only the files that have changed since the last full backup and does not reset their archive bits
- Incremental—Backs up only the files that have changed since the last full or incremental backup and resets their archive bits

The *full backup* is the most basic type of backup job, and copies the entire set of selected targets to the backup medium. You can perform a full backup every day, if you want to, or each time that you back up a particular computer. However, this practice can be impractical, for any of the following reasons:

- Too much data to back up—The hard disks on a high-end server or network can have a total storage capacity that adds up to thousands of gigabytes. Unless you intend to spend an enormous amount of money on tape drive and autochanger hardware, it is not possible to back up all of the data in every computer every day.
- Not enough time to perform the backups—Most administrators schedule backup jobs to occur at night, or whenever the organization is closed. Backing up during off hours makes it less likely for the backup job to skip files because they are locked open, and minimizes the impact of the system and network resources consumed by the backup process. For some organizations, the amount of time available to perform the backup is insufficient to back up the entire network, unless they use multiple high-speed backup drives.
- Too much redundant data—Much of the data stored on a typical computer's hard drive is static; it does not change every day. Application and operating system files never change, and some document files can go for long periods without users changing them. Backing up files like these every day means saving the same data to the backup medium over and over, which is a waste of time and storage space.

To save space on the backup media and shorten the backup time, many administrators perform full backups only once a week, or even less frequently. In between the full backups, they perform special types of filtered jobs that back up only the files that have recently been modified. An *incremental backup* is a job that backs up only the files that have changed since the last backup job of any kind. A *differential backup* is a job that backs up only the files that have changed since the last full backup. The backup software filters the files for these jobs using the archive attribute, also known as the *archive bit*, which every file on the computer possesses.

The archive bit does not actually modify a file's functionality, as the read-only and hidden attributes do; it is simply a marker that backup software uses to determine whether to back up each file or not. The state of the archive bit during a typical sequence of backup jobs is as follows:

1. When files are written to a computer's hard disk for the first time, their archive bits are activated, meaning that they are set to a value of 1.
2. During the first full backup performed on the computer, the software backs up the entire contents of the target disk, and also resets (that is, sets to a value of 0) the archive bit on all of the files. At this point, you have a complete backup of the disk, and none of the files on it has an active archive bit.
3. Whenever any application or process modifies a file on the target disk, the file system resets the archive bit to 1.
4. For the next backup, performing an incremental or differential job causes the backup software to scan the archive bits of all the files on the target disk and back up only the files with bits set to 1. At this point, you have a full backup of the entire disk and a backup of all the files that have changed since that full

backup. If a disaster should occur, causing the entire contents of the target disk to be lost, you can return it to its current state by performing a restore from the full backup, and then restoring the incremental or differential backup, allowing the changed versions of the files to overwrite the original versions.

Because in most cases incremental and differential jobs back up only part of the drive's contents, they run faster and take up less storage space than full backups. A typical network backup strategy consists of a full backup on one day of the week, and an incremental or differential job on each of the other days. With this arrangement, you can always restore the drive to a state no more than 24 hours old.

The difference between an incremental job and a differential job lies in the behavior of the **backup software** when it either resets or does not reset the archive bits of the files it backs up. Incremental jobs reset the archive bits, and differential jobs do not. Running incremental or differential jobs is often what makes it possible to automate your backup regimen without spending too much on hardware. If your full backup job totals 2000 GB, for example, you might be able to purchase an 800 GB magnetic tape drive. You'll have to manually insert two additional tapes during your full backup jobs, once a week, but you should be able to run incremental or differential jobs the rest of the week using only one tape for each one, which means that the jobs can run unattended.

USING INCREMENTAL BACKUPS

When you run an incremental backup job, you are only backing up the files that have changed since the last backup, whether it was a full backup or an incremental backup. Performing incrementals between your full backups uses the least amount of storage space, but it also lengthens the restore process. If you should have to restore an entire disk, you must first perform a restore from the last full backup, and then you must restore each of the incremental jobs you performed since the last full backup, in the order you performed them.

For example, consider the backup schedule shown in Table 12-1.

Table 12-1

Sample Incremental Backup Schedule

Day	Job Type	Files Included In Job
Sunday	Full	Data1.txt, Data2.txt, Data3.txt
Monday	Incremental	Data1.txt
Tuesday	Incremental	Data1.txt, Data3.txt
Wednesday	Incremental	Data1.txt, Data2.txt
Thursday	Incremental	Data1.txt, Data3.txt
Friday	Incremental	Data1.txt
Saturday	Incremental	Data1.txt

The Sunday backup is the only complete copy of the computer's disk, and each of the incrementals consists only of the files that have changed during the previous 24 hours. Because Data1.txt changes every day, it appears in every one of the incremental backups. The file's archive bit is set to 1 each time it changes, and each incremental backup resets the bit to 0 again. Data2.txt changes only once, on Wednesday, so it appears only in the full backup job and in Wednesday's incremental. Data3.txt changes twice, on Tuesday and Thursday, so it appears in the full backup and in Tuesday's and Thursday's incrementals.

If the computer's disk were to fail on Friday, causing all of its data to be lost, you would begin the restoration process by restoring the most recent Sunday full backup, and then you would restore the Monday, Tuesday, Wednesday, and Thursday incrementals that followed the full backup, in that order. The results of the restorations on the three data files would be as follows:

- Data1.txt: The original copy from the full restore would be overwritten by a newer copy during each incremental restore, leaving the newest (Thursday) version on the drive when the restoration process is complete.

- Data2.txt: The original copy from Sunday's full restore would remain on the drive until the restoration of the Wednesday incremental tape, at which time the newest (Wednesday) version would overwrite the Sunday version. The Wednesday version would be left on the drive when the restoration process is complete.

- Data3.txt: The original copy from Sunday's full restore would be overwritten twice, first by the version on the Tuesday incremental tape and then by the Thursday version, leaving the latest (Thursday) version on the drive when the restoration process is complete.

USING DIFFERENTIAL BACKUPS

If you were to perform the same sequence of backups using differential jobs instead of incrementals, the results would be like those in Table 12-2.

<table>
<tr><th colspan="3">Table 12-2</th></tr>
<tr><th colspan="3">Sample Differential Backup Schedule</th></tr>
<tr><th>DAY</th><th>JOB TYPE</th><th>FILES INCLUDED IN JOB</th></tr>
<tr><td>Sunday</td><td>Full</td><td>Data1.txt, Data2.txt, Data3.txt</td></tr>
<tr><td>Monday</td><td>Differential</td><td>Data1.txt</td></tr>
<tr><td>Tuesday</td><td>Differential</td><td>Data1.txt, Data3.txt</td></tr>
<tr><td>Wednesday</td><td>Differential</td><td>Data1.txt, Data2.txt, Data3.txt</td></tr>
<tr><td>Thursday</td><td>Differential</td><td>Data1.txt, Data2.txt, Data3.txt</td></tr>
<tr><td>Friday</td><td>Differential</td><td>Data1.txt, Data2.txt, Data3.txt</td></tr>
<tr><td>Saturday</td><td>Differential</td><td>Data1.txt, Data2.txt, Data3.txt</td></tr>
</table>

TAKE NOTE *

When restoring from incrementals, the order of the tapes you restore is crucial. You must restore the incrementals in the order they were written, or you might end up with old versions of files overwriting the newer versions.

Because the Data1.txt files changes every day, it appears in every differential job, just as it appeared in every incremental. However, because differential jobs do not reset the archive bits on the files they back up, once a file appears in a differential, it appears in every subsequent differential until the next full backup. Therefore, the Data2.txt file that first appears in the Wednesday incremental is also backed up on Thursday, Friday, and Saturday, because its archive bit is still set to 1. In the same way, the Data3.txt file that first appears in Tuesday's differential also appears in all of the subsequent differentials, but starting on Thursday, it is a newer version that is backed up each night. The archive bits for all three files are not reset until the next full backup, the following Sunday.

When you use differential backups, the jobs take a bit longer and they use a bit more storage space, because in some cases you are backing up the same files several days in a row. However, restoring from differentials is simpler and faster, because you have to restore only the last full backup and the most recent differential. If the drive in this example were to fail on a Saturday, you would have to restore only the full backup from the previous Sunday and the previous day's (Friday's) differential. The Friday tape would have the Data1.txt, Data2.txt, and Data3.txt files on it. The version of Data1.txt would be Friday's, Data2.txt would be Wednesday's version, and Data3.txt would be Thursday's version.

SCHEDULING JOBS

All backup products enable you to create a backup job and execute it immediately, but the key to automating a backup routine is being able to schedule jobs to execute unattended. Not all of the backup programs supplied with operating systems or designed for standalone computers support scheduling, but all full-featured backup software products do.

Most organizations perform incremental or differential backups daily and a full backup once a week. This arrangement provides a good compromise between sufficient protection and the amount of time and media devoted to backups. The ideal situation for a backup administrator is to have each daily incremental or differential job fit on a single tape. This enables the administrator to schedule the job to run unattended when the office is closed and the computers are idle so that all resources are available for backup, user productivity is not compromised, and there is no need to have someone change media. Once you have created the backup schedule, you can simply insert the correct tape into the drive each day.

Backup programs use various methods to automatically execute backup jobs. The Windows Server Backup program adds its jobs to the operating system's Task Scheduler, while other programs might supply their own program or service that runs continuously and triggers the jobs at the appropriate times. No matter which mechanism the backup software uses to launch jobs, however, the process of scheduling them is usually the same. You specify whether you want to execute the job once or repeatedly at a specified time each day, week, or month.

The idea of the scheduling feature is for the administrator to create a logical sequence of backup jobs that execute by themselves at regular intervals. After this is done, the only action required is to change the tape in the drive each day. If you have an autochanger, you can even eliminate this part of the job and create a backup job sequence that runs for weeks or months without any maintenance at all.

LOGGING BACKUP ACTIVITY

As a backup software product feeds data to the drive, it also keeps track of the software's activities. Most backup software products maintain a log of the backup process as it occurs. You can often specify a level of detail for the log, such as whether it should contain a complete list of every file backed up or just record the major events that occur during the job.

In most cases, a detailed log of your backup jobs is not necessary. This type of log typically contains a list of every file that the program has backed up, and since backup jobs can consist of many thousands of files, the detailed log can be very long and the important entries (such as errors) difficult to find. It is also important to keep an eye on the size of your log files, particularly when you configure them to maintain a high level of detail. These files can grow huge very quickly, and consume large amounts of disk space.

Periodically checking the logs is an essential part of administering a backup program. The logs tell you when selected files are skipped for any reason, such as when the files are locked open by an application or the computers on which they are stored are turned off. The logs also let you know when errors occur on either the backup drive or one of the computers involved in the backup process. Some software products can generate alerts when errors occur, notifying administrators by sending a status message to a network management console, by sending them an email message.

CATALOGING FILES

In addition to logging their activities, backup software programs also catalog the files they back up, facilitating the process of restoring files later. The catalog is essentially a database containing a list of every file that the software has backed up during each job. To restore files from the backup medium, you browse through the catalog and select the files, folders, or volumes that you want to restore. Different backup software products store the catalog in different ways. Some lower-end backup programs, such as those intended for standalone computers, store the catalog for each tape on the tape itself. The problem with this method is that you have to insert a tape into the drive to read the catalog and browse the files on that tape.

More elaborate backup software programs take a different approach by maintaining a database of the catalogs for all of your backup media on the computer where the backup software is installed. This database enables you to browse through the catalogs for all of your tapes and select any version of any file or folder for restoration. In some cases, you can view the contents of the database in several different ways, such as by the computer, volume, and folder where the files were originally located; by the backup job; or by the tape or other media name. After you make your selection, the program specifies which tape contains the file or folder; insert it into the drive, and the restore job proceeds.

The database feature can use a lot of the computer's disk space and processor cycles, but it greatly enhances the usability of the software, particularly in a network environment.

TAKE NOTE*

Backup software products that rely on a database typically store a copy of the database on your tapes as well as on the computer's hard drive. This is done so that if the computer you use to run the backups should suffer a disk failure, you can restore the database later. Many products also enable you to rebuild the database on a computer by reading the contents of a tape and assimilating its index into a new database file.

ROTATING MEDIA

Some fastidious administrators use new tapes for every backup job and store them all permanently. However, this practice can be extremely expensive. It is more common for administrators to reuse backup tapes. To do this properly, however, you must have a carefully planned media rotation scheme so that you don't inadvertently overwrite a tape you might need later. You can always create such a scheme yourself, but some backup software products do it for you.

One of the most common media rotation schemes is called the ***Grandfather-Father-Son method***. In this method, the terms *grandfather*, *father*, and *son* refer to monthly, weekly, and daily tapes, respectively. For daily backups, you have one set of "son" tapes that you reuse every week. For the weekly full backup, you have "father" tapes that you reuse every month. Then, every month, you perform an additional full backup to tapes in your "grandfather" set, which you reuse every year. This method enables you to perform a complete restore at any time, and maintains a year's history of your files. There are also other schemes that vary in complexity and utility, depending on the software product.

When the software program implements the rotation scheme, it provides a basic schedule for the jobs (which you can modify to have the jobs execute at specific times of the day), tells you what name to write on each tape as you use it, and once you begin to reuse tapes, tells you which tape to put in the drive for each job. The end result is that you maintain a perpetual record of your data while using the minimum number of tapes without fear of overwriting a tape you need.

PERFORMING RESTORES

Restoring data from your backups is, of course, the sole reason for making them in the first place. The ease with which you can locate the files you need to restore is an important feature of any backup software product. It is absolutely essential that you perform periodic test restores from your backup tapes or other media to ensure that you can get back any data that is lost. Even if all your jobs seem to complete successfully and your log files show that all of your data has been backed up, there is no more reliable test of a backup system than performing an actual restore. There are plenty of horror stories about administrators who dutifully perform their backups every day, only to find out when disaster strikes that all their carefully labeled tapes are blank due to a malfunctioning drive.

Although performing regular backups is usually thought of as protection against a disaster that causes you to lose an entire hard disk, the majority of the restore jobs you will perform in an enterprise environment are of one or a few files that a user has inadvertently deleted. As mentioned earlier, your backup software's cataloging capability is a critical part of the

X REF

The shadow copies feature in Windows Server 2008 can prevent the need for some of these minor restores. For more information on shadow copies, see Lesson 7, "Planning for High Availability."

restoration process. If a user needs to have one particular file restored and you have to insert tape after tape into the drive to locate it, everyone's time is wasted. A backup program with a database that lets you search for that particular file makes your job much easier and enables you to restore any file in minutes.

Restore jobs are similar to backup jobs, in that you select the files or folders that you want to restore, using a tree-based interface. When creating a restore job, a good backup software product typically enables you to configure the following parameters:

- File selection—You should be able to select any combination of files, folders, or volumes on any tape. Some software products enable you to switch between a media view, which displays the contents of each tape in the library, and a disk view, which displays your backup targets and a list of the multiple versions of each file available on your various tapes.
- Restore location—You should be able to restore your selected files to their original locations automatically, or specify an alternative location; you should also be able to re-create the original directory tree or dump all the files into a single folder.
- Overwrite options—When restoring files to their original locations, you should be able to specify rules for overwriting existing files with the same names, based on their dates or using other criteria.

Using Windows Server Backup

 THE BOTTOM LINE

Windows Server 2008 includes a backup software program that you can use to back up your volumes to an internal or external hard drive, to a writable DVD drive, or to a shared folder on the network.

The Windows Server Backup program included in Windows Server 2008 is a completely different product from the backup software supplied with earlier Windows versions. The program has different capabilities, a different interface, and most important, it uses a different format for the backup files it creates. This means that you cannot use Windows Server Backup to restore data from backups you made with the Windows Server 2003 Backup Utility program, or any other Windows backup software.

⊕ MORE INFORMATION

To perform restores from backups made with the Windows Server 2003 or Windows XP backup utilities, you can download a version of the Ntbackup.exe program from the Microsoft Download Center Web site at www.microsoft.com/downloads. This version of Ntbackup.exe is read-only, meaning that you can use it to perform restores from existing backups, but you cannot use it to create new backups.

Windows Server Backup is designed primarily to create backups of entire server volumes on an external hard disk drive. As a result, many of the backup software features discussed in the previous sections are absent from Windows Server Backup. Some of the most important factors that administrators must understand about Windows Server Backup are as follows:

- Limited drive support—Windows Server Backup does not support tape drives, and cannot back up to optical drives or network shares during a scheduled backup. The program is designed primarily for use with external hard disk drives, using a USB or IEEE 1394 connection.
- Limited target selection—Windows Server Backup can back up only entire volumes. You cannot select individual files and folders for backup, nor can you exclude specific files and folders. The only filtering available is a global incremental option.

- Limited scheduling—Windows Server Backup can schedule only a single job, and is limited to running the job either daily or multiple times per day. You cannot schedule a job for a future date, or specify an interval of more than 24 hours between jobs.

- Limited job types—Windows Server Backup does not enable you to perform full, incremental, and differential backups on a per-job basis. You can configure all of your backups to be either full or incremental, or select full or incremental for each target volume. The program does not support differential jobs.

- Different backup format—Windows Server Backup writes its backup files in VHD (Virtual Hard Disk) format, which makes them accessible to Windows Server 2008's Hyper-V virtual machine software, as well as the Microsoft Virtual PC products and Windows Vista's Complete PC backup utility.

- Dedicated backup disks—When you select a hard disk volume as a backup drive for a scheduled job, Windows Server Backup takes control of the volume, reformats it (destroying any existing data), and dedicates it for backup use. The drive no longer appears in Windows Explorer, and you cannot use it for any other purpose.

TAKE NOTE*

Many of the limitations of Windows Server Backup are addressed by another product, Microsoft System Center Data Protection Manager, which supports magnetic tape drives and is specifically designed to provide comprehensive backup services for Windows operating systems and Microsoft applications, such as SQL Server, Exchange, and SharePoint Services.

Windows Server Backup takes the form of a feature that you must install using the Server Manager console. Adding the feature installs the Windows Server Backup console, shown in Figure 12-2. If you also select Command-Line Tools (and its dependent, the PowerShell feature), you can manage your backups from the command prompt.

Figure 12-2

The Windows Server Backup console

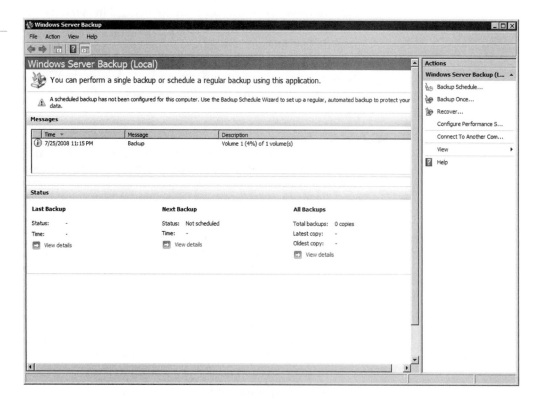

In addition to installing the Windows Server Backup feature, you must have a backup device accessible to the system, either a hard disk, an optical drive, or a network share. Once you have installed Windows Server Backup, you can begin creating your backup jobs.

Creating a Single Backup Job

Windows Server Backup can perform single, interactive backup jobs that begin immediately, or automated jobs that you schedule to commence at a later time.

In Windows Server Backup, single backup jobs provide more flexibility than scheduled ones, with the obvious disadvantage that someone must be there to create and start the job. You can use an optical disk drive or a network share for your backups, as well as a local hard disk. If the backup job requires more storage space than is available on a single optical disk, the program prompts you to insert another. However, if there is not enough space for the backup job on the selected hard disk, the job fails.

To create a single backup job using a local hard disk as the job destination, use the following procedure.

 CREATE A SINGLE BACKUP JOB

GET READY. Log on to Windows Server 2008. When the logon process is completed, close the Initial Configuration Tasks window and any other windows that appear.

1. Click **Start.** Then, click **Administrative Tools** > **Windows Server Backup.** The Windows Server Backup console appears.

2. In the actions pane, click **Backup Once.** The Backup Once Wizard appears, displaying the *Backup options* page, as shown in Figure 12-3.

Figure 12-3

The Backup options page of the Backup Once Wizard

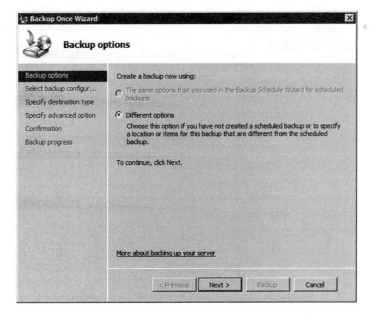

3. Click **Next** to accept the default Different Options option. The *Select backup configuration* page appears, as shown in Figure 12-4.

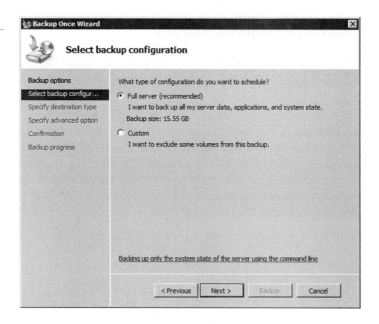

4. Select the **Custom** option and click **Next.** The *Select backup items* page appears, as shown in Figure 12-5.

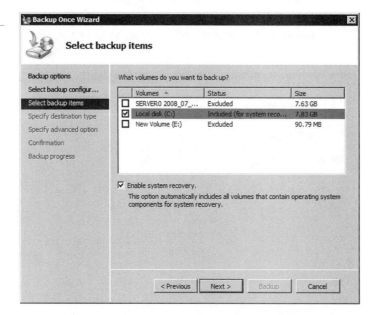

5. Select the volume(s) you want to back up. Leave the **Enable system recovery** checkbox selected and click **Next.** The *Specify destination type* page appears, as shown in Figure 12-6.

Figure 12-6

The Specify destination type
page of the Backup Once
Wizard

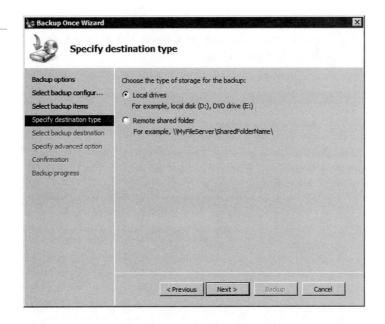

TAKE NOTE*

Selecting the Enable System Recovery checkbox causes Windows Server Backup to back up the system state, which consists of components that are unavailable to backup programs as normal files, because they are in use by the operating system. The system state includes the computer's boot files, the Windows registry, the COM+ class registration database, and any system files that are under Windows File Protection. The system state can also include certain role-specific files and databases, if those roles are installed on the computer, such as the Active Directory Domain Services and Active Directory Certificate Services databases, the SYSVOL directory, and the cluster service information. It is also possible to back up the computer's system state by itself, using the Wbadmin.exe program from the command prompt.

6. Leave the **Local drives** option selected and click **Next.** The *Select backup destination* page appears, as shown in Figure 12-7.

Figure 12-7

The Select backup destination
page of the Backup Once
Wizard

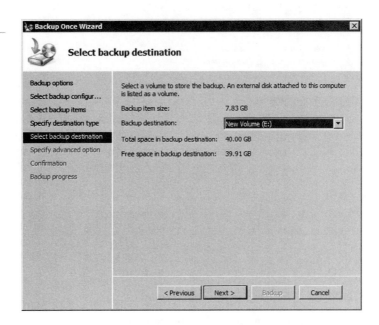

7. In the **Backup Destination** dropdown list, select the volume that you will use for your backup drive and click **Next.** The *Specify advanced option* page appears, as shown in Figure 12-8.

Figure 12-8

The Specify advanced option page of the Backup Once Wizard

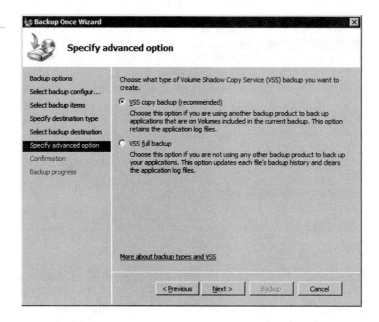

8. Leave the **VSS copy backup** option selected and click **Next.** The *Confirmation* page appears.

9. Click **Backup.** The *Backup progress* page appears, as shown in Figure 12-9, and the backup job begins.

Figure 12-9

The Backup progress page of the Backup Once Wizard

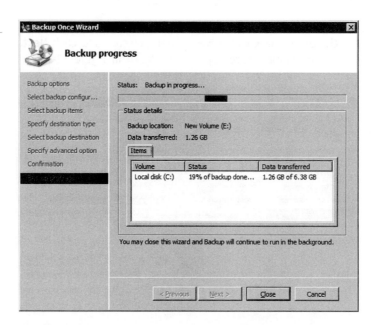

10. Click **Close.** The Backup Once Wizard closes.

CLOSE the Windows Server Backup console.

The backup job continues in the background, even after you close the wizard and the console.

Performing a Scheduled Backup

Windows Server backup makes it possible to schedule a backup job to execute at the same time(s) each day.

When you create a scheduled backup job, the options are somewhat different from a single, interactive job. First, you cannot use optical disks or network shares as backup drives; you must use a hard disk connected to the computer, either internal or external. Second, you cannot simply perform a backup to a file stored anywhere on the computer and manage it using Windows Explorer, as you would any other file. Windows Server Backup reformats the backup disk you select and uses it for backups exclusively.

To create a scheduled backup job, use the following procedure.

 CREATE A SCHEDULED BACKUP

GET READY. Log on to Windows Server 2008. When the logon process is completed, close the Initial Configuration Tasks window and any other windows that appear.

1. Click **Start**. Then, click **Administrative Tools** > **Windows Server Backup**. The Windows Server Backup console appears.
2. In the actions pane, click **Backup Schedule**. The Backup Schedule Wizard appears, displaying the *Getting started* page, as shown in Figure 12-10.

Figure 12-10

The Getting started page of the Backup Schedule Wizard

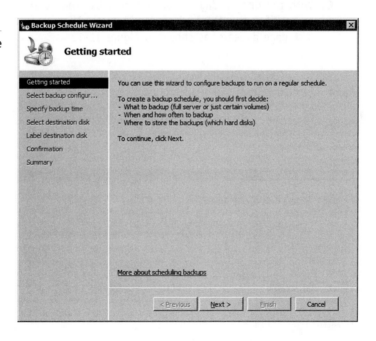

3. Click **Next**. The *Select backup configuration* page appears.
4. Select the **Custom** option and click **Next**. The *Select backup items* page appears.

TAKE NOTE*
Note that the Enable System Recovery checkbox does not appear on the Select backup items page, because scheduled jobs always back up the system state automatically.

5. Select the volume(s) you want to back up and click **Next.** The *Specify backup time* page appears, as shown in Figure 12-11.

Figure 12-11

The Specify backup time page of the Backup Schedule Wizard

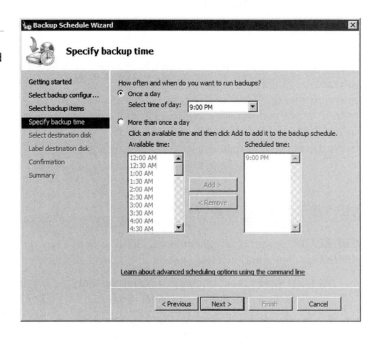

6. With the **Once a day** option selected, use the **Select time of day** dropdown list to specify when the backup should occur. Then, click **Next.** The *Select destination disk* page appears, as shown in Figure 12-12.

TAKE NOTE * For a computer running a volatile application, such as a Web server, you might want to select the More Than Once A Day option and select multiple times for the backup to occur each day.

Figure 12-12

The Select destination disk page of the Backup Schedule Wizard

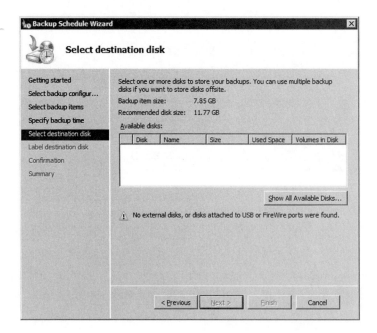

7. Select the disk you want to use for your backups. The Available Disks box lists only the external disks connected to the computer. To use an internal disk, you must click **Show All Available Disks** and select the disk(s) you want to add to the list from the Show All Available Disks dialog box.

TAKE NOTE*

If you select multiple disks on the Select destination disk page, Windows Server Backup will create identical copies of the backup files on each disk.

8. Click **Next.** A Windows Server Backup message box appears, informing you that the program will reformat the disk(s) you selected and dedicate them exclusively to backups. Click **Yes** to continue. The *Label destination disk* page appears, as shown in Figure 12-13.

Figure 12-13

The Label destination disk page of the Backup Schedule Wizard

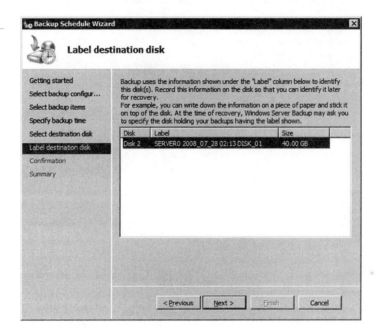

9. Use the name specified on this page to label the backup disk. Then, click **Next.** The *Confirmation* page appears.
10. Click **Finish.** The wizard formats the backup disk and schedules the backup job to begin at the time you specified.
11. Click **Close.** The wizard closes.

CLOSE the Windows Server Backup console.

Windows Server Backup allows you to schedule only one backup job, so the next time you start the Backup Schedule Wizard, your only options are to modify or stop the current backup job.

Configuring Incremental Backups

Windows Server Backup supports incremental jobs, but in a manner that is different from most other backup software products.

When Windows Server Backup takes control of a backup disk, it creates new, separate files for the backup job(s) it performs each day. The system retains the files for all of the old jobs until the disk is filled or 512 jobs are stored on the disk, whichever comes first. Then, the system begins deleting the oldest jobs as needed.

Unlike most backup software programs, Windows Server Backup does not enable you to specify a job type for each individual job you perform. You cannot choose to perform a full backup on Saturday, and an incremental or differential backup on each weekday, for example. As a result, the job strategies and tape rotation methods discussed earlier in this lesson do not apply here.

Windows Server Backup does support incremental backups, but only as a general setting that applies to all of your backup jobs. When you select Configure Performance Settings from the actions pane in the Windows Server Backup console, an Optimize Backup Performance dialog box appears, as shown in Figure 12-14.

Figure 12-14

The Optimize Backup Performance dialog box

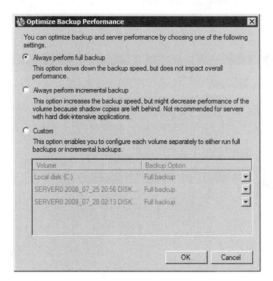

The Always Perform Full Backup option, which is the default setting, causes the program to copy every file on the selected volume(s) to the backup medium every time you perform a backup. This means that the program copies all of the operating system and application files on the volume(s), files which never change, to the backup disk over and over, possibly occupying a great deal of space to no useful end.

When you select the Always Perform Incremental Backup option, the program copies only the files that have changed since the previous backup. The first backup job is always a full backup, of course, but subsequent jobs use much less storage space, enabling the program to maintain a longer backup history. The Custom option enables you to specify whether to perform full or incremental backups for each of the volumes on the computer.

Performing a Restore

Windows Server Backup enables you to restore entire volumes or selected files, folders, and/or applications, using a wizard-based interface in the Windows Server Backup console.

Once you have completed at least one backup job, you can use the Windows Server Backup console to restore all or part of the data on your backup disk. Administrators should perform test restores at regular intervals, to ensure that the backups are completing correctly.

To perform a restore of selected files or folders, use the following procedure.

→ **PERFORM A RESTORE**

GET READY. Log on to Windows Server 2008. When the logon process is completed, close the Initial Configuration Tasks window and any other windows that appear.

1. Click **Start**. Then, click **Administrative Tools** > **Windows Server Backup.** The Windows Server Backup console appears.

2. In the actions pane, click **Recover.** The Recovery Wizard appears, displaying the *Getting started* page, as shown in Figure 12-15.

Figure 12-15

The Getting started page of the Recovery Wizard

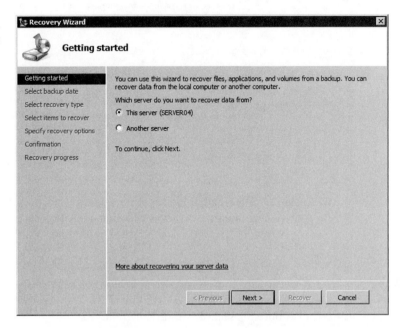

3. Leave the **This server** option selected and click **Next.** The *Select backup date* page appears, as shown in Figure 12-16.

Figure 12-16

The Select backup date page of the Recovery Wizard

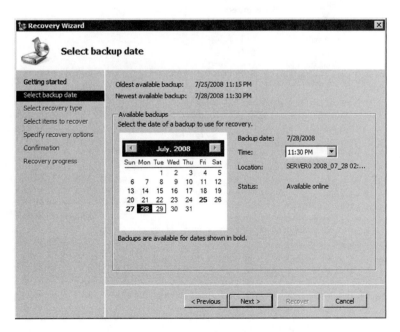

4. In the **Available backups** box, select the date of the backup you want to restore from, and if you performed more than one backup on that date, the time as well. Then, click **Next.** The *Select recovery type* page appears, as shown in Figure 12-17.

Figure 12-17

The Select recovery type page
of the Recovery Wizard

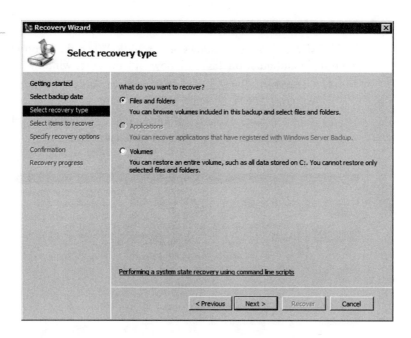

5. Leave the **Files and folders** option selected and click **Next.** The *Select items to recover* page appears, as shown in Figure 12-18.

TAKE NOTE The *Select items to recover* page enables you to restore entire volumes, as well as applications. When you back up a volume that contains applications that are Volume Shadow Copy Service (VSS) and Windows Server Backup–compliant, you can restore an entire application and its data, all at once, by selecting it in the wizard.

Figure 12-18

The Select items to recover
page of the Recovery Wizard

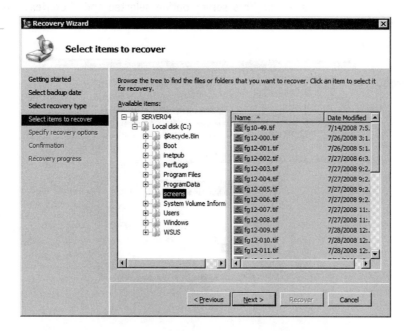

6. Expand the server folder and browse to the folder containing the files or subfolders you want to restore. Select the desired files and subfolders and click **Next.** The *Specify recovery options* page appears, as shown in Figure 12-19.

Figure 12-19

The Specify recovery options
page of the Recovery Wizard

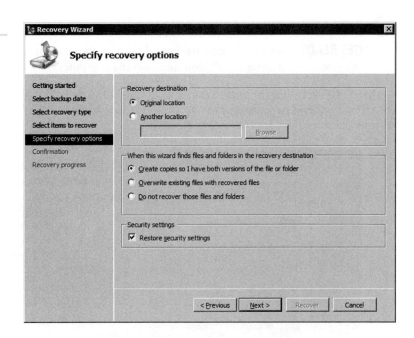

7. In the **Recovery destination** box, specify whether you want to restore the selections to their original location or to another location of your choice.

8. In the **When the wizard finds files and folders in the recovery destination** box, specify whether you want to copy, overwrite, or skip the existing files and folders.

9. In the **Security settings** box, specify whether you want to restore the access control lists of the selected files and folders. Then, click **Next.** The *Confirmation* page appears.

10. Click **Recover.** The wizard restores the selected files.

11. Click **Close.**

CLOSE the Windows Server Backup console.

Unlike most backup software products, the handling of incremental jobs in the restore process is completely invisible to the console operator. When you select a folder to restore, for example, the Recovery Wizard automatically accesses all of the previous jobs needed to locate the latest version of each file in the folder.

Restoring an Entire Server

If a disaster occurs in which all of a server's data is lost, or even just the volumes containing the boot and operating system files, obviously the server cannot start, Windows Server 2008 cannot load, and you cannot run the Windows Server Backup console to perform a restore. However, it is still possible to perform a full restoration of the server, as long as the backup drive is intact.

To perform a full server restore, you must boot the system using a Windows Server 2008 installation disk and access the backup disk using the Windows RE (Recovery Environment) interface. To perform a full server restore on a new computer from a backup on an external hard disk, use the following procedure.

⊕ **PERFORM A FULL SERVER RESTORE**

GET READY. Connect the external hard disk drive to the computer, if necessary. Then, insert a Windows Server 2008 installation disk into the computer's DVD drive and start the system.

1. Click **Next** to accept the default values in the language settings page. The *Install Windows* page appears, as shown in Figure 12-20.

Figure 12-20

The Install Windows page

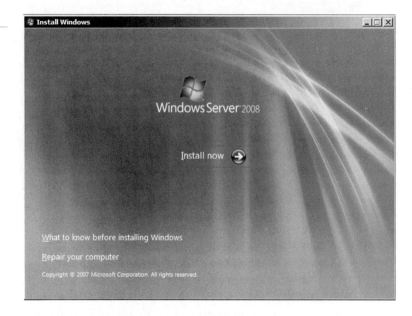

2. Click **Repair your computer.** The System Recovery Options dialog box appears, as shown in Figure 12-21.

Figure 12-21

The System Recovery Options dialog box

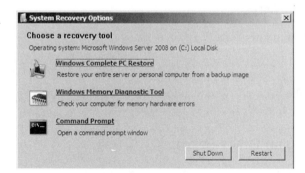

3. Click **Windows Complete PC Restore.** The Windows Complete PC Restore Wizard appears, as shown in Figure 12-22.

Figure 12-22

The Windows Complete PC
Restore Wizard

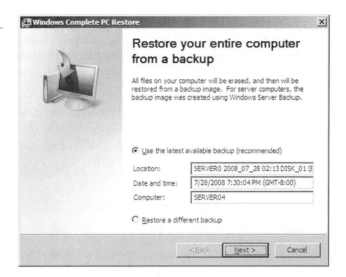

4. Click **Next** to restore from the latest available backup. The *Choose how to restore the backup* page appears, as shown in Figure 12-23.

Figure 12-23

The Choose how to restore the
backup page

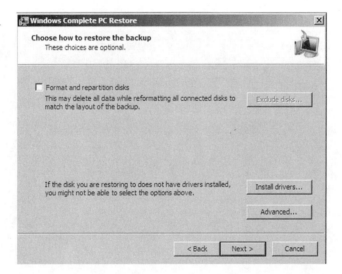

5. Select the **Format and repartition disks** checkbox and click **Next.** The final page of the wizard appears.

6. Click **Finish** to begin the restoration.

RESTART the computer after removing the disk from the DVD drive.

Once the process is completed, the system restarts using the files restored from the backup.

Backing Up and Recovering Active Directory

The Active Directory database is a crucial resource on most Windows networks, one that backup administrators must not ignore. However, backing up and restoring Active Directory is an exceptional process in nearly every way.

When you perform a scheduled backup of an Active Directory domain controller, or perform a single backup with the Enable system recovery checkbox selected, Windows Server Backup includes the system state as part of the job. The system state includes the Active Directory database, among other things.

Active Directory domains should have at least two domain controllers, and if that is the case and one of them fails or is lost, it should not be necessary to restore the Active Directory database from a backup. Instead, you can reinstall the Active Directory Domain Services role, make the computer a domain controller, and allow the replication process to rebuild the database on the new domain controller.

Performing a full server restoration includes the system state, and consequently the Active Directory database, but there might be occasions when you want to retrieve parts of Active Directory, such as objects you have inadvertently deleted.

It is possible to back up only the system state, but you must use the Wbadmin.exe command line tool with the following syntax:

```
wbadmin start SystemStateBackup -backuptarget:drive_letter
```

To restore just the system state from a backup, use the following command:

```
wbadmin Start SystemStateRecovery -versionMM/DD/YYYY-HH:MM
```

The MM/DD/YYYY-HH:MM variable specifies the version identifier for the backup from which you want to restore the system state. To list the version identifiers of the available backups, use the following command, as shown in Figure 12-24:

```
wbadmin get versions
```

Figure 12-24

Displaying backup version identifiers

UNDERSTANDING AUTHORITATIVE AND NON-AUTHORITATIVE RESTORES

It is important for the administrator to understand that there are two types of system state restores: authoritative and non-authoritative. When you open a Command Prompt window in a standard Windows session and restore the system state, you perform a ***non-authoritative restore.*** This means that the program will restore the Active Directory database to the exact state it was in at the time of the backup. However, the next time an Active Directory replication occurs, the other domain controllers will update the newly restored system with any changes that have occurred since the backup took place. This means that if you are trying to recover objects that you accidentally deleted, the replication process will cause the system to delete the newly restored objects.

To restore deleted objects, you must perform an ***authoritative restore,*** and to do this, you must restart the computer in ***Directory Services Restore Mode (DSRM)*** by pressing F8 during the boot process and selecting the appropriate entry from the Advanced Boot Options menu. After logging on using the Administrator account and the DSRM password specified during the operating system installation, you can perform the system state restore using Wbadmin.exe. Once the restoration of the system state is complete, you can use the Ntdsutil.exe tool to specify the objects that you want restored authoritatively.

BACKING UP AND RESTORING GROUP POLICY OBJECTS

Group policy objects (GPOs) are a special case. You cannot use the authoritative restore procedure to restore GPOs that you have deleted. To back up and restore GPOs, you must use the Group Policy Management console. When you right-click a GPO in the console and select Back Up from the context menu, a Back Up Group Policy Object dialog box appears, as shown in Figure 12-25, in which you can specify the location for the backup.

Figure 12-25

The Back Up Group Policy
Object dialog box

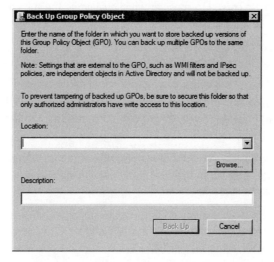

To restore a GPO, right-click the Group Policy Objects container and, from the context menu, select Manage Backups. The Manage Backups dialog box appears, as shown in Figure 12-26, in which you can select the GPO you want to recover and click the Restore button.

Figure 12-26

The Manage Backups
dialog box

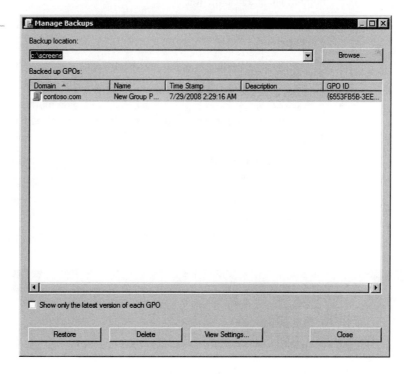

SUMMARY SKILL MATRIX

IN THIS LESSON YOU LEARNED:

- A backup is a copy of the data on a computer's hard disks, stored on another medium in case a hard drive fails. If a drive failure occurs, an administrator can repair or replace the drive, and then restore the data from the backup.

- The three main criteria to consider when evaluating the suitability of a storage device for backups are capacity, speed, and cost.

- It is possible to use a CD-ROM or DVD-ROM drive for backups. Most servers come equipped with a writable DVD-ROM drive, or can easily be retrofitted with one. The drives and media are both relatively inexpensive, and write speeds are reasonably fast.

- Magnetic tape is the traditional choice for server and network backups. Tape drives are well suited for backups; they are fast, they can hold a lot of data, they can archive that data indefinitely, and their media cost per gigabyte is low.

- The ever-increasing capacities of hard disk drives, along with their ever-decreasing prices per gigabyte, have led to their use as the primary backup medium for home users and small networks in recent years.

- Backup devices can use any of the standard computer interfaces, such as Parallel Advanced Technology Attachment (PATA), Serial ATA (SATA), USB, IEEE 1394, and Small Computer System Interface (SCSI).

- Depending on the type of backup device you select for your servers, a backup software product can be a convenience or an absolute necessity.

- Most backup software products include a collection of standard backup job types that are actually preset filter combinations. The most common of these job types are full, differential, and incremental.

- To reuse backup tapes, you must have a carefully planned media rotation scheme so that you don't inadvertently overwrite a tape you might need later.

- It is absolutely essential that you perform periodic test restores from your backup tapes or other media to ensure that you can get back any data that is lost.

- In Windows Server Backup, single backup jobs provide more flexibility than scheduled ones, with the obvious disadvantage that someone must be there to create and start the job.

- When you create a scheduled backup job, the options are somewhat different from a single, interactive job.

- When you perform a scheduled backup of an Active Directory domain controller, or perform a single backup with the Enable system recovery checkbox selected, Windows Server Backup includes the system state as part of the job.

Knowledge Assessment

Fill in the Blank

Complete the following exercise by filling in the blanks with the appropriate terms from this lesson.

1. When a magnetic tape drive receives data from the computer at too slow a speed, it must continually stop and start the tape, a condition known as _____.

2. By default, a recovery of the system state performed in a standard Windows session is a _____ restore.

3. In a business open during regular daytime hours, the time between 5:00 P.M. and 9:00 A.M. is known to backup administrators as the _____.

4. Magnetic tape drives that use _____ record data in diagonal stripes across the tape.

5. When you use a combination of _____ and _____ jobs, you will never need more than two tapes to perform a restore.

6. Incremental and differential jobs use _____ filtering to select files for backup.

7. One of the most common media rotation methods used by backup software products is the _____ method.

8. A device that automatically inserts tapes into a tape drive is called a _____ or a _____.

9. To perform an authoritative restore, you must restart the computer in _____.

10. The first backup job for any particular set of targets is always a _____ job.

Multiple Choice

Select one or more correct answers for each of the following questions.

1. To recover group policy objects that you have accidentally deleted, you must use which of the following tools?
   a. Server Manager
   b. Group Policy Management console
   c. Windows Server Backup console
   d. Wbadmin.exe

2. Which of the following backup job types does not reset the archive bits on the files that it copies to the backup medium?
   a. full
   b. incremental
   c. differential
   d. all of the above

3. Which of the following is the criterion most commonly used to filter files for backup jobs?
   a. file name
   b. file extension
   c. file size
   d. file attributes

4. What are the three elements in the Grandfather-Father-Son media rotation system?
   a. hard disk drives, DVD-ROM drives, and magnetic tape drives
   b. full, incremental, and differential backup jobs
   c. monthly, weekly, and daily backup jobs
   d. DAT, DLT, and LTO tape drives

5. Magnetic tape drives most commonly use which of the following drive interfaces?
   a. SCSI
   b. USB
   c. SATA
   d. IEEE 1394

6. Which of the following backup job types is not supported by the Windows Server Backup feature in Windows Server 2008?
   a. full
   b. incremental
   c. differential
   d. none of the above

7. Which of the following is the average data compression ratio typically used by backup drive manufacturers?
   a. 1:1
   b. 2:1
   c. 7:1
   d. 10:1

8. The best magnetic tape drives on the market can hold approximately how much data on a single tape?
   a. 10–20 GB
   b. 60–80 GB
   c. 200–400 GB
   d. 800–1000 GB

9. Optical disks are not a suitable backup medium for large capacity servers for which of the following reasons?
   a. insufficient disk capacity
   b. insufficient speed
   c. lack of backup software support
   d. all of the above

10. Which of the following devices can Windows Server Backup use for a backup drive?

    a. magnetic tape drives   **b.** optical disk drives

    c. external hard disk drives   **d.** remote network shares

Review Questions

1. How does a magnetic tape autoloader increase the overall storage capacity of a backup solution?

2. Give two reasons why is it best to perform backups when the organization is closed.

■ Case Scenarios

Scenario 12-1: Designing a Network Backup Solution

Alice is a consultant for a client who wants to install a new network backup system. The client's network has five servers containing company data, with a total capacity of 2000 GB. Roughly a third of the data consists of databases that are updated continually during business hours. The rest is archival data that seldom changes. The company works three shifts during the week, so there is a relatively small backup window of two hours, from 2:00 A.M. to 4:00 A.M. However, the IT department only works from 9:00 A.M. to 5:00 P.M. The company is closed on weekends. The client wants all new data to be protected every night. Alice is planning to purchase a magnetic tape drive for the client, as well as a comprehensive network backup software package. The tape drives Alice has been evaluating are as follows:

- A DDS 160 drive with a maximum capacity of 160 GB and a transfer speed of 6.9 MB/sec

- An SDLT 320 drive with a maximum capacity of 320 GB and a maximum transfer speed of 16 GB/sec

- An LTO Ultrium drive with a maximum capacity of 800 GB and a transfer speed of 120 MB/sec

Specify what types of backup jobs Alice should perform each night and which of the tape drives would enable the company to back up its servers with the greatest convenience.

Scenario 12-2: Recovering from a Disaster

Ralph is a server administrator for a company that uses the Grandfather-Father-Son media rotation method to back up its network. On arriving at the office on Friday morning, Ralph discovers that the hard disk on one of his servers has failed, causing all of its data to be lost. The first thing he does is to install a new hard disk drive into the server and install the operating system. Then, checking the backup logs, he sees that the last "grandfather" job was a full backup performed three weeks ago, on the first day of the month. The most recent "father" job was a full backup performed the previous Sunday. The "son" jobs are incremental backups that are performed every weeknight. All of the incrementals for that week completed successfully, except for Tuesday night's job, because Ralph failed to insert the appropriate tape into the backup drive. Describe the procedure Ralph must perform to restore all of the lost data on the failed disk, by specifying the tapes he must use and the order in which he must restore them.

MATRIX SKILL	SKILL NUMBER	LESSON NUMBER
Planning for Server Deployment		
Plan server installations and upgrades	1.1	1, 8
Plan for automated server deployment	1.2	1
Plan infrastructure services server roles	1.3	2, 3, 9
Plan application servers and services	1.4	4, 7
Plan file and print server roles	1.5	5
Planning for Server Management		
Plan server management strategies	2.1	10
Plan for delegated administration	2.2	10
Plan and implement group policy strategy	2.3	3, 12
Monitoring and Maintaining Servers		
Implement patch management strategy	3.1	10
Monitor servers for performance evaluation and optimization	3.2	11
Monitor and maintain security and policies	3.3	8, 9, 11
Planning Application and Data Provisioning		
Provision applications	4.1	4
Provision data	4.2	7
Planning for Business Continuity and High Availability		
Plan storage	5.1	6
Plan high availability	5.2	7
Plan for backup and recovery	5.3	12

The *Windows Server 2008 Administrator* title of the Microsoft Official Academic Course (MOAC) series includes two books: a textbook and a lab manual. The exercises in the lab manual are designed for classroom use under the supervision of an instructor or a lab aide.

■ Setting Up the Classroom

This course should be taught in a classroom containing networked computers where students can develop their skills through hands-on experience with Microsoft Windows Server 2008. The exercises in the lab manual require the computers to be installed and configured in a specific manner. Failure to adhere to the setup instructions in this document can produce unanticipated results when the students perform the exercises.

Classroom Configuration

The following configurations and naming conventions are used throughout the course and are required for completing the labs as outlined in the lab manual.

The classroom network consists entirely of computers running Windows Server 2008, including a single classroom server and a number of student servers. The classroom server performs several roles for the student servers, including the following:

- Active Directory Domain Services domain controller
- Domain Name System (DNS) server
- Dynamic Host Configuration Protocol (DHCP) server

Use the following information when setting up the classroom server:

- Active Directory domain name: contoso.com
- Computer name: ServerDC
- Fully qualified domain name (FQDN): ServerDC.contoso.com
- Administrator password: P@ssw0rd

The student computers are also servers running Windows Server 2008, which the students will join to the contoso.com domain. Each student computer in the domain is to be named Server##, where ## is a unique number assigned to each computer by the instructor. Each student server will also have a corresponding domain user account called Student##, where ## is the same number assigned to the computer.

As they work through the lab manual, the students will install and remove several different roles and features. In some of the exercises, students will initiate communication with another server on the network. To make this possible, the lab manual is designed to support the following three classroom configurations.

TAKE NOTE*

If you are using Web-hosted virtual machines in your classroom, you might not have to perform any of the setup procedures described in this document because the students will be able to access preconfigured virtual machines over the Web.

- Dedicated computers—Each student computer has a single instance of Windows Server 2008 installed. To complete the lab exercises that require interaction between two servers, you can provide each student with two computers or assign a lab partner to each student. In the latter case, each student will complete the exercise and provide the services required by his or her partner.

- Local virtual machines—Each student computer has a virtualization product—such as Microsoft Virtual PC—installed, enabling you to create two virtual machines, each running an instance of Windows Server 2008. With this configuration, each student can perform all of the exercises on one computer, using the two virtual machines to perform the required roles.

- Web-hosted virtual machines—Each student computer uses a Web browser to access two Windows Server 2008 virtual machines hosted by a commercial service on the Internet. With this configuration, each student can perform all of the exercises on one computer, using the two virtual machines to perform the required roles.

To support these classroom configurations, students must begin each lab in the manual with the same baseline operating system configuration on the student computers. Therefore, each lab begins with an exercise that sets up the server for that lab and, when necessary, concludes with an exercise that returns the server to the baseline configuration. Depending on your classroom configuration, the students might be able to skip the first and last exercises in each lab.

Classroom Server Requirements

The computer running Windows Server 2008 in the classroom requires the following hardware and software:

Hardware Requirements

- Processor: 1 GHz (minimum); 2 GHz or faster (recommended)
- RAM: 512 MB (minimum); 2 GB or more (recommended)
- Disk space requirements: 10 GB (minimum); 40 GB or more (recommended)
- DVD-ROM drive
- Super VGA (800 × 600) or higher-resolution monitor
- Keyboard and mouse (or other pointing device)
- One network interface adapter

Software Requirements

- Microsoft Windows Server 2008, Standard or Enterprise

Student Computer Requirements

Each student computer requires the following hardware and software:

Hardware Requirements

- Processor: 1 GHz (minimum); 2 GHz or faster (recommended)
- RAM: 512 MB (minimum); 2 GB or more (recommended)
- First hard drive: 50+ GB, sufficient disk space for one 40 GB system partition and at least 10 GB of unpartitioned space
- Second hard drive: 10+ GB with no partitions
- DVD-ROM drive
- Super VGA (800 × 600) or higher-resolution monitor
- Keyboard and mouse (or other pointing device)
- One network interface adapter

TAKE NOTE*

If you plan to create virtual machines on your student computers, each virtual machine must meet these hardware requirements.

Software Requirements

- Windows Server 2008, Standard or Enterprise

■ Classroom Server Setup Instructions

Before you begin, do the following:

- Read this entire document.
- Verify that you have the course materials provided on the instructor companion site and the installation disk for Microsoft Windows Server 2008.

WARNING By performing the following setup instructions, your computer's hard disks will be repartitioned and reformatted. You will lose all existing data on the system.

Installing Windows Server 2008

Using the following setup procedure, install Windows Server 2008 on ServerDC.

⊙ INSTALL WINDOWS SERVER 2008

1. Boot the computer from the Windows Server 2008 Installation disk. When you boot from the disk, the Windows Server 2008 Setup program starts automatically and the *Install Windows* page appears.
2. Modify the Language to install, Time and currency format, and Keyboard or input method settings, if necessary. Click **Next**.
3. Click **Install now**. The *Type your product key for activation* page appears.
4. Enter your product key in the Product key text box and click **Next**. The *Please read the license terms* page appears.

TAKE NOTE*

If you plan to use evaluation versions of Windows Server 2008 in the classroom, you can leave the Product key field blank and, in the Select the edition of Windows that you purchased window that subsequently appears, select Windows Server 2008 Enterprise (Full Installation) for the version you want to install.

5. Select the **I accept the license terms** checkbox and click **Next**. The *Which type of installation do you want?* page appears.
6. Click **Custom**. The *Where do you want to install Windows?* page appears.
7. Select the disk where you want to install Windows Server 2008 and click **Next**. The *Installing Windows* page appears.
8. When the installation process is complete, the computer restarts and prompts you to change the Administrator password. Click **OK**.
9. Key **P@sswOrd** in the New Password and Confirm Password text boxes and click the right arrow button. Then click **OK**. Windows Server 2008 starts and the Initial Configuration Tasks window appears.
10. Install any updates needed to keep the operating system current.

TAKE NOTE*

If your computer supports booting from CD/DVD, the computer might try to boot from the Windows Server 2008 disk after Windows Server 2008 Setup restarts. If this happens, you should be prompted to press a key to boot from the disk. However, if Setup restarts automatically, simply remove the disk and restart the computer.

PROCEED to the following section to continue the server configuration process.

Before you proceed with the server configuration, install any required updates to keep the operating system current. Use Automatic Updates, the Windows Update Website, or any other mechanism to locate, download, and install the updates.

Completing Post-Installation Tasks on ServerDC

After the installation is complete and the Initial Configuration Tasks window has appeared, complete the following procedures to prepare the computer to function as the classroom server.

PERFORMING INITIAL CONFIGURATION TASKS

Use the following procedure to prepare the server for the course.

⟶ PERFORM INITIAL CONFIGURATION TASKS

1. In the Initial Configuration Tasks window, click **Set time zone**. The Date and Time dialog box appears.
2. Verify that the date, time, and time zone shown in the dialog box are correct. If they are not, click **Change date and time** or **Change time zone** and correct them. Then click **OK**.
3. Click **Configure Networking**. The Network Connections window appears.
4. Right-click the **Local Area Connection** icon and, from the context menu, select **Properties**. The Local Area Connection Properties sheet appears.
5. Clear the **Internet Protocol Version 6 (TCP/IPv6)** checkbox.
6. Select **Internet Protocol Version 4 (TCP/IPv4)** and click **Properties**. The Internet Protocol Version 4 (TCP/IPv4) Properties sheet appears.
7. Configure the TCP/IP parameters using the following values:

   - IP Address: 10.1.1.100
   - Subnet Mask: 255.255.255.0
   - Preferred DNS Server: 127.0.0.1

> **TAKE NOTE** *
>
> The IP addresses supplied in this setup document and in the lab manual are suggestions. You can use any IP addresses for the computers in your classroom, as long as all of the systems are located on the same subnet.
>
> If the classroom network is connected to a school network or the Internet, you can specify the address of the router providing the network connection in the Default Gateway field. Otherwise, leave it blank.

8. Click **OK** twice to close the two Properties sheets. Close the Network Connections window.
9. In the Initial Configuration Tasks window, click **Provide computer name and domain**. The System Properties dialog box appears with the Computer Name tab selected.
10. Click **Change**. The Computer Name/Domain Changes dialog box appears.
11. In the Computer name text box, key **ServerDC** and click **OK**. A message box appears, prompting you to restart your computer.
12. Click **OK**, then click **Close** to close the System Properties dialog box. Another message box appears, informing you again that you must restart the computer.
13. Click **Restart Now**. The computer restarts.

The ServerDC computer must be an Active Directory domain controller. After the computer restarts, you can install the Active Directory Domain Services role and the Active Directory Domain Services Installation Wizard.

INSTALL ACTIVE DIRECTORY

To install Active Directory on ServerDC, use the following procedure.

INSTALL ACTIVE DIRECTORY

1. Log on with the local Administrator account, using the password **P@ssw0rd.**

2. When the Initial Configuration Tasks window appears, click **Add Roles.** The Add Roles Wizard appears.

3. Using the Add Roles Wizard, install the Active Directory Domain Services role.

4. When the role installation is complete, click the **Close this wizard and launch the Active Directory Domain Services Installation Wizard (dcpromo.exe)** link. The *Welcome To The Active Directory Installation Wizard* page appears.

5. Click **Next** to proceed with the Active Directory installation.

6. On the *Operating System Compatibility* page, click **Next.**

7. On the *Choose a Deployment Configuration* page, select **Create a new domain in a new forest** and click **Next.**

8. On the *Name the Forest Root Domain* page, key **contoso.com** and click **Next.**

9. On the *Set Forest Functional Level* page, select **Windows Server 2008** and click **Next.**

10. On the *Additional Domain Controller Options* page, verify that the **DNS server** checkbox is selected and click **Next.** A Static IP Assignment message box appears, warning you that the computer has a dynamically assigned IP address.

11. For the purposes of this manual, you can ignore the warning. Click **Yes, the computer will use a dynamically assigned IP address** to continue. A message box appears, warning you that the system cannot locate an existing DNS infrastructure.

12. Because you will be creating a new DNS infrastructure, you can ignore this warning and click **Yes.**

13. On the *Location for Database, Log Files, and SYSVOL* page, click **Next** to accept the default settings.

14. On the *Directory Services Restore Mode Administrator Password* page, key **P@ssw0rd** in the **Password** and **Confirm Password** text boxes and click **Next.**

15. On the *Summary* page, click **Next.**

16. When the installation process is complete, restart the server.

After the server restarts, it functions as the domain controller for the contoso.com domain. Students must log on to the domain in all of the lab exercises.

INSTALLING THE DHCP SERVER ROLE

To install the DHCP server on ServerDC, use the following procedure.

 INSTALL THE DHCP SERVER ROLE

1. Log on with the domain Administrator account using the password **P@ssw0rd.**

2. When the Initial Configuration Tasks window appears, click **Add Roles.** The Add Roles Wizard appears.

3. Using the Add Roles Wizard, install the DHCP Server role.

4. On the *Select Network Connection Bindings* page, click **Next** to accept the default settings.

5. On the *Specify IPv4 DNS Server Settings* page, click **Next** to accept the default settings.

6. On the *Specify IPv4 WINS Server Settings* page, click **Next** to accept the default settings.

7. On the *Add or Edit DHCP Scopes* page, click **Add.**

TAKE NOTE *

If the classroom network is connected to a school network or the Internet, you can specify the address of the router providing the network connection in the Default Gateway field. Otherwise, leave it blank.

8. In the Add Scope dialog box, create a scope using the following values:
   - Scope Name: Classroom
   - Starting IP Address: 10.1.1.101
   - Ending IP Address: 10.1.1.199
   - Subnet Mask: 255.255.255.0
   - Subnet Type: Wired
9. Select the **Activate this scope** checkbox and click **OK**. Then click **Next**.
10. On the *Configure DHCPv6 Stateless Mode* page, select the Disable DHCPv6 stateless mode for the server option and click **Next**.
11. On the *Authorize DHCP Server* page, click **Next** to accept the default settings.
12. On the *Confirm Installation Selections* page, click **Install**.

CLOSE the Initial Configuration Tasks window when the installation is complete.

After the DHCP role is installed, all student servers will obtain their IP addresses and other TCP/IP configuration settings via DHCP.

CREATING USER ACCOUNTS

Each student must have a domain user account called Student##, where ## is the same number as the computer the student is using. To create the student accounts, use the following procedure.

 CREATE USER ACCOUNTS

1. Click **Start**, and then select **Administrative Tools** > **Active Directory Users and Computers**. The Active Directory Users and Computers console appears.
2. Expand the contoso.com domain.
3. Right-click the **Users** container and select **New** > **User**. The New Object-User Wizard appears.
4. Key **Student##** in the **First Name** and **User Logon Name** text boxes, where ## is the number assigned to the first student computer in the classroom. Then click **Next**.
5. In the **Password** and **Confirm Password** text boxes, key **P@ssw0rd**.
6. Clear the **User Must Change Password At Next Logon** checkbox and select the **Password Never Expires** checkbox. Then click **Next**.
7. Click **Finish** to create the user account.
8. Repeat steps 3–7 to create a Student## user account for each computer in the classroom.
9. Right-click the **Users** container and select **New** > **Group**. The New Object-Group Wizard appears.
10. In the Group Name text box, key **Students**. Then click **Next**.
11. Click **Finish** to create the group.
12. In the Users container, double-click the Students group you just created. The Students Properties sheet appears.
13. Click the **Members** tab.
14. Click **Add**, key the name of the first Student## user you created, and click **OK**.
15. Repeat step 14 to add all the Student## accounts you created to the Students group.
16. Click **OK** to close the Students Properties sheet.

17. Using the same procedure, open the Properties sheet for the Domain Admins group and add the Students group to the Domain Admins group as a member.

CLOSE the Active Directory Users and Computers console.

The students will use these Student## accounts to log on to the domain as they complete the exercises in the lab manual. Their membership in the Students group provides domain administrator privileges, as well as local Administrator privileges on their individual servers.

PREPARING THE FILE SYSTEM

From the Microsoft Download Center Website at www.microsoft.com/downloads, download the following software packages:

- Windows Automated Installation Kit for Windows Server 2008
- Windows Server Update Services 3.0 SP1
- Microsoft Report Viewer Redistributable 2008

You will also need a Windows Server 2008 installation disk. Complete the following procedure to make these software resources modules available to the students and provide the students with storage on the classroom server.

 PREPARE THE FILE SYSTEM

1. On the server's C drive, create a new folder called \Install and three subfolders called \Install\WindowsAIK, \Install\WSUS3.0SP1, and \Install\WinSvr2008.

2. Burn the Windows Automated Installation Kit image file you downloaded to a DVD and copy the entire contents of the disk to the \Install\WindowsAIK folder.

3. Copy the entire contents of the Windows Server 2008 installation disk to the \Install\WinSvr2008 folder.

4. Copy the Windows Server Update Services 3.0 SP1 and Microsoft Report Viewer Redistributable 2008 packages you downloaded to the \Install\WSUS3.0SP1 folder.

5. Share the C:\Install folder using the share name Install, and then grant only the Allow Read share permission to the Everyone special identity.

6. Using Windows Explorer, grant the Students group the Allow Read, Allow Read & Execute, and Allow List Folder Contents NTFS permissions for the C:\Install folder.

7. Also on the server's C drive, create a new folder called \Students and copy the Lab Manual Worksheets from the book's instructor companion site to the C:\Students folder.

8. Grant the Students group the Allow Full Control NTFS permission for the C:\Students folder.

9. Share the C:\Students folder using the share name Students, and then grant the Everyone special identity and the Allow Full Control share permission.

CLOSE the Windows Explorer window.

These folders provide students with the additional software they need to complete the lab exercises and storage space to keep their lab worksheet files.

CONFIGURING FILE REDIRECTION

To complete the lab exercises, each student must be able to store files on the classroom server. Use Group Policy to redirect each user's Documents folder to the classroom server drive, using the following procedure.

 CONFIGURE FILE REDIRECTION

1. Click **Start**, and then select **Administrative Tools** > **Group Policy Management.** The Group Policy Management console appears.

2. In the scope (left) pane, expand the console tree to display and select the **Group Policy Objects** node under the contoso.com domain.

3. In the detail (right) pane, right-click the **Default Domain Policy** GPO and, from the context menu, select **Edit**. The Group Policy Management Editor window appears.

4. Navigate to the **User Configuration > Policies > Windows Settings > Folder Redirection** folder. Then, right-click the **Documents** subfolder and, from the context menu, select **Properties**. The Documents Properties sheet appears, displaying the Target tab.

5. From the **Setting** dropdown list, select **Basic – Redirect Everyone's folder to the same location.**

6. In the **Target Folder Location** box, verify that the default **Create a folder for each user under the root path** option is selected.

7. In the **Root Path** text box, key **\\ServerDC\Students.**

8. Click the **Settings** tab and clear the **Grant the user exclusive rights to Documents** checkbox.

9. Click **OK** to close the Documents Properties sheet.

CLOSE the Group Policy Management Editor and Group Policy Management consoles.

When students log on to their computers, their Documents folders will now be redirected.

INSTALLING AND CONFIGURING WSUS

To enable the students to install and use Windows Server Update Services, you will install WSUS on the classroom server. To install WSUS, you must have the Web Server (IIS) role installed, as shown in the following procedure.

 INSTALL THE WEB SERVER (IIS) ROLE

1. Click **Start**. Then click **Administrative Tools** > **Server Manager**. Click **Continue** in the User Account Control message box and the Server Manager console appears.

2. Select the **Roles** node and, in the detail pane, click **Add Roles**. The Add Roles Wizard appears.

3. Click **Next** to bypass the *Before You Begin page*. The *Select Server Roles page* appears.

4. Select the **Web Server (IIS)** check box and click **Next**. An Add Roles Wizard message box appears, listing the features that are required to add the Web Server (IIS) role.

5. Click **Add Required Features**, then click **Next**. The *Introduction to Web Server (IIS)* page appears.

6. Click **Next** to bypass the introductory page. The *Select Role Services* page appears.

7. Select the **ASP.NET** checkbox. An Add Roles Wizard message box appears, listing the role services and features that are required to add the ASP.NET role service.

8. Click **Add Required Role Services.**

9. Select the **Windows Authentication** and **IIS 6.0 Management Compatibility** checkboxes and click **Next**. The *Confirm Installation Selections* page appears.

10. Click **Install**. The wizard installs the role.

11. Click **Close.**

12. Close the Server Manager console.

Once you have installed the Web Server (IIS) role, you can proceed to install and configure WSUS, as shown in the following procedure.

 TAKE NOTE*

To complete this procedure, the computer must have access to the Internet. You can temporarily modify the TCP/IP configuration parameters, if necessary, to make this possible.

⊕ INSTALL AND CONFIGURE WSUS

1. Click **Start**. Then click **Run**. The Run dialog box appears.

2. In the Open text box, key **c:\install\wsus3.0sp1** and click **OK**. A Windows Explorer window appears, displaying the contents of the \wsus3.0sp1 folder.

3. Double-click the **ReportViewer** file. Click **Continue** in the User Account Control message box and the Microsoft Report Viewer Redistributable 2008 Setup wizard appears.

4. Click **Next** to bypass the Welcome page. The *End-User License Agreement* page appears.

5. Select the **I accept the terms of the License Agreement** checkbox and click **Install**. The wizard installs the software and the *Setup Complete* page appears.

6. Click **Finish**. The wizard closes.

7. In the Windows Explorer window, double-click the **WSUSSetup_30SP1_x86** file (or WSUSSetup_30SP1_x64, depending on which processor platform your computer is using). Click **Continue** in the User Account Control message box and the Windows Server Update Services 3.0 SP1 Setup Wizard appears.

8. Click **Next** to bypass the Welcome page. The *Installation Mode Selection* page appears.

9. Leave the **Full server installation including Administration Console** option selected and click **Next**. The *License Agreement* page appears.

10. Select **I accept the terms of the License agreement** and click **Next**. The *Select Update Source* page appears.

11. Leave the **Store updates locally** checkbox selected and, in the text box, key **C:\Updates** and click **Next**. The *Database Options* page appears.

12. Click **Next** to accept the default settings. The *Web Site Selection* page appears.

13. Leave the **Use the existing IIS Default Web site** option selected and click **Next**. The *Ready to Install Windows Server Update Services 3.0 SP1* page appears.

14. Click **Next**. The *Installing* page appears.

15. The wizard installs WSUS and the *Completing the Windows Server Update Services 3.0 SP1 Setup Wizard* page appears.

16. Click **Finish**. The Windows Server Update Services 3.0 SP1 Setup Wizard closes and the Windows Server Update Services Configuration Wizard appears.

17. Click **Next** to bypass the *Before You Begin* page. The *Join the Microsoft Update Improvement Program* page appears.

18. Clear the **Yes, I would like to join the Microsoft Update Improvement Program** checkbox and click **Next**. The *Choose Upstream Server* page appears.

19. Leave the **Synchronize from Microsoft Update** option selected and click **Next**. The *Specify Proxy Server* page appears.

20. Click **Next** to accept the default settings. The *Connect To Upstream Server* page appears.

21. Click **Start Connecting**. The wizard connects to the Microsoft Update site and downloads a list of available updates.

22. Click **Next**. The *Choose Languages* page appears.

23. Click **Next** to accept the default settings. The *Choose Products* page appears.

24. Clear the **Office** checkbox and the **Windows** checkbox.

25. Select all of the **Windows Server 2008** and **Windows Vista** checkboxes and click **Next**. The *Choose Classifications* page appears.

26. Click **Next** to accept the default selections. The *Set Sync Schedule* page appears.

27. Leave the **Synchronize manually** option selected and click **Next**. The *Finished* page appears.

28. Clear the **Launch the Windows Server Update Services Administration Console** and **Begin initial synchronization** checkboxes and click **Next**. The *What's* Next page appears.

29. Click **Finish**. The wizard closes.

30. Click **Start**. Then click **Administrative Tools** > **Microsoft Windows Server Update Services 3.0 SP1**. Click **Continue** in the User Account Control message box and the Update Services console appears.

31. In the scope (left) pane, select the **SERVER##** node.

32. In the detail pane, click **Synchronize now**.

33. Wait for the synchronization process to finish. This could take several minutes, depending on the speed of your Internet connection.

The computer is now ready to function as the classroom server. You can install the student servers.

■ Student Server Setup

The setup for the student computers depends on your classroom configuration. The result is a bare Windows Server 2008 installation, which students can configure. However, the tasks you must complete before the students arrive vary, as follows:

- Dedicated computers—If each student computer in your classroom will have a single copy of Windows Server 2008 installed on it, proceed directly to the following Installing Windows Server 2008 procedure.

- Local virtual machines—If you plan to use a virtualization product on the student computers to enable each system to run multiple copies of Windows Server 2008, first you must install the virtualization software on each computer according the manufacturer's instructions and create a virtual machine for each copy of Windows Server 2008 you plan to install. Then, install the operating system on each virtual machine, using the following Installing Windows Server 2008 procedure.

> **TAKE NOTE***
>
> Depending on the capabilities of your virtualization software and the type of licensing your school provides, you can perform a Windows Server 2008 installation on a single virtual machine and then clone multiple instances of that virtual machine, rather than perform each OS installation individually.

WARNING By performing the following setup instructions, your computer's hard disks will be repartitioned and reformatted. You will lose all existing data on the system.

- Web-hosted virtual machines—If your students will access virtual machines provided by a commercial service over the Web, then your classroom computers can run any operating system that provides the appropriate Web browser application. All of the operating systems are preinstalled, so you can skip the following procedure.

Using the following setup procedure, install Windows Server 2008 on the student computers.

⮕ INSTALL WINDOWS SERVER 2008

1. Boot the computer from the Windows Server 2008 Installation disk. When you boot from the disk, the Windows Server 2008 Setup program starts automatically, and the *Install Windows* page appears.

2. Modify the Language to install, Time and currency format, and Keyboard or input method settings, if necessary, and click **Next.**

3. Click **Install now.** The *Type your product key for activation* page appears.

4. Enter your product key in the **Product key** text box and click **Next.** The *Please read the license terms* page that appears.

> **TAKE NOTE***
>
> If you plan to use unregistered evaluation versions of Windows Server 2008 in the classroom, you can leave the Product key field blank and, in the Select the edition of Windows that you purchased window that subsequently appears, select Windows Server 2008 Enterprise (Full Installation) for the version you want to install.

5. Select the **I accept the license terms** checkbox and click **Next.** The *Which type of installation do you want?* page appears.

6. Click **Custom.** The *Where do you want to install Windows?* page appears.

7. Select the disk where you want to install Windows Server 2008 and click **Drive Options.**

8. Click **New.** In the **Size** text box, key **40000.** Click **Apply.**

9. Select the partition you just created and click **Next.** The *Installing Windows* page appears.

10. When the installation process is complete, the computer restarts and prompts you to change the Administrator password. Click **OK.**

> **TAKE NOTE***
>
> If your computer supports booting from CD/DVD, the computer might try to boot from the Windows Server 2008 disk after Windows Server 2008 Setup restarts. If this happens, you should be prompted to press a key to boot from the disk. However, if Setup restarts automatically, simply remove the disk and restart the computer.

11. Key **P@ssw0rd** in the New **Password** and **Confirm Password** text boxes and click the right arrow button. Then click **OK.** Windows Server 2008 starts and the Initial Configuration Tasks window appears.

12. Install any updates needed to keep the operating system current.

CLOSE the Initial Configuration Tasks window.

The computer is ready for a student to begin working through the lab manual. The student will perform all of the initial configuration tasks that the computer requires.

■ Creating Windows PE Disks

To complete the challenge in Lab 1, the students will need a Windows PE boot disk with the ImageX.exe program from the Windows Automated Installation Kit. You can choose to create an individual disk for each student, or require students to share a smaller number of disks.

To install the Windows AIK and create the disk, use the following procedure.

CREATE A WINDOWS PE BOOT DISK

GET READY. Log on to a Windows Server 2008 computer using an account with Administrative privileges. When the logon process is completed, close the Initial Configuration Tasks window or any other windows that appear.

1. Insert the Windows AIK disk you created earlier into the computer's DVD drive. A Welcome to Windows Automated Installation Kit window appears.

2. Click **Windows AIK Setup**. The Windows Automated Installation Kit Setup Wizard appears.

3. Click **Next** to bypass the *Welcome to the Windows Automated Installation Kit Setup Wizard* page. The *License Terms* page appears.

4. Select the **I Agree** option and click **Next**. The *Select Installation Folder* page appears.

5. Click **Next** to accept the default settings. The *Confirm Installation* page appears.

6. Click **Next** to begin the installation. The wizard installs the Windows AIK, and then the *Installation Complete* page appears.

7. Open Windows Explorer and create a new folder called C:\Images.

8. Open a Command Prompt window and switch to your PETools folder by keying the following command and pressing **Enter**:

    ```
    cd\Program Files\Windows AIK\Tools\PETools
    ```

9. Run the Copype.cmd script by keying the following command and pressing **Enter**. This command creates a WinPE folder on your local drive containing the Windows PE boot files. If you are running a 64-bit version of Windows on your technician computer, use the parameter amd64 or ia64, instead of x86.

    ```
    copype.cmd x86 c:\WinPE
    ```

10. Copy the ImageX.exe program to the Windows PE boot files folder by keying the following command and pressing **Enter**.

    ```
    copy "c:\Program Files\Windows AIK\Tools\x86\imagex.exe"
    c:\WinPE\iso\
    ```

11. Using Notepad, create a new text file containing the following instructions and save it to the C:\WinPE\iso folder, using the file name Wimscript.ini. ImageX.exe automatically searches for a file with this name when creating an image, and omits the files and folders in the [Exclusion List] section from the image it creates. These files are not needed in the image because Windows Server 2008 creates them automatically when it starts. The filespecs in the [CompressionExclusionList] section represent files that are already compressed, so it is not necessary for ImageX.exe to try to compress them again.

    ```
    [ExclusionList]

    ntfs.log

    hiberfil.sys

    pagefile.sys

    "System Volume Information"

    RECYCLER

    Windows\CSC


    [CompressionExclusionList]

    *.mp3
    ```

```
*.zip

*.cab

\WINDOWS\inf\*.pnf
```

12. Switch to your PETools folder by keying the following command and pressing **Enter**.

```
cd\program files\Windows AIK\Tools\x86
```

13. Create a Windows PE boot disk image by keying the following command and pressing **Enter**.

```
oscdimg -n -bc:\winpe\etfsboot.com c:\winpe\ISO c:\winpe\
winpe.iso
```

14. Burn the Winpe.iso image file in the C:\WinPE folder to a CD-ROM. This creates a Windows PE boot disk that students can use to start their computers.

15. Copy the Windows PE boot disk to create as many as you need for your students.

CLOSE all open windows on the computer.

80/20 rule In Dynamic Host Configuration Protocol, a method for splitting scopes between two DHCP servers, to provide fault tolerance.

A

access control entry (ACE) An entry in an object's access control list (ACL) that grants permissions to a user or group. Each ACE consists of a security principal (the name of the user, group, or computer being granted the permissions) and the specific permissions assigned to that security principal. When you manage permissions in any of the Windows Server 2008 permission systems, you are creating and modifying the ACEs in an ACL.

access control list (ACL) A collection of access control entries that defines the access that all users and groups have to an object.

actions pane The rightmost pane found in most preconfigured Microsoft Management Console windows, which contains context sensitive controls for the object(s) selected in the other panes.

Active Directory Domain Services Microsoft's Windows Server 2008 directory service that automates network management, such as user data, resources, and security.

answer file A text or XML file containing responses to the user prompts that typically appear during a Windows operating system installation. See also *unattend file*.

application A computer program designed to aid users in the performance of specific tasks.

application resilience The ability of an application to maintain its own availability by detecting outdated, corrupted, or missing files and automatically correcting the problem.

application services Software components that provide communications services, operating environments, or programming interfaces for specific applications.

Arbitrated loop (FC-AL) A Fibre Channel topology that consists of up to 127 devices, connected in a loop, similar to that of a token ring network. The loop can be physical, with each device connected to the next device, or virtual, with each device connected to a hub that implements the loop.

archive bit A file system attribute that backup software programs use as a marker to determine whether to back up a file.

ATA (Advanced Technology Attachment) A disk interface that uses parallel communications to connect multiple hard disk drives and other devices to a computer.

attributes In Active Directory, the individual properties that combine to form an object.

auditing The process by which administrators can track specific security-related events on a Windows Server 2008 computer.

authentication The process by which Windows Server 2008 verifies that the user matches the user account employed to gain access.

authoritative restore A restoration of the Active Directory database that overwrites existing objects and modifications on all domain controllers.

authorization The process of determining whether an identified user or process is permitted access to a resource and the user's appropriate level of access.

autoenrollment A security procedure in which a client application automatically issues a certificate enrollment request and sends it to a certification authority (CA), after which the CA then evaluates the request and issues or denies a certificate. When everything works properly, the entire process is invisible to the end user.

autoloader A single hardware device that contains one or more magnetic tape drives, as well as a robotic mechanism that inserts tapes into and removes them from the drives. See also *tape library*.

automatic allocation In Dynamic Host Configuration Protocol, a method by which a DHCP server permanently assigns an IP address to a client computer from a scope.

B

Background Intelligent Transfer Service (BITS) peer-caching A Windows Server 2008 component that enables computers to share their updates with each other on a peer-to-peer basis, rather than download them all from a WSUS server.

backup A copy of the data on a computer's hard disks, stored on another medium in case a hard drive fails.

backup targets In a backup software program, the files, folders, volumes, or disks that a user selects for copying to the backup medium.

backup window The amount of time available to perform backups.

baseline In Performance Monitor, a set of readings, captured under normal operating conditions, which you can save and compare to readings taken at a later time.

basic disk The default disk type in Windows Server 2008. A basic disk supports up to four partitions, typically three primary and one extended, with logical drives to organize data.

biometrics A group of technologies that enable computers to identify individuals based on physiological characteristics, such as fingerprints.

BitLocker Drive Encryption A Windows Server 2008 feature that can encrypt entire volumes, to prevent intruders from accessing their data.

block I/O access In storage area networking, a type of storage in which a computer accesses the stored data one block at a time.

boot image A single file with a .wim extension that contains all of the files needed to boot the computer and initiate an operating system installation.

bottleneck Occurs when a component is not providing an acceptable level of performance compared with the other components in the system.

C

caching-only server A Domain Name System server that has the ability to process incoming queries from resolvers and send its own queries to other

DNS servers on the Internet, but which is not the authoritative source for any domain and hosts no resource records of its own.

centralized authentication A security model in which all of the servers on a network rely on a single authority to authenticate users.

centralized DHCP infrastructure In Dynamic Host Configuration Protocol, a deployment model in which all of the DHCP servers are all placed in a single location, such as a server closet or data center, and a *DHCP relay agent* is installed on each subnet, to enable the broadcast traffic on each subnet to reach the DHCP servers.

certificate revocation list (CRL) A document maintained and published by a certification authority that lists certificates that have been revoked.

certificate templates Sets of rules and settings that define the format and content of a certificate based on the certificate's intended use.

certification authority (CA) A software component or a commercial service that issues digital certificates. Windows Server 2008 includes a CA as part of the Active Directory Certificate Services role.

Challenge Handshake Authentication Protocol (CHAP) An authentication protocol that uses MD5 hashing to encrypt user passwords, but does not support the encryption of connection data. The passwords it uses must also be stored in a reversibly encrypted format. As a result, CHAP provides relatively weak protection when compared to MS-CHAPv2.

channel In Event Viewer, a separate log devoted to a particular Windows component.

client access license (CAL) A document that grants a single client access to a specific software program, such as a Terminal Services server.

client-side caching A Remote Desktop Connection feature that enables a client to store screen elements that remain unchanged from one refresh to the next in a cache on the computer.

console An instance of the Microsoft Management Console application with one or more snap-ins installed.

container object In Active Directory, an object, such as a domain or organizational unit, that has leaf objects or other container objects as its subordinates.

convergence In network load balancing, a process in which a server is excluded from the cluster after it fails to generate five consecutive heartbeat messages.

copy-on-write data sharing A Windows Server 2008 Terminal Services memory management technique used by the operating system that, when a client attempts to write to a shared application file, creates a copy of that file, allocates it for the exclusive use of that client, and writes the changes to the copy.

Cryptographic Service Provider (CSP) A Windows Server 2008 component that generates public and private encryption keys for certificate requests.

D

data collector set In the Reliability and Performance Monitor console, a method for capturing counter data over a period of time, for later evaluation.

decentralized authentication A security model in which each server maintains its own list of users and their credentials.

Delegation of Control Wizard A tool in the Active Directory Users and Computers console that assigns permissions based on common administrative tasks.

delta CRLs Shorter lists of certificates that have been revoked since the last full certificate revocation list was published.

detail pane The middle or right pane of the Microsoft Management Console interface that displays the contents of the item selected in the scope pane.

DHCP relay agent A software component that receives the DHCP broadcast traffic on a subnet and then sends it on to particular DHCP servers on one or more other subnets.

dictionary attacks A password penetration technique in which a list of common passwords is encrypted, and the results compared with captured ciphertext.

differential backup A type of backup that saves only the data in the selected components that has changed since the last full backup, without resetting the archive bits.

digital certificate An electronic credential, issued by a certification authority (CA), which confirms the identity of the party to which it is issued.

direct-attached storage Hard disk drives and other storage media connected to a computer using one of the standard disk interfaces, as opposed to network-connected storage.

Directory Access Protocol (DAP) A communications protocol specified in the X.500 standard. Also progenitor of the *Lightweight Directory Access Protocol (LDAP)*.

directory schema An Active Directory component that specifies the attributes each type of object can possess, the type of data that can be stored in each attribute, and the object's place in the directory tree.

directory services Software components that store, organize, and supply information about a network and its resources.

Directory Services Restore Mode (DSRM) A Windows Server 2008 boot option that enables backup software products to perform authoritative restores.

disk duplexing A fault tolerance mechanism in which the computer stores duplicate data on two separate disks, each on a separate host adapter, so that the data remains available if one disk fails.

disk mirroring A fault tolerance mechanism in which the computer stores duplicate data on two separate disks so that the data remains available if a disk fails.

DiskPart.exe A Windows Server 2008 command line program that you can use to perform disk management tasks.

distributed DHCP infrastructure In Dynamic Host Configuration Protocol, a deployment model in which at least one DHCP server is installed on each of the network's subnets.

Distributed File System (DFS) A Windows Server 2008 File Services role service that includes two technologies: DFS Namespaces and DFS Replication. These technologies enable administrators to create virtual directories for shared network files and automatically copy files and folders between duplicate virtual directories.

DNS round robin A load-balancing technique in which you create an individual resource record for each terminal server in the server farm using the server's IP address and the name of the farm (instead of the server name). When clients attempt to establish a Terminal Services connection to the farm, DNS distributes the incoming name resolution requests among the IP addresses.

domain A set of network resources available for a group of users who can authenticate to the network to gain access to those resources.

domain controller A Windows server with Active Directory directory service installed. Each workstation computer joins the domain and is represented by a computer object. Administrators create user objects that represent human users. A domain differs from a workgroup because users log on to the domain once, rather than to each individual computer.

domain tree In Active Directory, an architectural element that consists of one or more domains that are part of the same contiguous namespace.

dynamic allocation In Dynamic Host Configuration Protocol, a method by which a DHCP server assigns an IP address to a client computer from a scope, or range of IP addresses, for a specified length of time.

dynamic disk The alternative to the basic disk type in Windows Server 2008. Dynamic disks can have an unlimited number of volumes using various configurations. The process of converting a basic disk to a dynamic disk creates a single partition that occupies the entire disk. You can create an unlimited number of volumes out of the space in that partition.

Dynamic Host Configuration Protocol (DHCP) A service that automatically configures the Internet Protocol (IP) address and other TCP/IP settings on network computers by assigning addresses from a pool (called a scope) and reclaiming them when they are no longer in use.

E

effective permissions A combination of allowed, denied, inherited, and explicitly assigned permissions that provides a composite view of a security principal's functional access to a resource.

enrollment The process by which a client requests a certificate and a certification authority generates one.

enterprise CA A certification authority that is integrated into the Windows Server 2008 Active Directory environment.

Event Viewer A Microsoft Management Console snap-in that provides access to the logs maintained by the Windows Server 2008 operating system.

events The fundamental unit of information that Windows uses to package information about system activities as they occur.

exit module A component used by a certification authority to determine how it should make new certificates available to their applicants.

Extensible Authentication Protocol (EAP) A shell protocol that provides a framework for the use of various types of authentication mechanisms.

Extensible Authentication Protocol—Transport Level Security (EAP-TLS) An authentication method that enables a server to support authentication with smart cards or other types of digital certificates.

extension snap-ins Microsoft Management Console modules that provide additional functionality to specific standalone snap-ins.

external drive array Hard disk drives and other storage media connected to a computer using a network medium, such as Ethernet or Fibre Channel.

F

failover cluster A collection of redundant servers configured to perform the same tasks so that if one server fails, another server can take its place almost immediately.

feature An individual Windows Server 2008 component designed to perform a specific administrative function.

Fibre Channel A high-speed serial networking technology that was originally designed for use with supercomputers, but is now associated primarily with storage area networking.

Fibre Channel Protocol (FCP) The protocol that Fibre Channel storage area networks use to transmit SCSI traffic between devices.

File Server Resource Manager (FSRM) A Microsoft Management Console snap-in containing tools that enable file server administrators to monitor and regulate their server storage.

file system An operating system component that provides a means for storing and organizing files so that users can easily locate them.

file-based I/O In storage area networking, a type of storage in which a computer accesses the stored data one file at a time.

firewall A software routine that acts as a virtual barrier between a computer and the attached network. A firewall is essentially a filter that enables certain types of incoming and outgoing traffic to pass through the barrier, while blocking other types.

forest In Active Directory, an architectural element that consists of one or more domain trees.

forest root domain In Active Directory, the first domain created in a forest.

forwarder A Domain Name System server that is configured to send the name resolution requests it receives from clients to another DNS server specified by an administrator using recursive, not iterative, queries.

full backup A backup job that copies all files to the storage medium and resets their archive bits.

full mesh topology In the Distributed File System, a replication scheme in which every member in a group replicates with every other member.

full zone transfer (AXFR) In Domain Name System, a type of zone transfer in which the server hosting the primary zone copies the entirety of the primary master zone database file to the secondary zone so that their resource records are identical. Compare with *incremental zone transfer (IXFR)*.

fully qualified domain name (FQDN) In Domain Name System, the complete DNS name for a particular computer, consisting at minimum of a host name, a second-level domain name, and a top-level domain name, written in that order and separated by periods.

G

global catalog A list of all the objects in an Active Directory forest and a subset of each object's attributes, used by domain controllers to locate and access the resources of other domains in the same forest.

globally unique identifier (GUID) partition table (GPT) You can use GPT as a boot disk if the computer's architecture provides support for an Extensible Firmware Interface (EFI)–based boot partition. Otherwise, you can use it as a non-bootable disk for data storage only. When used as a boot disk, it differs from the master boot record because platform operation critical data is located in partitions rather than unpartitioned or hidden sectors.

Grandfather-Father-Son method In backups, a media rotation method in which the terms *grandfather*, *father*, and *son* refer to monthly, weekly, and daily tapes, respectively.

H

hard quota In File Server Resource Manager, a limitation on user storage space that prohibits users from consuming any disk space beyond the allotted amount.

heartbeats In network load balancing, messages exchanged by cluster nodes to indicate their continued operation.

helical scanning In magnetic tape drives, a method of operation in which the heads are mounted on a rotating drum that records data in diagonal stripes across the tape.

host In TCP/IP, the network interface inside a computer or other device on a network.

host table In TCP/IP, a list of host names and their equivalent IP addresses, used for name resolution in the early days of the Internet.

hub/spoke topology In the Distributed File System, a replication scheme in which replication traffic is limited to specific pairs of members.

hybrid virtualization A type of virtualization in which a host OS shares access to the computer's processor with the virtual machine manager, with each taking the clock cycles it needs and passing control of the processor back to the other.

Hyper-V A Windows Server 2008 role that implements hypervisor virtualization on the computer.

hypervisor In virtualization, an abstraction layer that interacts directly with the computer's physical hardware.

I

image group In Windows Deployment Services, a collection of images that use a single set of files and the same security settings. Using an image group, you can apply updates and service packs to all of the files in the group in one process.

ImageX.exe A command line program, included in the Windows Automated Installation Kit, which can capture, transfer, modify, and deploy file-based images from the Windows PE environment.

incremental backup A type of backup that saves only the data in the selected components that has changed since the last full backup, while resetting the archive bits.

incremental zone transfer (IXFR) In Domain Name System, a type of zone transfer in which the server hosting the primary zone copies only records needed to synchronize the primary master zone database file with the secondary zone. Compare with *full zone transfer (AXFR)*.

infrastructure services Software components that provide support functions for network clients.

Initial Configuration Tasks The window that appears when you start a Windows Server 2008 computer for the first time after installing the operating system. This window presents a consolidated view of the post-installation tasks that, in previous Windows Server versions, you had to perform using various interfaces presented during and after the OS setup process.

install image A single file with a .wim extension that contains all of the files needed to install an operating system on a computer.

intermediate CAs Certification authorities that do not issue certificates to end users or computers; they issue certificates only to other subordinate CAs below them in the certification hierarchy.

Internet Storage Name Service (iSNS) In storage area networking, a software component that registers the presence of iSCSI initiators and targets on a SAN and responds to queries from iSNS clients.

IP (Internet Protocol) address A unique 32-bit numeric address used as an identifier for a device, such as a computer, on a TCP/IP network.

iSCSI initiator In storage area networking, a hardware or software device running on a computer that accesses the storage devices on the SAN.

iSCSI target In storage area networking, a component integrated into a drive array or computer that receives SCSI commands from the initiator and passes them to a storage device.

issuing CAs Certification authorities that provide certificates to end users and computers.

iterative query In Domain Name System, a name resolution request in which the DNS server immediately responds with the best information it possesses at the time. Compare with *recursive query*.

J

JBOD (Just a Bunch of Disks) A colloquial term for a drive array that is not configured to use RAID or any other type of special fault tolerance mechanism.

K

Kerberos A ticket-based authentication protocol used by Windows computers that are members of an Active Directory domain. Unlike NTLM, which involves only the IIS7 server and the client, Kerberos authentication involves an Active Directory domain controller as well.

Key Distribution Center (KDC) A Windows Server 2008 component, part of the Kerberos authentication protocol, that maintains a database of account information for all security principals in the domain.

L

Layer 2 Tunneling Protocol (L2TP) A virtual private networking protocol that relies on the IP security extensions (IPsec) for encryption.

leaf object In Active Directory, an object, such as a user or computer, that is incapable of containing any other object.

Lightweight Directory Access Protocol (LDAP) The standard communications protocol for directory service products, including Active Directory.

linear scanning In magnetic tape drives, a method of operation in which the drive draws the tape over stationary recording heads.

logical unit number (LUN) An identifier assigned to a specific component within a SCSI device, such as an individual disk drive in an array, which enables the SCSI host adapter to send commands to that component.

M

manual allocation In Dynamic Host Configuration Protocol, a method by which a DHCP server permanently assigns a specific IP address to a specific computer on the network.

master boot record (MBR) The default partition style used since Windows was released. Supports up to four primary partitions or three primary partitions and one extended partition, with unlimited logical drives on the extended partition.

master computer In Windows Automated Installation Kit, a fully installed and configured computer that serves as the model from which you will create answer files and images.

memory leak The result of a program allocating memory for use but not freeing up that memory when it is finished using it.

Microsoft Application Virtualization (App-V) 4.5 A product that virtualizes applications in such a way that they run on the client computer, not on the server.

Microsoft Assessment and Planning Solution Accelerator (MAP) A free tool that can perform hardware inventories on computers with no agent software required on the client side. MAP can then evaluate the hardware information and create reports that perform a variety of preinstallation tasks.

Microsoft Challenge Handshake Authentication Protocol Version 2 (MS-CHAPv2) An authentication protocol that uses a new encryption key for each connection and for each direction in which data is transmitted. MS-CHAPv2 is the strongest password-based authentication method supported by Windows Server 2008 Remote Access, and is selected by default.

Microsoft Deployment Toolkit (MDT) 2008 A free set of scripts, tools, and documentation that can help administrators to plan and perform large-scale deployments of operating systems and applications to new and existing computers on an enterprise network.

Microsoft Management Console (MMC) A Windows shell application that loads snap-ins that you can use to manage the local server or any other server on the network running the same role or feature.

Microsoft System Center Configuration Manager (SCCM) 2007 A network management product, designed for large enterprises, that administrators can use to deploy applications.

Microsoft System Center Essentials 2007 A network management product, designed for medium-sized organizations, that administrators can use to deploy applications.

Mstsc.exe The executable file for the Windows Remote Desktop Connection client, which you can run graphically, or from the command prompt.

multiple-master replication A technique in which duplicate copies of a file are updated on a regular basis, no matter which copy changes. For example, if a file is duplicated on four different servers, a user can access any of the four copies and modify the file as needed. The replication engine uses the changes made to the modified copy to update the other three copies. Compare to single master replication.

N

name resolution The process by which a Domain Name System server or other mechanism converts a host name into an IP address.

namespace In the Distributed File System, a virtual directory tree that contains references to shared folders located on network file servers. This directory tree does not exist as a true copy of the folders on different servers. Instead, it is a collection of references to the original folders, which users can browse like an actual server share.

network attached storage (NAS) A dedicated file server device, containing disk drives, that connects to a network and provides clients with direct, file-based access to storage resources. Unlike a storage area network, NAS devices include a rudimentary operating system and a file system implementation.

Network Level Authentication (NLA) A Terminal Services feature that confirms the user's identity with the Credential Security Service Provider (CredSSP) protocol before the client and server establish the Terminal Services connection.

network load balancing (NLB) A clustering technology in which a collection of identical servers run simultaneously, sharing incoming traffic equally among them.

non-authoritative restore A restoration of the Active Directory database in which the restored objects and modifications can be overwritten by replication traffic from other domain controllers.

NTFS permissions Controls access to the files and folders stored on disk volumes formatted with the NTFS file system. To access a file on the local system or over a network, a user must have the appropriate NTFS permissions.

O

Offline Files A Windows feature that enables client computers to maintain copies of server files on their local drives. If the computer's connection to the network is severed or interrupted, the client can continue to work with the local copies until network service is restored, at which time the client synchronizes its data with the data on the server.

organizational unit (OU) A container object that functions in a subordinate capacity to a domain, but without the complete separation of security policies.

P

partition style The method that Windows operating systems use to organize partitions on a disk. Two hard disk partition styles can be used in Windows Server 2008: master boot record (MBR) and GUID partition table (GPT).

Password Authentication Protocol (PAP) The least secure of the authentication protocols supported by Windows Server 2008 because it uses simple passwords for authentication, and transmits them in clear text.

Performance Monitor A tool in the Reliability and Performance Monitor console that displays system performance statistics in real time.

Point-to-Point Protocol (PPP) The data-link layer protocol used by Windows computers for remote access connections.

Point-to-Point Tunneling Protocol (PPTP) A virtual private networking protocol that takes advantage of the authentication, compression, and encryption mechanisms of PPP, tunneling the PPP frame within a Generic Routing Encapsulation (GRE) header and encrypting it with Microsoft Point-to-Point Encryption (MPPE), using encryption keys generated during the authentication process.

policy module A set of rules that a certification authority uses to determine whether it should approve the request, deny it, or mark it as pending for later review by an administrator.

port numbers In TCP/IP communications, the code numbers embedded in transport layer protocol headers that identify the applications that generated and will receive a particular message. The most common firewall rules use port numbers to specify the types of application traffic the computer is allowed to send and receive.

preboot execution environment (PXE) A network adapter feature that enables a computer to connect to a server on the network and download the boot files it needs to run, rather than booting from a local drive.

print device The hardware that produces hard copy documents on paper or other print media. Windows Vista supports *local print devices*—which are directly attached to the computer's parallel, serial, Universal Serial Bus (USB), or IEEE 1394 (FireWire) ports—and *network interface print devices*, which are connected to the network directly or through another computer.

print server A computer or standalone device that receives print jobs from clients and sends them to print devices that are attached locally or connected to the network.

printer The software interface through which a computer communicates with a print device. Windows Vista supports numerous interfaces, including parallel (LPT), serial (COM), USB, IEEE 1394, Infrared Data Access (IrDA), and Bluetooth ports. It also supports network printing services such as lpr, Internet Printing Protocol (IPP), and standard TCP/IP ports.

printer control language (PCL) A language understood by the printer. Each printer is associated with a printer driver that converts the commands generated by an application into the printer's PCL.

printer driver A device driver that converts the print jobs generated by applications into an appropriate string of commands for a specific print device. Printer drivers are designed for specific print devices and provide applications that access all of the print device's features.

private key In public key infrastructure (PKI), the secret key in a pair of keys. It is known only to the message or file recipient and used to decrypt the item. When a message is encrypted using the private key, only the public key can decrypt it. The ability to decrypt the message using the public key proves that the message originated from the holder of the private key.

program exception In Windows Firewall, a method for opening a communications port through the firewall. When you create a program exception, the specified port is open only while the program is running. When you terminate the program, the firewall closes the port.

Protected EAP (PEAP) An authentication protocol that uses Transport Level Security (TLS) to create an encrypted channel between a wireless client and an authentication server. The use of

PEAP is not supported for remote access clients in Windows Server 2008.

public key encryption See *public key infrastructure (PKI)*.

public key infrastructure (PKI) A security relationship in which participants are issued two keys: public and private. The participant keeps the private key secret, while the public key is freely available in the digital certificate. Data encrypted with the private key can be decrypted only using the public key and data encrypted with the public key can be decrypted only using the private key.

R

Read-Only Domain Controller (RODC) In Active Directory, a domain controller that supports only incoming replication traffic.

recursive query In Domain Name System, a name resolution request in which the DNS server takes full responsibility for resolving the name. If the server has no information about the name, it sends referrals to other DNS servers until it obtains the information it needs. Compare with *iterative query*.

Redundant Array of Independent Disks (RAID) A series of data storage technologies that use multiple disks to provide computers with increased storage, I/O performance, and/or fault tolerance.

referral The process by which one Domain Name System server sends a name resolution request to another DNS server.

Reliability and Performance snap-in A Microsoft Management Console module that displays system information on a continuous, real-time basis.

Reliability Monitor A tool in the Reliability and Performance snap-in that automatically tracks events that can have a negative effect on system stability and uses them to calculate a stability index.

Remote Authentication Dial In User Service (RADIUS) A centralized authentication service frequently used in organizations with multiple remote access servers.

Remote Desktop A limited Terminal Services implementation included with all Windows Server 2008 products that enables the computer to support up to two administrative connections.

Remote Desktop Connection A program running on a desktop computer that establishes a connection to a terminal server using Remote Desktop Protocol

(RDP) and displays a session window containing a desktop or application.

Remote Desktop Protocol (RDP) The protocol used to transmit screen information, keystrokes, and mouse movements between the Remote Desktop Connection client and a Remote Desktop or Terminal Services server.

Remote Differential Compression (RDC) In the Distributed File System, a protocol that conserves network bandwidth by detecting changes in files and transmitting only the modified data to the destination. This conserves bandwidth and greatly reduces the time needed for the replication process.

RemoteApp A Terminal Services feature that enables clients to run terminal server applications within individual, resizable windows.

replication group In the Distributed File System, a collection of servers, known as members, each of which contains a target for a particular DFS folder.

reservation In the Windows Dynamic Host Configuration Protocol implementation, a manually allocated IP address.

resolver In the Domain Name System, a client program that generates DNS queries and sends them to a DNS server for fulfillment.

Resource Overview A screen in the Reliability and Performance Monitor console that contains four real-time line graphs that display information about four of the server's main hardware components.

resource record In the Domain Name System, a unit of information that can contain host names, IP addresses, and other data.

reverse name resolution In the Domain Name System, the process by which a server converts an IP address into a DNS name.

role A collection of Windows Server 2008 modules and tools designed to perform specific tasks for network clients.

root CA The parent certification authority that issues certificates to the subordinate CAs beneath it. If a client trusts the root CA, it must also trust all the subordinate CAs that have been issued certificates by the root CA.

root name servers The highest-level DNS servers in the entire Domain Name System namespace. They maintain information about the top-level domains.

root zone method In Active Directory, a domain-naming strategy in which an organization uses its registered domain name for its Active Directory tree root domain. Compare with *subzone method*.

S

scope In the Dynamic Host Configuration Protocol, a pool of IP addresses that DHCP servers assign to clients.

scope pane The leftmost pane found in a Microsoft Management Console window, used for navigation between snap-ins, nodes, or folders.

secret key encryption A cryptographic system in which one character is substituted for another.

Secure Socket Tunneling Protocol (SSTP) A new virtual private networking protocol in Windows Server 2008 and Windows Vista that encapsulates PPP traffic using the Secure Sockets Layer (SSL) protocol.

security identifier (SID) A unique value assigned to every Active Directory object when it is created.

security principal The user, group, or computer to which an administrator assigns permissions.

serial ATA (SATA) A newer version of the ATA disk interface that uses serial instead of parallel communications, improves transmission speeds, and provides the ability to queue commands at the drive.

Server Core A Windows Server 2008 installation option that creates a stripped-down version of the operating system that relies primarily on the command prompt for user input. There is no Start menu, no desktop Explorer shell, no Microsoft Management Console, and virtually no graphical applications. All you see when you start the computer is a single window with a command prompt.

server farm A collection of identical servers used to balance a large incoming traffic load.

session In Terminal Services, a collection of client processes that form an individual user environment running on the server.

Session ID In Terminal Services, a unique identifier that a terminal server assigns to each client session to keep the processes for individual clients separate.

Shadow Copies A Windows Server 2008 feature that maintains a library containing multiple versions of selected files. Users can select a version of a file to restore as needed.

shoeshining In magnetic tape drives, a condition that occurs when the computer fails to deliver data to the drive at a sufficient rate, causing the unit to repeatedly stop and start the tape, which reduces its speed and its overall storage capacity.

simple volume Consists of space from a single disk. After you create a simple volume, you can extend it to multiple disks to create a spanned or striped volume if it is not a system volume or boot volume.

single instance storage A Windows technology that enables an image file to maintain a single copy of a particular operating system file and yet use it in multiple operating system images. This eliminates the need to store multiple copies of the same file.

single sign-on An environment in which users can access all network resources with a single set of credentials.

single master replication A technique in which duplicate copies of a file are updated on a regular basis from one master copy. For example, if a file is duplicated on four different servers, users can modify one copy and the replication engine propagates the changes to the other three copies. Compare with multiple master replication.

Small Computer System Interface (SCSI) A storage interface that enables computers to transfer data to multiple storage devices connected to a bus.

smart card A credit card–sized device that contains memory and embedded circuitry that enables it to store data, such as a public encryption key.

snap-ins Application modules that plug into the Microsoft Management Console interface, which you can use to configure operating system settings, applications, and services.

soft quota In File Server Resource Manager, a limitation on user storage space that allows the use of storage space beyond the allotted amount and sends an email notification to the user and/ or administrator.

spanned volume A method for combining the space from multiple (2 to 32) dynamic disks into a single large volume. If a single physical disk in the spanned volume fails, all the data in the volume is lost.

special permissions An element providing a security principal with a specific degree of access to a resource.

spooler A service running on a print server that temporarily stores print jobs until the print device can process them.

standalone CA A certification authority that does not use certificate templates or Active Directory. It stores its information locally.

standalone snap-ins A single tool that you can install directly into an empty Microsoft Management Console window. Standalone snap-ins appear in the first level directly beneath the console root in the console's scope pane.

standard permissions A common combination of special permissions used to provide a security principal with a level of access to a resource.

storage area network (SAN) A dedicated, high-speed network that connects block-based storage devices to servers. Unlike NAS devices, SANs do not provide a file system implementation. SANs require a server to provide clients with access to the storage resources.

striped volume A method for combining the space from multiple (2 to 32) dynamic disks into a single large volume. If a single physical disk in the striped volume fails, all the data in the volume is lost. A striped volume differs from a spanned volume in that the system writes data one stripe at a time to each successive disk in the volume.

subordinate CA A certification authority that has been issued a certificate by a root CA, which stands above it in the certification hierarchy.

subnet mask In TCP/IP networking, a 32-bit value that specifies which bits of an IP address form the network identifier and which bits form the host identifier.

subzone method In Active Directory, a domain-naming strategy in which an organization creates a subdomain beneath its registered Internet domain and uses that for its Active Directory tree root. Compare with *root zone method*.

Switched fabric (FC-SW) A Fibre Channel topology that consists of up to 16,777,216 (2^{24}) devices, each of which is connected to a Fibre Channel switch.

T

tape library A single hardware device that contains one or more magnetic tape drives, as well as a robotic mechanism that inserts tapes into and removes them from the drives. See also *autoloader*.

target In the Distributed File System, a physical folder on a shared server drive that is represented by a virtual directory in a DFS namespace.

technician computer In Windows Automated Installation Kit, the computer on which you install Windows Automated Installation Kit, create answer files, and manage the image deployment process.

terminal server farm A group of at least two servers running the Terminal Services role, working together to share a client load.

Terminal Services client access license (TS CAL) A document that grants a single client access to a specific software program, in this case, a Terminal Services server.

thin client A software program or hardware device that connects to a terminal server and accesses applications running on the server.

thin client computing A variation on the mainframe computing paradigm, in which clients function only as terminals, and servers do all of the application computing.

ticket granting tickets (TGTs) In Kerberos authentication, a credential issued by the Authentication Service that supplies valid authentication credentials. Whenever the client requires access to a new network resource, it must present its TGT to the Key Distribution Center.

trust chaining In a certification authority (CA) hierarchy, enables clients that trust the root CA to also trust certificates issued by any other CAs subordinate to the root.

Trusted Platform Module (TPM) A dedicated cryptographic processor chip that a Windows Server 2008 computer uses to store the BitLocker encryption keys.

trusts In Active Directory, relationships between domains that enable network resources in one domain to authorize users in another.

TS Licensing server A Terminal Services software component that issues client access licenses to Terminal Services clients on a network.

TS Session Broker A Terminal Services role service that maintains a database of client sessions and enables a disconnected client to reconnect to the same terminal server.

tunneling A networking technique in which one protocol is encapsulated within another protocol. In virtual private networking (VPN), an entire client/server session is tunneled within another protocol. Because the internal, or payload, protocol is carried by another protocol, it is protected from most standard forms of attack.

U

unattend file A text or XML file containing responses to the user prompts that typically appear during a Windows operating system installation. See also *answer file*.

V

VDS hardware provider In storage area networking, a software component that enables you to use the Storage Manager for SANs snap-in to manage LUNs on an external storage device.

virtual instance A guest OS installed on a virtual machine in a Windows Server 2008 computer using Hyper-V.

virtual machine manager (VMM) A virtualization software component that enables administrators to create and manage virtual machines on a computer.

virtual machine (VM) In virtualization, one of multiple separate operating environments on a single computer, in which you can install a separate copy of an operating system.

virtual private network (VPN) A technique for connecting to a network at a remote location using the Internet as a network medium.

virtual server A complete installation of an operating system that runs in a software environment emulating a physical computer.

virtualization The process of deploying and maintaining multiple instances of an operating system on a single computer.

W

Web enrollment A process by which clients submit certificate enrollment requests to a CA and receive the issued certificates using a Website created for that purpose.

Windows Automated Installation Kit (AIK) A free set of tools and documents that enable network administrators to plan, create, and deploy operating system image files to new computers on the network.

Windows Deployment Services (WDS) A role included with Windows Server 2008, which enables you to perform unattended installations of Windows Server 2008 and other operating systems on remote computers, using network-based boot and installation media.

Windows Installer 4.0 A Windows Server 2008 component that enables the system to install software packaged as files with a .msi extension.

Windows PE (Preinstallation Environment) 2.1 A subset of Windows Server 2008 that provides basic access to the computer's network and disk drives, making it possible to perform an in-place or a network installation. This eliminates DOS from the installation process by supplying its own preinstallation environment.

Windows RE (Recovery Environment) A command line operating system, similar to *Windows PE*, in which you can run diagnostic and recovery tools.

Windows Server Update Services (WSUS) A program that downloads updates from the Microsoft Update Website and stores them for administrative evaluation. An administrator can then select the updates to deploy and computers on the network download them using a reconfigured Automatic Updates client.

Windows System Image Manager (Windows SIM) A graphical utility that creates and modifies the answer files you can use to perform unattended operating system installations on remote computers.

witness disk In failover clustering, a shared storage medium that holds the cluster configuration database.

Z

zone In the Domain Name System, an administrative entity created on a DNS server to represent a discrete portion of the DNS namespace.

zone transfer In the Domain Name System, the process by which the server hosting the primary zone copies the primary master zone database file to the secondary zone so that their resource records are identical.

Index